past and present

Helen Miller Bailey

Frank H. Cruz

Howard R. Anderson
Consulting Editor

About the Authors and Editor

Helen Miller Bailey is Professor of History of
the Americas and Chairman of the Department
of Social Sciences at East Los Angeles Community College. Dr. Bailey has traveled widely
in Latin America and is the author of a number
of books on Latin American subjects.

Frank H. Cruz is Chairman of the Chicano
Studies Department at California State College, Long Beach. The first course on Latin
American Studies and Mexican History taught
in the Los Angeles City School District was
developed by Mr. Cruz, and much of the material in this book is based on that work.

Howard R. Anderson, consulting editor, is a
former president of the National Council for
the Social Studies. Dr. Anderson taught history
in the secondary schools of Michigan, Iowa,
and New York. He has also taught at the University of Iowa and at Cornell University, and
served as Provost of the University of Rochester.

Printed in the U.S.A.

Library of Congress Catalog Card Number: 78–174553

ISBN: 0–395–13373–4

Contents

List of Maps

Introduction

Does Latin America exist? In a recent magazine article a historian seriously raised this question. It may seem strange for such a question to be asked about a part of the world that has had so much said and written about it. But it is true that the exact meaning of the term *Latin America* is hard to pin down.

What is Latin America? To many people in the United States the term *Latin America* means vaguely "south of the border." Someone trying to define the term geographically could say that Latin America is an extremely large area reaching from the southern border of the United States almost to Antarctica. Politically the region includes 20 different nations—Mexico, nine republics in Central America and the Caribbean, and ten in South America. But this listing ignores four other independent nations in the tropical Western Hemisphere. These four until recently were British colonies. They are Guyana on the South American continent and three island-nations—Jamaica, Trinidad-Tobago, and Barbados. A number of other small territories in this part of the world still are controlled by European countries. How do these "non-Latin" territories figure in the definition of Latin America?

Latin languages gave Latin America its name. The expression *Latin America* reflects the fact that Latin was the common ancestor of the official languages of the 20 republics. These languages are Spanish, Portuguese, and French. The three languages were brought to the Americas after the European conquest in the 1500's. Along with their languages, European settlers brought their own ways of living to America. In this environment the Europeans encountered not only new conditions but also other cultures.

Indian peoples of the Western Hemisphere had developed rich civilizations long before the Europeans came. Still a third people participated in the blending of cultures—Africans who were forced to come to America as slaves. As the three peoples influenced each other, a new culture emerged. The Latin American culture of today is a blending of all three and is not just "Latin" as the name implies.

In fact, millions of people in Latin America still speak Indian languages as their native tongues. Some of these people speak *only* an Indian language; others speak Spanish or Portuguese as well. In Haiti, where French is the official language, most people speak a language that is more African than French.

Latin American culture extends north of "the border." One reason often given for studying Latin America is that it is our neighbor. But some of us in the United States *are* Latin Americans. Next to English, Spanish is the most widely spoken language in the United States. Many Spanish-speaking citizens of this country are of Mexican descent. They live chiefly in the southwestern states. Other Latin citizens of the United States are Puerto Ricans. They live not only on the island of Puerto Rico but also in New York City and many other parts of the eastern United States. In addition, large numbers of Cuban refugees and immigrants from Central and South America have come north to this country. Obviously it is not quite true to say that Latin America begins south of the United States border.

Latin America includes many lands and peoples. In still another way the term *Latin America* is misleading. Any single term applied to such a variety of peoples and lands would be unsatisfactory. Among the people of the southern Western Hemisphere are sophisticated residents of modern cities and isolated nomads who still follow Stone Age ways of living. Ranging between these extremes are people at all levels of cultural development and living very different kinds of lives.

The countries of Latin America themselves vary widely. Paraguay and Haiti are poor and have made little economic progress. But Argentina and Venezuela have advanced economies. Educational level is another example of contrast. In Uruguay practically everyone can read and write, while in Bolivia almost two-thirds of the population is illiterate. In geography, politics, racial background, and industrial development, there is endless variety. No one Latin American country is like any other.

But even *within* individual countries there are great extremes. Peru has many tiny Indian villages tucked away in high mountain valleys. The people of these villages live a way of life that has changed little over the centuries. They speak no Spanish and only rarely have contact with the up-to-date people of Lima, Peru's capital city. The historian Frank Tannenbaum said of the mountain villagers, "in look, manner, attitude, and belief these Peruvians are not part of the same world as Lima."

Why use the expression "Latin America"? How, after all this, can one justify the use of the term *Latin America*? The answer is another question: What other term is there to use? For want of any better expression, people are likely to keep on speaking and writing about *Latin America*.

Obviously Latin America does exist. And the amazingly varied peoples of this part of the world do share a common goal. They hope to overcome the many difficult problems that have grown out of long years of political disorder and economic neglect. As one writer has said, the common factor uniting the peoples of this region is "their sense of being part of the idea of Latin America, of the striving to break the shackles of underdevelopment, of the struggle to teach, to feed, to house, to decently employ and otherwise care for rapidly expanding populations." [1] At the same time they intend to preserve as much as possible of their unique and fascinating civilization.

[1] Tad Szulc, *Latin America* (New York: Atheneum, 1966), p. 16.

1

The Makers of Latin America: The Indians

Richly carved stone figures were discovered by John Lloyd Stephens among the ruins of Mayan temples in Central America. This drawing by Stephens' companion, Frederick Catherwood, depicted one of the Mayan sculptures found at Copán in Honduras. Thirteen feet high, the monument represents an ornately dressed figure with a monster-mask headdress. Stephens called it "one of the most elaborate specimens in the whole extent of the ruins. . . . On its sides are rows of hieroglyphics, which probably recite the history of this mysterious personage."

In 1839 a North American named John Lloyd Stephens set off on an exploring trip to Central America. Stephens had a keen interest in archeology and had already traveled a great deal in the Middle East and Greece, visiting the remains of ancient peoples. Having heard rumors of some strange ruins in Honduras, he decided to find out whether they existed. An artist named Frederick Catherwood agreed to go along and sketch anything of interest they might find.

Before long, Stephens, Catherwood, and a party of Indian guides and carriers were slashing their way through the "green sea" of the Honduras rain forest. The heat was stifling, mosquitoes swarmed, and the jungle trees and giant ferns were so thick they could hardly see where they were going. Stephens and Catherwood began to doubt that man could ever have lived in such a place.

But suddenly they came upon a stone wall. Then one of the Indians slashed away a mass of vines from a tall stone slab. To the amazement of the two white men, the slab was covered with beautifully intricate carving, like nothing they knew of anywhere else in the Americas. Soon they found more remarkable stone objects and remains of buildings covered with tangled vegetation. Stephens and Catherwood had discovered ruins of the stone city of Copán (koh-*pahn'*), once one of the leading temple centers of the Maya (*mah'* yuh) Indians.

"Nothing in the great romance of world history has impressed me more deeply than the appearance of this once so magnificent and gracious city," wrote Stephens about another Maya city he discovered. Stephens' account of his finds, illustrated with detailed drawings by Catherwood, was soon published. The book stirred up a storm of interest among historians and archeologists. Though some of the Spanish explorers of the 1500's had mentioned the Maya Indians in published accounts, awareness of the ancient cities had disappeared until Stephens made known his dramatic discoveries.

Now Copán and many other Maya ruins have been cleared of jungle growth. In a number of locations archeologists have uncovered and studied the remains of other ancient Indian cultures. As archeologists continue to study ancient remains, more will be learned about the people who built impressive civilizations in the Americas long before Europeans arrived in this part of the world.

1. The Origin of the American Indians

The American continents are often called the "New World." This name was given to the Western Hemisphere by Europeans who explored and colonized the Americas in the 1500's. Hundreds of centuries before that time, however, the Americas were a "new world" to other colonizers—people who were the ancestors of the American Indians.

American remains of prehistoric men are much less ancient than those found elsewhere in the world. Much has been written on recent discoveries of fossil man in East Africa. Scientific means of dating have shown that the most ancient African remains are some four million years old. Fossilized bones of other ancestors of modern man have been found in Europe, the Near East, Java, and China. These are less ancient than the African fossils but are still not as "human" in form as modern man.

The earliest human remains so far found in the Americas are much more recent. One of these finds was the skull of a woman unearthed in Texas. Methods of dating indicate that this woman died between 10,000 and 20,000 years ago. In Ohio archeologists found mastodon bones that had been cracked open by human beings. Apparently men had killed the big beast by hurling rocks at it and then had eaten its flesh and cracked the bones to get at the marrow. Archeologists have also found stone tools and weapons used by ancient Americans. One such weapon was discovered in a cave in New Mexico. It was buried in the ribs of a bison that lived some 10,000 years ago. In a desert in southern California scientists found chips of stone that were probably used as scraping instruments. Tests showed the stones to be at least 50,000 years old and perhaps even older. But all these remains are evidence that man came to America fairly "recently" in the history of the human race.

The earliest "Americans" migrated from Asia. It is now generally agreed that the ancestors of the American Indians migrated from Siberia (northeastern Asia). They probably crossed the Bering Strait before the last Ice Age. At that time the strait was a land-bridge above sea level, and the climate was warmer than it is now. Of course not all the Asian migrants crossed into America at the same time. Probably many groups wandered across the Bering Strait land-bridge over a period of ten or twenty thousand years.

These nomadic peoples spread out from Alaska into present-day Canada. As the Ice Age advanced, they gradually moved farther south. They had no idea of "exploring" a new continent. They were simply wandering in search of food. No doubt they hoped to find a place where there were large herds of bison and other game to kill with their spears. Apparently these people knew nothing about how to plant crops, although some probably gathered seeds from wild plants. There is no evidence that they brought any seed grains with them from Asia.

The development of corn was a significant accomplishment. It was probably between 6000 and 8000 years ago, somewhere in central Mexico, that Indians learned how to plant and harvest corn. This was a major development in history, for corn became a staple food throughout much of this hemisphere.

Gathering wild acorns or berries is a very different thing from deliberately planting seeds and waiting for them to grow into vegetables or grains. Beans, if left wet, will sprout,

and an observant person might think of planting the sprouts to get more beans. Then, if the biggest beans are selected for the next planting, the resulting crop may be even larger. Probably by some such process, carried on over many generations, ancient Indian peoples gradually improved a wild plant similar to corn. Today there is no wild corn growing anywhere in the Americas.

By perhaps 6000 years ago Mexican Indians had learned to plant and harvest corn in its modern form. In addition to corn, they grew beans, squash, and chili peppers. These formed their standard diet. From the Rio Grande to Nicaragua, many Latin Americans still eat as part of their daily meals the flat corn cakes known as *tortillas* (tor-*tee'* yahss). To prepare the corn, they use a stone grinder, called by the Aztec Indians a *metate* (may-*tah'* tay), and a handstone called a *mano* (*mah'* noh).

Agriculture led to permanent settlements and trade. Indians who knew how to plant and harvest no longer had to wander in search of food. They settled down in fertile valleys to tend the growing corn. As more of them began to stay permanently in these places, villages grew up. The Indians learned to use such tools as stone axes and wooden digging sticks. They also began to weave cloth and to fashion clay pots for cooking.

Eventually trade sprang up between some of the larger villages and towns. While some men farmed, others concentrated on weaving cloth or making decorated clay pots. Still other villagers set out on long journeys, taking with them bolts of cloth or loads of pots to trade in other areas. Much evidence of long-distance trade has turned up in the Americas. In Guatemala, turquoise has been found which could only have come from the upper Rio Grande region of New Mexico. Parrot feathers found in the Mesa Verde cliff dwellings in Colorado could only have come from distant tropical America.

(*Continued on page 8*)

Latin America — Natural Features

All varieties of land formation, climate, and vegetation are found in Latin America — mountains and hills, deserts, plateaus, tropical rain forests, temperate forests, and grassy plains. Pictured here are: (above) sand dunes in northern Peru; (left) an Amazon rain forest; (below) mountains in central Mexico. On the map on the facing page can be seen the regions of different vegetation. (The inset map shows the Valley of Mexico in Aztec times. Today most of the lakes have been filled in.)

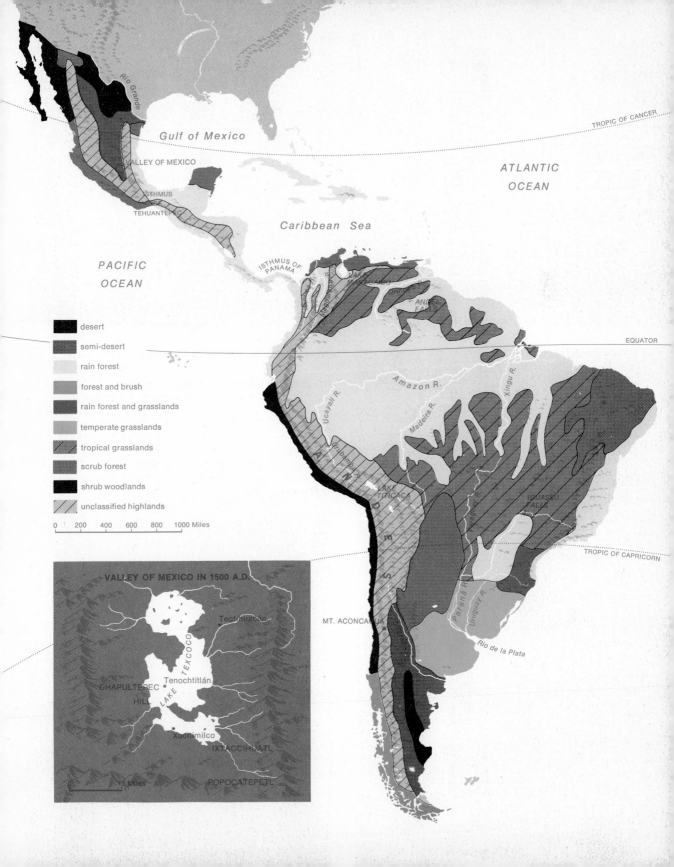

TROPIC OF CANCER

Gulf of Mexico

ATLANTIC

OCEAN

Rio Grande

VALLEY OF MEXICO

ISTHMUS

OF

TEHUANTEPEC

Caribbean Sea

PACIFIC

OCEAN

ISTHMUS OF
PANAMA

ANGEL
FALLS

EQUATOR

desert
semi-desert
rain forest
forest and brush
rain forest and grasslands
temperate grasslands
tropical grasslands
scrub forest
shrub woodlands
unclassified highlands

0   200   400   600   800   1000 Miles

Amazon R.

Ucayali R.

Madeira R.

Xingu R.

A
N
D
E
S
m
t
s

LAKE
TITICACA

IGUASSU
FALLS

TROPIC OF CAPRICORN

MT. ACONCAGUA

Paraná R.

Paraguay R.

Uruguay R.

Rio de la Plata

VALLEY OF MEXICO IN 1500 A.D.

Teotihuacán

CHAPULTEPEC
HILL

Tenochtitlán

LAKE TEXCOCO

Xochimilco

IXTACCIHUATL

POPOCATEPETL

0   15 Miles

Peoples learned from each other. As these things changed hands and passed north or south, those who traded often learned something from other peoples. One example of this cultural [1] exchange is the presence of certain common things in many of the ancient religious centers found in Mexico and Central America. These include tall pyramids that served as temple bases, with narrow steps leading to the top; large courts where a game something like basketball was played with a rubber ball; carvings of jaguar faces and quetzal bird feathers; and the worship of a rain god. There seems to have been little contact between Central and South America through the Isthmus of Panama.

THINKING ABOUT THIS SECTION

1. Explain or define the following words: fossil; Ice Age; cultural exchange.
2. How did the ancestors of the American Indians come to the Western Hemisphere?
3. How have scientists learned about "where, when, and how" prehistoric people lived in the Americas?
4. How did the American Indians change from hunters and food gatherers to planters? Why was this important?
5. What evidence is there in this section to support the view that long-distance trade was carried on in America long before 1492?

2. Early Indian Cultures in Mexico

Olmec culture may have been the oldest in Middle America. Archeologists have recently excavated ruins at the site called La Venta (lah *vayn'* tah) on the southern Gulf coast of Mexico. One of the most exciting findings was a pyramid made of mud and cobbled stones, with the marks of a wooden temple on top. Scientific dating methods have proved that wood in this temple was cut from live trees about 800 B.C. Archeologists now believe that this is probably the oldest temple so far discovered in the New World.

In the same general area archeologists have found large stone heads, some of them eight feet high. The "La Venta heads," as they are called, have pouting, babyish faces, wear "football helmets," and were carved without any bodies. The sculptors who made these heads

were an ancient people now called the Olmec. The great age of some of these remains and the evidence of their influence on later Indian peoples have caused some archeologists to call the Olmec civilization the "mother culture" of Middle America.[2]

The Olmec people influenced other Indian cultures. By comparing styles of pottery, sculpture, and architecture, archeologists can figure out which ancient cultures influenced others. Such a comparison shows that there was some connection between the Olmec Indians and the Mayas, the people who later built remarkable stone temple centers in Central America and the Yucatán (yoo-kah-*tahn'*) peninsula. Olmec influence also spread to peoples who lived in the valley of Oaxaca (wah-*hah'* kah), 300 miles south of Mexico City. Here people called

---

[1] In this book the word *culture* is used to mean the total way of life of a particular group or community, including social customs, government, economy, arts, religious beliefs, etc.

[2] *Middle America* includes Mexico, Central America, and the West Indies.

Zapotecs (*sah'* poh-tecks) and Mixtecs (meesh-*tecks'*) built beautiful temples faced with mosaic designs. Fine gold work has been uncovered in ancient graves in these locations. Archeologists working in Oaxaca have also unearthed stone ball courts similar to those found in ancient ruins elsewhere in Middle America.

Early people built a great city at Teotihuacán.
Corn-planting people seem to have lived in Mexico's central valley for thousands of years. The Valley of Mexico is a basin or cup in a mountainous region, about 7000 feet above sea level. It is a fertile area, ideal for growing corn and beans. Since the valley has no outlet, melting mountain snows pour down into it, creating many marshy lakes. The Indians built cities on islands in the lakes, on the shores, or nearby.

Olmec sculptors may have carved giant helmeted heads as portraits of chieftains or gods. This one was made from a stone weighing sixteen tons.

A place north of present-day Mexico City, called Teotihuacán (tay-oh-tee-wah-*kahn'*), was the site of an ancient culture of unknown origin. Visitors to Mexico City usually go to see the majestic Pyramid of the Sun at Teotihuacán. This man-made mountain is greater in size than any pyramid in Egypt. About a mile away is a smaller structure called the Pyramid of the Moon. Teotihuacán may have had more than 200,000 inhabitants in 600 A.D. If so, it was larger than any city in Europe at that time. About 650 A.D. the city was attacked, looted, and burned, and its people fled to other towns. Most archeologists believe that Teotihuacán was never occupied again.

Toltecs built a city at Tula. Perhaps 200 years later, a warlike people called Toltecs built a city at Tula to the north of the Valley of Mexico. From this site they waged war on other peoples of central Mexico. The Toltecs became famous for their military exploits. But all that they knew of architecture and crafts was apparently learned from the successors of the people who built Teotihuacán. One Toltec military chief was named Quetzalcoatl (kayt-sahl-*koh'* atl), or "Feathered Serpent." He may have been named after a god who was also called Quetzalcoatl. At some time the chieftain Quetzalcoatl was forced to leave Tula. He fought briefly with the people of various towns in the central valley, and then led an expedition to conquer the Maya people of the Yucatán peninsula. This happened about 1000 or 1100 A.D.

THINKING ABOUT THIS SECTION

1. Explain or define the following words: La Venta heads; Teotihuacán.

2. What kind of evidence suggests that the Olmec influenced other American Indians?

3. Look up "carbon dating" and report what archeologists can learn by using this research tool.

When Christopher Columbus first visited the Caribbean islands, he described the people that he saw there as "very handsome, of good stature, and of a tanned color with black hair." He wrote the Spanish queen that these "Indians" were "gentle people of great simplicity." On his next two voyages to the Caribbean he saw again these primitive Arawak (*ah′* rah-wahk) Indians and also some of their savage neighbors, the Caribs (*kah′* ribs). Then, on his fourth voyage Columbus passed a large canopied boat rowed by Indians wearing cotton clothes. Under the canopy lounged a richly dressed merchant. Columbus didn't know it, but this man was a Maya merchant taking bolts of brightly colored cloth to trade along the coast of Honduras.

Maya Indians built great stone cities. The Maya merchant seen by Columbus was a descendant of the people who had built Copán in Honduras and Tikal (tee-*kahl′*) and other cities in Guatemala. Still other Maya cities were Palenque (pah-*layn′* kay), Uxmal (ooz-*mahl′*), and Chichén Itzá (chih-*chayn′* eet-*sah′*), all located in what is now Mexico.

Actually these places were not cities in the sense of heavily populated areas. Rather they were religious centers with monumental pyramid-temples and graceful palaces. The people lived in little farm villages scattered around the religious center. When the time came to hold a ceremony, the people would troop into the city and gather around the great stone buildings. All these cities had probably been founded some time before 300 B.C.

Over the centuries the Maya people built up a remarkable civilization. Doubtless they learned much from earlier peoples of Middle America. But they elaborated on borrowed ideas and created a distinctive culture of their own.

It is true that the Mayas lacked certain things. They never invented a system of writing based on a phonetic alphabet. Moreover, they had no wheeled vehicles, beasts of burden, plows, iron tools, or oceangoing ships.[3] But the Mayas were fine artists, excelling in architecture, sculpture, weaving, and jewelry-making. They also knew much about astronomy, had worked out a complex system of mathematics, and had developed an elaborate religious society.

Maya remains have been studied. When Spanish explorers eventually came to Central America, they found the ancient Maya temples at Tikal and Copán. They casually noticed these imposing structures but moved on to look for fertile inhabited valleys. The existence of the cities was almost forgotten. Then, as told at the beginning of this chapter, John Lloyd Stephens made archeological "news" with his discovery of the Maya ruins. About a century later, archeologists began to study these ruins with modern scientific methods. It was once thought that Tikal was the oldest temple site in Latin America. But now older pyramids have been excavated at Teotihuacán and La Venta in Mexico. Tikal is still of great interest, however, especially for its elaborate dating stones.

Dating stones show Maya mathematical skill. The dating stones found at Tikal are proof of Maya knowledge of mathematics. The Maya numbering system was quite advanced. It was based on the numbers 20 and 400, just as ours is based on 10 and 100. Skilled Maya astronomers worked out a calendar based on a year of 365 days. In fact, their calendar has been proved slightly more accurate than the one we use today. At the Tikal temples astronomer-priests set up a marking stone for every 20 years and kept an accurate chronology, or record of events. These calendar stones were

[3] With one exception none of the American peoples possessed any of these things. The one exception was that the Incas had a beast of burden—the llama. (Also, some northern Indians used dogs to pull sleds.)

upright slabs, some as high as 30 feet. The chronological records were carved on them in a sort of picture writing.

Archeologists have cut cross-sections through some of the steep pyramids at Tikal. They have found that at the end of every 400-year cycle the Mayas destroyed the pyramids and buried the dating stones. Probably this was done at the command of religious leaders. Then builders used the rubble to construct temples that were larger and more elaborate than before. At the end of another 400 years all would be destroyed and rebuilt again.

Archeologists have figured out the count on the dating stones but not the picture writing. We are not sure how Maya dates correspond with ours, since we have no way of knowing when their "Year One" was. The best guess archeologists can make is that the Maya Year One was some event from the period 1000–800 B.C. If that is so, the last dating stones in this area were erected about 700 or 800 A.D.

City life flourished in Yucatán. Perhaps the largest Maya city built in Yucatán was Chichén Itzá. This name means "city at the wells where the Itzá tribe came to live." The ruins of once-magnificent structures may be seen at Chichén Itzá today. The largest of these buildings is an imposing square-based pyramid called *El Castillo* ("the Castle") by the Spanish. Steep stone steps on each side of the pyramid climb to a temple built on the top. As we might expect, such an important city had several of the stone ball courts. Carvings on the walls show players in action. These athletes had to hit a rubber ball with their elbows, hips, or knees and try to get it through stone or wooden rings 20 feet above the ground. The rings were not horizontal as in basketball but vertical. The sport seems to have had features of both basketball and soccer.

Across a wide plaza at Chichén Itzá stands another majestic temple-pyramid as high as a five-story building. Rows of carved columns stretch out from two sides of this pyramid to form a market square the size of several modern city blocks. Because carvings on the columns show men with swords, this pyramid is called the Temple of the Warriors.

When Chichén Itzá was a great city about 600 A.D., the market square must have been daily filled with merchants and shoppers. It served a population of 150,000 or 200,000. Some of these people lived in plaster and thatch houses along avenues leading to the holy temples and two great wells in the center of the city. People made pottery and cotton cloth at home and sold their wares in the central market, just as Indians do today in many parts of Mexico and Guatemala. At some booths traders offered carved jade from Guatemala, jewelry made of shells from the beaches 60 miles away, and brilliant headdresses for use on ceremonial days. These headdresses were made of feathers of turkeys or jungle birds. Traders from other towns could eat at restaurant stalls where women made hot tortillas on stone *metates* and served dark brown beans or perhaps venison.

Wall paintings show that women in Chichén Itzá wore long straight white dresses with rows of colorful embroidery around the square neck and the hem of the skirt. Women in Yucatán villages still wear dresses like this today. Men, especially those of the noble class, dressed more elaborately. They wore short pants of bright cotton, capes of deer or jaguar skin, and headdresses of jaguar skin and feathers. Ornaments of jade, coral, and feathers added to a colorful costume.

Priests were also astronomers. As mentioned earlier, the Mayas knew a great deal about astronomy. It was the priests who carried on the study of the sun and the night skies. They could probably foretell eclipses of the moon and sun. The priests at Chichén Itzá had an observatory, but they did not have the telescopes used by modern astronomers. The observatory, a round tower 41 feet high, still stands. Small peepholes in the thick walls point directly to positions of the sun and certain stars at the longest and shortest days of the year and

at the spring and fall equinoxes. Thus, the astronomer-priests kept track of the seasons and told the farmers when to plant and harvest corn.

Some knowledge of Maya religion has been preserved. Religion was the great force of the Maya culture. All life centered around the sacred ceremonies. Even astronomical calculations and various arts and crafts had religious significance. The priests had great influence over the affairs of the community and, in fact, were probably the ruling class.

After the Spanish conquest of Mexico, some of the Maya religious lore was written down in Spanish and thus preserved. One collection of ancient stories is called the *Popol Vuh* (pohpol' voo). It tells of many gods of rain and wind, crops and sun, illness and good health,

Today El Castillo, *the great pyramid of Chichén Itzá, looks like this (above). Though earlier Mayan temples stood on the same site, this pyramid was built by the Toltecs. Over the centuries the steps crumbled away, but those at the right have been restored and visitors can climb to the temple at the top. The sculptured figure seen at the right in this picture may have been an altar, where sacrifices were offered to the gods.*

(Right) Richly dressed aristocrats appear in this section of a wall painting lining the interior of a Maya temple discovered in southern Mexico in 1946. The figures may represent actual individuals, and the picture writing in the boxes above their heads probably identifies them, though decipherment is uncertain. Jade ornaments and quetzal feathers worn by the men symbolize their high status.

and the dances and ceremonies performed to please them. Another such manuscript is the *Book of Chilam Balam* (*chee′* lahm *bah′* lahm), a fascinating collection of prayers, legends, songs, and prophecies.

Early Maya sites were abandoned. For some reason, in the 700's or 800's A.D. the Mayas abandoned many of their great stone cities. The reason for the abandonment is a mystery. No one knows why the Maya people deserted the cities that they had built up over the centuries. Archeologists have found little evidence of destruction by war, earthquake, or forest fire.

One explanation may be that the land failed to feed the people. Modern Indians in this area prepare fields for planting corn in the same way that the ancient Mayas did. First, they slash down the thickest vegetation. Then they burn it off and thus clear the field for planting. After about five years of growing corn, the soil is worn out. The Indians then "slash and burn" another area and plant there, while jungle growth recovers the first field. In another few years the Indians clear other fields,

and so on. A small population could continue this without ever running out of land. But, as the number of people living around the ancient Maya centers steadily grew, the surrounding land probably failed to grow enough corn. Some authorities also think that epidemics may have killed off many people, or that wars crippled the cities. At any rate, the early Maya centers became ghost towns.

Toltec invaders brought changes to Yucatán. The Mayan civilization did not die out entirely, however. Maya legends and carvings dating from after 1150 A.D. show that a great change took place in Yucatán. By that time Toltec warriors had crossed from central Mexico to Yucatán in large canoes. The Toltecs conquered Chichén Itzá and remained in control there for about two centuries.

According to Maya legend, the Toltecs were led by a powerful bearded chieftain called Kukulcán, a name which, like Quetzalcoatl, means "Feathered Serpent." Kukulcán, the chieftain named Quetzalcoatl who left Tula (page 9), and the god who was also called Quetzalcoatl are all confused in the Indian

legends of Middle America, much to the puzzlement of modern historians.

The Toltec warriors brought new ideas of community organization to Yucatán. The early Maya communities had been independent "city-states" but had not fought much with each other. After the Toltec invasion, Chichén Itzá and two other cities formed a powerful league. Between them, they ruled the Yucatán peninsula. Eventually the three cities quarreled, and a series of exhausting wars followed.

War prisoners were sacrificed. The Toltec invaders practiced a brutal kind of religion. Human sacrifice was an essential part of their religious ceremonies. In fact, the Toltecs' chief purpose in waging war was to capture prisoners for sacrifice. Most prisoners were slaughtered in the temples on top of the pyramids. Others were hurled into deep wells. The deepest of the wells in Chichén Itzá was called the Well of Sacrifice and is still there to be seen today. It is a great natural pit measuring 150 to 190 feet across.

Before the Toltec invasion, the Maya people had sacrificed human beings only in time of desperate emergency. This might be an epidemic, a famine, or a long dry spell. The Toltecs, however, regularly sacrificed human beings. At the end of the dry season, before the rainy season began, the high priest would select victims and sacrifice them to the gods. In this way they hoped to please the gods and persuade them to send the rains.

The Maya civilization decayed. The series of wars fought by the Maya cities exhausted the people. Though the reason for the abandonment of the early Maya cities is still a mystery, we *do* know that warfare ruined the Yucatán culture after the time of the Toltecs. By the time the Spaniards came to America, the Yucatán people no longer maintained their proud cities. On holy days people still worshiped at the temple in Chichén Itzá, and they continued to sacrifice human victims to the rain god. But the temple was crumbling, and the people made no effort to repair it. Jungle growth had crept into the marketplace and the streets. Vines split apart the stone blocks of the buildings. No one remembered how to count the years by 20 and 400.

Thus, the great Maya civilization came to an end. Soon the Indians even stopped going to Chichén Itzá and the other large shrines. By 1600 all the ancient cities of Yucatán and Guatemala were covered by jungle and forgotten.

THINKING ABOUT THIS SECTION

1. Explain or define the following words: dating stones; picture writing; Quetzalcoatl.

2. What can be learned about Maya culture from remains found at such sites as Tikal? What were the great achievements of the people living there?

3. Why may the Mayas have abandoned their great temple centers?

4. Reconstruct Maya life in Chichén Itzá; describe architecture, religion, commerce, the role of the priests.

5. What changes in Maya life were introduced by the Toltecs?

4. The Aztecs, Heirs to the Early Peoples of Mexico

The Aztecs invaded the Valley of Mexico. Teotihuacán in central Mexico (page 9) had been a ghost city for almost a thousand years before the Spanish came to Middle America. The descendants of the people who had built that city lived in smaller communities around the lakes of the Valley of Mexico. Wandering tribesmen from the north constantly attacked these settlements. One of these tribes called themselves *Aztecs,* meaning "the people whose face nobody knows."

According to legend, one Aztec chief was named Tenoch. He was said to have dreamed that he would lead his people to a place where they would see an eagle sitting on a cactus plant in the middle of a lake. The eagle would hold a snake in its mouth. The story goes that the Aztecs *did* find such a place, and they settl d there and built a city called Tenochtitlán (tay-nohch-tee-*tlan'*), the "place of Tenoch." This is supposed to have happened about 1325 A.D., and the site is where Mexico City stands today. Actually the Aztecs had probably settled there at an earlier time. Another name by which the Aztecs called themselves was *Mexica.* Eventually the valley which they conquered came to be known as Mexico. Because of the old legend, the eagle, serpent, and cactus are now Mexico's national symbols and appear on the Mexican flag.

Aztec power grew. The invading Aztecs succeeded in dominating other peoples in the Valley of Mexico. The other Indians regarded the Aztecs as barbarians, but the Aztecs learned from more advanced cultures and soon built an impressive civilization.

About 1440 an Aztec chief named Moctezuma[4] came to power. Under Moctezuma I and the chiefs who followed him, the Aztecs conquered tribes to the north and to the south. The Aztecs did not wipe out the tribes they conquered. Instead, they allowed the defeated people some independence within a sort of "tribute empire." They forced their subjects to pay tribute in bolts of cotton cloth, deer hides, conch shells, and *cacao* (kah-*kah'* oh) beans (from which chocolate is made). The Aztecs also rounded up large numbers of prisoners. These victims were sacrificed on the temple-pyramids of Tenochtitlán. Naturally the subject peoples resented the demands of their Aztec conquerors.

[4] This is often spelled Mo*n*tezuma, but Mo*c*tezuma is regarded as a more accurate spelling.

Obsidian

The Aztecs' obsidian knives were as sharp as razor blades. Abundant quantities of obsidian, a glass formed by volcanic heat, were found by the Aztecs in the Valley of Mexico. Broken fragments of this hard and brittle material have dangerously sharp edges. Indian craftsmen learned how to chip off pieces of obsidian and to fashion them into knives, spearheads, and scalpels. They also made ornaments, such as vases, mirrors, and little figurines out of polished pieces of obsidian. Tiny bits of the glass, ground smooth, provided bright eyes for the Aztecs' stone idols.

Tenochtitlán was a metropolis. Much more is known about the Aztecs than the Mayas, because the Aztecs were the ruling people of Mexico at the time of the Spanish conquest. Spanish explorers, soldiers, and missionaries all wrote about the Aztecs. One Spanish soldier described Tenochtitlán as a city of perhaps 200,000 people. The city was built on islands in the middle of Lake Texcoco (tess-*koh'* koh) in the Valley of Mexico (map, page 7). Lake Texcoco was salty, but aqueducts carried water from fresh-water lakes into the city. Tenochtitlán's high temples shone in the sun like white towers. Most of the people lived in adobe houses, painted white with trimmings of bright colors, much like the houses in Mexican villages today. Because of the many small islands, the main streets of Tenochtitlán were canals, and canoes made their way from one island to another. Engineers had built several paved causeways to connect the island city with the mainland. Where canals cut through the causeways, removable bridges provided a way of crossing.

Tenochtitlán had several great marketplaces, much like the market in Chichén Itzá. One section of a market was given over to the sale of fruits and vegetables. Long lines of heavily laden canoes transported this produce along the city's canals. Merchants in other parts of the markets sold cloth and ready-to-wear clothing. Others specialized in reed sleeping mats and baskets made of grasses. There was also a "tools" section, where customers could find copper implements, sharp knives made of obsidian (volcanic glass), stone drilling tools, bone needles, and devices used in spinning cotton thread. Other booths sold ornaments— brilliant feathers and delicate jewelry of jade, shell, and turquoise. Articles were exchanged by barter, or customers could pay with cacao beans. These beans were used as a kind of money. The busy markets were filled with merchants and craftsmen showing their wares and milling housewives looking for bargains.

The Aztec monarch lived in splendor. When the Spanish came to Tenochtitlán in 1519, Moctezuma II, grandson of the first Moctezuma, reigned over the city. He lived in a splendid palace on Chapultepec (chah-*pool'* teh-peck) Hill. Both the royal family and the Aztec noblemen enjoyed a luxurious life. Moctezuma kept thousands of birds of colorful varieties in his gardens to provide plumage for the feathered cloaks of noblemen and warriors. The royal cooks roasted hundreds of turkeys every day to serve to the royal household. Daily runners brought fresh fish from the Gulf coast for Moctezuma's table. Other runners carried snow from the mountain slopes to cool fermented liquor made from a cactus plant called *maguey* (mah-*gay'*). Vegetables, fruits, and flowers to adorn the royal table were grown on mud-covered islands in the city's lakes. Some of these "floating gardens" remain for the modern visitor to see at Xochimilco (shoh-chee-*meel'* koh) outside Mexico City.

Aztec society was headed by a ruling class. A council of nobles had chosen Moctezuma from among the relatives of the previous chief to be head of the Aztec state. Called the Chief of Men, he was not really a king or emperor in the sense of a powerful ruler. Though he was regarded almost as a god, many nobles and military leaders had nearly as much actual

power. Wealthy merchants also were influential. The city was run by the elected leaders of 20 clans, or divisions of the community. Each clan had its own court, although Moctezuma served as head of the supreme court. Today many Mexican towns are divided into similar neighborhood units called *barrios* (*bah'* ree-ohss).

The warrior heads of the clans formed the most powerful class. The clan leaders or their families were granted the right to control extensive tracts of corn and bean fields outside the city. Villagers worked this land for the benefit of the landholder, or for the priests or the Chief of Men. The system of landholding resembled that of Spain in the 1500's. For this reason the Spaniards who came to America found it easy to get the Indian villagers to work for them.

Aztec young people were trained for their role in life. The Aztec young people were strictly educated. Since religion and war were matters of supreme importance, the education of sons of noblemen and rich merchants concentrated on these subjects. At the age of fifteen, the boys began to study at the "house of youth." There they learned how to use weapons. They were also instructed in Aztec history, arts and crafts, and religious rites and duties. Priests taught the young men rules of good conduct. These included such rules as "console the poor and unfortunate" and "never tell lies." Aztec boys from poor families had a better chance of rising to become army officers, landholders, or government officials than did boys living in Spain at the time.

Indians of Middle and South America Before the European Conquest

The routes on the inset map show how descendants of Asian migrants eventually spread over the American continents. The Indian groups labeled on the larger map were only the major ones. Throughout Indian America there was a countless variety of cultural groups and subgroups.

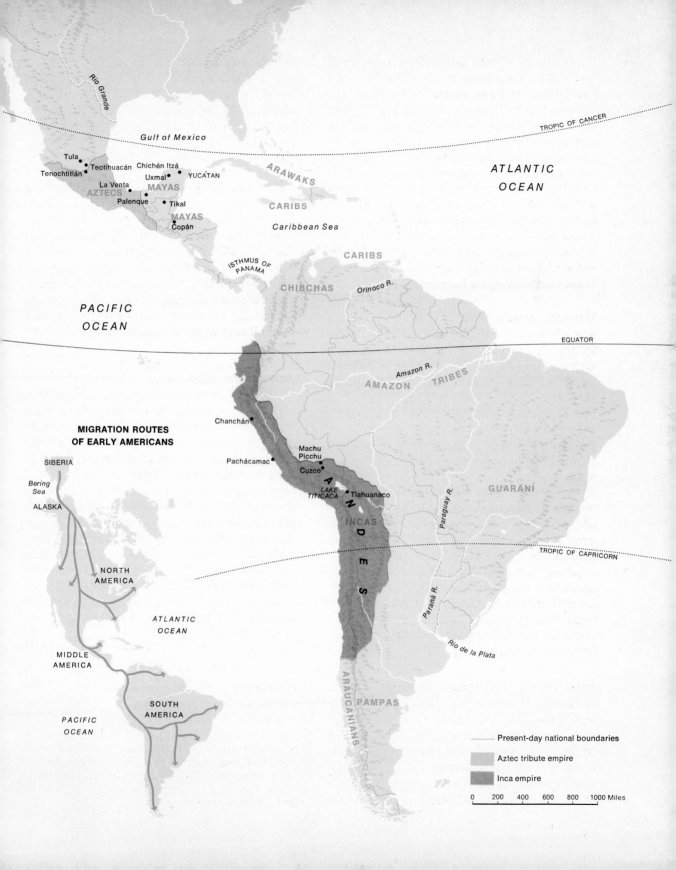

Rio Grande

Gulf of Mexico

TROPIC OF CANCER

ATLANTIC
OCEAN

Tula •
• Teotihuacán   Chichén Itzá
Tenochtitlán •   •
• Uxmal   • YUCATÁN
AZTECS   • La Venta   MAYAS
• Palenque   • Tikal
MAYAS
Copán •

ARAWAKS

CARIBS

Caribbean Sea

PACIFIC
OCEAN

ISTHMUS OF
PANAMA

CARIBS

CHIBCHAS

Orinoco R.

EQUATOR

Amazon R.

AMAZON   TRIBES

Chanchán •

MIGRATION ROUTES
OF EARLY AMERICANS

SIBERIA

Bering
Sea

ALASKA

NORTH
AMERICA

ATLANTIC
OCEAN

MIDDLE
AMERICA

PACIFIC
OCEAN

SOUTH
AMERICA

Pachácamac •

Machu
Picchu •
Cuzco •
LAKE
TITICACA   • Tiahuanaco

A
N
D
E
S

INCAS

GUARANÍ

Paraguay R.

Paraná R.

TROPIC OF CAPRICORN

Río de la Plata

ARAUCANIANS

PAMPAS

Present-day national boundaries

Aztec tribute empire

Inca empire

0   200   400   600   800   1000 Miles

In Aztec society, girls and women were more important than they were in Spain in 1500. Some young women trained to become priestesses who took part in temple ceremonies. Other women ran booths in the markets, oversaw the production and sale of crops, and organized the many tasks of the household. Girls were taught to be "pleasing." The advice of one Aztec mother to her daughter was: "My beloved daughter, . . . take care that your garments are decent and proper; and observe that you do not adorn yourself with much finery, since this is a mark of vanity and folly. When you speak, do not hurry your words from uneasiness, but speak deliberately and calmly." Aztec girls were also raised to be respectful daughters and faithful wives.

Young people were married through arrangements made by their parents, the girls at 16 and the boys at 20. A marriage feast would be held, with many presents and much drinking and dancing. When a child was born, it was given a name at a feast held in its honor. Wedding celebrations and baptismal parties in Mexico today combine Spanish and Aztec traditions.

Religion dominated Aztec life. As in other Middle American cultures, religion was all-important among the Aztecs. One authority has described it in this way: "Aztec religion, in purpose and practice, tried to attract those natural forces which are favorable to human existence and repulse those which are harmful. . . . The moral goals of [Christianity] were largely absent; the Aztec religion had no Saviour of mankind, no heaven or hell to reward or punish . . . human behavior." [5]

There were a great many Aztec gods, but the most important was Tlaloc (*tlah'* loc), the rain god. Since the Valley of Mexico has a long dry season, the arrival of the rainy season was essential for good crops. Like the Toltecs, the Aztecs believed that the rain god de-

manded many human sacrifices before he would permit the precious rain to fall on the dry fields. The war god was almost as important. Without success in war, the Aztecs would have no captives for sacrifice. The importance of the sacrifices and the enormous size of the sacred pyramids show the power the priests held over the people. There were more than 5000 priests in Tenochtitlán alone when the Spaniards came to Mexico.

The priests performed the sacrifices. The human sacrifices were carried out in elaborate ceremonies at the altars on the high pyramids. A captive was led up the steep stairs of the pyramid and thrown across the altar. There a priest cut open his chest with an obsidian knife and tore out the heart. Thousands of people were sacrificed every year. Apparently few resisted. The Aztecs believed the victims would be welcomed as honored guests by the gods to whom they were sacrificed.

But there was more to the Aztec religion than the offering of human sacrifices. Families brought gifts of flowers and food to the priests. Individuals fasted during the time of the sacrifices and prayed to the gods.

Priests also recorded the passage of time. The Aztec priests also kept track of the seasons and the years. Festivals and ceremonies marked the beginning of the different seasons. Watching the movement of the planets, the priests would advise on favorable or unfavorable periods for going on trading journeys, marrying off a daughter, or starting military expeditions.

The Aztec priests had probably learned astronomy indirectly from the Mayas. The Aztecs also counted by twenties rather than by tens. They divided the year into eighteen months of 20 days each, and saved 5 days at the end of every 360 for a period of repentance and then of feasting. A gigantic calendar stone, thirteen feet in diameter and weighing 20 tons, stood on the central pyramid in Tenochtitlán. Intricate picture writing inscribed on the stone told the Aztec history of the world.

[5] G. C. Vaillant, *Aztecs of Mexico* (Baltimore: Penguin Books, 1965), p. 176.

A gruesome illustration from an Aztec codex (below) shows a temple priest ripping the heart out of a war captive. At the foot of the temple lies another sacrificial victim. Right, this stone figure of a seated man suggests the skill of Aztec sculptors. The figure originally held a banner in its right hand, now broken, and probably was stationed at the head of a pyramid stairway.

Aztec history and legends were recorded. The Aztec picture writing had been developed in order to keep records of trade and tribute. Aztec scribes recorded the history of their people on long strips of paper made from the maguey plant and folded like a fan to make a book called a *codex* (*koh'* dex). A few of these *codices* (the plural of codex is pronounced *koh'* dih-seez) are still preserved.

In these Aztec manuscripts is found the story of how Tenochtitlán conquered the other cities of the Valley of Mexico. The Aztec chief in Tenochtitlán ordered the history books of all the other cities destroyed, since "they worshiped the wrong gods and gave credit to the wrong people." Thus the Aztec version became the "official" story. Many of the Aztec legends and poems were also passed from generation to generation by memory.

Aztec lore often told about the legendary figure named Quetzalcoatl in the Nahuatl (nah-*whah'* tl) language of the Aztecs. As we saw

earlier, this was the name of the Toltec chief who had led a band of warriors to Maya country several centuries before the Aztecs gained control of the Valley of Mexico. But Quetzalcoatl was also a god. One legend said that Quetzalcoatl, chieftain or god, promised to return at some future time to the central valley. In the 1500's, when the Spaniards arrived, the Mexican Indians still remembered this legend, and many believed that the Spanish commander must be the returning Quetzalcoatl.

After the Spaniards conquered Mexico, much Aztec lore was recorded in the Spanish language. Most of the story of Quetzalcoatl was written down by an Aztec who was a distant cousin of Moctezuma. This man was baptized a Christian and named Fernando de Alva, but he kept the surname of his grandfather, Ixtlilxochitl (eesh-tleel-*shoh'* cheetl). He translated many of the Aztec codices into Spanish. Ixtlilxochitl also translated many of the poems he knew by heart and some remembered by his great-uncles and other old Aztec people. Thanks to his efforts, much Aztec literature was preserved.

Indian culture is strong in Mexico today. The imprint of Aztec culture remains clearly visible in Mexico today. The Nahuatl language continues to be spoken by many Mexican citizens of Indian descent. Through a large part of the country, arts and crafts, house plans, home life, and market trade follow traditional Indian patterns. People in rural Mexican villages still eat beans and tortillas. Many women make their tortillas with *metates* that resemble tortilla-makers found in some of the oldest Indian ruins.

Not all of the Indians in present-day Mexico are descended from the Aztecs. In the state of Oaxaca in the south of Mexico, rural Indians still speak the Zapotecan language of people who built cities before the Toltecs and later paid tribute to Moctezuma. In the state of Michoacán (mee-choh-ah-*kahn'*), west of Mexico City, many Indians speak Tarascan, another language in which messages of tribute were sent to Moctezuma. Throughout Mexico today, from the Yaquis (*yah'* kees) in the west to the Mayas of Yucatán, many groups of Indians continue to follow traditional ways of life.

THINKING ABOUT THIS SECTION

1. Explain or define the following words: tribute empire; *barrios;* codex.

2. How were the Aztecs able to build an impressive civilization in such a short time?

3. Describe Tenochtitlán at the time of the Spanish conquest. In what ways was it a remarkable city?

4. From what different sources have we learned about Aztec civilization? Explain the value of each kind of source.

5. Report to the class on one of these aspects of Aztec life: religion; landholding; education; city government; arts and crafts; food; literature; engineering; commerce.

6. Explain the importance of Indian cultures in present-day Mexico.

5. The Incas of South America's West Coast

Remains of early civilizations have been found in Peru. In an oasis on the dry Pacific coast of Peru lie the adobe ruins of an ancient city with the name of Chanchán (chahn-*chahn'*). This city was built by a people called the Chimú (chee-*moo'*). Hundreds of years ago the Chimú developed an advanced culture and ruled a large nation. Aerial surveys show that Chanchán was an extensive city. Perhaps 50,000 people lived there. It must also have been a beautiful city, with lagoons, canals, green parks, and fine temples. Farmers grew food on a thousand square miles of corn land, irrigated from swift-flowing rivers.

In graves in this part of Peru, archeologists have found pitchers and bowls buried to assure the dead of food in the afterlife. Some of these clay objects are among the most remarkable pottery found in America, for they actually portray the dead individuals. Thousands of these portrait jugs have been unearthed on the Peruvian coast. Other graves in this area contain mummies wrapped in many yards of beautifully woven cotton or wool cloth. The dry coastal climate has preserved the mummies and their handsome robes for hundreds of years.

A few miles south of the modern city of Lima, Peru, there was once a city called Pachácamac (pah-*chah'* kah-mahk). Here was a large temple dedicated to the worship of the sun as a supreme god. Up in the high Andes, near the southeastern shore of Lake Titicaca (teetee-*kah'* kah), lie the ruins of another ancient city. Its floors and plazas are paved with large blocks of smooth stone. Mighty gateways once led to great temples or palaces. Bolivian Indians who live near this ruin today call the place Tiahuanaco (tyah-wah-*nah'* koh).

Inca history was handed down by memory. What became of the people who lived at Chanchán and Pachácamac and Tiahuanaco? They were conquered and absorbed into the empire of the powerful Incas. Like the Aztecs, the Incas were latecomers who learned from the cultures of other peoples. We know very little about the history of the early Peruvians. The Incas had no written language, not even a system of picture writing, such as the Mayas and Aztecs used. Inca history and legends were learned by heart, however, and passed down from generation to generation in the form of poetry.

From the accounts of Inca people who remembered this poetry and wrote it down in Spanish after the conquest, historians learned something of the background of the Inca civilization. But these accounts are often confusing and contradictory. A few Spaniards also recorded what they saw of Inca life and what they heard of the history of the people.

One of the most famous books about the Incas was written by a descendant of Indian nobility. Garcilaso de la Vega (gar-see-*lah'* soh day lah *vay'* gah) was the son of a Spanish captain and an Inca princess. From his mother's brothers, cousins of the last Inca ruler, Garcilaso learned Inca legends and history. His father had him educated in the Spanish language, and later Garcilaso went to Spain and became a military officer. When he was an old man, Garcilaso retired to a monastery and wrote down the stories of his mother's people as he remembered them.

According to the legends recorded by Garcilaso, the first Inca rulers were said to have been a brother and sister, who were created by the sun on an island in Lake Titicaca. This would suggest that the Incas borrowed from the people at Tiahuanaco. The Incas worshiped the sun, perhaps because they lived in a cold

This clay pot was molded into a realistic likeness of a one-eyed man by a craftsman of the Mochicas, a people who lived and ruled in northern Peru centuries before the Incas rose to power. Thousands of similar vases and jugs, all showing different individuals, have left a vivid record of Mochica life.

climate at high altitude and needed many days of sunshine for their crops. The Incas believed the sun god sent the first Inca rulers to the fertile highland valley of Cuzco (*koos'* koh), more than a hundred miles north of Lake Titicaca.

The Incas conquered other peoples. Historians think that Cuzco, the Inca capital city, was actually founded about 1200 A.D. For the next two centuries Inca territory remained fairly small. But in 1438 a ruler named Pachacuti (pah-chah-*koo'* tee) came to power. Sending out armies to conquer neighboring peoples, Pachacuti greatly expanded the Inca empire. By about 1470 the Inca empire was perhaps as large as modern Peru. Pachacuti's armies occupied the city and temple of Pachácamac and made it an Inca holy place. His son went north and conquered the Chimú kingdom, then followed mountain trails into Ecuador and conquered the Quitu (*kee' too*) people living near present-day Quito.

Inca rule was centralized. The Inca empire was remarkably unified, much more so than the Aztec tribute empire. The ruler, or Inca,[6] held supreme power. When the empire was at its height, the Inca's rule extended from the Pacific coast to the upper Amazon tributaries and from the present border of Ecuador and Colombia to northern Argentina and central Chile.

The system of government was fairly complicated. Once the Inca armies had conquered a people, Cuzco colonists were settled among them. The subjugated peoples soon learned to speak Quechua (*kay' choo-ah*), the language of Cuzco. All land belonged to the Inca emperor, but for purposes of farming it was divided equally among former enemies and Inca settlers. All were to work as tenants of the government. There were many officials of different ranks to see that each individual performed his duty to the state. People unable to work were cared for by the government.

Such a government, based on an all-powerful king and a people who willingly worked for him, provided a thorough-going "social security." No one starved in his old age; no teenager looked for a job. Of course, no one had much individual freedom either. Some historians think dependence on the government made the Inca people too passive, too willing to submit to authority. They were very easily conquered by the Spaniards.

Agriculture was the major activity. Agriculture was organized by the government to provide food for all. Every bit of hillside land was terraced and irrigated by mountain streams. (*Terraces* are small plots of earth on mountain slopes; the plots are lined with low stone walls to keep the earth in place.) Peruvian Indian

---

[6] The word *Inca* can apply either to the people themselves ("the Incas") or to the ruler ("the Inca").

Peruvian Potatoes

Like other American Indians, the people of pre-Columbian Peru ate corn, but their staple food was the white potato. The Indians would leave their small, gnarly potatoes out to freeze in the cold Andes nights. The potatoes were then thawed, smashed to a pulp, dried in sheets, and eaten like bread.

In the 1500's Spaniards who came to America took this valuable plant back to the homeland, and it soon was cultivated in other European countries. In Ireland the potato became the major food. Because Irish settlers introduced the potato into England's North American colonies, it became known there as the "Irish potato." Today in Peru and Bolivia descendants of the Incas still eat bread-like sheets of potatoes that have been frozen, thawed, and dried.

farmers still tend plots of land protected by Inca terrace walls.

Though all land was owned by the emperor, its allocation was controlled by the *ayllu* (*eye-lyoo'*) or local clan. State lands, however, were cultivated by the entire community, and harvested crops went into government storehouses. Government agents distributed food as it was needed to nonproducing citizens.

The Inca farmers used llamas as beasts of burden. These were the only large animals trained to work for the Indians anywhere in the New World. The guinea pig was also domesticated in the Andes and was raised by the hundreds of thousands for food. Wild duck was another source of meat. Corn from the coast and potatoes from the Andes were introduced throughout the empire. Peanuts were another major food crop. Fishing and the gathering of shellfish were important along the coast.

All people were expected to provide some service for the state. Each household in the Inca empire was required to contribute a certain amount of public work. This duty was known as the *mita* (*mee' tah*). Some men tended irrigation systems. Other men worked on the paved roads that connected all parts of the empire, even in the high Andes. One early Spanish traveler said of these highways: "Some of them extended over 1100 leagues along such dizzy and frightful abysses that, looking down, the sight failed. . . . The ascents were so steep and high that steps had to be cut from below to enable the ascent to be made." Suspension bridges carried the roads across such chasms. Swift runners followed the roads, rushing messages to the Inca's agents in remote corners of the empire.

Inca skills were highly developed. Workers who had special skills were excused from heavy labor. Weavers, for example, made clothing for the emperor and the nobility. Using cotton and the silky wool of a kind of llama called the *vicuña* (vih-*koon'* yuh), they wove many varieties of fine textiles. Some craftsmen made pottery, producing Chimú designs in thousands of copies. The stonework of Inca builders still amazes modern visitors to Peruvian ruins. Huge polished stones were fitted tightly together to make imposing structures. Other workers mined and smelted gold, silver, and copper. These metals went into decorations for the temples and were also used in jewelry worn by noblemen and priests. Certain towns that produced a particular item, like logs for temple fires, were free from the *mita*. Members of the Inca's court, including dancers and litter-bearers, were also excused from public duty. So too were professional soldiers.

Surgery was still another skill in which some Incas were specially trained. The Inca surgeons set broken bones, treated wounds, amputated limbs when necessary, and even did brain operations. Coca (from which the drug cocaine is made) was probably given to the patients as an anesthetic.

Education was provided by the state. There were no formal schools in Inca Peru. But young men of the noble class received training in warfare and instruction in religion. Other young men studied special skills, for example, the engineering techniques involved in building bridges and roads. Boys learned how to keep numerical accounts by making knotted cords called *quipus* (*kee'* pooz). These were used in sending reports about crops and herds of llamas. The Incas were a very practical people. One of their sayings was: "He who tries to count the stars and does not know how to count the marks and knots of the *quipus* ought to be held in derision."

Most girls had little schooling, but a few were selected for special training in religion, weaving, and cooking. Some of these "Chosen Women" became wives of nobles. Others were assigned to temples and had a role somewhat like that of nuns in a religious order.

The Incas had many gods. According to Inca religion, the emperor was descended from the sun. Inca priests are said to have lighted the holy fires at festival time by focusing the sun's light on a gold cup and producing a spark on a pile of dry straw. The Incas also prayed to gods of the moon, thunder, the earth, and the sea. Their prayers were similar to those of many other peoples in appealing for abundant harvests and good health. Other prayers were more formal and followed a traditional pattern of words.

The Inca people believed in confession of sin and in life after death. To a priest in his own *ayllu,* an Inca confessed sinful acts. The Inca religion provided for happy festival days at planting and harvest times and at weddings. At mass ceremonies all engaged couples were declared married in the name of the emperor. Then came individual ceremonies followed by days of merrymaking.

Inca religion was less bloodthirsty than that of the Aztecs. Human life was sacrificed only at times of great emergency (such as the illness of the emperor, or a plague, or a military defeat) or when a new emperor was installed. When a human sacrifice was carried out, the individual was usually a child, sometimes one of the candidates for the Chosen Women.

Inca structures still stand. When the Spaniards conquered the Inca city of Cuzco, they did not destroy it. The fine stone foundations of Inca buildings were used by the Spaniards as floors for the houses they built. A temple to the sun god became a Christian church and is still used today. The Inca house where Garcilaso de la Vega was born is now a modern museum. In the hills just above Cuzco is a mighty fortress built of fitted stones. Many stones from it were used in building Cuzco, both by the Incas and by the Spaniards. But the ruins are still an impressive sight.

The last Inca emperor was a young man set up by the Spaniards as a puppet ruler after they had killed the reigning monarch (page 81). This Inca and some of his followers managed to escape. In forbidding highlands near the Amazon headwaters, they occupied an early Inca fortress. Several thousand Indians lived in this region, free from Spanish domination. Eventually the fortress was abandoned. In 1911 an expedition went to search for this last Inca base. A hundred miles to the east of Cuzco, above the steep green canyon of the Urubamba River, the searchers found a spectacular ruin.

Below, a gigantic wall at the Inca fortress of Sacsahuamán shows the precise work of Inca masons. Huge stones, some nearly 20 feet high, were fitted tightly together without mortar, and have remained in place over the centuries. The Sacsahuamán fortress was built to protect the city of Cuzco. Left, silver figurines fashioned by Inca metalworkers included an alpaca, prized for its long wool, and a llama.

It was the Inca fortress, today called Machu Picchu (*mah′* choo *peek′* choo) for the mountain which towers over it.

Descendants of the Incas survive today. What of the descendants of the Incas? In the highlands of Peru, Ecuador, and Bolivia today live poor farmers and villagers who are of almost pure Indian descent. They speak the Quechua language or dialects of it. Some of them work in Bolivian silver and tin mines or copper mines in Peru. Only in recent years have the governments of these countries become concerned for the welfare of their Indian populations. It was in the 1940's that a Peruvian archeologist of Inca blood, Dr. Julio Tello (*tay′* yoh), began to interest his government in the study of the remains of the Inca civilization. Now ⸴ the government at Lima encourages tourists to visit Cuzco and Machu Picchu.

THINKING ABOUT THIS SECTION

1. Explain or define the following words: *ayllu; mita; quipu;* Quechua; terrace.
2. Describe some remains of pre-Inca civilizations still to be found in or near Peru.
3. What are our sources of information about the Incas? Explain and evaluate each.
4. Report on any of these aspects of Inca civilization: extent of the empire and how it was governed; public work and "social security"; roads and communications; domesticated animals and crops; arts and crafts; education; religion; architecture.
5. Compare the Aztec and Inca civilizations. Bring out similarities and differences.

6. Other South American Indian Peoples

The Araucanians of Chile. Inca influence reached far to the north and south of Peru. South of Lake Titicaca, in northern Chile, desert land extends for hundreds of miles. But knowledge of how to grow corn and how to use the llama spread across this desert to the central valley of Chile. There these ideas were adopted by a people called the Araucanians (ah-rau-*kahn′* yunz). When the Spaniards came to Chile after the conquest of Peru, the Araucanians fought them much more bravely than the Incas had. Today some 200,000 surviving Araucanians live on a reservation in the south of Chile. They consider themselves a "nation" and send their own representatives to the Chilean congress.

The Chibcha of Colombia. To the north of Quito, in what is today Colombia, lived peoples called the Chibcha (*cheeb′* chah). Though they did not build large stone cities, they had learned from the Andes Indians how to weave elaborate cotton textiles. They also mined gold and emeralds. The gold they used to decorate their houses. With the emeralds they made necklaces and even toys for their children. A king of the Chibcha people named Bogotá welcomed the Spaniards who came to his fertile valley in search of gold.

The Pampa of Argentina. On the plains of Argentina lived skin-clad nomadic Indians who called themselves the Pampa (*pahm′* pah). They caught wild llamas called *guanacos* (gwah-*nah′* kohz) with *bolas,* lassos weighted with stones. Apparently some Pampa Indians traded with peoples in the Andes, perhaps exchanging guanaco hides for silver ornaments. At any rate, the first Spaniards to reach this region found the Pampa wearing silver earrings.

Assuming that these Indians had mined the silver themselves, the Spaniards gave the Spanish name for silver, *plata* (*plah'* tah), to the whole region. Eventually this area was to be called Argentina, from the Latin word for silver, *argentum*. Actually, the Pampa Indians did not know how to mine or work any kind of metal.

The Guaraní of Paraguay. In Paraguay lived a people called the Guaraní (gwah-rah-*nee'*). These Indians planted corn and beans and built villages of thatched huts. Spanish missionaries who converted them learned the Guaraní language and developed a way of writing it. Today most of the people of Paraguay can still speak Guaraní, and it is taught as a required course in the schools of Paraguay. Of course, many Paraguayans also speak Spanish.

The Indians of Brazil and the Amazon basin. Guaraní was also the language of millions of Indians who roamed Brazil. These Indians lived on roots, small game, and fish. They peacefully welcomed the Portuguese explorers who came to Brazil. European efforts to enslave the nomadic Indians were unsuccessful. Unable to endure the hard work on the sugar plantations, many of these Indians died. Others ran away to the interior where few white men dared to go.

Today thousands of Indians live in the upper Amazon regions. Some of them, like the Jívaros (*hee'* vah-rohs) in eastern Ecuador, were said to be headhunters until recent times. Many of the Amazon Indians have probably never seen a white man. Others come to river ports on the Amazon tributaries to sell snake skins and blue butterfly wings for the tourist trade. For a century and a half the Brazilian government drove the Indians farther and farther into the interior and stole their lands. Only recently has the Brazilian government taken an interest in the welfare of the primitive Indians living in the backlands.

The European conquest of South America made little difference to the spear-carrying Ongwa Indians of the hot rain forests of southeastern Venezuela.

1. Explain or define the following words: *bola; guanaco.*

2. Who were the Araucanians and the Chibcha? Where did each live, and what had they learned from other Indian peoples?

3. Where did the Pampa live? What was the basis for trade between them and the Andes Indians?

4. Where did the Guaraní live? How did Guaraní become a written language?

5. Describe the changing relations over the centuries between Indians and whites in Brazil. Explain why there have been changes.

Summing Up

The first people to live in the New World were the ancestors of the American Indians. Most authorities believe that over a period of many centuries these migrants crossed the Bering Strait from Asia. The early Indians lived by hunting and seed-gathering. Probably they knew nothing of planting, weaving, or pottery-making. Searching for food, they fanned out through North America and moved southward through Central America into South America.

Perhaps the first Indians to plant corn and settle in villages lived in the Valley of Mexico. The idea of planting and harvesting grain made possible higher standards of living. In the Yucatán peninsula and northern Central America, the ancient Mayas built stone temple centers and achieved a high level of civilization.

Probably people living on the site of Mexico City were draining the marshy lakes and building stone temples there at about the same time. On the coast of Peru ancient Chimú people had begun to build at Chanchán.

Of all the Indian civilizations the Maya was the most advanced in terms of scientific and artistic achievements. But around 800 A.D., for unknown reasons, the Mayas abandoned their great stone cities. Some 300 years later the Maya people of Yucatán were conquered by invading Toltec warriors from the Valley of Mexico. These conquerors brought with them a religion that required human sacrifice. The need for captives to be sacrificed to the gods led to endless wars among the cities of Yucatán. By 1400 A.D. Maya civilization had decayed.

Meanwhile, wandering Aztec Indians had settled in the Valley of Mexico. They quickly learned from the Toltec peoples how to drain the lake area. As they adjusted to city life, they began to build imposing pyramids. While the Aztecs established a loose empire of peoples who paid tribute, the Incas of Peru conquered other civilized Indians in western South America and built up a tightly organized empire. The Mayas, Aztecs, and Incas all developed impressive civilizations. Especially notable were their accomplishments in astronomy and mathematics, engineering and architecture, crafts and fine arts, large-scale agriculture, and government.

Indian culture remains strong in many parts of Latin America today. Indian languages are still spoken, Indian customs survive, Indian crafts are practiced, and Indian history is taught with pride.

Indian faces and Christian images symbolize the blending of two cultures in a Guatemalan village.

2

The Makers of Latin America: The Europeans

CHAPTER FOCUS

1. The Historic Background of the Iberian People
2. Spain's Rise to Power
3. Portugal as an Exploring Nation
4. Contact Between Europe and America

Many Spanish American towns have names that combine Spanish and Indian words—like Santa Rosa de Copán in Honduras, or Santa Elena Quiché in Guatemala. The Spanish part of the name comes from a Catholic saint's day. Most of the residents may have more Indian than European ancestry, but their first names will probably be Spanish—Diego or Pablo, María or Lucita. And their last names will perhaps recall a region of Spain, a Spanish town, or the family name of a Spanish soldier who came with the conquerors. Those people who can read and write do so in Spanish.

When the town was founded, unless it was first an Indian village, it was laid out in squares similar to those of communities in Spain. The mayor is called an *alcalde* (ahl-*kahl′* day). He may have much the same powers and responsibilities as did the chief official of a town in medieval Spain. The biggest building in town is likely to be the church. It was probably built in Spanish colonial times and was modeled after a church in Seville, Córdoba, or some other city in Spain. In front of the church lies the *plaza* or central square. The houses around the plaza are built in the old Moorish style, with rooms opening through arches onto a central patio with a fountain in the center. The dwellings of the more prosperous citizens have roofs of terra cotta tiles made in the Spanish fashion.

On the saint's day associated with the name of the town, the people hold a religious festival. There may be a parade of colorful floats, much like those Christopher Columbus saw in Seville when he returned to Spain from the New World during Easter week in 1493. At dances the people dress up like the Muslim and Christian soldiers who fought each other in medieval Spain.

Outside the town, cows, sheep, and goats graze in pastures. They may be descendants of animals brought by the early Spanish settlers. Spanish explorers rode horses when they first penetrated the interior of America. Later, burros were introduced to carry loads, and teams of oxen were brought to plow the fields that Indians had worked with digging sticks. Around the little farmhouses outside the town are olive trees, grapevines, and orange trees. All of these originated in Spain. And the young man herding the goats may be playing a Spanish folk tune on a Spanish guitar.

Thus the Europeans who settled in Latin America brought with them not only their languages but also customs and practices. Even in the smallest towns, Spanish or Portuguese ways of life are mixed with those of the Mayas, the Aztecs, the Incas, or other American Indian peoples. To understand Latin America today, one must first know something about Spain and Portugal.

1. The Historic Background of the Iberian People

Spain and Portugal together are sometimes called *Iberia* (eye-*beer'* ee-uh). Side by side these two countries occupy the Iberian peninsula in southwestern Europe. This peninsula is less than half as large as Peru. In fact, the only South American countries that are smaller than Iberia are Ecuador, Uruguay, and Paraguay. But from that small part of Europe came the explorers and settlers who spread Iberian civilization across much of the Western Hemisphere.

Geography has handicapped the Iberian people. Nature has not been kind to the people of Iberia. Much of the soil in Spain and Portugal is dry or rocky and not very fertile. Rainfall may be either too heavy or too scanty. For centuries Iberian farmers have scratched out only a meager living from the land. Moreover, geo-

graphical features have tended to separate the people of different parts of Iberia from each other. The larger rivers are navigable only for a short way inland, and mountain barriers have discouraged travel. These handicaps of nature somewhat prepared the people of Spain and Portugal for dealing with similar geographical problems that they were to find in America.

The Iberian peninsula has been a crossroads. Just a short distance south of Spain lies North Africa. The body of water that divides Iberia and Africa is called the Strait of Gibraltar. This water passage narrows from about 23 miles to only 8 miles where the two land masses come closest. It is through the Strait of Gibraltar that ships pass from the Mediterranean into the Atlantic. Over the centuries many people from

Spanish and Portuguese in Latin America

There are some important differences between the Spanish spoken in Latin America and the language spoken in Spain. The former is called South American Spanish, and the latter Castilian Spanish. In South American Spanish, *c* or *z* is pronounced like *ss;* and *ll* is pronounced like *l* followed by the consonant *y.* In Castilian Spanish, *c* or *z* is pronounced *th;* the double *l* is pronounced *y.* Therefore, the pronoun *ella,* meaning "she," is pronounced *ay'* lyah in Latin America but *ay'* yah in Spain.

Portuguese, a first cousin of Spanish, is spoken in Brazil. It is much like the Portuguese heard in Portugal except for certain differences in sound and the addition of many words from Indian, African, and several European languages. Portuguese has nasal sounds similar to those in French. For instance, the *m* in *Belém* is pronounced with a nasal sound, something like *ng. São* (meaning "saint") sounds like *sow* with a nasal tone at the end. Some words having the same meaning are spelled differently in Portuguese and Spanish. The Spanish *n,* as in *señor* (sayn-*yor'),* becomes *nh* in the Portuguese *senhor;* and the Spanish *z,* as in *mestizo* (mee-*tee'* soh), becomes *ç* in the Portuguese *mestiço.*

North Africa and other Mediterranean lands have come to Spain on ships making this passage. People from northern Europe also invaded and overran Iberia at different times in history. As a result, the Iberians became a people of mixed descent. Among their forebears were Celts, Phoenicians, Greeks, Romans, and Germanic people called the Visigoths.

The latter people overran the Iberian peninsula at a time when the Roman Empire had decayed and could no longer protect outposts in various parts of western Europe. The Visigoths captured the Roman towns in Iberia, and their chieftains carved out small kingdoms for themselves. In time, these conquerors mixed with the earlier settlers and became converted to Christianity.

The Spanish and Portuguese languages developed. When Iberia had been a part of the Roman Empire, Roman soldiers and officials had brought the Latin language to this part of Europe. But with the collapse of the empire and the coming of the Visigoths, the language spoken in Iberia changed. The same thing happened in other parts of western Europe. In time, the languages spoken in what are now Spain and Portugal became different from those of France and Italy. By about 700 A.D. distinct dialects existed in Spain: Andalusian, Castilian, and Catalan. In the western part of the peninsula, the Portuguese developed their own language. Only Catholic churchmen still read, wrote, and spoke Latin.

Muslim influence came to Spain and Portugal. Far from Iberia, at the eastern end of the Mediterranean, a new religion was born in the 600's A.D. This religion was to become a powerful influence in Iberian history. Founded in Arabia by a prophet named Mohammed, the new faith was called Islam (*iz'* lahm). Mohammed preached the idea of one God and a moral code much like those of Judaism and Christianity. Followers of Islam were called Muslims. The Muslims in Arabia began wars of conquest which swept eastward into Asia and westward across North Africa. In 711 A.D., North African Muslims called Moors crossed the Strait of Gibraltar and invaded Europe. The Moors not only conquered Iberia but even for a time surged across the Pyrenees Mountains into France. In 732, they were driven back south of the Pyrenees.

Moorish culture flourished in Spain. In the southern two-thirds of Spain, the Moors built a powerful nation. By 800 A.D., the beautiful city of Córdoba was the Moorish capital city, under a ruler called a caliph. The Moors introduced cultural advances and an interest in science and scholarship. Universities were established at Córdoba, Seville, and Toledo. Learned professors taught algebra, astronomy, physics, and chemistry. Classes were conducted in the Arabic language, but lectures and writings were translated into Latin for Christian scholars who came there to study. The Moorish style of architecture was also introduced. As a result, curved arches, tiled roofs, and central enclosed patios became characteristic of Spanish buildings. Beautiful palaces were built in Seville (the Alcazar) and in Granada (the Alhambra).

Moorish farmers in Spain developed methods of irrigation which, centuries later, were combined with Indian practices to irrigate dry land in the New World. The Moors in Seville also cultivated and improved varieties of olives, figs, grapes, and oranges. Sugar cane, rice, and cotton were introduced, and fine textiles were woven from the cotton.

Muslim rule in Spain was tolerant of other religions. The Moors allowed Christians and Jews to practice their own religions, live where they pleased, own land, and carry on businesses. They were expected only to pay somewhat higher taxes than members of the Muslim faith. Jewish merchants advised the caliphs on finance, and Jewish professors taught at the universities. In Christian Europe at the time, Jews were cruelly persecuted.

Curved arches, lacy openwork, and colorful geometric designs make the Alcazar in Seville an outstanding example of Moorish influence in Spain.

THINKING ABOUT THIS SECTION

1. Explain or define the following words: Iberia; navigable river; dialect; caliph.
2. How did each of these peoples affect Iberian culture: Romans, Visigoths, Moors?
3. How were Christians and Jews treated in Moorish Spain?

2. Spain's Rise to Power

Christian kingdoms regained control of Spain from the Moors. Meanwhile, Christian kings ruled the small kingdoms of León, Castile, Navarre, and Aragon in the northern part of the peninsula. Through the centuries the people in these mountainous regions had continued to fight the Moors along their southern borders. Near the close of the eleventh century, Christians in the rest of western Europe began a series of wars called the Crusades, to recover the Holy Land (Palestine) from Muslim rule. But the Spanish Christian kingdoms never sent men to fight in these Crusades. Instead, they launched their own crusade against the Moors in the Iberian peninsula. By this time the caliph of Córdoba no longer ruled a united southern Spain. Disunity among the Moors helped the Spanish Christians to succeed in their crusade. In 1236 the king of Castile captured the Muslim capital of Córdoba. By 1250 the kingdom of Granada in the south had become the last Moorish stronghold in Spain.

Hidalgos became a proud upper class. Five hundred years of war against the Moors created a military class in Spain that was proud, haughty, and intolerant. The military man was held in high esteem in Christian Spain, while farming was scorned as a way of life fit only for "infidels" (that is, the Moors). Proud that they and their forebears fought for their religion, the Christian soldiers called themselves *hijos de algo,* "sons of somebody" in Spanish. This term came to be the Spanish word *hidalgo* (ee-*dahl'* goh), meaning a member of the lower nobility and a landowner.

The outlook of the *hidalgos* helps to explain much of what later happened when the Spanish came to the Americas. The *hidalgos* thought themselves too good to work with their hands. "I did not come to the New World to farm the soil like a peasant" declared the Spanish captain who conquered Mexico. All of the Spanish explorers in America looked for large Indian populations that could be subdued and forced to work for their new masters. Nor would *hidalgos* go into trade and become merchants as Jews had in the Moorish towns of Iberia. Because of this prejudice against work and trade, Latin America was to suffer for lack of skilled craftsmen and merchants throughout the colonial period.

The ancestors of the *hidalgos* had held small estates in the Christian kingdoms of northern Spain. As Moorish lands were conquered, the *hidalgos* acquired larger estates. Their lands were worked by peasants, as in the rest of Europe. This system of landownership, under which a few wealthy landholders controlled huge estates, was eventually introduced into the New World by the Spaniards. It was easily substituted for the Aztec and Inca pattern of clan ownership. Even today much of the land in Central and South America is owned by a few wealthy families and farmed by large numbers of poor tenants who are chiefly of Indian ancestry.

Isabella and Ferdinand united Castile and Aragon. Castile became the largest and most important Christian kingdom of the Iberian peninsula. In 1469 the heir to the throne of Castile was a handsome auburn-haired eighteen-year-old princess named Isabella. The king, her older brother, planned to have Isabella marry a king in northern Europe. But she had other ideas. Isabella sent a secret message offering her hand to the heir to the throne of Aragon. This prince was a young man named Ferdinand whom Isabella had never seen. Since Aragon was the second most powerful Christian kingdom in Spain, the Castilian princess recognized the importance of such a marriage. The young people met secretly and were married in a border town. Five years later, Isabella became queen of Castile and Ferdinand soon succeeded to the throne of Aragon.

Isabella wanted to unify Spain. Isabella was a devout Catholic. It was her mission, she firmly believed, to unify Spain and drive out the Moors and the Jews. With Ferdinand, she organized an all-out campaign against the Moors who still held Granada. In 1492 this last Moorish stronghold fell to Spanish forces. Now the two Spanish monarchs controlled all the peninsula except for Portugal and tiny Navarre.

Isabella launched several programs designed to unify the Spanish domain. She brought the great landlords under direct royal control, and limited the self-government that the larger towns had enjoyed. Royal law and government became supreme in all Spain. This concentration of royal power was to make possible the extension of Spanish government and culture into the New World.

Isabella also controlled religion. In Isabella's mind patriotism and the Catholic religion were one and the same thing. If the nation were to be unified, all Spaniards had to be "pure, true Catholics." Isabella set up a religious court called the Inquisition. Its purpose was to determine what was "pure and true" religion and to punish heretics, those who did not live up to the Inquisition's standards of purity and truth. In the course of their investigations, agents of the Inquisition tortured and put to death many people. Religious zeal was another Spanish trait that was greatly to affect the history of the New World after the conquest. But it is important to remember that punishment for religious belief was common throughout Europe at the time.

Following the defeat of Granada, Muslims and Jews in Spain were given the choice of becoming Christians or leaving the country. Many Muslims fled to Morocco, but a number of Moorish craftsmen and farm workers chose to stay in Spain. Most of the Jews chose to leave. They founded a number of Spanish-speaking Jewish communities in the eastern Mediterranean. The few Jews who stayed in Spain and became Christians were often hounded by the suspicious agents of the Inquisition.

Charles I inherited the throne of Spain. Before Isabella's death in 1504, both her son and oldest daughter had died. Only a daughter called Juana la Loca, or "Joanna the Mad," lived to be her heir. Juana's husband was heir to the throne of Austria. Their son, Isabella's grandson, was destined to be the most powerful ruler in all Europe. In 1516 he became King Charles I of Spain, and three years later he was crowned Emperor Charles V of the Holy Roman Empire. At the age of nineteen Charles ruled not only Spain and Austria but also the Netherlands, a large part of Italy, and several European duchies, as well as a huge domain claimed by Spanish conquerors in America.

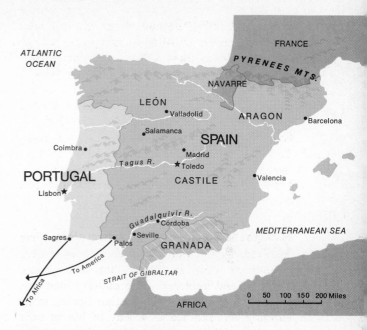

Spain and Portugal in 1492

In 1492 Queen Isabella conquered the Moorish kingdom of Granada and made it part of Spain.

Spanish culture reached its height during the Golden Age. The reigns of Charles I and his son Philip II (1556–1598) are called the Golden Age of Spain. During this period Spain was a great nation with powerful armies. In eastern Europe, Spanish armies fought and won battles against the Turks. From the new colonies in America shiploads of precious metals enriched the Spanish treasury. By this time the Caribbean Sea was a Spanish lake.

Spain's Golden Age was also a time of growing interest in learning. Queen Isabella had encouraged universities in the cities of Valencia, Valladolid, Seville, and Salamanca. At these universities young men prepared for careers in law and colonial administration.

Spanish literature and art flowered as never before. The outstanding book of the Golden Age was *Don Quixote* by Miguel de Cervantes (sehr-*vahn'* tayss). This great comic novel has remained popular throughout the ages and is still studied in Spanish and Latin American

The great artist Velázquez captured the self-assurance of a Spanish hidalgo in this painting of his part-African assistant, Juan de Pareja.

Spanish culture was to contribute to Latin America. Over the years the Spanish language, enriched with Indian words, became the language of half the New World. Latin America's Spanish heritage is also evident in such things as ways of government, laws, religion, the land-holding system, city life, and education. In agriculture, too, Spanish ways were transferred to the Americas as new crops like wheat, sugar cane, and cotton were introduced. And Spanish influences are strong in Latin American art, architecture, and music. Still other legacies were such character traits as the pride of the *hidalgos*. In all these ways the Spanish heritage came to Latin America.

THINKING ABOUT THIS SECTION

1. Explain or define the following words: Crusades; Inquisition; Golden Age of Spain.

2. How did centuries of warfare create the *hidalgo* class in Spain? What were its characteristics? What was the role of this class in the New World?

3. What plans did Isabella and Ferdinand have for Spain? To what extent were their plans achieved?

4. If you were to visit a Latin American country, what things that you might see, hear, read, or taste would reflect the Spanish heritage? The Indian heritage?

schools. Such artists as El Greco and Murillo (moo-*reel'* yoh) painted beautiful madonnas and angels for Spanish churches. Portraits of the royal family painted by Velázquez (vay-*lahss'* kayss) are among the great art treasures of Spain.

What did Spain give to the New World? This brief account suggests the main ways in which

3. Portugal as an Exploring Nation

Portuguese heritage, too, became solidly rooted in the New World. Though Portugal is the smaller of the two Iberian nations, it created the largest of the Latin American countries—Brazil.

Portugal became an independent kingdom in the 1100's. Like Spain, Portugal had fallen to Moorish conquerors. When Portugal threw off Moorish rule, it became part of the Christian kingdom of León. Then in the 1100's the Portuguese people won their independence. During the early 1400's, João I (zhoh-*ow'*) ruled Portugal. He drove the Muslims from the southern part of the country and built up his capital city at Lisbon.

The seafaring tradition was strong in Portugal. The city of Lisbon has one of the best ports on the Atlantic coast of Europe. Moreover, the

Today as in past centuries fishing boats are a common sight along the scenic coast of Portugal.

waters off the Portuguese coast are rich in fish. It was natural that people living along this coast should turn to the sea for their living. Much earlier than some other European peoples, Portuguese seamen ventured far from their home shores.

Henry the Navigator encouraged exploration. One of King João's younger sons had a keen interest in sailing and exploration. About 1420, Prince Henry the Navigator, as he is known today, founded a school of navigation at Sagres (*sah' gresh*) on the Portuguese coast. To this center came navigators, astronomers, map-makers, and ship captains. Prince Henry then began to send out his captains on a series of voyages to explore the Atlantic coast of Africa. As the captains returned from their voyages, the map-makers at Sagres drew accurate maps of their travels. The Portuguese navigators improved the compass and developed better methods of measuring distance by sighting the stars. Shipbuilders designed stronger and larger vessels, capable of making ever-longer voyages.

Prince Henry probably had several motives for taking an interest in exploration. One was certainly curiosity about lands that Europeans knew very little about. Religious zeal was another motive. The Portuguese had heard about a mysterious Christian ruler called Prester John. No one knew where his kingdom was located, but the Portuguese hoped they might find him in Africa. Since he was supposed to be extremely wealthy, they thought he would be a valuable ally in the Christian fight against Muslim power. During their search for Prester John, the Portuguese also intended to spread the Christian faith to any "heathen" peoples they might find.

But an interest in trade also drew the Portuguese farther and farther south along the African coast. This motive became even stronger as they reached parts of Africa where trade in gold, ivory, and slaves yielded increasing profits.

The Portuguese sailed around Africa to India. By the time of Prince Henry's death in 1460, Portuguese captains had reached the western bulge of Africa just north of the equator. Within a few years they crossed the equator and continued to venture farther south. Then, in 1488 the explorer Bartholomew Dias (*dee' ahss*) reached the southern tip of Africa, the Cape of Good Hope (map, page 52). Ten years later Vasco da Gama sailed around Africa and on to India. Returning to Lisbon with precious silks and spices, he made a huge profit on this voyage.

The Portuguese never found Prester John, but by the late 1400's finding a sea route to India was of much greater importance to them. Six years before da Gama's voyage, Columbus had sailed westward on an expedition sponsored by the Spanish rulers. Columbus claimed to have found islands somewhere off the coast of Asia. But da Gama's trip was hailed as a far greater accomplishment. The Portuguese now had a sure way to India itself.

Portugal entered an age of prosperity. Thus began a golden age for little Portugal. Vast wealth in jewels, silks, ivory, pepper, cinnamon, and cloves—all of them in great demand in Europe—came to Portugal from trade with the East. Lisbon became one of the richest cities of Europe. The University of Coimbra (*kweem'* bruh) was as famous for learning as the University of Salamanca in Spain. The Portuguese poet Luiz Vaz de Camões (kuh-*moinsh'*) told of the wonders of the East Indies in verses still read in modern Brazil. St. Francis Xavier, the great missionary, was sent by the Portuguese king to carry Christianity to India.

Brazil seemed less important than India. Two years after da Gama's voyage, the story of Portugal's claim to Brazil began. In 1500 a Portuguese ship captain named Pedro Cabral (kuh-*brahl'*) sailed south from Portugal in command of a spice-trading fleet. As he rounded the western bulge of Africa, he sailed too far to the west. Perhaps by chance, or perhaps on orders from the king, Cabral landed on the shoulder of Brazil and claimed the eastern coast of South America for Portugal (map, page 38). Because trade with the East was so profitable, the Portuguese took little interest in Brazil for some years. But eventually a Portuguese king encouraged some of his nobles to establish settlements on the Brazilian coast.

Portugal declined as a European power. Portugal's rich trade with India and the East Indies aroused the envy of other European kingdoms. By the early 1600's England, France, and Holland were building up their own trade with the East and competing with Portugal. Portugal was too small and poor to remain a great power. Much of the wealth that reached Portugal from the East was squandered. Moreover, poor soil, epidemics of plague, and overpopulation led many people to leave Portugal and migrate to Brazil and India.

To make matters worse, the royal family died out, and in 1580 Philip II of Spain took over the Portuguese throne. Spanish kings ruled Portugal for the next 60 years. Throughout this period the same sea powers that were competing with Portugal in the East threatened Spanish trade routes with America. The Spanish kings gave more attention to protecting Spanish America than to defending Portuguese Brazil.

In 1640 a Portuguese nobleman, the Duke of Braganza (brah-*gahn'* zah) led a revolt against Spanish rule. As King João IV, he established the Braganza dynasty in a newly independent Portugal. But the little country was never again to be among the top-ranking European powers. It had, however, made its language and traditions an important force in the New World.

THINKING ABOUT THIS SECTION

1. Explain or define the following words: Brazil; dynasty.

2. Why did the Portuguese become seafarers? Why did they begin to explore Africa's west coast? Why did they seek a route south of Africa to India?

3. Why did Portugal make rich profits from trade over the new all-water route to India?

4. Why was Portugal unable to maintain its near-monopoly on trade with India and the East Indies?

4. Contact Between Europe and America

In the last section we skipped ahead of the story of Columbus to tell what happened to Spain and Portugal in the 1500's and 1600's. It was, of course, back in 1492 that Columbus brought the two worlds of America and Europe into contact. What was the background of this historic voyage? What forces led Columbus to search for land to the west of Europe?

Europeans became interested in the rest of the world. By the 1400's Europeans were taking a far greater interest in the world than they had just a few centuries earlier. There were several reasons for this. Crusaders who had traveled to Palestine in the 1000's and 1100's had brought back to Europe silks, spices, and perfumes. Europeans were eager to get more of these luxury goods that came only from the East. Moreover, printing was invented in Europe during the 1450's. Books about foreign travels reached more Europeans and made them curious about distant lands. One such account was a book published about the travels of Marco Polo. In the 1200's this Venetian had traveled widely in the great Chinese Empire. Most Europeans found the story of Marco Polo's adventures in Asia fantastic and hard to believe. But the book was widely read.

Another significant development was a great increase in the power of kings. For long years western Europe had suffered constant warfare between feudal nobles. Now kings in western European countries were able to enforce law and order. They won support from merchants, who found it easier to carry on their business under peaceful conditions. Book-readers, merchants, and kings all took an interest in matters beyond the narrow limits of their own experience.

New trade routes were needed. There was a very practical reason for interest in the East— the hope of finding new trade routes. Most of the Eastern luxury goods that eventually reached Europe were carried by Muslim traders from Asia to ports on the Black Sea or the eastern Mediterranean. From there, Italian merchants brought the spices, silks, and other goods to European markets. But it annoyed the rulers in Spain, Portugal, France, and England that the Italians had a monopoly on this business. Why couldn't new trade routes be found that would lead directly to the countries where these goods originated? The western European kings knew that any nation finding a water route to the East could take over the trade in luxury goods and become rich. With their growing power and wealth, these rulers could afford to finance the search for such a route.

The question now was: In what direction should explorers start looking? By sailing around Africa from west to east, the Portuguese did find a water route to Asia. Other Europeans thought they could find Asia by sailing *west*.

Geographers knew the world was round. By the 1400's most educated men in Europe realized the world was round. One French scholar in the early 1400's wrote: "An ocean stretches from Spain to the eastern edge of India." He obviously knew nothing of the American continents, since he also wrote: "It is evident that this sea is navigable in a very few days if the wind be fair." Much later in the 1400's a German geographer constructed a model of the world as a globe. This globe showed Spain and China divided only by the Atlantic Ocean. The Pacific coast of China was located where one would expect to see North America's east coast. Another geographer assured Christopher Columbus in a letter that there was a "safe course for ships due west of Lisbon which will take you to the Chinese coast after 5000 miles."

Obviously none of these geographers knew how large the earth was or how far Asia extended eastward. And they knew nothing about the American continents. But they had no doubts that the world was round.

SAN SALVADOR

CUBA

Isabela, 1493
(abandoned)

YUCATÁN

Navidad, 1492
(abandoned)

Santo
Domingo
1496

PUERTO
RICO

HISPANIOLA

ATLANTIC OCEAN

Caribbean Sea

PANAMA

VENEZUELA

Orinoco R.

COLOMBIA

PACIFIC OCEAN

EQUATOR

Amazon R.

SOUTH
AMERICA

BRAZIL

→ Columbus, 1492

- - ► Vespucci, 1499(?)

► Cabral, 1500

► Balboa, 1513

- - ► Solis, 1516

► Magellan, 1519-1520

Paraná R.

Paraguay R.

COLUMBUS' LATER VOYAGES TO AMERICA

BAHAMAS

CUBA

ATLANTIC OCEAN

HISPANIOLA

JAMAICA

HONDURAS

Caribbean Sea

TRINIDAD

PANAMA

SOUTH AMERICA

Rio de la Plata

LINE OF DEMARCATION

→ Second voyage, 1493-1496

→ Third voyage, 1498-1500

→ Fourth voyage, 1502-1504

To Philippines

STRAIT OF MAGELLAN

Columbus trained as a seaman. Christopher Columbus had been born in Genoa, Italy, in 1451. He probably first went to sea during his late teens. When he was 25, he was shipwrecked off the coast of Portugal. He swam ashore and went to Lisbon to join his brother, a map-maker who was already living there. Soon Columbus was going to sea aboard Portuguese ships. On one voyage Columbus visited Bristol in England, where he no doubt heard stories of fishermen who sailed as far as Newfoundland to catch codfish. He may have made a trip to Iceland, though historians are not sure about this. Columbus also visited the coast of West Africa. These voyages provided valuable experience for a man eager to embark on a career of exploration.

Columbus sought backing from the Portuguese king. In 1479 Columbus married a young woman whose father was the governor of the Madeira Islands in the Atlantic, and for a time they lived in Madeira. Columbus also knew the Azores, islands located even farther west in the Atlantic. By the 1480's, Columbus was determined to make more ambitious voyages into the western ocean. He requested permission from the king of Portugal to sail beyond the Azores and seek a westward route to the Far East. But the king turned him down. About this time Columbus' wife died. Deciding to leave Portugal, Columbus went to Spain with his small son named Diego.

He next applied to Queen Isabella. Columbus lived for a time in a monastery in the town of Palos near Seville. The head of this monastery had studied astronomy and took an interest in the Genoese mariner's ideas. He introduced Columbus to an important shipowner who considered backing a voyage of exploration into the Atlantic. When the shipowner asked Queen

Early European Voyages to America

Note how the Line of Demarcation cut through eastern South America.

Isabella for permission, she refused. If any such expedition were to be sent out, the queen herself wanted to sponsor it.

Columbus then asked the queen directly for help. But she hesitated to say yes. Isabella's advisers warned her that Columbus' proposed voyage would be very expensive, and at this time the war with Granada was straining the nation's finances. But the queen granted Columbus a small salary to keep him from seeking another royal sponsor.

The queen sponsored the voyage. After six years Isabella finally decided to give her backing to an Atlantic expedition. She probably hoped to find a route to the East ahead of Portugal. Isabella did not go to any great personal expense to aid Columbus. She directed the town of Palos, where the merchants owed her money, to provide Columbus with two ships and crews. A family named Pinzon (peen-*thohn'*) provided two vessels called the *Niña* and the *Pinta*. Two Pinzon brothers joined the expedition as captains under Columbus' command. They never liked Columbus. They considered him a "foreigner" who spoke Spanish with a queer Genoese accent, and they resented the fact that he was in command. A third ship, the *Santa María,* was to serve as Columbus' flagship.

Queen Isabella promised great rewards if Columbus were successful. He was to have the title "Admiral of the Ocean Sea" and the right to pass this title on to his descendants. In addition, he was to be governor of all lands that he discovered and would receive one tenth of all the wealth that was ever to come from these lands. If Isabella had kept all these promises, Columbus and his heirs might have become rulers of most of Latin America. At the time, however, these were easy promises for Isabella to make. Columbus was not expected to "discover" more than a few islands. The real goal was to find a water route to Asia.

Land was first sighted in the Caribbean. During the long voyage Columbus showed great

An old sketch of Santo Domingo suggests how Spain's first city in the Americas looked about a century after its founding. Notice the governor's palace in the central plaza and the wall built for defense against land attacks. Pirate raids were also a danger.

skill in navigation and superb courage. The sailors from Palos were experienced seamen, but after being out of sight of land for six weeks, they were understandably worried. In fact, the crews were on the verge of mutiny when land was finally sighted before dawn on October 12, 1492. After daylight Columbus stepped ashore on the island of San Salvador in the Bahama Islands.

Columbus believed he had reached either the East Indies or islands off the coast of China. Throughout November he sailed along the shore of Cuba and then went on to another large island which he named Hispaniola, or "Little Spain." On Christmas Eve the *Santa María,* never a seaworthy ship, was wrecked on the northern shore of Hispaniola. Deciding that God must have meant for him to start a colony there, Columbus left most of the *Santa María*'s crew on that island. On New Year's Day the Admiral sailed for Spain with just the *Niña* and the *Pinta*. This first Spanish attempt at a colony in the New World failed. When Columbus returned to Hispaniola the next year, he found a fort that the men had built, but it was in ruins and empty.

Columbus received a hero's welcome. Arriving in Spain in March, 1493, Columbus attended

Easter Mass in the Cathedral at Seville. From there he rode across Spain to Barcelona, where he was to report to Isabella. Columbus had brought back with him six Caribbean Indians in native dress and several parrots in cages. Along the route from Seville to Barcelona, people flocked out to see the exciting procession. When Columbus arrived at the court, the king and queen invited him to sit down in their presence. This was the highest honor that could be shown a Spanish citizen of that time. The monarchs listened carefully to Columbus' story of his voyage to "Las Indias" ("the Indies"). Gold dust, collected by trading with the Indians, also interested the Spanish rulers.

Spain and Portugal agreed to divide non-Christian lands. The Spanish monarchs decided that they must protect their interests in these exciting discoveries. Queen Isabella immediately asked Pope Alexander VI to draw a line that would establish Spain's right to the distant lands to the west. The Pope, who was regarded by European rulers as a referee in such matters, agreed. After some adjustment the Treaty of Tordesillas (tor-thay-*see'* yahs) was accepted in 1494. It established a boundary along the north-south meridian 370 leagues (1175 miles) west of the Azores. The Line of Demarcation, as it came to be called, gave to Spain the sole right to non-Christian lands west of this meridian, and to Portugal the sole right to all such lands east of it. The fact that the line cut through the eastern bulge of South America later gave Portugal a solid claim to Brazil (map, page 38).

Columbus sailed again. In the months that followed, Isabella began preparations for Columbus' return to the Indies. This time he was to have a fleet of seventeen ships, and 1500 men were to go along as colonists. With them the colonists took cattle, horses, tools, seeds, and articles needed for religious services. Columbus, now "Admiral of the Ocean Sea," commanded the entire fleet.

Setting sail in September, 1493, the expedition reached the Caribbean two months later. After discovering several new islands, the Spaniards established a new town on the northern coast of Hispaniola. (In 1496 this settlement moved to the present site of Santo Domingo.) Leaving the colonists, Columbus began his search for the coast of China. He sailed along the southern coast of the island of Cuba, looking for evidence that it was part of Asia. As provisions ran low and the men started to grumble, the Admiral cut short the voyage and sailed for Spain.

On a third voyage, Columbus in 1498 discovered the island of Trinidad near the mouth of the Orinoco River. For the first time he saw the mainland of South America.

Isabella lost faith in Columbus. Meanwhile, the colony on Hispaniola had not prospered. Indians had been enslaved to do the work of the colony, but because the Spaniards treated them harshly and forced them to pay tribute in gold, the Indians ran away. The colonists quarreled among themselves and refused to grow food. Since the colony's purpose was to find gold and to serve as a station on the route to Asia, the colonists had no intention of becoming farmers. When Columbus visited Santo Domingo in 1498, he accused the colonists of laziness. They, in turn, resented the Admiral's efforts to make them work. The mutinous Spaniards even charged him with "cruelty and mismanagement." Shocked by the news from Hispaniola, Isabella sent an official to investigate conditions in the colony.

This official, already prejudiced against Columbus, was angered to find that the Admiral had hanged the ringleaders of a mutiny. He had Columbus arrested and sent him back to Spain in chains. By this time Isabella felt that Columbus had brought Spain nothing but expense and trouble. His three voyages had produced only a little gold. He had not reached China, and the colony in Hispaniola was a failure. Although Isabella freed Columbus, she canceled his title of governor and forbade him to visit Santo Domingo. The queen then sent out new officials and more colonists to Santo Domingo, and the colony got off to a fresh start.

On a fourth voyage Columbus reached Panama.
By 1502 Isabella was willing to outfit another expedition for Columbus. She allowed him four ships and 150 men to "find a strait through these islands." On this expedition his younger son Ferdinand, fourteen years old, went along as a cabin boy. Ferdinand's book about his father's life is a valuable source of information for modern scholars. This fourth voyage took Columbus along the coast of Central America from Honduras to Panama. On the return trip a storm forced Columbus onto the coast of Jamaica. He and his crew remained there, marooned, for more than a year.

In November, 1504, Columbus at last returned to Spain, only to find that his patroness Isabella was dying. Exhausted and bitter, Columbus himself had less than two years to live. Much of this time he spent in trying to collect money owed him by King Ferdinand.

Columbus' achievements are recognized today.
By the time of his death, Columbus was almost a forgotten man. But gradually his achievements began to be recognized. In navigation and seamanship his skill was probably unsurpassed in his time. The route which he pioneered from Spain to the Caribbean was followed as long as the Atlantic was crossed by sailing ships. Columbus failed as an administrator, but his courage in exploring unknown seas cannot be questioned. And, although he himself never realized the full importance of his voyages, he had brought Europeans into permanent contact with the Americas.

Exploration continued in the islands and along mainland coasts.
After Columbus other explorers filled in the gaps in European knowledge of the Caribbean and the coasts of Central and South America. One such explorer was Americus Vespucci (ves-poo' chih), after whom the Americas were named. On several trips (at least one for Spain and another for Portugal), Vespucci explored along the coast of Brazil. The coasts of Venezuela and Colombia also became fairly well-known to European navigators. In 1513 a Spanish captain named Vasco Nuñez de Balboa organized an expedition of Spaniards and Indians and crossed the Isthmus of Panama. After struggling through dense jungle and fighting off hostile Indians for three weeks, Balboa reached the crest of a mountain ridge. Looking southward from that high point, he became the first European to lay eyes on the Pacific Ocean from the American shore. Balboa called this ocean the "South Sea."

Solis found the Plata estuary.
Explorers continued to look for a water passage through the American land mass. Among them was a Spaniard named Juan de Solis (sohl' eess), who sailed the year after news of Balboa's discovery reached Spain. Cruising southward along the Atlantic coast of South America, he reached the great salt-water estuary now called the Rio de la Plata (plah' tah). Certain that he had found a strait that would lead him to Balboa's ocean, Solis sailed a hundred miles inland. There, to his disappointment, he found that the passage became fresh water. When he went ashore to claim the land for Spain, wild Pampa Indians killed and ate Solis and seven of his men. Survivors of the crew returned to Spain to tell the story.

Magellan proved the world was round.
The search for a strait through America was carried on by a Portuguese sea captain named Ferdinand Magellan. He had seen service in the Portuguese trade with India, Malaya, and perhaps the East Indies. When Magellan returned to Portugal from the East, he had expected promotion and new assignments. Instead, he fell into disfavor with the king. Magellan then offered his services to Spain. He told the teen-aged king, Charles I, that the salt-water passage reported by Solis' men *must* be a strait leading to the South Sea. Magellan was sure that the islands he himself had visited in Asia must lie

Columbus might have seen the ancestors of these Cuna Indians while sailing along islands off the Caribbean coast of Panama.

tober, 1520, his fleet entered the strait which now bears his name. For 38 days the ships fought their way through the cold and fog of this gale-swept passage. At last they sailed out onto a calm, sunny ocean, which Magellan thankfully named the Pacific ("peaceful"). Several months later he and his men, reduced to eating rats and sawdust, landed on an island in the Philippines. A Malay slave boy who had accompanied Magellan since his Portuguese service was able to talk with the people. Magellan then knew he had reached Asia.

Magellan died in the Philippines. Magellan did not live to complete his history-making voyage. He was killed in a skirmish with Filipino natives. Only one of his ships, the *Victoria,* finally returned to Spain in September, 1522. Of the original 270 members of the expedition, only 18 worn-out survivors manned the *Victoria* as it sailed into port.

The news told by this tattered crew caused great excitement in Spain. The Spaniards now realized they could claim a great "new world" whose fringes they had been exploring since 1492. Moreover, an ocean vaster than anyone ever imagined lay between these lands and Asia. It was clear that there could be no quick passage westward from Europe to the riches of the East. The best policy for Spain was to concentrate on developing the huge region claimed by right of discovery and the Treaty of Tordesillas.

The American discoveries brought changes to Europe. For the Spanish people, and eventually for all Europeans, the discovery and colonization of America was to have a deep and lasting effect. For one thing, a flood of wealth was to pour into the Spanish treasury. Spanish ships probably carried home from the Americas more silver and gold than the whole world had found since the time of the ancient Egyptians. The Spanish kings spent much of this wealth on building fleets of ships, equipping large armies, and fighting wars. As other countries of Europe helped provision the Spanish fleets

just beyond. Charles I hoped that the East Indies might come within the area allotted to Spain by the Line of Demarcation. So, eager to beat out the Portuguese, the Spanish king agreed to finance an expedition for Magellan.

Magellan's fleet of five ships sailed from Spain in September, 1519. In two months it reached Brazil and then turned southward. After exploring the Plata estuary, Magellan realized it was not a passage to Asia. Returning to the coast, he ordered his fleet to continue southward. Meanwhile, Spanish members of the expedition distrusted Magellan as a foreigner. In fact, one captain deserted and sailed his ship back to Spain. There he reported that Magellan was lost in the cold Antarctic waters.

But Magellan survived the freezing, stormy weather at the tip of South America. In Oc-

and armies, *their* commerce and industries began to flourish. But little was done to improve Spain's agriculture and industries. As a result of this neglect, Spanish power and prestige would eventually decline.

To balance this picture, we must give credit to both Spain and Portugal for their brilliant achievements in exploration. As one historian has said, "the sons of Iberia taught the world the most stupendous geography lesson it has ever had in any half-century of recorded history." The mere knowledge that two great continents lay across the Atlantic brought an entirely new outlook to the people of Europe.

THINKING ABOUT THIS SECTION

1. Explain or define the following words: Marco Polo; Line of Demarcation; Hispaniola.

2. What conditions in western Europe during the 1400's contributed to a growing interest in voyages of exploration?

3. What factors might cause a sea captain to believe that he could reach China by sailing westward from Europe?

4. Why was Queen Isabella ready to back Columbus in 1492? What promises did she make?

5. Why did the queen want a line of demarcation giving Spain exclusive rights to non-Christian lands west of it? Why did Portugal agree to such a line?

6. Why did the queen begin to lose faith in Columbus after 1498?

7. What instructions were given Columbus on his fourth voyage? What were the goals of Balboa and Solis? What did each achieve?

8. Why was Magellan eager to undertake a westward voyage? What facts were established by his expedition?

Summing Up

Spain and Portugal were the colonizers of most of Latin America. The two nations are neighbors on the Iberian peninsula, separated from the rest of western Europe by the high Pyrenees.

Most of the soil of Iberia is poor and rainfall is uncertain. But for centuries peasant farmers have managed to scratch out a living. In ancient times a succession of peoples lived in the Iberian peninsula, including Celts, Phoenicians, Greeks, and Romans. After invading Germanic tribes brought an end to Roman rule, small Christian kingdoms grew up. But they were soon overrun by Muslims, called Moors, from North Africa.

Centuries of Moorish rule brought benefits to the southern part of the peninsula—improved agriculture, prosperous industry, liberal government, and an interest in learning. The Catholic Europeans who held onto the northern part of the peninsula were also affected by the Moorish presence. They became intolerant of other religions, scornful of manual labor, and proud of military exploits. The small Christian kingdoms in the north continued to make war on the Moors, and in 1492 Queen Isabella ousted the Muslims from their last Iberian stronghold.

Meanwhile, new forces had stimulated Europeans to look outward. A curiosity about the rest of the world, the greater power and wealth of kings, and the desire to find a new water route to the East resulted in voyages of exploration. Portugal led the way in charting a route around Africa to India. From Columbus' discovery of Hispaniola in 1492 to the round-the-world voyage of Magellan's expedition thirty years later, Spain's explorers added much to European knowledge of the world. By the Treaty of Tordesillas, Portugal and Spain agreed to divide the non-Christian world between them.

Years later, a half-century of union with Spain saw Portugal's interests take second place to those of Spain. The period of glory as colonizing world powers did not last long for either Spain or Portugal. But their influence on the future of the Americas was immense. The Iberian contributions to Latin America can be seen not only in the languages and names of the people but also in forms of government, legal and landholding systems, religion, customs and outlook, agriculture, and the arts.

A black man, Estevanico, was one of the first Spanish-speaking explorers in what is now the southwestern United States. This modern mural painting shows Estevanico as he tried to learn something from Indians about legendary cities that Spaniards of the 1500's dreamed of finding in New Mexico.

3

The Makers of Latin America: The Africans

American Indians, Europeans, and Africans are the ancestors of the people of modern Latin America. Of these three, only the Africans came to the Americas against their will. The slave trade which brought millions of Africans to the Americas was one of the largest forced migrations in human history.

Black men had come to the New World, however, long before the transatlantic slave trade became "big business" in the 1600's and 1700's. In fact, blacks accompanied the earliest European explorers to America. Historians believe that one of Columbus' sailors in 1492 was a black man. Blacks also took part in the expeditions of Balboa, Cortés, Pizarro, and many other explorers.

The best-known of the black men who came to America with the early Spaniards was Estevanico (ays-tay-*vah'* nee-koh), who became

45

an explorer in his own right. Estevanico was the slave of a Spanish captain who was shipwrecked on the coast of Texas in 1528. The resourceful Estevanico and three other survivors wandered for eight years through Texas and regions to the west. Eventually they found their way back to Mexico. Later, Estevanico led an expedition into what is now New Mexico, searching for rich cities described by the Indians. Thus, a black man was one of the first Spanish-speaking explorers in what later became the southwestern United States.

Today probably more than 50 million people in the Western Hemisphere are descendants of black Africans. Of these, over 20 million live in the United States and a large number in Brazil. French-speaking Haiti is the only Negro republic in Latin America. Other areas with large black populations are Cuba, the Dominican Republic, Trinidad, Jamaica, Puerto Rico, and the Virgin Islands. Many black people also live in the port cities of Colombia, Venezuela, and Panama and on the banana plantations of the Central American coast. In spite of the cruel conditions of their arrival and early life in the Americas, Africans and their descendants contributed greatly to the development of the New World.

1. West Africa Before the Arrival of Europeans

North Africa has been an important part of the Mediterranean world since ancient times. One of the world's earliest civilizations developed in Egypt. In the western Mediterranean the North African city of Carthage became the leading sea power of ancient times. With the defeat of Carthage, Rome began to build an empire that rimmed the Mediterranean. Some of Rome's richest provinces were in North Africa. Centuries later this region became part of the Muslim Empire.

North African merchants traded with people south of the Sahara. Between the Mediterranean coast and the grasslands and rain forests of central and southern Africa lies the vast scorching Sahara. This man-killing desert has always made north-south travel difficult. Nevertheless, since ancient times there had been some exchange of goods between the Mediterranean region and the area south of the Sahara.

By 800 A.D. merchants with large camel caravans were crossing the Sahara to trade with people in the *sudan,* the grassland region south of the desert. At this time the leading kingdom of the sudan was Ghana (*gah'* nah). This kingdom did not have strictly defined borders, but it roughly covered the region drained by the Niger and Senegal rivers.[1] Most of the people lived in villages. Skilled crafts, farming, and trade were important in the economy.

Ghana became a wealthy empire. As a thriving trade developed with Arab merchants, Ghana grew into a wealthy empire. Gold mined in regions farther south contributed to Ghana's prosperity. Other goods exchanged with the Arabs were salt from the Sahara, ivory, cloth, and copper. Ghana also became a military power. According to an Arab writer of the eleventh century, one Ghana king had an army of 200,000 warriors equipped with bows and arrows and iron-tipped spears.

Ghana was followed by other powerful empires. Ghana's great wealth attracted invaders, and by 1100 the empire had crumbled. During the next few centuries a succession of other kingdoms rose and fell in the sudan. Some of them, especially Mali (*mah'* lee) and Songhai (sahn-*guy'*), became empires as great as Ghana had been.

[1] The *modern* African nation called Ghana lies farther south.

Muslim culture influenced West Africa. Over the centuries of contact there was much cultural exchange between the Arabs and the West Africans. In West African towns members of the upper classes learned to read and write Arabic. (Centuries later, Portuguese slave-owners, who often could not write themselves, were surprised to find that some of their West African slaves could read and write in Arabic.) Several of the West African kings became Muslims. One emperor of Mali went on a pilgrimage to Mecca, the Muslim holy city, and "astonished the Arabs there with his wealth and luxury." A university in the West African city of Timbuktu attracted scholars from throughout the Muslim world.

Arab influence also reached the Guinea coast. Most of the Africans who eventually were taken as slaves to the Americas came from the coastal region south of the western sudan. This region is called the Guinea (*ghin′* ee) coast. Foreign traders gave specific names to different parts of Guinea: the Grain Coast, the Ivory

The clay-walled houses of Kano (below), an ancient market town in what is now Nigeria, provide cool dwellings in a hot climate. Over many centuries caravan merchants exchanged goods in Kano and also introduced Islamic ideas. Still today the Kano people are mostly Muslim. Left, studying the Arabic language is a young man of Kano. He has copied a passage from the Koran, the sacred writings of the Muslim religion.

Coast, the Gold Coast, and the Slave Coast. These names show what especially interested traders in the particular areas. Most of the Guinea coast was thickly forested, and Arab merchants and travelers seldom visited this part of Africa. Their camel caravans could penetrate the desert but not the hot, humid tropical forests. By the 1200's, however, the Arab-influenced cultures of the western sudan had reached Guinea.

Yoruba people founded cities in Guinea. After about 1000 A.D. a people called the Yoruba founded a number of independent city-states on the Guinea coast. Probably the earliest Yoruba town was Ife (*ee'* fay). Fine craftsmen, the people of Ife created jewelry from shells and stones and fashioned terra cotta dishes and figurines. By the time Arab traders reached this area, the Ife people were casting lifelike portrait heads out of bronze.

Benin became a leading city-state. One of the most important Yoruba centers was the city of Benin (beh-*neen'*), located near one of the branches of the Niger River. Benin became the capital of a kingdom of the same name. In 1602, Benin was visited by a Dutchman who described the city:

The town seems to be very great. When you enter into it, you go into a great broad street, not paved, which seems to be seven or eight times broader than [a main] street in Amsterdam. . . . When you are in the great street . . . , you see many great streets on the sides thereof. . . . The houses in this town stand in good order, one close and even with the other, as the houses in Holland stand. . . .

The king's court is very great. . . . I saw the stable where his best horses stood. . . . It seems that the king has many soldiers. He has also many gentlemen, who when they come to the court ride upon horses. . . . There are also many men slaves seen in the town that carry water, yams, and palm-wine . . . for the king.[2]

[2] Quoted in Roland Oliver and J. D. Fage, *A Short History of Africa* (Baltimore: Penguin Books, 1969), pp. 106–107.

The king of Benin, called the Oba (*oh'* bah), commanded great power, and his people treated him as a representative of God on earth. His palace had many rooms and courtyards decorated with beautifully worked bronze figures and plaques, works of art that are treasured today. The Dutch traveler wrote that the people of Benin had "good laws and a well-organized police. They live on good terms with the Dutch and other foreigners who come to trade with them, and show them a thousand marks of friendship."

Benin prospered from trade. Benin and other important trading towns of the Guinea coast were linked to each other and to the western sudan and North Africa by a network of trade routes. Since the Oba of Benin and other Yoruba kings were wealthy, they could afford luxuries. In trade with other peoples, Benin obtained gold and copper jewelry, handsome cotton fabrics, metal cutlasses and armor, and well-trained horses.

In return, the people of Benin traded ivory secured from forest regions farther south where elephants were common. They also traded salt derived from sea water. Kola nuts, which furnished a mild narcotic permitted by the Muslim religion, came from the coast and were sent inland to the sudan peoples. Ingots of iron and copper, leather bags of gold dust from the Gold Coast, and carefully weighed packages of salt all served as money. Cowry shells from the Indian Ocean found their way across Africa and also served as a sort of international money.

African societies and cultures were complex. It is clear from accounts of life in West Africa before the European slave trade began that peoples of the western sudan and the Guinea coast had built flourishing civilizations. Their farming methods were as good as those of the Spanish and Portuguese. Some of them raised cattle, and many of them used horses. From a very early date they knew how to forge and cast iron, and they also used copper. The West Africans built fine cities, to which Arab traders brought Muslim culture as well as trade goods.

Society and government. The family was the most important unit in African societies. Usually the family consisted of many blood relatives and relatives by marriage as well. The oldest member of such a family was highly respected and acted as the chief or "headman." A council of these headmen often governed the smaller communities. Where kingdoms or empires developed, the headmen bowed to the authority of a powerful ruler. The king had a professional army to enforce his rule, and all people of the kingdom served him.

Slavery. Slavery was common in West African societies. Most slaves were condemned criminals, prisoners of war, or poor people who were sold into bondage to pay off debts. It was fairly easy for a slave to win his freedom. Slaves could own and farm their own plots of land. From the profits of their produce they could buy their freedom. A slave also could inherit money and use it for this purpose. In some areas a male slave might gain freedom by marrying his master's daughter. Once freed, slaves entered into the life of the community and were not treated differently from other people. Bondage in West Africa was much milder than the slavery that was to develop in the Americas.

Religion. Religion influenced every aspect of life in West Africa. Ancestor worship was tied in with the importance of the family. Spirits of ancestors were regarded as members of the community and were believed to take an active interest in the family's and community's well-being. Like many other religions, those of Africa included the idea of a Supreme Being or Creator. He was worshiped indirectly through the ancestors of a community or through the lesser gods of nature. These gods were believed to be present in such natural elements as trees, mountains, rivers, snakes, and thunder and lightning. Like Europeans who lived before the age of science, Africans believed in the supernatural and in good and bad magic.

A Benin craftsman fashioned this bronze head portraying a queen.

As mentioned earlier, rulers of some West African kingdoms adopted the Muslim religion after contact with the Arabs. Often the peoples ruled by these kings did not become Muslims but kept their own religious practices. Though Christianity came to North Africa very early, it was not known in West Africa until the 1500's.

Literature. African peoples did not develop systems of writing of their own. One reason for this may have been the large number of different languages, each spoken by a small group of people. Nevertheless, many African cultures had a body of literature which was handed down by word of mouth, much like the stories of the Incas. A number of the royal courts had "rememberers" who recited long ritual poems from memory during religious celebrations. These poems told of the history of the people, their traditional glories, the origin of the king's ancestors, and victories in war. The recitations also included proverbs, traditional laws, and folk stories. African scholars who learned Arabic wrote down some of this literature and thus preserved it.

Art. West African artists produced works of the highest quality. Today masterpieces created by African sculptors, weavers, potters, and jewelmakers are treasured by museums throughout the world. Though art objects were made for the royal courts, art was chiefly a form of religious expression.

Musicians and dancers often performed in religious ceremonies. Visitors to West African towns described the intense enthusiasm of the religious dances, which were accompanied by singing and complex rhythms beat out by drummers. These rhythms helped create an emotional atmosphere in which the people could feel closer to the power or "life force" of their religion. The ceremonial dances were not spontaneous but followed a very strict ritual. Only trained dancers took part. Other dances, however, were held for recreation or to celebrate the beginning of a hunt. Everyone might dance in these. The musicians who accompanied the dancers played harps, flutes, and marimbas in addition to the drums.

THINKING ABOUT THIS SECTION

1. Explain or define the following words: sudan; Ghana; Benin; Ife.
2. What contacts were there between southern Europe and North Africa in ancient times? What was the role of the Arabs in the trade between North Africa and the sudan?
3. Why did powerful kingdoms develop in the sudan? along the Guinea coast?
4. How have we learned about advanced civilizations in West Africa? What similarities do you see between these and the American Indian civilizations described in Chapter 1? What differences?

2. The African Slave Trade

Slavery has existed throughout history. Since earliest times and probably in every part of the world, people have enslaved other human beings. In ancient societies most slaves were prisoners of war. But convicts, debtors, political enemies, and unwanted children were sometimes sold into slavery. The Egyptian pharaohs enslaved the people of Israel and other peoples captured in war. The ancient Greeks used slave labor to build their impressive temples. In writing about conquered cities, Greek historians often noted that the cities' populations were "sold into slavery."

Slavery was also common in the Roman Empire. It has been estimated that more than a third of the inhabitants of the Roman Empire were either slaves from birth or were sold into slavery. The Romans enslaved not only Greeks and other Europeans but also Asians and North Africans. During the feudal period that followed the fall of the Roman Empire, most European peasants became serfs who could not leave the estate to which they belonged. Serfdom made the older form of bondage less important, but slavery was still practiced. After the rise of Islam, Muslims enslaved Christians, and Christians in turn enslaved Muslims.

The Portuguese voyages to Africa led to the slave trade. By the 1440's the Portuguese ship captains sent out by Henry the Navigator to explore the West African coast had reached the mouth of the Senegal River. It was here on the Senegal coast that one of Prince Henry's captains traded for ten young blacks who probably were already the slaves of an Arab merchant. The Portuguese took the black slaves home to Lisbon. Some of them were presented to the king as a gift. Others were sold. Prince Henry always made a point of having Africans baptized into the Catholic faith as soon as they landed in Portugal. He regarded the trade in black slaves as a good thing because it brought new souls to his religion.

By the 1470's the Portuguese had reached the Gold Coast. From here the Europeans shipped a few slaves back to Lisbon, but they also found rich supplies of gold. The Portuguese merchants set up a trading post and fort (called a "castle") at Elmina (el-*mee'* nah) on the Gold Coast. Here gold and other products could be stored and guarded until ships arrived to transport them to Portugal. Another post was built on the island of São Tomé (*sah'* oon too-*may'*) in the Gulf of Guinea. At both of these stations the Portuguese carried on a busy trade in gold, cloth, ivory, and slaves.

African slaves became servants in Portugal. Most of the Africans sent to Portugal had been farm workers or servants belonging to African kings or traders. In Portugal their new owners treated them much as they did any other servants. This is clear from the following account by a Portuguese writer of the time: "As our people . . . saw how [the Africans] came in unto the law of Christ with a good will, they made no difference between them and free servants, born in our own country. But those whom they saw fitted for managing property they set free and married to [Portuguese] women. . . . And some widows of good family who bought . . . female slaves either adopted them or left them a portion of their estate by will so that in the future they married right well. . . ."

By the time Europeans began sailing to the New World, black African slavery was well-established in both Portugal and Spain. The total number of slaves in Europe remained small, chiefly because there was no great need for additional labor.

The Portuguese extended their slave trade southward. Meanwhile, the Portuguese had established relations with an African kingdom called Kongo, along the Congo River. The king of Portugal sent Catholic missionaries to Kongo in 1491. These missionaries succeeded in converting the ruler (called the *Manikongo*), his family, and several members

European ambassadors kneeled as they were received by the king of Kongo in the early 1600's.

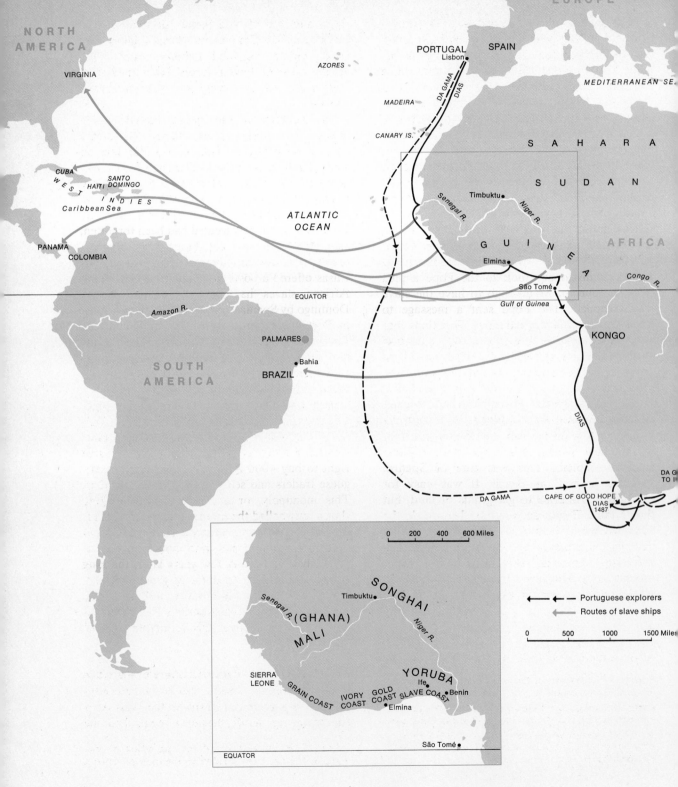

NORTH
AMERICA

VIRGINIA

AZORES

EUROPE

PORTUGAL   SPAIN
        Lisbon

MEDITERRANEAN SE

MADEIRA

CANARY IS.

S A H A R A

S U D A N

CUBA   SANTO
        DOMINGO
    HAITI
W E S T   I N D I E S
Caribbean Sea

ATLANTIC
OCEAN

Timbuktu

Senegal R.

Niger R.

G U I N E A

AFRICA

PANAMA
COLOMBIA

Elmina

São Tomé

Congo R.

EQUATOR

Gulf of Guinea

Amazon R.

PALMARES

KONGO

SOUTH
AMERICA

BRAZIL   Bahia

DA GAMA
TO IN

DIAS

DA GAMA

CAPE OF GOOD HOPE
DIAS
1487

0   200   400   600 Miles

SONGHAI

Timbuktu

Senegal R.   (GHANA)

Niger R.

M A L I

SIERRA
LEONE

YORUBA

GRAIN COAST

IVORY
COAST

GOLD
COAST   SLAVE COAST

Ife
Benin

Elmina

São Tomé

EQUATOR

◄— — —   Portuguese explorers

◄——   Routes of slave ships

0   500   1000   1500 Miles

of the Kongo nobility to Christianity. The crown prince, baptized with the name Alfonso, was sent to Portugal for his education. Alfonso became king of Kongo in 1507 and ruled, still a Christian, until his death 36 years later.

By the 1530's, however, Portugal was becoming increasingly interested in the slave trade. Plantation owners in Brazil needed slave labor to work their fields. To get more slaves, Portuguese traders forced King Alfonso of Kongo to make war on people to the south of his realm. These Africans in turn made war on Kongo. Many black Christians from Kongo were captured as prisoners of war, sold into slavery, and transported to Brazil. The Kongo people bitterly resented the slave trade. In the 1630's a missionary took to the Pope a plea from the current Manikongo to have the slave trade stopped. The Pope sent a message to Lisbon protesting the selling of Christians into slavery in America. Portugal at this time was ruled by the king of Spain. His answer in effect said that he could do nothing about the slave trade.

African slaves were introduced into Spanish America. A growing demand for cheap labor in the New World caused the African slave trade to expand. This was true of Spanish America as well as Brazil. It was easy for hidalgos in America to get grants of land, but they had no European peasants there to do the farm work for them. The most obvious solution was to exploit the Indians. In many parts of Latin America, however, Indian labor proved unsatisfactory. European settlers in Brazil and the West Indies especially needed

Africa and the Transatlantic Slave Trade

Portuguese explorers of the late 1400's made the West African coast known to Europeans. Later Europeans began the transatlantic trade that carried millions of Africans against their will to the Americas. Note that slave ships headed for Brazil had a much shorter voyage than those sailing to the West Indies or North America.

large numbers of field hands for their plantations. But the Indians in these regions had been hunters and food gatherers rather than settled farmers. Under forced labor they sickened and died, ran away, or even committed suicide.

The suffering of the Indians on Hispaniola shocked a Spanish priest named Bartolomé de Las Casas (lahss *kah'* sahss). He himself was a landowner in Santo Domingo for a time. In 1517 Las Casas returned to Spain to see young King Charles I. The command of the king's grandmother, Queen Isabella, that the Indians be humanely treated had been forgotten, said Las Casas. In fact, he charged, Spanish cruelty would soon leave no Indians alive. Las Casas offered a possible solution. Several black African slaves had been brought to Santo Domingo by Spaniards who had purchased them in Portuguese ports. According to Father Las Casas, they were hard workers. They knew how to hoe, plant, and harvest crops in a tropical climate, and they seemed strong enough to survive such work day after day.

The urging of Las Casas and other missionaries persuaded the Spanish king that African slaves should be shipped to the Caribbean.[3] Charles granted one of his courtiers the sole right to buy 4000 Africans a year from Portuguese traders and sell them in the West Indies. This monopoly, or exclusive right of selling slaves, was called the *asiento* (ah-see-*ayn'* toh).

The Spanish courtier soon sold the *asiento* to Genoese merchants who bought slaves in the Lisbon market. A few years later, the king granted the *asiento* to different groups of merchants, from other countries as well as Spain. Still later in the colonial period, European nations fought wars over this profitable right of *asiento*.

Other countries demanded a share of the slave trade. During the 1500's the Portuguese controlled the purchase of slaves on the West African coast. Spaniards, however, controlled the

[3] Las Casas later regretted the suggestion he had made to Charles I and advocated abolition of slavery.

importation of Portuguese-sold slaves into the Spanish colonies in the New World. Nevertheless, other Europeans were entering the slave trade as smugglers or as pirates. Holland, France, Denmark, and England all wanted a share of the rich slave trade.

Holland. In the 1630's the Dutch West India Company took over part of the coast of Brazil without strong protest from the Portuguese. The Dutch also claimed the islands of Curaçao (koo-rah-*sah'* oh) and Aruba (ah-*roo'* bah) in the Caribbean. By 1642 aggressive Dutchmen had ousted the Portuguese slave traders from their trading posts on the Gold Coast of Africa. Vessels of the Dutch West India Company brazenly smuggled African slaves into Spanish ports in America. Thus, the Dutch gained the major share of the transatlantic slave trade.

By the early 1700's, however, the Dutch had almost abandoned the slave trade. They had taken over much of Portugal's trade with the East Indies and were finding commerce in that area more profitable than the slave trade.

France. French pirates came to the Caribbean to prey on Spanish ships. They eventually established themselves in western Hispaniola, the area today called Haiti. These pirates captured slave ships and smuggled the slaves into Spanish ports for illegal sale. Some of the Africans the pirates put to work raising crops and tending cattle in Haiti.

Around 1700, Haiti became an official French colony. The French king allotted lands along the coast and in fertile valleys to rich Frenchmen. With the growth of the plantation system in Haiti, the demand for slaves increased greatly. To meet this demand, the French arranged for the Portuguese to send 40,000 slaves from central Africa to Haiti every year. This was the "legal" number. Actually, the slave traders probably shipped three times that many to the French colony.

Denmark. Denmark also took part in the slave trade. A Danish West Indies Company settled the Virgin Islands and developed large sugar plantations. Only a few Danes settled in these islands. They purchased large numbers of slaves from Spanish markets in Cuba and Santo Domingo and from the English in Jamaica. Some Danish ships brought slaves directly from Africa, trading "illegally" at the various slave stations on the coast.

England. The first Englishman known to have brought slaves to America was a captain named John Hawkins. On a voyage to Guinea in 1562 he picked up 300 Africans in a coastal raid. Hawkins crossed the Atlantic and sold the Africans in Santo Domingo for a cargo of hides, sugar, and pearls. Queen Elizabeth of England called his voyage "detestable." But when she heard about Hawkins' profits, she helped him finance a second trip. This time Hawkins commanded a squadron of four ships. When they reached Sierra Leone (south of Senegal), the Englishmen landed and spent several days burning villages and kidnapping Africans. Hawkins eventually sold his cargo of slaves in Venezuela. From this voyage he returned to England a rich man.

Many other English captains raided the African coast for slaves and smuggled them into Spanish colonies or sold them to English colonists in North America. About a century after Hawkins, Englishmen founded the Royal African Company (1672). The English king himself invested in it. This company soon earned large profits from the slave trade along the West African coast. It supplied slaves for the English sugar islands of Barbados and Jamaica (which had been taken from the Spaniards) and also for the North American colonies.

The English came to dominate the trade. In the 1700's English control of the slave trade became supreme. War had broken out in Europe over who should succeed to the throne of Spain. This War of the Spanish Succession ended in 1713. Under the terms of the peace treaty, England received the coveted *asiento,* the legal right to sell African slaves in the Spanish colonies.

More slaves than ever before were now shipped to the New World. Jamaica became

Domingo. Throughout the 1700's an average of about 57,000 Africans were sold every year in American slave markets.

Slave ships brought great profits. In spite of the high death rate among slaves during the transatlantic voyage, dealers made tremendous profits from the "traffic in human flesh." The price paid for slaves bought from kings or local raiders in Africa varied, depending on the supply available. During the 1700's the average price per slave rose from about ten British pounds to fifteen. This was paid in iron bars, gold dust, European cloth, muskets, gunpowder, or rum.

Merchants in the English city of Liverpool were especially active in the slave trade during the 1700's. In fact, they grew rich from their investments in slave ships. New docks built for the slaving vessels made Liverpool one of the world's great ports. Profits from the slave trade were invested in machinery and factories and helped make England the world's leading industrial country.

The international slave trade was abolished. The lack of any feeling of guilt about the buying and selling of human beings was shared by Arabs, Europeans, and Africans. Some Portuguese in the 1400's and 1500's had justified slavery as a means of converting blacks to Christianity, but slave traders soon lost any concern for the souls of their victims. The traders and merchants generally treated the slaves like animals.

Even in the 1500's, however, a few individuals had questioned the morality of slavery and protested against the cruelties of slave traders. By the late 1700's reformers in several countries were demanding that the trade be stopped. In 1807 British reformers succeeded in getting a law passed that prohibited British subjects from taking part in the slave trade. The following year the United States officially abolished the trade. Holland and France also outlawed it. And Spain and Portugal, at Britain's urging, agreed to end the slave traffic north of the

A man firing a gun was the subject of this work by a West African artist of the late 1500's. Guns became more and more common in West Africa as European traders exchanged weapons for slaves.

the largest slave market in the Americas. Spanish merchants from South America went to Jamaica to buy slaves, or bought them directly from cargoes carried by "legal" English ships to Havana, Porto Bello in Panama, Cartagena (kar-tah-*hay'* nah) in Colombia, or Santo equator. In the 1820's British treaties with newly independent Brazil and other countries allowed British naval vessels to stop and search vessels suspected of carrying slaves.

Illegal trade continued. Unfortunately there was no way of enforcing these treaties and laws. British ships could not possibly have patroled the entire West African coast and the south Atlantic as well. Moreover, planters still felt they needed more slaves, the governments involved were too weak to enforce laws against slaving, and most people ignored the moral question. So the slave trade continued illegally into the later 1800's.

In Brazil the importation of slaves became illegal in 1830. But smugglers continued to sell slaves to work on the sugar, tobacco, cotton, and coffee plantations. A British consul in Brazil estimated that a million slaves were smuggled into that country between 1830 and 1852.

The slave trade crippled the West African kingdoms. Historians have only recently recognized what a devastating effect the slave trade had on Africa. Figures are very uncertain, but perhaps six million men and women were lost from West Africa alone. The slave trade also weakened the economies of the African countries. The African kings knew that European traders were interested in just one commodity—slaves. To get the European goods they wanted, the Africans could offer only human cargo in exchange. Interest in crafts or agricultural improvement, therefore, died out in the African states. Some of the African kings tried to prohibit slave trading in their own domains, but they failed to keep out the determined slave merchants.

The guns that the Europeans traded for slaves did little to promote peaceful relations between the African kingdoms. Many African peoples warred on each other to get prisoners to sell for even more guns. Meanwhile, coastal towns were destroyed in clashes between the different European traders. Cities farther inland declined as the economy suffered, and kingdoms began to break up. The resulting disorder made it easier for Europeans in later times to conquer and colonize in Africa.

THINKING ABOUT THIS SECTION

1. Explain or define the following words: Manikongo; *asiento;* Las Casas; trading post.
2. Why did Portugal develop trade with the West African coast? Why did it begin to import slaves from Africa?
3. Why were African slaves taken by Europeans to America? What evidence is there that the slave trade was highly profitable for Europeans?
4. How was the slave trade disastrous for the West African kingdoms?
5. For centuries Arabs, Europeans, and Africans seemed to feel no guilt about buying and selling human beings. How could this be?

3. The Transporting of the Slaves from Africa to America

Since slave traders kept no accurate records, it is impossible to say exactly how many Africans came to the New World. But historians have estimated that over eleven million people were captured or purchased in Africa for the transatlantic trade. Probably more than nine million of these Africans survived the harrowing ocean voyage. An estimated two million Africans died on the way to America.

Most slaves were captives before being sold to European traders. Most Africans who were sold to European traders had first been enslaved by other Africans. Seldom did Europeans themselves go inland from the African coast to seize victims. Instead they purchased slaves from local kings, usually through middlemen.

The majority of slaves had lost their freedom through being captured in wars waged by local rulers. Often these wars were fought for the sole purpose of taking prisoners to sell to European slavers. Other slaves, especially children, had been kidnapped and sold to merchants. Also, people were often sold by native chiefs as punishment for crimes, even very minor ones. In fact, a chief occasionally declared some common act to be a "crime," just so that "guilty" people could be seized and sold. In time of famine a local ruler might sell a whole village, or starving people might sell themselves.

Sometimes, when a local chieftain failed to deliver the number of slaves he had promised a European agent, the white trader would enslave the chieftain himself and all his family. This possibility made the kings along the coast doubly anxious to provide large numbers of captives to the slave merchants.

Captured slaves were marched to the coast. From hundreds of miles inland long lines of slaves chained together were marched to the West African coast by Arab raiders. These collections of slaves were called *coffles*. The local kings along the Guinea coast bought the coffles. A king could sell the slaves who had survived the march for double the cost of the gold dust or salt he paid the Arabs for them. From the European slavers the king obtained highly valued European goods: brandy and rum, guns, woolens, cottons, and other items.

A Scottish explorer named Mungo Park described the march of one slave coffle to the Atlantic coast. In 1795 Park traveled to the coast in company with Arab traders who had collected this coffle. There were 73 slaves, all roped together in a long line. The grueling journey lasted two months. Along the way several of the slaves tried to commit suicide, and one was stung to death by a swarm of bees. All of the slaves suffered terribly from

hunger and thirst. At times elephants and lions attacked them. The coffle passed through many villages that had been burned in slave raids. Park reported the following incident in a town where the coffle spent the night:

Here one of the slaves belonging to the coffle, who had traveled with great difficulty for the last three days, was found unable to proceed any farther. His master . . . proposed therefore to exchange him for a young slave girl, belonging to one of the townspeople. The poor girl was ignorant of her fate until the bundles were all tied up in the morning, and the coffle ready to depart. Coming with some other young women to see the coffle set out, her master took her by the hand and delivered her to the [slave trader]. Never was a face of serenity more suddenly changed into one of the deepest distress. The terror she [showed] on having the load put upon her head, and the rope fastened round her neck, and the sorrow with which she bade adieu to her companions were truly affecting.[4]

When the coffle arrived at the coast, it was learned that no vessel had called for several months. The slave driver put the Africans to work planting a crop while waiting for a ship. Mungo Park arranged for his own passage with a Yankee captain who exchanged his cargo of rum and tobacco for 130 slaves. During the voyage across the Atlantic, Park talked to the slaves in their own language. He found that about one fifth of them had been recently captured in war. The rest had already been slaves when they were sold to an Arab trader. But they too had once been prisoners of war.

The slave ships loaded their cargoes at stations along the African coast. The trading companies and merchants of various nations maintained agents at several points along the West African coast. These agents were called *factors* by the English, and their headquarters came to be called *factories*. The factors carried on their business with the consent of the local king. They were often as brutal as the rest of

[4] Mungo Park, *Travels in the Interior Districts of Africa* (New York, 1800), pp. 345–346.

57

Captains of the slave ships crowded the Africans into close quarters, with little regard for health or comfort (left). Slaves who survived the ocean voyage were sold in New World markets (below).

the participants in the trade. A factor would herd newly purchased slaves into a *barracoon,* a sort of barracks. The slaves were inspected for disease and then branded with the company's brand. They were fed a mush made of corn, bananas, and yams.

When a slave ship arrived, the captain might not find enough slaves to meet his needs. Sometimes he had to wait several weeks or even months to get a full cargo. Often a ship visited several factories in search of cargo. The factor loaded the Africans into canoes or barges that would carry them out to the slave ship. Since there were few good harbors along the coast, this was often a rough trip for the slaves.

Many of the slaves from the interior had never seen the ocean before. Desperate by this time, some threw themselves into the sea rather than go aboard the strange ships. No fellow African had ever returned to tell what happened after boarding the ships, and the white captain and crew did not speak African languages. There was no one to tell the prisoners that they were going to work as field hands and not be eaten. The belief that the whites were cannibals who were buying the Africans for food lasted for three centuries.

One African named Olaudah Equiano (ek-wee-*ah'* noh) was captured in Benin when he was eleven years old. He was shipped to Barbados, sold, and taken first to Virginia and then to England. After learning to write English, he published an account of his life as a slave. Following is Equiano's description of going aboard the slave ship:

The first object which saluted my eyes when I arrived on the coast was the sea and a slave ship, which was then riding at anchor. . . . These filled me with astonishment, which was soon converted into terror. . . . When I was carried on board, I was immediately handled and tossed up, to see if I were sound, by some of the crew; and I was now persuaded that I had gotten into a world of bad spirits, and that they were going to kill me. Their complexions too, differing so much from ours, their long hair, and the language they spoke, which was very different from any I had ever heard, united to confirm me in this belief. . . .

When I looked round the ship too and saw a large [cauldron] boiling, and a multitude of black people of every description chained together, every one of their faces expressing dejection and sorrow, I no longer doubted of my fate. . . . I asked them if we were not to be eaten by those white men with horrible looks, red faces, and long hair.[5]

The ocean voyage was an even worse ordeal. The horrors of the voyage across the Atlantic were also described by Equiano:

I was soon put down under the decks. There I received such a salutation in my nostrils as I had never experienced in my life; so that, with the loathsomeness of the stench and crying together, I became so sick and low that I was not able to eat. . . . Two of the white men offered me eatables; and, on my refusing to eat, one of them held me fast by the hands, and laid me across, I think, the windlass and tied my feet while the other flogged me severely. . . . I would have jumped over the side, but I could not. . . . I [saw] some of these poor African prisoners

[5] From Philip D. Curtin, editor, *Africa Remembered: Narratives by West Africans from the Era of the Slave Trade* (Madison: The University of Wisconsin Press; © 1967 by the Regents of the University of Wisconsin), pp. 92, 93, 95, 96–97.

most severely cut for attempting to do so, and hourly whipped for not eating. . . .

The closeness of the place and the heat of the climate, added to the number in the ship, which was so crowded that each had scarcely room to turn himself, almost suffocated us. . . . This . . . brought on a sickness amongst the slaves, of which many died. . . .

The adults on most slave ships were kept below deck, chained to the floor. Each had a space about as big as a coffin. Some slave captains kept these decks clean by having slave "trustees" wash them out with sea water. Others reasoned, "Crowd them in closely, throw them food, and enough will survive to yield a handsome profit." To avoid mutiny, captains were careful not to fill their vessels with captives who spoke the same language. There were many records of seaboard mutinies over the centuries. Sometime a ship was taken over by the slaves. Since the mutineers had no seafaring knowledge, they could not sail the ship back to Africa. But they preferred death at sea to the unknown dangers that lay ahead.

There were heavy losses from sickness. The poor diet (rough corn or barley without meat or fresh vegetables), the bad water, and the unsanitary, crowded conditions made many slaves sick. Those who seemed to be dying or showed signs of a contagious disease were tossed overboard, dead or not. Smallpox was particularly dreaded. Any slave who developed the sores of smallpox was thrown into the ocean. Some of the slaves seemed to die not so much from physical causes as from despair.

Slaves were sold at ports in the New World. A large number of slaves were sold in the West Indian islands and then resold elsewhere, particularly to the English colonies. Olaudah Equiano was taken to Barbados. He described what happened when the ship arrived:

Many merchants and planters now came on board. . . . They put us in separate parcels and examined us attentively. They also made us jump. . . . [We cried so much] that at last the white people got some old slaves from the land to pacify us. They told us we were not to be eaten, but to work, and were soon to go on land where we should see many of our country people. This report eased us much; and sure enough, soon after we landed, there came to us Africans of all languages. We were conducted immediately to the merchant's yard, where we were all pent up together like so many sheep in a fold. . . .

We were not many days in the merchant's custody before we were sold after their usual manner, which is this: on a signal given (as the beat of a drum), the buyers rush at once into the yard where the slaves are confined, and make choice of that parcel they like best. . . . In this manner, without scruple, are relations and friends separated, most of them never to see each other again.

Equiano was more fortunate than other slaves, since he was not sold to a sugar-plantation owner. A Virginia slave trader bought him and several of his shipmates. They were later sold to officers in the British navy as personal servants. Equiano learned to read and write English and was eventually bought by a Quaker, who set him free. He later became active in the British antislavery movement. Thus, his experience was unusual in the history of slavery. But his account of his capture and voyage to America reveals the feelings of those millions of Africans who never had a chance to write their own stories.

Africans were trained for slavery. In the Caribbean the Africans experienced a process called "seasoning." Whether they were to remain in the islands or be sent to the mainland, all Africans were "seasoned" or "trained" for life in slavery. As part of this process the new slaves were put to work alongside veteran slaves. But "seasoning" also meant "breaking in," or forcing the slaves to accept the rigidly controlled life they would now have to lead. A number of Africans were killed during this harsh experience. Even more died from disease, inadequate food, unfamiliar climate, and despair. Many committed suicide.

THINKING ABOUT THIS SECTION

1. Explain or define the following words: coffle; factor; "seasoning."

2. What was the role of each of these in transforming Africans into New World slaves: African rulers, Arab raiders, slave drivers, European traders?

3. Why was Olaudah Equiano terrified when taken aboard the slave ship? when he was auctioned in America? How was he reassured?

4. For what various reasons was the transatlantic voyage a hideous and dangerous experience for the slaves? Could nothing be done about these reasons?

4. Black Slavery in Latin America

Why did the slave trade become such a big business? And what was life like for the tremendous numbers of Africans shipped to Latin America?

The slaves worked the plantations. The need for cheap labor provided the motive for the slave trade. The white settlers in America had found that no amount of harsh treatment could force the Indians to become satisfactory mine and field workers. As large-scale agriculture developed in the West Indies and Brazil, Eu-

ropeans demanded more and more black workers from Africa.

By the mid-1600's sugar cane had become the chief crop grown in the Caribbean. Because of the great demand for sugar in Europe, this crop yielded huge profits. Strong, hard-working people were needed to clear and plant the fields, to tend the growing cane, and to operate the cane-grinding mills. Slaves also worked on plantations growing cacao, rice, and cotton, and they tended fields of tobacco, vegetables, and fruits. They did the heavy labor on the docks

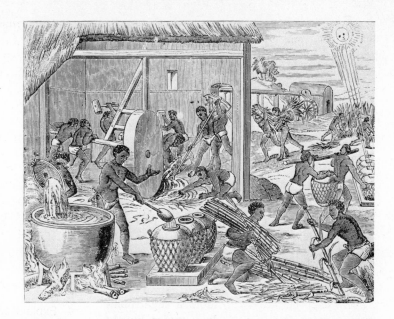

An old engraving showed the many tasks done by slaves on a Caribbean sugar plantation of the 1500's. Probably the hardest work was turning the heavy stone that crushed the cane.

of port cities and in mines and quarries. Slaves were also used as personal servants.

Slavery in the Caribbean was brutal. Slavery in all the Caribbean islands was harsh, whether under French, Spanish, English, Dutch, or Danish masters. Some of the owners enjoyed a good life in Europe and paid overseers to supervise the slaves on their New World plantations. Since the owners were interested only in profits, they cared little how the overseers treated the slaves. Men and women, both young and old, labored eighteen hours every day during the sugar harvest. Because of the heavy work required of the slave women, few babies were born alive, and few children survived infancy. Better treatment would have lengthened the lives of the plantation slaves. But the European owners and managers considered it "better business" to work the slaves hard and buy fresh ones to replace those who died of exhaustion.

Since slaves far outnumbered the Europeans on most of the Caribbean islands, the governments adopted "black codes," or laws to control the slaves. Some of these laws were meant to protect the slaves, but they were often ignored. On the other hand, laws that required

stiff punishment for any "misconduct" were rigidly enforced. Despite such controls, many mutinies broke out. A number of slaves died struggling for freedom, but a few managed to escape. In Cuba and Hispaniola runaway slaves escaped in large numbers. Their descendants lived for generations in the hilly inland regions.

In Haiti the life of the slaves was as wretched as anywhere in the Caribbean. By the late 1700's absentee plantation owners were making enormous fortunes. Managers of plantations in Haiti paid low prices for blacks from central Africa, worked them to death, and then imported more. They kept the slaves in chain gangs, making sure that none spoke a language understood by the others. The slaves were allowed little family or personal life. Haitian slaves were more than ready to join the largest and most successful of slave revolts in the 1790's (Chapter 7).

Slavery in Brazil was different. Brazil, too, became dependent on sugar plantations worked by slave labor. The Brazilian Indians along the coast, where the Portuguese first settled, were "children of the forest." As nomads living on tropical forest products, they knew little of plowing and planting. To make the colony profitable, the Portuguese government imported African slaves.

Like the Caribbean slaves, most slaves in Brazil suffered harsh treatment. The class structure in Brazil was rigid, and slaves ranked lower than anyone else. Yet in the Brazilian plantation society, conditions were different. Some slaves became personal servants, craftsmen, and skilled workers. For these blacks life was not so wretched as it was for plantation workers. Moreover, Africans in Brazil were regarded as people with souls. The law required slaves to receive instruction in the Catholic faith. They were baptized, attended church, and took part in religious ceremonies.

Some Brazilian slaves were able to buy their freedom or were granted it when their masters died. In fact, the freeing of slaves was encouraged in Brazil, particularly after an owner's death or when a faithful slave reached a certain age. Teaching slaves to read and write was not illegal as it was in the English colonies. Many children of Portuguese masters and female slaves were freed at birth or when they grew up. Some were even sent to Portugal to study at the university in Coimbra. In short, slaves in Brazil had the status of human beings entitled to certain rights.

Another factor in the difference between Brazilian and Caribbean slavery was the vast size of the Portuguese colony. In Brazil there was no population pressure as there was in the Caribbean islands. The Portuguese had less fear of being outnumbered and overrun by mutinous slaves.

Brazilian slaves rebelled. Even so, in Brazil as elsewhere, blacks sometimes rose up against their white masters. In some towns Muslim Africans sought each other out and organized uprisings. When these failed, some of the slaves killed themselves rather than surrender to the Portuguese. A small number of the Muslim slaves managed to buy ships and sail back to West Africa.

Brazilian slaves also escaped into the forests, where they organized their own communities. Some of these communities united to form a state called Palmares (pahl-*mah'* rays). The people of Palmares maintained their independence from the coastal government for nearly half a century. They had their own king and army and an efficient government. About 20,000 black people lived in Palmares when it was conquered by a Portuguese army in 1697. Most of them were sold back into slavery.

Slavery existed throughout Latin America. Although most slaves were held in the Caribbean islands and Brazil, they were to be found in all parts of Latin America. In Central America slaves worked on plantations and cattle ranches. Perhaps the largest number of slaves in Spanish South America lived in Colombia, Venezuela, and Ecuador. Throughout Latin America, Africans took part in the exploration of frontier regions. Many blacks were absorbed into the general population.

What was the status of the slave? Spanish law, like Portuguese, recognized that slaves had certain legal rights. Under Spanish law, slaves were supposed to be baptized and adequately fed and clothed. But these laws were not always obeyed. In the Caribbean, laws requiring humane treatment of slaves were obviously ignored. On the mainland, however, slaves were in general treated less harshly. This was especially true of areas where they were fewer in number than the white population and therefore not considered a threat.

Race relations took a different direction than in North America. In both the Spanish and Portuguese colonies, marriage between all the races was more common than in the English colonies. As a result, a large percentage of Latin American people are of mixed descent. Various terms are used to refer to Latin Americans of mixed ancestry. Many of these terms are in common use while others are considered insults. The most frequently used terms in Spanish America are *mestizo* (mes-*tee'* soh), meaning someone of Indian and white descent,

African culture remains strong in Brazilian cities today. Here throngs of black Brazilians celebrate a festival honoring Yemanja, an African sea-goddess.

and *mulatto* (moo-*lah'* toh), meaning someone of Negro and white descent. In Brazil the word *mestiço* (pronounced like mestizo) generally means anyone of mixed ancestry, though it is often applied to a person of white and black parentage. *Mameluco* (mah-may-*loo'* koh) is the Brazilian term for the offspring of Indian and white parents.

There is no question that slavery was as cruel in Latin America as it was in the English colonies. Nevertheless, in Latin America the slave's humanity was not denied, as it was in North America. The difference between slavery in Latin America and in the English colonies can be summed up in one statement by the historian Frank Tannenbaum: "The question of the slave's fitness for freedom never arose, and the freed Negro was a free man, not a freedman."

The "hybrid" nature of Latin American society probably contributed to the fact that race prejudice did not become as intense as it did in the United States. Race prejudice certainly exists in Latin America. But racial background is less important than social status. Manners, dress, and occupation outweigh skin color in determining a person's level on the social ladder. Moreover, in Latin America, race prejudice less often takes the form of segregation.

Black people influenced the whole of Latin American life. The African heritage played a large part in shaping the culture that developed in Latin America. In the history of some Latin American nations black people have taken a far more active role than the native population. The arts, music, literature, cooking, politics, and family life are only a few of the many aspects of culture that reflect African influence. Latin American culture is the product of both its native and its pioneering peoples—Indians, Spanish and Portuguese, and Africans.

1. Explain or define the following words: overseer; black codes; Palmares; mestizo.

2. Contrast slavery in the Caribbean islands and in Brazil. How do you account for the differences? How had slavery been different in the West African kingdoms? in Portugal in the late 1400's? Explain why, in each case.

3. Under Spanish law, what were the legal rights of slaves? Why were these legal provisions ignored more often in the Caribbean islands than on the mainland?

4. Why did race prejudice develop to a greater degree in English-speaking North America than in Latin America?

Summing Up

Over 50 million Latin Americans are descended from people who were enslaved in Africa and shipped to the New World for sale as laborers. Slavery is as old as the human race. But probably never before had such huge numbers of people been sent as slaves to a part of the world so far from their homeland.

Since most Europeans knew little about Africa during the years of the slave trade, they often assumed that African peoples had no cultures or nations of their own. But in recent years American and European historians have learned more about the history of West Africa.

They have found that kingdoms in this part of Africa were extensive and well-organized and had developed high levels of civilization. Cities like Benin were thriving centers of commerce.

By the early 1500's, Europeans had begun to buy slaves along the coast of West Africa for shipment across the Atlantic. Over the next three centuries the greediness of African kings and European and Arab slave traders robbed West Africa of its best young people and halted the development of the nations of that region.

Most of those Africans who survived the terrible voyage across the Atlantic were put to work on the plantations and in the mines of the New World. In the hot Caribbean ports they also did many other kinds of heavy work. Where few Europeans came to live and only overseers were sent to run the plantations, as in Haiti, the population today is still mostly black. A large portion of the slave population also lived in Brazil. Though life for a slave was grim everywhere, slavery in the Caribbean was much harsher than in Brazil and on the Spanish mainland.

In both the Portuguese and Spanish legal systems, the slave was recognized as a person entitled to human rights. Though slaves were at the bottom of the social scale in both Latin America and the English colonies, it was easier in Latin America for them to win freedom and gain acceptance as full members of the community. Throughout Latin America, the African heritage contributed to the formation of a new culture.

4

The European Conquest

Gold ornaments made by Indian craftsmen were eagerly collected by the Spanish soldiers who came to America. Indifferent to the beauty of the goldwork, the Spaniards melted much of it down. Fortunately, some of the Indian treasures, like this Colombian pendant representing a winged god, were overlooked by the European invaders.

CHAPTER FOCUS

1. Cortés in Mexico
2. Conquests South and North from Mexico City
3. Pizarro in Peru
4. Spanish Explorations in Other Regions of South America
5. The Portuguese on the Brazilian Coast

One of the stories that lured European adventurers into the interior of South America was the legend of *El Dorado* (el doh-*rah'* doh), "the Golden King." According to the story, this wealthy Indian king once a year (some said every day) was anointed with beeswax or gum and then sprinkled with precious gold dust. In a stately ceremony the king's subjects rowed *El Dorado* to the middle of a lake, where he dove into the water and washed off the gold. His subjects also threw golden trinkets into the lake as offerings to their gods.

The European thirst for riches led explorer after explorer to search for the mysterious *El Dorado*. Not only Spaniards sought the Golden King. The Englishman Walter Raleigh also ventured up the Orinoco River, hoping to find the source of the legend. No one ever found *El Dorado*. Recently, however, golden treasure discovered in a lake in Colombia suggests that the legend may have been based on fact. There is gold dust in the mud at the bottom of this lake. But the cost of bringing the mud up and separating the gold would be too great to make the effort worthwhile.

Though the Spaniards never found *El Dorado,* they did find fantastic riches in other parts of the New World. As a result, the empires of the Aztecs in Mexico and the Incas in Peru were conquered and destroyed. Their rulers were killed, their armies overcome, and their people put to work for the *conquistadores* (kohn-keess-tah-*doh'* rayss), as the Spanish conquerors were called. Elsewhere in the Americas, the restless soldiers of Spain continued to seek new empires and more golden treasure. Some of them tried to follow Queen Isabella's command to Christianize the Indians they conquered, and this was the chief concern of the priests who accompanied the *conquistadores.* On the heels of these trail-blazers came other priests and also settlers. Missions and towns were founded. In 1500, Santo Domingo was the only Spanish settlement in Latin America. Within a century the Spaniards had founded many towns from Chile to Mexico. Meanwhile, Portuguese settlements were planted on the Brazilian coast.

1. Cortés in Mexico

After starting a colony at Santo Domingo, the Spanish gave their attention to Cuba. By 1514 *conquistadores* had made that island an outpost of Spanish power.

An expedition to Mexico was planned. Diego Velásquez (vay-*lahss'* kayss), the governor of the new Spanish colony of Cuba, had heard reports of cities on the Yucatán peninsula. An expedition sent out by Velásquez to investigate the reports failed miserably. Fierce assaults by the Indians drove back the Spaniards who tried to land on the Yucatán coast. Less than half of the men got back to Cuba. A second expedition returned to Cuba with the news that civilized people lived along the coast of Yucatán and also inland. The Spaniard who led this expedition reported to Velásquez that some of the Indians had pointed to the sunset and indicated that gold was to be found in that direction.

Cortés was ordered to explore Mexico. Velásquez then decided to send a third expedition to explore farther inland. He named Hernando Cortés (cor-*tez'*) to lead this daring venture. Cortés had been born in Spain, the son of well-to-do parents. At the age of nineteen he left Spain to seek adventure in Santo Domingo. Like many other Spaniards, Cortés hoped to find gold in the New World. On Santo Domingo he received an allotment of land with Indians to do the work, but he was bored by life there. Cortés had welcomed the opportunity to serve under Velásquez in the conquest of Cuba.

Cortés was 33 years old when chosen by the governor of Cuba to lead an expedition into Mexico. Courageous and ambitious, Cortés was also a fair man, respected by those he led. Throughout his exploits he was to show remarkable talent for leadership and military strategy. Velásquez gave Cortés the task of organizing the expedition. Cortés rounded up eleven ships and enlisted some 500 soldiers and 100 sailors. One of the soldiers was Bernal Díaz (*dee'* ahs), a young man who had gone on the earlier expeditions to Yucatán. Bernal Díaz survived many adventures in the New World and lived to be 80 years old. Late in life, he wrote a book giving an eyewitness account of Spanish exploits in Mexico.

Cortés loaded his ships with supplies, several small cannon, gunpowder, and sixteen horses.

In his account, Bernal Díaz carefully lists all the horses. These animals were precious, since they had to be brought all the way from Spain. Both cannon and horses were to give the Spaniards a great advantage in fighting the Indians, who had neither. This advantage was especially effective against those Indians who encountered cannon and horses for the first time.

Several landings were made along the coast. Before Cortés left Cuba, Velásquez began to have second thoughts. Feeling that Cortés was acting too independently, Velásquez decided to fire him. But before the governor could act, Cortés ordered his ships to sail for Mexico. His first anchorage was at the island of Cozumel (koh-soo-*mel'*), off the east coast of Yucatán. Here the Spaniards picked up a Spanish priest who had survived a shipwreck years before and had become the slave of an Indian chieftain. This priest, named Aguilar (ah-gwee-*lar'*), had escaped and rowed out to Cozumel after hearing that the Spaniards had landed there. He told Cortés all that he knew about Mexico and joined the expedition to act as an interpreter.

Farther along the coast the Spaniards made a second stop for fresh water. Here Cortés and his men fought the first of many battles with Indian warriors. After turning back the assault, Cortés assured the Mayan *caciques* (kah-*seeks'*) or chieftains that he came in peace. While talking with them, he had his men fire the cannon and caused his horse to rear. Bernal Díaz says in his book that the *caciques* were terrified and from then on paid great respect to the Spaniards and gave them presents.

Marina joined the Spaniards. Among the gifts were 20 slaves, one of them a beautiful young woman called Marina by the Spaniards. She had been born an Aztec noblewoman in the highlands of Mexico. Her stepfather had sold her as a slave to the coastal Mayan people. As a child she had spoken Nahuatl, the language of the Aztecs, and as a young slave she had

This portrait of Cortés shows how he looked when he first came to the New World.

learned a Mayan dialect. Aguilar immediately saw her value as an interpreter. As the Spaniards advanced inland, Cortés would tell Aguilar in Spanish what he wanted to say to the Indians. Aguilar translated into Mayan for Marina, and she in turn communicated with the Nahuatl-speaking people. Marina soon learned Spanish and then interpreted directly between Spanish and Aztec leaders. She gave her loyalty to the Spaniards but apparently was respected and admired by Spaniards and Indians alike. The Indians called her Malinche (mah-*leen'* chay).

Marina became Cortés' common-law wife and bore him a son, whom Cortés had legally baptized as Martín Cortés. Although Cortés later married a young noblewoman when he returned to Spain, he provided for Marina and their son.

Cortés founded the city of Veracruz. Sailing northwest along the Mexican coast, the Spaniards watched for a good port and, when they found one, landed on the beach. Cortés began to plan a new town for this site and named it Villa Rica de la Vera Cruz ("rich town of the true cross"). By declaring Veracruz (as it came to be called) a new colony and by making himself mayor of the town, Cortés could claim to be independent of his enemy, the governor of Cuba. By this time some of the men who were more loyal to Velásquez than to Cortés were grumbling and demanding that the expedition return to Cuba. Using both threats and promises of great wealth, Cortés persuaded the reluctant men to push on.

The Spaniards learned more about the Mexican Indians. Leaving 150 men to garrison Veracruz, Cortés led the rest of the Spaniards north along the coast to Cempoala (sem-poh-ah' lah). This was the largest city the Spaniards had yet seen in the New World. Through the interpreters Cortés learned that many of the tribes between Cempoala and Mexico City were dominated by the Aztecs. The Indians resented having to send tribute and sacrificial victims to the Aztec ruler. But, they said, Moctezuma was a very powerful king. All feared him and believed he could never be defeated. According to Díaz, Cortés replied "that he would see to it that they were relieved of their burdens."

In Cempoala, as elsewhere, the Spaniards were shocked at the Indian religion and its demands of human sacrifice. Spanish soldiers mounted the great stairway to one of the temples, pulled down and burned the idols, and erected a Christian altar. A Spanish priest even baptized some of the Indians.

Cortés burned his ships. Meanwhile, some of the Spaniards were secretly plotting a return to Cuba. When Cortés found out about it, he ordered all of his ships burned. Now the men had no choice but to follow him inland. Cortés realized that Velásquez probably considered him a rebel. Typically, Cortés went over the Cuban governor's head and wrote directly to the Spanish king. He sent Charles I gold and other treasure the Spaniards had found in

Mexico. Cortés did not hear from the king for some time. Nevertheless, Cortés proceeded on his own. He knew that if he found more rich treasure and conquered a new land for Spain, Charles would not quibble over "legality."

The Spaniards won allies. The ruler of Cempoala gave Cortés warriors, guides, and other men to carry supplies. In August, 1519, the Spaniards and their new allies left Cempoala and advanced inland. Soon they came to the city of Tlaxcala (tlahs-kah' lah), capital of a kingdom which had managed to stay independent of the Aztecs. In a clash with Tlaxcalan warriors the Spaniards encountered the strongest resistance they had yet faced. After defeating the Tlaxcalans, Cortés took them on as allies. These Indians remained valuable companions throughout the Mexican campaign.

Cortés and the combined army of Spaniards and Indians now marched to Cholula (choh-loo' lah). This city was the site of a massive sacred pyramid. Although the Cholulans seemed friendly, Marina found out that they were plotting to ambush the Spaniards. She told Cortés, who acted swiftly. The Spaniards massacred hundreds of Cholulans, destroyed the temple on top of the city's pyramid, and replaced it with a Christian church. News of this action spread to other Indians, who began to realize that the fair-skinned strangers could be dangerous enemies.

Knowledge of the conquest comes from both Spanish and Aztec sources. Most accounts of the conquest of Mexico reflect the Spanish point of view. Bernal Díaz, other Spaniards, and Cortés himself, in his letters to the king, told their own stories of the conquest. After more than four centuries these chronicles still make dramatic reading. But it is well to remember that the men who wrote them naturally told their own side of the story. The Spaniards all believed they were justified in conquering

European Exploration and Conquest

MEXICO

Gulf of Mexico

ATLANTIC OCEAN

Mexico City
Veracruz
YUCATÁN *Cozumel I.* CUBA
Santiago

Santo Domingo

Caribbean Sea

Guatemala

LINE OF DEMARCATION

Santa Marta
Cartagena
Panama Darién
Cauca R.
Magdalena R.
Orinoco R.

PACIFIC OCEAN

Cali
Bogotá
Popayán

Quito

Amazon R.

Túmbes

Cajamarca

PERU SOUTH AMERICA BRAZIL

Olinda
Recife

Bahia

Rimac R. Lima
Callao
Pachácamac Cuzco

Paraguay R.

Cortés, 1519
Cortés' captains, 1520's–1530's
Pizarro, 1530–1532
Almagro, 1535–1536
Orellana, 1541–1542
Valdivia, 1540–1553
Belalcázar, 1538–1539
Quesada, 1536–1539
Federmann, 1536–1539
Ayolas, 1537

Asunción
Tucumán Paraná R.

Rio de Janeiro
São Vicente

Córdoba
Santa Fe

Valparaiso Buenos Aires
Santiago *Rio de la Plata*

Bio-Bio R.

CORTÉS' ROUTE ACROSS MEXICO

*Gulf
of
Mexico*

Tenochtitlán
(Mexico City)

Tlaxcala Cempoala

Cholula Veracruz

0   20   40   60 Miles

0   200   400   600   800   1000 Miles

the Aztecs and destroying the Indians' government and religion.

Equally dramatic, though less well-known, are the Aztec chronicles of the conquest. In these writings we see the Spanish conquest from the viewpoint of the people whose civilization was destroyed. Some of the Aztecs who lived through these events recorded their experiences in the folded paper books called codices. A very few of these codices still exist. Other survivors of the conquest told their stories to a missionary, Father Sahagún, who came to Mexico after the conquest. He wrote these accounts down in Spanish. The Indian Fernando de Alva Ixtlilxochitl also recorded stories told by his aged uncles who had fought the Spaniards (page 19). Many of the Aztec records have been collected in a book called in English *The Broken Spears*. This title was suggested by an Aztec poem lamenting the destruction of Mexico:

> Broken spears lie in the roads;
> We have torn our hair in our grief.
> The houses are roofless now,
> And their walls are red with blood.

This verse and much of the quoted material in the following pages are from *The Broken Spears*.[1]

Moctezuma knew the Spaniards were approaching. First reports of the Spaniards' arrival off Yucatán had reached Moctezuma, the Aztec chief, from messengers. They had seen "two towers or small mountains floating on the waves of the sea. . . . [The people] have very light skin, much lighter than ours. They all have long beards, and their hair comes only to their ears." Moctezuma's efficient communications system brought news of the Spaniards' approach through Tlaxcala.

[1] *The Broken Spears,* ed. Miguel Leon-Portilla, pp. xxxv, 16, 17, 25, 29, 30, 61, 64, 66, 74, 76, 77, 84–85, 107, 109. Copyright © 1962 by the Beacon Press; originally published under the title *Visión de los Vencidos,* copyright © 1959 by Universidad Nacional Autonoma de Mexico. Reprinted by permission of Beacon Press.

The Aztecs believed in the legend of Quetzalcoatl's return (page 19), and Moctezuma apparently thought Cortés might well be this god, though he was not quite sure. Moctezuma ordered his messengers to bear gifts to the strangers: gold and turquoise masks and necklaces, shields, and other ornaments decorated with shells and quetzal feathers. Moctezuma said to the messengers: "Go now, without delay. Do reverence to our lord the god. Say to him: 'Your deputy, Moctezuma, has sent us to you. Here are the presents with which he welcomes you home to Mexico.' "

Though he sent presents to the strangers, Moctezuma was not overjoyed at their arrival. While the messengers were gone, said an Aztec scribe, he "could neither sleep nor eat. . . . He sighed almost every moment. He was lost in despair, in the deepest gloom and sorrow. . . . He said: 'What will happen to us?' "

Cortés was delighted with the gifts brought by Moctezuma's messengers. But he shot off the cannon to impress them. The messengers hurried back to Tenochtitlán and reported to Moctezuma: "A thing like a ball of stone comes out of its entrails; it comes out shooting sparks and raining fire." They also described the Spaniards' horses: "Their deer carry them on their backs wherever they wish to go. These deer, our lord, are as tall as the roof of a house."

According to the Aztec chronicles, Moctezuma was alarmed by this news. He sent another party of envoys to Cortés, this time with magicians and wizards who were instructed to cast evil spells on the foreigners. Moctezuma also sent the Spaniards more presents. Clearly the Aztec leader was uncertain how to treat the approaching strangers. As for the Spaniards, the rich presents simply made them more determined to find the source of this wealth.

As the Spaniards advanced toward Tenochtitlán, Moctezuma called a conference of courtiers and relatives. One of his brothers warned: "I pray to our gods that you will not let the strangers into your house. They will cast you

Tenochtitlan.

Marina translates as Cortés and Moctezuma meet in this Indian portrayal of the first encounter of the two leaders. At the foot of the picture the Indian artist showed some of Moctezuma's gifts to the Spaniards, including birds and a roped deer.

out of it and overthrow your rule, and when you try to recover what you have lost, it will be too late." In spite of this advice, Moctezuma reluctantly decided to welcome the Spaniards to Tenochtitlán.

Cortés received a friendly welcome. By early November the Spaniards were fast approaching the beautiful Valley of Mexico, with its lakes and cities. Fertile and prosperous, the valley was the seat of a civilization more advanced than any the Spaniards had yet seen. From the pine forests of the mountains the Spaniards began their descent to the cornfields and the lake-shore towns. Along the way the Spaniards had been joined by more Indian allies. These people complained about the Aztec tax-gatherers, who, said Bernal Díaz, "robbed them of all they possessed."

When the Spaniards came to the lakes, crowds of Indians rowed out in canoes to see the white "gods" and their horses, the enormous "deer." As the Spaniards marched along the southern causeway which led across the water into the Aztec capital city, they marveled at what they saw. Bernal Díaz writes:

Gazing on such wonderful sights, we did not know what to say, or whether what appeared before us was real, for on one side, on the land, there were great cities, and in the lake ever so many more, and the lake itself was crowded with canoes, and in the causeway were many bridges at intervals, and in front of us stood the great City of Mexico, and we—we did not even number four hundred soldiers! And we well remembered the words and warnings . . . that had been given [by Indian allies] that we should beware of entering Mexico, where they would kill us, as soon as they had us inside.[2]

In a sedan chair carried by four men and accompanied by many noble attendants, Moctezuma himself came to greet Cortés. The Aztec chief was splendidly dressed in robes of quetzal feathers and silver and gold embroidery.

Moctezuma greeted Cortés, according to an Aztec scribe, in these words: "Our lord, you are weary. The journey has tired you, but now you have arrived on the earth. You have come to your city, Mexico. You have come here to

[2] Bernal Díaz del Castillo, *The Discovery and Conquest of Mexico,* tr. A. P. Maudslay (New York: Farrar, Straus and Cudahy, 1956), p. 192.

sit on your throne again. This was foretold by the kings who governed your city, and now it has taken place. . . . Rest now, and take possession of your royal houses." After Marina translated this, Cortés told her to answer: "We have come to your house in Mexico as friends. There is nothing to fear." Moctezuma provided living quarters in the city for the Spaniards and ordered that they be supplied with anything they needed. He also gave them more presents of gold.

Cortés gained power over Moctezuma. The Spaniards spent the next week relaxing in their quarters but wondering uneasily what might happen next. Cortés decided to strengthen his position by bringing the Aztec leader completely within his power. Moctezuma is a puzzling figure. He commanded a large army of well-trained warriors. A word from him at any time would have hurled these men into a fierce attack on the Spaniards. But instead he allowed the small band of strangers to march all the way across Mexico and into his capital city.

Now Cortés took advantage of Moctezuma's uncertainty. He persuaded the Aztec ruler to move into the quarters provided for the Spaniards. Thus Moctezuma became a hostage. Though still surrounded by luxury and treated like royalty, Moctezuma was in effect a prisoner. He still could have resisted. Many of his nobles were eager, in fact, to attack the Spaniards. Perhaps Moctezuma still thought the Spaniards might be gods. At any rate, he seems to have felt that he could not oppose Cortés. By this time, said an Aztec chronicler, the Indian chiefs were angry with Moctezuma "and no longer revered or respected him." There followed a strange six months of apparently peaceful relations. But under the surface tension mounted on both sides. Meanwhile, the Spaniards spent their time collecting gold and other treasure.

Cortés returned to the coast. In May, 1520, word reached Cortés that a thousand Spaniards under Captain Panfilo de Narváez (nar-

vah′ ayss) had landed on the coast north of Veracruz. Cortés had no choice but to leave Tenochtitlán and meet this force sent by the governor of Cuba. Only about 150 Spanish soldiers remained in Tenochtitlán under the command of a young and impetuous captain named Pedro de Alvarado. With the rest of his men, Cortés hurried off to the coast. Taking Narváez's more numerous troops by surprise, he won a quick battle with them. Cortés had little difficulty persuading the defeated soldiers to return with him to Tenochtitlán.

Fighting had broken out. The Spaniards returned to a strangely silent Tenochtitlán. No Indians came to greet them on the causeways. Cortés soon learned the reason. During his absence the young Aztec warriors had asked permission to celebrate one of their festivals. Alvarado had granted permission but became suspicious of the preparations for warlike dances. The festivities were held in a courtyard outside the Spanish quarters. One of the Aztec writers gave this version of what happened:

The great captains, the bravest warriors, danced at the head of the files to guide the others. . . . The others called to them: "Come, comrades, show us how brave you are! Dance with all your hearts!" At this moment in the fiesta, when the dance was loveliest and when song was linked to song, the Spaniards were seized with an urge to kill the celebrants. . . . They attacked the man who was drumming and cut off his arms. . . . They attacked all the celebrants, stabbing them, spearing them, striking them with their swords. . . . When the news of this massacre was heard outside the Sacred Patio, a great cry went up: "Mexicanos, come running! Bring your spears and shields! The strangers have murdered our warriors!"

In the battle that followed, the Aztecs drove the Spaniards back into their quarters. When Cortés arrived, he found the Spanish soldiers in a state of siege. He cursed Alvarado and called him a madman. The Spaniards launched several attacks against the Aztec forces in an unsuccessful effort to regain control of the city. Cortés at last realized that he and his men would have to fight their way out of Tenochtitlán. He forced or persuaded Moctezuma to appear on the roof of one of the Spanish-occupied buildings. The unhappy Moctezuma pleaded with the angry crowd to let the Spaniards leave the city. But the Indians hurled stones and insults at their former leader. A few days later Moctezuma died, probably of injuries from the stones but perhaps also of a crushed spirit. Some accounts say the Spaniards strangled him.

The Spaniards escaped but suffered heavy losses. The Spaniards planned their escape for the night of June 30, 1520. Cortés urged his men to leave behind most of their booty, pointing out that the added weight would slow down their escape. Bernal Díaz took with him only four pieces of jade. The Spaniards decided to leave the city over the short western causeway. They built a portable wooden bridge and took it with them for crossing the canals that cut through the causeway. The Spaniards were discovered, so the Aztec story goes, by a Mexican woman who was drawing water from one of the canals. She cried: "Mexicanos, come running! They are crossing the canal! Our enemies are escaping!"

An Aztec priest shouted the alarm from the top of the pyramid, and the Mexican warriors attacked the Spaniards. The wooden bridge stuck fast at the first canal across the causeway, and the Spaniards could not move it to cover the second canal. As the men dashed ahead to get out of the city, they fell into the open water. Those who escaped had to cross the canal over the drowned bodies of their comrades. Others were captured by the Aztecs. The losses suffered on this nightmarish flight were so heavy that the Spaniards afterward remembered it as *La Noche Triste*, "The Night of Sorrows."

Some distance from the city Cortés halted to regroup his forces and count his losses. He was thankful to find that Marina was safe, as well as three men who knew how to make powder and cannonballs. Several experienced shipbuilders and many of those who had been with him since the landing at Veracruz also escaped. Moreover, they still had several cannon and horses. But it was a sorry band of survivors that limped back toward Tlaxcala. After several skirmishes with Aztec spearmen, the Spaniards finally reached safety in that city.

Smallpox broke out in the Aztec capital. The Aztecs exulted over their victory. But the Spaniards had unknowingly left an evil ally in the city. An epidemic of smallpox, a disease new to the Americas, broke out. It had been brought to Mexico by a sick man who came with Narváez. The Aztecs inside the city began to fall ill. They had no resistance to smallpox and no idea of how to treat it. One of the first to die was a younger brother of Moctezuma who had succeeded him as chief of the state.

Hundreds of the Aztecs died in the epidemic. Finally the survivors rallied and chose a new chief. He was a nephew of Moctezuma, a young man of great courage named Cuahtemoc (kwah-*tem'* ok). Today Cuahtemoc is a national hero of Mexico.

Cortés prepared to return to Tenochtitlán. Meanwhile, Cortés was regrouping his forces in Tlaxcala. Many of his men wanted to return to Cuba. But Cortés was determined to conquer Tenochtitlán. He still had received no word from the Spanish king. For all Cortés knew, he might be clamped into chains if he returned to Cuba or Spain. But if he returned as the conqueror of Mexico, with rich treasure to give to the king, it would be a different story. Cortés convinced his soldiers that they must follow him, and he found new allies among the Indians. Equally important, gunpowder, cannon, and supplies intended for Narváez's expedition reached him from Cuba.

For his second expedition to the Aztec capital, Cortés decided to build a fleet of boats. With these, he could attack Tenochtitlán from the lakes surrounding the city. Carpenters set

Aztec arrows were no match for Spanish cannon, as can be seen in this Indian drawing of the attack on Tenochtitlán.

to work cutting and shaping parts which could be fitted together later to make small sailing ships called *brigantines*. After completing his arrangements, Cortés ordered the return march to begin. Indians and Spaniards carried the unassembled parts of the boats over the mountains and down to Texcoco, on the other side of the lake from Tenochtitlán. Here the Spaniards assembled the brigantines and mounted the cannon on the decks. With this invasion fleet, the Spaniards bombarded the Indian city and swept the lake clean of Aztec boats.

The Spaniards besieged Tenochtitlán. Then began an eight-day siege of the city. The Spaniards landed from the brigantines to fight the Aztec warriors, who resisted fiercely. An Aztec historian described conditions in Tenochtitlán:

The Spanish blockade caused great anguish in the city. The people were tormented by hunger, and many starved to death. There was no fresh water to drink,[3] only stagnant water and the brine of the lake, and many people died of dysentery. The only food was lizards, swallows, corncobs, and the salt grasses of the lake. . . . We were so weakened by hunger that, little by little, the enemy forced us to retreat.

Block by block, burning and destroying as they went, the Spaniards took the city from the weakened people. Cuahtemoc, the popular young leader, was captured and had no choice but to surrender the city.

Mexico City was founded on the ruins of the Aztec capital. The surrender took place in August, 1521. Cortés' men hunted in the ruins of Tenochtitlán for the treasure they had abandoned on La Noche Triste, but little of it was found. Cortés immediately began the work of clearing and rebuilding the city. Already the

[3] The Spaniards had cut the aqueduct which brought fresh water into Tenochtitlán.

soldiers were calling it Mexico City. The Spaniards destroyed the great pyramid and began to build a cathedral on the same site. Aztec noblemen who were willing to become Christians were given land and houses in the city. Spanish soldiers took Aztec noblewomen as their wives and settled down in houses built for them by Indian slave laborers.

Spanish control was expanded. Cortés' officers spread out into the surrounding countryside. With their native allies they quelled those Indians who still resisted. Village lands were allotted to Cortés' soldiers, and Indian farmers were ordered to work for the Spaniards.

Cortés sent out one of his officers, Cristobal de Olid, to Honduras, southeast from Mexico. Later, Cortés received word that Olid had declared himself independent of his commander and was ruling a colony he had founded there. Cortés could not allow such a challenge to his authority. He decided to go to Honduras and deal with Olid in person.

On the overland march, part of it through dense jungle, the Spaniards suffered an endless series of hardships. With him Cortés took Cuahtemoc. The Spanish commander had feared that the Aztec leader might start a rebellion if left in Mexico City. When Cortés heard rumors that Cuahtemoc was plotting to massacre the Spaniards, he ordered the young chief hanged. This "execution" earned the *conquistador* the hatred of all the Indians.

The Spaniards reached Olid's town at last, only to find Olid's men had mutinied and killed him. News of uprisings in Mexico City compelled Cortés to return to the capital. There he carried on with the business of organizing Spain's new colony.

Cortés was denied the rule of Mexico. In 1529 Cortés returned to Spain after an absence of a quarter-century. He was greeted warmly and given many honors. Charles I made Cortés a noble, granted him large tracts of land, and encouraged him to explore the Pacific coast of Mexico. But Cortés was not allowed to rule the empire he had conquered. The king had already begun consolidating the new lands under his own control, and Cortés was too independent for the royal peace of mind. Instead of naming Cortés governor of Mexico, Charles arranged for a committee of judges to represent royal authority in the new domain. Cortés was, however, given the title of captain-general.

The disappointed Cortés returned to New Spain, as Mexico was now called, in 1530. Nine years later he again traveled to Spain to press his claims. At the royal court he was received courteously but coldly. The conqueror of Mexico never went back to the New World. Cortés died in Spain in 1547.

THINKING ABOUT THIS SECTION

1. Explain or define the following words: *conquistador;* Bernal Díaz; causeway; Veracruz; *The Broken Spears;* quetzal.

2. Why did the governor of Cuba decide to send an expedition to Mexico? How did Cortés learn something about the Mexican Indians before reaching the site of Veracruz?

3. How did Cortés make sure that the Spanish soldiers would follow him in his advance through Mexico? How did Cortés win Indian allies?

4. Evaluate Moctezuma's policy in dealing with the Spaniards. Why did he think that they might be gods?

5. Evaluate Cortés' strategy in each of the following situations: dealing with Moctezuma; dealing with the expedition commanded by Narváez; reacting to the situation that developed in the Aztec capital during his absence.

6. Why was Cortés determined to recapture Tenochtitlán? What was his plan? Why did it succeed?

7. How did Cortés make the Aztec capital over into a Spanish city? How did he provide land for his men? How did he treat the Aztecs?

8. What was the Spanish king's plan for ruling Mexico? Explain his reasons.

9. If your ancestors had lived in the Valley of Mexico before the coming of the Spaniards, what would be your reaction to the conquest?

Spaniards continued to be drawn by the lure of treasure in America. But they were also looking for a water passage through the new land mass, and they were expanding the territory claimed for the Spanish Crown.

Alvarado conquered Guatemala. In the years following his conquest of the Aztec capital city, Cortés organized several expeditions to explore regions to the north and south. He assigned Pedro de Alvarado to lead one of these expeditions. Alvarado was a dashing, handsome young man, but he also had a cruel streak, as the attack on the Aztec dancers had shown. In 1523 Cortés sent him with a party of Spaniards and Indian allies to explore what is now Central America. Alvarado led his expedition into the mountain valleys of Guatemala. This was the home of a branch of the Mayan Indians. The different tribal groups in Guatemala had built walled towns around small stone temples in traditional Mayan fashion.

Because the different towns had long been fighting each other, Alvarado had little trouble conquering them all. The Spanish soldiers were allotted huge tracts of land and stayed to farm only the more fertile valleys. Meanwhile, Alvarado founded a new city, also called Guatemala, to serve as capital of the new colony.

Alvarado traveled north and south seeking adventure and riches. Pedro de Alvarado was too ambitious and restless to stay long in Guatemala. For a while he returned to Spain. Then, in 1534 he heard of the conquests of the Pizarro brothers in the land of the Incas and the fantastic wealth they had found there. Alvarado decided to look for some of that gold for himself. Sailing from the west coast of Guatemala, he landed on the Ecuador coast only to find other Spaniards already there. Alvarado sold his ships and supplies for silver bars worth a fortune and returned to Guatemala.

Alvarado's restless imagination was next attracted by tales of the "Seven Cities of Cíbola" (*see'* boh-lah). These cities, said to be built of solid silver, supposedly lay far to the north of Mexico. But before Alvarado could set off in search of them, the viceroy at Mexico City enlisted his aid in subduing an Indian uprising. In this campaign Alvarado was killed when a horse slipped and crushed him.

Silver was discovered in the north. To the west of Mexico City, one of the first non-Aztec tribes conquered by the Spaniards were the Tarascans. These Indians were glad to throw off the Aztec yoke. North of the Tarascans the men of Cortés found the valley of Jalisco (hah-*leess'* koh). The Spaniards decided that its broad acres could be used for cattle grazing. One morning, after camping overnight on a large rock, some herdsmen found globules of pure silver under the coals of their campfire. This incident led to the discovery of the silver lodes of north-central Mexico. Eventually the Spaniards developed many mines in this region.

A Spanish official named Nuño de Guzmán (gooss-*mahn'*) became a governor in the mining area. Guzmán soon won a reputation for cruelty and corruption. In savage raids Guzmán and his men destroyed towns and captured Indians, who were sold into slavery and forced to work in the silver mines. Guzmán was removed from power in 1536, but the effects of his "reign of terror" continued to be felt. The desperate Indians rose in rebellion in 1541. The governor in Mexico City finally managed to put down this uprising, and the Indian rebels were enslaved.

THINKING ABOUT THIS SECTION

1. What were the major reasons that caused Spaniards to explore both south and north from Mexico City?

2. What types of settlement were established in Guatemala? in north-central Mexico?

It was another famous *conquistador,* Francisco Pizarro (pih-*sar'* roh), who added the great Inca empire to Spain's domain in the Americas. Pizarro was among the mixed lot of adventurers and soldiers of fortune who had crossed the Isthmus of Panama with Balboa in 1513.

Balboa planned to explore southward. When Balboa stood on the Pacific shore of the isthmus, he had called the vast body of water that stretched before him the "South Sea." But he had suspected that it was the Indian Ocean. Balboa's Indian guides tried to tell him about the "silver king" of Peru who ruled a land far to the south. They also showed him drawings of llamas, the Incas' valuable domesticated animals. Thinking that the animals in the drawings were camels, Balboa decided that the Indians were describing Persia or Arabia. He began to make plans for building a fleet of boats on Panama's Pacific coast and exploring to the south.

Pizarro hoped to take over Balboa's plans. If Balboa had plans, so did Pizarro. Francisco Pizarro was about 45 years old at the time. He had been born in northern Spain, the son of a soldier. As a young man, he left Spain and took passage to Santo Domingo. Since his family had no social importance, Pizarro was not given any grant of land in the New World. Instead of settling down in Santo Domingo, he joined expeditions exploring the mainland. Pizarro was ambitious to take over for himself the exploration of the coast south of the Isthmus of Panama.

Balboa was executed. In 1513 the Spanish king had decided to replace Balboa as governor of Darién (dah-*ryayn'*), the settlement on the Caribbean coast of the isthmus. The new governor was Pedro Arias de Avila, commonly called Pedrarias (pay-*drah'* ree-ahss). Charging that Balboa's activity on the Pacific was illegal, Pedrarias seized the four boats that

Balboa had ordered built. Actually Pedrarias, a ruthless man, was jealous of Balboa and had made this charge just to have an excuse for arresting him. Francisco Pizarro was among the soldiers who arrested Balboa and witnessed his execution for treason in 1517. But Pizarro was not able to take immediate advantage of Balboa's death. Another captain took over Balboa's ships and sailed south along the South American west coast. He brought back stories of a land of great riches.

Pizarro and Almagro joined forces. Determined to find this land, Pizarro in 1523 formed a partnership with Diego de Almagro (ahl-*mah'* groh), another soldier of fortune. During the next few years two expeditions sent out by Pizarro and Almagro tried to reach the Peruvian coast. On the second attempt Pizarro himself was one of fourteen men who survived shipwreck on an island off the coast of Ecuador.

After months of hardship, a ship from Panama finally reached the castaways, and Pizarro set out again, heading southward. At Túmbes (*toom'* bayss), a prosperous Inca town in northern Peru, the Spaniards traded for golden vessels and fine cloth made of llama wool. Pizarro also captured a teen-aged Inca boy, whom the Spaniards called Felipillo (fay-lee-*pee'* yoh), or "Little Philip." This boy was later to serve as an interpreter in Pizarro's invasion of Peru. But Felipillo never learned Spanish very well and was not the skillful interpreter that Marina had been for Cortés.

Pizarro sought help from the king. By now, Pizarro and Almagro had run out of money. In 1528 Pizarro returned to Spain, hoping to get support from the king. As proof of the existence of the rich Inca empire, he showed Charles I the golden objects from Túmbes. The king authorized Pizarro to organize a large expedition but offered neither funds nor soldiers. These Pizarro would have to raise for himself. By the terms of the royal decree, Pizarro was to have the right of conquest over territory from Túmbes south for 600 miles.

Pizarro organized another expedition. After his audience with the king, Pizarro visited his old home in northern Spain. His older half-brother, Hernando Pizarro, was heir to their father's land. But, attracted by the stories of riches in America, he decided to join Francisco. Hernando's son, Pedro Pizarro, came along. Three other half-brothers, Juan and Gonzalo Pizarro and Martín de Alcántara, also joined the expedition and brought with them horses and equipment. Pizarro recruited still other soldiers of fortune in northern Spain and more when he returned to Panama. One of these was a young man named Hernando de Soto.

With a force of 180 men and 27 horses, Pizarro set sail from Panama late in 1530 and headed for Túmbes. Almagro was to follow after raising additional forces. On arriving at Túmbes, the Spaniards took over the city with little opposition. Pizarro decided to march inland without waiting for Almagro.

The Inca empire had been weakened by civil war. During the events of the following year Pizarro was greatly aided by dissension within the Inca empire. Two sons of an Inca ruler who had died seven years earlier were rivals for control of the kingdom. Civil war had resulted. One of the sons, Atahualpa (ah-tah-*wahl'* pah), won the war and imprisoned his half-brother rival, named Huáscar. When Pizarro heard of this, Atahualpa and his courtiers were celebrating at a hot springs resort called Cajamarca (kah-hah-*mar'* kah), south of Túmbes.

Pizarro sought the Inca ruler at Cajamarca. Leaving forces to guard the ships and hold the coast, Pizarro climbed the difficult Andean trail with a little over a hundred men. The march took 45 days. In mid-November, 1532, Pizarro reached Cajamarca. Having heard of the Spaniards' coming, Atahualpa was curious to see the white men. He had no fear of them, since he had an army of some 30,000 warriors stationed nearby.

The meeting with Atahualpa ended in violence. The meeting of Atahualpa and Pizarro and the events that followed were not described by any Inca eyewitness. Garcilaso de la Vega, who recorded so much of Inca history (page 21), was born later. Though Garcilaso wrote an account of the Spanish conquest, he did not see these events for himself. But we do have an account written by a Spanish eyewitness. Young Pedro Pizarro later wrote down what he had seen at Cajamarca.

The Spaniards had found the city empty, for Atahualpa and his courtiers were relaxing at the hot springs nearby. When the Inca ruler heard that the Spaniards had arrived, he returned to the city with his attendants. Pedro Pizarro wrote afterwards that "our knees trembled as we saw so many approach."

Atahualpa, magnificently dressed, entered the town square on a golden throne carried by servants. Throngs of Indian courtiers, also in splendid garments, accompanied the Inca ruler. Using Felipillo as an interpreter, Pizarro's chaplain made a long speech. He declared that the king of Spain claimed all of the Inca domain, that the Pope held authority over all rulers on earth, and that the true God was the Christian God. The Spanish priest then held out a prayer book to emphasize what he had just said. According to Spanish accounts, Atahualpa answered scornfully that he was greater than any other "prince on earth" and threw the prayer book to the ground. But Garcilaso de la Vega reported that the Inca's reply was courteous, that he pointed out the need for a better interpreter, and that the prayer book simply fell. Garcilaso also said of the official report that Pizarro later sent to the Spanish king:

All these declarations were invented by the Spanish general [Pizarro] and his captains to be included in the official report. . . . They took great pains to arrange the facts, leaving out every-

Atahualpa, attended by a huge army of Inca warriors (above), and Pizarro, with only a small band of soldiers (right), came face to face in a dramatic meeting at Cajamarca. Though far outnumbered, the Spaniards were victorious in the fighting that broke out. (Note the very different portrayals of the Inca town in these old prints, both done by European artists.)

thing that did not [add] to their honor, and adding what seemed more favorable to them. . . . They wanted their feats to be rewarded and for that, they had to gild them, glaze, and enhance them, as best they could.[4]

At any rate, the Spaniards at this point fired on the crowd, apparently using some action of the Inca ruler's as an excuse to attack. Stunned by this sudden attack and the strange sound of gunfire, the Indian warriors offered little resistance. Thousands of Indians were killed. Not one Spaniard was badly injured, and the day ended with Atahualpa a prisoner.

Atahualpa offered to pay ransom. In captivity the Inca ruler became better acquainted with the Spaniards. Hernando de Soto, set to guard him, struck up a friendship and taught Atahualpa to play chess. But the Inca ruler soon realized that what the Spaniards wanted was gold. To gain his freedom, Atahualpa offered to give them enough gold to fill a large room as high as he could reach. He further agreed to fill the room twice over with silver. Pizarro accepted the fantastic offer. During the next two months the treasure was collected from all over Peru. Most of it consisted of temple vessels and works of art.

Three Spanish officers journeyed with Inca messengers to Cuzco, the Inca capital city. According to Garcilaso, "they were struck by the city's majesty, by the size of its temples and the wealth of its palaces. . . . And they were also greatly surprised to see so many people, so many merchants and shops. . . ." When Atahualpa heard about the warm welcome given the Spaniards in Cuzco, he ordered Huáscar killed in prison. He may have feared that his half-brother's followers in Cuzco would side with the Spaniards.

Meanwhile, Almagro and his men by this time had reached Cajamarca. Almagro agreed

with Pizarro's men that they should get rid of Atahualpa. They wanted to remain masters of Peru, and they felt that the Inca ruler was a burden on their hands. Even though the entire ransom had been paid, the Spaniards accused Atahualpa of plotting an uprising against them and had him strangled.

The Spaniards quarreled over the Inca riches. The huge ransom stirred up trouble among the Spaniards. One-fifth of it, mostly in large ornate pieces of gold, was sent to the king. This was the "royal fifth," the king's legal share of any wealth found by Spanish explorers. Indian goldsmiths were then put to work melting down the rest of the treasure into gold and silver bars. The artistry that had fashioned exquisite goblets, trays, vases, and jewelry was thus destroyed. Pizarro and his brothers kept a third of the gold and silver bars for themselves. They allotted another third to the men who had come to Peru with Pizarro. This left only the remaining third of the treasure for the latecomers, Almagro and his men. Jealousy and resentment soon began to divide the two groups of Spaniards. Reckless gambling started among the soldiers, moreover, and discipline broke down.

Pizarro and his men spread Spanish control to other cities. Hoping to stop the quarrels, Pizarro sent out expeditions to explore and conquer outlying parts of the Inca empire. A lieutenant named Belalcázar (bay-lahl-*kah'* sar) conquered Quito (*kee'* toh) and founded a Spanish city there. Pizarro himself led a small army to Cuzco. The royal Inca city, still full of wealth, was plundered and then reorganized as a Spanish municipality.

From Cuzco, Pizarro moved on to Pachácamac on the coast. There, also, the Inca temple was stripped of gold and silver. While in this area, Pizarro decided to found a new city to serve as the capital of the colonial empire. He chose a site on the Rimac (ree-*mahk'*) River near the harbor now called Callao (kah-*yah'* oh). The city was laid out in a regular

[4] *The Incas: The Royal Commentaries of the Inca Garcilaso de la Vega,* translated by Maria Jolas from the critical, annotated French edition of Alain Gheerbrant (New York: The Orion Press, 1961), p. 341.

plan, and Inca villagers were put to work constructing buildings. The Spaniards called the city Lima (*lee'* mah). This was probably a careless pronunciation of Rimac.

Almagro explored Chile. Meanwhile, the quarrel between the Pizarro and Almagro factions had flared up again in a dispute over rights to the spoils of Cuzco. Word arrived from Spain that the king had granted Almagro rights to territory south of the area earlier granted to Pizarro (page 78). This helped somewhat to ease tensions. Almagro now set out on a journey southward to see what lay in the regions granted to him. Naturally he and his men hoped to find more cities of gold. But the difficult journey across deserts in western Bolivia and northern Chile ended in bitter disappointment. They found no wealth, only poor Araucanian Indians living in adobe huts.

An Inca rebellion was put down. In Cuzco, the Pizarro brothers sought to win over the followers of Atahualpa's half-brother by making his young brother, Manco Capac, a puppet emperor. Manco soon began to realize that this was a humiliating role. At a time when Francisco Pizarro was settling Lima and Almagro was off in the south, the puppet ruler called on his people to rebel. The Indians, resentful of Spanish pillaging and cruelty, laid siege to the Spaniards inside Cuzco. But when Almagro returned from Chile, his men swept aside the weakened Indian forces and ended the siege.

The Pizarros eliminated their rival. The showdown between the two Spanish factions came when Almagro challenged the followers of Pizarro to an open battle. In 1538 the two factions fought a bloody tournament on a field outside Cuzco. Pizarro's men won and took Almagro prisoner. Hernando Pizarro had him executed by strangling. In vain, the defeated Almagro had pleaded, "I was the first ladder by which you and your brothers mounted up."

Manco Capac escaped capture. Meanwhile, Manco had escaped to a mountain fortress in

Roofs of grass thatch once covered the stone houses of Machu Picchu, the mountain hideaway of the last Inca emperor. From nearby peaks lookouts kept watch for enemies. Abandoned and for several centuries almost forgotten, Machu Picchu was rediscovered by archeologists in 1911.

the eastern Andes (page 24). There he held court as emperor, ruling over nearby villages and ordering occasional raids against the Spanish. Twenty-six years after Manco's death, a Spanish force captured his son and heir, **Tupac Amaru.** This last Inca leader was taken to Cuzco and in 1571 was executed for treason.

Pizarro ruled New Castile. After the battle with the "men of Almagro," the Pizarro brothers seemed to be in complete control of Peru. From 1538 to 1540 Francisco made his headquarters in Cuzco, working to restore order to New Castile, as the colonial domain was called. Like Cortés in Mexico, Pizarro sent out trusted lieutenants to extend the area under Spanish control.

As for the other Pizarros, Juan had died in the Inca revolt. Pedro, the nephew, became a government clerk in Cuzco and began writing his account of the conquest of Peru. Gonzalo Pizarro was named governor of Quito and was assigned to lead an expedition eastward across the Andes. He was to search for the gold of *El Dorado* but also for a rumored grove of cinnamon trees. The Pizarro brothers were well aware that trade in spices could be very profitable.

Hernando Pizarro returned to Spain with a load of gold and silver bars. Charles I had heard about the execution of Almagro. Influenced by Almagro partisans, the king had old Hernando put in prison. After 20 years, he was finally released and died a few years later. Said to be a hundred years old, he was the only one of the Pizarro brothers to die a natural death.

"Kid" Almagro sought revenge. Meanwhile, Almagro's son by an Indian wife yearned to avenge his father's death. Eighteen years old at the time of his father's execution, he became known as *Almagro El Chico,* or "Kid" Almagro. Together with other Almagro partisans, he plotted to assassinate Francisco Pizarro, who had returned to Lima in 1540. In June, 1541, young Almagro and his henchmen

stabbed both Francisco and his half-brother Martín de Alcántara to death in Francisco's house. (Today, Pizarro's body, mummified by the dry climate, lies in a glass case in the cathedral at Lima.)

"Kid" Almagro was now in charge at Lima. He failed, however, to win much popular support. A governor-general arrived in Peru with soldiers and with authority to break up "Kid" Almagro's gang. This he succeeded in doing with the backing of the Pizarrist faction.

Gonzalo Pizarro ruled for a while. But when still another royal governor came to Peru, the Spanish soldiers who had been given land by the Pizarros rallied around Gonzalo Pizarro. These Pizarrist forces met and defeated the Spanish regular troops in a battle at Quito in 1546. The Pizarrists beheaded the new governor. Gonzalo Pizarro then ruled Peru as if he were king.

In 1547 came yet another royal governor and more Spanish troops. The Pizarrist forces were scattered, and in 1548 Gonzalo was executed. The rule of the Pizarro brothers came to an end sixteen years after it had started. But their legacy of chaotic government and abuse of the Indians was to burden Peru for many years afterward.

THINKING ABOUT THIS SECTION

1. Explain or define the following words: royal fifth; puppet emperor.

2. What reasons did Francisco Pizarro have for thinking there was a rich land south of Panama? How did he organize an expedition to conquer it? What circumstances made this venture a success?

3. Why is it difficult to know exactly what happened at the Cajamarca massacre? Why did the Spaniards execute Atahualpa?

4. Why did the Spaniards quarrel among themselves? What was the result?

5. How was Peru finally brought under the control of the royal Spanish government?

The travels and exploits of other *conquistadores* spread Spanish rule to many parts of South America.

Gonzalo Pizarro reached the headwaters of the Amazon.

Gonzalo Pizarro's search for the cinnamon forest led to an amazing feat of exploration. In 1541 Gonzalo had set out from Quito with some 200 Spaniards and 4000 Indians. He also took along great numbers of llamas to carry supplies. One of his captains was an able man named Francisco de Orellana (oh-ray-*yah'* nah). This expedition turned out to be a nightmare. After struggling across icy passes in the Andes, the Spaniards followed swift streams down to green rain forests. Here the climate changed to suffocating heat, and many of the highland Indians died from the sudden change. In these remote regions the Spaniards actually found some cinnamon trees, but by this time they were more concerned with finding food to keep from starving. The llamas had died or strayed or had already been killed and eaten, and the desperate men were eating reptiles and jungle vines and leaves. Finally, Gonzalo Pizarro ordered the men to build a boat and sent out a scouting party under Orellana to explore a nearby river. When Orellana failed to return, Pizarro cursed him as a traitor and decided to make his way back to Quito.

Orellana explored the length of the Amazon.

Orellana had found it impossible to turn back against the current of the swift-flowing river. His boat had finally reached a wide stream flowing eastward into still another river. At one point along the broad river, the Spaniards later claimed, they fought female Indian warriors. Remembering the ancient Greek legend about women warriors called Amazons, Orellana gave the river the name *Amazon*.

Meanwhile, Orellana's men had built a bigger boat, using nails forged from armor and weapons. Eight months after leaving Gonzalo Pizarro, they reached the mouth of the Amazon River and sailed out into the Atlantic. Heading northwestward, they finally landed on an island off the northern coast of South America. Here they found a Spanish settlement where they recovered from the ordeal of their amazing voyage across the continent.

When Orellana returned to Spain, he persuaded the king to finance further exploration of the Amazon. But Orellana died before the expedition started.

Valdivia conquered Chile.

Far to the south, one of Francisco Pizarro's men, Pedro de Valdivia (vahl-*dee'* vyah), led an expedition into Chile. He planned to settle the land that Almagro had found so disappointing. Valdivia and his men

A stamp issued by Peru in 1942 commemorated the 400th anniversary of Orellana's exploration of the Amazon. Compare the old map featured on the stamp with the modern map on page 69. What inaccuracies are most obvious on the old map?

crossed the barren desert of northern Chile and after eleven months reached the pleasant central valley. Here, in 1541, he founded the city of Santiago and the port of Valparaiso. Farms were started and an aqueduct built to bring spring water into the settlement.

At first the local Indians seemed peaceful. But within six months after the founding of Santiago, the Araucanians lashed out against the Spaniards. They burned the town and slaughtered all the Spaniards they could find. Over the next few years Valdivia and the surviving Spaniards fought off repeated Indian attacks while rebuilding Santiago.

Lautaro led an Araucanian uprising. Valdivia had captured an Araucanian boy named Lautaro (lau-*tah'* roh) and taught him how to ride and care for the Spaniards' horses. While working for the Spaniards, Lautaro secretly organized other young Araucanians and taught them how to handle horses. Meanwhile, Lautaro planned a revolt.

Finally the young Araucanian leader escaped from the Spaniards. In 1553 he organized guerrilla bands far to the south. There Valdivia and a force of mounted Spaniards pursued the Indians. Lautaro's guerrillas lured the heavily armed Spaniards into a swamp. The Indians easily killed off the floundering Spaniards and rode away with their horses. Over the next four years Lautaro and his guerrillas kept up the fight against Spanish control until he was killed and his bands exiled south of the Bío-Bío (*bee'* oh-*bee'* oh) River. But the name "Lautaro" has been a password for South American patriots ever since.

Belalcázar sought El Dorado. Another of Pizarro's men who became an explorer was Sebastian de Belalcázar, who had conquered the city of Quito (page 80). Like Gonzalo Pizarro, he was intrigued by the stories of cinnamon forests and *El Dorado*. With his share of the Peruvian treasure, Belalcázar organized a big expedition. From Quito, he marched north to the valley of the Cauca (*cow'* kah) River,

founding the settlements of Cali (*kah'* lee) and Popayán (poh-pah-*yahn'*) on the way. These were in what is now Colombia. Turning eastward, he followed Indian trails to the fertile valley of the Chibchas, ruled by King Bogotá (page 25).

Several expeditions met in Bogotá. When Belalcázar arrived in this valley in 1539, he found that two other groups of Europeans were there ahead of him. One was led by Jiménez de Quesada (kay-*sah'* dah). He had been sent by the Spanish king to govern the new towns of Santa Marta and Cartagena on the coast of Colombia. With 900 men Quesada had made his way south along the Magdalena River in search of *El Dorado*. After months of fever, starvation, and other hardships, only 166 of his men remained alive. Finally, with the guidance of friendly Indians, the expedition had reached the domain of King Bogotá. It was indeed a land of riches. Bogotá's subjects lived in houses decorated with discs of gold, and their children played "marbles" with emeralds. Taking possession of the rich valley, Quesada's men recovered their strength and idled through the winter months of 1538.

Meanwhile, the Spanish king had granted permission to a group of German bankers to found colonies in Venezuela. The Germans hoped to find gold and Indians to sell as slaves. In 1536 one of their agents, Nikolaus Federmann, led an expedition south from the Venezuelan coast. He and his men crossed several tributaries of the Orinoco River and reached its headwaters in the snows of the Andes. Two and a half years after they had started, this party also reached the valley of Bogotá.

Discovery rights were settled peacefully. Federmann and his exhausted Germans had no sooner reached Bogotá than they met Belalcázar's force coming up from the south. Quesada, of course, was already there. The three leaders agreed to ask the Spanish Crown to settle the question of territorial rights. After resting, all three expeditions loaded up with emeralds and set out for Cartagena on the coast. Then the three leaders all sailed on the same ship to Spain.

Quesada was made Marshal of New Granada (the name given to this new colonial domain). He returned to the Bogotá valley, where he lived as a wealthy man and leader of the town council. As for the Germans, the king ruled that the emeralds they had collected were adequate reward for their efforts. Belalcázar was named Captain-General of the upper Cauca. Spanish settlers returned with him to build up his towns of Cali and Popayán.

A colony was founded in the Plata region.
While European explorers were moving into South America from the Pacific and Caribbean coasts, others were penetrating the region of the Rio de la Plata on the southern Atlantic coast. Juan de Solis, the first Spaniard to see the Plata mouth, had been killed by cannibals (page 42). Members of his crew who got back to Spain reported that the wild Pampa Indians had silver earrings. This suggested to the Spanish that the Plata region might provide a route to the land of the Incas. In 1536, after the Pizarros had conquered Peru, a rich nobleman named Pedro de Mendoza came to the Plata mouth at his own expense. His huge expedition included a dozen ships, about 1500 settlers, and several hundred cattle and horses. Choosing a pleasant site on the south bank of the Plata estuary, Mendoza founded a town and named it after a shrine in Spain, *Santa Maria de Buenos Aires,* "Our Lady of the Cool Breeze."

Like other Spaniards who came to the New World, Mendoza's colonists expected to recruit Indians to work for them. At first, the nomadic Indians were friendly, exchanging fish and game for cloth and beads. But the Indians tired of being expected to provide for the Spaniards' needs. They began to attack their would-be masters.

To make matters worse, most of the cattle and horses escaped into the open grasslands. Soon lack of food became a serious problem.

In fact, some of the desperate colonists were said to have resorted to cannibalism.

Asunción was a more successful settlement.
The disgusted Mendoza gave up and set sail for Spain but died on the way home. His second-in-command, Juan Ayolas (ah-*yoh'* lahss), had taken a party of colonists and sailed up the Plata from Buenos Aires. They hoped to find a better site for a settlement and, if possible, a route to Peru. Nearly a thousand miles inland on the Paraguay River, Ayolas found villages of friendly Guaraní Indians in what is now Paraguay. Here in 1537 Ayolas founded a town called Asunción (ah-soon-*syohn'*), the first permanent Spanish settlement in this area. After founding the colony, Ayolas set out in search of a route to Peru but died on the way.

From the frontier outpost depicted in this old sketch eventually grew the modern city of Buenos Aires.

In 1541 the rest of the colonists at Buenos Aires moved upriver to Asunción, and the settlement at the Plata mouth lay abandoned. Horses and cattle that could not be captured were left behind at Buenos Aires. Running wild, these animals thrived on the rich pasture of the Argentine plains.

Buenos Aires was refounded. Paraguay needed a seaport, however. So eventually an official named Juan de Garay (gah-*rah'* ee) was appointed to start a new colony at Buenos Aires. For this mission he chose mostly young men born in Asunción. Thus, Buenos Aires, the metropolis of modern Argentina, was settled in 1580 by Paraguayan youths of mixed Spanish and Indian parentage. These settlers planted crops and herded cattle themselves instead of forcing Indians to work for them. They made money by shipping hides to Spain. Garay lived to become governor of other new towns of the southern area—Tucumán, Santa Fe, and Córdoba. With Garay ends the story of the first generation of Spanish conquistadors.

THINKING ABOUT THIS SECTION

1. Explain or define the following words: Lautaro; New Granada.
2. How did Orellana come to explore the Amazon? Why was his trip an amazing achievement?
3. Why were the Araucanians able to offer far stiffer opposition to the Spaniards than the more numerous and wealthier Incas?
4. Why did several expeditions seek the realm of King Bogotá?
5. What problems had to be overcome by the Spaniards who tried to settle in the Plata region? How successful were these settlements?
6. In general, what was the Spanish attitude toward the property rights of Indians? Did the Aztecs and Incas respect the rights of tribes that they conquered? Explain.

5. The Portuguese on the Brazilian Coast

Meanwhile, the Portuguese were slow in exploring their claims in what is now Brazil. Chapter 2 told how Pedro Cabral had touched on the coast of Brazil while on his way to Africa. Portuguese kings thereafter claimed the whole eastern coast of South America from north of the Amazon mouth to Uruguay. This claim was also supported by the Line of Demarcation, which had been agreed to by Spain and Portugal some years before Cabral's landing in Brazil.

Interest in Brazil at first was slight. In agreeing to the Line of Demarcation, Portugal's chief interest had been in keeping Spain away from the profitable spice trade in the East Indies. For some time after Cabral's landing the Portuguese king took little interest in Brazil. The king did grant a few merchants permission to explore for trade goods. They found a tree with bright-colored bark which produced a red dye when boiled. Ships came occasionally to Brazil to cut this dyewood, called *brazilwood.*

Caramurú became the first European settler in Brazil. From time to time survivors of shipwrecks came ashore on the Brazil coast. Other sailors were marooned there as punishment for mutiny. One castaway was Diogo Alvares (dee-*oh'* go ahl-*vahr'* esh), a Portuguese who in 1503 came ashore at a bay near what became the city of Bahia (bah-*ee'* ah), now called Salvador. Alvares managed to save his musket and some ammunition. As Indians approached him on the beach, he shot his musket into the air. Because of the flash of flame and thunderous noise, the Indians called him Caramurú (kah-rah-moo-*roo'*), or "Man of Lightning."

Caramurú became leader of the Indians who found him and eventually the chieftain of a large tribe. After 20 years he was a man of great influence with many wives and children. When the Portuguese government finally became interested in colonizing Brazil, Caramurú and his many descendants helped the settlers who came to Bahia. Bahians today are proud if they can claim descent from him. Another tiny settlement got started farther north on the coast, at Recife (ray-*see'* fay) in what is now the state of Pernambuco (pair-nahm-*boo'* koh).

The Souzas promoted settlement in Brazil. For a time the kings of Portugal considered Brazil "a wretched business." The dyewood trade seemed insignificant compared to Portugal's rich Asian trade. But several things began to stimulate Portuguese interest in Brazil. In the 1520's stories of Pizarro's plans to invade the Inca empire reached the new king of Portugal, João III. He suspected that Spain might try to occupy the Brazilian coast as well. France too was a possible threat, since French traders were setting up small trading stations on the South American coast. Moreover, the brazil-wood trade was proving more profitable than had been expected. For all these reasons João III decided to start an official colony in Brazil.

The king chose Martím Afonso de Souza (*soo'* zah), a member of the royal court, to start the new town. With five ships and 400 men Souza arrived on the southern Brazilian coast in 1531. He founded a settlement near what is now the city of Santos and called it São Vicente (sown vih-*sayn'* tay).

Even before Souza returned to Portugal with a favorable report, the king had decided to sponsor more settlements on the coast of Brazil. But since he did not want to spend royal funds on colonizing, he asked individual rich men to become proprietors. Each of these men would colonize a section of the Brazilian coast at his own expense and would pay taxes to the king. The proprietors would, however, keep any profits for themselves and their heirs. More than a century later, the king of England followed a similar plan when he granted land in eastern North America to various English noblemen.

The donatários settled towns. The Portuguese noblemen who were assigned such grants in Brazil during the 1530's were called *donatários* (doh-nah-*tah'* ree-ohs). Each *donatário* received a section of land extending some 50 miles along the coast and inland for an indefinite distance. The *donatário* transported his own settlers, raised and paid soldiers, coped with the Indians, built houses, paid missionaries, and even provided ships for trade with the mother country. Most of these ventures failed. The Portuguese proprietors had not expected to find either tropical climate or mountainous country so close to the beaches. They could not get the Indians to work for them, and the European settlers were unruly. Only Souza and one other *donatário* made financial successes of their colonies, chiefly because they had large fortunes to invest in these ventures. Nevertheless, by the mid-1500's there were about fifteen fortified towns along the Brazilian coast.

Government was centralized in Brazil. To unite the various settlements, King João III in 1549 appointed another member of the Souza family, Thomé de Souza, to be governor-general of Brazil. Bahia was made the capital. At royal expense, more than a thousand additional colonists were sent to Bahia, shipbuilding yards were started, and Jesuit missionaries arrived. The Jesuits established missions to convert Indians. In 1565 a Portuguese town was founded on the bay where Rio de Janeiro (*ree'* oo duh zhuh-*nay'* roo) stands today. French traders had settled a few years earlier at this site, but the Portuguese drove them away.

The Brazilian colony developed. A Portuguese historian who visited Brazil wrote in 1576 that Bahia had 62 churches and 47 sugar mills. The town of Olinda (near Recife) was so prosperous, he said, that wealthy men "ate their meals with a fork and set their tables with silver and fine porcelain." By 1600 there were probably close to 100,000 people in the Portuguese communities of Brazil. About a fourth of the population consisted of black slaves. Sugar had become Brazil's leading export.

The settlement of Brazil cannot be called a "conquest" in the same sense that Mexico and Peru were conquered. The Portuguese did not have to fight and subdue an organized Indian state. In fact, in many parts of Brazil there were few or no Indians. Nevertheless, in Brazil, as in the Spanish-occupied areas, Indians were exploited and enslaved. But the settlement of Brazil was gradual and, compared to the bloody campaigns in Mexico and Peru, peaceful. As Portuguese power faded during the 1600's, the mother country came to depend more and more on the slave trade with the New World, and with Brazil especially, as a source of wealth.

THINKING ABOUT THIS SECTION

1. Explain or define the following words: brazil-wood; *donatário.*

2. Why were the Portuguese about 1500 not greatly interested in colonizing their holdings in South America? Why did this attitude begin to change in the 1520's? What plan of colonization did the Portuguese king adopt?

3. What were the chief characteristics of Portuguese colonization of Brazil? In general, how was it different from Spanish colonization?

Summing Up

In the early 1500's, Spanish adventurers set out from the original base at Santo Domingo to explore the other Caribbean islands, the Isthmus of Panama, and the Gulf coast of Mexico. The success of Cortés's expedition opened up the mainland of Mexico to Spanish conquest. Months of fighting ended in tragedy for the Aztecs. After the Spanish demolished Tenochtitlán, Mexico City began to rise from the ruins of the Indian city. Lieutenants of Cortés explored to the north and south. As silver was discovered in northern Mexico, that land began to fill in with Spanish mining towns. Indians were forced to work in the mines and to grow food for the Spaniards.

The Pizarro brothers, bringing despair to the Incas, conquered Peru and sent men north to Ecuador and southeastward into Bolivia. Many modern cities of South America's west coast had their beginnings during this period. Other Spaniards settled in Chile, explored the Amazon, and found the way to Bogotá. Far to the south, in an area that Spain considered almost worthless, colonists established a foothold far inland up the Paraguay River. Later settlers held the mouth of the Rio de la Plata for Spain by founding a permanent colony at Buenos Aires.

Meanwhile, Portugal slowly rooted its authority along the coast of Brazil south of the bulge of the continent. At first, individual proprietors settled parcels of land granted to them by the king. Eventually a royal government was organized over all the new towns. As in the Spanish colonies, European colonization came about at heavy cost to the native Americans. Wherever a European settlement was planted, the Indians were enslaved and their civilizations destroyed.

The massive fortification that impressed Antonio de Ulloa in the 1730's still surrounds Cartagena today. From sentry boxes on the thick wall, guards in the old days stared out to sea watching for pirate sails on the horizon. Looking inland from the wall, present-day visitors to Cartagena can see narrow streets, weathered churches, and cobbled plazas.

Life in Colonial Latin America

CHAPTER FOCUS

1. Spanish Cities and Towns in America
2. Government and Society in the Spanish Colonies
3. The Economy of the Spanish Colonies
4. Trade Between the Colonies and Spain
5. Religion, Education, and the Arts in Spanish America
6. Colonial Life in Brazil

In 1735 the king of Spain assigned a young naval officer to accompany a group of French scientists visiting the Spanish colonies in the New World. The scientists were planning to measure the size of the earth at the equator. The young officer, nineteen-year-old Antonio de Ulloa (ool-*yoh'* ah), was to serve as an interpreter. The king also instructed him to report on conditions in the colonies. "I was overjoyed at this appointment," Ulloa later wrote. "My instructions were to keep careful records, to draw plans of cities, harbors and forts, to take useful sightings at sea. I must supply the king with details on soil, plants, handicrafts, and people in the colonies, including both Spaniards and Indians."

Ulloa's first stop in the New World was Cartagena (in Colombia). He began his report by describing this "well laid out city." He was especially impressed by the fortifications at Cartagena. From there Ulloa had hoped to go overland to Quito, but found that the French surveying instruments were too delicate for a long mountain trip by mule. So he had a chance to visit the great yearly trade fair at Porto Bello (now Portobelo) on the Caribbean coast of Panama. Once a year Spanish ships loaded with European wares arrived at Porto Bello. In a burst of activity merchants traded the goods for gold, silver, and other American products. Ulloa described how the fair stirred up the town of Porto Bello:

He who has seen this place during the *tiempo muerto,* or "dead time," solitary, poor, and [silent], the harbor quite empty, and every place wearing a melancholy aspect, must be filled with astonishment at the sudden change, to see the bustling multitudes, every house crowded, the square and streets encumbered with bales and chests of gold and silver of all kinds; the harbor full of ships and vessels, some bringing . . . the goods of Peru, as cacao, quinquina [quinine bark, and] vicuña wool. . . . others coming from Cartagena, loaded with provisions; and thus a spot, at all other times detested for its [unhealthy] qualities, becomes the [center] of the riches of the old and new world, and the scene of one of the most considerable branches of commerce on the whole earth.[1]

Crossing the Isthmus of Panama by river-boat and then by mule, Ulloa found "elegant" stone houses in Panama City. Ulloa then sailed for Guayaquil (gwah-yah-*keel'*), a seaport in what is now Ecuador. There, he reported, "ladies . . . wear the finest dresses, ruffled with the richest lace, for there is so much profit from the trade with Panama in cacao beans." The trip north to Quito had to be made by mule anyway, but the scientific instruments arrived safely.

In Quito the condition of the Indians disturbed Ulloa. Of all the inhabitants of the city he found the native people to be the "most poor, miserable, and distressed." He devoted an entire chapter of his report to the Indians of Quito, and urged that more of them be taught Spanish.

Ulloa stayed in the New World nine years. When his account of his trip was published, the book won readers all over western Europe. Many years later Ulloa returned to Peru as a governor and also served briefly as governor of New Orleans (page 126). During his later life he lived in Madrid and wrote books on the geography and wild life of the Western Hemisphere. Antonio de Ulloa's report on his early trip is still a very readable source of information on life in the Spanish colonies during the eighteenth century.

1. Spanish Cities and Towns in America

The first thing many of the explorers did in the New World was establish a town. As the mayor of a town, a *conquistador* acquired more prestige. Since Roman times, most towns in Spain had been laid out with the streets in squares. By Queen Isabella's time all Spanish cities had a central plaza in front of a large Catholic church. But not all towns in the New World were built on the Spanish pattern. In fact, they differed in a variety of ways.

Mexico City. In 1700, when neither Boston nor Philadelphia had more than 10,000 people, Mexico City had a population of about 100,000. The large cathedral on the *Zócalo* or central square was surrounded by the homes of the mayor and other high officials and by govern-

[1] Jorge de Juan and Antonio de Ulloa, *A Voyage to South America* (abridged) (New York: Alfred A. Knopf, 1964), p. 56.

In the 1600's Mexico City still was a cluster of islands in the lakes of the Valley of Mexico. Causeways connected the city with the mainland, just as in Aztec times. Notice the central plaza.

ment buildings. These red stone buildings are still standing. Many churches were scattered throughout the city, and there were also large convents and monasteries. The typical house of a well-to-do Spaniard was likely to be three stories high and built around a square patio. Each patio had a tile fountain and gardens. On top of Chapultepec Hill, where Moctezuma had once lived, stood the viceroy's palace. Water fountains flowed at almost every street intersection, and the streets were paved with cobblestones.

Lima and other towns in Peru. Lima, unlike Mexico City, was an entirely new city, since it had not been founded on the site of an existing Indian community. By 1620, before Boston had even been founded, Lima had 4000 stone houses. Arches surrounded the city's large central square, and an aqueduct carried melted snow-water from the mountains down to the town. The Spanish noblemen of Lima lived in great mansions with balconies extending out over the streets. Dressed in the latest European fashions, the wealthy Peruvians drove about in open carriages with coachmen in splendid uniforms.

Every day long mule trains carried goods into Lima. The mules were loaded with cloth woven by Indians in Cuzco or silver bars from the mining towns of what is now Bolivia. Into the port of Callao, on the Pacific coast just outside Lima, came ships from Panama to exchange Spanish goods for the silver bars and other local products.

Guatemala City and Antigua. The city founded by Alvarado in Guatemala (page 76) had been destroyed by earthquake and floods in the 1540's. A new Guatemala City grew up in a mountain valley where the climate was like spring. In 1773 this city was called "third in magnificence among Spanish colonial capitals." But that year earthquakes shook the area for weeks. Frightened people moved from their houses out into the open country and prayed for safety. When the news reached the king in Spain, he ordered the settlement moved to a site 60 miles away, where present-day Guatemala City is now located. Today the old town is called Antigua (an-*tee'* gwah). Some Spanish-speaking families moved back to Antigua in the 1800's but many of the houses have never been repaired.

Walled towns and mountain towns. Perhaps the best-fortified city in the Spanish colonies was Cartagena near the mouth of the Magdalena River in Colombia. Its high walls were built by black slaves to protect the town from English pirates. Inside the walls there still stand old Spanish houses with carved balconies. San Juan, Puerto Rico, had walls almost as high and a fort which is today a United States national monument. Bogotá and Quito in their mountain valleys had no fear of English pirates. Each developed as a center of culture—Bogotá, of poetry and books; Quito, of painting and church architecture.

Towns of the Plata region. Asunción (Paraguay) and Buenos Aires (Argentina) were remote frontier settlements. Although Asunción was important in the early colonial period, it was not on any main trading route. Compared to sophisticated Mexico City, Asunción was provincial. Ladies complained that there was no "society" and spent their time "in sewing, weaving, gardening, and taking care of babies and ducks."

Buenos Aires, on the Plata estuary, could have been a thriving port city. Instead, it was a poor, backward town. It had no direct contact with Spain since the king had ordered that all trade go by way of the Isthmus of Panama. Goods sent from Spain to Buenos Aires had to be carried from Panama to Lima, across the Andes by muleback, and then in wagons across the pampa (the grassy heartland of what is now Argentina). This was a trip of many months. In the 1650's, Buenos Aires had only "four hundred roofed houses," that is, houses covered with tile rather than thatch. There were only "sixteen horse-drawn coaches in all the town." About 4000 people, mostly mestizos, lived there.

Other towns. By the 1700's there were hundreds of other towns in the Spanish colonies. Life for well-to-do people was often more pleasant and cleaner than in towns of the same size in Europe. Gardens were larger, water was better, there was greater variety in food, and winters were shorter and milder. Life for the poor was hard. But it was probably no worse than for the poor peasants or city dwellers of Europe. When the German scientist Alexander von Humboldt visited Mexico City in 1803, he was disturbed to see how Indian workers had to live. Even so, he wrote that they did not live as "meanly as peasants of North Europe."

THINKING ABOUT THIS SECTION

1. Explain the following words: Porto Bello; *tiempo muerto.*

2. Compare Mexico City in 1700 with Tenochtitlán before it was destroyed by the Spanish conquerors. How do you account for similarities and differences?

3. Contrast Latin American cities and cities in the English colonies in America during the early 1700's. Why were the Latin American cities larger?

4. During the 1600's how did goods from Spain reach Buenos Aires? Why? What was the effect on Buenos Aires?

---

2. Government and Society in the Spanish Colonies

There had never been an empire in history like the one that Spain ruled in America. Spain's colonial possessions lay far from the mother country, across the Atlantic Ocean. They included islands and a vast expanse of mainland territory. Some of the towns and cities were thousands of miles apart. Travel between them was far from easy, for they were separated by deserts, mountains, and tropical rain forests. But Spain had to develop a workable government for these colonies.

Agencies were set up to govern the colonies. In 1493 Queen Isabella had appointed a bishop, Juan de Fonseca, as an adviser to Columbus in the settlement of Santo Domingo. As more towns were founded on the Caribbean islands and the Isthmus of Panama, the bishop set up an agency to regulate New World trade and shipping. This agency was called the *Casa de Contratación* (*kah'* sah day kohn-trah-tah-*syohn'*), or Board of Trade.

Bishop Fonseca remained in charge of colonial affairs until his death in 1524. Charles I then established a Council of the Indies to handle the work involved in governing the colonies. The members of the Council were leading attorneys, university professors, or relatives of the king. To advise them, these men employed map-makers, historians, and mathematicians. Each member of the Council had a variety of duties. He served on committees, wrote decrees for the king's signature, made appointments, censored books, balanced accounts, and consulted on military activities. The Council also heard legal cases referred to it from colonial courts.

The Council issued laws. The Council of the Indies worked out a code of laws for the American colonies. These laws were designed to benefit the mother country. Every phase of colonial life was subject to orders from Spain. Year after year, as new regulations were added

to the code, the laws became confusing and some even contradicted others. Moreover, through the centuries conditions changed, so that laws could not always be applied. Many laws were disregarded, sometimes intentionally and sometimes through ignorance. In 1681, nearly two centuries after Columbus came to America, all the rules and regulations were reorganized in a more orderly code of laws.

The king appointed viceroys to rule in his name. Cortés, Pizarro, and other early *conquistadores* held great power in the lands they conquered. As told in Chapter 4, Cortés had hoped that Charles I would appoint him governor of Mexico. But the king was reluctant to place royal authority in the hands of so independent a man. Instead he named a board of judges to rule in Mexico City. Then, in 1535, Charles ordered a man called Antonio de Mendoza to govern Mexico with the title of *viceroy* ("acting king"). As a direct royal representative, the viceroy had authority to hold court and to rule in the king's name. During most of the colonial period there were two viceroys: one for Peru, with headquarters at Lima, and one for New Spain, centered in Mexico City.

For fifteen years Mendoza ruled in Mexico City. By the end of this term the viceroy's rule extended over central and north Mexico, Central America, and the Caribbean islands. Mendoza proved so successful in this assignment that he was sent to Peru on the same kind of job. But he died after serving only ten months in Lima. He was replaced by Francisco de Toledo, an able administrator who tried to improve conditions for the Indians.

The viceroys governed with the help of the audiencias. Lima and Mexico City became the twin capitals of Spanish America, a colonial domain many times larger than Spain itself. The Council of the Indies received reports from the viceroys and appointed new ones every three to five years. Courts called *audiencias* (ow-*dyen'* syahss) were also established in Mexico City and in Lima. The judges of the *audiencia* assisted the viceroy, heard cases in which his judgments were appealed, and acted as a governing body when he was abroad. Eventually, *audiencias* were set up in Quito, Santiago de Cuba, Havana, Guatemala City, Bogotá, Buenos Aires, Cuzco, and Caracas as well.

The viceroys had great prestige. Whenever a new viceroy came to Lima, his arrival was celebrated with parades, dinner parties at the homes of wealthy families, five days of bullfighting, and special religious services. It would be three months before he could get down to government business. The records and reports sent by the viceroys, the *audiencias*, and other officials to Spain were carefully preserved. Today these papers are housed in a building in Seville and continue to be studied by historians interested in colonial Spanish America.

Mayors and councilmen ran local government. Since Spaniards did not vote for officials in Spain, those who migrated to the colonies did not expect to have a voice in choosing their governors there. But the farther a town was from Mexico City or Lima, the more chance there was for some degree of self-government. Towns had city councils called *cabildos* (kah-*beel'* dohss). These councils were made up of *regidores* (ray-hee-*doh'* rayss) or city councilmen and were presided over by a mayor or *alcalde* (ahl-*kahl'* day). In frontier settlements all Spanish landholders voted in elections to choose *alcaldes* and *regidores*. But after a century or so these jobs began to be handed down from father to son. Thus, the little beginnings of democracy came to an end. Poor Spaniards, mestizos, Indians, and blacks had no voice in the government.

Some changes were made in the colonial government. By the 1700's the Spanish colonies were some two centuries old. Many changes

had taken place in the colonies, but the system of government had failed to keep up. The colonial government had grown clumsy and outmoded. To strengthen Spain's colonial empire, King Philip V started a program of reorganization. Because he was a member of the Bourbon family, the changes made by Philip and his successors are called the *Bourbon reforms*.

Among these changes were the creation of two new viceroyalties, New Granada and La Plata (map, page 96). Certain subdivisions of the viceroyalties were called *captaincies-general*. After this, Guatemala, Venezuela, Cuba, and Chile were all ruled by captains-general. A new kind of official, called an *intendent*, was appointed to assist the viceroys and captains-general in governing frontier regions. But these reforms came too late. By the early 1800's some colonial leaders were demanding that royal power be limited (Chapter 7).

People born in Spain were the aristocrats of Spanish America. Social standing was very important in Spanish America, just as it was in Spain and everywhere else in Europe at the time. Spaniards appointed to serve as officials in the American provinces were always chosen from the nobility. These people did not intend to settle permanently in the colonies. Viceroys served for three to five years. Their families, other relatives, and scores of assistants came with them to America and usually returned to Spain when the term of service was over. Many officials got their appointments because the king or a member of the Council of the Indies owed them or their families a favor. Most officials returned to Spain wealthier than when they had left. Bishops and other high-ranking churchmen were also Spanish-born.

The Spaniards born in Spain considered themselves superior to other people in America. Not only did they look down on the Indians, the blacks, and people of mixed ancestry. They also took a haughty attitude toward Spaniards born in the New World, no matter how wealthy the latter might be. The permanent settlers in Spanish America called persons born in Spain *peninsulares* (pen-in-soo-*lah'* rayss), meaning that they had been born in the Iberian peninsula. Toward the later part of the colonial period the Americans came to resent the *peninsulares*. In Mexico the haughty Spaniards were called *gachupines* (gah-choo-*pee'* nayss), "those who wear spurs." This term implied that the Spaniards dealt with their "inferiors" as an arrogant horseman might mistreat a horse.

American-born whites were called creoles.
In the English colonies of North America people of almost any nationality were allowed to settle. But in Spain's colonies only Spanish Catholics, hand-picked by government agents, were welcome. Foreigners, people of Jewish or Moorish descent, heretics, and people whose loyalty seemed questionable were barred from the colonies. Spanish men who were cleared for settlement often brought along wives from Spain. Any of their children born in the New World had lower social rank than the Spanish-born parents. This was true even if the children inherited or acquired great wealth. American-born Spaniards were called *criollos,* or

creoles. Many creoles were envious of the privileges of the *peninsulares*. Often they copied Spanish ways and tried to pass as Spanish-born.

Mestizos formed the bulk of the population.
The mestizos, of mixed Spanish and Indian descent, soon formed the largest racial group in colonial Latin America. Since few Spanish women came to Mexico or Peru during the first years after the conquest, many Spanish soldiers took Indian wives. Their sons, like Martín Cortés, were given their fathers' names.

Another such person was Garcilaso de la Vega, who recorded Inca legends and history (page 21). His mother was an Inca princess who became a Christian, and his father was a Spanish captain. As *Doña,* or "Lady," Isabella, the Indian princess presided over a large house built by the captain in Cuzco. Young Garcilaso was taught by a Spanish tutor, but he also spent many hours learning Inca lore. Then, when the father was 50, he visited Spain and brought back to Peru a young Spanish bride. Garcilaso's mother was no longer considered a Doña, and Garcilaso was suddenly only a "half-breed."

Indians, mestizos, and creoles mingled at city markets in colonial Spanish America.

VICEROYALTY OF NEW SPAIN

St. Augustine

Gulf of Mexico

Zacatecas
Guadalajara
Guanajuato
Mexico
Taxco
Veracruz

Captaincy General of Havana

CUBA

Santiago

HAITI

PUERTO RICO

Santo Domingo

San Juan

Antigua
Guatemala

Captaincy General of Guatemala

JAMAICA (Br.)

Caribbean Sea

Captaincy General of Caracas

TRINIDAD

Porto Bello
Cartagena

Caracas

Panama City

Bogotá

Orinoco R.

VICEROYALTY OF NEW GRANADA (1718)

GUIANA

Quito
Guayaquil

Amazon R.

Belém

VICEROYALTY OF PERU

Lima
Callao
Cuzco

LAKE TITICACA

Recife

(UNEXPLORED)

Bahia

Potosí

MINAS GERAIS

Ouro Preto

Asunción

São Paulo
São Vicente
Santos

Rio de Janeiro

Tucumán

Córdoba

Paraná R.

Valparaiso
Santiago
Mendoza

Buenos Aires

Rio de la Plata

Captaincy General of Chile

VICEROYALTY OF LA PLATA (1776)

ATLANTIC OCEAN

PACIFIC OCEAN

	Spanish territory
	Portuguese territory
	French territory
	Dutch territory

0   200   400   600   800   1000 Miles

Though he became a soldier of Spain himself, all his father's lands were inherited by the children born to the Spanish wife.

Obviously any mestizo had reason to feel insecure. But few mestizos were even as fortunate as Garcilaso. Their Spanish fathers often ignored or forgot them; their mothers' tribes would not accept them. Over the years the number of mestizos grew large. Few of them owned land. Many of them formed a sort of "lower middle class," working as farmers, shopkeepers, and craftsmen, or serving in the army.

Royal policy failed to protect the Indians. Queen Isabella had given Columbus strict instructions to Christianize the native people of Santo Domingo and to "train them to useful tasks." Protection of the Indians and their conversion to Christianity continued to be royal policy after Isabella's time. But this policy failed to take into account the Spaniards' need for laborers. In forcing the Indians to work for them, the Spanish colonists soon lost sight of their obligation to protect these people.

During the early colonial period, groups of Indians were assigned or "entrusted" to Spanish landholders. In return for "training in village life," the landholder could require the Indians to work on his property. This system came to be called the *encomienda* (en-koh-*myen'* dah). Though in theory the landholder was supposed to protect the Indians, actually they were often treated like slaves.

The *encomendero* (en-koh-men-*day'* roh), as the Spaniard was called, could demand tribute as well as work from the Indians. One observer wrote of tribute demands in New Spain

Colonial Latin America

The Viceroyalty of La Plata was originally part of Peru, and the Viceroyalty of New Granada was originally part of New Spain. New Spain extended far north into what is now United States territory. Chapter 6 will tell about that part of the Spanish empire. Note that the interior of Brazil was unexplored. Only coastal Brazil was settled by the Portuguese, and the vast interior remained unknown to white men for many years.

about 1540: "The tributes were so [heavy] that [the Indians] had scarcely paid one when they were obliged to pay another. They sold their children and their lands to moneylenders in order to meet their obligations; and when they were unable to do so, many died because of it, some under torture and some in cruel prisons."

With this kind of treatment the native populations in the lands colonized by Spain rapidly died out. To ease the lot of the Indians, Charles I in the early 1540's ordered certain reforms. The New Laws, as the reforms were called, abolished Indian slavery and forbade absentee landlords to use Indians as farm workers. Furthermore, no more *encomiendas* were to be granted. Actually the New Laws were never enforced. But throughout colonial history the Spanish government worried about abuse of the Indians. Governors in the New World always assured officials in Spain that conditions were improving. But the Indians were still treated harshly.

Most Indians continued to live in villages. At the time of the Spanish conquest, most Indians in Mexico and Peru were already living in villages or towns. Under Spanish rule the Indians of these communities were often allowed to run their own local affairs. Some Indian villages were not assigned to work for any particular *encomendero*. In these cases they had to send tribute (usually in crops) to the nearest Spanish official. The villages also had to send to a labor center a certain number of young people to serve as workers. This "drafting" of Indians for hard labor was called the *repartimiento* (ray-par-tih-*myen'* toh) or *mita* (*mee'* tah) in Peru. The *repartimiento* provided workers for the mines and handcraft centers.

In villages near larger towns or cities, or on trails leading to the ports, Indians learned to speak Spanish and began to dress more like European peasants. Among these people many Indian ways died out. In more distant areas Indian villages changed very little. The people continued to speak their own languages, even in church services held by Spanish missionaries. But in almost all the Indian villages some European ways were adopted. Tiles instead of thatch were used for roofing. The villagers kept herds of sheep and goats, and oxen and burros were used in farm work. None of these animals were native to America; they all came from Europe.

On the remote frontiers, far from Mexico City or Lima, nomadic Indians were almost untouched by European influence. Even today in the lands of the Amazon tributaries of Brazil some Indian tribes have never heard the Portuguese language.

Black people became another important group. On the Caribbean plantations, on the Isthmus of Panama, and at ports like Veracruz and Cartagena, the heavy work was done by black slaves from Africa. The story of their role in colonial Latin America was told in Chapter 3. European traders continued to ship Africans to America by the hundreds of thousands. Though laws existed for the protection of the slaves, these regulations, like the ones concerning Indian rights, were largely ignored. Even blacks who became free still were treated unfairly.

THINKING ABOUT THIS SECTION

1. Explain or define the following words: *Casa de Contratación;* captaincy-general; intendent; *peninsulares; criollos; repartimiento.*

2. English colonies in North America prospered because of the mother country's "salutary neglect." What does this mean? Could the same be said of Spanish America?

3. What was the role of each of these in Spanish America: Council of the Indies, king, viceroy, *audiencia?*

4. What was the role of each of these in local government: *alcalde, regidores, cabildo?* Was local government democratic?

5. Contrast the policies of Spain and England concerning immigration to the colonies in America. How did the differences affect the colonies of each country?

6. How did the status of Garcilaso and his mother change after his father married a Spanish woman? Why were mestizos an insecure group in colonial society?

7. How did the relations of Indians to their *encomendero* differ in theory and in practice? Why?

8. To what extent did native American villagers retain old ways? adopt new ways?

3. The Economy of the Spanish Colonies

New and old crops were grown in colonial Latin America. From the first the Spanish rulers had encouraged farmers to migrate to America. Those Spaniards who intended to settle and farm brought along with them domestic animals —cows, burros, horses, pigs, sheep, and goats. They also introduced new plants. Olive trees were planted, and grapevines were set out. Both olives and wine became important products in Peru. The Spaniards also introduced orange and fig trees, wheat, and sugar cane.

Meanwhile, the Indians continued to grow many native crops. Corn and beans were still the staple foods in many areas. The descendants of the Incas ate potatoes, although the Spaniards seldom did. The Indians adopted some of the Spanish foods, learning, for example, to make cheese from the milk of cows and goats. Two plants cultivated by the Indians were to provide important export crops for the Spanish colonists. These were tobacco and cacao beans.

Livestock was raised. The Spanish farmers carried on kinds of activities that were suitable to the part of America where they settled. On the plains of northern Mexico and in Argentina and parts of Venezuela and Chile, cattle raising became a way of life. Cattle raisers were called *rancheros* and their land holdings *ranchos*. The Indians who worked as cowboys on these ranches were called *vaqueros* (vah-*kay'* rohss) in Mexico, *gauchos* (*gow'* chohss) in Argentina, and *llaneros* (yah-*nay'* rohss) in Venezuela. On horseback the cowboys rounded up the herds of cattle. In Mexico they drove the herds long distances to markets where the animals were bought as food for mining towns. In Argentina the cattle were important chiefly for their hides. The meat would spoil if shipped long distances, and cattle could not be driven over the dangerous Andes trails to Lima. Many Spanish words used on the *ranchos* passed into English: *lasso, corral, rodeo, buckaroo* (from *vaquero*), and *ranch* itself.

In the Andes, sheep-raising was more profitable, for wool could be spun and woven into cloth by skillful Inca weavers. Raising mules was also profitable. Thousands of Indians and mestizos made their living as mule-drivers.

Plantations grew export crops. In the tropical lowlands of the Caribbean islands and along the coast of Venezuela and Colombia, plantation agriculture was carried on. Here black workers grew sugar cane, tobacco, and cacao for export to Spain. Before white men came to America sugar had been considered a luxury in Europe. But large-scale production on the American plantations made sugar much less expensive. Its use then became common. Tobacco and cacao also were in great demand in Europe. It was fashionable for high-born ladies to have a cup of chocolate (made from cacao beans) for breakfast every morning. European men learned to take snuff (a powdered form of tobacco) and to smoke pipes.

Spanish landowners were powerful. The system of land ownership that developed in the Spanish colonies persists to this day in parts of Latin America. The earliest conquerors had been authorized to grant large tracts of land to their soldiers. The fact that Indian tribes had owned much of this land was ignored. Later, the king gave town councils, governors, and viceroys the right to make such land grants. After the mid-1500's land was more often sold by the Crown.

The large estates held by Spanish settlers were called *haciendas* (ah-*syen'* dahss) or *estancias* in the Plata region and *fundos* in Chile. Since land was a major source of wealth and prestige, the large landholders formed the creole aristocracy, just as in Spain itself the aristocrats were landowners. The *hacendado* (ah-sayn-*dah'* doh), as the landholder was called, often controlled the local government as well. In fact, he ruled like a little king on his own territory.

The *encomienda* system forced the Indians to work for the landholders. Sometimes the Indian laborers or *peons* were allowed little plots of land for their own use. In these cases the Indians had to pay the *hacendado,* either by giving him a share of their crops, or working a certain number of days on his land, or both. Regardless of the form of payment required, the peons usually found themselves in debt to the *hacendado.* Rarely did they ever manage to pay off the debt. Thus, they found themselves bound to the hacienda with little hope of ever improving their lot. This kind of peonage is still a problem in parts of Latin America.

Silver mines yielded huge profits. Mining was next in importance to agriculture in the economy of colonial Spanish America. By the early 1600's gold supplies had dwindled. The rich silver mines of Mexico, however, were producing twice the wealth that gold had yielded earlier. A fifth of this wealth was earmarked for the royal treasury. The rest of the profits went to private individuals who had been granted the right to operate the mines. Zacatecas, Guanajuato, and Taxco[2] were the leading silver towns in Mexico. The richest

[2] These names are pronounced as follows: Zacatecas (sah-kah-*tay'* kahss), Guanajuato (gwah-nah-*hwah'* toh), and Taxco (*tahss'* koh).

Mining and weaving had been occupations of the Indians long before the Spanish conquest and continued to be afterward. Left, a cutaway view of a mine, from a book published in 1590, showed how Indians dug out gold ore from the interior of a mountain. Below, the creation of colorful fabrics is a tradition carried on by Guatemalan weavers today.

single mine in Spanish America was Potosí (poh-toh-*see'*), in what is now Bolivia. Potosí was a typical mining town, with gamblers, dance halls, and gunmen.

Gold continued to be extracted in some areas, especially in Colombia. Other metals were also mined. Copper was an important export from Chile, Cuba, Haiti, and Venezuela.

In the early years the Spaniards had simply taken gold and silver from the Indians. Then the Spaniards took over the operation of the ore-producing areas. But the Indian workers continued to follow the traditional practice of collecting the ore near the surface. By the mid-1500's, however, more complicated operations had replaced the simpler methods. Deep pits were dug into the earth, and workers used rope ladders to climb down into them. Pick and shovel were used to loosen the ore. The Indians strapped baskets loaded with ore to their backs and climbed to the surface. The ore was then crushed by teams of oxen pulling grinding stones. In silver mining, mercury (quicksilver)

was poured over the crushed ore to dissolve the silver. The mercury was then boiled off in vapor. The pure silver that remained was poured into molds. As it cooled, it formed bars of a standard size.

From Callao, the port for Lima, small coastal vessels carried the silver bars to Panama City. Slaves reloaded the silver onto mules for transportation across the Isthmus. At Porto Bello on the Caribbean side, the silver was picked up by ships bound for Spain. Meanwhile, mule trains and oxcarts trundled loads of silver from northern Mexico to the port of Veracruz.

Miners led a hard life. Work in the mines was exhausting and dangerous. The Indians who mined the ore were treated even more like slaves than were the peons on the haciendas. Some miners received no wages themselves. Instead, payment for their work was made to their tribe or *cacique*. Not only were the miners overworked and poorly fed; often they were crippled or killed in accidents. Because of the overcrowded conditions in which they worked and lived, they had little resistance to disease. Writing about the mines in Mexico, Alexander von Humboldt said that the Indians were "considered as beasts of burden. . . . [They] remain loaded with a weight of from 225 to 350 pounds for a space of six hours. . . . During this time they ascend and descend several thousands of steps in pits of an inclination [slope] of 45 degrees."

Potosí was one of the worst places for Indians to work in the entire New World. When *caciques* in the Andean villages rounded up youths to be sent off as workers in the Potosí mines, their families wept. They knew the young men would never return.

Indians also worked as craftsmen. In the towns Indians and mestizos worked as servants, potters, and weavers, and also made articles of leather and metal. The most important handcraft products were textiles. The conquerors placed a high value on the fine cloth

---

The Black Legend

For years Spain was accused by other countries of having been unusually cruel toward its American colonies, especially in its treatment of the Indians. This traditional belief in Spain's "wickedness" came to be called the *leyenda negra,* or "black legend." Actually Spanish rule was probably no worse than that of other colonial powers. Conquerors are seldom "kind" to the people they rule.

A famous Spanish historian, Salvador de Madariaga, suggested that the "black legend" reflected jealousy on the part of other nations. Nationalistic feeling, wrote Madariaga, made it necessary for other nations "to blacken Spain." "Spain had to be wrong so that France, Holland, and England, and later the United States, could be right." It should also be pointed out that the "black legend" ignored the many contributions made by Spanish culture to Latin American civilization.

---

woven by native Americans. Aztec or Zapotecan weavers soon learned to work with sheep's wool as well as with the cotton they had always used. In addition to blankets and shawls for themselves, they made coats and cloaks for the Spaniards.

Cloth woven by the Peruvian Indians was of better quality than textiles made in Spain. Ladies in Lima complained that "fine materials brought from Spain rotted and faded on the long sea journey." When the Spanish colonies began to trade with the Philippines, American weavers used raw silk from China in making velvets and taffetas.

Like the miners, the weavers were exploited. An Indian chieftain might be ordered to send young men and women to work in textile workshops as well as in the mines. Supposedly the young people had to work there for only two years. But since no records were kept, they were seldom released. The weavers toiled at the looms from dawn to dark seven days a week. The Council of the Indies passed laws intended to stop the exploitation of Indian weavers, but the viceroys seldom enforced these regulations.

The Indians and mestizos learned other crafts from the Spaniards and made changes in traditional American crafts. Spanish ironworkers, leather craftsmen, and tile-makers who emigrated to America taught their skills to the Indians. The Indian workers often were able to improve on the Spanish methods. Richly colored glazed tiles decorated houses in colonial Latin America. Fine saddles studded with silver and leather clothing embroidered with gold braid were popular among young aristocrats. Indian pottery, different in each region, was decorated with shiny glazes. A glassblower from Venice who settled in Guadalajara (gwah-dah-lah-*hah'* rah) taught a few mestizo families to make blown-glass pitchers and plates of a bright blue color. Thus, the Spanish colonies profited from the fine work of Indian and mestizo craftsmen.

Creoles also worked in the crafts. Many of them formed their own organizations, called craft guilds. These guilds barred Indians and blacks from membership, and some also barred mestizos.

THINKING ABOUT THIS SECTION

1. Explain or define the following words: *ranchero;* hacienda.

2. What were the contributions of the Indians to Latin American agriculture? What were the contributions of the Spanish? What crops were chiefly grown on plantations?

3. Explain the relationship between an *hacendado* and his peons. Why was it difficult for a peon to get ahead? Were there greater opportunities in the English colonies in North America? Why?

4. How did methods of mining in Spanish America change during the 1500's? Why?

4. Trade Between the Colonies and Spain

Trade was controlled by the government. Spain had a strict policy concerning trade with the colonies. Like other colonial powers, Spain believed that the colonies existed for the benefit of the mother country. It was expected that the colonies would produce raw materials needed in Spain and would buy manufactured goods shipped by Spanish merchants.

All goods shipped to and from Spanish America had to be carried in Spanish vessels, and these ships had to leave from the ports of Cadiz or Seville. Only the *Casa de Contratación* (the Board of Trade) could approve such shipping. Moreover, for a long time Spanish trading ships called at only a very few ports in the New World. Once a year a fleet of trading ships sailed to Porto Bello on the Isthmus of Panama, stopping first at Cartagena in Colombia. Another fleet sailed each year to Veracruz in Mexico, with a stop at Havana, Cuba. Merchants in Spanish America could secure imported goods only at those ports. And the ships brought only goods that had been authorized by royal license.

When a fleet arrived in America, a month-long fair would be held, as described by Antonio de Ulloa at the beginning of this chapter. Among the luxury goods brought to America were French laces and tapestries, linens from Holland, North African rugs and shawls, and Italian gold work and jewelry. The ships also brought foods that Spaniards particularly enjoyed, such as olives and sardines. Other imports included hardware, books, dishes, and pens and paper. At the fairs, agents for the Seville merchants did a lively business exchanging Old World commodities for silver bars and hides, textiles, and cacao beans.

The monopoly on trade held by a few Caribbean ports imposed hardships on the rest of the American provinces. Since no Spanish ships could trade at Buenos Aires or Valparaiso, for example, all goods to and from those remote towns had to be shipped by way of Panama. This naturally slowed the economic growth of these places.

In the long run the policy was bad for Spain too. Because so much wealth from the New World flowed into the mother country, Spain had the money to buy what it needed in other countries. As a result, Spanish industry declined, while manufacturers in northern Europe flourished on business from Spanish customers. Spain also squandered its wealth on long wars against the Turks, the English, and the French. The administration and defense of the colonies was another major expense.

Englishmen raided Spanish ships and ports. In 1588 Spain had suffered a humiliating defeat. Spain had sent a great fleet (the Spanish Armada) to invade England. But this invasion force was fought to a standstill by English seamen and then wrecked by a great storm. A hero for the English in that encounter was Francis Drake. Years earlier Drake had shown his scorn for Spanish power in the Caribbean. He had attacked Cartagena, Havana, and San Juan, and then sailed around South America to raid Valparaiso and Lima's port of Callao. Drake even reached the coast of northern California before starting westward across the Pacific to return to England.

Other English "sea-dogs" continued to plunder Spanish ships and ports for two centuries. The fortifications at Cartagena, Veracruz, San Juan, and Havana were strengthened. But English pirates holed up on small islands in the Caribbean and watched for Spanish ships

that strayed from convoys. French pirates, based in Haiti, also preyed on Spanish vessels

Smuggling was widespread. The strictness of the Spanish trade policy encouraged people to try to get around the government controls. Smuggling was one way of doing this. Many English, French, and Dutch merchants made fortunes in illegal trading with Spanish America. Ignoring Spanish regulations, they sailed into colonial ports with such goods as cloth, weapons, tools, books, and paper. Often they were welcomed by colonial officials who took bribes from the foreign smugglers.

Trade became freer. Partly because of an increase in smuggling, the profits of the Spanish trade fleets declined. Finally, the Bourbon kings of the 1700's abolished the fleet system. Goods bound for the colonies no longer had to be shipped only from Seville or Cadiz. Spanish merchants now could send out their wares in their own ships.

In the American provinces a new class of merchants began to prosper. Trade between the different colonies became easier. And some remote towns developed into busy trade centers. Goods from Europe were even shipped directly to Buenos Aires, and hides and other cattle products (though not meat) were sent from there to Spain. Enjoying their new prosperity, colonial merchants became more and more critical of Spanish merchants and even the king's tax collectors. In the early 1800's this resentment was to be an important factor in the movement for independence.

THINKING ABOUT THIS SECTION

1. How was trade carried on between Spain and Spanish America? Why did this policy hurt both?
2. What is "smuggling"? Why was it widespread in Spanish America? How were trade and merchants in the colonies affected by the abolishing of the fleet system?

From the time of Queen Isabella, Spain was committed to a policy of converting the Indians to the Catholic faith. Some *conquistadores* and later Spanish rulers did not pursue this policy with as much zeal as Isabella. Nevertheless, missionaries were always more important in the Spanish colonies than were parish priests or monks.

The Crown administered the Catholic Church in Spanish America. Soon after the conquest, the Catholic Church was established in all the colonized areas. The Crown took charge of spreading the Catholic faith in the New World. The Spanish ruler appointed bishops and missionaries, and the churches were supported by the government. But wealthy Spaniards gave huge gifts of land and gold and silver to the Church.

Spain was not much affected by the rising tide of Protestantism in Europe. Muslims and Jews were still persecuted in Spain during the mid-1500's, and the Catholic Church was very strict in its treatment of "heretics." The government took care to send dedicated churchmen to the colonies to spread the faith.

Missionaries became active. Priests had sailed to America with the earliest Spanish explorers and *conquistadores*. After the conquest of Mexico and Peru, great numbers of missionaries came from Spain to spread the Catholic faith among the native Americans. These early missionaries were members of two leading *orders* (organized religious societies), the Franciscans and the Dominicans. During the 1600's another order, the Jesuits, became the most active missionary order in Latin America. All three orders set up schools, founded hospitals, instructed the Indians in Christianity, and explored frontier regions.

Jesuit missions flourished in Paraguay. The most successful missions in the Americas were those founded by Jesuits among the Guaraní Indians in what is now Paraguay. The Spanish king, hoping to keep the Portuguese out of the area, authorized the Jesuits to organize a chain of missions in the vicinity of the Paraná River.

By the early 1700's the Jesuits were operating 30 large Guaraní communities. Under Jesuit direction the Indian residents of the missions grew grapes, oranges, olives, sugar cane, and corn, and raised thousands of head of livestock. On each mission the land, buildings, and equipment belonged to the community as a whole. The Jesuit fathers learned the Guaraní language and developed a way of writing it. The mission Indians learned to operate printing presses and printed a number of books in Guaraní. This attempt to preserve an Indian language was unusual in the Spanish colonies and helps to explain why Guaraní is still widely used in Paraguay.

During the early years of these missions, the Jesuits and their Indian charges were plagued by Portuguese slave raiders from Brazil. Perhaps 60,000 Guaranís were kidnapped and sold into slavery. Later, as the missions prospered, they were better able to defend themselves against slave raids. But then their Spanish neighbors began to make trouble. Spanish landowners were jealous of the missions' prosperity. They also resented the fact that they could not exploit the Indians on the missions as a source of labor. Finally, the Spanish government itself began to charge the Jesuits with not showing respect for royal authority.

The Jesuits were expelled from America. In 1767 the Spanish king suddenly ordered all the Jesuits out of Spanish America. Spanish officials thought the Jesuits had become too powerful and that their going would be good for the colonies. But the forced departure of the Jesuits was a severe blow to the missions in Paraguay. Government officials who took over the management of the mission communities failed to run them efficiently. The Indians themselves had never been allowed a voice in

A Spanish friar of the 1650's drew this picture of missionaries preaching to Indian converts, baptizing an Indian baby, and hearing a confession.

the running of the communities. They soon deserted the missions. Some ran off to live in the forests. Other became peons on large Spanish estates. The mission buildings were soon abandoned, and the orange and olive trees grew wild.

Town life centered around the church. In the Spanish villages and towns as well as in the missions, life was strongly influenced by the Church. Every Spanish community had its own church, usually the largest building in the settlement. In the larger towns and cities there was a church in each neighborhood.

Every church was named for a saint or a holiday. On the day celebrated in honor of a particular saint, special festivals were held at the churches named for that saint. The festivals or *fiestas* included performances by dancers dressed as *conquistadores,* ancient Indians, Muslim warriors, or wild animals. Many of these dances had Spanish origins. Other dances had been performed by the Indians for centuries before the coming of the white man. By 1600 the dancing had become a traditional part of Christian fiestas.

The Church played an important part at every stage of an individual's life, beginning with baptism. Parents held a baptismal party in honor of a new baby. A godmother and a godfather stood up for the child at his baptism. They become the co-parents or *compadres* (kohm-*pah'* drayss) of the baby's parents, a relationship as close as that of sisters and brothers. The godparents took an interest in their godchild throughout his life. Children who attended schools were taught by priests or monks. If a young man was a good student or took an interest in social work, he might become a priest himself and teach in a university or serve in missions and hospitals. When young people married, there was a big church wedding with godparents sponsoring the party. The men of the town belonged to religious brotherhoods which sponsored charities and kept the church in good repair. When someone died, a priest said a funeral mass, and the body was buried in holy ground. The life of a woman was even more closely tied to the church than that of a man. If she did not marry, she entered a convent. Married women's church clubs and nuns' societies did charity work, such as caring for orphans, the sick, and the homeless.

Local shrines were revered. Just as the Spanish Catholic Church had its shrines, so did the Catholic Church in America. One of these shrines was that of the Virgin of Guadalupe (gwah-dah-*loo'* pay) in Mexico. According to tradition, in 1531 an Aztec Indian named Juan Diego had a vision. While picking cactus apples on Guadalupe Hill near Mexico City, he believed that he saw the Virgin Mary. She asked him to tell the bishop to build a church on that hill. To prove that she had been there, she turned the cactus apples into roses. When Juan picked the roses and carried them in his blanket, a painting of a brown-skinned Indian Virgin appeared on the blanket. The Church authorities accepted the appearance of this picture as a miracle, and a church was built at Guadalupe to house a shrine. Here the picture is still preserved. Because of her Indian features, the Virgin of Guadalupe especially appealed to the Indians and mestizos of Mexico.

The shrine at Guadalupe and others like it aided the Spanish priests in converting Indians to Christianity. On Lake Titicaca in South America the shrine of an ancient pre-Inca goddess became the home of a statue of the Virgin Mary brought from Spain. It is called the Virgin of Copacabana. Outside Buenos Aires there is a little town called Luján (loo-*hahn'*) which also has a shrine. In 1630 a statue of the Virgin was loaded on an oxcart in Buenos Aires for transport to an inland town. At Luján the oxcart broke down. When the statue was moved to another cart, it stuck in the mud. Then the statue was transferred to a third cart, but the oxen bolted. The drivers insisted that the Virgin wanted to stay in Luján. A church was built there for the statue, and many Argentines still make pilgrimages to this shrine.

Indian conversion often meant a blending of old and new. Catholic priests and missionaries baptized great numbers of Indians into the Christian faith. In many areas the conquering soldiers had destroyed the Indians' temples and idols. This destruction shook the faith of many Indians in the power of their native religions. The Catholic faith often helped relieve the sense of insecurity that resulted.

But many of the Indians who accepted Christianity did not completely give up their old religions. Millions of Indians were "converted" to Christianity. Only a very few of these converts received the individual teaching needed for full understanding of a new faith. The Indians often merged old religious festivals and rituals with Christian festivals and practices. Sometimes they substituted the names of Christian saints for those of their former gods. Many Catholic churches were built on the foundations of ancient temples. Today in Guatemala or Cuzco or Quito, Indian worshipers in Christian churches still recite Indian-language prayers that were said to ancient gods centuries ago.

The Inquisition was less harsh in America than in Spain. One of the duties of the Catholic Church in America was to exercise control over religious belief. This was done in the name of the Spanish Crown. Such control meant that the Church had authority to regulate education and any expression of thought, written or spoken.

Chapter 2 told how the Inquisition was established in Spain to root out any signs of lack of faith. Agents of the Inquisition also came to the colonies to search out and punish any "freethinkers" or heretics among the Spanish settlers. The Inquisition had no authority over Indians, however.

In the New World the activities of the Inquisition were mild in comparison with its persecutions in Spain. During the whole colonial period probably fewer than a hundred persons were executed for heresy in Spanish America, while thousands were put to death in Spain. Of course, settlers had been carefully screened before their migration to America. No one who was suspected of heretical views was permitted to settle in the colonies.

Education was a responsibility of the Church. Education in colonial Spanish America was limited to the upper classes. Probably fewer than 10 per cent of the people could read and write. The idea that all people were entitled to free public education was unheard of in Spain or its colonies, or anywhere else in the world at that time. Education at all levels was controlled by the Church. The few primary schools were run by priests, but there were no high schools. Young men who planned to study at a university were first tutored by private teachers or priests. Higher education was regarded as unsuitable for young women.

Universities were founded. Long before Harvard and Yale were founded in the English colonies, a number of universities in the Spanish New World had been started. In fact, only 32 years after Cortés' conquest, a university had opened in Mexico City. Courses at this institution were the same as those offered at the University of Salamanca, then regarded as the best in Spain. By 1600 the university in Mexico City had 24 professors. Two of them specialized in the languages of Mexican Indians. In the 1550's a university was also founded in Lima. By the end of the colonial period, 25 colleges and universities had opened their doors to students in Spanish America.

Books at first had to be imported from Spain. Books were expensive in the Spanish colonies, especially in the early years since they had to be imported from Spain. Only books approved by the Church and by the Council of the Indies could enter the colonies. At first, most of the imported volumes were religious writings for use in the missions. But, as the number of educated people increased in the colonies, so did the demand for a variety of books. *Don Quixote* became as popular in the colonies as in Spain, and other novels and books of plays and poetry were also read.

Printing started very early in the colonies. Mexico City had a printing press by the 1530's. Most books printed in Mexico in the 1500's were religious works used in teaching the Indians. As in Spain, few magazines or newspapers were printed until after 1700.

Many colonial books dealt with the conquest. Most of the early authors in the Spanish colonies dealt with the events of the conquest. Soldiers, explorers, and priests published poems or chronicles glorifying Spanish exploits. One of these was probably the longest poem in the Spanish language. *Elegies of the Illustrious Men of the Indies,* 150,000 lines long, was written in praise of the conquering Spaniards by a priest raised in the Caribbean islands. But another epic poem, *La Araucania,* dealt with Lautaro and his brave Araucanian fighters. This famous poem was written by a Spanish soldier named Ercilla (ehr-*theel'* yah).

Sor Juana was a brilliant poet. One of the most remarkable writers of the colonial period was the Mexican poet called Sor Juana de la Cruz ("Sister Joan of the Cross"). In a society where women were thought to be inferior beings, the beautiful young Sor Juana (*hwah'* nah) astonished learned men with her brilliant intellect. While still only a child, Juana pleaded to be allowed to attend the university in Mexico City. Juana was barred from the university but continued to study on her own. As a lady-in-waiting to the wife of the viceroy, she impressed men of importance and learning. At the age of sixteen she decided to become a nun. Her restless mind led her to study science, mathematics, music, and literature. In fact, as she wrote in an autobiographical account, "I studied everything that God created, and all this universal machine [the world] served me as a textbook. . . . I looked at and wondered about everything, so that even the people I spoke to, and what they said to me, aroused a thousand speculations in [my mind]." But Sor Juana's greatest achievement was an outpouring of lyrical poetry, still regarded as the colonial period's finest contribution to literature.

A few Spanish-Americans made scientific studies. During the 1700's in Spanish America, as in Europe and the English colonies of North America, educated men were taking a greater interest in science. One of these was a scientist in Peru named Pedro de Peralta Barnuevo (pay-*rahl'* tah bar-*nway'* voh). As a mathematician, Peralta taught at the university in Lima for many years. He was also a skilled engineer, astronomer, and geographer. At a time when little was known about measuring latitude, he figured out Lima's exact distance from the equator.

Another scientist of distinction was José Celestino Mutis (*moo'* tis). He had come to Bogotá from Spain in 1762 to serve as physician to a new viceroy. Amazed at the variety of tropical plants in Colombia, he decided to stay in America and study botany. With the aid of a royal grant, Mutis hired artists to make careful drawings of several thousand different plants. These paintings were sent to the king in Madrid, and there they are still preserved. Mutis also founded an astronomical observatory.

Colonial art stressed religious themes. Religious influence was very strong in the arts of colonial Spanish America. Anyone who visits Latin American churches dating from the colonial period can see the work of many fine artists. The names of most of these artists are no longer known, but they were probably Spanish monks or Christianized Indians. In building the churches and decorating their walls and altars, the artists imitated the art of Spain. Nevertheless, it can be seen that these are American works of art. For example, in some of the wall paintings and sculptures done by native artists, Christ is portrayed with Indian features.

Indian, African, and European influences are reflected in Latin American music. The music of Latin America, so popular throughout the hemisphere today, had its roots in colonial times. Indian village musicians performed on drums and pipes that had originated in ancient times. Black slaves brought new rhythms and dances from Africa. From Spain came the chants and the choruses of the Catholic Church and Iberian folk songs and dances. Thus, rhythms and melodies from three continents blended in the rich heritage of Latin American music.

THINKING ABOUT THIS SECTION

1. Explain or define the following words: *compadres;* Virgin of Guadalupe; Sor Juana.

2. How did the Jesuit missions in Paraguay help the Guaraní Indians? What people were hostile to these missions? Why?

3. What were the functions of the Church in the Spanish towns and villages in America? In what ways did the Church seek to meet the needs of the Indians?

4. What evidence is there that learning was held in high esteem in Spanish America? What classes of society were most directly involved in education?

5. What was the subject matter of much of the literature and art that was produced in Spanish America?

Brazil slowly expanded inland. Chapter 4 told how the Portuguese got a slower start in American colonization than the Spanish. During the 1500's life in Brazil centered chiefly around sugar plantations in fertile coastal areas. Natural obstacles and a small population discouraged movement inland. As in the Spanish colonies, it was often Jesuit missionaries who first penetrated remote areas in Brazil. The Jesuits set up missions in the wilderness and brought together communities of Indians. Soon other Portuguese pioneers began to follow rivers into the interior, seeking good lands on which to raise livestock.

The bandeirantes raided missions. Among the frontiersmen in Brazil were also bands of slave-hunting *bandeirantes* (bahn-day-*rahn'* tesh). (Their name probably comes from the *bandeira,* or banner, carried by each group.) The lawless *bandeirantes* scaled the steep mountains behind the settlement at Santos and spread inland to the Paraná River, looking for gold or for Indians to enslave. Many of their victims they found in the Guaraní villages and the Spanish Jesuit missions. Because they explored new regions and extended the borders of Brazil, the *bandeirantes* are often presented as heroes in Brazilian history, just as some outlaws of the North American West have become heroic figures.

São Paulo was founded. In an effort to control the *bandeirantes,* the Portuguese king ordered colonists from Santos to found a new inland settlement. This outpost was combined with a Jesuit Indian mission and renamed São Paulo (sown-*pow'* loo). The energetic *paulistas* ("men of São Paulo") continued to spread out as frontiersmen, establishing a pioneer tradition that modern *paulistas* still prize. From its beginning as a small trading post, São Paulo was to grow into one of the world's largest cities.

Mining developed. Wherever they roamed, the *bandeirantes* were on the lookout for mineral wealth as well as slaves. In the early 1700's they discovered gold northwest of Rio de Janeiro. Gold seekers swarmed to the area called Minas Gerais (*mee'* nah zheh-*rice'*), or "General Mines." Rough mining camps grew up, like those in Mexico and Bolivia. Some Indians and black slaves found enough gold to buy their freedom. Soon diamonds were also discovered.

Since the gold-bearing ore was black rock, the chief mining camp was called Ouro Preto (*oh'* roo *pray'* too), or "Black Gold" in Portuguese. By the 1750's Ouro Preto had grown into a wealthy town of ornate houses and churches. Today Ouro Preto is preserved as an example of a Portuguese colonial town, much like Williamsburg in Virginia or Taxco in Mexico.

For a time Portugal had a Spanish ruler. Chapter 4 told how the Portuguese king had granted land to a number of individual proprietors. Partly because of this system of individual settlements, the central government in Brazil was never very strong, even after the king appointed a governor-general in the mid-1500's. Then, in 1580, Philip II of Spain took over control of Portugal. He and two succeeding Spanish kings ruled Portugal as a sister kingdom to Spain until 1640.

The Dutch occupied part of the Brazilian coast. Unfortunately for the Portuguese, this meant that the enemies of Spain also became enemies of Portugal. The Dutch soon took advantage of Portuguese weakness in Brazil. For years the Dutch West India Company had been trading at the port of Recife. In the 1630's a Dutch fleet completely took over Recife. Spreading northward along the coast, the Dutch occupied territory from Recife almost to the mouth of the Amazon. The settlements in this area prospered under the Dutch. Jews fleeing from the Spanish Inquisition were welcomed as settlers.

Eventually, however, the Brazilians revolted against Dutch rule. Although by this time a Portuguese king again ruled in Lisbon, no help came from Portugal. On their own the settlers raised an army that included Indians, free blacks, and Portuguese and for some thirteen years fought to drive out the Dutch. A leading hero of this war for freedom was a black named Henrique Dias. Finally in 1654 the Portuguese regained control. But the long struggle, without aid from the mother country, had aroused in the north Brazilians the first stirrings of nationalism.

Portuguese rule was restored. The Portuguese king made some effort to strengthen royal rule in the colony but without much success. Portuguese control of Brazil continued to be less strict than that of Spain in its colonies. A viceroy replaced the governor-general, with headquarters at Bahia. In 1763, to provide a more central location for the seat of government, the Portuguese moved the viceroy to Rio de Janeiro. But the change did little to strengthen the colonial government. The real problem was the change that had taken place in the mother country. Once a world power, Portugal had lost its wealth and prestige and was in no position to govern a huge American colony. Brazil increasingly came to be ruled by the great plantation owners.

A succession of products dominated Brazilian trade. During the 1500's sugar was the chief export from Brazil. In fact, by the end of that century the Brazilian plantations were the world's leading producer of sugar. Over the next two centuries a series of other products became important. After gold was discovered, it took first place in Brazilian exports. Then, in the 1700's cotton became the country's leading commodity in foreign trade. But in the early 1800's North American plantations took over leadership in the world cotton market. During all this time, of course, sugar continued to be a major export, and cattle products, tobacco, and cacao beans also contributed to Brazilian prosperity. Not until the 1800's did coffee become important.

Social divisions were less rigid in Brazil than in Spanish America. Unlike Spanish aristocrats, the great Portuguese landowners did not congregate in the cities. As a result, towns and cities played a less important role in colonial Brazil. Since Portugal allowed people of all kinds to emigrate to Brazil, there were more poor and middle-class Europeans in the Brazilian towns than in Spanish towns. These whites mixed freely with both Indians and Africans. By the second or third generation Brazilians of mixed descent usually lived in better circumstances than their black or Indian ancestors had. Although Brazil had different social classes, people were not strictly "locked in" at one social level.

Life along the Brazilian coast centered around the big sugar plantations. Here the cane was cut and then ground in crude mills to make cakes of brown sugar. The plantations were self-sufficient. In fact, one writer has described the typical plantation of this area as "a colony in itself." The plantation included the "big house" where the master's family lived, the slave quarters, a sugar mill, various shops where skilled slaves made useful articles, a chapel, and cemetery. The rest of the land was divided into canefields, plots for food crops, woodlands, and pastures.

These plantations resembled those in the southern English colonies of North America. Yet there was a difference. As in the English colonies, plantation society in Brazil was clearly divided into masters and slaves. But there was much more interaction between the two groups in the Portuguese colony. In Brazil all the children — white and black — played together, and all received religious instruction. Masters and slaves joined in religious services and festivals. Many laws protected slaves from cruel masters and enabled them to gain their freedom in various ways. The slaves' right to earn money and inherit land was recognized. As a result of these and other factors, color lines became less sharp in Brazil than elsewhere in America.

Women had a low position. In Brazil, as in the Spanish colonies (and in the mother countries), women had a low status. They were regarded primarily as childbearers and, in the case of slaves and other poor women, as manual laborers. Among the landholder class, women were responsible for carrying out the religious duties of the family. While the head of the plantation respected his wife, she had to remain in the background, unseen.

Jesuits were leaders in education and literature. Religion and education were other aspects of life that were similar in the Spanish and Portuguese colonies. The Church, particularly the Jesuits, controlled education in Brazil. Mission schools were founded in most coastal towns and farther inland as well. In the 1700's the Jesuits were expelled from Brazil as they were from Spain. But by that time they had set up nine secondary schools. Most children of landowners, however, were instructed by private tutors or family chaplains. Since there were no universities in colonial Brazil, sons of wealthy families often went to Portugal for higher education.

The earliest writings about Brazil were the work of two dedicated Jesuit missionaries. Father Manoel da Nóbrega (*noh′* bray-gah) was one of the first Jesuits to come to the New World. Nóbrega did his utmost to protect the Indians from the raids of the *bandeirantes*. In the São Paulo area he founded schools for the Indians and in other ways worked to improve their lot. He wrote plays, histories, and poetry in Guaraní for the Indians to read.

A Jesuit who joined Nóbrega in this work was José de Anchieta (ahn-chee-*ay′* tah), only 20 years old when he came to Brazil. Suffering from tuberculosis, he expected to die within a few months. But he regained his

In the early 1800's the Brazilian mulatto sculptor called "Aleijadinho" created his masterpiece—a group of twelve statues of biblical figures carved in green soapstone for a church in Minas Gerais. Pictured here is the head of his statue of Isaiah.

health in Brazil's mild climate and lived to be 64. Anchieta also prepared books for the Indians and wrote accounts of Brazilian life for readers in Portugal. Anchieta has been called the "father of Brazilian literature."

Apart from these writings, colonial Brazil produced little literature that is remembered. The major exceptions are two long poems that rank high in Brazilian literature. One by Basilio da Gama, called *O Uruguay,* dealt with the Guaraní Indians. The other, *O Caramurú* by José de Santa Rita Durão (thoo-*rown′*), told about the shipwrecked Portuguese who became an Indian chieftain (page 87).

Brazilians contributed to art and music. In the arts generally, colonial Brazil did not equal the achievements of Spanish America. Yet the most notable artist of all colonial Latin America was a Brazilian. The sculptor Antonio

Francisco Lisbõa (leess-*boh'* ah) was the son of a Portuguese carpenter in Ouro Preto and a slave mother. A hunchback, he was called Aleijadinho (ah-lay-hah-*deen'* yoh), or "the little cripple Alexander." When leprosy and rheumatism attacked his fingers, he had to work with chisels tied to his hands. Despite these handicaps, he produced masterpieces of sculpture. His statues of Christ and his gigantic lifelike figures of Old Testament prophets may still be seen in churches in Salvador and the old mining towns of Minas Gerais.

The most famous music of colonial Brazil consisted of the old slave songs which are still heard at carnival time. The rhythms and melodies of two continents mingled in these songs of the people. Brazilian folk songs have often been used by modern composers as themes in both popular and serious music.

THINKING ABOUT THIS SECTION

1. Explain or define the following words: *bandeirantes; paulistas.*

2. Note on the map on page 96 that the early Portuguese colonies hugged the Atlantic coast. Why was the expansion into the interior slow in Brazil?

3. How did Portugal's changing fortunes affect Brazil? Give examples.

4. During the first three centuries after European settlement, what were the chief sources of wealth in Brazil? Why did the importance of these change?

5. Why were cities less important in Brazil than in Spanish America? How were social divisions different in the two colonial areas? Contrast Brazilian plantation life with that of the southern English colonies.

Summing Up

By the end of the 1700's, Latin America had many thriving cities and towns. The Spanish colonies were ruled by the monarch. The chief agents of the royal government were the Council of the Indies, the viceroys, the *audiencias,* and (later) the intendents.

Colonial society was divided into distinct classes. At the top were the Spaniards born in Spain. Ranking just below them were the creoles, Spanish people born in America. Then there were the millions of mestizos, or people of mixed Indian and Spanish descent. At the bottom of the social scale were Indians and black slaves. It was the mestizos, Indians, and slaves who did the hard work that made the colonies prosperous.

Agriculture and mining were the major economic activities. Domestic animals had been introduced by the Europeans, and sugar cane, tobacco, and cacao became valuable export crops. Precious metals, especially silver, yielded Spain great wealth from its colonies. Although trade was strictly regulated to benefit the mother country, widespread smuggling brought non-Spanish goods into the colonies. During the 1700's the Bourbon rulers did away with the more restrictive trade policies.

The king controlled the Catholic Church in Spanish America. Missionaries converted the Indians, founded schools, and opened up frontier regions. In the settled areas, social life centered around the local church, and religion was important in every phase of life. Thus, education was a domain of the Church, and priests served as professors at the universities that were founded in Mexico City, Lima, and other colonial cities.

Life in the Portuguese colony of Brazil was similar but more easy-going. Very little of the deep interior was explored, and the areas around São Paulo and Ouro Preto long were frontier settlements. The great sugar plantations dominated Brazilian life. In the 1700's a gold rush brought miners to Ouro Preto. For a while, cotton became an important export. Though Brazilian society was also divided into classes, life for people of mixed ancestry was easier than in the Spanish colonies.

6

Spanish Roots in the United States

CHAPTER FOCUS

1. Early Explorations of the Spanish Borderlands
2. Spanish Settlements in Florida
3. Early Settlements on the North Mexican Frontier
4. Life Along the Northern Frontier to 1800

So far, this book has dealt with the European conquest and settlement of Middle and South America. But Spanish expansion did not come to a halt at the Rio Grande. Explorers pushed northward into what is now the United States, and five of this country's states — California, Arizona, New Mexico, Texas, and Florida — were settled by Spanish-speaking people. These areas in the United States that were once Spanish colonies are sometimes called the "Spanish borderlands."

The Spanish heritage is reflected in many place names in these five states. Such names as San Francisco, San Diego, Santa Barbara, and San Antonio were given to missions founded on particular saints' days. Monterey was the name of a viceroy in Mexico City. El Paso was a pass where the Rio Grande breaks through the mountains. Albuquerque was named after a cousin of the Spanish king. In 1781 the Spanish founded a town called *Nuestra Señora la Reina de Los Angeles* ("Our

From the rancheros and vaqueros of northern Mexico came the traditions and equipment that were later adopted by English-speaking cattlemen in the southwestern United States.

Lady the Queen of the Angels"). Today, of course, we call it Los Angeles.

In other ways, also, the Spanish influence is clear. Cattle ranching spread from northern Mexico into what is now the southwestern United States. Techniques and equipment developed by the Mexican ranchers became part of ranch life in this country. The roundup and the rodeo, branding, the western saddle, and the lasso were all contributions of Spanish-Mexican ranchers. Knowledge of how to irrigate dry lands also spread northward.

Today more than a fifth of the people living in the southwestern United States have Spanish last names, and many of them speak Spanish at home. Spanish and Mexican food, music, and dances are enjoyed by people throughout the United States, and houses and other buildings reflect the old Spanish mission architecture. Fashion designers have copied gaucho styles of clothing and Mexican jewelry. A variety of Spanish words have entered the English language. *Corral, patio, avocado, adobe, siesta,* and *fiesta* are just a few of the many familiar words of Spanish origin.

A later chapter will say much more about the Spanish-speaking people of the southwestern United States today. This chapter tells how that region and Florida bcame the "Spanish borderlands."

1. Early Explorations of the Spanish Borderlands

Spanish explorers were drawn into the borderlands by two dreams. One was the hope of discovering "another Mexico" — another land rich in gold. But they also hoped to find a waterway that was supposed to cut through North America from east to west. Such a waterway would provide a shorter and easier route for trade with Asia. Naturally the Spanish wanted to find this route before any other European power.

Ponce de León explored the Florida coast. One of the earliest Spaniards to explore in what is now the United States was Ponce de León (*pohn'* say day lay-*ohn'*), the first Spanish governor of Puerto Rico. Ponce de León had heard fanciful stories of a land to the north called Bimini. The waters of a certain fountain in Bimini, it was said, would make old men young again. Ponce de León set out to look for this Fountain of Youth in 1513.

Sailing north from the Caribbean islands, Ponce de León landed on the eastern coast of Florida. He touched several spots on the coast, at one point rounding what is now Cape Kennedy. Ponce de León gave the peninsula (which he thought an island) the name of Florida, meaning in Spanish "the flowering place." But he did not find the Fountain of Youth.

Narváez led an expedition to Florida. Eventually, another Spaniard sailed to Florida, this time hoping to find rich Indian cities. He was Panfilo de Narváez, the captain who had been sent to Mexico in 1520 to arrest Cortés. Narváez arrived at Tampa Bay on Florida's west coast in the spring of 1528 and led a party inland. Included in this band were a captain named Cabeza de Vaca (kah-*bay'* sah day *vah'* kah) and an African called Estevanico (page 45). Half of Narváez's men remained aboard the ships and cruised northward, looking for a good harbor. If they found one, they were supposed to wait there for the overland party. Meanwhile, Narváez and his men moved far to the north, looking for cities. But they found only a village of huts near the site of modern Tallahassee. Disappointed, they turned back, only to find no sign of their companions. The men on the ships, certain that their leader was lost, had sailed for Cuba.

The survivors of Narváez's expedition were shipwrecked off Texas. Narváez decided that the expedition had to make its way to Mexico by water. He had no idea that Mexico was more than a thousand miles away. The men began to cut down trees in order to build boats. Day by day they killed their horses, ate the flesh, and saved the hides to make the boats watertight. Sails were fashioned from shirts, and the fibers of palmetto plants were used to make ropes and bindings. At last, in this "horsehide fleet" of five boats, the 200 men set out to sea.

At the mouth of the Mississippi in November, 1528, the mighty current swamped four of the boats, and Narváez was among those who were lost at sea. Eighty survivors were cast ashore near what is now Galveston, Texas. Indians gathering shellfish found the castaways sprawled on the beach. Although the Indians fed the sick and starving men, only fifteen lived through the winter. Among those who managed to stay alive were Estevanico and Cabeza de Vaca.

Estevanico and Cabeza de Vaca finally reached Mexico. Each of the surviving Spaniards became the slave of a different Indian clan. These nomadic Indians made their living by collecting shellfish and seasonal fruits. During the next few years the surviving Spaniards saw each other only when the clans met to gather pecans in the fall and prickly pears in the summer. At each meeting Cabeza de Vaca urged the others to join him in a dash for freedom. But a dash to where? For six years the others refused to follow him into the unknown.

Finally, only four remained alive. These four —Estevanico, Cabeza de Vaca, and two others —made their escape. Heading west and then south, they trudged on, posing as wandering medicine men. In 1536, eight years after building the boats in Florida, the four men came upon a party of slave-hunting Spaniards on the west coast of Mexico. By water and on foot, they had crossed from the eastern Gulf of Mexico to the Pacific and had survived a journey of incredible length and difficulty.

Estevanico set out for Cíbola. In Mexico, Cabeza de Vaca and Estevanico told about the towns of the Pueblo (*pweb'* loh) Indians. They themselves had not seen these towns, but Indians had told them that the Pueblos lived in houses three stories high. To many Spaniards the description seemed to fit the fabled "Seven Cities of Cíbola," which were supposed to be rich in silver and gold (page 76).

In 1539 Estevanico led an expedition northward in search of Cíbola. Somewhere on this journey into what is now New Mexico, Estevanico lost his life, probably a victim of hostile Indians. A priest named Friar Marcos returned to Mexico from the expedition and told some "tall" tales. From a plateau, he said, he had seen in the distance a city "larger than the city of Mexico."

Coronado continued the search. This report stirred up excitement in the capital of New Spain. The viceroy lost little time in raising a large force to send north. To lead the expedition, he chose a wealthy young nobleman named Francisco Vásquez de Coronado. In 1540 Coronado started north with a large party of Spaniards and Indians. At the same time the viceroy ordered a fleet of three ships to sail up the Gulf of California. These ships reached the mouth of the Colorado River. But the shallowness of the river and the desert country on each side decided the captain to turn back. He never made any contact with Coronado's men.

On reaching western New Mexico, Coronado found Pueblo Indians living in adobe dwellings several stories high. But these communities were obviously not the silver cities of Cíbola. One of the Spaniards wrote: "When they saw the first village, such were the curses that [Coronado's men] hurled at Friar Marcos

Coronado found no rich cities in North America, but he probably saw villages of grass huts like this one built by Wichita Indians in what is now Kansas.

his men covered territory in what are now the states of Arizona, New Mexico, Texas, Oklahoma, and Kansas. None of them found any gold, nor did they find a water route to the Pacific.

In a report that he later wrote to the king, Coronado described one "province" as being the "best I have ever seen for producing all the products of Spain, for besides the land itself being very fat and black and being very well-watered by the rivulets and springs and rivers, I found prunes like those of Spain and nuts and very good sweet grapes and mulberries." But it was precious metals the king had hoped to hear about. Coronado's report discouraged further exploration of the country north of the Rio Grande.

De Soto traveled from Florida to the Mississippi River. Meanwhile, at about the same time, Hernando de Soto was moving across what was eventually to become the southeastern United States. De Soto had served with Pizarro in Peru (page 78). Later he asked and won royal permission to seek gold in Florida. With a large expedition, de Soto sailed from Cuba in 1539. He landed in the vicinity of Tampa Bay and advanced into the interior.

At each Indian village he came to, de Soto heard tales of gold somewhere a little farther on. At one town in Georgia, a rich chieftainess presented him with a gift of pearls. The ungrateful Spaniard made her a slave and continued searching for precious metals. Over three years de Soto's expedition covered much of what is now the southeastern United States. But the Spaniards found no gold. By the spring of 1542 the exhausted men were marching south, hoping to reach the Gulf coast. Sick with fever, de Soto died near the Mississippi River.

About half the men who had landed in Florida remained alive. These survivors built seven boats, sailed down the Mississippi into the Gulf, and finally landed on the coast of Mexico. They had found neither riches nor a

that I pray God may protect him from them. It is a little crowded village, looking as if it had been crumpled all up together." Enraged at finding no treasure, Coronado and his men slaughtered many of the Indians.

The search failed. The Indians managed to get rid of Coronado by describing more prosperous towns farther away. From the upper Rio Grande, Coronado headed east into the Great Plains. There he found nomadic Indians who hunted immense herds of what he described as "humpbacked cows." These, of course, were the American buffalo or bison. Coronado sent out small scouting parties to explore in various directions. One of these, heading west, came upon the yawning chasm of the Grand Canyon of the Colorado River. Another party scouted east into Texas. All together, Coronado and

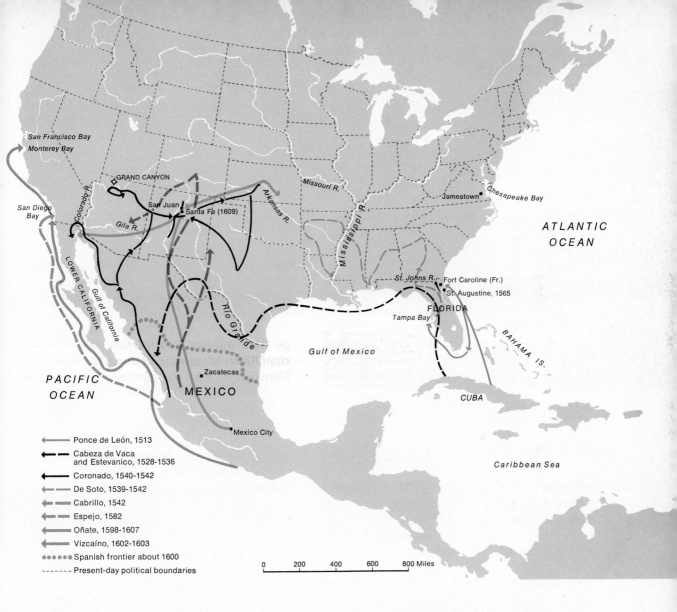

San Francisco Bay
Monterey Bay

San Diego Bay

GRAND CANYON

Colorado R.

San Juan

Gila R.

Santa Fe (1609)

Arkansas R.

Missouri R.

Jamestown

Chesapeake Bay

ATLANTIC OCEAN

LOWER CALIFORNIA

Gulf of California

Rio Grande

Mississippi R.

St. Johns R.

Fort Caroline (Fr.)

St. Augustine, 1565

FLORIDA

Tampa Bay

BAHAMA IS.

PACIFIC OCEAN

Gulf of Mexico

Zacatecas

MEXICO

CUBA

Mexico City

Caribbean Sea

Ponce de León, 1513
Cabeza de Vaca and Estevanico, 1528-1536
Coronado, 1540-1542
De Soto, 1539-1542
Cabrillo, 1542
Espejo, 1582
Oñate, 1598-1607
Vizcaíno, 1602-1603
Spanish frontier about 1600
Present-day political boundaries

0   200   400   600   800 Miles

waterway to Asia. Like Coronado's, this expedition was regarded as a failure.

Knowledge of North America had been expanded. Actually, of course, these two tremendous journeys yielded a "gold mine" of information about parts of America never before seen by white men. As a noted historian has pointed out, Coronado and de Soto had made known to Europeans "nearly a third of the area now contained in the United States, and

The Spanish Borderlands to About 1600

in several respects had changed current ideas regarding the entire land mass of North America and its geographical relation to the rest of the globe." [1]

[1] Herbert Eugene Bolton, *Coronado, Knight of Pueblos and Plains* (Albuquerque: The University of New Mexico Press, 1949), pp. 397–398.

The Pacific coast was explored. Meanwhile, exploration was adding to knowledge of the California coast. Ships sent out by Hernando Cortés explored Lower California and the Gulf of California. The Spaniards at first had thought Lower California was an island. But one of the explorers sent out by Cortés became convinced that this long strip of land was a peninsula.

In 1542 another captain searched along the California coast for the outlet of the waterway that was supposed to cut across the continent. This captain was Juan Rodriguez Cabrillo (kah-*bree'* yoh). After a long sail up the western coast of Lower California, Cabrillo and his men landed at San Diego Bay. They continued up the coast, but heavy fog in the San Francisco area prevented them from seeing the great bay there. On the return voyage, Cabrillo fell from a mast and broke an arm.

An infection developed and he soon died. In the following year, his first mate turned northward again and sailed as far as present-day Oregon. He laid claim for Spain to the entire Pacific coast of North America. But Charles I was busy with wars in Europe and took little interest in this region.

THINKING ABOUT THIS SECTION

1. Explain or define the following words: borderlands; Lower California; Pueblos.

2. During the 1500's what were Spanish explorers seeking in the regions that today are the southern and southwestern United States (map, page 117)? What did they accomplish?

3. Give examples of the following from this section: (a) rumors or myths that were exploded; (b) extraordinary courage and perseverance; (c) unusual inventiveness.

2. Spanish Settlements in Florida

England and France challenged Spanish power. After the 1550's Spain's position of power in the New World was increasingly challenged by England and France. In North America, French explorers had claimed the entire St. Lawrence valley. English pirates waylaid Spanish treasure ships and burned Spanish towns in the New World. By the 1560's Philip II had decided that Spain must hold Florida. Between this strategic peninsula and the Bahama Islands lay the main route of Spanish ships on their way to Europe.

Spanish missionaries visited Florida. Florida had not been neglected by the missionaries. A brave priest called Friar Luis Cancer (kahn-*sair'*) went to Florida without soldiers or arms, hoping to win the Indians to Christianity. He and three other missionaries landed near Tampa Bay in 1549. There they found a Spaniard who

had lost his way from de Soto's expedition and been enslaved by Indians. Warning that the Indians now hated all white men, he urged Friar Luis to leave Florida. But the determined missionary ignored this advice and was soon killed by the Indians.

The Spanish king sponsored settlement in Florida. Once Philip II realized the advantage of holding Florida, he decided to start a colony there. It would provide a haven for Spanish ships that were caught in hurricanes off the coast or were trying to escape from English pirates. In 1559 an expedition of 1500 colonists and soldiers sailed north under the command of an officer who had served with Coronado. One group of colonists landed at what is now Pensacola on the northern Gulf coast of Florida. Another party landed on the coast of South Carolina. But both these colonies were soon abandoned. The Spaniards were unwilling to grow food themselves, and the Indians were hostile.

French activity forced the Spanish king to try colonizing Florida a second time. Though France was a Catholic country, its government had permitted a group of French Protestants to start a colony on the Atlantic coast of north Florida, at the mouth of the St. Johns River. (This is about where Jacksonville is now situated.) Alarmed at this news, Philip II of Spain hurriedly ordered another expedition to set out for Florida. To lead the expedition, he chose Pedro Menéndez de Avilés (meh-*nehn′* dayss day ah-vee-*layss′*), a naval officer who had fought French pirates at sea.

Menéndez de Avilés enlisted a band of 500 men to go to Florida. Some of these men took along their wives and families. Also included in the colonizing party were 500 African slaves. This was probably the first large number of black people to go to what is now United States soil. The expedition sailed in 1565.

The Spaniards drove out the French. Menéndez de Avilés landed his colonists on the coast a little way south of the St. Johns River. At a nearby Indian village he drove the natives out of their communal ceremonial hall and turned the building into a fort. This was the beginning of St. Augustine, the first European town in what is now the United States. From this base Menéndez de Avilés marched north to the French settlement at the St. Johns River. Attacking early in the morning, the Spaniards slaughtered most of the sleeping Frenchmen. The Spaniards also massacred the survivors of a French shipwreck. Menéndez de Avilés was praised by Philip II for these "patriotic" acts. Two years later the French took their revenge. A French raiding party attacked the Spaniards who now held the post at the St. Johns River. All the Spaniards were killed.

St. Augustine survived. Life in the little Spanish colony at St. Augustine was not easy. The Indians, thoroughly hating the Europeans by now,

Like many other native Americans, Florida Indians in the 1500's raised corn and beans. This drawing from a 1591 book about Florida showed Indian men breaking up the earth and women planting seeds.

were a constant danger. Food was always short. Moreover, that enemy of the Spanish, Francis Drake himself, had boldly sailed into the harbor and set fire to the town. Philip II sent out more colonists, determined to hold the "Florida coast" as far north as Chesapeake Bay. It was not until 1607 that the English established a successful colony on the Atlantic coast of North America. This was the colony of Jamestown in what is now Virginia.

Spain held Florida until 1819. Spanish missionaries had little success in founding other settlements in Florida. Pensacola, where an early settlement had been abandoned, was again settled in 1698, long after Philip's day. In 1763, after a great colonial war won by the English, Spain ceded Florida to England. By way of compensation Spain received from France the city of New Orleans and French territory west of the Mississippi. France and Spain both sided with the thirteen English colonies in the American Revolutionary War. At the close of that war (1783), Britain restored Florida to Spain. Then, in 1819 Spain ceded Florida to the United States.

THINKING ABOUT THIS SECTION

1. Why did Florida become important to Spain? What steps were taken to hold it?

2. Florida eventually became a pawn traded back and forth in various peace settlements between the great colonial powers of the 1700's. Use Florida's history to show how this was so.

3. Early Settlements on the North Mexican Frontier

In the west the Spanish pushed northward the Mexican frontier. On the heels of the explorers followed missionaries, ranchers, and settlers.

Missionaries followed Coronado into New Mexico. Franciscan missionaries were among the earliest Europeans to venture into the borderlands north of the Rio Grande. In 1581, about 40 years after Coronado, Spanish missionaries visited the Pueblo towns in New Mexico. Two of the Franciscans founded a mission nearby but were killed by Indians.

Espejo led a rescue party. Learning of this attack and hoping to find the missionaries still alive, a soldier named Antonio de Espejo (es-*pay'* hoh) led a rescue party north from Mexico. But rumors of a lake of gold drew Espejo westward into Arizona. There he found Hopi Indians who grew cotton. Espejo traded with the Hopi for 4000 cotton blankets. He also discovered veins of gold and silver, but these were not to be developed until much later.

Oñate led settlers into New Mexico. Rumors that Francis Drake had found a strait through North America revived Spain's interest in strengthening its claim to territory north of the Rio Grande. The viceroy in Mexico selected Juan de Oñate (ohn-*yah'* tay) to lead a colonizing party northward. Oñate was a wealthy man from the silver-mining town of Zacatecas. Other men of wealth in Zacatecas also invested in the expedition.

In 1598 more than a hundred soldier-settlers and their families set out from Mexico City. They took with them African and Indian slaves, several thousand horses and cattle, and 80 wagons carrying baggage. On reaching the Rio Grande, Oñate founded a settlement about where El Paso, Texas, and Juárez, Mexico, lie on opposite sides of the river today. Continuing northward along the river, Oñate took possession of an Indian town. This settlement, just north of present-day Santa Fe, he named San Juan. A Catholic church built by the Spaniards at San Juan became the first permanent Christian church north of the Rio Grande. Chiefs from nearby Indian towns came to San Juan to swear allegiance to the king of Spain.

The New Mexico settlement seemed a failure. Over the next three years, Oñate explored New Mexico and northeastern Arizona. He searched for gold and also kept an eye out for the fabled strait to the Pacific. He hoped as well to capture and tame young buffalo calves. Leading a scouting party to the east, Oñate advanced as far as the site of present-day Wichita, Kansas. Here the discouraged Spaniards retreated from hostile Indians. They failed to find any gold or the strait through North America. Nor did they capture any buffalo.

When Oñate returned to his colony, he found it in trouble. The year had been very dry, and food supplies had run short. Many of the settlers had gone back to Mexico. The ruthless Oñate confiscated Indian stores of corn. Since this was the seed corn for the next year's planting, the Indians faced starvation. One of the missionaries wrote about Oñate: "He has butchered many Indians, . . . and he has committed thefts, sackings, and other atrocities. I pray that God may grant him the grace to do penance for all his deeds."

On another exploring trip, Oñate crossed the desert to the Colorado River and followed the river south to the Gulf of California. But he had no more success on this trip than on his earlier explorations. Moreover, he had lost his entire fortune as well as the funds invested by his Zacatecas backers. In 1607, Oñate returned to Mexico in disgrace.

Santa Fe became headquarters for the New Mexico colony. But some colonists remained at the El Paso settlement, and a few soldiers and missionaries held on at the settlements farther north. A new governor, Pedro de Peralta, decided to move all the scattered settlers to the site of Santa Fe and founded a town there in 1609. By 1630 this new capital was the headquarters for 25 missions and some 60,000 Christianized Indians. About the people of one mission, a Spanish priest reported: "These Indians are very dexterous in reading, writing, and playing on all kinds of instruments and are skilled in all the crafts, thanks to the great industry of the friars who converted them."

Spanish interest in the Philippines led to further exploration of the Pacific coast. Meanwhile, interest in the California coast had revived as a result of Spain's occupation of the Philippines. Magellan had claimed these islands for Spain. From this Pacific base, the Spanish hoped to find trade as profitable as Portugal's Asian spice trade.

Spanish ship captains soon found they could reach the Philippines by sailing west across the Pacific from Mexico. But ocean winds and currents prevented them from returning eastward over this route. Their only alternative was to sail west from the Philippines into the Indian Ocean and continue around Africa to Spain. This route, however, was controlled by the Portuguese.

Finally in the 1560's a Spanish captain found a way of getting back to Mexico from the Philippines. By sailing a *northward* route from the islands, a ship could cross the Pacific to Oregon or northern California and then sail south to Mexico. Ocean currents made this a sure way of returning from the Philippines. But it was a very long voyage. The viceroy of New Spain realized that a harbor on the California coast was needed as a way-station for ships homeward bound from the Philippines. There weary sailors could take on fresh water and food before continuing their voyage.

Vizcaíno explored the California coast. The viceroy appointed a merchant named Sebastian Vizcaíno (vees-kah-*een′* oh) to find the best spot for the California base. Using Cabrillo's charts, Vizcaíno rediscovered San Diego Bay in 1602 and continued northward. He spotted another bay which seemed to offer a good location for a base, and he named it Monterey. After sailing almost to Oregon, Vizcaíno returned to Mexico and reported that he had found an excellent harbor. Like Cabrillo, he had failed to see San Francisco Bay, the best harbor on the California coast.

Unfortunately Philip II had died shortly before Vizcaíno's voyage. The next king considered territorial expansion a waste of time and money. Vizcaíno's map and report were filed away in the government archives, and for 160 years nothing was done to extend Spanish settlement along the California coast.

THINKING ABOUT THIS SECTION

1. In the late 1500's Antonio de Espejo found veins of gold and silver in what is now Arizona. Why were these not mined until much later?

2. Evaluate Oñate as an explorer and a colonizer.

3. Why did possession of the Philippines make Spain interested in the California coast?

Under Pedro de Peralta and the governors who followed him, the Santa Fe settlement seemed to be doing all right. It was hardly a prosperous community, but 3000 Spanish-speaking settlers made Santa Fe the largest settlement north of Zacatecas. The local Indians, however, grew more and more restless under Spanish rule.

The Pueblo Indians rebelled. Santa Fe was an isolated outpost, hundreds of miles from Mexico City and surrounded by Indian villages. Many of the Spanish settlers were lawless men escaping from justice. They forced the Indians to work for them. When crops were bad, the white settlers took the food and left the Indians to starve. Nomadic Apaches constantly raided the Pueblo villages, and the Spanish soldiers did little to defend their Indian neighbors. The Pueblo Indians also resented the missionaries' efforts to convert them to Christianity. They still preferred their traditional religion.

A leader among the Indian medicine men was a man named Popé (poh-*pay'*). For five years Popé quietly planned a revolt. Finally, in 1680, the Indians of the villages around Santa Fe rose up against the Spanish settlers. Four hundred Spaniards were killed. The rest fled south to the El Paso area.

The Spanish reconquered New Mexico. Once again, the Pueblo Indians controlled New Mexico. The usually peaceful corn farmers had succeeded in driving out the white men. But their triumph did not last long. In 1692 the viceroy sent a military force to restore Spanish rule in New Mexico. The Spaniards conquered village after village, and by 1697 most of the Indians had surrendered. Many were killed or enslaved. Several hundred settlers, both Spanish and mestizo, returned to Santa Fe. The missions, mostly of the Franciscan order, were rebuilt. Under the Franciscans' direction, the mission Indians grew corn, beans, and wheat on irrigated land and raised cattle and sheep.

The missionaries hoped to teach Spanish ways to the Indians. The settlement of the Spanish borderlands was quite different from the settlement of eastern North America by English-speaking people. As pioneers advanced westward from the English colonies along the Atlantic coast, the Indians were driven from their lands and forced to move westward also. But in the northward expansion from Mexico the Indians were not displaced. Rather the missionaries sought to bring the Indians (at least those who were not nomadic) within the Spanish community and to teach them Spanish ways. The missionaries also did their best to protect the Indians from exploitation by dishonest Spaniards.

The chief purpose of the missionaries, of course, was to spread the Catholic faith. But in working for this goal they had to do many other things as well. When the missionaries arrived in a new region, they either built a mission near an existing Indian town, or they founded a new mission community. They gathered together as many Indians as they could and tried to teach them Spanish. Great stress was placed on teaching better methods of agriculture and of raising livestock. Useful crafts were also taught. But the Indians were seldom allowed to manage things by themselves.

Sometimes a mission had to defend itself against raiding Indians. Thick walls helped protect the buildings of a typical mission. But *presidios* or forts manned by Spanish soldiers were often built nearby. In fact, the missionaries found the presence of the soldiers helpful, not only in defending the mission from attack but also in disciplining the mission Indians. One priest wrote frankly about this problem:

It is seen every day that in missions where there are no soldiers, there is no success, for the Indians, being children of fear, are more strongly appealed to by the glistening of the sword than by the voice of five missionaries. Soldiers are necessary to defend the Indians from the enemy, and to keep an eye on the mission Indians, now

San Xavier del Bac, still standing near Tucson, Arizona, is the best-known of the missions founded by Eusebio Kino (below, right), the pioneering Jesuit father who explored southern Arizona.

to encourage them, now to carry news to the nearest *presidio* in case of trouble.[2]

Missionaries and ranchers clashed. As Spanish ranchers moved into New Mexico, they clashed with the missionaries over the use of land. The ranchers wanted the best lands as pasture for their sheep and cattle, while the missionaries thought fields should be irrigated and used for growing food crops. Trade was another point of conflict. Once a year caravans of wagons lumbered into Santa Fe loaded with goods from Mexico City. The Franciscans wanted the caravans to bring supplies needed by the missions, while government officials and ranchers in Santa Fe had their own ideas about what kinds of goods should be brought in. Still another issue was treatment of the Indians.

[2] Quoted in Herbert Eugene Bolton, *Bolton and the Spanish Borderlands*, ed. John Francis Bannon (Norman, Okla.: University of Oklahoma Press, 1964), p. 202.

As in other parts of Spanish America, settlers and missions competed for Indian labor.

New Mexico grew slowly. The New Mexico settlers faced other problems. Comanche and Apache Indians continued to raid settlements.

Also, a few French explorers and trappers moved into New Mexico from the north. But the Spanish colony slowly grew. In 1706 Albuquerque was founded on the trail to Mexico City. By 1821, when Mexico won independence from Spain, New Mexico had some 30,000 settlers. The missionaries claimed some 60,000 Indians as "Christians." But Indian life had changed very little. Today the Pueblo people still preserve many traditional ways.

Jesuits founded missions and ranches in Arizona and Lower California.

While the Franciscans built missions in New Mexico, the Jesuits extended Spanish influence along Mexico's west coast. A Jesuit of Italian descent, Eusebio Kino (*kee'* noh), pioneered in Arizona and Lower California. This remarkable man has been called "superb missionary, church-builder, explorer, and ranchman." In the late 1680's, Father Kino and a few companions headed into what is now Arizona, riding on horseback and driving cattle to stock new missions. Among several missions that they founded was one called San Xavier del Bac, near the present city of Tucson.

In exploring the country Father Kino rode along the Gila (*hee'* luh) River down to its junction with the Colorado River. Traveling from the mouth of the Gila south along the Colorado to the Gulf of California, Kino definitely proved that Lower California was part of the mainland. The map that he drew of this region served later explorers for more than a century.

Some of Father Kino's companions founded missions in Lower California. They arranged for cattle, sheep, and horses to be sent across to them by boat. The livestock that Kino and the other Jesuits brought to Arizona and Lower California multiplied rapidly. Some horses and cattle ran wild. Other horses were captured by Indians living outside the missions. Before the coming of the Spanish, the nomadic Apaches and Comanches had done their wandering on foot. But by the time English-speaking pioneers crossed the plains many years later, these Indians had become skilled horsemen.

When Father Kino died in 1711, he had founded some twenty towns and explored thousands of miles of country previously unknown to white men. He showed tolerance for Indian ways and, in return, won the respect of these native Americans. This was a major factor in his successful missionary effort.

Tucson was founded.

After the Jesuits were expelled from Spanish America in 1767, Father Kino's missions were maintained by Franciscans. To protect the mission at San Xavier del Bac from Apache raids, Spanish soldiers in 1776 built a walled town a few miles to the north. It was on the site of an Indian village, the name of which the Spaniards wrote down as Tucson. Mexican colonists went north to live within Tucson's adobe walls. Thus began the first Spanish "city" in Arizona.

Early explorers followed the Texas coast.

About the same time that Father Kino was active in Arizona, missionaries were also moving into Texas. Probably the first white man to touch the Gulf coast of Texas was Alonso de Pineda (pee-*nay'* thah) almost two centuries earlier. Sailing along the northern Gulf coast in 1519, this Spanish explorer failed to find what he was looking for—a waterway to the Pacific. But Pineda did discover the mouth of the Mississippi River. Moreover, he charted the whole northern coast of the Gulf of Mexico, from Florida to Tampico, Mexico.

A few years later, the survivors of Narváez's unlucky expedition reached the Texas coast. Both Coronado and de Soto also crossed parts of Texas. But neither of these journeys resulted in colonization. Occasionally agents seeking workers for Mexican silver mines made raids across the Rio Grande to capture Indians. The first white settlement in what is now Texas was in the El Paso area, then considered part of New Mexico.

The following labels appear on the map:

TREATY LINE 1819

Missouri R.

UNITED STATES

San Francisco
San José
Santa Clara
Monterey
San Luis Obispo
Santa Barbara
Los Angeles
San Diego

Colorado R.

Independence

Taos
Santa Fe
Albuquerque

Arkansas R.

Red R.

ATLANTIC OCEAN

Gila R.
Tucson
San Xavier del Bac
Tubac

El Paso

SONORA

Chihuahua

LOWER CALIFORNIA

Gulf of California

San Antonio R.
San Antonio

Mississippi R.

Sabine R.

Mobile
Biloxi
New Orleans
Pensacola

St. Augustine

FLORIDA
CEDED BY SPAIN
TO U.S., 1819

MEXICO

Rio Grande

Gulf of Mexico

PACIFIC OCEAN

Caribbean Sea

Legend:

←·—·— Kino, late 1600's
←———— Alonso de León, 1689-1690
←———— Portolá and Serra, 1769
←———— Anza, 1774
←— — — Anza, 1775-1776
———— Santa Fe Trail
░░░░ Louisiana Purchase, 1803
- - - - Present-day political boundaries

0   200   400   600   800 Miles

The French showed interest in Texas. At this time the name "Texas" was generally applied to territory between the mouth of the Rio Grande and the mouth of the Mississippi and extending for an unlimited distance into the interior. It was explorations by the French that finally aroused Spanish interest in this area. The explorer La Salle claimed the mouth of the Mississippi for France in 1682. Two years later he returned to the Gulf of Mexico to start a town at the mouth of the Mississippi.

The Spanish Borderlands by the Early 1800's

Compare with the map on page 117 to see how Spain's holdings in North America expanded after 1600.

This time, however, he could not find the mouth of the great river. La Salle landed his colonists several hundred miles to the west of his intended destination and set out into the wilderness. The unlucky explorer was murdered by his own men.

125

The Spanish moved in to stop the French.
The Spanish authorities had no idea that La Salle had failed. They knew only that the French were somewhere on the Texas coast, planning a colony. The news caused a sensation in Mexico. A Spanish expedition under Alonso de León described "the province of Texas" as "large and fertile" and having a "fine climate." León's favorable report, rivalry with the French, and the missionary impulse—all stimulated Spanish interest in Texas. On several trips, León escorted missionaries into the new province, and in 1690 a frontier post was founded.

The French, however, were not ready to be counted out of the Gulf area. Over the next few years they settled bases at several spots on the Gulf coast east of the Mississippi River. These included Biloxi (1699) and Mobile (1711). From these bases French explorers and fur traders probed into the interior.

Spanish missions were founded in Texas. The viceroy at Mexico City sent out several expeditions of missionaries, soldiers, and settlers to strengthen Spain's hold on Texas. Mission outposts were planted from the San Antonio River to the Red River in what is today Louisiana. In 1718, soldiers with families settled at the site where the city of San Antonio now stands. Several years later, more families came to San Antonio all the way from the Spanish-owned Canary Islands in the Atlantic Ocean. The frontier remained thinly settled, however, partly because of raids by Comanche and Apache Indians.

Louisiana became a Spanish colony. In the same year that San Antonio was founded, the French founded a trading post at New Orleans, about a hundred miles above the mouth of the Mississippi River. In the huge region north of New Orleans and west of the river, Spanish and French claims overlapped. La Salle had given the name "Louisiana" to the entire Mississippi-Missouri basin, in honor of the French king, Louis XIV. French frontiersmen

and fur traders in Louisiana occasionally wandered far enough south to give concern to outposts on the Spanish frontier. The viceroy at Mexico City continued to worry over every report of French fur trappers south of the Missouri River.

Finally, in 1763 the rivalry over Louisiana was settled. That year marked the end of colonial wars between the French and the British in North America. By the terms of the peace treaty, France turned over to Spain not only New Orleans but all French claims to territory west of the Mississippi. Now the huge Louisiana territory was solidly Spanish.

O'Reilly put down a rebellion in New Orleans. To govern Spain's new seaport on the Mississippi, the Spanish king sent Antonio de Ulloa. This was the same man who, many years before, had traveled throughout the Spanish colonies and written a famous book about his experiences there (page 89). Soon after Ulloa arrived in New Orleans, the French settlers, resentful of Spanish control, forced the distinguished governor to leave the city.

The Spanish king was not about to tolerate such rebellious behavior. He sent another governor, Alejandro O'Reilly. (He had been born in Ireland.) In 1769 O'Reilly entered the port of New Orleans with a squadron of 24 ships and several hundred soldiers. Overawing the settlers with this show of force, O'Reilly had no trouble establishing Spanish authority. The leaders of the rebellion were tried and executed. Settlers who wanted to return to France were permitted to do so, but most chose to stay in New Orleans. O'Reilly encouraged French fur traders to continue bringing beaver skins down the river to New Orleans. He also sent out expeditions to establish trade routes with San Antonio and Santa Fe. For almost 40 years Spanish control unified the region from the Mississippi to the Colorado River.

Napoleon regained Louisiana and sold it to the United States. To understand what happened next in Louisiana, we must take into account revolutionary changes in Europe. During the late 1700's, Europe was thrown into a state of confusion by the French Revolution. After the monarchy was overthrown in France, Napoleon Bonaparte rose to power. In 1800 he "persuaded" Spain to return Louisiana to France. Recovering Louisiana was only a part of a much bigger scheme dreamed up by the French dictator. Napoleon planned to re-establish France as a major colonial power in the New World. The island colony of Haiti was to be the base for winning control of the entire Caribbean. Haiti's rich sugar plantations would pour profits into the French treasury. Louisiana would provide food and other supplies for the island colonies. But it would also serve as a market for French manufactures and as an outpost of settlement in North America.

Within three years, however, Napoleon abandoned the whole idea. In Haiti a determined rebellion by freed black slaves and the ravages of yellow fever forced out the French army that Napoleon had sent to the island. Moreover, France was facing war with Great Britain. Knowing that the United States was interested in buying New Orleans, Napoleon decided to sell all of Louisiana. His offer was quickly accepted, and in August, 1803, the people of New Orleans learned that their city was to become part of the English-speaking United States. Louisiana's western boundary was rather indefinite at this time. By a treaty worked out in 1819, Spain and the United States agreed to a boundary that clearly separated Louisiana Territory from Spanish Mexico (map, page 125).

Spain sought to strengthen its control of Upper California.

California was to be the last Spanish colonial frontier. In the 1760's, Charles III of Spain had appointed a statesman named José de Gálvez to study Spanish rule in the regions of northern Mexico. The king also asked Gálvez to suggest how Spain could best hold the Texas-New Mexico-California frontier. At this time Russia had an outpost in Alaska, and Russian fur traders were moving south along the Pacific coast. Gálvez urged the king to secure his hold in Upper California (the present-day state) by founding missions there. The missions, he said, should be supported by *presidios,* and settlers should then follow. This, of course, was the typical pattern of Spanish frontier settlement.

Father Serra founded California missions.

Named to lead the missionaries into Upper California was the Franciscan Father Junípero Serra (*sehr'* rah). As a young man, Father Serra had come to Mexico to take up missionary work. In Mexico he learned all the things that a missionary on the frontier had to know—how to make bricks from clay, build arcades and towers for churches, plant orchards and vineyards, and tan hides and care for cattle. He was overjoyed at being assigned to lead missionaries into Upper California. After a long journey on foot to San Diego Bay, Father Serra founded there the first mission (1769) in what is now the state of California. He and his Franciscan companions established 21 missions in California by the early 1820's. Today many of these sites are important cities—Santa Clara, Santa Barbara, San José, San Francisco, and San Diego among them.

To the Indians, Father Serra and the other missionaries taught the useful skills they themselves had learned. The Indians also built beautiful churches. But, as was the case in other missions, the Indians had no opportunity to become self-sufficient members of Spanish communities.

Portolá explored California.

Father Serra's northward trek had been part of a colonizing expedition led by Captain Gaspar de Portolá. The captain hoped to find Monterey Bay, which Vizcaíno had praised almost 170 years earlier. In July, 1769, Portolá left Father Serra at the mission station in San Diego. With a small party of soldiers and Indians, Portolá rode north. After many days, he reached Monterey Bay. But he had been expecting a much larger bay. Disappointed, he continued up the coast.

Some of his men, while hunting for game, rode up a knoll and suddenly saw below them a great sheet of water. Finally, white men had found San Francisco Bay, the finest harbor on the California coast. One of the Spaniards said of the bay: "It is a very large and fine harbor, such that not only all the navy of our most Catholic Majesty but those of all Europe could take shelter in it."

On the journey back to San Diego, Portolá's men almost starved. At San Diego the situation was no better. The supplies were almost used up, many of the colonists had died of hunger, and the remainder were sick. Portolá was ready to abandon the whole California enterprise, bay or no bay. But Father Serra insisted that they wait just a little longer for a supply ship. One finally did arrive from Mexico, thus saving the venture from failure. In 1770 Serra and Portolá traveled north to Monterey. There the captain established a *presidio,* and the Franciscan founded a mission called San Carlos.

Anza opened an overland route from Arizona to California. When news of the Monterey mission and of the discovery of the great bay reached the viceroy at Mexico City, he ordered all the church bells rung in celebration. But there remained the problem of how to get supplies to the remote California missions. What was needed was a land route to Upper California from the cattle-rich missions in Sonora (the northwestern part of present-day Mexico) and Arizona.

The man chosen to search out such a route was Juan Batista de Anza, commander of a fort at Tubac in Arizona. A frontiersman, Anza knew the western deserts well. In 1774, with a small band of soldiers, loaded mules, and herds of cattle, Anza started out over a trail followed by Father Kino many years before, down the Gila River to the Colorado. The chief of the nomadic Yuma Indians helped Anza's party cross the Colorado River in return for a ribbon sash and a necklace of Spanish coins. Then the party wandered for days in the desert

Many California cities had their beginnings in the mission communities founded by Junípero Serra and his Franciscan companions. This statue of Father Serra represents the state of California in Statuary Hall in the Capitol Building, Washington, D.C. Right, an 1847 drawing of San Francisco shows the settlement that grew up near one of the Franciscan missions.

that is now the irrigated Imperial Valley of California. They eventually crossed the mountains east of the site of modern Riverside, California. After a trip of 700 miles, Anza's party came out at the mission at San Gabriel, near what is now Los Angeles.

San Francisco was founded. The next step in holding the California coast against the Russians was to recruit settlers for a town at San Francisco Bay. Anza returned to Sonora for this purpose, but he found few people willing to go. Anza offered to pay them in advance with livestock, rations, clothing, and miscellaneous other articles. He finally rounded up 30 families, all of them Sonora mestizos or converted Arizona Indians. They set out from Tubac in October, 1775, and reached San Francisco Bay in March, 1776, having covered well over a thousand miles. Only one person died along the way, an incredibly low casualty rate for such a journey. At San Francisco, a *presidio* and mission were founded. (About the same time, on the eastern coast of the North American continent, English-speaking Americans were declaring their independence from Great Britain.)

Other settlers started Los Angeles. In 1781 a similar group of Mexican families founded Los Angeles. The eleven families who migrated to Los Angeles included Indians, mestizos, and mulattos. Each family received a grant of land, two cows, two mares, two oxen, and two sheep, as well as tools and clothing.

Spanish settlers in California prospered. The "founding fathers" of both San Francisco and Los Angeles were soon joined by mission Indians, Spanish soldiers who received large land grants as their pay, and mestizo *vaqueros* who did the work on these land grants. Compared to some other Spanish frontier settlements, life was easy in California. Cattle and horses multiplied. Cuttings of grape vines and fig, orange, and olive trees were transplanted from the missions to the ranches.

California was not governed as a separate province. Since it was considered a part of Mexico, it was ruled by the viceroy at Mexico City. Spain held California for four decades after the founding of San Francisco and Los Angeles. When Mexico broke away from Spain in 1821, California and the other borderlands became part of independent Mexico.

THINKING ABOUT THIS SECTION

1. Explain or define the following words: mission; *presidio;* Apaches.

2. Compare the map on page 117 with the one on page 125 to see how Spanish settlement spread during the 1600's and 1700's. What were some of the reasons for this expansion?

3. Contrast the Spanish policy toward Indians in the Southwest with that of English settlers along the Atlantic coast. Why was each policy adopted? What were the advantages of each for whites? for Indians?

4. Why did Spanish missionaries and ranchers disagree about land use?

5. Why did Spanish and French interests clash in the lower Mississippi valley? What came of this conflict?

6. Describe the role of each of these men in the Spanish colonization of California: Portolá; Serra; Anza.

Summing Up

Spanish expansion in the Americas did not stop short at what is now the border between Mexico and the United States. Soon after Cortés' conquest of Mexico, Spanish explorers pushed north into regions that are now United States territory. These soldier-adventurers were searching for "another Mexico," a civilized Indian nation that would yield riches in gold. They also hoped to find a navigable water passage through North America. But another motive was to hold frontier lands against the approaches of foreign powers. At different times and places this foreign threat was represented by France, England, Russia, and eventually the United States.

Drawn by these motives, Spanish explorers penetrated the wilderness in much of what is now the southern United States. In the east Spaniards founded St. Augustine, Florida, the oldest European settlement in United States territory. In the west, four states — New Mexico, Arizona, Texas, and California — were settled by Spanish-speaking people from Mexico. Many frontier missions and *presidios* in these states have grown into modern towns and cities.

The leaders in the colonization process were the Spanish missionaries who marched along with the explorers or followed close behind. Since the missionaries were intent on bringing the Catholic faith to the native Americans, conversion was their chief goal. But in the course of this work they also blazed trails into regions unknown to white men, laid the foundations of new communities, and introduced new agricultural techniques. The missions were, in effect, schools for the Indians. Instead of driving the native people out of Spanish-occupied lands, the missionaries tried to make the Indians members of Spanish communities.

7

The Independence Movements in Latin America

"What the patriots wanted in numbers was made up by enthusiasm" said an eyewitness patriot officer about the Battle of Ayacucho, fought in 1824 in a Peruvian valley 11,000 feet above sea level. Though heavily outnumbered, the patriot army at Ayacucho won a decisive victory over royalist forces, thus breaking Spain's hold on Peru and ensuring independence for all of Spanish South America.

By the late 1700's many creoles in Latin America felt restless under Spanish rule. One of these was a young landowner named Antonio Nariño (nah-*reen'* yoh). The son of a well-to-do exporter in New Granada (modern Colombia), Nariño had attended the university in Bogotá. There he studied law and learned English and French. Nariño and many of his friends, also sons of creole merchants, resented Spain's control of colonial trade. These young men felt frustrated too because there were few opportunities for creoles to serve in the colonial government. The Spanish-born *peninsulares* always had an advantage in social standing, economic opportunities, and appointment to high office.

In 1776, while Nariño was still a boy, the English colonies in North America had issued a Declaration of Independence. In stirring words the English colonists had affirmed the equality of all men and declared their right to overthrow a tyrannical government. Probably Antonio Nariño heard little about this at the time. But when he was 24, a meeting of people's representatives in France adopted a Declaration of the Rights of Man. This dramatic statement expressed much the same ideas as had been stated in the document written by the North American colonists.

Since the Declaration of the Rights of Man denounced the French monarchy, rulers all over Europe called it radical. The Spanish government forbade anyone in the American colonies to read such dangerous words. But friends of Nariño smuggled a copy of the Declaration into Bogotá. The young creole translated its fiery words into Spanish. Secretly using a small hand press, Nariño printed many copies of his translation on cheap wrapping paper. This paper was used in wrapping samples of chocolate and twists of tobacco that were distributed through his father's business. Thus, in spite of Spanish censorship, revolutionary ideas were circulated.

Eventually, the Spanish authorities arrested Nariño. Besides the French papers, they also found in his possession writings by North American revolutionaries, including Thomas Jefferson and Alexander Hamilton. Following a trial, Nariño was sentenced to a long term in prison.

Nariño's defiance of censorship did not touch off a rebellion against Spain in New Granada. But his example was an inspiration to later leaders. Within a very few years creoles throughout Spanish America were to rise up against the colonial authorities. In fact, Nariño escaped from prison and returned to his homeland in time to help Simón Bolívar work for independence.

1. The First Independent Nation—Haiti

French ideas of liberty spread to Haiti. The first Latin Americans to win independence were the people of the French colony of Haiti. In 1789, when revolution broke out in France, the population of Haiti included 28,000 Europeans, 22,000 mulattos (most of them freedmen), and over 400,000 black slaves. The Europeans in Haiti had grown wealthy from the profits of the sugar plantations. But their prosperity depended on ruthless exploitation of the slaves at the bottom of the rigid class system. Although many mulatto freedmen had received some education, they were denied the rights and opportunities of white men.

A Haitian mulatto named Vincent Ogé (oh-*zhay'*) was in Paris when the French National Assembly adopted the Declaration of the Rights of Man. He returned to Haiti to declare "liberty, equality, and fraternity" for himself and other freedmen. This kind of talk outraged the French authorities. Ogé was tortured to death in the plaza of Port-au-Prince (*port'*-oh-*prans'*), the Haitian capital city. The slaves were forced to watch him die.

Haitians rebelled. But the execution of Ogé could not stifle the cry for freedom. To the slaves of Haiti the French Declaration meant one thing — release from bondage. When revolt broke out in 1791, it spread like wildfire from plantation to plantation. A former slave, Toussaint L'Ouverture (too-*san'* loo-vehr-*tyoor'*), emerged as leader of the rebellion. He hoped to draw up a constitution for Haiti, restore order, and make the country a sort of "sister state" to the new France that had rid itself of its king.

Toussaint took charge. Toussaint organized an army of ex-slaves, ousted the French offi-

Toussaint L'Ouverture emerged as leader of the Haitian quest for independence. Born a slave, he proved to be a skilled military commander and able statesman.

friendly relations with the leaders of the new French republic.

Napoleon tried to reconquer Haiti. The man who became ruler of France in 1799, however, had little regard for Toussaint. Napoleon Bonaparte, the ambitious French dictator, had a scheme to re-establish a colonial empire in America. As the first step in this plan, described in Chapter 6, Napoleon sent a large army to Haiti. But great numbers of the French soldiers fell victim to yellow fever. The general in command of the French army himself died, though not before he had lured Toussaint into a trap and taken him prisoner. The Haitian leader was sent to Europe, where he died in prison.

Haiti became independent. Meanwhile, rebellion flared up against the French occupation. Badly weakened by the yellow fever epidemic, the French army left Haiti in 1803. Among the chief officers of the Haitian forces had been Jean-Jacques Dessalines (dess-ah-*leen'*), the son of an African chief, and Henri Christophe (crees-*toff'*), an ex-slave. After Toussaint's removal, Dessalines took over as commander-in-chief of the Haitian army. On the first day of 1804 he declared Haiti an independent black nation. Two years later Dessalines was assassinated and Henri Christophe became ruler of Haiti.

Christophe felt sure that Napoleon would someday launch another invasion of Haiti. To prepare for this attack, Christophe had a monumental fortification built high on a mountain. The ruins of this fort, called the Citadel, are still an impressive sight. For several years after Napoleon was defeated in Europe, Christophe kept teams of workers laboring on the Citadel. But the French never came back to Haiti.

Henri Christophe had himself crowned as king. His ambition was to turn Haiti into a strong and prosperous state. Stern measures were used in forcing his subjects to labor on the sugar and coffee plantations. Christophe

cials, and established himself in power. But he faced enormous problems. The former slaves had stopped working on the plantations, and there was confusion throughout Haiti. Moreover, Spanish forces remained in Santo Domingo on the eastern end of the island. This situation posed a constant threat to Toussaint.

Nevertheless, this capable leader took measures to restore order. He wrote a constitution, appointed officials, and insisted that the people resume work on the plantations. He also invaded and temporarily occupied Santo Domingo. Visitors from the United States and England called Toussaint "a true leader, intensely just and upright." And he maintained planned to export the plantation products and use the profits to build roads and schools and to improve Haiti's port. But the Haitian people resented the harsh rule of their king. In 1820, when Henri Christophe was paralyzed by a stroke, rebellion broke out against the weakened leader. Realizing that the end was near, Christophe had just enough strength to shoot himself with a silver bullet specially cast for this purpose.

THINKING ABOUT THIS SECTION

1. Explain or define the following words: "sister state"; Citadel.
2. Why did the slave revolt in Haiti bring to an end the island's flourishing plantation economy?
3. In what ways did Toussaint try to establish order in Haiti?
4. Why did Napoleon's plan to conquer Haiti fail?

2. The Stirrings of Revolution in Spanish America

At the time of the Haitian revolution and for some years afterward, Spain continued to hold a large empire in South and Middle America. It was in 1810 that young creoles in Venezuela began to plot an uprising. Within fifteen years of that uprising, Spain was to lose almost all its American domain. What caused the great Spanish empire to collapse so quickly? Obviously, tremendous forces must have been at work.

Various forces led to upheaval in the Spanish colonies. No one thing can be singled out as "the cause" of the revolutions that broke up the Spanish empire. But several important factors can be identified. As noted earlier, one was the spread of revolutionary ideas to Latin America. In France the monarchy had been overthrown, and in North America the English colonies had won their independence. To Latin Americans who wanted freedom from Spain, these happenings made revolution seem possible.

In Spanish America the revolutionary spirit took hold chiefly among a small group of creoles. Actually these creoles were the least oppressed of all the people in the Spanish colonies. And many of them had little concern for the mestizos, mulattos, Indians, and blacks who far outnumbered them. Few of the non-white people were even aware of the revolutionary ideas that were smuggled in from Europe, and they took little part in the revolutions plotted by the creoles.

Jealousy of the *peninsulares* was another factor that stirred up rebellious feelings among the creoles. The creoles resented the special privileges of the Spanish-born people who came to America, and they felt hemmed in by Spanish attempts to control trade and manufacturing in the colonies. By the late 1700's the Bourbon reforms had eased some of the stricter controls. But the creoles thought these reforms had not gone far enough. Though many creole merchants were prosperous, they were sure they could do much better if allowed to trade with other European countries besides Spain.

Finally, the creoles by this time felt more "American" than "Spanish." They continued to declare their loyalty to the Spanish king, at least at the beginning of the revolutionary movements. But this loyalty was to the monarchy rather than to Spain itself. America was the creoles' homeland, and, as Americans, their interests were different from those of Spain.

Miranda was the first to call for change. A few outstanding men took the lead in the movements for independence in Spanish America. One of the earliest was a Venezuelan creole who has been called "the morning star of independence." In the 1780's Francisco de Miranda had fought as an officer in the Spanish army against England. While stationed in the West Indies, he was court-martialed on charges of smuggling and spying, and he retired from the army. Miranda was later cleared of the charges. But he felt that he had been treated unfairly because of his creole birth.

While traveling in North America and Europe, Miranda met many political leaders with forward-looking views. He also served in the French revolutionary army. Miranda began to dream of liberating South America from Spanish rule. He cherished the idea of creating a single huge independent nation in South America.

In 1806 Miranda made his strike for freedom. With help from sympathetic North Americans, he organized a small army and sailed to Venezuela. His little invasion force landed at the town of Coro, prepared to lead the people in an uprising. To Miranda's dismay, not a single Venezuelan joined him. The people had no interest in revolt. In fact, Miranda was lucky to escape with his life when the people of Coro welcomed the arrival of Spanish troops a few days later. Miranda returned to London. But four years later many Venezuelans were to welcome him back as a great patriot. By then, events in Spain had triggered an uprising in Venezuela.

Napoleon ousted the Spanish rulers. In 1808 Napoleon had invaded Spain and arrested both Charles IV (who had already given up the throne) and his son and heir, Ferdinand VII. Napoleon installed his own brother Joseph as king of Spain. The people in Spain rebelled. They formed *juntas* (*hoon'* tahs), or committees, to carry on guerrilla warfare against the French invaders.

Meanwhile, in the Spanish colonies the people felt equally outraged at the upstart Napoleon. In city after city the colonists rioted, calling for "our old king or none!" Other groups declared their loyalty to the son of the old king. They paraded with banners showing his picture labeled *Fernando el Deseado,* or "Ferdinand the Desired One." In many localities the colonists followed the example of the people in Spain and formed juntas to govern in the name of the Spanish king. Most of these juntas, at least at first, did not urge independence from Spain. Their members were simply determined not to be ruled by Napoleon.

THINKING ABOUT THIS SECTION

1. Explain or define the following words: junta; guerrilla.
2. Why were some creoles becoming interested in independence during the early 1800's?
3. What was the reaction in the Spanish colonies to Napoleon's action in putting his brother on the Spanish throne?

3. The Winning of Independence in South America

Creoles in Caracas formed a junta. Typical of the anti-French protests was the one in Caracas, capital city of the captaincy-general of Venezuela. A group of wealthy young creoles formed a junta. Some of them were fervent royalists (supporters of the Spanish king). Others were more interested in reform. At any rate, in 1810 the creole junta ousted Spanish

officials and set up a new government in Caracas. One member of this junta was Simón Bolívar (boh-*lee'* vahr).

Bolívar became an outstanding leader. Simón Bolívar was to win fame as "the Liberator of South America." His story has been called one of "courage, wisdom, romance, and tragedy."

Bolívar was born in 1783 in Caracas. He was heir to a large fortune but was left an orphan at an early age. Interest in the ideals of the French Revolution was aroused in him by his tutors. When Bolívar was sixteen, he went to Spain where an uncle presented him at the royal court. The young man felt that he was snubbed because he was a creole. But he won as his wife a young noblewoman, who returned with him to Caracas. Within a few months his bride was dead of malaria. Years later he wrote that his wife's death had changed his destiny. If she had lived, he might well have been content with life as a prosperous landowner.

Bolívar was a short, dark man with "large and penetrating eyes." He seems to have inspired all who knew him. When he began the drive for independence, people of all kinds — Indians, mestizo cowboys, freed slaves, English soldiers, and rich creoles — volunteered to serve with him. Military men admired his skill in battle and his genius for strategy. Those close to Bolívar found his energy and endurance unlimited. He could ride all day and dance all night. He was generous to a fault, caring little for personal property. In fact, almost his entire fortune was spent on the wars for independence. Though ambitious and perhaps too vain, he was a serious thinker and writer. As will be seen later, his chief concern was for the future of Latin America.

The Caracas junta called for independence. Bolívar was chosen by the Caracas junta to seek help in England for the patriotic cause. Though he failed in this mission, he did persuade Francisco de Miranda to return to Venezuela. This time the white-haired Miranda received an enthusiastic welcome. Together Bolívar, Miranda, and the other junta members worked to rally the people to the cause of independence. On July 5, 1811, the junta declared Venezuela independent from Spain, and Miranda was chosen to lead the new government. Thus, Venezuela became the first South American republic.

Miranda's life ended unhappily. The young republic soon suffered two heavy blows, however. Early in 1812 a severe earthquake shook Caracas, killing and injuring thousands. Priests declared that God was punishing the Venezuelans for challenging royal authority. Just a few months later a strong Spanish army won a victory over the Venezuelan patriot forces. Miranda, apparently feeling that the situation was hopeless, signed a treaty with the Spanish commander. He then tried to escape to a British ship, taking with him the funds of the ill-fated republic. Miranda insisted afterwards that he had intended to use the funds in efforts to keep the republic alive.

But Bolívar evidently believed that Miranda was betraying the cause and allowed him to fall into the hands of the Spanish. Miranda was taken as a prisoner to Spain, where he died in a dungeon four years later. Historians still are not clear who was in the right in this tragic affair. A growing jealousy between the two Venezuelan leaders apparently played a part in the story.

Bolívar carried on the struggle. Venezuela was again a Spanish colony, and Bolívar, who had been allowed to leave the country, was an exile. Much of this period in exile he spent in New Granada. There, as in Venezuela, a junta had declared an independent republic. Antonio Nariño, having made his escape (page 132), was one of those leading the struggle against the Spanish in New Granada.

In 1813 Bolívar returned to Venezuela with a small army and seized Caracas. A second republic was declared. Bolívar promised a "war to the death" against the Spanish and their loyalist sympathizers. Thus, the struggle became a civil war as well as a revolution.

The restored Spanish king tried to crush the rebellions. Meanwhile, events in Europe were working against Bolívar. In 1814 Napoleon was overthrown, and Ferdinand VII returned to the throne of Spain. Now that the legal monarch was restored to power, many Latin

Americans declared their loyalty to Spain. But others, having tasted independence, were sorry to see the old system back in force. Moreover, the new king was proving to be stern and dictatorial. Determined to wipe out any sign of rebellion, Ferdinand sent large armies to enforce Spanish rule in the New World.

Bolívar again became an exile. When Caracas again fell to Spanish forces, Bolívar took refuge on the British island of Jamaica. There, in 1815, he made plans for the future of South America. In his famous "Jamaica Letter," Bolívar stated some of his ideas. He realized that the people of Latin America, unlike those of the United States, had no experience in self-government. So he believed that a president would need greater powers than in the United States. Bolívar also realized that Latin America was too large and its peoples were too varied in culture to be united under a single government. He suggested that Central America become a single nation and that Venezuela and New Granada might unite under the name of "Colombia."

Bolívar returned to the mainland. From Jamaica, Bolívar visited Haiti, where he was welcomed by a president who ruled in the southern part of the country. Eventually Bolívar returned to South America, and by 1817 had made his base in eastern Venezuela. At his headquarters in a town named Angostura (now Ciudad Bolívar), on the Orinoco River, Bolívar made plans for liberating northern South America. He decided against attacking Caracas, since it was strongly defended by Spanish forces. Instead, the daring leader planned to march across the high Andes and surprise the Spaniards in New Granada.

A decisive victory was won at Boyacá. By now Bolívar had assembled an army that included several thousand volunteer soldiers from Europe. He had also won over many of the tough *llaneros* (yah-*nay'* rohss), the cowboys of the Orinoco plains. Neither the Europeans nor the *llaneros* were experienced mountain climbers, nor were they used to the thin air of high altitudes. Nevertheless, in marching across the Andes, Bolívar's men scaled some of the roughest land on earth. An Englishman who took part in the march wrote: "The plainsmen regarded these stupendous heights with astonishment and terror, and marveled at the existence of a land so different from their own. As they ascended, each new elevation increased their surprise, for what they had taken for the last peak was only the beginning of other and still loftier mountains."

Hundreds of men died from cold and hunger on this grueling march, but their determined leader urged the survivors on. Finally they reached the plains area outside the city of Bogotá. There, in August, 1819, Bolívar's army met the enemy and won a decisive victory. The defeat of Spanish forces in the Battle of Boyacá marked the end of Spain's power in New Granada.

Gran Colombia was formed. Within two years Bolívar had also driven the Spanish out of Venezuela. The Liberator then formed a new nation called the Republic of Gran Colombia ("Great Colombia"). It was made up of Venezuela, Colombia (including Panama), and Ecuador. Bolívar reluctantly became president of Gran Colombia, while Francisco de Paula Santander, a Colombian general, was made vice-president. But Santander actually governed, since Bolívar preferred to continue fighting until all of South America was freed from Spanish rule.

The spirit of independence took hold in Buenos Aires. While Bolívar was leading the revolutions in Venezuela and New Granada, the independence movement was also taking hold in southern Spanish America. Until the later 1700's, Spain had shown little interest in the colonies of the Plata region. Partly for that reason the spirit of independence had fertile ground on which to flourish there. Moreover, in the early 1800's the creoles of Buenos

Aires had driven off two British expeditions that tried to occupy the town. This success convinced the *porteños* (as the "port dwellers" of Buenos Aires were called) that they could manage their own affairs without supervision from Europe.

Even so, when Napoleon invaded Spain in 1808, the *porteños* were as outraged as creoles elsewhere in Spanish America. They ousted an unpopular viceroy and by 1810 had formed a junta to run Buenos Aires. This junta wanted to annex all the other provinces that had been part of the Viceroyalty of La Plata. Many of these provinces went along with the idea. But Paraguay and the province that is now Uruguay refused. Local wars fought over this issue continued for years.

The Plata provinces formed a new state. The river port of Rosario and the foothill towns of Córdoba, Tucumán, and Mendoza were wary of *porteño* leadership. Nevertheless, they agreed to join with Buenos Aires in a loose federation called the United Provinces of La Plata. In 1816, this new state was proclaimed at a meeting held in Tucumán.

San Martín offered his services. Several years before this, one of the great heroes of South American independence had entered the picture. José de San Martín (*sahn' mar-teen'*) was born in 1778 at a mission on the Uruguay River. His father was a Spanish official in that frontier region. When the boy was seven, the family returned to Spain. There José attended military school and became an officer in the army.

In 1812, when he was 34 years old, San Martín decided to return to the land of his birth. Sympathetic toward the spirit of independence, he offered his services to the Buenos Aires junta. Like Bolívar, San Martín seems to have had a remarkable personality. Though quieter and more modest than Bolívar, the Argentine liberator also had the power to inspire loyalty.

San Martín prepared an army. The Buenos Aires government asked San Martín to organize an army in Mendoza. This town was located in the Andes foothills east of Santiago, Chile. San Martín's long-range goal was to attack the Spanish forces in Peru, where royal power was strongest. Until the Spanish were driven out of Peru, the continent would never be free. San Martín planned, therefore, to build an effective army in Mendoza, cross the Andes, and free Chile. From there he would move his forces up the coast and attack Lima from the sea.

For several years San Martín gave all his energies to the job of preparing his army. He had little co-operation from the quarrelsome government in Buenos Aires. But in Mendoza he found enthusiastic supporters. Though separated from Chile by some of the highest mountains in the world, the people of Mendoza feared an invasion by Spanish forces on the west coast. For more than two years Mendoza patriots worked closely with San Martín. The men made cannon, muskets, and special shoes for the mules and horses that would have to cross the rugged Andes. Women spun and wove cloth for uniforms and knapsacks, and they dried strips of beef as rations for the soldiers.

O'Higgins became an ally. Also offering their help were Chilean refugees under the leadership of Bernardo O'Higgins. The "Liberator of Chile," as O'Higgins came to be known, was the son of a Chilean viceroy of Irish parentage. After the patriot army he commanded was defeated in Chile, O'Higgins and 3000 men had made their way across the Andes to Mendoza.

San Martín crossed the Andes. After months of preparation, San Martín and his army of 5000 men were ready to challenge the forbidding Andes. Their route lay along passes at an altitude of more than 12,000 feet. Dragging their cannon on sleds, the men toiled up the steep mountain trails. Nearly half of their mules and horses were lost. San Martín himself described the determination of his men:

The greater part of the army suffered from lack of oxygen, as a result of which several soldiers died, besides others who succumbed to the intense cold. Everyone was convinced that the obstacles which had been overcome did not leave the slightest hope for retreat. But, on the other hand, there reigned a great confidence among the ranks, . . . [and] keen rivalry among the different units.[1]

Thanks to San Martín's careful planning, the army made it through.

Victory in Chile opened the way to Peru. Officers of the Spanish forces in Chile had heard rumors of the preparations at Mendoza. But they refused to believe that such a daring campaign would be attempted. In February, 1817, San Martín's army surprised and easily defeated the Spanish forces at Chacabuco, a small town outside Santiago. San Martín and O'Higgins entered Santiago two days later. The grateful people of the city made O'Higgins ruler of the new republic of Chile, after San Martín had refused the honor. Chilean independence was insured in 1818 by a decisive victory won by San Martín's army in the Battle of Maipú (my-*poo'*).

The way was now clear for an assault on Peru, Spain's chief stronghold in America. San Martín began plans to move his army up the coast to Lima. Though money was short, he managed to buy a few ships and thus assembled the first South American navy. In August, 1820, his forces boarded the little fleet at the port of Valparaiso. After a long sea voyage, the soldiers landed in southern Peru.

Lima was a conservative stronghold. San Martín did not expect that the Peruvians would rush to join his forces and declare their independence from Spain. The oppressed Indians and mestizos had heard little, if anything, about the "rights of man" that had been proclaimed in France. Lima, moreover, was full of Spanish and creole aristocrats who were content with their easy life. No patriotic junta had been organized in Lima during the stirring days of 1810. The Spanish viceroy, backed by loyal troops, had retained power in Peru throughout the period when Napoleon controlled Spain.

San Martín was cautious, therefore, in approaching Lima. To hotheads who urged action, he replied: "What good would Lima do me if its inhabitants were hostile politically?" But public opinion in Lima slowly turned in favor of independence. Moreover, the viceroy soon received the alarming news that Spain had no plans for sending reinforcements to Peru. He and the worried aristocrats fled into the interior.

San Martín entered Lima. Thus, the city was left open for San Martín to make a peaceful entry in July, 1821. Peruvian independence was proclaimed, and in the city plaza San Martín addressed the people of Lima. He said, "All I want is that this country should be managed by itself alone." He told them that when they had established a government, he would leave. In spite of these words, some accused San Martín of wanting to make himself king. This suspicion stemmed from the fact that he assumed dictatorial powers under the title of "Protector of Peru." Other problems developed. Agents of the Peruvian aristocrats were enlisting young men in Lima to join the royalist forces in the mountains. Meanwhile, San Martín's army was dwindling as a result of desertions and a yellow fever epidemic.

A historic meeting took place at Guayaquil. Meanwhile, in the north, Bolívar had won his stunning victory at Boyacá and had formed the nation of Gran Colombia. Hoping they could work together in the independence effort, the

---

[1] Quoted in Ricardo Rojas, *San Martín, Knight of the Andes,* Herschel Brickell and Carlos Videla, trs. (New York: Doubleday, 1945), p. 108. Reprinted by permission.

Best-known of the remarkable men who led the drive for independence were José de San Martín (top) and Simón Bolívar (bottom). Both men were determined to free South America from European control, and the names of both became symbolic of the liberation movement.

two leaders agreed to meet. The rendezvous was to be at the port of Guayaquil, in what is now Ecuador.

"I have been looking forward to this moment all my life; and only the moment of embracing Your Excellency and joining our flags can be more satisfactory to me. . . . I am on my way to fulfill my promise of uniting the Empire of the Incas to the Empire of Freedom." So Bolívar wrote in one of the last letters he sent to San Martín before the two men met in July, 1822.

But a letter written by San Martín to Bolívar *after* their meeting sounds very different: "The results of our interview are not those which I foresaw for a quick end of the war. Unfortunately I am completely convinced that either you have not deemed sincere my offer to serve under your orders with the forces at my command, or my person is embarrassing for you." [2]

What really happened during the two days that South America's two great leaders conferred? Since the meeting was secret, no one knows for certain. But it is clear that the meeting was not one of warm agreement. Even before this, there had been an element of rivalry between the two men. Moreover, they were entirely different in personality: Bolívar more flamboyant, and San Martín more reserved. Perhaps, too, there were hard feelings over Ecuador. San Martín had wanted to add this region to Peru, but Bolívar had already persuaded the Quito provinces to join Gran Colombia.

Neither man talked much about the meeting afterward. It is only from letters written later that historians can guess at what was said. San

[2] Both letters quoted in *San Martín, Knight of the Andes,* pp. 198 and 207. Reprinted by permission.

Martín did accept Ecuador's annexation to Gran Colombia. From a letter written by Bolívar, however, it appears that he and San Martín clashed over the form of government Peru should have. The Argentinian, said Bolívar, "stated that this government should not be democratic, as democracy did not suit Peru; and . . . he said that an independent, unattached prince should be brought from Europe to rule Peru." Bolívar firmly rejected the idea of a monarchy. Some historians have suggested that San Martín asked Bolívar for military aid and was turned down. It is very likely that the two men disagreed on several issues.

San Martín withdrew. At any rate, on the second night of the meeting, San Martín quietly boarded ship and left for Peru. In his letter to Bolívar, he said:

My decision has . . . been made. I have called the First Congress of Peru for the 20th of next month, and on the day after its installation I shall embark for Chile, satisfied that my presence is the only obstacle which prevents you from coming to Peru with the army at your command. For me it would have been the acme of happiness to end the war of independence under the orders of a general to whom America owes its freedom. Destiny orders it otherwise, and one must resign oneself to it. [3]

San Martín was true to his word. In a speech to the Congress in Lima, he resigned his position as Protector of Peru. The way to Peru was now open for Bolívar.

San Martín sailed back to Chile, where he told the disappointed O'Higgins: "As my youth was sacrificed in the service of Spain and my middle age in the service of my native land, I believe that I have the right to dispose of my old age." San Martín then returned to Mendoza. Families there accused him of abandoning their sons, the soldiers he had left behind in Peru. Finding no peace in Buenos Aires

[3] Quoted in *San Martín, Knight of the Andes,* p. 208. Reprinted by permission.

either, he sailed for France. There he lived quietly until his death in 1850. Only after he died was San Martín honored in Argentina and Chile as the hero of the liberation movement.

Bolívar drove the Spanish from Peru. A year after the meeting at Guayaquil, Bolívar entered Lima in triumph. But Peru was still in a state of disorder, as different factions fought for control. Meanwhile, Spanish forces remained in the mountains. Bolívar spent almost a year training and equipping his army. Then he moved against the enemy, defeating a Spanish force in August, 1824. In the decisive battle fought at Ayacucho four months later, the revolutionary forces were led by Bolívar's ablest general, Antonio José de Sucre (*soo´ kreh*). Peru, the last Spanish stronghold, had finally been won.

Bolivia was liberated. In 1825 Sucre marched his troops into the far northern part of what had been the Viceroyalty of La Plata and expelled the royalists from that area as well. Independence was proclaimed, and the new nation was named the Republic of Bolívar. This name was later changed to Bolivia.

Bolívar's hopes ended in disappointment. Bolívar devoted the rest of his life to plans for the new nations. Most of these ideas ended in failure and disappointment. In 1826 he called a meeting to be held in Panama, at which he hoped to lay the foundation for an international league of American states. But only four of the newly independent nations sent delegates. Bolívar then turned his attention to another international plan, the Federation of the Andes. This was to include Gran Colombia, Peru, and Bolivia. But, far from uniting, the new nations began to fight among themselves. Bolívar's desperate efforts could not save his federation. By 1830 even Gran Colombia had split into three nations: Colombia, Venezuela, and Ecuador.

Not long before Bolívar's death in 1830 he wrote: "There is no good faith in America,

UNITED STATES

MEXICO

Gulf of Mexico

Guadalajara
Dolores
Guanajuato
★ Mexico

Acapulco

CUBA (Sp.)

SANTO
DOMINGO
(indep. 1844)

PUERTO RICO (Sp.)

BR. HOND.

JAMAICA
(Br.)

HAITI

GUATEMALA
HONDURAS
EL SALVADOR
NICARAGUA

UNITED PROVINCES OF
CENTRAL AMERICA

COSTA
RICA

PANAMA
(Col.)

Coro
Caracas ★
Ciudad
Bolívar

VENEZUELA

BR. NETH. FR.

GUIANA

Boyacá
×
★ Bogotá

COLOMBIA

G
R
A
N

C
O
L
O
M
B
I
A

★ Quito

Guayaquil

ECUADOR

EMPIRE OF BRAZIL

(UNEXPLORED)

PERU

Lima ★

× Ayacucho

BOLIVIA

★
Sucre

PARAGUAY

Asunción
★

Rio de Janeiro ●

*ATLANTIC
OCEAN*

*PACIFIC
OCEAN*

Tucumán ●

Córdoba ●
Rosario ●

Chacabuco
Valparaiso ●
×
Santiago ●
× **Maipú**

Mendoza ●

Buenos Aires ●

★ Montevideo

URUGUAY

UNITED PROVINCES
OF
LA PLATA

CHILE

(UNSETTLED
BY
EUROPEANS)

FALKLAND IS.
(occupied by Br., 1833)

0   200   400   600   800   1000 Miles

nor among the nations of America. Treaties are scraps of paper; constitutions, printed matter; elections, battles; freedom, anarchy; and life, a torment." Bolívar had good reason for disillusionment. Chaos and corruption plagued the government of Gran Colombia; the constitution was disregarded; his dream of unity, or even co-operation, was dead. Bolívar's efforts to check disorder had led some people to condemn him. Many of his old revolutionary friends felt betrayed because he had made himself virtually a dictator in Colombia. But Bolívar felt this was necessary to save the new nation from overwhelming problems.

Brazil's independence completed the formation of new nations in South America. Brazilian independence was achieved with little bloodshed. In 1808 Napoleon tried to seize the Portuguese king as he had the king of Spain. But the Portuguese royal family escaped and sailed to Brazil under the protection of the British fleet. In Rio de Janeiro, the royal court received a warm welcome. Rio became the capital of both the mother country and the colony.

When Napoleon was defeated in Europe, King João VI had no intention of returning to Lisbon. He preferred life in Brazil. But in 1821 an uprising in Portugal threatened to overthrow the monarchy. Reluctantly the king sailed for Lisbon. He left his 23-year-old son, Pedro, as *regent* of Brazil. Pedro, in other words, was to rule in João's name. Before

leaving, the king advised his son: "If Brazil goes its own way, let it be with you, rather than with some of those adventurers."

It soon became clear, however, that the Lisbon government meant to reduce Brazil to its former position as a dependent colony. In 1822, with the support of Brazilian patriots, Pedro acted on his father's advice. The prince declared Brazil independent and took for himself the title of Emperor Pedro I. With little fighting the last Portuguese troops were forced out of Brazil. This was the only South American country to adopt a monarchy as its form of government following independence.

THINKING ABOUT THIS SECTION

1. Explain or define the following words: royalist; *llanero;* Gran Colombia; regent.
2. Why was the revolutionary movement led by Bolívar from 1819 to 1821 successful whereas earlier efforts had failed?
3. How did the people of Buenos Aires achieve independence? How was the federation called the United Provinces of La Plata formed?
4. How did San Martín liberate Chile?
5. What problems confronted San Martín when he sought to liberate Peru? What was the role of Bolívar in the liberation of Peru and Ecuador?
6. Why did Bolívar become disillusioned by developments in Latin America?
7. By what steps did Brazil achieve independence?

4. The Independence Movement in Mexico

The revolution in Mexico took a far different course from independence movements elsewhere in Latin America. For one thing, it began not in the leading city but in a provincial town. Moreover, it was started by a Catholic priest leading not the creoles but mestizos and Indians.

Latin America After Independence

To see how Latin American national boundaries have changed since the late 1820's, look ahead at the map in Chapter 17.

A loyalist junta was formed in Mexico City. Mexico City, like Lima, was a center of loyalist sympathy during the turbulent days after Napoleon's invasion of Spain. When news of the Spanish king's arrest reached Mexico, Spanish officials formed a junta and declared allegiance to King Ferdinand. This junta was dominated by *gachupines,* as natives of Spain were called in Mexico. The *gachupines* suspected the viceroy of favoring independence for New Spain. So the junta threw him out and chose a new viceroy. The Spanish-born aristocrats remained in control of Mexico City. But in the provinces creole leaders, long resentful of the Spanish, began secretly to talk about independence. One of these men was a parish priest named Miguel Hidalgo (ee-*dahl'* goh).

Father Hidalgo hoped for reform. Hidalgo, the son of a ranch manager, had become a priest at the age of 26. He was interested in the new ideas of the times, including developments in revolutionary France. More than once, Hidalgo was investigated by the Inquisition.

In 1803, when he was 50 years old, Hidalgo became the parish priest of Dolores, a small country town north of Mexico City. Feeling a deep sympathy for the oppressed Indians, he tried to help them. Some he taught to read and write. Father Hidalgo also showed the Indians how to manufacture various small articles. By selling these, he thought they might make enough money to buy farm land of their own. Needless to say, the wealthy absentee landlords opposed these efforts.

Hidalgo called for revolt. By 1810 Hidalgo was an active leader in a creole conspiracy to overthrow the Spanish authorities. The conspirators were secretly collecting weapons. When Hidalgo learned that the Spanish had discovered the plot, he decided to strike at once. On September 16, 1810, he rang the bell in the plaza of Dolores and then spoke to the assembled townspeople. "My friends," the priest said, "we have no choice but to attack the Spaniards now. Will you make the effort to get back from the hated Spaniards the

land stolen from your forefathers three centuries ago?" Hidalgo's revolutionary appeal became known as the "Cry of Dolores," or *Grito de Dolores.* Every year its anniversary is still celebrated throughout Mexico.

Father Hidalgo armed his Indian and mestizo followers, and together they set out to liberate Mexico. The rebels carried the banner of the Virgin of Guadalupe as they marched toward the city of Guanajuato, a rich mining center. By the time they reached the gates of the city, their number had grown to 50,000. The terrified creoles of Guanajuato took refuge in a large grain warehouse. Hidalgo's frenzied followers easily broke through the city gates. Once inside, they were joined by local Indians and mestizos. The rebels looted the fine houses and finally broke into the warehouse. Most of the people inside were massacred. The plundering of Guanajuato continued for several days, as Father Hidalgo was unable to stop it.

When news reached Mexico City that a "wild mob of drunken Indians" was killing aristocrats in towns to the north, the Spanish garrison fortified all northern routes to the capital. Father Hidalgo hesitated to attack Mexico City with his untrained, poorly armed followers. Hearing that he had many sympathizers in Guadalajara, he moved his "independence army" to that town.

Hidalgo hoped to establish a reform government. In Guadalajara, Hidalgo formed a government and made plans to summon a congress. He wrote: "Our lawmakers will treat us all like brothers, they will do away with poverty. The richest products of our fertile soils will be for the use of all of us." Father Hidalgo also issued an order freeing slaves in Mexico. Thus, he was probably the first independence leader in Spanish America to strike at slavery.

But Hidalgo's plans — whether for reform, government, or winning the revolution — were vague and impractical. He had hoped that enthusiasm would bring success, and seemed not to realize that such a movement called for discipline, organization, and skilled military leadership.

Hidalgo was captured. The viceroy and his Spanish generals did not intend to let this "people's revolt" succeed. In January, 1811, a large Spanish force, with cavalry and cannon, advanced on the ragged army outside Guadalajara. The rebels were completely routed. Father Hidalgo was captured and executed.

Morelos tried to keep the movement alive. Another priest, José Maria Morelos (moh-*ray'* lohss), took over leadership of the revolutionary movement. From his headquarters in the hills above Acapulco he called a congress of rebels who had escaped capture. This little congress met and declared independence from Spain in 1813. For nearly a year the rebel congress worked at writing a constitution. Meanwhile, Morelos's guerrilla forces won control of most of southern Mexico. But in 1815 a creole officer in the royalist army discovered the location of Morelos's secret headquarters. This officer, Agustín de Iturbide (ee-toor-*bee'* day), led an attack on the mountain outpost. Morelos fled but was soon captured and executed. Since the rebel congress had been broken up by Spanish assaults, it seemed that the independence movement in Mexico was dead.

Liberal reforms in Spain caused conservatives in Mexico to favor independence. But within a few years events in Spain touched off a new independence movement in Mexico. This time leadership came from a very different source. When Ferdinand VII returned to the Spanish throne, he turned out to be a tyrant. In 1820 there was a violent reaction in Spain. Liberals gained control of the Spanish government and introduced reforms. This turn of events alarmed the conservative Spaniards and creoles in Mexico City. Rather than allow the colonial government to be dominated by men who had imprisoned the king in Spain, they started a move for independence.

Miguel Hidalgo, a man of courage and compassion, dared to lead a "people's revolt" against Spanish power in Mexico.

Ironically it was Agustín de Iturbide who soon emerged as leader of a conservative junta set up to rule Mexico until a king could be chosen. This junta asked the government in Spain to allow Ferdinand to become king of

Mexico. But the liberal government refused to consider the proposal. Iturbide and his forces then declared Mexico independent. Soldiers paraded through the streets of Mexico City, shouting "Emperor Agustín the First!" A congress called by Iturbide himself rubber-stamped this choice, and so this military officer was crowned emperor of independent Mexico in 1822.

Iturbide's rule was short. But Iturbide soon became unpopular with conservatives and liberals alike. He and his court led an extravagant life, and the Spanish aristocrats scorned him as an upstart. Independence leaders who earlier had co-operated with him withdrew their support. In less than a year "Emperor Agustín" was forced to give up his throne and go into exile.

In 1823 a new constitution established a federal republic in Mexico. A president was inaugurated the next year. When Iturbide tried to return to Mexico, he was arrested, quickly tried for treason, and shot.

Central America became independent. As Emperor of Mexico, Iturbide had sent troops into Central America and declared it a part of his domain. After his fall from power a congress met in Guatemala City. Representing the different towns of Central America, this congress declared the area independent of Mexico. A new state was formed — the United Provinces of Central America. But quarrels over various issues soon led to civil war. In the late 1830's the federation broke up into the separate nations of Nicaragua, Costa Rica, El Salvador, Honduras, and Guatemala.

THINKING ABOUT THIS SECTION

1. Explain or define the following words: *gachupines; Grito de Dolores.*
2. Contrast the reactions of Mexican *gachupines* and of creoles like Hidalgo to Napoleon's plans for Spain. Why did Hidalgo's revolt fail?
3. Why did Mexican conservatives advocate independence after 1820? What was the result?

5. An Evaluation of the Independence Movements

A number of independent nations emerged. By 1830 eleven independent republics had replaced what had been a great Spanish empire only 20 years before. But all of these nations faced a difficult future. Torn by quarreling, Gran Colombia had split into Colombia, Ecuador, and Venezuela. Peru was in a state of chaos. Ambitious politicians in Chile had exiled Bernardo O'Higgins from the country he had founded. Bolivia, named after the great liberator, had already driven out the first of a long series of ousted presidents. Farther south, in the Plata region Uruguay was resisting

invasions from Brazil, Britain, and Buenos Aires. Paraguay remained isolated under an eccentric dictator. Power struggles divided the United Provinces of La Plata (Argentina).

By this time Mexico was an unstable republic. The United Provinces of Central America had achieved independence from Mexico but it collapsed into five separate states within a few years. Panama remained a province of Colombia. Only Cuba and Puerto Rico were still in Spanish hands. In addition to the new nations of Spanish America there were Brazil, an independent monarchy, and Haiti, at this time master of the entire island of Hispaniola.

What did independence mean for the new countries? All the new nations got off to a bad start. While part of the Spanish empire, none of the people in these countries had had much experience in self-government. As Bolívar said, Spain had kept the people of America "in a state of permanent childhood with regard to public affairs." Following independence, popular rule was not established in the new nations. Perhaps it would not have worked in countries where so few could read and write.

The leadership of most of the new countries was drawn from the creole upper classes. Even these men had held only minor offices under Spanish rule. Now that they controlled the new independent nations, they had no intention of allowing the lower classes to participate in the governments. Bolívar himself had not believed the people ready for democracy.

Orderly government emerged in hardly any of the new nations. Idealistic constitutions were adopted only to be ignored. In most countries military dictators took control. Some of these men were well-meaning; others were selfish tyrants. But in either case their word was law. Revolution rather than election became the accepted way of bringing a new government into power.

Under creole rule there was little change in the social order of the new countries. In some areas Indians and blacks were even worse off than before the revolutions. Some progress was made toward the abolition of slavery. But, as economic and social injustices continued, no real middle class developed.

The Church, however, was deeply affected by the revolutions. Although it survived as an institution, many of its best leaders were lost when the *peninsulares* returned to Spain. In some countries the new governments took over much Church property and wealth. The Church had been chiefly responsible for education during the colonial period. Now that churchmen had less influence and money, education suffered. It was, of course, the common people who chiefly felt this blow.

Economic problems plagued the new countries. During the turmoil of the revolutions farming and trade had been disrupted. Many of the Spanish merchants closed their businesses in America and returned to Europe. In a very real sense Latin America continued to have a "colonial economy." The new countries exported raw materials and bought manufactured goods from Europe or the United States. Thus, none of them developed a balanced economy, that is, one that included manufacturing as well as the sale of natural resources. During the colonial period there had been little trade between the different provinces of Spanish America, and this pattern continued after independence. One reason was that many of the countries produced the same raw materials for export.

Obviously the new countries of Latin America started off with much greater handicaps than faced the United States when it won independence from Great Britain. Moreover, Latin America's problems were to continue for a long time. As later chapters will show, problems stemming from the colonial past still plague these countries today.

George Pendle, an Englishman who has studied Latin America, has summed up the positive side of the achievement of independence:

Yet the emancipation of Spanish America—together with the nonviolent attainment of independence by Brazil—was, as the discovery had been, one of the formative events in the history of the world. It not only marked a further stage in the shift from a Mediterranean to an Atlantic civilization. It opened an enormous region to trade and immigration, and it brought into existence a number of new states which thereafter would have to be taken into account by statesmen of other parts of the world in the conduct of diplomacy and strategy.[4]

[4] George Pendle, *A History of Latin America* (Baltimore: Penguin Books, 1967), p. 86.

1. Locate the independent Latin American countries on the map on page 142. How do you explain the break-up of the Spanish colonial domain into a number of nations?

2. Why did revolution not lead to democracy in Latin America?

3. What is a "colonial economy"? Why did the Latin American countries continue to have such an economy even after independence?

4. What other problems plagued the new countries?

5. According to George Pendle, what was the positive side to the "emancipation of Latin America"?

Summing Up

When Napoleon imprisoned the Spanish king and crown prince in 1808, he set off a chain of events that was to end in independence for the peoples of Spanish America. Certain influences had already prepared the way for the independence movements. Chief among these were (1) the spread of French revolutionary ideas; (2) the examples set by the revolutions in France and the United States; (3) the creoles' jealousy of the *peninsulares;* (4) the creole belief that the Bourbon reforms of the late 1700's had not gone far enough; and (5) a growing feeling of patriotism.

Following Napoleon's arrest of the Spanish royalty, creoles formed juntas in the major Latin American cities. Feelings of loyalty to the Spanish king soon gave way to the decision to seek independence. Two outstanding leaders emerged to lead the independence movements in South America. Through brilliant military campaigns and inspired leadership, Simón Bolívar and José de San Martín between them liberated all of Spanish South America from European rule.

In Mexico, an uprising of the Indians and mestizos led by Father Hidalgo ended in failure. The drive for independence was taken over by the conservative Iturbide and resulted in independence in 1822.

In French Haiti the independence movement took the form of a revolt by oppressed slaves and mulattos. In Portuguese Brazil, on the other hand, independence was won peacefully and a monarchy was established.

The new nations plunged into a state of chaos almost before independence became a fact. Bolívar, who had worked for unity among the new nations, saw his own government fall apart before his death. None of the new nations had the experience, stable government, and healthy economy needed to face the future with confidence.

Outstanding Leaders of the Nineteenth Century

CHAPTER FOCUS

1. Common Problems of the New Nations
2. Three Dominant Leaders in Mexican History
3. Pedro II, Emperor of Brazil
4. Important Leaders in Argentina and Chile

An American woman living in Mexico City in 1840 described a revolution in letters she wrote to relatives:

July 15, 1840. Revolution in Mexico! . . . The storm which has for some time been brewing has burst forth at last. . . . At two this morning, [two generals] joined by the fifth battalion . . . took up arms, set off for the palace, surprised the president in his bed, and took him prisoner. . . . Some say that it will all end in a few hours—others that it will be a long and bloody contest. Some are assured that it will merely end in a change of ministry—others, that Santa Anna will come on directly and [take over] the presidency. . . .

July 21. After passing a sleepless night, listening to the roaring of cannon, and figuring to ourselves the devastation that must have taken place, we find to our amazement that nothing decisive has occurred. The noise last night was mere

"The Napoleon of the West" Antonio Lopez de Santa Anna liked to call himself, but this Mexican general and president came to symbolize the worst traits of Latin American caudillos of the nineteenth century. The picture above is a daguerreotype of Santa Anna, taken around 1850.

skirmishing, and half the cannons were fired in the air.

July 26. The tranquillity of the people during all this period is astonishing. In what other city in the world would they not have taken part with one or the other side? Shops shut, workmen out of employment, thousands of idle people—yet no riot, no confusion, apparently no impatience. Groups of people collect on the streets, or stand talking before their doors and speculate upon probabilities. [They] await the decision of their military chiefs, as if it were a judgment from heaven, from which it [would be] both useless and impious to appeal.[1]

Probably it *was* useless for the people of Mexico City to do anything more than talk about a "palace revolution." Government in Mexico after the winning of independence was disorderly and unstable. Throughout Spanish America, after the departure of the Spaniards, the well-to-do creoles took over as a ruling class. Many of the creoles who came out on top in the confused struggles for power were military officers.

Individual loyalty to a military leader was a tradition that survived the chaos of this period. Men of many classes had followed Bolívar and San Martín and Morelos. It was easy to transfer this loyalty to new military leaders who emerged in the 1820's and 1830's. In fact, in most Latin American countries it became an accepted fact that no leader could remain in power without the support of the army. Such leaders were, in effect, military dictators. They were called *caudillos* (cow-*dee'* yohss, Spanish for "chief"). Bolívar himself has been called the first of the *caudillos*. Strong-man rule was so characteristic of Latin American government in the 1800's that the period is spoken of as the age of *caudillismo* (cow-dee-*yeess'* moh). This tradition of *caudillismo* became so strong that it extended into the twentieth century as well.

One way of studying the first century of independence in Latin America is to examine the careers of leading *caudillos*. In personality and character they covered a wide range. A few were well-meaning and able. Others were selfish and irresponsible. A good many fell somewhere between these extremes. Unstable government and hard times enabled *caudillos* to dominate this era.

1. Common Problems of the New Nations

The last chapter described some of the handicaps that burdened the new nations of Latin America as they faced the future. While each country was to develop differently, certain conflicts troubled all of them.

Federalism or centralism? One of these conflicts concerned the division of power between national government and provinces or states. Most Latin American countries had little unity at this time. Clusters of population were isolated from each other by geographic barriers.

People in remote villages might have little or no contact with the capital city of the country within whose borders they happened to live. It is not surprising that a government based in a capital city had trouble exerting control over back-country regions.

In any of the countries those who favored strengthening the government centered in the capital city were called *centralists*. Many of the centralists (though there were exceptions) were creoles living in the cities. Their opponents were called *federalists*.[2] Naturally many regional *caudillos* held to the federalist view

[1] Fanny Calderón de la Barca, *Life in Mexico During a Residence of Two Years in That Country* (Boston: Little and Brown, 1843), pp. 348–349, 364, and 378.

[2] In United States history the term *federalism* has the opposite meaning. Federalists in this country favored a strong central government.

that the separate provinces within a country should keep a large measure of power. Important in the ranks of the federalists were mestizos in the provinces. They were jealous and suspicious of the new creole ruling class in the cities.

The conflict between centralists and federalists was often simply a struggle for power rather than a basic disagreement over principle. In many cases, when a federalist *caudillo* gained control of a national government, he became an ardent centralist (even though he might still give lip service to the theory of federalism).

Liberalism or conservatism? Tied in with the federalist-centralist argument was a clash between liberal and conservative viewpoints. The liberals included mestizos who distrusted powerful creoles. Other liberals were merchants who hoped for fewer restrictions in trade, intellectuals who resented the privileges of the Church, and opponents of the military class. Liberals, therefore, in general favored change.

The ranks of the conservatives included creole aristocrats and wealthy landlords who saw no need to change traditional patterns of life. High-ranking churchmen and military officers also sided with the conservatives.

Political parties developed. Political parties often grew up around the liberal and conservative viewpoints. Among the issues that divided liberal and conservative parties were the breaking up of huge estates, higher taxation on land, separation of Church and state, improvements in education and social services, and civilian rather than military control of the government. In general, the liberals favored these points, while the conservatives opposed them. But differences between liberal and conservative parties were often not clear-cut. Personal advantage rather than principle often determined which party an individual would support. Some persons shuttled back and forth between the parties, as first one and then another seemed to offer greater advantage.

All of the political parties, liberal or conservative, declared their faith in constitutional government. And the liberals often expressed idealistic hopes of democracy. Yet both sides relied on *caudillos* and "strong-man" tactics in seeking to control the national governments.

THINKING ABOUT THIS SECTION

1. Explain or define the following words: *caudillo;* "strong-man" tactics.

2. Contrast the views on government of centralists and federalists in Latin America. Were most *caudillos* likely to be centralists or federalists? Why?

3. What were the major issues that divided liberals and conservatives? What stand were liberals likely to take on each of these issues? What kinds of people were generally liberals? conservatives? Why?

2. Three Dominant Leaders in Mexican History

Mexico's history in the years following independence is an unhappy story of seesaw struggles for power between different factions. *Caudillos* played starring roles in this chaotic period.

Santa Anna built up personal power. The dominant figure in the early years of independent Mexico was a man who has been called the "supreme egotist." Antonio Lopez de Santa Anna was the son of a wealthy creole plantation owner in the state of Veracruz. As a boy, he idolized the French emperor Napoleon. His choice of a military career was probably influenced by this hero worship. Santa Anna entered the Spanish army as a teen-ager and fought against Hidalgo's rebels in 1810. Ten years later he was an officer in command of the Spanish forces in the port of Veracruz.

When Iturbide took over the independence movement in Mexico, Santa Anna made several switches in loyalty with an agility that was to become typical. First, as a Spanish officer, Santa Anna fought against Iturbide. Then he joined Iturbide. After Iturbide became emperor, Santa Anna started plotting against him and led the revolt that resulted in Iturbide's downfall.

In the new republic that was organized, Santa Anna became commander-in-chief of the army. When he defeated a Spanish force sent from Cuba, Santa Anna won fame as a popular military hero. In 1833 he led his troops into Mexico City and had himself "elected" president. Over the next 20 years Santa Anna served six different times in the presidency. Whenever serious trouble threatened, he would retire to his plantation or go off with the army, leaving the current vice-president in charge. When the vice-president failed to deal with the problem, Santa Anna would rush back to the capital to "save the country."

Although Santa Anna had led the revolt that resulted in the birth of the republic, he admitted afterwards that he "scarcely knew the meaning of the word republic." He held no views on the conflict between liberalism and conservatism or on any other serious issue. Santa Anna was the supreme opportunist. If it seemed to be to his advantage, he would turn in an instant against a person or cause he had been supporting. Although the people cheered him after each military victory, individuals who had to deal with Santa Anna mistrusted and feared him.

In addition to power itself, Santa Anna loved the trappings of power. Dramatic appearances, cheering crowds, lavish display, and titles and decorations were far more important to him than his country's welfare. At times Santa Anna's vanity became comical. Having lost a leg in a skirmish with French soldiers, he ordered the leg buried with military honors.

North Americans settled in Texas. Latin American historians can find few words of apology for Santa Anna. But the fact that Mexico was badly ruled in the 1830's and 1840's does not dim their bitterness over the actions of the United States during the same period. They feel that the United States government took advantage of Mexico's weakness. Many historians in the United States share this view.

The trouble started with Texas. Before Mexico won its independence, Spain had granted United States citizens permission to settle in the Texas borderlands. By the 1820's the lure of cheap land had brought thousands of English-speaking settlers into this region. The Mexican government became alarmed, as these newcomers ignored Mexican laws. Many of the settlers came from the slave states of the southern United States. Since they planned to grow cotton in Texas, they brought along large numbers of slaves. This practice continued despite the fact that Mexico had abolished slavery. Also, the new settlers often staked out land claims that overlapped with earlier claims. In 1830 the government at Mexico City forbade any more United States citizens to settle in Texas. But the Mexican army was not strong enough to enforce this ban.

Texas separated from Mexico. In 1835 the English-speaking settlers in Texas rebelled against Mexican rule. Early the next year they declared Texan independence. The rebels mustered a small army and asked for help from the United States. Mexico refused to recognize the independence of Texas.

Santa Anna marched north with an army to crush the revolt. In San Antonio he found that 150 men had fortified a mission called the Alamo. For two weeks the Mexican troops laid siege to the Alamo, but the Texans refused to surrender. Finally Santa Anna ordered his men to storm the mission, and all its defenders were slaughtered. From the Mexican point of view the defenders of the Alamo were rebels.

Mexican boundary in 1821
U.S. attacks on Mexico

U.S. States Carved Out of Lands Lost by Mexico:

Texas Annexation, 1845

Mexican Cession, 1848

Gadsden Purchase, 1853

Mexico after 1853

Mexico Loses the Borderlands

But in the United States they have been honored as martyrs for freedom.

A few weeks later Texans avenged the fall of the Alamo. Near the mouth of the San Jacinto River a Texan force commanded by Sam Houston won a decisive victory. Six hundred Mexicans were killed in the battle, and Santa Anna was captured. In return for his freedom the Mexican commander signed a treaty which recognized Texas as an independent nation. He then went into exile. But the Mexican government refused to accept Santa Anna's treaty. Moreover, Mexico threatened to declare war if the United States annexed Texas. From 1836 to 1845 Texas was an independent republic.

The United States annexed Texas. This was a time when many citizens of the United States believed it was their country's destiny to expand to the Pacific. They saw the annexation of Texas as a logical step in this "natural" expansion. In 1845 the United States Congress adopted a resolution providing for the annexation of Texas. The official view of the United States was that an independent nation had joined the Union of its own free will. But Mexicans charged that the United States had seized territory that was rightfully a part of Mexico.

War began. War fever ran high in both countries. Fighting finally broke out in disputed territory between the Rio Grande and the Nueces (noo-*ay'* sess) River (map, page 153). The United States claimed that the Rio Grande was the boundary between Texas and Mexico, while Mexico held that Texas never had extended beyond the Nueces River. In April, 1846, forces of the two countries clashed in the disputed area. When news of the fighting reached Washington in May, the United States declared war on Mexico.

Santa Anna led the Mexican forces. Late that summer Santa Anna was allowed by the United States to return from exile in Cuba through a blockade of Mexican ports. He had led the United States government to believe that once in power he might negotiate a peace settlement. Instead, Santa Anna took command of the Mexican forces and marched north to meet the invading North Americans. At Buena Vista, Santa Anna's troops fought an army commanded by General Zachary Taylor. The Mexicans suffered heavy casualties from the artillery fire of Taylor's forces. Santa Anna withdrew his men during the night and returned to Mexico City. There he showed two captured United States flags as "proof" of his claim that he had defeated the enemy.

The fall of Mexico City ended the war. But the United States' campaign against Mexico could not be halted by strategic withdrawals on the part of Santa Anna. Early in 1847 General Winfield Scott occupied the Mexican port of Veracruz with an army of 10,000 men and advanced toward Mexico City. By September, Scott had reached Chapultepec, the ancient castle and fort on a hill above the capital city. Among the defenders of Chapultepec were cadets from a nearby military academy. Officials of the school had ordered the teen-aged students to leave Chapultepec, but some of them refused to go. In the fierce fighting which marked the United States' attack on the heights, the boys fought to the death. Ever since, these cadets have been honored as *Los Niños Héroes* ("the boy heroes") by the Mexican people.

The day after taking Chapultepec, Scott entered Mexico City. Santa Anna fled with his troops. Even after the city fell, Mexican citizens continued firing on the United States soldiers from houses and rooftops. Meanwhile, in the borderlands North American forces had taken possession of New Mexico and California (Chapter 15).

Mexico lost a vast territory. Mexican forces had fought bravely, but they were poorly armed and suffered from inept leadership. In February, 1848, the Treaty of Guadalupe-Hidalgo officially ended the war. Mexico recognized the United States' claim to Texas and also ceded half its territory to its northern neighbor. From the enormous Mexican Cession were eventually carved the states of California, Nevada, and Utah as well as parts of Arizona, New Mexico, Colorado, and Wyoming. In return, Mexico received fifteen million dollars from the United States.

The war had been a disaster for Mexico. The people felt crushed and defeated. Their government had been shown up as weak and corrupt, their economy was shattered, and they felt humiliated by the loss of half their territory.

Santa Anna became dictator. Over the next few years Mexico continued to be torn by local revolts and financial problems. In 1853 conservatives seized control of the government and invited Santa Anna to return from exile. Santa Anna soon made himself an absolute dictator, taking the title of "Most Serene Highness." Suppressing all criticism, he exiled his enemies. Santa Anna outdid Iturbide in lavish expenditures on his "court." Short of cash, he agreed to sell more territory to the United States. This was the strip of land in southern Arizona and New Mexico known as the Gadsden Purchase. He also sold Yucatán Indians to Cuban plantation owners for 25 pesos each.

Santa Anna was driven from power. In little over a year the Mexicans had enough of Santa Anna. Rebellion spread quickly, and once again he was forced to leave Mexico. Years later, in 1874, Santa Anna was allowed to return to Mexico, but by that time he was an old man. Two years later he died, a poor and obscure figure. It was tragic for Mexico that during a time when responsible leadership was desperately needed, the vain and selfish Santa Anna dominated the scene.

A liberal trend was opposed by conservatives. Santa Anna's ouster in 1855 was part of a liberal movement in Mexico. Over the next 20 years, known as the era of *La Reforma,* liberals tried to chart a new course for Mexico.

Among the conservatives who opposed reform were wealthy creoles who owned much of the land worked by Indian peons. The great estates were handed down from father to oldest son; younger sons became army officers or high Church officials. These three groups— the large landowners, army officers, and churchmen— formed a privileged class which evaded taxes and ignored laws. Military officers and members of the clergy even had the right to be tried in their own courts rather than in the regular national courts. Naturally the conservatives supported Santa Anna or any other leader who promised to keep this situation unchanged. But growing opposition to special privilege swelled the ranks of the liberals.

Benito Juárez was of humble origin. The man who emerged as leader of the liberals was a Zapotecan Indian. Benito Juárez (*hwah' rayss*) was born in a mountain village in the state of Oaxaca. Orphaned at the age of three, he went to live with his uncle. One day when he was twelve, some Indian muleteers camped in his uncle's sheep pasture on the way to Oaxaca City, 40 miles away. They told the boy about the "city," which Benito had never seen. After they left, Benito found that they had stolen a sheep. Rather than tell his uncle about the theft, the boy left on foot and went to the city himself.

In Oaxaca, Benito stayed with a family for whom his sister was working. A relative of this family, a Franciscan priest, befriended the boy and helped him get some schooling. At the age of fifteen Juárez entered a seminary to train for the priesthood. Seven years later, however, he began studying law, while working as a waiter to pay his way. After completing his studies, Juárez carried on a small law practice for some years. Many of his cases were complaints brought by poor Indians against unfair landlords.

Santa Anna and Juárez were enemies. Juárez's first political experience was a term served in the national congress. In 1847 he became governor of the state of Oaxaca. As governor, he refused to give refuge to Santa Anna, who was fleeing from Mexico City after its fall to United States forces. Santa Anna claimed that Juárez "could not forgive me because he once waited on me at table in Oaxaca, with his feet bare on the floor." When Santa Anna had regained power in 1853, one of the first persons he imprisoned was Juárez, who had strongly opposed his return. Eventually Juárez was released from prison and went into exile in New Orleans.

Reforms were adopted but civil war broke out. When Santa Anna was ousted in 1855, Juárez returned to Mexico and worked with other liberal leaders who now controlled the government. As part of the *La Reforma* movement, the liberals announced several important measures. One law forced the Church to sell all its lands that were not used for religious purposes. Another, called *Ley Juárez* ("law of Juárez"), required cases involving clergymen and military officers to be tried in the regular courts. In 1857 a new constitution was adopted that included these and other measures designed to end special privileges. The outraged conservatives denounced Juárez as an enemy of the Church.

When army officers overthrew the reform government, Juárez and other liberal leaders had to flee from Mexico City. In Veracruz they set up a government and declared Juárez president. Three years of civil war followed, as the conservatives battled the liberal forces who supported the Constitution of 1857. This War of the Reform (1858–1860) was a bitterly fought conflict, with massacres carried out by both sides. Though the conservatives had better trained troops, the liberals had far greater support among the people.

Liberals regained control of the government. Eventually the liberals took Mexico City, and in 1861 Juárez was legally elected president. He became the first Indian to serve as a head of state anywhere in Latin America after the European conquest.

Juárez faced a difficult situation. The new government's financial problems were enormous. Moreover, conservative forces were carrying on guerrilla warfare in the mountains around Mexico City. Added to these problems was the threat of interference from Europe.

The French tried to take over Mexico. During the civil war the Mexican government had borrowed large sums in Europe. Juárez's new government was so short of cash that it could not pay these debts. In an effort to collect the money owed them, Britain, Spain, and France jointly landed troops at Veracruz in 1862. The British and Spanish troops soon left, but the French remained and advanced inland. Near the city of Puebla they were driven back by a band of Mexican peasants. The battle of *Cinco de Mayo* ("Fifth of May") was the last big victory won by the liberal forces for nearly four years.

Meanwhile, the French ruler, Napoleon III (a nephew of the first Napoleon), had thought up a scheme for making Mexico a French "puppet" state. Napoleon hoped to safeguard the rights of the Church in Mexico and also to prevent possible United States expansion. Under his plan an Austrian archduke named Maximilian would become "Emperor" of Mexico. Napoleon believed that Mexican conservatives would welcome a member of European royalty as their ruler.

When Maximilian and his wife Carlota arrived in Mexico City in 1864, they were warmly received by the clergy and the wealthy creoles. Maximilian was a handsome young man, sincere and well-meaning. But he had no understanding of the situation in Mexico. He had been led to believe that the Mexican people wanted him to save the country from the liberals. Once in Mexico, Maximilian soon realized that there was something to be said for the liberal reforms. When he refused to restore the property lost by the Church, conservatives began to turn against him. Unfortunately for Maximilian, his liberal sympathies failed to win the support of the Mexican reformers. Meanwhile, Juárez had set up headquarters in a town on the Rio Grande. (Today this town is called Ciudad Juárez.) There he began raising a large patriot army.

Maximilian was overthrown. Napoleon III soon lost interest in his scheme for Mexico and called home most of the French troops supporting Maximilian. One reason was that the French ruler was having troubles in Europe. But another reason for his change of mind was that the United States had demanded the withdrawal of the French forces. The betrayed Maximilian decided to stay on in Mexico even though the French emperor had abandoned him. In a desperate move Maximilian took command of the few troops left to him and marched north to meet Juárez's army. In a battle near Querétaro (kay-ray′ tah-roh) the patriot army was victorious. Maximilian was captured, tried for treason, and executed by a firing squad in June, 1867.

Juárez, restored to power, faced a hopeless task. Juárez returned quietly to Mexico City.

A giant portrait of Benito Juárez is featured in this mural painting by the modern Mexican artist José Clemente Orozco. Other figures in the mural are caricatures of military and clerical conservatives.

He was to serve five more years as president before his death in 1872. During this time he tried to carry out further reforms: abolition of special privileges in the courts, separation of Church and state, the establishment of free compulsory education, and the holding of democratic elections. But lack of money was an overwhelming handicap, and gradually Juárez lost support. Even the liberals deserted him, as his rule became more and more dictatorial. Juárez believed in democracy. But, like any *caudillo,* he found it necessary to use dictatorial powers in order to get things done. Nevertheless, to the Mexican people Juárez is still a hero. They remember him as the young Indian who became president and devoted his life to the welfare of his country.

Díaz seized power. Still another strong Mexican leader provides an interesting contrast to both Santa Anna and Juárez. Porfirio Díaz (*dee' ahss*), a mestizo, became a military hero at the battle of Cinco de Mayo. By 1867, when Maximilian's rule ended, Díaz was a leading general. Ten years later he headed a revolt which ousted the president who had followed Juárez. Leading his army into Mexico City, Díaz had himself

named president. Meanwhile, he had already taken over the estates of some wealthy conservatives, thus becoming a rich *hacendado.*

Although he had sided with the liberals against the French, Díaz had little sympathy for reformers. His goal was to restore peace and order to Mexico. To bring this about, he ruled Mexico with an iron hand. Díaz was careful to keep the loyalty of the army, since he needed its support. Local leaders were bribed to accept his authority. Those who followed an independent course were shot or mysteriously disappeared. Díaz also silenced all opposition in the press, and an efficient and brutal police force imposed "law and order."

At the end of four years in office, Díaz set up a "stooge" to serve one term, and then he returned to the presidency himself in 1884. Four years later he decided not to bother with another puppet president. Díaz remained in the presidency until 1911.

Some economic progress was made. Mexico was a desperately poor country when Díaz came to power. Under his rule the country did make some economic progress. Díaz invited foreign companies to build railroads in Mexico,

A cartoon of the 1890's showed Porfirio Díaz placing on his own head "the crown of authority." Though an elected president, Díaz reigned as an absolute ruler.

and electricity was installed in Mexico City. When oil was discovered near Tampico, the Mexican president invited North American and British companies to develop this resource. By 1900 millions of barrels of Mexican oil were entering the channels of world trade.

The plight of the people worsened. But the Mexican people did not benefit from these developments. In fact, many of them were worse off. Foreign-owned companies exploited Mexico's mineral resources and ran its textile factories and public utilities. The profits from these industries were spent abroad and did Mexico little good. Moreover, Díaz allowed the foreign companies to pay little or no taxes. Even in employment foreigners were favored over Mexicans. Well-paid jobs went to foreign technicians, while Mexican laborers earned only a few cents a day. Nothing was done to train Mexicans for the better jobs.

Díaz also allowed oil interests to take over lands that Indian communities had held by custom from ancient times. He ruled that if no villager could show a deed to a tract of land,

anyone who promised to "improve" that tract might claim it. Left homeless, thousands of Indians became tenants on large estates.

On the large haciendas the lot of Indian tenants was hardly different from that of slaves. They lived in miserable huts and received a tiny wage or a small share of the crops. Each hacienda had its own store, where the peons had to buy whatever they needed. Since they could buy only on credit, the amounts they owed the store were charged against their future wages. By going into debt, the peons became tied to the hacienda for life.

Porfirio Díaz was affectionately called *Tata* (*tah'* tah), or "Grandpa," by his friends. But liberals charged that under his regime Mexico was a "mother to the foreigner and stepmother to the Mexican." His rule did produce some economic gains, and his achievement in establishing peace won praise from foreign observers. But his policies bled the Mexican people, for they made Mexico a "colony" for foreign business interests. Finally, in 1911 the Mexican people overthrew Díaz (Chapter 9).

THINKING ABOUT THIS SECTION

1. Explain or define the following words: *Los Niños Héroes; La Reforma; Ley Juárez; Cinco de Mayo.*

2. Evaluate the goals and achievements of Santa Anna, Juárez, and Díaz. Which do you think did most for Mexico? Why?

3. Contrast the views that students in this country and in Mexico might take of the following: the movement for independence in Texas; causes of the war between Mexico and the United States; the Treaty of Guadalupe-Hidalgo.

4. What were the causes of the War of the Reform? What was its outcome? Why was Maximilian's role in the conflict between Mexican liberals and conservatives a tragic one?

5. Although Mexico made economic progress under Díaz, the plight of the Mexican people worsened. How could this have been so?

3. Pedro II, Emperor of Brazil

The first Brazilian emperor was unpopular.
Personal rule took a far different course in Brazil. When Brazil declared its independence from Portugal in 1822, Pedro I, the son of João VI, became emperor. Pedro I meant well, but he was not a successful leader. He exiled an able prime minister for supporting a liberal constitution. Pedro then had conservatives write another constitution, which was adopted. But soon the emperor was ignoring this constitution and taking more power into his own hands. Many Brazilians also resented the fact that Pedro awarded high government posts to Portuguese who had remained in Brazil.

Pedro became even more unpopular when Brazil lost Uruguay. This region on the east bank of the Plata estuary had long been an object of rivalry, first between the Spanish and the Portuguese and then between Argentina and Brazil. After much fighting, Uruguay was recognized as an independent buffer state in 1828.

The growing hostility of the Brazilian people soon forced Pedro to abdicate the throne. In 1831 he sailed for Portugal, leaving his five-year-old son, also named Pedro, to be ruler of Brazil.

Pedro II was trained to be emperor. Since the little emperor's mother was dead, he was now without parents. But he was left in good hands. A series of capable regents managed the country until the emperor would be old enough to rule for himself. Meanwhile, those in charge of the boy's education planned it with great care. Tutors prepared the prince for the important role he would eventually have. When he was six, he began to study German, French, and English. Pedro eventually learned to speak fourteen languages well. With his wide range of interests and natural abilities, Pedro II was easily the best-educated ruler in nineteenth-century Latin America.

Strife threatened Brazilian unity. During Pedro's boyhood Brazil was hardly a unified nation. The regents found it difficult to hold the country together during years of factional quarrels and provincial revolts. Some monarchists wanted Pedro I to return as emperor. Other Brazilians called for the founding of a republic. And conservatives and liberals clashed over many issues.

Brazil at this time had three main regions of settlement: the towns along the coast, São Paulo about forty miles inland, and Minas Gerais still farther inland. In the deep interior was wild country that Brazilian authority had never reached. The national government was centered in Rio de Janeiro, then a city of about 100,000 people. A series of rebellions raged in both north and south throughout the period of the regency.

Pedro became emperor in fact as well as in name. In 1840, when Pedro was fourteen, liberal leaders urged that he be formally crowned. As a symbol of central authority, Pedro seemed to provide the best hope for establishing Brazilian unity. The prince declared himself "willing to rule," and in 1841 the coronation ceremony took place.

Pedro II proved to be an able ruler, honest, intelligent, and truly concerned for the welfare of the Brazilian people. As a grown man, the handsome emperor presented an imposing appearance. He was six feet three inches tall, and wore a long full beard. Pedro married an Italian princess three years older than he. Quick-witted and good-humored, the queen proved to be an ideal wife for the serious young man. They had two daughters, of whom the older, Princess Isabel, was educated to be Pedro's heir. The royal family lived simply, showing little interest in elaborate court ceremony.

Pedro's wide-ranging interests led him to travel in Europe and the United States. Wherever he went, he sought out scientists, philosophers, educators, and writers. The American poet Longfellow wrote after a visit with Pedro: "He wants to see the great world as a simple traveler, not as a king. He is a hearty, genial, noble person, very liberal in his views." At home the emperor took a keen interest in education. "If I were not an emperor," Pedro once said, "I should like to be a schoolteacher." There was a great need for such an interest in Brazil, for only a tiny percentage of children received any schooling.

Pedro was a powerful but just ruler. The Brazilian emperor was sincere in wanting to rule wisely and justly. But he also believed in ruling with a strong hand, and he had the power to do this, since he could dissolve the Brazilian congress at will. Yet, for the most part, Pedro allowed the congress to meet regularly. Although the great majority of the Brazilian people had no voice in the government, they did have individual liberties, such as freedom of speech. Few other Latin Americans at that time enjoyed as much freedom.

Brazil made progress toward unity and prosperity. One of Pedro's first tasks as emperor was to put down uprisings in the provinces. By 1848 this had been done, and centralized government became a reality. During Pedro's long reign of 48 years Brazil fought only two foreign wars, both of them disputes over boundaries with Argentina and Paraguay. The second of these wars was particularly costly, in both lives and money. Pedro realized that it was more profitable to give his attention to peaceful development at home.

During Pedro's reign, sugar continued to be a major export, but the planting of coffee trees was encouraged. Gradually coffee replaced sugar as the country's leading crop. Cotton, tobacco, and livestock products also were important exports. Pedro took a special interest in Brazil's pampa region of Rio Grande do Sul, bordering Uruguay. With his encouragement many immigrants from Italy and Germany settled there on small land-holdings and raised livestock. During the 1850's, the high point of Pedro's reign, Brazil enjoyed a period of unusual prosperity.

Brazil profited from a boom in rubber. The discovery of new uses for rubber contributed to Brazilian prosperity during Pedro's reign. Rubber had been known in America long before the coming of Europeans. But little use had been found for it other than for making bouncing balls. A new market developed when it was discovered that rubber could be blended with fibers to make waterproof fabrics. But the boom in rubber really began when Charles Goodyear invented the process of vulcanization. This process, basically one of heating, kept rubber from getting sticky in hot weather and brittle in cold. The demand for rubber skyrocketed as a great variety of uses were found for it.

Since the Amazon basin was at this time the only known source of rubber, Brazil had a monopoly on the international supply. Indians searched out the wild rubber trees and tapped them for their juice, called *latex*. Merchants shipped the raw rubber down-river to the port of Belém (beh-*laym'*), which became the world's chief market for this commodity. Over five million pounds of rubber were exported from Belém in the single year of 1853. Halfway up the Amazon, rubber trading made the river port of Manaus (mah-*noush'*) a boom town.

To preserve the Brazilian monopoly, Pedro II forbade the export of seeds or cuttings from the rubber trees. But Brazil's monopoly came to an end in the 1870's when British botanists smuggled out some seedlings and planted them in Malaya. Even so, Brazilian rubber "barons" continued to make fortunes. Finally, in the early 1900's the Brazilian rubber boom collapsed as Asian rubber began to take over the market.

Mauá promoted industrialization. The leading figure in Brazil's economic development was the Baron of Mauá, a financier and industrialist. Mauá was responsible for most of Brazil's modernizing improvements during Pedro's reign. Brazil would always have a colonial economy, Mauá pointed out, as long as it depended on the export of raw products and failed to develop industry. He also recognized the

The huge numbers of slaves owned by the sugar planters of nineteenth-century Brazil are suggested by the picture above, showing a slave "muster" or gathering at a single plantation. Left, millions of trees growing wild in the Amazon rain forest yielded the latex that made rubber a booming industry. To tap the trees, workers cut gashes in the bark and attached cups to catch the draining latex. The latex was made into solid rubber by smoking it over a fire.

great need for transportation and communication systems, especially in a country the size of Brazil. This "baron of industry" built up a great banking empire and, with the help of British capital, financed the construction of railroads, ports, canals, telegraph lines, and factories. All these activities, in turn, created a demand for European immigrant labor. Despite industrial advances, however, Brazil continued to rely on products that came from the land for its principal exports.

Opposition to slavery grew. During the later years of Pedro's reign slavery became an increasingly controversial issue. The emperor was strongly opposed to human bondage. But in the sugar-raising areas of Brazil the plantation system depended on slavery. Because the large landholders were a powerful force in Brazilian politics, Pedro faced a dilemma. He feared the consequences if all the slaves were freed at once.

As one way of combating slavery Pedro encouraged European immigrants to settle in Brazil and become a new labor force. He also urged individual Brazilians to free their slaves. But more and more Brazilians were beginning to think that slavery should be totally abolished. In 1871 the Brazilian congress passed the Law of Free Birth. This law provided that all children born to slave mothers after that time were to be free. They were, however, to serve as "apprentices" to their mothers' masters until the age of 21. The law also freed slaves belonging to the national government and established a fund to buy freedom for other slaves.

Since this law was only a compromise measure, it failed to satisfy many abolitionists. A young politician named Joaquim Nabuco (nah-boo′ koh) became an eloquent spokesman for the antislavery movement. In a stirring book called *Abolition,* Nabuco presented both social and political reasons for ending human bondage. Several black Brazilian leaders joined Nabuco in his crusade, and together they persuaded a number of local governments to abolish slavery. By the 1880's slave-owners in Brazil were releasing large numbers of slaves. Encouraged by the abolition campaign, other slaves deserted plantations. When called on by the landowners to hunt down the runaways, army officers refused. Clearly slavery could not last much longer under these conditions.

Slavery was abolished. Pedro II, now in his sixties, was seriously ill. In 1887 he traveled to Europe for medical treatment, leaving his daughter, Princess Isabel, to rule in his place. The next year, the Brazilian congress passed a bill immediately freeing all the slaves, by now numbering about 700,000. Princess Isabel gladly signed the measure into law. When the emperor received the news in Europe, he cabled his daughter: "My blessings and congratulations to everybody!" In Brazil a five-day holiday was declared to celebrate the emancipation law. A United States diplomat in Rio remarked that Brazil had done quickly and easily something that had taken the United States four years of civil war to bring about.

Pedro II was overthrown. Though Pedro was out of the country when the emancipation bill was adopted, the plantation owners blamed him for the loss of their slaves. For various reasons other groups were also dissatisfied with the monarchy. Within the Catholic Church there was resentment of Pedro's liberal policies. Army officers felt bitter over their lack of political power. Many liberals simply wanted to do away with the monarchy and make Brazil a republic. When Pedro returned to Brazil, he did little to halt the rising tide of opposition.

In 1889 Pedro was overthrown by a rather strange combination of army officers and republicans. Early one morning, before people knew what was happening, the conspirators put the royal family on board a ship in Rio's harbor. Pedro and his family were sent into exile in Portugal. Both the emperor and his wife soon died, heartsick over their banishment from their homeland.

Meanwhile, Brazil had been declared a republic. Over the next few years a series of men held the presidency as army officers and civilians plotted against each other. Brazil's finances grew chaotic under a wasteful government, and uprisings broke out in the provinces. Fortunately, Pedro's long reign had given the nation a legacy of stability. This helped Brazil survive its first rocky years as a republic (Chapter 14).

THINKING ABOUT THIS SECTION

1. Explain or define the following words: buffer state; monarchist; Belém.
2. What problems faced the young Emperor Pedro II in the 1840's?
3. Why did the issue of slavery pose a difficult problem in Brazil? Contrast the way in which slavery was ended in that country and in the United States.
4. How was Pedro II overthrown? What problems troubled the republic of Brazil in its early years?

4. Important Leaders in Argentina and Chile

During the 1800's "strong men" dominated political life in the important countries of Argentina and Chile.

ARGENTINA

Gauchos lived a rough life on the pampa. A major theme in Argentine history in the years following independence was the conflict between the pampa and the city of Buenos Aires. The pampa—the great plains region—was the heart of Argentina. It was destined to become one of the great beef-producing areas of the world. On the pampa lived the rough and lawless *gauchos,* the cowboys who made their living off the huge herds of wild cattle. Most of the gauchos were mestizos, though some were blacks or whites. Riding horses they had captured and tamed, the gauchos ran down and killed the wild cattle, stripped them of their hides, and left the carcasses on the pampa. Eventually landholders fenced in the plains, established great ranches, and hired the gauchos to round up the cattle and brand them. Thus, life in the Argentine pampa resembled that on the western plains of North America.

The gauchos scorned settled community life and distrusted city people. Usually they slept on the ground in the open air. Beef cooked over a campfire was almost their only food. The fiercely independent gauchos were staunch supporters of any provincial *caudillo* who could win their loyalty.

Porteños and gauchos disliked each other. In complete contrast to the pampa style of living was life in the growing city of Buenos Aires, at least among the middle and upper classes. The well-to-do *porteños* enjoyed the refinements of a European city and looked down on people in the provinces. Thus, two factions emerged in Argentina. One included the city merchants and growing numbers of the European immigrants who settled in Buenos Aires. These people, called the *unitarios* (oo-nee-*tahr'* ee-ohss), favored a centralist government, with Buenos Aires as the seat of power. The *caudillos* in the provinces and their followers, however, were suspicious of any concentration of power in Buenos Aires. They wanted a federalist government, in which provincial leaders would have a powerful role. For 23 years (1829–1852) the Argentine federalists controlled the nation. Their leader was a dictator named Rosas (*roh'* sahss).

Rosas won power with gaucho support. The son of a well-to-do landholder, Juan Manuel de Rosas had grown up on a cattle ranch.

Argentina's gauchos spent their lives in the saddle chasing and roping wild cattle on the pampa.

Popular with the gauchos and ranchers, he soon became a leader. Rosas organized cattle breeders and businessmen who dealt in livestock products and soon secured a monopoly on the cattle market. With economic power in his hands he found it easy to gain political power as well. Backed by an army of gauchos, Rosas became governor of Buenos Aires province in 1829. Within six years he was president—actually dictator—of the nation.

A description of Rosas and the loyalty he inspired was provided by the English naturalist Charles Darwin, who visited South America in 1832. Darwin wrote that Rosas was a "perfect horseman, who can drop from a crossbar above a gate onto the back of a wild horse plunging through, and keep his seat without saddle or bridle." Rosas had "unbounded popularity," said Darwin. The Englishman told about meeting a gaucho who had been tried for murder and acquitted. According to the gaucho, his victim had "spoken disrespectfully of General Rosas, so I killed him!" This reason for the killing seemed to satisfy the court.

Rosas held total power. Rosas called himself a "federalist," but no government could have been more centralized than his. To consolidate his power, he set out to eliminate the *unitarios* who opposed him. During this reign of terror thousands were imprisoned and many were executed. Even schoolchildren were taught to denounce the *unitarios*. Since Rosas' name meant "rosy-red," his private army wore bright red sashes and silk shirts. Ordinary citizens too had to wear something red.

Rosas allowed little power to any group in the country. Though he claimed to be a champion of the Catholic Church, he exiled priests and bishops who opposed him. Portraits of

Rosas and his wife were carried in religious parades and even placed on altars. Schools were closed, and professors were exiled. Newspapers printed in Buenos Aires were strictly censored. Rosas discouraged European immigration and allowed land to become even more concentrated in the hands of large landowners. He also involved Argentina in a series of costly wars with other countries.

A coalition overthrew Rosas. Rosas' enemies finally joined forces to bring about the *caudillo*'s downfall. Spearheading this effort were young Argentine intellectuals who lived in exile in neighboring countries. They agreed to back a provincial *caudillo* named Urquiza (oor-*kees'* sah), who was a former henchman of Rosas'. With aid from other Argentines and some Uruguayan and Brazilian troops, they succeeded in ousting the dictator in 1852. Rosas had been a ruthless tyrant, but, by holding the Argentine provinces together, he did help unify the nation.

Domingo Sarmiento wanted to modernize Argentina. During the second half of the 1800's, Argentina was to make great strides, especially under the presidency of Domingo Sarmiento (sar-*myen'* toh). Sarmiento was born in 1811 in a small town near the Chilean border. Though poor, his parents were ambitious for their son. By the age of five he already knew how to read, and when he started school, he was an excellent student. Since his parents could not afford higher education for their son, Sarmiento became a storekeeper at the age of sixteen. On being drafted into the militia, he protested. The local *caudillo,* Facundo Quiroga (kee-*roh'* gah), had him arrested, and Sarmiento spent a short term in prison.

Determined to fight *caudillismo* government, Sarmiento joined *unitario* forces opposing Rosas and saw some military action. But in 1831 he had to go into exile in Chile. To support himself, he worked as a schoolteacher, as a store clerk, and then in the mines of northern Chile. In his spare time Sarmiento continued

his studies, learning English and reading widely in that language.

After the death of the *caudillo* Quiroga, Sarmiento returned to Argentina. In his native province he founded a school for young women and started publishing a newspaper in which he aired his progressive ideas. The local governor soon cracked down on the young reformer, and again Sarmiento sought refuge in Chile. While in exile, Sarmiento wrote an outspoken book called *El Facundo,* in which he bitterly attacked *caudillo* government. The book was aimed at Rosas, then firmly in control of Argentina. The Chilean government, perhaps wanting to get this blunt young man out of the way, sent Sarmiento to study educational systems in Europe and the United States. In the United States he met the educator Horace Mann, and the two became firm friends. Sarmiento had a warm regard for the United States. Later, he was to urge Argentinians to "North Americanize" their country.

Meanwhile, after the overthrow of Rosas, Buenos Aires province had seceded from the rest of Argentina. But by 1862 all the Argentine provinces were again unified under a central government, and Buenos Aires was recognized as the capital city of the nation. By this time Sarmiento was back in Argentina. As governor of his native province, he at last held a position that enabled him to carry out his many ideas for reform. These involved changes not only in education but also in government, landownership, and social services. Some of his programs seemed too new and different, however, and did not work out. In 1864 Sarmiento was appointed Argentine Minister to the United States.

The war with Paraguay was costly. That same year marked the beginning of a terribly wasteful war. A Paraguayan dictator picked quarrels with Argentina and Brazil, chiefly over the buffer state of Uruguay, which was regarded as a Brazilian "satellite." Weak Paraguay had little chance against the combined forces of its three neighbors. The war turned into a nightmare

The pampa frontier was slowly pushed back as pioneer farmers settled and raised corn and wheat. At first horses and oxen were used for transportation, but in the late 1800's railroad lines were laid.

as both sides suffered terrible losses. After five years of cruel fighting Paraguay had lost half its population. For Argentina the war was much less of a disaster than it was for Paraguay. Even so, Argentina suffered from the drain on its manpower and resources.

Sarmiento became president. Towards the end of the Paraguayan War, Sarmiento was elected president of Argentina. He had done no active campaigning. In fact, at the time of the election he was out of the country, returning from the United States. When asked for a political program, Sarmiento had said: "My program is in twenty years of life, actions, and writings." He owed his election to support from landholders and middle-class citizens who wanted an end to the war.

Argentina entered a period of economic expansion and modernization. Sarmiento served as president for a term of six years (1868–1874). During his presidency the country continued to face difficult problems, including widespread poverty, yellow fever epidemics,

and Indian revolts in the interior. But Sarmiento's driving energy accomplished many things. When he took office, there were only 30,000 children in school throughout Argentina. By the end of his presidency more than three times as many were attending school. Sarmiento also founded colleges of science, mining, and agriculture and for training teachers.

President Sarmiento also built railroads into the pampa and encouraged European immigrants to settle on farms in that region. As the plains were fenced in with barbed wire, tenant farmers of Italian descent raised wheat and corn on land where wild cattle had once roamed. Towns began to grow up on the pampa, each one with a school. Telegraph lines speeded communication, and hospitals and public libraries were built. Trade, both foreign and domestic, was expanded, and the port of Buenos Aires was modernized. Many immigrants settled in Buenos Aires and other cities, and helped to expand the middle class.

An evaluation of Sarmiento is difficult. After his presidency, Sarmiento served as a senator and then as minister of education in Buenos Aires. Despite his accomplishments, he was a controversial figure. Many Argentines resented his too forceful methods and his lack of patience with the people. Sarmiento was vain and self-righteous and seldom willing to compromise. In spite of his respect for the "rule of law," he often acted high-handedly, using the very tactics for which he condemned the *caudillos*. There is no doubt, however, that Sarmiento was responsible for countless improvements in Argentine life.

Economic progress continued. In the years after Sarmiento the Argentine economy continued to develop. The introduction of refrigeration in packing plants and ships revolutionized the beef-cattle industry in the 1880's. Now refrigerated meat could be shipped to England, which soon became Argentina's best customer. The livestock industry expanded tremendously, profits soared, and cattlemen grew wealthy.

Indian life was destroyed. As in the United States, expansion into the frontier regions in Argentina came at the expense of native people. For years unconquered Indians had fiercely resisted white settlement in southern Argentina. In 1879–1880 a military expedition was sent into the southern pampa with orders to wipe out Indian resistance. The Argentine troops destroyed Indian villages, killed many of the people, and captured others. Some of the survivors were confined on a reservation. A number of young Indians were sent to Buenos Aires, where they became indentured servants. This "War of the Desert," as it was called, eliminated Indian power on the Argentine frontier.

CHILE

Chile in the 1830's provided an example of still another "strong man" type—a businessman who became a dictator.

Chile prospered. Chile enjoyed greater prosperity and more stable government than most Latin American countries in the nineteenth century. The struggle for independence had caused less disruption in Chile than in many other countries. Wealthy Chilean landowners soon took charge of the government and saw to it that the new nation was run efficiently. The Araucanian Indians were subdued and forced to live on reservations in the south. Natural resources, especially minerals, contributed to Chile's prosperity. But agriculture was backward. In fact, food had to be imported to feed the Chilean population.

Portales ruled from "behind the scenes." In the years following independence both liberal and conservative political parties developed in Chile. The conservatives won power in 1830, and Diego Portales (por-*tah′* layss) emerged as the conservative "strong man." Portales came from a well-to-do creole family in Santiago. After studying law, he went into business and quickly prospered. In politics too he was rapidly successful but preferred to work behind the scenes. Portales never held the office of president. While serving in various positions in the presidential cabinet, he carefully and thoroughly drew all power into his hands. As dictator of Chile, Portales silenced the opposition. He believed in complete centralization of authority and had only contempt for liberal principles and democracy. The haughty Portales was not popular, but he cared little for the common man. "The people," said Portales, "must be given both bread and blows."

Portales promoted economic development. Portales was, however, able and honest. And he was ambitious for Chile. Many of his policies were designed to increase Chilean prosperity. He encouraged foreign investment in the mines of the northern deserts, which yielded gold, copper, and valuable nitrates. Also, he improved the harbor of Valparaiso and in other ways promoted trade. The majority of Chileans did not benefit directly from these policies, but the great landholders and businessmen did. They and the high army officers gave Portales their full support.

Portales was also ambitious for Chile to expand, especially at the expense of Peru, since that country competed with Chile for trade on South America's west coast. When Peru and Bolivia joined in a federation in 1836, Portales started a war against Peru. Chile won the war and succeeded in breaking up the Peru-Bolivia Confederation. But two years before the war ended in 1839, Portales was assassinated by a revolutionist. Portales' supporters maintained control of Chile, however, and continued his policies for some years afterward.

THINKING ABOUT THIS SECTION

1. Explain or define the following words: *gauchos; porteños; unitarios.*

2. Why did the *gauchos* and the *porteños* not see eye to eye? What type of national government did each favor? Why?

3. How did Rosas come to power? What led to his downfall? What part did he play in Argentina's unification?

4. What were Sarmiento's goals for his country? What did he achieve? What difficulties did he have to deal with?

5. What kind of government was established in Chile after independence? What were Portales' goals for the nation? How was he different from rulers like Juárez and Sarmiento?

6. After reading about the strong men who rose to power in various Latin American countries, what are your conclusions about why they came to power? How well did they serve their countries?

Summing Up

All of the Latin American nations were beset with problems as they started out on the path of independence. Government was the most bewildering problem. The great majority of people were illiterate and had no idea of what was involved in self-government. Well-to-do creoles, though themselves lacking in political experience, generally became the ruling class in each country. As different factions battled for control, *caudillos* backed by military force often took power into their own hands and imposed their will on entire countries. Though many *caudillos* called themselves federalists as opposed to centralists, a *caudillo* who gained control of a national government would centralize authority in his own hands.

Some *caudillos,* like Santa Anna, were little more than selfish rascals. But even thoughtful leaders who believed in constitutional government often felt obliged to assume powers that were not legally theirs. Notable examples of this type of leader were Juárez and Sarmiento. A happy example of personal rule was that of Pedro II of Brazil, who was generous to his subjects and took a deep interest in his country's welfare.

Poverty continued to be an enormous problem throughout Latin America. Unscrupulous *caudillos* raided national treasuries, leaving little money for programs of economic development. Some leaders, such as Díaz in Mexico and Portales in Chile, attacked the economic problem by inviting foreign businessmen to invest in their countries. But foreign investment benefited only a few Latin Americans. In some areas it actually worsened conditions for the great mass of poor people.

Brazil, Argentina, and Chile were better off than their neighbors during the nineteenth century. In these three countries immigrants from Europe helped form a middle class, and some modernization of farming, mining, and transportation systems was accomplished. But in these countries, as in the rest of Latin America, serious problems remained unsolved.

Mexico's rural people still face a hard life, but for those like the family above, the outlook is brighter than it was for the peasants of the early 1900's. This family lives in the village of Tamápaz (state of San Luis Potosí), about 200 miles north of Mexico City. The husband makes a living buying and selling livestock, and is also the only policeman in Tamápaz.

The Latin American Nations: Mexico

CHAPTER FOCUS

1. Mexico's Natural Setting
2. The Grass-roots Revolution, 1910–1920
3. Presidents of Mexico Since 1920
4. City Life and the New Prosperity
5. The Problems of Rural Mexico
6. Education and the Arts in Modern Mexico

The following story was told about Lázaro Cárdenas, president of Mexico in the 1930's:

One morning while dispatching business in the capital, his secretary laid a list of urgent matters, and a telegram, before him. The list said: *Bank reserves dangerously low.* "Tell the Treasurer," said Cárdenas.

Agricultural production failing. "Tell the Minister of Agriculture."

Railways bankrupt. "Tell the Minister of Communications."

Serious message from Washington. "Tell Foreign Affairs."

Then he opened the telegram, which read: "My corn is dried up, my burro died, my sow was stolen, my baby is sick. Signed, Pedro Juan, village of Huitzlipituzco."

"Order the presidential train at once," said Cárdenas. "I am leaving for Huitzlipituzco." [1]

[1] Anita Brenner, *The Wind That Swept Mexico* (New York: Harper, 1943), p. 85.

169

What a change from the days of Porfirio Díaz! That president regarded the peasants of Mexico with contempt if he ever thought about them at all. But Cárdenas had a very different outlook. Even though this story about Cárdenas may have been just an affectionate joke, it suggests the deep concern he felt for the long-suffering peasants of Mexico.

After Díaz was overthrown in 1910, Mexico went through a period of upheaval much like the troubles that had plagued the country in the years after independence. But this upheaval was different. After a decade of turmoil reforms began to get under way in an orderly manner. Moreover, greater attention was paid to the wretched lot of the peasants.

Mexico para los Mexicanos!—"Mexico for the Mexicans!"—expresses the spirit that took hold as Mexico and its people began to work out their problems. This chapter will describe the progress that Mexicans have made toward this goal.

1. Mexico's Natural Setting

Mexico has been called a "miniature continent." The great variety in scenery and climate make it a fascinating country to visit. But some of Mexico's geographical features have made life difficult for the people who live there.

Mexico has three climates. Much of Mexico lies within the tropics and therefore is much closer to the equator than the United States. Usually, the nearer a country lies to the equator, the less its average temperatures will vary. But this is true only if the land is fairly level. When a country has many "ups and downs," as does Mexico, there are great variations in climate.

Mexico's coastal lowlands on both the Caribbean and the Pacific are called *tierra caliente* (*tyeh'* rah kahl-*yen'* tay), or "hot land." Along the Caribbean coast this is a region of heavy rainfall, large trees, and thick vegetation. In fact, much of it can be called jungle. Most of Mexico's Pacific coast is also *tierra caliente*. But north of the Tropic of Cancer this coast has too little rainfall for jungle growth. In fact, the peninsula of Lower California, lying across the Gulf of California from mainland Mexico, is desert.

Much of the heartland of Mexico is a great plateau, which broadens as it reaches north toward Texas. A large part of this plateau lies from 3000 to 6000 feet above sea level. Because of this altitude, the air is cool, even though much of the area is within the tropical zone. The Mexicans call this climate *tierra templada* (tem-*plah'* dah), or "temperate land." Climbing higher into the mountains, one reaches *tierra fría* (*free'* ah), "cold land," where the weather is chilly all year round. Since *tierra templada* is the most comfortable of the three climate zones, that is where the majority of Mexicans have always lived.

Mexico is crossed by mountain ranges. The mountains that seem to dominate Mexico are part of the great range, or *cordillera* (cor-dee-*yay'* rah), which extends from Alaska to the southern tip of South America. In Mexico these mountains form the broad Sierra Madre range. This separates into two ridges, one eastern and one western. South of Oaxaca the two ridges come together in the narrow neck of land called the Isthmus of Tehuantepec (teh-*wan'* teh-pek). The hills are low in this part of Mexico. But the *cordillera* becomes higher as the isthmus widens and continues into Guatemala.

Volcanoes have made rich soil in the central valley. Some of the mountains in the valley of Mexico, where the capital city is located, are volcanic. Two famous volcanic peaks have names given them long ago by the Indians.

Mount Popocatepetl (poh-*poh′* kah-*tay′* petl) has a perfect snow-capped cone, and Mount Ixtaccihuatl (*ees′* tahk-*see′* wah-tl) is a long ridge of snow nicknamed "the sleeping woman." The threat of volcanic eruption has always made life a little uncertain for the people living in this valley. But ash and lava from the volcanoes have made the soil fertile. The central valley is one of the most productive farming regions in Mexico.

Mexico has little good farming land. Water has always been a problem for the Mexican people. In a large part of the northern plateau rainfall is too scanty for good farming. Also, the northern end of the Yucatán peninsula is semidesert. On the other hand, farther south in Yucatán are thick rain forests. Here the steaming heat and swarming mosquitoes are almost intolerable. Moreover, the heavy rain washes away minerals from the ground surface, leaving the soil unfertile. Obviously much of Mexico's land is too dry or too wet for good farming. Also, extensive areas are too steep. Soil experts have estimated that only 14 per cent of Mexico's land can be used for agriculture. But in recent years the government has increased farm acreage by irrigating thirsty lands.

Natural barriers make transportation difficult. Geographical factors have also hampered transportation and communication in Mexico. The high mountain barriers have tended to isolate people and make the building of roads and railroads difficult. Moreover, there are few navigable rivers. On the west coast, rivers run swiftly from the mountains to the Pacific during the rainy season from May to September. But they dry to rivulets in the rainless months from September to May. Nor does Mexico have many deep-sea harbors. Despite the country's long coastlines on both the Pacific and Caribbean, Veracruz is really the only good port.

Mexico has rich mineral deposits. For the people who have had to make their living from the soil, Mexico has been a very poor country.

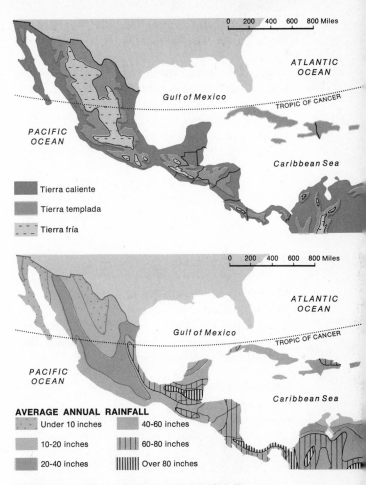

Tierra caliente

Tierra templada

Tierra fría

AVERAGE ANNUAL RAINFALL

Under 10 inches — 40-60 inches

10-20 inches — 60-80 inches

20-40 inches — Over 80 inches

Middle America — Climate and Rainfall

Note in the top map the regions of different climate. The bottom map shows the average yearly rainfall in different parts of Middle America. Seasonal variations in rainfall are also important. In some areas nearly all of the year's rainfall may come within a few summer months. Almost no part of Mexico has adequate rainfall through all seasons of the year.

But in mineral resources Mexico is rich. Though its silver mines have been worked for centuries, Mexico is still one of the world's leading producers of silver. There are also good deposits of copper, lead, zinc, and iron. Mexico's oil industry has grown as geologists continue to find new oil reserves. Industry has also steadily expanded.

171

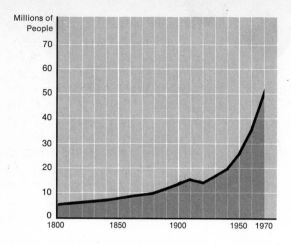

Millions of People

Mexico's Population, 1800–1970

lived in clusters of small rural communities. Often the people of the tiny villages had little or no contact with people of other areas. Now that transportation systems have improved, this situation is changing. Since the 1900's, moreover, there has been a drift from the countryside to the cities. In recent years the rapid growth of population has speeded up this movement. By 1940, Mexico's population was 20 million; ten years later it had reached 26 million; and now it has passed the 50-million mark. This spectacular increase poses a problem. Even with new irrigation projects, can Mexico's limited farmland provide enough food for a rapidly growing population?

Agriculture remains important. Despite the importance of mining and industry, most Mexicans still make their living from farming. Since ancient times, corn and beans have been the staple foods of the people of Mexico. Other grains, cotton, sugar cane, coffee, and fruits are important commercial crops. Cattle and sheep are raised on the dry northern plateau.

People are moving from rural regions to the cities as the population increases. For centuries the majority of the Mexican people have

THINKING ABOUT THIS SECTION

1. Explain or define the following words: *tierra caliente; tierra templada; tierra fría.*
2. How have geographical conditions affected Mexico's climate? agriculture? transportation? (In answering, make use of the maps on pages 7 and 171.)
3. What problems are created by Mexico's rapid increase in population?
4. Why are mining and industry important in Mexico's economy? What changes in patterns of living are related to the country's industrial expansion?

2. The Grass-roots Revolution, 1910–1920

Mexico today is one of the most dynamic countries in Latin America. Well-planned programs have overcome obstacles and improved the quality of life for many Mexicans. And the effort is a continuing one. Mexico's tragic history during the 1800's makes this achievement all the more striking. How could things change so much? The key lies in the Mexican Revolution of 1910–1920, called by one historian "the wind that swept Mexico." More than any other revolutionary movement in Latin Amer-

ica, the Mexican Revolution brought about major changes for the better.

Reform-minded Mexicans opposed Díaz. By 1910, Porfirio Díaz had ruled Mexico for more than 30 years. Foreign investors, large landowners, and Díaz's personal friends had prospered during this period. But the lot of the poor was miserable. Indian and mestizo farmers lost their lands and were reduced to peons. Workers received tiny wages for hard labor, and efforts to improve their situation were ruthlessly suppressed.

To many Mexicans who hoped for reform, the problem of land ownership seemed to be of crucial importance. Fewer than three thousand families owned nearly half of Mexico. Over 90 per cent of the ten million Mexican farmers owned *no* land. Reformers thought the land should be divided into small plots and sold to farm workers on easy-payment plans.

Reformers also criticized the foreign ownership of factories, oil wells, and mines. They wanted the Mexican government to take over the industries owned by foreign companies. They believed that industrial workers should get better pay and be allowed to form unions. Still other goals of liberal reformers were to reduce the power of the army and the Catholic Church and to provide free education for all children. In particular, they wanted to take education out of the hands of the Church and make it the government's responsibility.

Madero touched off the Revolution. Mexicans interested in reform became convinced that change was impossible as long as Díaz ruled the country. But the reformers had no well-organized plan for getting rid of him. In fact, the Revolution started in a haphazard way. In 1908, Díaz had startled everyone when, in an interview with a North American magazine writer, he said that perhaps Mexico needed an opposition political party. This was exciting news for Mexican liberals. They wondered if Díaz was thinking about retiring. One daring liberal named Francisco Madero (mah-*day'* roh) even announced that he would run for the presidency in 1910. No candidate had opposed Porfirio Díaz in a presidential election since 1888.

But, shortly before the election was held, Díaz threw Madero into jail. After the election, Díaz announced the results. To no one's surprise, he himself won millions of votes while Madero received only 196. Madero was released from jail, and Díaz began his eighth term as "elected" president.

Madero was a small and apparently mild man. But he was also stubborn. From Texas, where he had gone to live in exile, Madero issued a manifesto called the "Plan of San Luis Potosí." In this document he claimed that the election had not been fair, demanded Díaz's resignation, and urged the Mexican people to rebel. Responding to this call for revolution, guerrilla bands sprang up all over northern Mexico. Madero's popularity grew rapidly, and in May, 1911, the people of Mexico City forced President Díaz to resign. The ex-dictator fled to Veracruz, where he boarded a ship for France.

Madero's government was ineffective. Madero, now a popular hero, entered Mexico City in June and received a warm welcome from the people. Soon he was elected president of Mexico. The people sang:

No más trabajo, y mucho dinero,
Frijoles para todos, Viva Madero!

(No more work, and lots of money,
Beans for everybody, long live Madero!)

But Madero's government lasted only a little more than a year. A weak leader, he was unable to cope with conflicting demands from various groups. All the reform leaders had wanted to get rid of Díaz. But once the dictator was gone, they fought among themselves.

Civil war resulted. The years 1911–1920 were an especially unhappy period in Mexican history. The country became a bloody battlefield as men left their villages to join the forces of one leader or another. Women and children tried to harvest the corn by themselves or followed the rebel bands that their men had joined. From the scattered guerrilla groups, competing revolutionary armies were formed. Hundreds of thousands of people died as civil war raged.

Huerta overthrew Madero. Many of the revolutionary leaders despised Madero's weakness, and they turned against him. Felix Díaz, a

Emiliano Zapata (top) became a legendary hero among Mexican peasants. Above are pictured a few of the many women who took an active part in the revolution.

nephew of the ousted dictator, gained control of the army. In desperation Madero ordered a general, Victoriano Huerta (*hwair'* tah), to put down the rebellious army. In February, 1913, Mexico City suffered what came to be known as the "Tragic Ten Days" of fighting. The forces of Díaz and Huerta fought each other in the streets, but many more civilians than soldiers were slaughtered. Finally, Huerta betrayed Madero by joining forces with Felix Díaz. Huerta declared himself president and ordered Madero taken into "protective custody." Madero was then murdered by prison guards.

Other revolutionary leaders forced out Huerta. Huerta's corrupt rule was a throwback to the days of Porfirio Díaz. Before long, other leaders agreed that Huerta must go. Several important revolutionary figures emerged during this period. The strongest was Venustiano Carranza (kah-*rahn'* zah). His most loyal supporter was Alvaro Obregón (oh-bray-*gohn'*), a *caudillo* from the state of Sonora. Two other famous revolutionists took little part in later constitutional development in Mexico. But they became folk heroes to the Mexican people and to people of Mexican descent in the United States Southwest. Their names were Emiliano Zapata (sah-*pah'* tah) and Pancho Villa (*vee'* yah).

Emiliano Zapata. When Zapata was a boy in the state of Morelos, the lands of his village had been seized by one of Díaz's friends. During the revolutionary period Zapata became a popular leader and formed an army of landless peasants. With the slogan *Tierra y libertad!* ("Land and liberty!"), he called for land to be returned to the peasants.

In the white cotton clothing of a peon, wearing a white sombrero and riding a white horse, Zapata fought at the head of his guerrilla forces. They burnt haciendas, murdered landlords, and farmed the lands they seized. At least they were not cruel just for the sake of cruelty. When Zapata's men entered Mexico City, the townspeople feared they would all be murdered. But Zapata's "boys" simply wandered around and humbly asked housewives for tortillas.

Of all the leaders in the Mexican Revolution, Zapata was the least ambitious. He never tried to declare himself president. When other political leaders promised to carry out land reforms, he retired to Morelos. But his spirit caught the imagination of rural Mexicans, and his ideas had to be adopted by any leader who sought popular support. Betrayed by Carranza, Zapata was assassinated in 1919. The people of Morelos insisted that his restless ghost still rode a white horse in the mountains at night.

Pancho Villa. An equally dramatic leader was Francisco ("Pancho") Villa, called by some the Robin Hood of the northern cattle country. Villa was a poor cattle herder in the state of Durango. After attacking a ranch foreman, he had escaped into the hills. There Villa became head of a band of cattle thieves. In support of Madero, Villa gathered together an army of thousands of cowboys and outlaws. When Madero was killed, Villa kept his army intact and soon began quarreling with other revolutionary leaders.

Accusing the United States of intervening in Mexican affairs, Villa crossed the border with a band of guerrillas and "shot up" the town of Columbus, New Mexico, killing nineteen people. United States cavalry pursued Villa, but he skillfully eluded them in the cactus and sagebrush land of northern Mexico. In 1920 leaders in the Mexican government talked Villa into "retiring" by offering him an hacienda in Durango. Three years later he was murdered in a private quarrel.

A new constitution was adopted. Meanwhile, Carranza had taken Mexico City and ousted Huerta. Carranza proved to be a cautious president. In 1917 he was pressured into calling together a constitutional convention. The constitution adopted by this convention proved to be one of the most significant documents in Latin American history. It contained the usual liberal provisions found in many Latin American constitutions: representative government, a president ineligible for re-election, and a legislature made up of two houses. But the Mexican constitution also called for a number of far-reaching reforms.

Sweeping changes were written into the new constitution. Article 27 of the constitution struck at foreign ownership of Mexican oil wells and mines. This article was based on the old Spanish tradition that all mineral rights belonged to the king. The constitution declared that the Mexican government had inherited the Spanish king's ownership of mineral resources. Therefore, foreign companies that exploited Mexican resources would have to obey the regulations of Mexico's government. For example, they would have to pay fair taxes and hire Mexican workers at decent wages. Another article of the constitution allowed the Mexican president to take over mines and oil wells if the government's regulations were violated. Clearly the days of Porfirio Díaz, friend of foreign businessmen, were over.

Complete separation of Church and state was called for in other articles of the constitution. Schools were to be run by the government rather than by the Catholic Church. The Church could not own land, make money in business, or take part in politics.

The constitution also established certain rights for workers. These included an eight-hour day, a minimum wage[2], and the right to join unions and to strike. Child labor was outlawed. Any laborer hurt in an accident on his job was to receive compensation.

Finally, the constitution called for agrarian reform. This reform provided that large haciendas be broken up into small plots for distribution to landless peasants. The landholders whose property was taken were to be paid by the government.

The constitution provided a blueprint for future action. The history of Mexico after 1917 is the story of how the provisions of the new constitution were put into effect. The changes it called for were so drastic that they could not

[2] A minimum wage is the lowest wage that an employer may legally pay a worker.

possibly have been accomplished overnight. Moreover, various presidents interpreted the constitution differently. Some took a greater interest than others in carrying out its provisions. A few presidents wanted to make changes rapidly, while others preferred to move slowly. And certain presidents emphasized one goal in particular, such as agrarian reform. The problems dealt with in the constitution have not yet been completely solved.

Carranza was forced out of power. Carranza was the first president to serve under the new constitution. He had little interest in bringing about the changes called for. Hardly anything was done about land distribution, and trade unions were suppressed. Moreover, the government became increasingly corrupt. As Carranza's power dwindled, Obregón became his chief rival. A popular figure, Obregón had fought in the guerrilla clashes in the north, losing his right arm as a result. He was supported by a new union organization, the Regional Confederation of Mexican Labor. This was

called CROM from its Spanish initials. With the support of the army, Obregón ousted Carranza in 1920 and took over the government. Carranza tried to escape into the mountains but was captured and killed.

THINKING ABOUT THIS SECTION

1. Explain or define the following words: Plan of San Luis Potosí; *Tierra y libertad;* agrarian reform; CROM.

2. What were the major goals urged by Mexican reformers during the early 1900's? Explain the importance of each of these goals.

3. Why were the years from 1911 to 1920 a tragic period in Mexico's history?

4. Who were the leading personalities of the revolutionary period? How did they differ in their methods and in their goals? To what extent was each successful?

5. What major reforms were called for in the constitution adopted in 1917? Why were all its provisions not carried out at once?

3. Presidents of Mexico Since 1920

Obregón brought about some reforms. Alvaro Obregón was as much a dictator as earlier Mexican presidents. But he was an able leader and made a start at carrying out some of the reforms promised by the constitution. Most notable was progress made in public education, with the building of many new elementary schools. Also, Obregón's support of CROM led to higher wages and better working conditions for Mexican laborers. During Obregón's term of office three million acres of land were distributed. But this was only a tiny fraction of the acreage held by the great landholders. Some peasants created their own "land reform." They banded together and attacked and occupied large haciendas. Then they farmed the land for their own use.

Obregón managed to stabilize Mexico's relations with the United States. After 1917, officials in Washington had feared that United States-owned companies would lose their Mexican mines and oil wells. But after Obregón made promises of "good will and fair-mindedness," the United States recognized his government. That is, it acknowledged Obregón's government as the legal government of Mexico.

Calles continued reform programs. Since Obregón was not eligible for re-election in 1924, he arranged to have one of his supporters elected to the presidency that year. President Plutarco Elias Calles (*kahl'* yayss) generally followed the course set by Obregón, but he speeded up agrarian reform. During his presidency eight million acres were distributed to more than 1500 villages. Progress was also made in education and public health.

Catholics protested restrictions on the Church.

Relations between Church and government became the major problem of Calles' presidency. Powerful Catholic churchmen had opposed the constitution's restrictions on the Church. Calles was the first president really to enforce these restrictions. Besides closing Church-run schools and many churches, Calles set a limit on the number of priests. In protest, the Church "went on strike." Priests refused to say Mass or perform marriages, baptisms, and burial services. In some states Church officials and devout Mexicans organized guerrilla bands. One rebel group was called the *Cristeros* because of its battle cry *Viva Cristo Rey!* ("Long Live Christ the King!"). The *Cristeros* burned government schools and murdered teachers. Calles' armies retaliated with attacks on Catholics. This bloody conflict continued into the 1930's.

After Obregón's death, Calles continued in power.

As the 1928 election approached, Calles and Obregón had the law changed to allow a former president to serve a second term. This cleared the way for Obregón to return to the presidency. But just two weeks after he won the election, Obregón was assassinated.

Calles could not succeed himself as president. But from 1928 to 1934, he was the "power behind the throne" while three puppet presidents held office. Meanwhile, Calles held an important position in the National Revolutionary Party (PNR), Mexico's only effective political party. During these years Calles became more conservative. Land distribution almost came to an end, and, since Calles did not support CROM, labor made no progress. Hopes for democracy faded. Some leaders within the PNR grew impatient and came to oppose Calles.

Cárdenas put new spirit into the Revolution.

To satisfy reformers, Calles picked a liberal, Lázaro Cárdenas (*kar'* day-nahss), to run for president in 1934. But Cárdenas had no intention of becoming another puppet. Once in office, he made clear his hope of reviving the Revolution. In a test of strength between Calles and Cárdenas, the latter won. Cárdenas had the ex-dictator sent into exile in the United States.

Lázaro Cárdenas was a mestizo who in 1913, at the age of eighteen, had joined the revolutionary forces. Within seven years he had risen to the rank of general. Cárdenas was dedicated to Zapata's ideal of land for the peasants. After becoming governor of the state of Michoacán, he broke up a number of large estates and distributed the land to peons. He completely won the hearts of the poor Indians. When Cárdenas ran for president, city people sneeringly said, "He smells of *petate*." (*Petates* are straw sleeping mats used by rural Indians and mestizos.) Since half the population slept on *petates*, this gibe only made him more popular.

Land distribution was stepped up.

As president, Cárdenas traveled to country villages to see conditions for himself. His willingness to listen to the complaints of the poorest peons gave rise to the anecdote told at the beginning of this chapter. During his administration, 47 million acres of land were distributed to 12,000 villages. This was more land than had been distributed during all the previous administrations. Cárdenas' government also started rural schools and taught the peasants better farming methods. Government projects brought piped water into remote villages.

Cárdenas favored a community system of landholding, in which the people of a village held the land in common. On the *ejido* (ay-hee' doh), or co-operative farm, the villagers worked the land together and divided the crops or the profits from selling the crops. The government set up a National Bank of Ejidal Credit. From this bank an *ejido* could borrow money for seed, farm machinery, or an irrigation project. By the time Cárdenas left office, more than half of the Mexican people were members of *ejidos*.

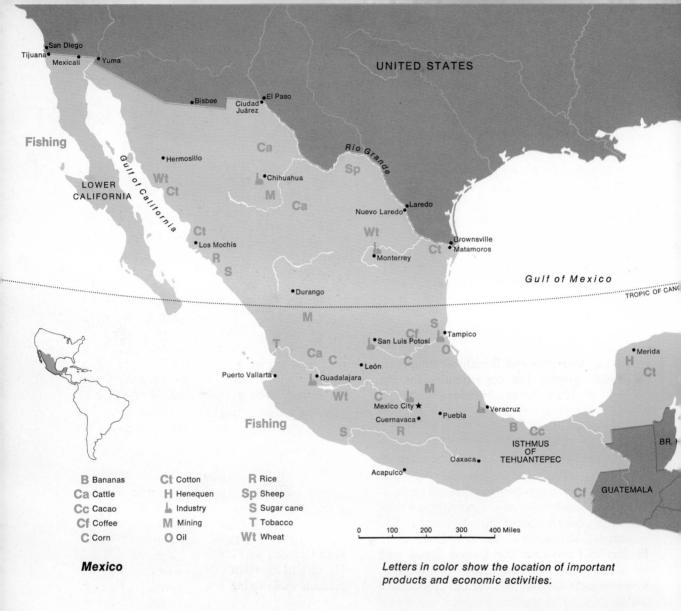

Mexico

B   Bananas
Ca Cattle
Cc Cacao
Cf Coffee
C   Corn
Ct Cotton
H   Henequen
    Industry
M   Mining
O   Oil
R   Rice
Sp Sheep
S   Sugar cane
T   Tobacco
Wt Wheat

0   100   200   300   400 Miles

Letters in color show the location of important products and economic activities.

A few *ejidos* became model farms, but they were the exception. Not all of the *ejidos* were efficiently managed, and some were exploited for personal gain by local politicians. As a result, the *ejido* program remained controversial. Moreover, production was disappointing. Mexico continued to import food, even though two-thirds of its people worked in agriculture.

Cárdenas nationalized the oil industry. Cárdenas' most dramatic action was the take-over of Mexico's oil resources. Oil workers had

formed a union and demanded higher pay and better working conditions. When the foreign-owned oil companies refused to meet these demands, Cárdenas appointed an arbitration board to settle the dispute. After examining the financial records of the companies, the board ordered a pay raise. But the companies fought this decision. Finally, Cárdenas took over or *expropriated* the oil fields. Expropriation meant that the oil wells and refineries now belonged to the Mexican government. The government, however, intended to pay the companies for the property. The day that Cárdenas nationalized the oil wells—March 18, 1938—is still celebrated in Mexico as Expropriation Day.

The North American oil companies hoped that the United States government would pressure Cárdenas into returning the oil property. But President Franklin D. Roosevelt refused to interfere. In a final settlement the Mexican government agreed to pay the oil companies 24 million dollars. Within ten years the entire sum was paid.

Cárdenas created a government agency to run the oil fields. Its petroleum products are sold under the brand name *Pemex*. Pemex is the only gasoline sold in Mexico. Gradually, as young Mexicans were trained to become technicians and managers, Pemex no longer needed to hire foreigners. The Mexican example led American and British oil companies to provide greater job opportunities for the citizens of other Latin American countries where the companies had operations.

Avila Camacho stressed closer relations with the United States. Under Cárdenas' successor, Manuel Avila Camacho (*ah'* vee-lah kah-*mah'* choh), Mexico entered World War II on the side of the United States. Some Mexicans were surprised to find themselves an ally of their old enemy. Mexico sent an air squadron to the Pacific, and provided the United States with valuable raw materials needed to fight the war. The United States and Mexico also co-operated in building a highway to speed the movement of supplies. This road later became part of the Pan American Highway system. During the war years thousands of Mexican farm laborers crossed the border to harvest crops in the United States.

Avila Camacho was much more conservative than Cárdenas. During his presidency (1940–1946) the bitterness between the government and religious leaders disappeared. One achievement of his term was the launching of a nationwide campaign to teach illiterate adults to read and write (page 186).

Alemán promoted industry. Miguel Alemán (ah-lay-*mahn'*), president of Mexico from 1946 to 1952, stressed modernization and industrialization. During his term many large-scale construction projects were started—bridges, highways, irrigation systems, flood-control plans, and universities. Alemán brought in new industries, including automobile assembly plants and textile and plastics factories. His irrigation projects were controlled by great dams that produced hydroelectric power. Alemán also encouraged tourism and investment. But foreign investors were subject to Mexican law.

In agriculture Alemán favored private ownership of farmland over the *ejido*. During his presidency the program of land distribution came to a halt. This president was often criticized for favoring industry over agriculture at the expense of both workers and peasants. While the rich grew richer and dazzling new buildings sprang up in Mexico City, the peon continued his struggle with poverty. Towards the end of Alemán's term, moreover, it became clear that corruption and graft had seeped throughout his administration.

Quiet progress was made under Ruiz Cortines. In 1952 the leaders of Mexico's only effective political party (now called the PRI) chose Adolfo Ruiz Cortines (roo-*eess'* kor-*tee'* nehss) to run for president. A quiet, moderate man, Ruiz Cortines won office in a peaceful election. He carried on Alemán's goal of industrial expansion while trying also to balance the budget and rid the government of corruption. Industry continued to prosper. To modernize agriculture, the government encouraged the use of fertilizers, machinery, and crop rotation. Land distribution went on for some villages.

A notable advance during Ruiz Cortines' term in office was the granting of full citizenship rights to Mexican women. In 1958, for the first time in Mexican history, women were able to vote in the presidential election.

New problems arose during the 1950's with the rapid growth of cities. Both jobs and housing were scarce for the country people who flocked to urban areas. Workers became restless as wages failed to keep up with the rising cost of living. Many of these problems were tackled by the able Secretary of Labor, Adolfo López Mateos (*loh′ pehss mah-tay′ ohss*).

López Mateos gave new emphasis to the problems of labor. In 1958 López Mateos became president. He made clear his views on the country's needs in a statement made at the time of his inauguration: "Mexico must create national wealth from capital, outside capital if necessary, to make jobs for an additional one million Mexicans a year. The human factors involved, that is, whether the worker gets enough to eat and whether his malaria is cured, are the responsibilities of modern capitalism."

By this time the plight of the peons who had left the land and moved to the cities had become a critical problem. Around Mexico City slums mushroomed, making the area of the city twice as big as in 1900. These jobless city dwellers lived in wretched poverty.

To create more jobs for Mexican labor, López Mateos vigorously promoted the expansion of industry. United States automobile manufacturers built assembly plants in Mexico and hired thousands of local workers. Mexican steel mills made many of the automobile parts, which before had been imported from the United States. A growing number of Mexicans could afford to buy these Mexican-made cars. As the demand for Pemex products doubled, more workers were hired in the oil fields and refineries. Various other industries grew up, including electrical-appliance factories, fruit canneries, and food-freezing plants. López Mateos also successfully settled many labor disputes between workers and management. When his term as president ended in 1964, he could say: "Mexico is becoming a modern industrial nation."

Prosperity continued under Díaz Ordaz. On that note of optimism Mexico in 1964 elected its next president, Gustavo Díaz Ordaz (*dee′ ahss or-dahss′*), the son of a post-office worker. During his presidency Mexico continued on a course of dynamic economic growth. At the close of Díaz's term in office, the *New York Times* said of Mexico: "From poverty near the level of the poorest Asian countries in 1930, . . . this country has accomplished one of the most successful development programs among developing countries." A major factor in this achievement was Mexico's political stability. Though there still was no effective two-party system, opposition parties were at least permitted to carry on political activity. Elections, moreover, were much more peaceful than in the old days.

Student unrest built up. But in the 1960's Mexico's political system began to be questioned. There was a growing feeling, especially among students and intellectuals, that political reform was necessary. The students demanded a greater voice in university affairs and a freer political atmosphere. They also charged the police with using brutal methods in breaking up campus protests. In 1968 anti-government demonstrations at two universities erupted into full-scale battles between armed students and troops. Many people were injured or killed. More than a hundred students, professors, and left-wing activists were jailed.

Relations with the United States are cordial. In recent years Mexico has shown increased self-confidence in its foreign policy. For example, it has disagreed with its powerful northern neighbor on such issues as Cuba under Castro. But relations between Mexico and the United States are friendly. Presidents of the two countries have met on a number of occasions, and the two governments have agreed to several treaties which settled old problems. These peaceful agreements concerned such things as fishing rights in offshore areas, the use of water in certain rivers, and boundary disputes.

Tall buildings, car-filled streets, and park-like plazas are typical of modern Mexico City (above). Mexico's urban middle class now enjoys greater opportunities as the result of industrial expansion. Right, this skilled technician works in the Mexican plant of a United States record manufacturer.

Echeverría Alvarez took office. In 1970 Mexico's official political party chose as its presidential candidate Luis Echeverría Alvarez, a member of the presidential cabinet in the previous administration. As expected, Echeverría (ay-chay-veh-*ree'* ah) won easily, since opposition parties still offer no threat in national elections. The new president promised that the welfare of rural people would be of major concern during his administration. In his inaugural address Echeverría said that the Mexican Revolution would "continue in force until the very poorest have attained an adequate standard of living."

THINKING ABOUT THIS SECTION

1. Explain or define the following words: *Cristeros;* PNR; *ejido.*
2. Why did Cárdenas nationalize Mexico's oil industry? What was the reaction in Mexico? in the United States? How has the industry fared since 1938?
3. Since 1920, what have Mexico's presidents done about land distribution? the promotion of industry? women's rights?
4. Describe Mexico's relations with the United States since the 1930's.

4. City Life and the New Prosperity

The expansion of urban areas is the most dramatic feature of Mexican life today. One of the great world capitals, Mexico City has a population of seven million and continues to grow. This huge city is the political, economic, and cultural center of the nation. A blend of old and new, it is changing fast.

Mexico City is a dynamic metropolis. Much evidence of Mexico City's past remains. There are suburbs with ancient Indian names like Texcoco and Xochimilco. The city's cathedral is the one which Cortés ordered built on the site of the Aztec pyramid-temple. At the Church of the Virgin of Guadalupe visitors from all parts of Mexico come to see the picture of the brown-skinned Virgin. In the older neighborhoods there is a Spanish colonial church every three or four blocks.

When city engineers started building a subway in 1968, pre-Conquest Indian pottery, building stones, and bones were unearthed. The ancient Americans had built their city on islands in lakes that covered the bowl-like valley. Though the lakes have been drained, the land is still swampy. As a result, Mexico City has been sinking several inches every year. Mexican engineers use modern methods of drainage and construction in coping with this problem. In spite of the gradual settling and the danger of earthquakes, downtown Mexico has become a cluster of skyscrapers.

Change is all around in Mexico City. Modern tourist hotels and large shopping centers are evidence of growing prosperity. Many members of the growing middle class live in houses and apartments in the suburbs that surround the city.

Slums are a problem. In stark contrast to these suburbs are the shanty towns on Mexico City's outskirts. City authorities are hard put to provide adequate electricity and drinking water for the people who stream in from the country to live in these slum communities. Few of the slum residents have had a chance to learn useful job skills, though a small number find work in the booming new factories. These people are not without hope, however. In the new Mexico it is possible for people to get ahead.

Mexico has other large cities. Mexico has a number of large modern cities. Next in size to the capital city is Guadalajara, with over a million people. About twenty other cities have more than 100,000 people each. Government-owned railroad lines connect Mexico's cities. Mexican airlines fly tourists and Mexican businessmen and government officials between the urban centers.

The tourist industry is vital to Mexican prosperity. In recent years tourism has earned more income for Mexico than all its exports combined. Acapulco, with fine beaches and scenic rocky coves, has long been a vacation spot for visitors from the United States and Europe. A newer tourist favorite is Puerto Vallarta. As late as 1963 this little fishing port had no road connection with the rest of Mexico, but now many visitors enjoy the water sports and the charms of the village. Improved roads, stable government, good drinking water, and modern motels and hotels make Mexico an attractive vacation area for the growing numbers of tourists from the United States and Europe. Newly prosperous Mexicans themselves also enjoy the beaches and other resorts.

THINKING ABOUT THIS SECTION

1. Why can Mexico City be called a city of contrasts?
2. Why have cities in Mexico experienced rapid population growth?
3. Why is tourism booming in Mexico? What effect does this have on the country?

5. The Problems of Rural Mexico

Many Mexicans still live in poverty. Mexico's impressive economic growth has chiefly benefited the middle-class and well-to-do people. Mexicans who work on the land, however, still make only a very meager living. More than a million rural families have a cash income of less than a hundred dollars a year.

More peasants now own a little land. Every president since Obregón has tried to bring about some improvement for the people of rural Mexico. Land taken from large haciendas was distributed to peasants, often in plots as small as five acres. But much of this land was poor and unproductive. To support their families, the peasant farmers had to do something else, such as weave blankets, raise goats for market, make charcoal, or work for wages on larger farms for part of the year. Recently, with government encouragement, Mexico's small farmers have begun to raise cash crops in addition to the corn and beans needed by their own families. By selling crops of sugar cane, cotton, and sisal (used in making rope), the farmers can earn a little cash income.

A mechanized farm community contrasts with a traditional farm community. By comparing two actual towns, one can see how modern ways have affected rural life in Mexico.

LOS MOCHIS

Typical of the new Mexico is the town of Los Mochis (lohss *moh'* cheess). Modern agricultural techniques have made this community prosperous. Hardly a town at all in 1950, Los Mochis today has banks, modern hospitals, and an airfield. It is the terminal of a railroad running from Chihuahua to the Pacific and of a bus line that operates on the West Coast Highway.

Los Mochis is the center of a new irrigation project using the water of the Fuerte (*fwehr'* teh) River. Formerly this river overflowed its banks in the rainy season but disappeared in the dry season. Now its waters are stored for

Mechanization has increased yield on some of Mexico's farms and plantations. Here loading machines aid workers in clearing sugar-cane fields on Mexico's Gulf coast.

use the year round. The farmers of Los Mochis send huge amounts of tomatoes, lettuce, and other vegetables to the United States. Some of this produce is shipped by air and sold at high prices in midwinter. The irrigated valley also grows high-quality cotton, which is picked by machinery. At a nearby coastal village a port is being built. When it is completed, Los Mochis cotton will be shipped directly to Japan.

The people of Los Mochis own plots of land ranging from a hundred to a thousand acres. Those who do not own land can earn up to 20 dollars a day operating tractors and harvest machinery on the larger farms. Few farm workers migrate from Los Mochis to the United States to pick crops, since they can make good money in their home town. As evidence of this, the young men ride motorcycles instead of burros.

SANTA CRUZ ETLA

More typical of Mexican farm communities is the village of Santa Cruz Etla, in Oaxaca state. Here, 30 families, with a total of some 150 people, live on hilly land along a mountain

brook. Each family owns less than five acres. If more than one son survives childhood, the oldest son inherits the land. The younger sons work in a tile factory in Oaxaca City or become road repairmen on the Pan American Highway. Some may go to Mexico City and live in the shanty towns while looking for jobs as unskilled laborers.

The sons who stay in Santa Cruz Etla grow corn and beans, plowing their small acreage with teams of oxen. At planting and harvest times men, women, and children all work in the fields. During the rest of the year the men go into the forest hills to cut firewood. This they burn slowly under green brush until it becomes charcoal. They can earn a little cash by selling the charcoal in nearby towns. But in the larger towns electricity and gas are gradually replacing charcoal as fuel. In another ten years there may be no market for charcoal.

Santa Cruz Etla gets its water from a mountain brook which runs through many cowyards. Formerly the death toll from diseases caused by impure water was very high, especially among small children. Now the people have learned to boil drinking water, and outhouses are built some distance from the brook. A deep well has been dug to supply water during the dry season.

Some other improvements have come to Santa Cruz Etla. Every child has been vaccinated against smallpox, and a state malaria control program has wiped out disease-carrying mosquitoes. By community effort, an old ox-cart trail has been improved. Now trucks can drive into the village to pick up loads of charcoal, and a bus comes once a week to take the women to Saturday market in Oaxaca City. With the money sent home by younger sons working in the city, families have replaced dirt floors with cement, and thatch roofs with tile.

The people also pay part of the salary of the teacher who holds classes in the little school. But the village still has no electricity and no hope of getting it soon.

THINKING ABOUT THIS SECTION

1. Why do many of Mexico's small farmers have an extremely low cash income? How has the government tried to improve their situation?
2. Contrast life in Los Mochis and Santa Cruz Etla. Why is the first community prosperous? Can the latter "catch up" with Los Mochis? Why?

6. Education and the Arts in Modern Mexico

EDUCATION

After the Revolution more schools were built. In the days of Porfirio Díaz rural Mexicans had little or no chance to go to school. In fact, the government discouraged education for the peasants. It was thought that ignorant people were more easily controlled. One of the goals of Zapata and other revolutionary leaders was free public education for every Mexican child. The Constitution of 1917 supported this goal, but Mexico is still trying to make it a reality.

In the 1920's President Obregón appointed a well-known educator, named José Vasconcelos (vahss-kohn-*say′* lohss), to broaden Mexico's educational system. Plans were made available so that villages could build their own schoolhouses. These plans were made up of pictures and diagrams that illiterate people could understand. Hundreds of such schools were built all over Mexico. Teams of enthusiastic young men and women traveled to remote villages to teach in the new schools.

Many children leave school at an early age. Today schools in rural Mexico offer four grades,

and about one fourth of the village schools go through the fifth or sixth grades. But the dropout rate is very high. By the time a boy is twelve years old, he is needed by his father for herding goats, plowing, or cutting firewood. Girls drop out of school even earlier. At ten or younger they can help their mothers care for babies or grind corn for tortillas.

There are schools too for the children of the rural families who have moved to city slums. But few families of rural origin can send their children to high school. Secondary schools require expensive textbooks and uniforms, all of which must be provided by the family. When a rural family moves to the city, children over the age of twelve usually look for work.

Middle-class children attend high schools. City families that can afford it send their sons, and often their daughters as well, to high schools. Some of these schools offer college preparatory courses, but there are commercial and trade schools as well. Many city families send their young people to Catholic high schools. These schools, separate for girls and boys, prepare students for the Catholic colleges.

Several institutions offer higher education.
Graduates of public and Catholic high schools may attend the National University of Mexico. This university has one of the largest and most beautiful campuses in the world. But its 70,000 students are handicapped by a shortage of teachers, laboratory facilities, and library books. Students have been demanding a voice in the running of the university. After graduation liberal-arts students may have difficulty finding good positions. There is much greater demand for graduates of technical institutes.

Adult education is encouraged. In 1944, President Avila Camacho launched a campaign against illiteracy. The "Each One Teach One" program was aimed at teaching all illiterate adults in Mexico to read. A primer was prepared with which any literate person could teach others to read and write. Its lessons dealt with farmers plowing and women cooking tortillas, activities familiar to all rural Mexicans. Every literate adult was urged to teach someone else to read and write. In some towns, adults could not buy a bus ticket unless they could prove they were either teaching someone to read or learning themselves. By 1950 some two million adults had learned to read in this campaign. After this first drive, the campaign was continued in the rural and city schools. Today Mexico has one of the highest literacy rates in Latin America.

THE ARTS

Before the Revolution of 1910 most Mexican artists imitated the work of Spanish and Italian painters. But the Revolution made many artists more conscious of their Mexican background. This changed outlook resulted in the creation of some of the New World's finest works of art.

Mexican muralists are outstanding. When José Vasconcelos was Minister of Education in the 1920's, he arranged for Mexican artists to provide large mural paintings for the walls of several government buildings. The artists who did these remarkable paintings were Diego Rivera, José Clemente Orozco, and David Siqueiros.[3]

Rivera became the best-known of these men. Working with very bright colors, he depicted the Indian heritage of Mexico. In enormous murals in the courtyard of a government building in Mexico City, Rivera showed Indian tribes in regional costumes. On the walls of the Cortés Palace in Cuernavaca, Rivera painted the story of the Aztec resistance to the Spanish conquest. Because of his Communist leanings, this artist was a controversial figure during his lifetime. Nevertheless, most Mexicans take great pride in his murals.

Today Mexican artists are turning away from purely Mexican themes to a wider range of subjects. But the government continues to commission murals for new public buildings and provides scholarships for art students.

Indian crafts also contribute to Mexico's art. José Vasconcelos once said, "We wish to make Mexico the cultural center of the Western Hemisphere as the United States is the industrial center." With this goal he encouraged a revival of the traditional Indian arts and crafts. Among the fine products of Indian craftsmanship are hand-woven wool blankets, wood carvings, leather work, lacquered plates, hand-blown blue glass pitchers, terra cotta pottery, and silver filigree. Such articles as these have made Mexico the leading center for native handicrafts in Latin America.

Other Mexican arts flourish. Other art forms as well display the creativity of modern Mexican artists. One of the New World's most distinguished composers is Carlos Chávez (*chah' vayss*), a mestizo who learned folk themes from his Indian mother. In his compositions for symphony orchestras, Chávez used these themes and other melodies that he himself recorded at Indian fiestas in remote villages.

[3] These names are pronounced as follows: Rivera (ree-*vay'* rah), Orozco (oh-*rohss'* koh), and Siqueiros (see-*kay'* rohss).

The Ballet Folklorico captures the beauty and excitement of traditional Mexican dances. Above, this dancer re-creates the Yaqui Indians' Deer Dance. Since ancient times the Yaquis have performed this dance as a ritual before their men set out on the hunt. Also pictured on this page are two scenes from the mural paintings in which Diego Rivera portrayed Mexico's Indian heritage. The two murals represented here were based on the Tarascan culture (top, right) and the Totonac (bottom, right).

Chávez founded the Mexico City Symphony and served as its conductor.

North Americans and Europeans have had a chance to hear Mexican folk music and see native dancing in the authentic performances of the touring company called the Ballet Folklorico. Motion pictures too are produced in Mexico. The Mexican film industry is the largest in Latin America. It distributes hundreds of Spanish-language films to the rest of Latin America and to communities of Spanish-speaking people in the United States.

Novelists took themes from the Revolution. The Mexican Revolution freed writers as well as artists from the domination of foreign influences. Mariano Azuela (ah-*sway'* lah) was a young Mexican doctor who led a guerrilla band in the early years of the Revolution. In 1916 he wrote a novel based on his experiences called *Los de abajo*. The novel has been translated into English with the title *The Underdogs*. More than any other work, it shows the desperation and frustration of the peons who fought in the Revolution. It is still one of the most widely read novels in the Spanish language.

Gregorio López y Fuentes (*loh'* pehss ee *fwen'* tayss) was already writing novels and newspaper pieces when at the age of 20 he was caught up in the Revolution. Perhaps López Fuentes' best-known book was *El Indio* (*The Indian*). It described the day-by-day life of Indian farming people like those who live in Santa Cruz Etla.

Martín Luis Guzmán (gooss-*mahn'*) was a young newspaperman who rode with Villa's army from the first days of the Revolution. In two books, *El águila y la serpiente* (*The Eagle and the Serpent*) and *La sombra del caudillo* (*The Shadow of the Chieftain*), he told the exciting story of Villa's campaigns.

Like modern artists, Mexican writers in more recent years have turned their attention away from the Revolution. Though they still value their heritage, they now take greater interest in Mexico as a modern nation. And, like the serious writers of all countries, they explore the problems of modern man in a complex world.

THINKING ABOUT THIS SECTION

1. What was the Mexican government's attitude toward education in the late 1800's? Why? What has it been during the last 50 years? Why?

2. Why do many children drop out of Mexico's rural schools after a few grades?

3. Why do many students attend commercial and trade schools and technical institutes?

4. Following the Revolution of 1910 what themes were stressed by Mexican artists and writers? Why?

5. Why was there a revival of Indian arts and crafts in Mexico? of folk music and native dancing?

Summing Up

"The wind that swept Mexico" brought about the most significant revolutionary movement in Latin American history. Though chaos followed the overthrow of Díaz, order was finally restored and important reforms were outlined in the Constitution of 1917. This landmark document asserted Mexico's right to its own mineral wealth, separated Church and state, provided for agrarian reform, and established workers' rights.

Over the years many of these reforms have been carried out. Just as important is the sense of national achievement and confidence that has emerged in the Mexican nation. In works of outstanding quality Mexican artists vividly expressed this feeling of national consciousness as well as a new interest in the country's Indian heritage.

A new middle class came into being along with Mexico's economic development. The oil industry, now owned by the Mexican government, is one of the world's leading producers of petroleum. Other industries also contribute to growing prosperity. With the irrigation of arid lands and the use of more efficient farming practices, agricultural production has steadily increased.

Mexico's new prosperity has done very little, however, to improve life for most peasants. Many barely raise enough food to feed their own families. The growing numbers who stream to the cities looking for jobs are no better off. Aware of the plight of these people, the Mexican government has tried to provide more opportunities for education. But the soaring growth of population makes it difficult to raise standards of living.

In recent years opposition has grown to the political system, under which personal leadership has dominated the Mexican government. In the words of Frank Tannenbaum, "the leader is taken to be the whole government, and the people expect him to behave as if he were the whole government. . . . How to change this psychological dependency upon leadership, so deeply ingrained, is the great riddle in the contemporary political life of the country."

The Latin American Nations: The Central American Republics

CHAPTER FOCUS

1. Common Features of the Six Republics
2. Guatemala
3. Honduras
4. El Salvador
5. Nicaragua
6. Costa Rica
7. Panama

Volcanic eruption is a threat that many Central Americans live with every day of their lives. In 1770 ashes and lava suddenly spewed forth from a peak in western El Salvador, and within a few weeks a volcanic cone had formed. As the picture shows, this volcano, called Izalco, is still active. Izalco's smoke and fire can be seen from ships far out in the Pacific Ocean.

Bridging the two American continents is the narrow ribbon of land called Central America. Here lie the six republics of Guatemala, Honduras, El Salvador, Nicaragua, Costa Rica, and Panama. (British Honduras, west of Guatemala, is a colony of Great Britain.) All together, the six nations of Central America form an area much smaller than the state of Texas. It seems logical that these nations should consider the idea of joining together into a larger, stronger federation. And indeed this idea has kept bobbing up in Central American history.

In the days of Spain's colonial empire, Central America (except for Panama) was governed as the Captaincy-General of Guatemala. Then, as told in Chapter 7, this area became part of the empire of the Mexican dictator Agustín de Iturbide.

After the fall of Iturbide in the early 1820's, the rich creoles of Central America declared their independence of "Spain, or Mexico, or any other power." They formed the United Provinces of Central America and wrote a constitution. But from the outset this federation suffered from disunity. Guatemalan landowners dominated the government, which was centered at Guatemala City, and the creoles of the smaller provinces were jealous. It was the old story of federalism versus centralism that comes up so often in Latin American history. There was also quarreling, and even actual fighting, over the question of government support for the Catholic Church. As in other Latin American republics at this time, the great majority of the population—mestizos, Indians, and blacks—had no voice in the government.

In 1830 Honduran and Salvadorian creoles managed to win control of the federation's government. They installed a young Honduran creole named Francisco Morazán (moh-rah-

sahn') as president. But Morazán's friends and supporters resented having to go all the way to Guatemala City for meetings of the Central American congress. Wild and rugged country made travel between all the provinces of the federation difficult and dangerous.

Quarreling among the members of the little federation grew more and more intense. The conservative landowners were very religious, and when Morazán tried to keep Church leaders out of politics, the tottering federation dissolved. The five member-states became separate republics. (Panama was still part of Colombia.) In 1842 Morazán tried to raise an army to reunite Central America. But Costa Rican conservatives resented his efforts to recruit soldiers in their country, and they had Morazán executed by a firing squad.

Today the nations of Central America share common problems, but each of the nations is different from the others. The citizens of each are intensely proud of their own country. Even so, Francisco Morazán is honored in all the republics as an early hero of Central American history.

1. Common Features of the Six Republics

Central America has three geographic regions. Among the things that the six nations of Central America have in common is geography. All of this area has a two-season climate; heavy rains alternate with summer heat. But altitude and other factors affect the climate. Dominating Central America are the mountains that sweep down from Mexico and continue into South America. On each side of the mountain chain is a coastal region. Thus, Central America has three geographic divisions.

1. *The Caribbean coast.* Along the Caribbean coast is a broad band of *tierra caliente,* where humidity is high and rainfall heavy (map, page 171). Steaming rain forests and lush undergrowth discouraged settlement in early times. Moreover, disease can be a serious problem in the extensive swamplands. For the

most part, early Europeans left this area to pirates, who, among their other activities, cut dyewoods for trading. Today forest products are still harvested in some coastal areas. But throughout Central America sections of the coastal forest have been cleared for plantations. Crops of bananas, cacao, rubber, and coconuts are grown.

2. *The highland interior.* Because the climate is more comfortable in the interior highlands, Central Americans have tended to settle there rather than on the coasts. In the valleys, basins, and plateaus of *tierra templada* are the major cities (except for seaports). Coffee trees thrive in this climate.

3. *The Pacific coast.* The Pacific coastlands of Central America are also *tierra caliente,* but they are quite different from the Caribbean

lowlands. For one thing, the Pacific plain is narrower. In fact, mountains in some places descend abruptly to the shore. Also, the Pacific coastlands are less rainy and so have less plant growth. Much of the land has been eroded by floods that pour down from the highlands. Although these coastlands were easier to settle than the Caribbean, settlement was never heavy. In recent years cotton has become an important crop along the Pacific lowlands.

Central America suffers from poor transportation. Transportation has always been a headache in Central America. The steep terrain and thick rain forests have tended to isolate people. In fact, only in recent decades were the six capital cities connected by good roads. These roads are part of the Pan American Highway system that extends from the United States to southern South America. Only one section of the Highway has not yet been built. The bottleneck is the "Darien gap," a dense rain forest in Panama and northwestern Colombia. A route through this gap has been planned. But construction has been delayed.

Coastal transportation in Central America also has its difficulties. There are some good ports on the Caribbean coast, but linking them with the inland cities has been a problem. On the Pacific side there are fewer ports for ocean-going ships. Airplane travel has become important. It not only connects the cities of the six countries but provides links with the outside world.

Volcanoes are active. Volcanic eruptions are still another problem that has plagued Central America. There are at least 21 active volcanoes, many of them in Nicaragua and El Salvador. Near Managua, Nicaragua, workmen digging for a sewer line found footprints in a wide slab of rock. At some time thousands of years ago, seventeen barefoot people and several small animals ran in terror over a flow of mud caused by an erupting volcano. Heat from the volcano hardened the mud into rock, thus preserving the footprints. In modern times, the volcanoes continue to "blow off." In the early 1960's, San José (*sahn'* hoh-*say'*), the capital of Costa Rica, was covered by two inches of ash every day from an eruption of the volcano Irazú (ee-rah-*soo'*). The ashes were swept away daily by the persistent Costa Ricans, and they protected themselves with umbrellas whenever they went outdoors. But ashes were more than just a nuisance, for they killed plants and animals and destroyed houses. Finally the rain of ashes ended, but there has been talk of moving the capital city to a safer location.

Two good things can be said for the volcanoes. Over the centuries volcanic ash has built up fertile soil. Also, the volcanoes attract tourists, and that always helps a country's economy.

Central Americans depend on tropical agriculture. The Central American republics are agricultural countries. A great many small farmers grow crops for their own use and for sale in local markets. Foreign investment has made possible the large-scale plantations that raise bananas and coffee for export. But Central American coffee has to compete in the world market with Brazilian, Colombian, and African coffee. The banana industry has been hurt by plant disease, and the United States-owned fruit companies are resented by many Central Americans. In many fertile little valleys, farmers grow cacao beans, sugar, and rice and also raise livestock. But their output has not been large enough to profit from foreign sales.

Industry has been slow in getting started in Central America, chiefly because of the small size and meager resources of the countries. In the 1960's, however, the Central American Common Market enabled a number of small industries to get started (page 195).

Most of the Central American populations are racially mixed. There are great differences in population from country to country. Over 90 per cent of the Costa Ricans are white. In Guatemala, on the other hand, most of the people are Indian or of a mestizo type in which

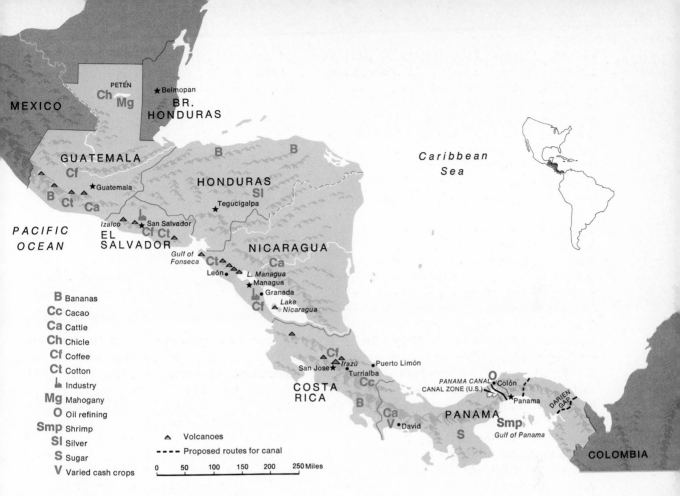

The following labels appear on the map:

MEXICO

PETÉN
★ Belmopan
Ch Mg
BR. HONDURAS

GUATEMALA
Cf
★ Guatemala
B
Ct Ca

B
HONDURAS
Sl
★ Tegucigalpa

B

Caribbean Sea

Izalco
★ San Salvador
Cf Ct
EL SALVADOR
Gulf of Fonseca
Ct

NICARAGUA
Ca
León •
L. Managua
★ Managua
• Granada
Lake Nicaragua
Cf

PACIFIC OCEAN

Cf
Irazú
San Jose ★
Turrialba
• Puerto Limón
COSTA RICA
Cc
B
Ca
V • David

PANAMA CANAL
CANAL ZONE (U.S.)
O • Colón
• Panama
DARIEN GAP
PANAMA
Smp
S
Gulf of Panama

COLOMBIA

Legend:

B Bananas
Cc Cacao
Ca Cattle
Ch Chicle
Cf Coffee
Ct Cotton
⌐ Industry
Mg Mahogany
O Oil refining
Smp Shrimp
Sl Silver
S Sugar
V Varied cash crops

▲ Volcanoes
- - - Proposed routes for canal

0 50 100 150 200 250 Miles

Central America

The crops indicated by colored letters are chiefly grown for commercial use. Throughout Central America many small farmers also raise corn, beans, rice, and manioc for their own use or for local sale.

Indian ancestry is strongest. In the other four countries most people are mestizos. There are black minorities in Costa Rica, Honduras, Nicaragua, and Panama. These Negroes are chiefly descendants of workers from the British Caribbean islands. In the early 1900's they were encouraged to migrate to Central America's east coast. Intermarrying with the descendants of slaves who were already there, the English-speaking blacks became a large under-privileged class. They have not been encouraged to vote or go to school, and they generally live in shanty housing. In Panama unfair treatment has been especially serious for black people.

There are sharp divisions between wealthy and poor. Regardless of racial make-up, in all these countries whites have dominated for centuries. In colonial times there were Spanish overlords. When independence was won, creoles seized power and became the ruling class. Since then, wealthy white landowners and high-ranking army officers have generally controlled the governments. Central America has great contrasts of wealth and poverty. Living standards for the majority of the people are among the lowest in this hemisphere.

Most of the people are rural. Between 60 and 65 per cent of the Central American people live on the land, not in cities or large towns. Most of these rural folk lead lives of drudgery. Some raise barely enough food for themselves and their families on small patches of exhausted soil. Others work on estates owned by wealthy individuals or on plantations owned by foreign companies. The ownership of land in Central America is very unevenly distributed (except in Costa Rica). Only a few hundred families own most of the productive land. A sizeable part of the land on these great estates is not even used.

Population is growing fast. Adding to the problem of poverty is a population explosion. Better sanitation methods have made it possible for many more babies to survive infancy and grow to adulthood. As a result, the Central American populations have one of the fastest growth rates in the world. This situation can only mean greater poverty and social tensions in an area with limited resources.

Discontent is increasing. The younger sons of rural families often leave home to seek a less dreary existence in the cities. There they live in slums, seldom find good jobs, and grow restless and bitter. For children there are seldom enough schools, either in the farm villages or in the city slums. As a rule, only young people from middle- and upper-class families have a chance to get an education. But even among those who complete high school and go on to the small national universities, dissatisfaction with social and political conditions is mounting. Student militants are active in every one of these nations.

Democracy exists in theory but not in practice. Poor transportation, rigid social systems, and widespread poverty are all factors that work against democracy. The democratic ideal is supposedly a goal in the Central American countries. Nevertheless, most of the governments have been dictatorships. (Again, Costa Rica is an exception.) All of the countries call themselves republics, and they all have fine-sounding constitutions. They choose their presidents in elections, and they have congresses that meet in the capital cities.

But Latin American *caudillos* use these democratic procedures for their own purposes. For example, when an election is held, supporters of the government in power often count the votes. Not surprisingly, the candidates favored by the government tend to win. Also, most of the Central American constitutions allow the presidents to suspend personal liberties, such as freedom of speech, when an emergency threatens the nation. So, by declaring a "state of emergency," a dictator-president can legally silence and even arrest his critics and opponents.

A common market was formed. After the break-up of the United Provinces, the idea of union never quite died out. Every so often there would be an attempt to unite the Central American nations, but with little success. Then, in the early 1960's, a giant step was taken toward Central American co-operation. All of the nations except Panama agreed to work together in planning for economic improvement. As a first step, they decided to form a *common market*. The basic idea of a common market is to reduce or even remove import taxes, or tariffs, on goods exchanged between the member countries.

It might be well at this point to review how tariffs work. If Country A imports shoes from Country B, Country A normally requires payment of a tariff on the shoes. This raises the price of the imported shoes, since the shoe stores have to charge enough to make up for the cost of the tariff. As a result, shoes made within Country A and sold in that country have a price advantage over similar-quality shoes imported from Country B.

If Countries A and B form a common market, however, they might agree to reduce the tariff on each other's shoes, or they might remove the tariff barrier entirely. If the latter is done, shoes made in either country can then sell at the same price within both.

Dr. Pedro Delgado, a Guatemalan economist, clearly stated the case for a Central American common market: "Our five nations average two million people each. They cannot possibly find the resources to develop their economies if they work separately. So we must combine." This is what the five countries decided to do. By forming a common market, they enlarged the tariff-free market for their manufactured products. Obviously the countries cannot sell bananas and coffee to each other. But for manufactured items the five countries together provide a good-sized market.

Again consider Countries A and B and their shoes. After reducing their trade barriers in a common market, Country A continues making shoes while Country B decides to concentrate on making bicycles. The manufacturers of both these articles now have a larger number of potential customers within the common-market area. Since sales are greater, the manufacturers expand their businesses and hire additional workers. More people now earn wages and so can afford to buy an extra pair of shoes or a bicycle. Still other businessmen, including some from foreign nations, are attracted to set up new industries. They create even more jobs, and more consumers become able to buy.

Progress was made. Something like this is what happened in Central America after the common market was started in the early 1960's. Tire factories were started in Guatemala, shoe factories in El Salvador, cement plants in Costa Rica, and meat-packing plants in Nicaragua. The dollar value of trade among the five member nations more than tripled from 1963 to 1969.

Other kinds of co-operation were also involved. To finance the new industries, a Central American Bank was created. The Bank has helped finance the construction of village-to-market roads in areas where only mule and foot trails existed before. The common market even has an educational committee. It has distributed free textbooks to many children in the five countries.

The common market was endangered. The Central American Common Market seemed to offer an excellent model for other Latin American regions to follow. Unfortunately, however, after several years of steady progress a quarrel between two of the members threatened to tear apart the organization. Relations between Honduras and El Salvador were badly strained after a war fought in 1969. The two countries refused to trade with each other, and this confused matters for the whole market area. Once again, the traditional inability of the Central Americans to work together threatened what was a promising co-operative effort.

THINKING ABOUT THIS SECTION

1. Explain or define the following words: Darien gap; common market.

2. Why did the federation formed by five Central American states in the 1820's soon fall apart? Are the factors which led to the break-up of the federation still important today?

3. What are some ways in which natural features have made life difficult for the people of Central America?

4. Why has discontent been increasing in Central America? Why can it be said that democracy exists in theory rather than practice in most Central American nations?

5. Why has there been little industrial development in Central America? How has a common market helped the economies of the member states?

Most Guatemalans live in the highlands. Guatemala is the northernmost of the Central American republics. Though second largest of the six countries in area, it has the greatest population. Guatemala has three regions. In the north is a big area called the Petén (peh-*tayn'*) where many Mayan ruins have been found. The Petén is a richly forested region, and, as yet, very few people live there. For years the Petén was chiefly important for mahogany and chicle. (Chicle, the gum of a wild tree, is used in making chewing gum.) Since oil has been discovered in the Petén, more development is likely.

A second major zone in Guatemala is the lowland strip along the Pacific coast. A United States-owned business, the United Fruit Company, developed large-scale banana plantations in this region. Since the 1950's, many Guatemalan farmers have settled here. Cotton has become a major crop and livestock are also raised.

It is in the highland region, running across Guatemala from Mexico to Honduras, that over half of the Guatemalans live. Valleys, volcanic peaks, and glistening lakes make this a region of great beauty. The climate is mild all year round, and conditions are ideal for growing coffee, the country's major export. The Indian people who live in the high country farm small plots of land planted in corn and beans. In the *tierra fría* of the higher altitudes, wheat, barley, and potatoes are cultivated. The small Indian villages of this region have changed little since colonial times.

Indian life survives in Guatemala. The Indian heritage remains so strong in Guatemala that it has been called a country of two cultures—the Indian and the *Ladino* (lah-*dee'* noh). The term *Ladino* is applied to anyone who follows a "Latinized" way of life, regardless of racial descent. When an Indian leaves his village, begins to wear western-style clothing, and speaks Spanish, he has become a *Ladino*. The number of Guatemalan Indians classified as *Ladinos* is steadily increasing. But many continue to live the traditional life.

Well-known to many North Americans are the beautiful textile patterns of the spinners and weavers of the Guatemalan hill towns. Each town has its traditional design, and the Indians of each town have their own distinctive clothes. In one village the men may wear red and white striped cotton pants, and in another they wear blue and white pants. Today, however, a growing number of Indian men wear blue jeans and zippered factory-made jackets. Most women still wear bright hand-made costumes.

Among these Mayan people of the Guatemalan highlands, several different native languages are spoken. This handicaps any efforts to bring schooling to the Indian villages. Few Indians speak or understand more than one of these languages, and hardly any know Spanish. It is difficult to find Spanish-speaking teachers who also know the Mayan languages.

Almost all of the highland Indians are farmers. They may own little plots of their own, or the villages may hold the land as community farms. Though the Indians are skillful farmers, they seldom earn much cash from their crops. In order to make a little money, they may work for a time on coffee plantations in the lower valleys.

Many Indians are dissatisfied with old ways. A number of the young Indians have grown tired of the age-old cycle of poverty. After seeing something of modern life, they are no longer satisfied with traditional ways. Younger sons especially, since they do not inherit land, are likely to go to Guatemala City and become *Ladinos*. But without special skills they cannot find jobs that pay decent wages. Many of these young men follow militant leaders who demand a greater role in the government, more land for Indian farmers, and better schooling for Indian children. The following comment made by a young Guatemalan suggests the changing out-

Over the centuries Indian culture has remained strong in Guatemala. Many descendants of the Mayas continue to pray to ancient gods in traditional rituals.

look in one Indian family: "My father says that reading and writing in Spanish can only be to serve the *Ladinos* because that is their language, but I know that without Spanish we Indians will never get our rights." [1] The impact of these new demands, together with the quickening pace of economic and social change, has given Guatemala the stormiest politics of any of the Central American countries in recent years.

In the mid-1900's the government started reform programs. Government in nineteenth-century Guatemala followed the pattern of much of the rest of Latin America. Military *caudillos* ruled the country. Actually this pattern continued into the 1900's. By the 1940's, however, Guatemalans who wanted social and political change were making themselves heard. When a dictator was overthrown in 1944, these liberals secured control of the government. They wrote a new constitution patterned after

[1] Quoted in *The New York Times*, August 22, 1970.

Mexico's 1917 constitution. The presidents elected to lead the new government, first Juan José Arévalo (ah-*ray'* vah-loh) and then Jacobo Arbenz, called for programs of wide-ranging reform. The government took over unused land from big property-holders and distributed it to Indian farmers. Some of this land was taken from Guatemalan property-owners, but much was seized from the United Fruit Company. This action was popular among Guatemalan nationalists since there was widespread resentment against the big North American company.

Communist influence was charged. Under both Arévalo and Arbenz, some Communists held positions in the Guatemalan government. Conservatives charged that Communist influence was growing stronger, especially during Arbenz's administration. This alarmed the United States government. In 1954 a Guatemalan colonel led an army of exiles across the Honduran border and seized control of Guatemala City, thus overthrowing President Arbenz. It is generally believed that the Guatemalan exiles had aid from the United States in carrying out this revolution.

The colonel who led the rebellion, Castillo Armas, promised to be a "middle-of-the-road" president and to give seized land back to the former owners. Some land distribution was carried out under Castillo Armas, but in a more moderate form. The emphasis was on resettling small farmers on unused land. In other respects the government reverted to dictatorial rule. The prisons were crowded with critics of the government. After three years in office Castillo Armas was assassinated.

Disorder continues in Guatemala. The nation was then ruled by a *junta* until an election was held in 1958. The new president was ardently anti-Communist. In fact, he allowed exiles from Communist Cuba to train on Guatemalan soil with United States assistance. It was this band of Cuban exiles who attempted the Bay of Pigs invasion in 1961 (Chapter 17).

Rioting and other violence kept Guatemala in turmoil in the early 1960's. Finally another *junta* ousted the president and took over the government. Since then, several presidents have held office in Guatemala but have done little to halt political violence. Guerrilla terrorists, claiming to be champions of the masses, have kidnapped and assassinated foreign officials and diplomats. In turn, right-wing vigilantes have murdered people connected with left-wing politics. There is little hope for a better future as long as Guatemala continues to be plagued by violence.

THINKING ABOUT THIS SECTION

1. Explain or define the following words: Petén; *Ladino.*
2. Compare Guatemala's three regions in terms of climate, resources and crops, and ways of living.
3. What efforts to bring about reform were made after 1944? With what success? Why has this country been plagued with violence and disorder?

3. Honduras

Geography has tended to isolate Honduras. Honduras got its name from Christopher Columbus. He found the water off the Caribbean coast so deep that he used the Spanish word for "depths" in naming the land. Geography has made travel to and within this country difficult. Rugged mountain ranges extend eastward from Guatemala across most of Honduras. Though it has a long Caribbean coast, there are few good ports. On the Pacific side Honduras has only a narrow wedge of land along the Gulf of Fonseca, a body of water shared with El Salvador and Nicaragua. Swamps and forests cover the lowlands bordering on this Gulf.

Most Hondurans live on the central plateau, a region of high ridges and deep valleys. Tegucigalpa (teh-*goo'* sih-*gahl'* pah), the capital city, lies in this region. This city has the doubt-ful distinction of being the only Central American capital not on any railroad line. Moreover, the Pan American Highway circles around the Gulf of Fonseca so that only a tiny stretch of it lies within Honduras. A branch road, however, now connects the Highway with Tegucigalpa. Efficient air service also keeps the city in touch with the rest of the world.

On the northern coast is Honduras's most important economic region. Here jungle lowlands have been converted into banana plantations.

Banana production dominates the economy. In a region where all the countries are poor Honduras is the least developed of all. More than any other of the Central American countries, Honduras depends on the export of ba-

Bananas flourish in the hot, humid tierra caliente *of the Central American coast. The picture at right shows how bananas are harvested on a United Fruit Company plantation in Honduras. Some Central American countries encourage industry, hoping to get away from dependence on agricultural exports. Below, right, a textile worker in El Salvador checks loom spindles.*

nanas. Some Hondurans work in small silver mines in the mountains, and others gather hardwoods for export. Coffee, moreover, is growing in importance. But bananas continue to be the mainstay of the country's economy. Here, as elsewhere in Central America, many small farmers grow staple food crops for their own use.

Bananas were first brought to the New World from Africa in the 1500's. They flourished in the hot, damp coastlands of the Caribbean. Today, of course, bananas are a favorite fruit in the United States and many other countries. To supply the demand, banana production has become a tremendous industry in Central America.

When a new banana plantation is started, workers clear away jungle growth and set out shoots of banana roots in rows. These shoots grow into plants from 10 to 25 feet tall. The plant is not a tree with a trunk but rather a tight mass of overlapping layers of leaves. Each plant produces a long purple flower. When the

petals fall off, the central stamen of the flower has many tiny yellow branchlets. Each of these branchlets grows into a banana. By the time a bunch is ready to pick, it may have 60 to 80 bananas.

Most of the banana plantations lie near the coast and have rail connections with a port. The bananas are not cut until a ship comes into port. Then, teams of workers hurry to cut the green bananas and get them down to the ship before they can ripen in the hot sun. Bruised or ripened bananas are not loaded because they would soon spoil, even in the ship's refrigerated hold. Bananas sold in the United States ripen in warehouses before they reach supermarkets and grocery stores.

North American businesses monopolized the banana industry. Two companies owned by United States businessmen have dominated the Caribbean banana industry. The United Fruit Company is the biggest of these. In the Caribbean the name of this company, sometimes shortened to UFCo, has become a symbol of United States influence. For this reason the United Fruit Company is often the target of bitter words from Central American nationalists.

One can understand the resentment of people who feel that foreign companies have made fortunes by exploiting their countries' resources. At the same time it should be pointed out that the United Fruit Company has done much to bolster local economies. Hondurans working for the banana companies live far better than they would in the nearby jungle towns. Workers are well-paid by Central American standards. Moreover, the company provides modern housing, schools, and medical care for the workers and their families. UFCo has also planted various other crops, including sugar cane, hemp, and coconuts. This helps to reduce local dependence on the banana industry. More important, in recent years UFCo has sold land to independent local planters. These planters are advised by company experts but grow their own bananas. The company then buys the fruit and ships it off to market. Thus, the Hondurans

have a greater stake in their country's economy. In the words of one observer, "the desire for freedom to make one's own mistakes is a very basic urge, not only in Latin America, but throughout the underdeveloped world. In the 1960's the banana companies have recognized this point of view." [2]

Honduras has had little experience with democracy. During the stormy days after independence, Honduras had its share of revolutions and military bosses. The rule of *caudillos* continued into recent times. Hampering political growth was the fact that the Hondurans developed little sense of nationhood. Geography divided their country into clusters of isolated communities. Another handicap was the large amount of influence wielded by the North American fruit companies in Honduran political life. But the banana interests no longer control the country. In 1971 Honduras held its first direct election for president in almost 40 years. The new administration launched a "National Unity Plan" with the goal of building a democratic system.

Relations between Honduras and El Salvador have been hostile. Honduras was badly upset by its war with El Salvador in 1969. Supposedly the cause of the war was a dispute over the boundary between the two countries. But this dispute had been going on for a century. Other tensions actually touched off the war. About 300,000 Salvadorians had crossed the border to work in Honduras, which is less densely settled than El Salvador. Many of these Salvadorians were skilled workers and earned good wages in Honduras. Lower-paid Hondurans resented the outsiders. El Salvador in turn charged that some of its citizens living in Honduras were being mistreated.

Intense rivalry over a soccer match also added to the growing hostility. In play-offs for the Central American championship, Honduras and

[2] Preston James, *Latin America* (New York: The Odyssey Press, 1969), p. 168.

El Salvador tied for first place. When the Salvadorian team won the final game, Hondurans took out their anger on the Salvadorians living in their country. To defend these people, the president of El Salvador sent troops into Honduras. Fighting lasted for several weeks. Though the Organization of American States finally arranged a truce, bitterness continued between the two countries.

THINKING ABOUT THIS SECTION

1. Why has the United Fruit Company been bitterly attacked by Central American nationalists? What can be said on the side of the company?

2. What were the causes of tension between Honduras and El Salvador? Why does this tension pose a serious problem?

4. El Salvador

El Salvador is small and crowded. Tucked in between Guatemala and Honduras is El Salvador, the smallest of the Central American republics. This nation is about the size of the state of Massachusetts. El Salvador (meaning "The Savior") faces only the Pacific; it is the only Central American nation with no Caribbean coast. El Salvador has very little flat land but is not as rugged as Honduras's mountain belt. Several volcanoes rise above the sunny green valleys and plateaus. Most of the land is fertile. The capital, San Salvador ("Holy Savior"), is a very modern city. Earthquakes have destroyed the city so often that it has had to be rebuilt several times.

El Salvador is not only the smallest country in Central America; it is also the most crowded. That is why so many Salvadorians moved to Honduras. Some Latin American countries do not use large portions of their land. But the Salvadorians make use of every bit of territory. The population is growing rapidly, and the pressure of overcrowding steadily mounts.

Coffee and cotton are important, but industry is growing. Coffee has long been El Salvador's most important product. But, to escape dependence on a single export, the government has encouraged the planting of other crops. Today cotton is an important export. Industry too is growing. In fact, El Salvador ranks as Central America's most industrialized nation. The new jobs created by industry are important in a country where there is no more cropland for additional farmers.

El Salvador is a mestizo country but has been dominated by white millionaires. Most of the people of El Salvador are mestizos. Perhaps a fifth of the population has all-Indian ancestry, but these Salvadorians have given up the traditional Indian way of life. They speak Spanish and take part in the modern economy. Much of the land is owned by small independent farmers. Over 80 per cent of the coffee lands, however, are the property of wealthy families of European descent. This group of millionaires is called the *Catorce Grande* (kah-*tor'* say *grahn'* day)—the "Big Fourteen."

Military rulers have seen the need for reform. Much of El Salvador's early history centered around the efforts of its people to remain independent of Guatemalan dictators. Up to about the 1930's the government was controlled by the *Catorce Grande*. Since then, military officers have been more powerful. The most recent of these military presidents have recognized the need for modern changes. Despite strong resistance from the old families, El Salvador has made some progress in providing needed public services for its people. With full employment, diversified agriculture, and expanding industry, El Salvador showed impressive economic growth during the 1960's.

THINKING ABOUT THIS SECTION

1. Why is El Salvador building up its industry?

2. How are the Indians of El Salvador different from those of Guatemala?

3. How has El Salvador's government changed in recent years?

5. Nicaragua

Lakes and volcanoes are important in Nicaraguan geography. Nicaragua is larger than Guatemala but has a smaller population. In fact, it has even fewer people than little El Salvador. As in most other Central American countries, there are three geographic regions. Nicaragua's Caribbean coast is mostly rain forest. Rainfall along this coast is so heavy that banana production has not been profitable. A highland region, extending south from Honduras, has a healthy climate but is thinly settled.

The majority of Nicaraguans live near two large lakes in the Pacific lowlands—Lakes Nicaragua and Managua (mah-*nah'* gwah). The capital city, also named Managua, is situated on the shore of the latter lake. Like many cities of Central America, the city of Managua lies near volcanoes that are still active. In 1931 a large part of the city was destroyed by a terrible earthquake that resulted from volcanic action. Since then, Managua has been rebuilt.

The Nicaraguan people depend on agriculture. Three-fourths of the Nicaraguans are mestizos. There are minorities of blacks and whites and a very few Indians. As in other Central American countries, small farmers raise their daily food—corn, rice, and beans—on little plots of land. For export income Nicaragua depends on three C's—cotton, coffee, and cattle. In recent years much of the cotton has been bought by Japanese textile manufacturers. As a result, Nicaragua is less dependent on United States purchases than it used to be. Another economic change is the steady growth of light industry since the late 1950's.

North Americans meddled in Nicaraguan affairs. Ever since Spanish colonial times, people have talked about building a canal across Nicaragua. Lake Nicaragua drains into a river which empties into the Caribbean. This natural waterway seems to offer an ideal route for a canal. Much of Nicaraguan history has centered around interest in the idea.

In the 1850's a North American businessman named Cornelius Vanderbilt exploited this route across Nicaragua. Gold had been discovered in California in 1849, and many would-be miners from the eastern United States traveled to the West Coast by way of Central America. Vanderbilt provided them with transportation. His steamships loaded passengers in New York City or New Orleans and carried them to Nicaragua. In canoes they traveled upriver to Lake Nicaragua, where they transferred to steamboats.

After crossing the lake, the gold-seekers boarded stagecoaches which carried them to a port on the Pacific coast. There a ship loaded the passengers for the voyage to California.

Another North American, named William Walker, also played a part in Nicaraguan history. Walker, born in Tennessee, was well-educated but an adventurer and a pirate at heart. A rivalry between two cities gave him a chance to gain power in Nicaragua. For years these cities, León and Granada, had been struggling for control of the country. In the early 1850's the people of León invited Walker to help them defeat Granada. With a band of adventurers Walker arrived in Nicaragua, captured one of Vanderbilt's steamboats on Lake Nicaragua, and defeated Granada. Next, this North American had himself "elected" president of Nicaragua.

Vanderbilt, however, moved quickly to oust the intruder. He persuaded the Costa Ricans and other Central Americans to take joint action against Walker. After ruling for only a few months, Walker was defeated by the Central American allies but managed to escape. Within a few years he returned to Central America with hopes of reconquering Nicaragua. In 1860 Walker was captured in Honduras and executed. The rivalry between León and Granada was settled by making a third city, Managua, the capital.

United States forces occupied Nicaragua. Foreign interest continued to complicate Nicaraguan politics. In 1893 a tyrant named Zelaya came to power. He started trouble with the other Central American nations by trying to organize a federation dominated by himself. It was rumored that he was trying to interest Great Britain and even Japan in the construction of a canal. Zelaya's enemies, with United States backing, forced him into exile in 1909. Conditions in Nicaragua were so chaotic that three years later the United States landed marines and took financial control. From then until 1933, United States forces almost continuously occupied Nicaragua.

Meanwhile, the United States remained interested in a possible canal across Nicaragua, even though it had opened the Panama Canal in 1914. In 1916 a treaty was agreed to by the United States and Nicaragua. The treaty declared that the United States had the sole right to build a canal across Nicaragua. In 1970, however, Nicaragua ended this agreement.

Sandino defied the Yankees. Many Nicaraguans resented the intervention of the United States into their national affairs. Even after order was restored, guerrilla resistance continued in the hills. One rebel leader, Augusto Sandino, became a hero throughout Central America. North American newspapers and conservatives in Managua called Sandino a bandit. He and his men, after all, raided mountain villages and kidnapped women. But Nicaraguan nationalists regarded Sandino as a hero because he defied Yankee power. In 1934, after United States forces had left Nicaragua, Sandino agreed to come down out of the hills and make a truce with the Managua government. A banquet was even held in his honor at the presidential palace. Within a few hours after leaving this banquet, Sandino was cut down by assassins armed with machine guns. The man often accused of planning this murder was Anastasio Somoza (soh-*moh'* sah), the commander of the Nicaraguan army.

The Somoza family controlled Nicaragua. Before long, Somoza had become the "strong man" of Nicaragua. From 1937 until his assassination in 1956, Somoza ruled the country as if it were his private estate. He made a fortune by controlling the cattle industry and more than a hundred business enterprises. But Somoza was not as ruthless as some Central American dictators. In fact, he did not even think of himself as a dictator. A great friend of the United States, Somoza once visited President Franklin D. Roosevelt at the White House. Later the Nicaraguan ruler explained his views on democracy to a newspaper writer: "Now, as I told FDR, democracy down here is like a baby, and nobody gives a baby everything to eat right away. I'm giving them liberty, but in my own style. If you give a baby a hot tamale, you kill him."

After Somoza's death, his sons continued the family regime. Under Luis Somoza and then Anastasio ("Tachito") Somoza, Nicaragua enjoyed economic growth, social progress, and a certain amount of freedom of speech. But some Nicaraguans began to demand more. In 1970 militant members of a "Sandinist Liberation Movement" clashed with the Nicaraguan army.

THINKING ABOUT THIS SECTION

1. Contrast the crops raised by Nicaragua's small farmers with the crops that are exported by that country.

2. Why did the United States become interested in Nicaragua in the early 1900's? Why did it send troops into Nicaragua? What was the reaction among the people of the country?

3. What do you think of Somoza's views on democracy for the Nicaraguans?

6. Costa Rica

Except for El Salvador, Costa Rica is the smallest of the Central American nations, but it stands first in democracy and in the well-being of its people.

Costa Rica has highlands and coastal plains. The greater number of Costa Ricans live on the fertile central plateau, an area surrounded by volcanoes. As noted earlier, some of these volcanoes are still active. Economically, Costa Rica (meaning "rich coast") is a land of "firsts." It was in the Costa Rican hills that the first successful coffee plantations were established in Central America. In the 1820's the government gave free land to people who would set out coffee trees and cultivate them. The result was a boom in coffee agriculture. Today coffee and bananas are Costa Rica's chief exports.

Bananas were another "first." The Caribbean coast of Costa Rica was the first site chosen by a North American fruit company for banana production. This company later merged with others to form the giant United Fruit Company. By the early 1900's more bananas were shipped out from Costa Rica's Caribbean port of Puerto Limón (*pwehr'* toh lee-*mohn'*) than from any other port in the world. Eventually a disease all but wiped out the crop. The United Fruit Company then abandoned its eastern Costa Rican plantations and concentrated on other Central American locations. On the southern Pacific coast of Costa Rica, however, bananas are still a major crop.

A tradition of equality developed. Most Costa Ricans are of European descent, though some also have Indian ancestry. A good many of them live in and around the capital city of San José, in the central highland valley. San José has a modern appearance, wide shady streets, and pleasant parks. The school system is unusually good for a Central American country. In fact, in percentage of literate citizens Costa Rica ranks with countries like Mexico and Argentina.

Costa Rica is free of the great gap which divides the people of other Central American countries into rich and poor. One explanation for this tradition of equality is found in the area's early history. When the Spaniards first came to Central America, they found no gold in Costa Rica, nor was there a large Indian population to exploit. The Spaniards who settled in Costa Rica were more interested in building homes than in getting rich quick. Unlike the *conquistadores* they did not scorn manual labor. The Spanish farmers received small pieces of land and worked the soil themselves. Still today the majority of Costa Rican farmers own and work their own property. There

Costa Rican schoolgirls receive vegetable seeds for planting gardens. The goal is better nutrition, for which a great need exists throughout Central America.

are wealthy families in Costa Rica, but they do not dominate the country's life.

Pioneer farmers are moving into frontier lands.

Costa Rica's population is growing rapidly. But, unlike El Salvador, Costa Rica has an abundance of undeveloped land. In recent years many small farmers have moved into pioneer lands never before cultivated. Newly built roads enable them to market their crops. The resettlement program has helped to relieve pressure on the fast-growing cities.

Blacks have met with discrimination.

There is one flaw in Costa Rica's claim to social equality. When banana plantations were started on the Caribbean coast, the fruit company brought in black workers from the British West Indies to clear the land and gather the harvest. Some white Costa Ricans resented the English-speaking newcomers. In those days a railroad provided the only transportation between Puerto Limón, where many of the blacks settled, and San José. The black workers were not allowed to ride on the train. This was a way of keeping them out of the highland towns and cities. Now a highway connects San José and Puerto Limón. Many of the children and grandchildren of the original banana workers are small shopkeepers and union leaders in Puerto Limón. They own automobiles and drive over to San José whenever they please. But among many people of Spanish descent there is still prejudice against black Costa Ricans.

The democratic tradition is strong. Few countries anywhere in Latin America have shown as much political stability as Costa Rica. After independence, the little nation had its dictators, but in 1889 the Costa Ricans held the first free and honest election in all of Latin America. The democratic tradition successfully took root.

This is not to say that politics have always been peaceful in Costa Rica. There have been attempted revolutions and an occasional lapse from democratic government. In 1948, for example, a civil war broke out. A revolutionary junta gained power and put through some drastic reforms. For one thing, the army was abolished. Still today Costa Rica has only a police force to keep order. The junta also increased taxes for the rich, gave women the vote, and began new social welfare measures.

Figueres led a reform program. The leader of this junta was José Figueres Ferrer (fee-*gehr'* ayss fehr-*rehr'*), called "Don Pepe" (*pay' pay'*) by the Costa Ricans. After putting through these reforms, Figueres turned over the government to an elected president. In 1953 he himself was elected to the presidency. Figueres persuaded the United Fruit Company to pay a much larger share of its profits to the Costa Rican government. He did not try to force the company out of business, for he realized that his country benefited from its efficient, large-

scale operations. Figueres did, however, nationalize electric-power plants and railroads and encouraged a variety of local economic enterprises. Meanwhile, he had to cope with an invasion threat from President Somoza of Nicaragua.

Figueres also had enemies at home, and in 1958 they helped defeat the candidate he had favored to succeed him in the presidency. The election was a fair and honest one. Figueres commented: "I consider our defeat as a contribution, in a way, to democracy in Latin America. It is not customary for a party in power to lose an election." In 1970 the Costa Ricans elected Figueres to another term as president.

THINKING ABOUT THIS SECTION

1. What made it possible for a tradition of democracy to develop in Costa Rica? What is the flaw in this country's record of social equality? How do you account for it?

2. Compare the policy of Jacobo Arbenz in Guatemala (page 197) and that of José Figueres in Costa Rica in dealing with the United Fruit Company. Why might each have acted as he did?

3. Interpret this remark made by Figueres: "It is not customary [in Latin America] for a party in power to lose an election."

7. Panama

Panama occupies the narrowest part of Central America. The narrowest part of the strip of land connecting the two American continents is the Isthmus of Panama. This isthmus runs generally east-west, not north-south. Therefore, the border of Panama and Costa Rica lies about 400 miles *west* of Panama's border with Colombia. The width of the isthmus varies from 30 to 120 miles.

The presence of the Canal Zone affects Panamanian life. To the people of the United States, the word "Panama" suggests the Canal and the Zone through which it runs. But to the people of the isthmus, it is the name of their country. The republic of Panama is sliced in two by the United States-operated Canal Zone. At the two ends of the Canal Zone lie Panama's two largest cities—Panama City (the capital) and Colón (koh-*lohn'*). Many Panamanians work in the Zone. Others sell goods and services to the North Americans, called Zonians, who live there, and to the seamen and travelers who pass through this "crossroads of the world." Thus, many Panamanians are dependent on the North American presence for their livelihood.

Outside the Zone agriculture is the most important activity. Panama has hills and mountains, forests, and low coastlands. As in other Central American countries, the Caribbean coast is swampy and was originally covered with tropical rain forest. If the isthmus had not had strategic importance as a gateway to the colonies, the Spaniards might not have settled such an unhealthful area. Today the Caribbean coast has many banana plantations.

Large numbers of Panamanians live in villages and isolated farms in the valleys and highlands of the interior. These small farmers grow crops of rice, corn, bananas, and manioc for local consumption. In the rest of the nation there is much unused land, but a large part of it is no good for agriculture. One of the more prosperous areas reaches from the Costa Rican border to the city of David (dah-*veed'*). Here cattle graze, and modern methods are used in growing abundant food crops. Eastern Panama is tropical rain forest so dense that it has blocked construction of the last link in the Pan American Highway.

Bananas grown by a subsidiary of the United Fruit Company are Panama's leading export crop. The Gulf of Panama, on the Pacific side, is the source of another important export— shrimp. In the 1960's, Panama also began to sell petroleum products to foreign customers.

The population includes peoples from many lands. Even before the building of the Panama Canal, but especially since then, people from all over the world have crossed the Americas at this narrow neck of land. As a result, Panama's population includes a variety of Europeans and Asians as well as native Americans and West Indian blacks. Many of the West Indians are descendants of laborers brought in during the early 1900's to build the Panama Canal. When the Canal was finished, United States officials failed to keep their promise to help the English-speaking West Indians go home. The blacks stayed on in Panama, seldom finding good jobs, crowded in bad housing, and discriminated against by the Panamanians.

Panamanians were unhappy as part of Colombia. "How beautiful it would be if the Isthmus of Panama [became] . . . the site of a world capital!" wrote Simón Bolívar in 1814. But far from becoming the capital of a great American confederation, Panama found itself part of Colombia after that country won independence from Spain. More than once during the 1800's, the people in Panama City announced their independence from the government in Bogotá. But each time the Panamanians quarreled among themselves and the rebellion failed.

A railroad was built across the isthmus. The California gold rush brought many travelers to Panama as well as to Nicaragua. In the 1850's, Colombia granted a North American engineer the right to build a railroad across the isthmus. He finished it in 1855, just about the time William Walker was harassing Vanderbilt's lake-and-stage route across Nicaragua. But when a transcontinental railroad was built across the United States, the isthmus railroad lost most of its business.

Interest in a canal increased. It was in the late 1870's that someone actually started digging a canal across the Isthmus of Panama. A French engineer named Ferdinand de Lesseps had just built the Suez Canal in Egypt. He and his company bought from Colombia the right to build a canal in Panama. Construction started in 1879. But the task proved far more difficult than in Egypt. The terrain was rugged and insect-borne diseases took a terrible toll of life. De Lesseps spent a fortune and 40,000 laborers died before the project was abandoned after eight years of work.

Central American leaders are often military "strong men." Below, Anastasio Somoza ruled Nicaragua for years. General Omar Torrijos, shown above talking with students, took over in Panama in 1969 and sought popular support by claiming sovereignty over the Canal Zone.

Soon the Spanish-American War quickened United States interest in a canal across Central America. The United States had become a world power with possessions in both the Pacific and the Caribbean. Clearly its navy needed a faster route between Atlantic and Pacific than the long passage around the southern tip of South America. In 1903 a treaty was worked out with Colombia that would give the United States the right to build a canal in Panama. But the Colombian senate declared that the price offered by the United States was too low and refused to accept the treaty.

Theodore Roosevelt helped Panama win independence. Since the Panamanians were eager to have the canal built, they were angry that the Colombian government had turned down the treaty. Leaders in Panama City proclaimed independence from Colombia. United States warships appeared at Colón harbor and prevented Colombian troops from crossing the isthmus to put down the revolt. Only three days after the rebellion, moreover, President Theodore Roosevelt of the United States recognized the new republic of Panama. By making possible the secession of Panama, the United States angered not only the Colombians but people throughout Latin America.

The Panamanians, however, were now assured that they would have their canal, or rather that the United States would build *its* canal through their country. For a down payment of ten million dollars and a yearly rent of 250,000 dollars, Panama leased to the United States the ten-mile-wide Canal Zone. It was agreed that the two cities, Panama City and Colón, would not be considered part of the Zone. Since the original agreement, the yearly rent has been increased several times. The United States now pays Panama about two million dollars a year.

The building of the canal was an engineering triumph. The United States lost no time in starting work on the canal. Army engineers began surveying and planning. Laborers were hired, a railroad was built, and supplies and equipment were shipped to Panama. For ten years, thousands of men worked on the canal. The difficulties were enormous. Mountains of rock had to be blasted out with dynamite, and massive amounts of earth had to be moved. Landslides were a frequent danger. Since different sections of the canal lie at different levels, a system of locks had to be built. The locks enable ships to be raised or lowered to the different levels. Finally, in 1914 the canal was opened to ship traffic. Since then, ships of all nations have saved thousands of miles by using the canal instead of making the long trip around Cape Horn.

Another canal is needed. Today the Panama Canal has more traffic than it can handle efficiently. Ships occasionally have to wait two days for their turn, and some modern oil tankers are too large to pass through the canal. Engineers have studied the possibility of building another canal across the isthmus, but Panama and the United States will have to ratify a new treaty before a second canal can be started.

Panama was dominated by the United States. After 1903 Panama was officially an independent republic, but actually it was under United States domination. The treaty that Panama had signed with the United States gave the North American giant the right to intervene in Panamanian affairs to protect the canal. In 1939 the United States gave up this right of intervention, but its officials still tended to treat Panama like a dependency.

For several reasons the Panamanians have felt bitter toward the United States. (1) They resent the contrast between the high living standard of United States citizens who live in the Canal Zone and the widespread poverty in their own country. (2) Panamanians working in the Canal Zone have been paid less than United States citizens for the same kind of work. In still other ways they have been discriminated against by United States citizens and officials in the Canal Zone. (3) The yearly rent paid by the United States is only a fraction of the tolls that ships pay for use of the canal. Feeling that the canal is their "natural resource," the Panamanians want a greater share of the income from these tolls.

For all these reasons the canal became a symbol of Panamanian nationalism and hostility toward the United States. At times this hostility has boiled over into anti-Yankee demonstrations.

Panama has had no experience of democracy. Meanwhile, the Panamanians have had little chance to build a democratic government. Most of the people are poor and without political influence, and until very recently illiteracy was high. For years a few wealthy families ran the country. The members of these families not only controlled the government but owned a large amount of land and a great many business enterprises as well. In the late 1960's the rule of the old families was overthrown, and a military dictatorship of middle-class background took charge in Panama.

THINKING ABOUT THIS SECTION

1. Explain or define the following words: Canal Zone; right of intervention.

2. Why did Spain become interested in Panama during the 1500's? Why did the railroad built across Panama in 1855 lose most of its business in the later 1800's?

3. Why did the United States succeed in building a canal across Panama after earlier efforts had failed? What was the Latin American reaction to Theodore Roosevelt's role in Panama's secession from Colombia? Why?

4. Try to put yourself in the shoes of a Panamanian in evaluating the reasons given for Panamanian bitterness toward the United States. Would you expect the Panamanians to change their view if it was pointed out that economic conditions in their country would probably be less good if the United States had not built the canal? Explain.

Summing Up

Central America is one of the least developed regions of Latin America. The countries are small, dependent on tropical agriculture, and (except for Costa Rica) lacking in democratic experience. Most of the people have had little opportunity to educate themselves or improve their condition. The majority are small farmers who grow basic food crops for their own use or for sale in local markets. Export crops have generally been grown by large planters, including the United Fruit Company, a North American business.

In the 1960's the Central American Common Market held out hopes for economic progress. Because products manufactured in one country could be sold tariff-free in the other countries, industry was encouraged. But hostility between El Salvador and Honduras strained relations within the free-trade area and weakened prospects for growth. A population explosion also threatens economic stability since Central America has limited resources.

Central America lies very close to North America, and United States power and influence have unavoidably been felt in these small countries. Several times the United States intervened in Central American republics to stabilize financial conditions or to restore order. In Panama the United States took a special role. First, it enabled the Panamanians to gain independence from Colombia, and then it built the canal across the Isthmus. The United States continues to operate the canal and has sole responsibility for its defense.

The Canal Zone in Panama and the activities of the United Fruit Company have been special targets for anti-Yankee nationalists in Central America. To these nationalists, the benefits that have come to Central America from the North American presence are outweighed by the unfairness of not having full control of their countries' destinies.

11

Sugar cane has been raised on the Caribbean islands since the earliest days of Spanish occupation. Conditions on the islands are ideal for its growth, and the crop requires little care. At harvest time, however, teams of field hands must work fast to cut the stalks, since they should be crushed while still fresh and sweet. Because their countries depend so heavily on exports of this crop, sugar cane has been regarded as both a blessing and a curse by the Caribbean islanders.

The Latin American Nations: The Latin West Indies

CHAPTER FOCUS

1. The Caribbean Islands
2. Cuba
3. The Dominican Republic
4. Haiti

After his first voyage to the western Atlantic, Columbus returned to the beautiful Spanish province of Andalusia at Easter time, 1493. He was asked by Queen Isabella to describe the "Indies islands" that he had discovered. Columbus told the queen, "They were like April in Andalusia." He was talking about the Bahamas, Hispaniola, and Cuba. These are part of a long chain of islands, now called the West Indies, extending from Florida to the island of Trinidad off the coast of Venezuela.

In the early days of European colonization these islands became major ports, since the trade winds carried sailing vessels from Europe across the Atlantic directly to the Caribbean. Columbus himself came to America by this fast route. On homeward voyages he sailed north of the islands, following the Gulf Stream to the east of Florida, and then crossing the Atlantic to Spain. Later explorers used the

Caribbean islands as steppingstones to the American continents.

Today two large islands in the West Indies are the home of three Latin American nations—Cuba, the Dominican Republic, and Haiti. The latter two share the island of Hispaniola. Soon after their discovery by Columbus, Cuba and Hispaniola were settled by Spaniards. The western end of Hispaniola, now Haiti, was neglected by Spain. A haven for French pirates, it be-

came a French possession around 1700. Both Cuba and Hispaniola yielded rich profits from sugar cane planted and harvested by African slaves. Now Cuba, the Dominican Republic, and Haiti have many citizens of African descent. Except for Mexico, these three countries lie closer to North America than any other of the Latin American nations. Their location has made them of special interest to the people of the United States.

1. The Caribbean Islands

The islands have certain features in common. Most of the West Indies islands are the peaks of underwater mountains. Some of the smaller islands, however, are formed of coral and sand. Though the majority of the islands lie within the tropics, they have a pleasant climate. Average temperatures range from the 70's to mid-80's. From about May to October, the islands have a rainy season. Hurricanes often hit the West Indies during the later part of this period. Born in the Atlantic, these dangerous storms sweep across the ocean into the Caribbean. The southern West Indies generally escape hurricanes, but western Cuba and Hispaniola are often hard-hit by the savage storms.

Fertile soil is perhaps the most precious of the islands' natural resources. A variety of tropical crops are grown, among them sugar cane, fruits, and coffee. Some of the islands also have valuable mineral resources.

The larger islands are called the Greater Antilles. The four largest islands of the West Indies lie in the western part of the chain. Called the Greater Antilles (an-*til'* eez), they are Cuba, Hispaniola, Puerto Rico, and Jamaica. Cuba and Hispaniola are the main subjects of this chapter. Puerto Rico will be described in Chapter 16. Jamaica, though today independent, was long a British colony and so is not generally considered part of Latin America.

Most of the Lesser Antilles are territories of European nations. The smaller islands in the Caribbean are called the Lesser Antilles. Columbus visited many of these islands and named them for Spanish shrines and holy days. One island Columbus called "the place of the beards" because of long strands of moss hanging from the trees. It became known as Barbados (bar-*bay'* dohss), from the Spanish adjective *barbudo* meaning "bearded." On another island Columbus saw three mountains of about the same height. He called that island Trinidad, the Spanish word for "Trinity."

Today most of the islands of the Lesser Antilles are still controlled, more or less, by European nations. The majority are associated with Great Britain. But Barbados and Trinidad (with Tobago) became independent nations in the 1960's. The United States Virgin Islands are also part of the Lesser Antilles.

The older islands of the Lesser Antilles chain are sometimes called the "low" islands, since the greater part of them is beneath the sea. In general, they have limited resources. On those islands that receive little rainfall, the people make their living from fishing or raising cattle, sheep, and goats. Where rainfall is adequate, there are large sugar-cane plantations.

The "high" islands are those which are more mountainous and have active volcanoes. Water is generally plentiful on these islands, since they have lakes and enjoy abundant rainfall. Each island has traditionally specialized in a single crop. These range over a variety of products, including sugar, cotton, limes, arrowroot, and spices. The tourist trade is important to many of the Lesser Antilles.

The Bahamas are a third group of islands. North of the Greater Antilles and east of Florida lies a third group of islands, the Bahamas. It was on one of these islands that Columbus made his first landing in the Americas. Now they are a British dependency, officially called the Commonwealth of the Bahamas. Winter visitors from the United States have made the Bahamas a thriving resort area.

THINKING ABOUT THIS SECTION

1. Which islands are included in the Greater Antilles? What are the Lesser Antilles? the Bahamas?
2. What features do many of these islands have in common?

2. Cuba

GEOGRAPHY AND ECONOMY

Cuba is the largest of the Antilles. With an area a little smaller than that of Pennsylvania, Cuba is the largest island in the Caribbean. From east to west, it is about 760 miles long, a distance greater than from New York City to Chicago. The island's average north-south width is 50 to 60 miles. Cuba lies only 90 miles from Florida, a very short distance by air.

Cuba is such a beautiful island that the Spaniards called it the "Pearl of the Antilles." Rich soil, a good climate, and plenty of rainfall make it a perfect place for growing sugar cane and tobacco. There are mountains in the eastern and western ends of the island, but over half of Cuba's land area is flat enough that farm vehicles can be used in cultivating fields. Most of this land is devoted to raising sugar cane. In the foothills and sandy plains of the westernmost province, the highly prized Cuban tobacco is grown. Cattle raising, fishing, mining, and light industry also contribute to the nation's income.

The island is indented with a number of good harbors. One of these, Guantánamo (gwan-*tahn'* uh-moh) Bay, is leased by the United States as a naval base. Though the United States and Cuba have not had diplomatic relations since 1961, the United States continues to maintain this base.

One of Cuba's finest harbors is that of Havana, the capital city. With over a million people, Havana is the island's largest city and chief port. At the other end of the island is Santiago, the second largest city. For many years before Fidel Castro came to power, Havana was a popular stop for winter cruise ships from North America.

Cubans are of European or African descent. Over half of the Cuban population is urban. About three-fourths of the people are white, and the rest are mostly black or mulatto. During the early years of Spanish rule, so many native Cubans died from forced labor or European diseases that the Indian strain has disappeared from Cuba. There is a small Chinese population on the island.

Sugar is all-important to Cuba. Cuba produces more sugar than any other country in the world. Just as for other "single-crop" countries, this is both a blessing and a curse. A high price for sugar means prosperity; a low price,

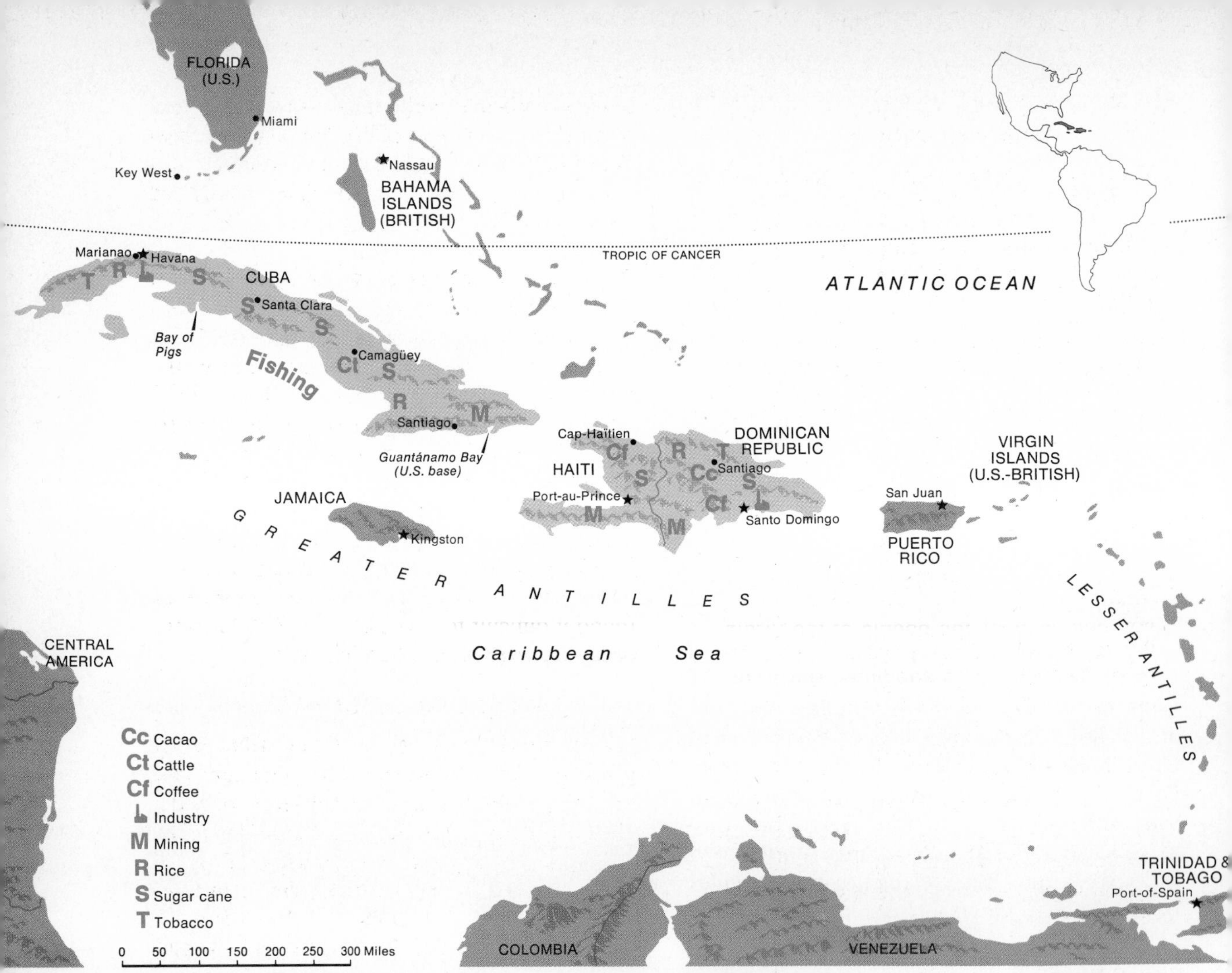
FLORIDA (U.S.)
Miami
Key West
Nassau
BAHAMA ISLANDS (BRITISH)
TROPIC OF CANCER
ATLANTIC OCEAN
Marianao
Havana
CUBA
Santa Clara
Bay of Pigs
Fishing
Camagüey
Santiago
Guantánamo Bay (U.S. base)
Cap-Haïtien
HAITI
DOMINICAN REPUBLIC
Santiago
Port-au-Prince
Santo Domingo
VIRGIN ISLANDS (U.S.-BRITISH)
San Juan
PUERTO RICO
JAMAICA
Kingston
GREATER ANTILLES
LESSER ANTILLES
Caribbean Sea
CENTRAL AMERICA
Cc Cacao
Ct Cattle
Cf Coffee
Industry
M Mining
R Rice
S Sugar cane
T Tobacco
0 50 100 150 200 250 300 Miles
COLOMBIA
VENEZUELA
TRINIDAD & TOBAGO
Port-of-Spain

The Caribbean Republics

The crops shown on the map are chiefly for export. As in Central America and elsewhere throughout Latin America, many small farmers grow food crops for their own use or for sale in local markets.

disaster. For years Cuba's economy has depended on the size of the cane harvest and on foreign sale of the sugar. The current government has encouraged the raising of cattle and some planting of other crops. But Cuba still devotes so much of its land to sugar cane that it cannot grow enough food for its people.

For a long time Cuba's sugar industry was dominated by North American businessmen. Cuban sugar imported by the United States was subject to a much lower duty than sugar from Brazil or the British West Indies, and therefore most of the Cuban crop was sold to United States markets. Cuba, in turn, imported most of its manufactured goods from the United States. Cubans felt that their country was almost a "colony" of the North American sugar companies.

Sugar cane was harvested by hand and crushed in mills. The North American companies ran the Cuban sugar industry efficiently. The plantations were more like factories than farms. Cuttings of the cane were planted at the beginning of the summer rainy season. During the dry season the cane matured and sweetened. Then from about January to June was the harvest season. Gangs of field hands, called *guajiros* (gwah-*hee'* rohss), moved along the rows of cane, stripping the long leaves off the stalks. The leaves were left on the ground to rot and fertilize the next crop. Other *guajiros* followed the first group of workers. With long knives they cut the stalks close to the ground and loaded them on oxcarts or small railroad cars to be taken to the mills.

At the sugar mills, called *centrales* (sehn-*trah'* layss), the sweet juice was pressed out of the cane. By boiling, the juice was reduced to a mixture of raw sugar crystals and syrup. The crystals were then bagged for shipment to refineries in the United States. There they would be processed into white table sugar. The syrup was made into molasses. Today sugar production still follows much the same routine. But Communist countries, rather than the United States, now buy Cuba's sugar.

Guajiros were out of work for half the year. Efficient use of labor has always been a problem in the sugar industry. The United States companies installed modern machinery in the *centrales,* thus speeding the extraction of juice from the cane. But large numbers of workers were still needed in the fields during the harvest period. From about June to December, on the other hand, was the "dead time," or *tiempo muerto,* when there was little work to be done. The *guajiros* were paid only during the months when they worked. Since wages were low, they found it difficult to save money, and the months of lay-off were always hard times.

POLITICAL HISTORY

The Spanish held on to Cuba after other colonies won independence. Except for Panama, Cuba has a shorter history of independence than any of the other Latin American republics. Throughout the turbulent days of the independence movements, the island remained a Spanish colony. In fact, Spanish aristocrats from cities like Bogotá and Caracas settled there as exiles. In governing Cuba, Spain seemed to have learned nothing from the loss of its other colonies. Large armies were stationed on the island to enforce strict rule. Through dishonest tax collection and other forms of corruption, the Spanish governors made fortunes for themselves. As each governor retired, a new one arrived to "feather his nest." During the 1800's Havana was a dirty and neglected city, with many beggars in the unpaved streets. But the Spanish aristocrats lived a pleasant existence and were hardly aware of the poverty of most of the people.

Cubans sought independence. Some brave Cubans dared to criticize Spanish rule. One of these was a black man who made his living by carving tortoise-shell combs. Under the pen-name of Plácido (*plah'* see-thoh), he wrote protest poetry and circulated it secretly. Only if his poems were read, he said, could he "face the rifles, freed from bondage." In 1844 Plácido did "face the rifles." The Spanish government arrested the poet, charged him with planning a slave revolt, and executed him.

But Plácido's spirit lived on. Patriotic Cubans began to raise a guerrilla army. Independence and liberation of the slaves were the goals of the barefoot and poorly armed guerrillas. One of the rebel leaders was an ex-slave named Antonio Maceo (mah-*say'* oh). His guerrillas rode through the canefields at night, burned sugar mills and storehouses, and terrorized Spanish landowners. For ten years (1868–1878) guerrilla armies carried on a rebellion called the Ten Years' War. Spain promised reforms, but conditions remained much the same. Maceo and other guerrilla leaders went into exile. Not until 1885 was slavery abolished in Cuba, years after it had ended in the rest of Spanish-speaking America.

By 1890 even conservative Cuban merchants and planters were becoming disgusted with Spanish taxation and restrictions. More and more Cubans became willing to back an independence movement. Soon *Cuba Libre!* ("Free Cuba!") began to be heard throughout the island. A veteran of the Ten Years' War, Tomás Estrada Palma, had formed a government-in-exile in New York City and was raising funds for another rebellion. In Jamaica, Antonio Maceo was also collecting supplies. These veterans were joined by an idealistic Cuban poet named José Martí.

Martí was to become one of Cuba's most popular heroes. At the age of sixteen, he had been imprisoned for protesting Spanish rule. After his release, Martí was barred from Cuba. He worked as a journalist in Mexico, Central America, and the United States. In New York City he joined with other Cuban exiles in planning the campaign to free Cuba.

Early in 1895 Martí and Maceo sailed to Cuba in a small boat. Landing secretly, they launched a new guerrilla war. In the first week of fighting, the patriot cause suffered a heavy blow when Martí was shot by a Spanish sniper. A few weeks later Maceo was also killed. The Spanish governor believed that the Cuban revolt could be easily crushed. But volunteer forces continued to land, bringing new supplies and encouragement to the patriots. Two hundred thousand Spanish soldiers, led by General Valeriano Weyler, arrived from Spain to wipe out the rebellion.

General Weyler's name became a synonym for cruelty. To prevent Cuban villagers from helping the guerrillas, the Spanish general forced hundreds of thousands of rural people into concentration camps. These camps were so badly run that lack of sanitation resulted in thousands of deaths from disease. Moreover, on Weyler's orders, Spanish soldiers destroyed crops and cattle. Food became scarce in the camps and also in the cities. Fifty thousand starved to death in Havana alone. The Cubans hated Weyler, and accounts of his methods angered people around the world. In New York City, newspapers called Weyler "the Butcher."

Independence was won. From 1895 to 1898, Cuban guerrillas fought the Spanish forces. Then in April, 1898, the United States declared war against Spain. Within a few months the fighting was over, and before the end of the year a peace treaty was signed. By this treaty Spain recognized the independence of Cuba. President William McKinley had promised that the island would not become a United States possession. But United States forces stayed in Cuba until 1902. Many Cubans resented this, for they felt that their own heroes had been winning the war against Spain and had needed no help from the United States.

Cuba needed help. Cuba had been in a frightful state when the war ended. Savage fighting had devastated the island. People were homeless, hungry, and ill. Fields were unplanted, towns lay in ruins, and there was no effective government. Under United States occupation, order was restored. Food was given out, and seed and cattle were distributed to farmers. Public works programs resulted in new roads and water and sewage systems. Hospitals and schools were also built, and thousands of Cuban children attended school for the first time.

Yellow fever was controlled. Out of the Cuban struggle for independence came an important advance in medical science. During the war more United States soldiers had died of yellow fever and malaria than from wounds. For years a Havana doctor named Carlos Finlay had insisted that mosquitoes carried yellow fever, but the Spanish government had ignored him. One person who did listen to Dr. Finlay was Walter Reed, a scientist from the United States. Reed was sent to Cuba in 1900 to find a way of controlling yellow fever and ridding the army camps of this dreaded disease. Through a series of experiments, Reed and other army doctors proved that Finlay's theory was correct. The United States army then drained swampy areas to get rid of the mosquitoes' breeding places. Methods used in Cuba served as a model for controlling yellow fever and malaria in other tropical countries.

A Cuban government was organized. But Cuba needed a government. At first, since matters were so confused, the United States army commander, Leonard Wood, ruled the island. Soon elections were held for delegates to a constitutional convention. In 1901 a constitution providing for a republican form of government was adopted, and Tomás Estrada Palma was elected Cuba's first president. The United States left the island in 1902, but it insisted on keeping the right to intervene.

Cuba failed to achieve democracy. The new republic started out free of many of the handicaps that plagued other nations in Latin America. Cuba had no jealous neighbors, no tradition of *caudillismo* or regionalism, no great mountain barrier dividing its territory, and little racial or social tension. Moreover, a popular hero had taken office as president.

Nevertheless, Cuba faced difficult problems, many of them the result of years of colonial misrule and lack of experience in self-government. As one historian has pointed out, Cuba "had become a republic, but it lacked citizens. Certainly the people were nationalistic enough, as they had demonstrated in the independence struggle. Yet they had a tradition of nearly four centuries under Spain which caused them to regard the government as something to defy or exploit." [1] Unfortunately, Cuba never learned how to make democratic government work.

President Estrada Palma was an honest man who tried hard to give Cuba good government. But several presidents were more interested in enriching themselves. Just as under Spanish rule, theft of public funds became an accepted way of life for public officials. Meanwhile, Cuba's economic health depended on the world price of sugar. But profits went to the sugar-company stockholders who lived in the United States.

Batista ruled from behind the scenes. In 1933 Fulgencio Batista (bah-*tees'* tah) emerged on the scene. For most of the following quarter-century he was to dominate Cuban politics. Batista came from a *guajiro* family of mixed Spanish, Indian, African, and Chinese ancestry. At the age of 20 he had joined the Cuban army and taught himself to read and write. He soon rose to the rank of sergeant and secretly organized a society of non-commissioned officers. Batista succeeded in winning the support of most enlisted men.

One night in 1933 Sergeant Batista arrested the army chief of staff and occupied his office. He then removed other high army officers and took over Havana. Within a few days the president resigned, and Batista took charge of all of Cuba. The new dictator promoted himself to the rank of colonel but did not take the title

[1] John Edwin Fagg, *Cuba, Haiti, and the Dominican Republic* (Englewood Cliffs, N. J.: Prentice-Hall, Inc., 1965), p. 55.

of president. Batista was content to be a backstage power, ruling Cuba through a series of "puppet presidents."

From 1933 to 1944, Batista controlled Cuba. He raised the pay of soldiers and increased literacy in the ranks. Education for children was also stressed. In an effort to win over the *guajiros,* Batista forced the sugar companies to improve working conditions and raise wages. Tenant farmers were guaranteed a fair share of the crops.

By 1940 Batista was tired of working behind the scenes and ran for the presidency himself. At this time popular with the Cuban people, he won easily. Four years of prosperity followed, chiefly because of the high price of sugar during World War II. In 1944 the candidate chosen by Batista to be his successor was defeated in a fair election. Batista, by this time a millionaire, retired to live comfortably in Miami, Florida.

Batista imposed harsh rule. Batista's "retirement" lasted for eight years. In 1952 he returned to Cuba and announced that he would run for president. But before the election even took place, Batista organized his old friends and henchmen and seized power in Havana. Since Communist influence had grown among Cuban workers, Batista was able to convince the United States government that Communism posed a great threat to Cuba. The United States recognized Batista's government and sent Cuba technical and military aid. In 1954, Batista staged a presidential election in which he was the only candidate. Thus he won a "legal" four-year term.

Batista then imposed a harsh dictatorship on Cuba. In fact, Cuba became a police state as Batista abolished constitutional rights and ruled by military force. His opponents were imprisoned, tortured, and killed. Though the country was fairly prosperous during the 1950's, Cubans who had cheered Batista in earlier years turned against him. Students rioted in protest against the government, and an underground opposition gathered strength.

A rebel movement got under way. One rebel leader was Fidel Castro. Fidel and his younger brother Raúl were university graduates, the sons of a well-to-do Cuban family. On July 26, 1953, the 26-year-old Fidel led a small group of students in an attack on a military barracks near Santiago. Other uprisings took place elsewhere in Cuba at the same time. The revolt failed. Many of the rebels were killed, while Fidel and Raúl were captured and sentenced to fifteen years in prison. In 1955, however, the Castro brothers were pardoned and allowed to go to Mexico. Still determined to overthrow Batista, they continued planning revolution. They called their campaign the "26th of July Movement."

Castro established a revolutionary base in the Cuban mountains. In Mexico the Castro brothers were joined by Ernesto "Che" Guevara (*chay' geh-vahr' ah*), a young doctor from Argentina, and other young Cuban exiles. They trained in guerrilla warfare and managed to raise funds in the United States, where anti-Batista feeling was strong. Rashly, Fidel announced that he would land in Cuba in late 1956.

In December of that year, on an old yacht named the *Granma,* the Castro brothers, Che Guevara, and 79 other men left Mexico and landed in southeastern Cuba. Since Batista knew of their plans, he had armed forces ready and waiting for them. Only twelve of the conspirators, including Fidel, Raúl, and Che escaped the ambush and went into hiding in the mountains. Soon other anti-Batista Cubans joined them, and their camp became headquarters for an active guerrilla movement. Batista claimed that Castro was dead. Secretly, however, a reporter from the *New York Times* made his way to the mountain hideout. In a dramatic newspaper story he announced to the world that Fidel was alive and confidently planning to overthrow Batista.

Batista was forced out. For two years Castro's growing band of guerrillas waged a campaign of harassment. The rebels burned sugar mills, cut communications, kidnapped United States businessmen, threatened assassinations, and even bombed schools and theaters. Batista struck back by rounding up suspected rebel sympathizers. The dictator's henchmen tortured and murdered thousands. Middle-class Cubans began to give their support to Castro, as Batista's tyranny grew more ruthless. Even soldiers of the Cuban army deserted to join the guerrillas. By December, 1958, two years after the landing of *Granma,* the Castro rebels were advancing across the island towards Havana. Batista declared a "state of emergency," but time had run out for the Cuban dictator. On New Year's Eve, Batista, his family, and aides fled to the Dominican Republic. The 26th of July Movement had succeeded.

Castro took control of Cuba. In their mountain hideout the Castro brothers and Che had grown long hair and whiskers. Now beards became a symbol of the revolutionary spirit. Dressed in shabby rough clothes, with his beard flowing, Fidel arrived in Havana riding on top of an American-made tank that had been captured from the Batista forces. Crowds went wild with enthusiasm. More sedate citizens, happy that Batista was gone, also welcomed the young men who seemed to be freedom-loving idealists.

Castro apparently had no long-range plans for a new government. A judge named Urrutia was appointed "acting president," but he was soon replaced. Brother Raúl became commander-in-chief of the armed forces, and Che was named economic adviser. At first Fidel took no official position, but within a few months he gave himself the title of premier. Other members of the 26th of July Movement replaced Batista officials still in Cuba.

Fidel had promised his followers that Batista's aides and supporters would be punished. In the early weeks of 1959 some 550 men who had worked for the dictator were arrested, quickly tried, and executed. These executions shocked many people in other countries.

Castro and the United States became enemies. Would-be sympathizers in the United States were also startled by Castro's growing hostility to their country. In radio broadcasts Fidel shouted words of hatred for the United States, accusing it of economic aggression against Cuba. He declared that Cuba was a "socialist state," words intended to alarm the United States government. Moreover, Castro seized Cuban property and businesses owned by United States interests. The owners were not paid for their property.

In the words of the journalist Tad Szulc, by early 1960 "Castro had decided that his future was with Moscow, not Washington." About this time the Soviet Union began to give Cuba economic aid. Soon Soviet technicians and advisers were streaming into Cuba. The United States government finally lost patience with Castro. President Dwight Eisenhower stopped trade with Cuba, ended purchases of the island's sugar, and broke off diplomatic relations. Castro then became dependent on Communist countries to buy Cuba's main income crop. According to Tad Szulc, "Whatever the reasons, the Soviet presence in Cuba was established early in 1960, sucking that Caribbean island and the rest of Latin America into the cold war. The United States began to consider Cuba and all Latin America in terms of the East-West struggle." [2]

The most dramatic events in the new hostility between Cuba and the United States were still to come. The Bay of Pigs invasion attempt and the missile crisis are discussed in Chapter 17, since they are part of the fuller story of the United States' relations with Latin America. But it is important to note here that, by capturing the Bay of Pigs invaders, Castro won a great propaganda victory. Little Cuba had defeated an invading expedition supported and financed by the giant United States. This incident strengthened Fidel at home and made him popular with all Latin Americans who resented North American power. Throughout the

[2] Tad Szulc, *Latin America* (New York: Atheneum, 1966), p. 109.

Western Hemisphere, *fidelismo* (fee-del-*eess'* moh) came to mean a new kind of grass-roots revolutionary spirit, aimed chiefly against United States influence. People in South America, Santo Domingo, and Panama demonstrated in the streets, shouting "Fidel! Fidel!" They also yelled "Yanqui, go home!"

Che Guevara, too, captured the imagination of restless rebels. In 1967 Che was killed in Bolivia while trying to start a revolution there. But he remained an idol for rebellious young people all over the world.

At home Castro had successes and failures.
Under Castro the Cuban people have not fared as well as they had hoped during the happy celebrating of New Year's Day, 1959. But not all this disappointment can be blamed on Castro. For one thing, Cuba has not yet escaped from its dependence on sugar. Several times the sugar crop almost failed. Bad weather was partly to blame, but mismanagement and lack of parts for repairing machinery were also factors. In the early 1960's, Castro had hopes of making Cuba over into an industrial nation. But Cuba's Communist friends failed to deliver promised equipment. By itself Cuba had neither the financial resources nor the raw materials to develop industry. Disappointed, Castro returned to an emphasis on producing as much sugar cane as possible. Urban workers were sent into the canefields to work alongside the *guajiros* in harvesting the cane. Students and volunteers from abroad also helped. But sugar harvests have failed to meet Castro's production goals.

All large agricultural holdings, not just those owned by foreigners, were confiscated by Castro's government. But there was little distribution of land to small farmers. Instead, large holdings were turned into state-owned farms. Factories are also run by the Cuban government.

The workers and rural people seem to have profited by Fidel's programs. The *guajiros* are

Fidel Castro (left) overthrew the dictator Batista but failed to give Cuba democratic government. Many Cubans chose to leave the island on airlift flights sponsored by the United States. Far left, Cuban refugees land at Miami, Florida.

no longer jobless for half the year. During the slack season in the fields they serve in Castro's army, train for other jobs, or even go to school. There are better housing, more schools, and effective public health programs. In the words of one historian, "It could be fairly admitted that [Castro] had improved the status of the Negroes and, for the first time, had enforced rigid standards of personal honesty among government employees. The hotels, luxury resorts, and beaches were now available to the common man. The lower classes thought themselves better off, and probably were, while the middle classes by mid-1960 were scarcely suffering. Massive efforts to reduce illiteracy and to provide technical training pointed to the upgrading of the population's skills." [3]

But there are shortages of food and other consumer items in Cuba. Because so many workers and farmers leave their regular jobs to cut sugar cane at harvest time, output of manufactured goods and staple crops has declined. Though probably no one goes hungry, Cuba must import great quantities of food. Both food and other consumer items are rationed, and many shop windows are empty.

Meanwhile, Cuba is no nearer to achieving democracy than it was under Batista. Opposition is silenced, and the elections promised by Castro have never been held. Soon after taking power, Castro announced that his revolution had already achieved "pure democracy." "It was pure, he explained, because what the revolutionary government was doing in terms of agrarian reform and urban reform had the unanimous support of the nation as shown by the applause of the crowds. Subsequently an official slogan was unveiled. 'We've already elected Fidel!' it proclaimed." [4] One reason given by Castro for postponing an election was that democratic debate would delay putting his programs into action.

Many Cubans emigrated. The stifling of freedom was especially disappointing to middle-class Cubans—the professional people, skilled workers, and small businessmen. At first, they welcomed Castro, believing he would bring freedom as well as reform to Cuba. But when Castro's government punished critics, postponed elections, and took over private property without payment to owners, they were disillusioned and many left the island. Since 1958, more than half a million Cubans have migrated to the United States. Most have settled in Miami, Florida, and other cities of the eastern seacoast.

[3] John Edwin Fagg, *Cuba, Haiti, and the Dominican Republic*, p. 105.

[4] Tad Szulc, *Latin America*, p. 73.

1. Explain or define the following words: Guantánamo Bay; *guajiro;* 26th of July Movement; *fidelismo.*

2. What is Cuba's chief source of national income? Before Castro came to power, why did many Cubans feel that their country was dominated by the United States?

3. How is sugar cane harvested and processed? Why do the canefields not need full-time workers through the year? How has this affected Cuba's agricultural workers?

4. In governing Cuba, why did it seem that Spain had learned nothing from losing its mainland colonies? How did Cuba win independence?

5. What problems faced by other Latin American nations did *not* burden Cuba after independence? Why, nevertheless, did it fail to achieve democracy and prosperity?

6. By 1958 how might most Cubans have regarded Batista and Castro? Explain.

7. Why did pro-Castro feeling decline in the United States? Why did Castro become increasingly dependent on Communist support?

8. How does the Cuban economy operate under Castro? What groups have benefited from Castro's programs? have not been helped or have been hurt? Why was Castro unable to industrialize Cuba?

9. Why has *fidelismo* had wide appeal in Latin America? Compare the Mexican and Cuban revolutions. How did each begin, what course did each take, and what were the results?

3. The Dominican Republic

GEOGRAPHY AND ECONOMY

Between Cuba and Puerto Rico lies the island of Hispaniola. It was on this island that Santo Domingo, the first European city in the Americas, was founded. Today Hispaniola is divided between two uneasy neighbors, the Dominican Republic and Haiti.

Hispaniola is a rugged island. According to an old story, a king once asked an admiral what Hispaniola was like. The admiral crumpled up a piece of paper and held it out to the king. "This, sire, is Hispaniola," he said. Hispaniola is much more "crumpled" than Cuba. Several mountain ranges cross the island, reaching a peak of just over 10,000 feet in the Dominican Republic. Scattered between these ranges are valleys and basins. (One is 150 feet *below* sea level.) The amount of rainfall varies greatly on Hispaniola. Some places are very wet, and others are dry. In lowland pockets, extremely high temperatures have been recorded.

The Dominican Republic lies in eastern Hispaniola. Of the two nations that occupy Hispaniola, the Dominican Republic is much the larger. It covers the eastern two-thirds of the island. This is an area about the size of the states of Vermont and New Hampshire combined. More significant than total size is the fact that the Dominicans have much more fertile and level land than their neighbors, the Haitians. This has made for jealousy and tension between the two countries.

Some two-thirds of the Dominican people are of mixed European and African descent. There are small minorities of whites and blacks and a few orientals. As in Cuba, the native Indians long ago disappeared from the population.

Most of the Dominican people live in two areas. One is a fertile valley in the north, known as the nation's "food basket." The other is centered around the capital city, Santo Domingo, in the southeastern lowlands.

The economy is agricultural. Sugar cane, coffee, tobacco, cacao, and rice are grown as export crops in the Dominican Republic. Many small farmers also grow corn and manioc for their own use. There is some mining, chiefly of bauxite, and a little industry. The country is heavily dependent on the United States as a customer. Over 80 per cent of its exports are bought by North American markets. Unfortunately the country's violent past has discouraged North American tourists from vacationing on the beautiful Dominican beaches.

POLITICAL HISTORY

The 1800's were a stormy period in Dominican history. By late colonial times Santo Domingo had so declined in importance that it was of little interest to the mother country. In fact, in 1795 Spain gave up its part of the island of Hispaniola to France. Many Spaniards and creoles left the island after this. Chapter 7 told how the Haitians under Toussaint drove out the French from the western end of Hispaniola. For a while the Haitians even took over the former Spanish colony at the eastern end.

The French emperor Napoleon stepped into Hispaniola in the early 1800's. But, when he was defeated in Europe, Spanish rule was restored to Santo Domingo. As independence movements gathered strength, the Spanish-speaking people of Santo Domingo proclaimed a republic. In 1822, however, troops from Haiti easily reoccupied the eastern end of the island. For the next 22 years Haitians controlled Santo Domingo. The harshness of Haitian rule made for a bitterness that continues to this day. During a civil war in Haiti the Dominicans managed to regain their independence. But they remained fearful of their neighbors to the west.

From 1844 to 1916 Dominican history was a confused story of one dictator after another. At times independence seemed less important to the Dominicans than finding security under the protection of some strong power. In the 1860's one dictator actually persuaded the once-hated mother country, Spain, to accept Santo Domingo as a colony again. Spanish rule lasted for only four years, however. Faced with problems at home, the Spanish ruler failed to suppress revolts on the island. In 1865 Spanish troops left the island, and the Dominican Republic was restored.

To raise money, the next Dominican president tried to sell the United States a large bay for use as a naval base. Another president offered the entire nation to the United States. President Ulysses S. Grant was willing to consider the idea, but the United States Senate would not approve it.

In 1882 one of the harshest dictators in Dominican history came to power. Ulises Heureaux (uhr-*oh'*) ruled the nation with an iron hand for seventeen years. Although Heureaux was ruthless toward his enemies, he at least gave the Dominican Republic a period of stable rule. But he borrowed heavily from foreign companies and plunged the nation deeply into debt. Chaos followed Heureaux's death by assassination in 1899.

The United States intervened in Dominican affairs. When Theodore Roosevelt became president of the United States, he took an interest in developments in the Dominican Republic. For one thing, he was concerned about the safety of investments made by United States citizens in that country. Also, he suspected that European nations might be tempted to occupy the Dominican Republic to collect debts owed their citizens. In 1905, therefore, Roosevelt sent United States officials to manage Dominican financial affairs. The Dominican government consented to this arrangement. Over the next few years the Dominican presidency changed hands several times. None of the men who held office found a way to establish a stable government.

Meanwhile, the United States government continued to keep an eye on Dominican affairs. Then, in 1916, another United States president, Woodrow Wilson, ordered marines landed in the Dominican Republic to put down political disturbances and restore order. For eight years United States marine officers ran the country.

According to one historian, most of these officers were "unwilling and not particularly qualified for the task." But some improvements were made in education and public health. Deaths from yellow fever were greatly reduced by the draining of swamps. Roads were built and the nation's finances put in better order.

But the Dominicans resented the United States' occupation. They charged that the United States officers were running the island for the benefit of foreign interests, and they protested against tight censorship. The occupation was humiliating for the proud Dominicans. Both countries were glad to end the arrangement in 1924.

The "Era of Trujillo" spanned three decades.
In 1930 a revolt brought a new "strong" man to power. The next 31 years marked the "Era of Trujillo," as Rafael Trujillo (troo-*hee'* yoh) himself proclaimed it. Born to a poor mulatto family, Trujillo had risen rapidly after joining the Dominican army. Tough, able, and shrewd, he became head of the army and then used that position to seize the government.

A few months after his take-over, a severe hurricane gave Trujillo a chance to win the gratitude of the Dominicans and international prestige as well. The storm devastated the city of Santo Domingo. Trujillo organized quick help for homeless and injured people, stopped panic, and began rebuilding the city. His skillful handling of the emergency assured Trujillo of solid support for his programs. Over the next few years he paid off the national debt, balanced the budget, began public-health programs, and started new schools. But at the same time Trujillo's family built up huge private fortunes.

Trujillo used stern military force to impose his will. He alone, surrounded by members of his family, was the Dominican government. With brutal efficiency he had his opponents and critics jailed, tortured, and executed. Some enemies who sought safety in other countries were murdered by Trujillo's hired assassins. He even quarreled with the Catholic Church and

expelled 50 priests from the island. Trujillo claimed that any Dominican who opposed him was a "Communist." Eventually he proudly declared that there were no "Communists" left in his country. An egotist, the dictator demanded constant praise and cringing loyalty from his aides and officials. He even ordered historic old Santo Domingo renamed Ciudad Trujillo.

One of the dictator's most brutal acts was an attack in 1937 on Haitians working on Dominican sugar plantations. Dominican workers resented competition from Haitians who crossed the boundary line to cut cane. Apparently seeking public favor, Trujillo ordered his army to move against the Haitian migrants. Several thousand helpless workers were slaughtered.

Trujillo was unpopular in Latin America.
Other Latin American nations distrusted Trujillo. Cruel dictatorships were nothing new in Latin America, but Trujillo's was regarded as one of the most evil in a long time. By 1960 several Latin American countries were openly expressing disapproval. Venezuela asked the Organization of American States (OAS) to investigate Trujillo's tyranny. Soon afterward, Trujillo's agents made an unsuccessful attempt on the life of the Venezuelan president. Meanwhile, Fidel Castro aided Dominican leftists who had formed an underground "liberation" movement. By the end of 1960 most of the OAS member nations, including the United States, had condemned the Dominican Republic. (The United States continued, however, to buy Dominican sugar.)

Disorder followed Trujillo's death.
In the end it was officers of Trujillo's own army who brought his long reign to a close. In May, 1961, three officers ambushed and shot the 69-year-old dictator as he was driving along a lonely country road. For a few months there was a struggle for power between Trujillo's playboy son, Rafael, Jr., and the puppet president, Joaquin Balaguer (bah-lah-*gehr'*). Young Rafael and his relatives were discouraged, however,

Crowds of cheering Dominicans followed armed rebel leaders as they marched through the streets of Santo Domingo during the 1965 civil war.

when United States warships appeared off the Dominican coast. They realized that the powerful northern neighbor was no longer friendly to the Trujillo family. Finally, all the Trujillos fled the country to live comfortably abroad on their millions.

After the Trujillos left, a number of political parties took shape in the Dominican Republic. In 1962 free elections were held in that country for the first time in 38 years. Juan Bosch was elected president. Bosch was well known as a writer and an intellectual. For many years he had been living in exile and teaching at Latin American universities. As president, he hoped to bring democratic reforms and social justice to Dominican life.

For one thing, Bosch planned to break up the big estates formerly owned by the Trujillos and to distribute the land to peasant farmers. But this was prevented by the well-to-do families from whom the Trujillos had grabbed the land

years before. Moreover, many government workers, military officers, policemen, and tax collectors were hold-overs from the Trujillo regime. They blocked Bosch's plans and accused him of being "soft on Communism." After only seven months in office, Bosch was ousted by military leaders.

Civil war erupted. A junta of officers and businessmen then took over. Though they promised that free elections would be held in the fall of 1965, dissatisfied Dominicans could not wait. In April of that year a revolt led by Bosch sympathizers exploded in Santo Domingo. The situation turned into a civil war between mostly conservatives on one side and liberals and left-wing elements on the other side. United States President Lyndon Johnson soon ordered 20,000 marines and paratroopers into Santo Domingo. At first Johnson declared that he only wanted to protect the lives of United States citizens in Santo Domingo. But it soon became clear that he had feared a Communist take-over of the rebellion.

President Johnson was widely criticized for having sent forces to the Dominican Republic.

This action had contradicted recent statements that the United States government would not interfere in the affairs of other American nations. To make the action more acceptable, Johnson asked other Western Hemisphere nations to form an inter-American peacekeeping force. By a narrow vote the Organization of American States agreed to this request. Several nations contributed soldiers, and together these men formed a peace mission that restored calm to Santo Domingo. The fuller story of this joint effort is told in Chapter 17.

Order was finally restored. After fighting finally halted in Santo Domingo, all factions agreed to accept a provisional president. Then, an election was held in mid-1966. Joaquin Balaguer defeated Juan Bosch and became president. Soon afterward the inter-American peace force withdrew from the Dominican Republic. Through the rest of the 1960's the country enjoyed relative calm and order, though political agitation continued. President Balaguer, who emphasized the need for economic progress, was elected to a second term in 1970. It remains to be seen whether the Dominican Republic can make its way in the world without yielding again to strong-man rule.

THINKING ABOUT THIS SECTION

1. Unlike many islands of the West Indies, neither the Dominican Republic nor Cuba can count on a large income from tourism. Why is this so?

2. Why are the Dominican Republic and Haiti not friendly neighbors? Why has the United States at times intervened in Dominican affairs? What has been the Dominican reaction? Why?

3. How did Trujillo come to power? Why was he unpopular elsewhere in Latin America? How did the Trujillo regime come to an end?

4. What were the plans of President Bosch for the Dominican Republic? What was the outcome?

5. Why was the United States criticized for landing troops in the Dominican Republic in 1965? How has the Dominican Republic fared since then?

4. Haiti

GEOGRAPHY, ECONOMY, AND CULTURE

Haiti is an agricultural country but lacks good land. Haiti, even more mountainous than the Dominican Republic, is a strikingly beautiful country. But it is also a poor one. Though the Haitians depend on agriculture for their living, about two-thirds of the land is not good for farming. Most of the people are peasant farmers who try to make the most of tiny patches of land on eroded hills and steep slopes. Of the level land much is planted in sugar cane and coffee. These two crops, together with bauxite ore, are exported by Haiti. But Haiti makes very little money from foreign trade. In fact, Haiti has a lower average yearly income per person than any other country in the Western Hemisphere. With so little money Haiti cannot afford to spend much on education. As a result, illiteracy is high.

Haiti is a black nation. As in the other Caribbean republics, the native population of Haiti perished soon after the European conquerors arrived centuries ago. Now most of the Haitian people are of African ancestry. They are descendents of the slaves imported by the French to work on the sugar plantations. About 5 per cent of Haiti's population is of mixed white and black descent. Port-au-Prince (*port'* oh-*prans'*), the capital, has a few hundred thousand people. There are some other towns, but the majority of Haitians live in rural areas.

Despite grinding poverty and a low level of education, personal independence is a strong tradition in Haiti. Preston James has written about this trait: "The Haitian has one strongly held state-idea—that his government must keep Haiti free, and that the people of Haiti must be shielded from any authority. . . . No government in Haiti would last long if it should attempt to use force in changing the way of living of the individual peasant." [5]

African and French elements have merged in Haitian culture. During colonial times many Haitian mulattos had been educated in France. When the blacks and mulattos rose up and drove the French out of Haiti, these mulattos took over as the ruling class. Still a large gap divides Haiti's educated, French-speaking, mulatto aristocracy from the rest of the people. The members of this aristocracy seem to take little or no interest in efforts to improve life for their fellow Haitians.

The life of the Haitian peasants has not changed much over the years of independence. They speak not French but a language called *creole* that mingles French and African elements with words borrowed from other languages. The African heritage is also reflected in the voodoo religion practiced by many Haitians. Magical rites and dancing suggest the kinship between voodoo and ancient West African religions (page 49). Roman Catholicism is the official religion in Haiti, however.

Haitian art has won recognition. Since the 1950's, the outside world has taken an interest in Haiti's unique culture. In 1949 a fair was held to celebrate the 200th anniversary of the founding of Port-au-Prince. Tourists who visited the fair discovered the impressive work of Haitian primitive artists.[6] Much of this art focused on the African slave theme. A few Haitian "voodoo" artists were asked to paint the story of the life of Jesus for a large church in Port-au-Prince. They created striking murals done in brilliant colors on the church's white plaster walls. All the characters in the story were portrayed as black Haitian villagers. Modern artists of other countries traveled to Haiti to see these artists at work, and reproductions of the paintings sold widely in the United States. Touring Haitian dance companies have also found appreciative audiences in North America.

POLITICAL HISTORY

A century of disorder followed independence. The story of Haiti's violent revolt against the French overlords is told in Chapter 7. Even before Henri Christophe's death, a mulatto named Jean Pierre Boyer (bwah-*yay'*) had ruled in southern Haiti. After Christophe's suicide Boyer extended his authority throughout Haiti. It was Boyer who sent forces into Santo Domingo and for a time occupied the Spanish-speaking part of the island.

During Boyer's rule of Haiti the Paris-educated mulattos built up their power in Port-au-Prince. Black Haitians continued to live in primitive villages, and bandits controlled much of the interior. There was constant tension between the black peasants and the mulattos. Meanwhile, as the Haitian plantations were neglected, the economy suffered. Coffee beans picked from wild bushes provided a small cash crop. But sugar cane must be harvested at just the right time. Since the harvest was neglected, Haiti soon had no sugar to export.

In 1843, Haitian mulattos forced Boyer into exile. From this time until 1915, Haiti averaged about one new dictator every three years. Confusion and violence reigned as would-be rulers plotted to overthrow the current resident of the presidential palace in Port-au-Prince. Some dictators borrowed money from European bankers and wasted it in extravagant spending. Since Haiti was unable to repay these debts, European governments threatened to take action to collect the money.

The United States stepped into Haiti. As in the neighboring Dominican Republic, the United

[5] Preston James, *Latin America* (New York: Odyssey Press, 1969), p. 277.

[6] The word *primitive* when applied to art does not mean "uncivilized." Primitive artists are self-taught, and their work usually deals with unsophisticated folk themes.

Terraced fields (above) show how Haitian farmers make heavy use of hillsides. Soil erosion is a serious problem in a country without much level land. Left, a notable example of Haitian primitive painting is The Farm by the artist Toussaint Auguste. On the facing page is a photograph of the two Duvaliers, father and son, taken only a few months before the death of "Papa Doc."

States government decided to take a hand in Haitian affairs. In 1915 United States marines landed in Haiti and took control of Port-au-Prince. Like the Dominicans, the Haitian people resented having their country run by foreigners. They especially hated a system of forced labor that was introduced. The United States officers regarded this unpaid labor as a substitute for taxes, but to the Haitians it seemed like a return to slavery. Furthermore, many of the United States marines and soldiers treated the Haitians like inferiors. In the backlands, peasant guerrillas rose in revolt against the occupation. Many lives were lost before the marines crushed this uprising.

The United States occupation was ended. By the late 1920's the United States government looked forward to ending the Haitian occupation. It was President Franklin Roosevelt who finally ordered the United States forces to leave Haiti in 1934. The Haitians celebrated the end of the occupation as if it were a second winning of independence.

Haiti had a hostile neighbor. By the mid-1930's the Haitian government had to contend with Rafael Trujillo, the Dominican dictator. Haitian migrant workers had crossed the boundary to take jobs on Dominican sugar plantations. As told earlier, Trujillo authorized a "purge" of these Haitians, and thousands were killed. The two countries almost went to war over this massacre. But when the United States protested to Trujillo, he agreed to pay Haiti "damages" of 550,000 dollars. Thus he indirectly admitted his guilt.

Duvalier took over Haiti. In the years following the United States occupation, Haiti failed to find a way of making peaceful changes in government. A series of presidents held office. Then, in 1957 François Duvalier (doo-val-yay') rose to power. Duvalier was a doctor who came from a black middle-class family. He had studied at the University of Haiti and for a short time in the United States. Duvalier had worked in Haitian public-health programs for some 20 years before entering politics. In the presidency Duvalier at first seemed to bring new hope for Haiti. The country people fondly called him "Papa Doc."

But Duvalier soon showed that he intended to rule in the tradition of Haitian dictatorships. Once a reform-minded young doctor, Duvalier had become a bitter middle-aged man who despised his opponents and allowed no criticism. The Haitian dictator once said of himself: "I am an exceptional man, the kind the country could produce once every half-century. I am the personification of the Haitian people, and only God can take my power from me." Duvalier created a private army of thugs called the *Tonton Macoute* (*tohn' tohn'* mah-*coot'*, creole for "bogeymen"). These terrorists dealt brutally with anyone whose loyalty to "Papa Doc" was suspect. Haitian officials claimed that Duvalier was beloved by the people. But since no opposition was permitted, the truth was difficult to find. Meanwhile, Haiti seemed cut off from the mainstream of modern Latin American development.

Duvalier was succeeded by his son. In 1971 an era of Haitian history apparently came to an end when Duvalier died. Even before his death was announced to the public, his nineteen-year-old son was sworn in as the next president of Haiti. Jean-Claude Duvalier declared in a broadcast to the nation that he would continue his father's work with the "same fierce energy." But it remained to be seen whether the young inexperienced leader could hold the country together.

THINKING ABOUT THIS SECTION

1. Explain or define the following words: creole language; "primitive" art; *Tonton Macoute*.

2. Compare the Dominican Republic and Haiti. Consider area, population, natural features, economy, and government.

3. How did Haiti come to have a mulatto aristocracy? What evidence supports the view that Haitian culture is a blend of African and French elements?

4. Why did United States forces occupy Haiti in the early 1900's? What was the reaction among Haitians?

5. Why were Haiti's relations with the Dominican Republic strained during the Trujillo regime?

6. How did the Duvalier regime maintain itself in power?

Summing Up

Developments in the Caribbean island republics are of great concern to the United States. Except for Mexico, these three republics are closer to this country than any other Latin American nations. By fighting Spain in the 1890's the United States took a part in the Cuban independence movement. During the early years of this century the United States in one way or another intervened in the affairs of all three of the island nations. Moreover, in Cuba, North American business interests had large investments. Today the United States is concerned with the close link between Cuba and other Communist countries and the possible spread of Castro-type Communism to other areas of Latin America. Whether the influence of the United States in the Caribbean area has been for good or ill remains an unanswered question.

On both Cuba and Hispaniola few Indians survived the early years of European control. Thus, the work on the sugar plantations was done by slaves imported from Africa. In Haiti the slaves and free mulattos drove out the French land-owning class in Latin America's first revolution for independence, leaving the new nation with a population almost entirely of African origin. Haiti's unique culture remains a blend of French and African elements. Among the mulatto aristocrats the French heritage prevails, while African traditions are strong among the black majority. In Cuba and the Dominican Republic the white landowning class remained in control after independence, though each country had large numbers of mulattos and blacks. The Castro revolution introduced a Communist system in Cuba. In the Dominican Republic well-to-do whites remain in control of the government.

All three of these countries share a tropical location, and all have an agricultural economy. But the level of prosperity varies greatly. Haiti has little to export, and many of its people live in poverty. Though both Cuba and the Dominican Republic have some light industry, their chief source of income is the exporting of sugar. Both suffer the problems that handicap any country relying so heavily on a single export.

All three of these republics have lived under harsh dictatorships. Resentment of the Batista regime led to Cuban acceptance of Fidel Castro. The Trujillo dictatorship in the Dominican Republic was one of the longest in Latin American history and one of the harshest. In Haiti, Duvalier had total power and allowed no opposition. With a heritage of economic problems, unstable government, lack of democracy, and resentment against the United States, these three nations face an uncertain future.

12

The Latin American Nations: The Northern Andean Republics

These children survived the terrible earthquake that shook northern Peru in 1970. Rubble from ruined houses filled the narrow streets of their town.

CHAPTER FOCUS

1. Colombia
2. Venezuela
3. Peru
4. Bolivia
5. Ecuador

In 1970 a fearful earthquake devastated huge areas of mountainous northern Peru. Some 50,000 people lost their lives and probably 800,000 were left homeless. The number of victims could only be guessed at. Not even the Peruvian government had accurate population figures for the remote Indian villages of this region.

In the days following the earthquake, airplane spotters could see survivors of isolated villages huddled on mountaintops. Dozens of countries quickly offered aid. But efforts to reach the survivors were slowed by mountain barriers, bad weather, and flooding. Finally, relief operations got under way. It then became clear that there were problems other than earthquake damage.

Some relief helicopters sent by the United States flew in canned goods, powdered milk, and plastic knives and forks to the mountain villages. But many of the Indians had never seen such articles. They had nothing to open the cans with and saw no point in mixing the white powder with drinking water. They kept the donated materials, however, to trade for "useful" goods once roads were opened to local towns.[1]

Medical teams also flew into the stricken areas. They discovered that few of the mountain Indians had ever had professional medical care. The doctors and nurses found a far greater need for treatment of basic health problems and long-term illnesses than for tending earthquake victims.

Larger towns in less remote regions of Peru were also hard-hit by the earthquake. Months afterward, little had been done to replace ruined houses and public buildings. One reason was that the government tried to prevent rebuilding with the traditional adobe bricks made of mud. Structures of this material collapse too easily in earthquakes. But many Peruvians could not afford to build dwellings of stronger materials. So, to provide themselves with shelter, they pieced together shacks made of cardboard, strips of metal, and other odds and ends.

As foreign journalists reported what they saw in northern Peru, outsiders became aware of the staggering problems that confront this country even in "normal" times. Poverty, ignorance, poor health, lack of communication, social strife, and inefficient government trouble all the republics of northern South America. In response to growing pressure, important steps have been taken to improve ways of living, especially in Venezuela and Colombia. But in those countries, and more especially in Peru, Bolivia, and Ecuador, there is still a long way to go.

1. Colombia

GEOGRAPHY, ECONOMY, AND CULTURE

Colombia has been called the "gateway to South America," since it is here that the narrow strip of Central America joins the southern continent. In area Colombia is a little larger than the three states of New Mexico, Texas, and Louisiana put together.

Colombia has two main regions. The country can be divided into two regions—the mountainous west and the plains in the east. Three ridges of the Andes reach from southwestern Colombia north almost to the Caribbean coast. Between these ridges run the country's two great rivers—the Cauca (*cow'* kah) and the Magdalena. The Cauca runs through a fertile valley thickly planted with coffee trees. The broader, more sluggish Magdalena, navigable for 815 miles, flows through tropical forests. Colombia is the only South American country having both Caribbean and Pacific coasts. Since most of it lies just north of the equator and rainfall is plentiful, its coastal lowlands have a hot and humid climate.

Grassy plains called *llanos* (*yah'* nohss) cover the undeveloped eastern region of Colombia. A long finger of Colombian territory reaches south to the Amazon. Thus, Colombia is one of the nations interested in plans for developing the Amazon basin.

Three peoples have formed Colombia's population. Probably more than half of Colombia's people are of mestizo descent. In port cities on both Caribbean and Pacific coasts, there are

[1] Reported in *The New Republic*, September 19, 1970.

large black populations. Colombia's Indians generally live in the southern and eastern forest areas.

Most of the people live in the west. Though the eastern plains make up three-fifths of Colombia's territory, only a tiny percentage of the country's people live there. Over 95 per cent of the Colombians live in the fertile valleys and plateaus of the western region. About half of the people are town and city dwellers.

Colombia has a number of cities. The major city in Colombia is Bogotá, the capital. Bogotá is not far from the equator, but since it has an altitude of a mile and a half above sea level, its climate is cool and pleasant. The city has a mixture of old Spanish buildings and modern structures of glass and steel.

Nineteen other cities in Colombia have passed the 100,000 mark in population. In the Cauca valley are Medellín (may-thay-*yeen'*) and Cali (*kah'* lee), both of which ship coffee down-river to Caribbean ports. Using cheap hydroelectric power generated along tributaries of the Cauca, these two cities are also busy manufacturing centers. Along the Caribbean coast Colombia has three major ports—the old Spanish cities of Cartagena and Santa Marta and the more modern Barranquilla (bah-rahn-*kee'* yah). As in other parts of South America, migration from rural areas swells the city populations.

Air travel is important. Because of the mountains in western Colombia, transportation has always been an enormous problem. To go from Cartagena to Bogotá by river used to take anywhere from 8 to 30 days. Now that airlines link the Colombian cities, the trip takes only an hour. But air travel is expensive for freight. A slowly growing network of usable roads is improving the transportation of goods. Though there is weekly air service to the Amazon outpost of Leticia in southern Colombia, there are still no roads or railroads to this remote part of the country.

B Bananas	**L** Livestock (sheep & cattle)
Ca Cattle	**M** Mining
Cc Cacao	**O** Oil
Cf Coffee	**R** Rice
Ct Cotton	**S** Sugar cane
I Industry	**T** Tobacco

The Northern Andean Countries

Colombia's coffee is grown chiefly on the Andean slopes of the western part of the country. Left, coffee farmers weigh their crop. Far to the southeast is the Colombian town of Leticia, an Amazon riverport. Right, a seaplane lands in the river near Leticia. Throughout South America, air travel provides the easiest way of reaching remote areas.

Colombia is seeking to diversify its economy. Coffee is "king" in the Colombian economy. The volcanic soil of the mountain slopes is ideal for growing coffee trees, especially in the Cauca valley. Many coffee farmers own their own small plots and thus are better off than many coffee workers elsewhere in Latin America.

But Colombia is making a strong effort to get away from its dependence on coffee. Other important crops are cotton, tobacco, and sugar cane. Manufacturing provides jobs for a growing number of skilled workers and white-collar employees. As a result, a middle class is steadily emerging. Colombia is also developing its oil reserves. Already Colombian oil fields yield enough for national needs and for export as well.

Progress is being made in education. Along with the expansion of Colombia's middle class, progress is being made in education. Until the 1950's schooling was generally for the children of the privileged few. Today this situation has changed, as more and more children are going to school. But much work is needed

to make up for lost time. For one thing, there is a shortage of trained teachers. Moreover, many of the primary-grade students are older than students at the same level in other countries. In a recent year one-fourth of the first-grade students in Colombia were between the ages of ten and fourteen. A number of children cannot attend school at all because they have to work.

Another problem is that many students who manage to get a few years of schooling have no further use for what they learn. They may live in homes and communities where illiteracy is the rule, and where there are few newspapers or books. After they leave school, they may forget their reading and writing skills just through lack of practice. Educational problems of this sort are not Colombia's alone. They are typical of all Latin American countries where illiteracy is widespread.

POLITICAL HISTORY

Quarrels plagued nineteenth-century Colombia. Chapter 7 told how Colombia, Venezuela, Ecuador, and Panama had all been part of

234

Bolívar's republic of Gran Colombia. When Gran Colombia fell apart, Panama remained part of Colombia. Like many of the other countries, Colombia in the 1800's had a difficult time working out a stable government. There was a sharp division between Conservatives and Liberals. Basically the former wanted a centralized government, limited voting rights, and continued privileges for the wealthy and for the Catholic Church. The Liberals tended to favor federalism (page 150), wider voting rights, and the separation of church and state. The question of the status of the Catholic Church continued to be a major source of conflict in Colombia.

Colombia resented the loss of Panama. From 1899 to 1902 a violent Liberal revolt against the government in power tore through the country. The next year Colombia suffered another blow when Panama seceded. Colombia was unable to stop this secession because United States warships prevented Colombian troops from reaching the area (page 209). The reaction in Colombia was anger and humiliation. In 1909

a president of Colombia tried to accept two and a half million dollars from the United States in exchange for recognizing Panama's independence. But resentment on the part of the Colombian people forced him to resign. Eventually the United States agreed to pay Colombia 25 million dollars. Meanwhile, "Remember Panama!" continued to be a slogan in Colombia.

Conditions improved in the 1920's and 1930's. North American businessmen encouraged the mending of relations with Colombia. Colombian oil reserves made the country too valuable a neighbor to be neglected. Investments and loans from the United States, as well as trade between the two countries, brought money into Colombia. Growing prosperity helped to heal the wounds from the long period of quarreling and civil war. Despite falling coffee prices in the early 1930's, Colombia made progress toward national unity and a more democratic system.

When World War II broke out, the Allies needed the co-operation of Colombia. If enemy airplanes had been allowed to use bases in Colombia, they could easily have bombed the

As in the United States, Latin American political candidates compete for voters' attention. Here a Colombian citizen considers rival candidates.

vital Panama Canal. But the president of Colombia gave his country's support to the United States, and in 1943 Colombia declared war against the Axis powers.

"La violencia" ravaged Colombia.
In the late 1940's, Colombia again was torn by disorder.

Conflict between the extreme wings of the Conservatives and Liberals kept the country in turmoil. While an inter-American conference was meeting at Bogotá in 1948, a popular left-wing leader was assassinated. Rioting mobs lynched the assassin and rampaged through Bogotá for several days.

Rioting soon spread to the countryside, where it took the form of rural wars fought between villages that considered themselves "Liberal" or "Conservative." Much of the violence was simply banditry, without any political meaning. Throughout the country organized groups of bandits attacked people who ventured outside the cities. Sometimes the bandits invaded towns and kidnapped people. This period of bloodshed and disorder lasted for years and became known as *la violencia*.

Many observers saw *la violencia* as a social revolution that burst out of long years of poverty and frustration. *"La violencia* is fed by the sons of farmers," wrote one observer. "Faced with the prospect of having to leave the tiny family plot and struggle for a job among the unemployed in the cities, many prefer to go back into the depths of the mountains and enlist in bands of desperadoes." [2] Others charged that the movement had Communist backing or at least the support of Fidel Castro, the Cuban dictator who hoped to spread revolution throughout South America.

From 1948 into the 1960's *la violencia* ravaged Colombia. This turmoil weakened confidence in democratic government. Some Colombians felt that the only way to prevent a complete breakdown in government was to restrict personal freedoms. One dictatorship was overthrown in 1953 by military officers led by General Gustavo Rojas Pinilla. Rojas (*roh' hahss*) restored order but proved to be a cruel dictator himself.

After four years of tyrannical rule, leaders of both Liberals and Conservatives decided to work together to get rid of Rojas. They formed a

[2] Gary MacEoin, *Life World Library: Colombia and Venezuela and the Guianas* (New York: Time Incorporated, 1965), p. 87.

National Front (*Frente Nacional*) and agreed that the presidency would alternate between the two parties. Rojas was forced out, and in 1958 a Liberal president, Alberto Lleras Camargo (*yair'* ahss kah-*mar'* goh), was installed after a free and peaceful election. Lleras Camargo worked hard to bring order to Colombia and also started economic and educational reforms. Under succeeding presidents these reform programs were continued.

Thus, for a time at least, Colombia breathed free from the burden of disorder and was able to give attention to other problems. The ex-dictator Rojas, however, remained on the scene as a troublemaker and a possible threat to democratic government. Moreover, occasional rioting in the cities showed that *la violencia* was not entirely a thing of the past.

THINKING ABOUT THIS SECTION

1. Explain or define the following words: *llanos; la violencia; Frente Nacional.*

2. Why does western Colombia have many more people than the larger eastern region? Why is air transportation important in Colombia? What rivers are important? Why? Why is Colombia trying to diversify its economy?

3. How might a Colombian view Panama's secession from Colombia and the United States' acquisition of the Canal Zone? What is your reaction?

4. What factors have been suggested as possible causes of the violence that ravaged Colombia for years? Which of these do you think was most responsible? Why has there been less violence in recent years?

2. Venezuela

GEOGRAPHY, CULTURE, AND ECONOMY

Venezuela is crossed by the Orinoco River. From northern Colombia the farthest eastern arm of the Andes extends into neighboring Venezuela, one of the middle-sized countries of South America. In Venezuela the mountains become hills near the hot, humid plain bordering the Gulf of Maracaibo (mah-rah-*ky'* boh) on the Caribbean coast. A more rugged chain of the Andes forms ridges and valleys around Caracas (kah-*rah'* kahss), the capital city of Venezuela. East of Caracas, hills extend southward like fingers into the Orinoco River valley. Almost unexplored by the Spanish, this great valley of tropical forests and *llanos,* or grassy plains, has only recently begun to be developed. The wide Orinoco flows across Venezuela all the way to the Atlantic. Some of the river's tributaries have their sources in the snowy peaks of Colombia.

South of the Orinoco is hilly land called the Guiana Highlands. The interior of this region has seen little exploration. In fact, white men were long unaware that the world's highest waterfall, Angel Falls, existed here. It was discovered from the air in the 1930's. Now Venezuela is developing new industries on the northern edge of the Guiana Highlands.

Venezuela's population is largely urban. About three-fourths of Venezuela's people live in towns and cities. By far the largest of the urban centers is dynamic, modern Caracas. This city lies in a mountain valley ten miles from the Caribbean coast. With an elevation of about 3000 feet, the city has a healthful climate. Like other large cities in South America, Caracas has streamlined skyscrapers in the downtown area and hillside slums built by rural migrants on the outskirts. A superhighway cuts through rugged land to connect Caracas with the harbor and airport at La Guaira (lah *gwy'* rah). Many North American tourists vacation in Caracas and the nearby Caribbean resorts. Maracaibo, the second largest city, is an oil town. In the east, rich iron-ore deposits have made Ciudad Bolívar a boom town. Paved highways and airline systems connect all the population centers of Venezuela. Railroads are less important.

The population includes three racial strains. In racial make-up Venezuela's population resembles that of Colombia. Mestizos account for an estimated 65 per cent of the people. The rest are European, black, Indian, or of mixed descent. Also as in Colombia, the great majority of the people live in the western, more developed part of the country. In recent years, however, industrial growth in the eastern Orinoco valley has attracted many people.

The level of education is rising. In education, too, there is a similarity between Colombia and Venezuela. But Venezuela's efforts to provide schools and teachers for its children are even more determined than Colombia's. For the first time many Venezuelan rural districts now have schools for their children. Venezuela also provides classes for adults who want to learn to read and write. But the population is growing so fast that the government finds it difficult to keep up with educational needs.

College education is free in Venezuela, and there are seven universities. The students are active in shaping university policies and influencing national politics.

Venezuela's economy is "taking off." Economists say that Venezuela has entered the "take-off" stage. What they mean is that old obstacles to economic progress have given way, allowing modernization of both industry and agriculture to surge ahead. In order to "take off," a country must also have a great demand for skilled workers, a growing number of consumers able to buy new products, and an over-all expansion of urban life. Mexico and Argentina are Latin American countries that have already "taken off."

Oil is of major importance. Venezuela can thank its booming oil industry for the new prosperity. Foreign companies began to drill for oil

A forest of oil derricks in Lake Maracaibo (left) dramatizes the importance of Venezuela's oil industry. In eastern Venezuela a growing steel industry has created additional jobs for workers and technicians (right).

in the region of Lake Maracaibo in 1917. Dutch, North American, and English companies invested millions of dollars in these oil lands and also built refineries. Now oil derricks line the shore of Lake Maracaibo and rise like a "forest" from the lake itself. The derricks are set in long rows and are connected by catwalks. Workers go from one section to another in speedboats.

The oil companies in Venezuela learned a lesson from Mexico's take-over of oil properties in 1938. The foreign owners have been willing to pay large royalties and taxes to the Venezuelan government. In fact, the government is guaranteed an amount equal to the companies' profits. Any new oil reserves that are discovered become Venezuelan property. The government has put its oil income into new schools, public-health programs, highways, housing, and other useful projects.

The oil companies also have introduced generous labor policies. Employees are paid good wages and can train for better jobs. The companies provide model housing, schools, hospitals, and recreation centers for workers and their families. The skilled workers, technicians, and managers of the oil industry form part of Venezuela's growing middle class.

Oil profits help to develop other industries. The Venezuelans realize, however, that some day (not soon) their oil may be used up. Wisely looking ahead, they follow a policy called "sowing the oil." In other words, oil income is used to create other profitable enterprises. New industries manufacture chemicals, synthetic rubber and fibers, and a variety of consumer items. By creating new jobs, this industrial expansion contributes to the "taking off" of the Venezuelan economy.

The mining of iron ore is also booming. For a long time it was known that eastern Venezuela had rich deposits of iron ore. But it was only after World War II that United States steel companies began mining ore in the Orinoco valley near Ciudad Bolívar. Like the foreign-owned oil companies, the steel producers treat their Venezuelan workers well.

In the 1950's the Venezuelan government began to develop other industries in this area, using hydroelectric power generated by waterfalls in the Orinoco tributaries. A government-owned steel plant processes local ore, and there is also a North-American-owned aluminum plant. For a long time the eastern Orinoco valley was a wilderness. Now it is booming. The development of this area will ensure Venezuelan prosperity when the Maracaibo oil fields are exhausted.

Agriculture also contributes to the economy. All this emphasis on industry does not mean that agriculture is neglected. After oil and iron ore, Venezuela's main export items are coffee and cacao. Cattle raising is important on the grassy *llanos*. But weather conditions keep this region from becoming a major livestock producer. In the winter the plains are very dry and in the summer they are often flooded. Finding adequate forage for the cattle is a problem.

Oil profits have also been used by the government for land distribution. Acreage has been bought up from large property holders, divided into plots, and sold on credit to landless tenants. The government sees to it that the new farmers get seed, equipment, irrigation if needed, and assistance in marketing their crops. Abundant harvests have proved the success of this policy. Though wheat is imported, almost all of the nation's other food needs are now met by Venezuelan farmers.

POLITICAL HISTORY

Independent Venezuela suffered poor government. Venezuela was another large country that broke away from Bolívar's ill-fated Gran Colombian federation. During the 1800's, Venezuela's history was marked by turmoil and corruption as regional *caudillos* warred with each other. The Venezuelan people had little sense of national unity.

Gómez dominated Venezuela. In 1908 a dictator came to power who strengthened central authority but at a great price to the Venezuelan people. This dictator was a soldier of Indian ancestry named Juan Vicente Gómez (*goh'* mayss). "All Venezuela is my cattle ranch," he said. Gómez ruthlessly silenced opposition and ruled with an iron hand. He gave army officers just enough power to make sure of their complete support. When Gómez died of old age in 1935, the people of Caracas at first carefully refused to believe the announcement. After they were sure that he was buried, they danced in the streets to celebrate.

Venezuelan presidents secured oil profits from foreign companies. It was during Gómez's reign that the "black gold" of Lake Maracaibo began to pour out profits. Gómez allowed the foreign oil companies to drill for oil, but he taxed them heavily. Thus, though he kept much of the money for himself, he started the practice of charging the foreign businessmen for their exploitation of Venezuelan oil.

Later presidents saw the oil revenue as a source of benefit for all Venezuelans. In the late 1930's the idea of "sowing the oil" was first discussed, though little was accomplished. In 1947 a well-known novelist, Rómulo Gallegos (gahl-*yay'* gohss), was elected president. He began to work out a plan under which taxes levied on the oil companies would pay for welfare and education. But in 1948, while Gallegos was visiting the United States, the army overthrew his government.

Pérez Jiménez took over. A general named Marcos Pérez Jiménez (*pehr'* ess hee-*may'* nayss) next ruled Venezuela. This dictator used the oil income to modernize Caracas. But he also squandered much money on spendthrift projects. While Pérez Jiménez and his friends prospered, the mass of the people had little share in Venezuela's oil wealth. As discontent built up, underground leaders organized opposition. Fighting in the streets of Caracas finally forced Pérez Jiménez to resign in 1958. For a few months the exiled dictator lived in Miami, Florida. Resentment over this was

Better health care for Venezuelan families has been a goal of recent governments. Here a family leaves one of the clinics that have been built with the country's oil profits.

one reason why a crowd threw stones at Vice-President Richard Nixon when he visited Caracas that year.

Betancourt started basic reforms. In a democratic election Rómulo Betancourt (bay-tahn-*koor'*) won office as president. The new president faced a staggering array of problems that had built up over years of neglect and corrupt rule. Despite opposition from both radicals and conservatives, Betancourt's reform programs were largely successful. Oil revenues were put to good use. New housing and schools were built, public-health programs were started, and industry was encouraged. Also, the land reform program got under way.

Communist agitation became a problem. In 1963, for the first time in Venezuelan history, a legally elected president (Betancourt) completed his full term and turned over the government to another legally elected president (Raúl Leoni). But, under both of these presidents, Venezuela was plagued with violence plotted by left-wing extremists. Many of these revolutionaries were supporters of Fidel Castro. Their goal was to overthrow a government that did not approve of Castro's Communist rule in Cuba. During a particularly severe wave of terrorism, the Venezuelan government for a time suspended constitutional rights.

In 1968 Rafael Caldera was elected president of Venezuela. After inauguration he adopted a policy of leniency toward the guerrillas. Instead of fighting them, he offered them free airline tickets to other countries. The guerrilla movement soon faded out. Some said that the movement had simply run its course. Others believed that revolutionaries had little chance of winning much support in a country as prosperous as Venezuela.

THINKING ABOUT THIS SECTION

1. Explain or define the following words: "take-off" stage in the economy; "sowing the oil."

2. Why have most of Venezuela's people lived in the country's western region? Why is the population largely urban? Why are people moving into the eastern Orinoco valley?

3. How is oil important to Venezuela's economy? What arrangements have been made with foreign owners to protect Venezuela's interests? How have the country's oil profits been used?

4. What happened to the left-wing guerrilla movement in Venezuela?

GEOGRAPHY, ECONOMY, AND CULTURE

The three other countries to be described in this chapter share an Indian heritage that sets them apart from Colombia and Venezuela. The largest of these Indian nations in the northern Andes is Peru.

Peru has three regions. Along Peru's Pacific coast stretches mile after mile of dry sandy plain. Brown, barren mountains rise from this desert, occasionally sending a spur down to the ocean. It is a cold ocean current (called the Peru Current) flowing north from the Antarctic that keeps the Pacific coast of both Peru and Chile very dry. Rain seldom falls along Peru's entire coastal region. Only where rivers of melted snow rush down from the nearby Andes are there oases where men can live comfortably on the Peruvian coast. "From the air," reports one writer, "a traveler sees the forty or so oases as bright green stains on an otherwise endless strip of dun-colored sand." These "green stains" make the desert coast Peru's most productive agricultural region. Westerly winds blowing across the cold ocean current reduce the tropical heat of the coast to comfortable temperatures.

Running alongside the narrow coastal strip is the great mountain belt of Peru. The Andean highlands and valleys of Peru and Bolivia form one of the highest inhabited regions in the world. In fact, a mining camp found at an elevation of 17,500 feet in Peru is believed to be the world's highest permanent human habitation. Water from melted snow irrigates mountain valleys that have been farmed since long before the days of the Incas.

The rest of Peru lies east of the mountains. Thick forests, some of them never visited by white men, cover much of the slopes and tropical lowlands of this region. In northeastern Peru the Andes plunge down to the Amazon plain.

Lima is the major city. About half of the Peruvian people live in cities and towns. Many handsome colonial buildings still stand in Lima, the capital city, along with some very modern structures. The University of San Marcos in Lima is one of the oldest universities in the

0 200 400 600 800 Miles

EQUATOR

TROPIC OF CAPRICORN

PACIFIC
OCEAN

ATLANTIC
OCEAN

AVERAGE ANNUAL RAINFALL

Under 10 inches

10-20 inches

20-40 inches

40-60 inches

60-80 inches

Over 80 inches

South America — Rainfall

A belt of desert stretches along South America's Pacific coast. Note the great difference in rainfall between northern and southern Chile. Heavy rainfall, low altitude, and a location along the equator combine to give the Amazon basin a hot, steamy climate, while drought plagues a large area in eastern Brazil.

Adaptation to Life in the High Andes

The Andean Indians live at such high altitudes that their bodies have adapted to the oxygen-thin air. Visitors from lower altitudes often get sick in the Andes because their tissues become starved for oxygen. The Indians, however, have hearts that are larger than normal and pump more blood. They have many more red blood cells too. It is these cells which carry oxygen to all parts of the body. The Indians also have larger lungs than low-altitude people and breathe more deeply and rapidly. They are so adjusted to the high altitude that they suffer if they move to a lower altitude. When Bolivia fought a war with Paraguay in the 1930's, Andean Indians were recruited into the Bolivian army. But the Indians sickened and died when they were taken to fight in the hot lowland Chaco of northern Paraguay. The sudden descent to a low altitude was too great a shock for their high-altitude-adapted bodies.

Western Hemisphere. In recent years it has been the scene of violent student demonstrations. Many Indians from the Andes come to Lima in search of wage-paying jobs. Overcrowding and lack of sanitation are staggering problems in Lima's slums.

Just eight miles west of Lima is Peru's major seaport, Callao (kah-*yah'* oh). The chief city of southern Peru is Arequipa (ah-ray-*kee'* pah), a leading wool market. Cuzco, the ancient Inca capital, remains a center of Indian life. Its people live in houses built on earthquake-proof foundations laid by the Incas centuries ago. At an elevation of 11,000 feet, the air in Cuzco is thin and chilly. Tourists often suffer from "mountain sickness," caused by lack of oxygen.

In eastern Peru the Amazon river-port of Iquitos (ee-*kee'* tohss), is the major town. Until recently Iquitos had closer commercial ties with Brazil than with western Peru. Ocean-going vessels steamed up the Amazon to Iquitos, a distance of more than 2000 miles from

the Atlantic. In the days before the airplane, the 600-mile overland journey between Iquitos and Lima was long and rugged. A recently completed road now makes travel easier between these two Peruvian cities.

Geography complicates travel. Like other Latin American countries, Peru for centuries consisted of isolated islands of population. Many small communities had no contact with the outside. This is still true of some Indian villages in remote Andean highlands. But in recent years a road-building campaign has linked more and more Peruvian towns and cities. Now Peru is co-operating with other Andean nations in building a "Forest Road" along the eastern edge of the mountain range. Side roads will branch out from the Forest Road into communities along the way. Air transportation is important in a country so handicapped by geography as Peru. In the eastern region rivers provide another means of transportation.

Mining and fishing are important in Peru's economy. Agriculture is the mainstay of Peru's mountain Indian villages. But "modern" Peru's economy depends on a variety of activities—agriculture, fishing, mining, and manufacturing. Peru's fishing fleets catch more fish than those of any other country in the world. Much of the catch is processed into a mealy substance rich in protein and used as feed for livestock. The exporting of fish meal is a vital part of Peru's foreign trade. Other major exports are copper, silver, iron ore, sugar, and cotton. Oil resources are being developed along the northern coast and on the eastern mountain slopes.

Peruvians are mostly mestizos and Indians. About a tenth of Peru's population is of totally European descent. For centuries this minority dominated Peru's national affairs. These aristocrats owned most of the land and controlled the wealth. The rest of the population is divided about equally between mestizos and Indians. The difference between Indians and mestizos depends more on way of life than on ancestors.

Peru's thriving fish industry provides jobs for thousands of people. Many fishermen are Indians who have left their mountain homes to live on the coast.

In all of the Andean countries an Indian who begins wearing "western" clothes and speaking Spanish, and who leaves his native community to live in a town or city, is usually regarded as a mestizo.

The mountain Indians have a bleak existence. The contrast between life in coastal Peru and in the primitive mountain communities is startling. Coastal towns are "modern," while the highland Indian villages have changed only slowly through the centuries. As told in Chapter 1, the Andean Indians were once ruled by the colonizing Incas. The Inca empire included many different culture groups. Today the population of the Andean highlands remains varied, both in language and customs. The chief languages spoken by Andean peoples in Peru, Ecuador, and Bolivia are Quechua and Aymara. But there are countless dialects of these languages, and very few of the highland Indians speak Spanish.

Despite the differences, it is possible to sketch out a general description of life in the Andean communities. Existence is harsh for the Indians. Their small houses are made of unbaked adobe bricks, with thatch or tile roofs and no windows. None of the houses have electricity or plumbing. There is not even a chimney, though a fire burns between a few bricks on the earth floor. A few mats or animal skins are the only furnishings. Meals consist of potatoes, turnips, corn, or manioc. Occasionally there may be a little smoked or salted meat. Many of the Indians chew coca leaves, the raw material from which the drug cocaine is manufactured. The coca dulls the feelings of cold, hunger, and exhaustion that are ever-present in their lives.

The Indians wear home-made woolen clothing, designed for protection from the sun and cold. The clothing of each village differs in some identifiable way from that of other communities. Common to most, however, is the tight-fitting cap worn by the men and the "derby" hat worn by the women. Some men wear sandals made from old automobile tires.

Throughout the bleak highlands of the Andean countries many Indians live in houses like this.

The Indians grow their own food on small hillside plots. Crude digging sticks may be the only farm tools. On the higher slopes, sheep graze. Women and children care for the flocks, spin wool into thread, and weave cloth.

Until very recently, not many Indians owned their own land. Most of them toiled long hours on haciendas owned by large landholders. As part of their pay, the Indians were allowed to work small patches of the least fertile land for their own use. They often had to carry out certain services, without pay, for the landholder. In many ways their life resembled that of serfs on a medieval manor.

The mountain villages are small, and schools and medical services are usually inadequate. Facing a bare plaza there may be an adobe church. But months may go by without a visit from the priest, since several villages often share his services. If the priest arrives, on Sunday the women and children attend a mass given in the local Indian dialect. Indian religious practices of ancient origin may be mixed in with the Christian service.

The people of a village choose a mayor or *alcalde*. He often sits with other members of the village council on the church steps. The council decides on the time for plowing, plans religious festivals, and handles whatever relations the village has with the distant provincial government. But actually the owner of the local hacienda has more to say about village affairs than the mayor or the council.

Several times a year the villagers go to market in the nearest town. During this visit a few of them may be recruited to work in copper mines or in oil fields. By taking such jobs, they hope to earn a little cash. Though few want to leave their villages permanently, more and more Indians are migrating to the cities. How to integrate these highland Indians into modern society is a major challenge in all the Andean countries.

APRA tried to help the Indians. The Andean Indians have lived in poverty for centuries. Since they have no political or economic influence, there seemed to be no way for them to help themselves. Moreover, until recently neither governments nor well-to-do people in the Andean nations took any interest in Indian problems. In fact, other groups looked down on the Indians as inferiors.

In the 1920's a political party founded in Peru took up the cause of the Indians. This was the *Alianza Popular Revolucionaria Americana,* called APRA. One of APRA's goals was to free the Indians from their serflike existence. The *apristas* (APRA members) urged that land be nationalized and distributed to the Indian villages. The *apristas* also stressed education for Indian children and campaigned against alcoholism and coca addiction. Still another APRA goal was labor legislation to protect Indian workers in both urban and rural areas.

The *apristas* failed to win the presidency in Peru, but their influence with the voters forced the government to start improvements. Reform parties in Colombia and Bolivia also made an issue of the neglect of Indian problems.

THE VICOS PROJECT

With outside encouragement, some Indian communities have begun to introduce modern improvements. One notable attempt at social change took place at Vicos (*vee'* kohss), a valley hacienda 250 miles north of Lima. Here, with the co-operation of the Peruvian government, social scientists from Cornell University studied the reaction of Indians to the introduction of modern ways of life.

The Vicos Indians were dominated by the patrón. When the Cornell team arrived in 1952, about a fifth of the 35,000 rocky acres at Vicos were being used. On the lower slopes, corn, potatoes, barley, wheat, and beans were grown. Cattle and sheep grazed higher up. Over 300 families raised barely enough food for themselves on their small plots. The land in Vicos belonged to the government, which leased it to the person who offered the highest rent for it. For the use of the land the Indians paid the leaseholder or *patrón* (pah-*trohn'*) three days of labor every week. They also had to provide free domestic service whenever the *patrón* demanded it. Moreover, the *patrón* could use the Indians' farm animals without charge. Except

in religious matters the *patrón* was judge and jury in everything concerning the village.

The Cornell team respected the Indians' culture. The goals of the Cornell experiment were to improve agriculture, nutrition and health, and education at Vicos. But the Cornell people did not want to force change on the villagers. Dr. Allan Holmberg, who headed the Cornell team, described the approach that was used: "Every effort was made to tackle each problem in terms of understanding and respecting the local culture. [This is] the only basis on which lasting changes can be understood [and accepted] by the community." [3] Since the elders of the community held the respect of the people, the Cornell team generally worked through them. But the people, or their elected representatives, shared in making decisions.

Changes were introduced gradually. One of the first changes was an agreement with the *patrón* that villagers would no longer have to give free domestic service. Instead, the *patrón* was to hire workers and pay them regular wages. A more significant change came about when a number of families agreed to try more modern ways of farming. New supplies, including better seed, were bought on credit. The Indians learned to fertilize the soil, to weed and cultivate the crop effectively, and to use insecticides.

It had taken courage for the Indians to change their time-honored farming methods. By experimenting, they were risking the chance of smaller crops, which could have meant famine. But the improvements resulted in a bigger harvest. Surplus produce was sold to pay off debts and buy more supplies and different kinds of food. The success of the farmers who had adopted the new techniques persuaded others to try them. The Vicos community soon grew far more potatoes than any other village in the region.

The Cornell team found that the Indians resisted the idea of education. Though there was

[3] *Social Change in Latin America Today* (New York: Vintage Books, 1960), p. 82.

a run-down schoolhouse, the local teacher made no serious effort to instruct the pupils. Of some 350 children, only 15 or 20 boys attended the school. They often spent the school day doing household chores for the teacher. Moreover, the *patrón* was opposed to schooling for the Indian children.

The Cornell team persuaded the Indian villagers to build a new schoolhouse and got the Peruvian government to send better teachers. A school lunch program was started. For many children this alone was good reason to attend school regularly. Soon there were two schools: one for boys and one for girls. Never before had girls in Vicos gone to school. As traditional attitudes slowly changed, the villagers accepted the value of education. Within a few years more than 200 students were being taught by seven teachers. An adult education program also got under way. A new clinic taught hygiene and simple medical practices to the people at Vicos.

The Vicos community became self-sufficient. In 1956 the Vicos villagers bought the land they had farmed for generations. A loan from the Peruvian government made the purchase possible. No longer did the villagers have to give three days of labor a week to a *patrón*. As landowners they were masters of their own lives, and they showed new self-respect and confidence as they began to run their own affairs. The Cornell University staff left Vicos in 1957. The community by then could manage by itself. Other village self-help programs got under way, using the Vicos project as a model.

POLITICAL HISTORY

Dictators ruled Peru after independence. During the 1800's government in Peru was chaotic or dictatorial or both. Throughout the colonial period, and after independence, a small class of aristocrats dominated the country. There was no chance for democratic government in a country where the social structure was so rigid, poverty and illiteracy were widespread, and population centers had little or no contact with each other.

APRA urged reforms. In 1924 a young reformer named Víctor Raúl Haya de la Torre (*ah' yah day lah tor' ray*) started the APRA movement in protest against military rule in Peru. As noted earlier, APRA supported land distribution and justice for the Indians. The movement also favored nationalization of industry and the passage of social security laws, and was opposed to Communism.

Haya de la Torre had been exiled in 1920 for leading student demonstrations in Lima. For years afterward he was in and out of Peru, occasionally in prison. But he continued his fight for social equality and against dictatorship. Haya spent some time in Mexico and became enthusiastic about the Indian revival there.

In 1930 Haya de la Torre ran for president of Peru and probably won the most votes in the election. But a candidate backed by the army was declared the winner. The next year thousands of *apristas* were machine-gunned by troops in the town of Trujillo. This massacre had been authorized by the president. "The reactionaries irrigated the country with blood. We will irrigate it with water," said Haya de la Torre.

In the mid-1940's a combination of political parties ran the government, and APRA had three members in the cabinet. But when a conservative newspaper editor was murdered, the *apristas* were blamed and their party outlawed. Haya escaped arrest by taking refuge in the Colombian embassy in Lima. For three years he stayed there as a house guest, but was finally permitted to leave the country. He spent the next three years in Europe supporting himself by teaching Spanish. When Haya de la Torre returned to Peru in 1957, he found that the long years of agitation were having some effect. The APRA party was now legal, and many of Haya's reform ideas were actually getting under way. In 1962 Haya won the most votes in a three-way presidential election. But officers of the Peruvian army said, "We will never let Haya de la Torre be president of Peru." The generals sent tanks to take over the presidential palace and called off the election.

Belaúnde sponsored reforms. In 1963 a popular reformer named Fernando Belaúnde Terry was elected president of Peru. Belaúnde (bay-lah-*oon'* day) was the candidate of a new Popular Action Party which favored many of APRA's ideas. During the first two years of his term, this energetic president traveled throughout Peru by car, truck, motor launch, and mule. He urged the "reconquest of the difficult geography of Peru by the Peruvians themselves."

Belaúnde accomplished a good deal. It was he who planned the Forest Road along the Amazon foothills. He also divided up large estates that were not being farmed efficiently and promised to pay the owners over a 20-year period. The lands were distributed to Indian families, who were shown how to improve their farming methods. Indians willing to migrate to the eastern region beyond the Andes were resettled there with government aid. Students and army officers were sent to teach in Indian schools and to show villagers how to build roads. Health programs were also introduced. Loans from the United States enabled President Belaúnde to go a long way toward carrying out APRA's ideas.

A new kind of military dictatorship seized power. In 1968, a year before his term was to end, Belaúnde was overthrown by army officers. The men who carried out this revolt and took over Peru's government represented a new kind of army dictatorship in Latin America.

Many of the young officers oppose the traditional aristocracy and favor land distribution and welfare programs. They say that Peru is taking a "new path between capitalism and Communism." In other words, they want to nationalize Peruvian business and industry while avoiding the extremes of Communism. One of the military government's first steps was to seize an oil field and refinery owned by a United States corporation. Other foreign investments in Peru have been restricted. Nationalist policies like these have won support among the Peruvians, but some experts think they handicap economic growth. Meanwhile, democracy suffers as the military government limits personal freedoms and controls the press.

THINKING ABOUT THIS SECTION

1. Explain or define the following words: Peru Current; Forest Road; APRA; patrón.

2. How is western Peru different from the land to the east? Why are minerals and fishing more important than agriculture in Peru's economy?

3. About 10 per cent of Peru's people are white; the rest are mestizo and Indian. Yet the minority has owned most of the land, controlled most of the wealth, and dominated national affairs. How was this possible? What was the result?

4. What has the life of the Andean Indians been like? In answering, consider food, clothing, shelter, occupations, health, education, public services, and contact with other people. What conclusions can you draw from the Vicos project?

5. What conclusions can you draw from the efforts made to block Haya de la Torre from becoming president of Peru? from the election of Belaúnde and his reform efforts? from the army dictatorship established in 1968?

4. Bolivia

GEOGRAPHY, ECONOMY, AND CULTURE

Bolivia is divided by the Andes. Bolivia is so high that it is sometimes called the "roof of South America." The lofty Andes range cuts the country in two. To the west of the Andes is a high plateau called the *altiplano*. North and east of the mountains, lowlands reach down to large tributaries of the Amazon and Plata river systems. Both drought and floods have discouraged people from settling in eastern Bolivia. Nevertheless, the government is trying to develop this region. Bolivia has no seacoast, though by treaty with Chile it may use two of that country's seaports. Bolivia is often thought of as a "small" country, but its area is larger than the combined area of France and Spain.

Lying across the boundary between southern Peru and Bolivia is the world's highest large lake. Lake Titicaca (tee-tee-*kah'* kah), 12,500 feet above sea level, is the largest body of fresh water in the Americas south of the Great Lakes. Its barren shores and cool waters make one forget that it lies within the tropics.

Southeast of Lake Titicaca lies Bolivia's capital and only large city, La Paz (lah *pahss'*). This city is so high that here, as in Cuzco, visitors often have trouble breathing. Sucre (*soo'* kreh), the home of the Bolivian supreme court, is a secondary national capital. It too is a mountain city, though at a lower altitude than La Paz. Newer towns lie in the foothills extending down into the eastern lowlands. But Bolivia's rough terrain discourages the building of roads and railroads.

Construction is difficult in terrain like this, but Bolivia now has a road reaching from La Paz into the eastern lowlands.

Tin dominates Bolivian foreign trade. Bolivia is one of the poorest countries in Latin America. Yet it has a wealth of undeveloped mineral deposits. "A beggar sitting on a chair of gold" is what some people have called Bolivia. The Bolivians are not unaware of their underground treasure. But the minerals are worthless without machinery and money to mine them and railroads and highways to take them to market. Even though mining dominates Bolivia's economy, the country has not yet really exploited its resources.

During colonial times the Bolivian mines yielded much of the silver that was sent to Spain. But silver mining fell off as the richest ores were exhausted. A little before 1900, deposits of tin were discovered. At this time the United States and Europe were beginning to use tin in the canned-food industry. The growing de-

mand made tin mining profitable. Since then, tin has been the mainstay of the Bolivian economy. But Bolivia also exports other metals and is trying to develop its oil fields as well. Like any country that depends heavily on a single export, Bolivia is at the mercy of the world market. When the price of tin slumps, all of Bolivia suffers.

Only a tiny percentage of the Bolivian people work in mining, and there is very little manufacturing. The great majority of the country's workers are farmers. Most of the crops are used by the farm people themselves or go to local markets. Bolivia has to import much food for its city populations.

Bolivia is an Indian country. Over half of the Bolivian people are Indian. About a third are mestizo, and there is a small minority of white people. As in the other Indian countries of the Andes, a great gap has divided the wealthy minority and the Indian masses. For years the Indians of Bolivia lived the bleak sort of existence described on pages 244–245. But since 1952 the government has divided up many large estates to provide small farms for rural people. Both mine workers and Indian farmers have insisted on a more important role in Bolivian national affairs. But poverty remains a basic fact in Bolivia, and well over half the people are illiterate. A country as poor as Bolivia has little money to spend on education.

POLITICAL HISTORY

Disorder followed independence. Bolivia's political history has been turbulent since the country's birth. During the first century of independence there were more than 180 revolutions and other political crises. Probably the worst thing that happened to Bolivia during this period was a war fought with Chile in the early 1880's. In this War of the Pacific, Bolivia lost valuable nitrate lands and a strip of coastal territory. During the early 1900's the tin boom brought prosperity to Bolivian businessmen. But this prosperity came to an end with the depression of the 1930's. The senseless Chaco War with Paraguay (page 274) made matters worse.

One of the heroes of the Chaco War became president of Bolivia. Germán Busch, half Indian and half German, hoped to improve conditions for the downtrodden people of his country. Busch was responsible for a new constitution which called for improvement of education, the legalization of miners' unions, and government ownership of the mines. But Busch faced strong opposition from the most powerful interests in Bolivia—the landowners, tin-mine operators, and foreign investors. Busch died suddenly in 1939. It is still uncertain whether he took his own life or was murdered.

The next president of Bolivia had little sympathy with Busch's aims. Nevertheless, the tin miners were able to organize. In 1942 their union called strikes to protest low wages and harsh working conditions. The government sent troops to break the strikes, and scores of miners were shot down. In 1946 a bloody rebellion overthrew the military government.

The 1952 revolution marked a turning point. Finally, in 1951 a legal election was held in Bolivia. A professor of economics named Víctor Paz Estenssoro (*pahss'* es-ten-*sor'* oh) received the most votes for president. He was the candidate of a leftist political party called MNR (*Movimiento Nacional Revolucionario*). But the army refused to allow Paz to take office. In 1952 the MNR and student and labor leaders joined forces in a bloody revolt against the military junta then in power. The MNR took over and installed Paz Estenssoro as president.

Under Paz Estenssoro the Bolivian government set out on a program of far-reaching changes. The three largest tin-mining companies were made the property of the government. All adults, literate and illiterate, men and women, received the right to vote. Large estates were divided into small plots and distributed to farm workers. Paz Estenssoro also tried to develop industry in Bolivia. But little could be accomplished in a country so poor in financial resources and lacking skilled workers.

Turmoil continued. In its 1952 revolution Bolivia had made a sharp break with the past. Nevertheless, the country's traditional political confusion went on. Democracy as we know it seemed almost impossible in a country so beset with deep-rooted problems. Moreover, radical leaders in the miners' unions began to use terrorist tactics. In trying to control this violence, Paz Estenssoro finally declared martial law (rule by military force). But in 1964 the army forced Paz into exile, and General René Barrientos took over as president. He ruled with a heavy hand, breaking up demonstrations and imprisoning agitators. In 1966 Barrientos was confirmed as president in an election. Many Bolivians feared that he would halt the reform programs. The reforms were slowed down, but they did not end entirely.

Bolivian women carried signs in the streets of La Paz in 1969 to show support for their government's nationalization of oil fields developed by a United States company.

"Che" Guevara was captured in Bolivia. Meanwhile, Fidel Castro and the Cuban Communists tried to organize an underground movement in Bolivia. Castro's comrade Ernesto "Che" Guevara secretly traveled to the Bolivian backlands. Guevara and Bolivian guerrillas who joined him hoped that the miners and peasants would rally behind their revolutionary movement. But they failed to gain much support. In 1967 Guevara and his guerrilla followers were captured, and the Cuban leader was shot to death by Bolivian army officers.

The Bolivian government remains unstable. In 1969 President Barrientos was killed in a helicopter crash. Over the new few years several "palace revolts" resulted in a steady turnover in the presidency. One president was Juan José Torres (*tor'* rehss). Torres' military government appeared to be of the new nationalist type that had gained power in Peru. But his radical programs made conservatives fear that he was aiming to make Bolivia another Cuba. In 1971 Torres was overthrown, and a coali-

tion of conservative army officers and middle-class civilians installed a new military president.

THINKING ABOUT THIS SECTION

1. Explain or define the following words: altiplano; War of the Pacific; MNR.

2. How has Bolivia's terrain been a handicap to its people? What role have mineral resources played in Bolivia's economy? Why has it been impossible for Bolivia to exploit its mineral wealth fully?

3. Look at the map on page 142 that shows Latin America just after independence was won. Notice that Bolivia then had land on the Pacific coast. In the war with Chile, Bolivia lost its seacoast. What has this meant for Bolivia? Why is it important for a country to have direct access to the sea?

4. What reforms were urged by Germán Busch? What changes were started by Paz Estenssoro? What problems made progress difficult?

Ecuador is also divided by the mountains. The remaining Andean nation, Ecuador, is one of the smallest South American countries. Only Uruguay has less territory. As its name suggests, Ecuador is crossed by the equator, just north of the capital city, Quito (*kee'* toh). But Quito's altitude of more than 9000 feet above sea level keeps the city cool and pleasant. Looking down on the capital is the world's highest active volcano, Cotopaxi. Since Quito was the city of the Quitu Indians before their conquest by the Incas, it claims to be the oldest capital in the Western Hemisphere. Large numbers of Quitu Indians, wearing felt hats and bright blue or red ponchos, still stream into the city to sell beans and fruits in the markets.

Like Peru and Bolivia, Ecuador has three main regions. The mountain slopes of Ecuador's Andes region are rugged and barren. There is no green growth except in the valleys where Indian farmers grow their food. East of the Andes, humid forested land slopes down into the Amazon basin. Little has been done to develop this part of Ecuador. Along the Pacific coast are narrow lowlands that are wet in the north but increasingly dry to the south. Coastal Ecuador is dominated by the port of Guayaquil (gwah-yah-*keel'*), the largest city in the country. Slower-paced Quito seems old-fashioned in contrast with busy, sprawling Guayaquil.

Ecuador exports tropical products. Along the coast lie the plantations that produce Ecuador's major exports—bananas, coffee, and cacao. The country's prosperity depends on the world demand for these products and the health of the plants that grow them. Some rice is also grown for export. Small quantities of minerals are mined, and oil reserves recently discovered in Ecuador's Amazon region are being developed by foreign companies. Some Ecuadorians talk about becoming "another Venezuela."

The population includes a variety of peoples. Ecuador's population resembles that of Peru and Bolivia, with one difference. About 10 per cent of the people in Ecuador are Negroes and mulattos, mostly living on the northern coast. People of European origin and those mestizos who have adopted "modern" ways chiefly live in the cities and coastal area. Wealthy white Ecuadorians have dominated the country's political and economic affairs. As in the other Andean countries, the Indians have long been the poorest and least privileged members of society.

In the eastern lowland region live primitive forest Indians. A tribe called the Jívaros (*hee'* vah-rohs) are famous as headhunters who shrink the heads of their victims. Another of these Amazon tribes, the Aucas, have fiercely resisted any contact with white men. A few Christian missionaries, however, have dared to live among them.

Among Ecuador's highland Indians, the Otavalo people are best-known. By Indian standards, the Otavalo Indians are well-off. Skilled weavers, they have a steady market for their woolen blankets, ponchos, and tweed fabrics. Not only Ecuadorians but people of other countries as well buy the fine materials woven in Otavalo. But most of the highland Indians are poor farmers. Many work as tenants on large estates, though a number of Indian communities own land.

Most of the people are poor and unskilled. Like Bolivia, Ecuador has little money to spend on education or other programs that might help its people improve their lot. About a third of the population is estimated to be illiterate, though the proportion is much higher than that in the highland and eastern regions. As in other countries, many Indians and mestizos migrate to the cities in search of wage-paying jobs. Guayaquil, which attracts most of these restless people, has some of the worst slums in South America.

Ecuador has been held back by internal strife. Ecuador is a country troubled by divisions. In

The Galápagos Islands

One part of Ecuador lies far out in the Pacific Ocean, 650 miles to the west of South America. This is the cluster of about 60 islands called the Galápagos (gah-*lah'* pah-gohss). Desolate and rocky, these islands are chiefly known for their unique wild life, especially giant tortoises and large iguana lizards. When the English scientist Charles Darwin visited the Galápagos in the 1830's, no people lived there and the animals seemed almost unafraid of him. Now about 3000 people live on the islands. Some of them staff a satellite-tracking station. There is also a wildlife sanctuary in the Galápagos for the protection of some of the rare species of reptiles.

addition to geographical differences and unrest among the poor, there are other factors that divide the nation. Quito and Guayaquil have a long-standing dislike of each other. Their physical separation is partly to blame. Before the 1900's there was not even a good road connecting the two cities. But their antagonism has also been part of a lack of co-operation between the mountain region and the coastal area. One historian has explained how this hostility has retarded progress in Ecuador:

The lack of roads, the racial contrasts . . . , the tropical diseases on the coast, all worked in favor of isolation and against a free interchange of populations, goods, and money. Thus the coast got used to living with its back turned to the sierra [mountain] hinterland. . . . Foreign trade made the coast completely dependent on the fluctuations [ups and downs] of the world markets.

[Quito,] in the sierra, on the other hand, lived as if the outside world might not have existed but for the fact that the government income was mainly derived from import and export duties raised on the coast, though largely spent in the sierra. A strong central government . . . was impossible because of the same obstacles.[4]

[4] Lilo Linke, *Ecuador: Country of Contrasts* (London and New York: Oxford University Press, 1954), pp. 116–117.

Like so many of the Latin American countries, Ecuador after independence entered a time of confusion and bad government. But, unlike Venezuela or Peru, Ecuador has experienced no dramatic shift in direction. As noted in the passage just quoted, the central government has seldom been strong enough to make the country an efficient political unit. In fact, few presidents of Ecuador have ever completed a full term in office.

Galo Plaza Lasso attempted reform. One president who did successfully finish his four-year term was Galo Plaza Lasso. As a young man, Galo Plaza (*plah'* sah) studied at colleges in the United States. Though his father was wealthy, he paid his own way by working in a factory. When Galo Plaza returned to Ecuador, he made his family estate the most efficient farm in the country. After his election as president in 1948, he hoped to modernize agriculture throughout Ecuador and thereby raise standards of living. He also encouraged mining and industry. Moreover, Galo Plaza tried to strengthen democracy. In the 1952 election all literate Ecuadorians could vote, and the balloting was secret. In his last speech as president, Galo Plaza said that one of the things most satisfying to him was having proved it was possible to govern Ecuador "freely and democratically."

After his presidency, Galo Plaza became an international figure. For a while he served as a United Nations trouble-shooter in the Middle East. In 1968 he was chosen Secretary General of the Organization of American States.

Velasco declared a dictatorship. Since 1952 Ecuador's political situation has been less stable. The man who followed Galo Plaza as president was José María Velasco Ibarra, a conservative lawyer who had already served in the presidency several times. After him, several politicians were in and out of the presidency. But in 1968 Velasco was re-elected at a time when Ecuador was experiencing widespread unrest.

Two years later, with the support of the army, Velasco declared himself a dictator. This action was necessary, he claimed, to restore order.

---

1. What tropical products are exported by Ecuador? In what part of the country are these raised? Why may the eastern region become much more important to the country's economy?

2. How does the population of Ecuador differ from that of Bolivia? Why are the Otavalo Indians more prosperous than most Andes Indians?

3. How has the traditional hostility between Quito and Guayaquil slowed down progress in Ecuador?

4. What were Galo Plaza's goals for Ecuador?

Galo Plaza Lasso is seen here with Indian farmers on his hacienda celebrating a harvest festival. This talented Ecuadorian has at various times been a full-time rancher, amateur bullfighter, ambassador to the United States, member of Ecuador's senate, president of his country, and Secretary General of the Organization of American States.

Summing Up

Colombia, Venezuela, Peru, Bolivia, and Ecuador lie in northern South America. For years each of these countries consisted of isolated clusters of population divided by geographical barriers and social and cultural differences. Lack of unity hindered the growth of orderly government and efficient national economies.

Though all five of these countries have abundant natural resources, the economies of Colombia and Venezuela are more advanced than those of the other three. The Colombians and Venezuelans have made significant progress in reducing dependence on a single export and in developing industry.

Bolivia, Peru, and Ecuador are Indian countries in which a majority of the people still live in non-Spanish-speaking villages remote from the stream of modern life. The Indian populations have enjoyed none of the benefits of their countries' natural wealth, and many have lived like feudal serfs on large estates owned by absentee landlords. They have had no part in the money economy and few have had any education.

Recently, however, the old social order has begun to crumble. Various groups, such as miners and farm workers, have demanded greater opportunities. Agrarian reform and the nationalization of mineral resources and industries are two ways in which these countries have sought to improve the lot of their people.

All of these nations have had stormy political histories. Though a belief in social justice is developing, practical democracy has not yet been achieved.

13

A street scene in downtown Buenos Aires in many ways resembles the business section of a North American city. One obvious difference is the absence of traffic jams. Argentina has a much lower percentage of cars in relation to its population than the United States.

The Latin American Nations: Southern South America

CHAPTER FOCUS

1. Argentina
2. Chile
3. Uruguay
4. Paraguay

The Latin American countries farthest from the United States are those that lie in the southern triangle of South America—Argentina, Chile, Uruguay, and Paraguay. The first three of these countries are in many ways more like the United States than any other Latin American nations. The majority of people in Argentina, Uruguay, and Chile dress like North Americans and enjoy a fairly comfortable standard of living. The climate of these countries is mostly temperate, and many of the people live in busy, modern cities. Literacy rates are among the highest in Latin America. As in the United States, many European immigrants have settled in these countries, and it is not unusual for people to have German, Irish, and Italian names.

Because these countries lie south of the equator, their seasons are the opposite of those of the United States. In southern South America, January is a summer month and July is a winter month. Yet these countries do not experience the extremes in temperatures that are characteristic of the northern United States. Instead, the summers are long and the winters generally mild. The reason for this is the effect of the two oceans that border the southern triangle of South America. Masses of cold air from Antarctica cross southern South America just as Arctic blasts chill North America. But by the time the polar air masses reach Argentina and Chile, they have crossed wide expanses of water and this has made them less cold. Even at the southernmost tip of South America the temperature averages above 32 degrees in the coldest month.

It is convenient to group Argentina, Chile, Uruguay, and Paraguay together, since they occupy the southern end of South America. But these four countries cover an enormous amount of land, and there are great differences between them, not only in natural features but also in cultures, politics, and economies.

1. Argentina

GEOGRAPHY, ECONOMY, AND CULTURE

Argentina has a variety of regions. Earlier chapters told about the Rio de la Plata, the great salt-water estuary that lies on the south Atlantic coast between Argentina and Uruguay. Prairie land with rich black soil stretches from the Plata estuary west into Argentina and east into Uruguay. In Argentina, this prairie land forms the heartland pampa, probably the finest pasture land in the world. It is this land that made possible Argentina's great livestock industry. To the west the Argentine pampa is drier and to the east it is wetter. In the eastern region live two-thirds of the Argentine people, many of them clustered in or around Buenos Aires, the huge capital city.

It would be a mistake, however, to think of Argentina as being all pampa. The second largest Latin American country, Argentina is almost six times as large as Spain and has several distinct regions. In western Argentina the towering Andes mark the long border with Chile. These mountains dwindle to hills in the far south. Among the Argentine foothills of the Andean barrier lie several cities in oases where mountain streams bring life-giving water. Toward the north along the mountain barrier the land is almost a desert.

Northeastern Argentina is part of a lowland plain which extends into Paraguay. Called the Chaco (*chah'* koh), this plain is often flooded in summer and dry in winter. Agriculture is difficult, but the harvesting of hardwoods is profitable. One tree that grows in the Chaco is so hard that it is called the *quebracho* (kay-*brah'* choh), "the axe-breaker."

A strip of Argentine territory reaches north from the Plata estuary between the Paraná and Uruguay rivers. In this warm and humid region, there are rain forests but also grassy plains where livestock is raised and a variety of crops are grown.

Southern Argentina is the region called Patagonia, reaching to the tip of the South American continent. On the grasslands of this bleak and windswept plateau graze huge flocks of sheep. Though Patagonia includes more than one-fourth of Argentina's land area, only 1 or 2 per cent of the people live there. The tip of Argentina is only 600 miles from Antarctica. Yet winters in Patagonia are not severe. As explained above, temperatures in this region are affected by the two oceans that close in on the tapering land.

Most Argentines are of European descent. The great majority of Argentina's people are of

Spanish or Italian descent. Perhaps 3 per cent of the Argentines are mestizo or Indian. Though Africans were brought to Argentina in colonial times, their descendants have merged into the general population.

About a third of the people live in Buenos Aires. About 70 per cent of the Argentine people live in and around the nation's towns and cities. The largest of the cities, of course, is Buenos Aires. The population of Greater Buenos Aires, which includes the areas clustered around the core city, exceeds eight million. Lying inland on the Plata estuary, Buenos Aires is the port for Argentina's livestock products. Deep channels have been dredged in the Plata to permit ocean freighters to dock at this port.

Buenos Aires strikes North American visitors as having a European atmosphere. There are many old mansions but also large modern buildings, fashionable stores, and sidewalk cafés. The aristocrats of Buenos Aires are the members of about 200 families of old creole stock. Some of them are of Italian or English ancestry. Most of these families made their fortunes raising cattle on large estates on the pampa. Today the wealthy Argentines maintain their country homes but also have luxurious apartments in Buenos Aires. They travel in Europe, speak French and English as well as Spanish, and follow international fashions in dress, music, and the theater. Rapid industrial growth has also created a well-to-do business class in Buenos Aires.

Argentina has a sizeable middle class, but few of the white-collar workers in Buenos Aires own cars. Since large numbers of them live in the suburbs, they ride to work on buses and subway trains. The office workers are not well-paid and prices are high. To make ends meet, many of them hold more than one job.

Many of the laborers in Buenos Aires work in the packing houses that process beef for export, or on the docks where meat is loaded onto

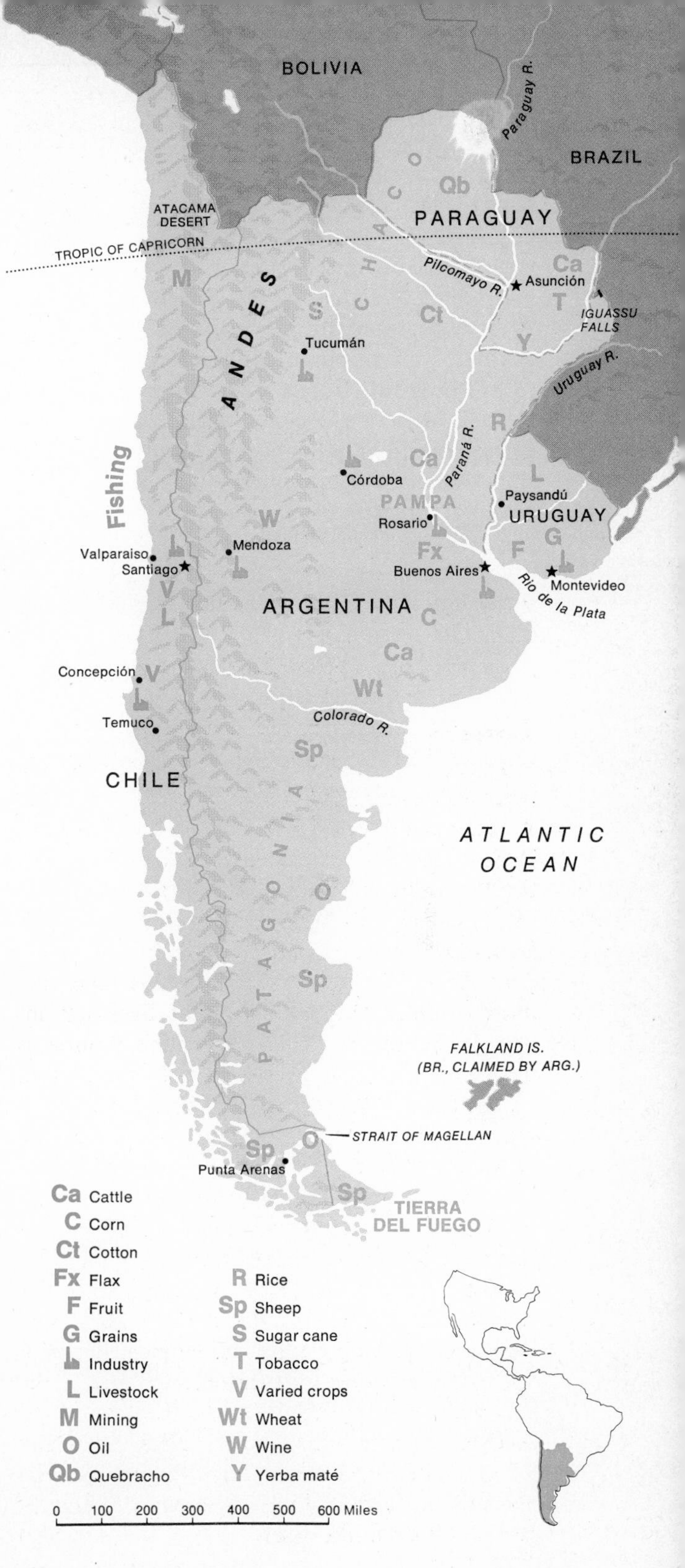

refrigerated ships. These workers are among the best-paid in Latin America. They belong to powerful unions and enjoy generous social security benefits. Paid vacations enable them to visit the beaches of Mar del Plata, a popular resort south of Buenos Aires.

Finding adequate living space in Buenos Aires is a problem for workers of all kinds. A continued housing shortage forces many people to live in crowded flats. Like other large cities in Latin America, Buenos Aires has its slums where poor families manage to survive in makeshift dwellings. The city has built some public housing projects in an effort to relieve the problem.

Other cities are of medium size. Argentine life seems to focus on Buenos Aires. No other Argentine city approaches this metropolis in size. But the other cities should not be overlooked. Rosario, the second largest urban center, is one of the world's major grain-shipping ports. Ocean-going ships steam from the Plata estuary into the Paraná River to load wheat at Rosario. In the foothills of the Andes lies Córdoba, once a center of Spanish colonial culture. This city now has an important automobile industry. Two other large cities, Tucumán and Mendoza, also lie in the western foothills. Tucumán, close to the tropics, is the center of a sugar-cane growing region. Mendoza lies about 500 miles west of Buenos Aires in a valley that produces wine grapes.

Rural people fare less well than urban workers. The farm workers of Argentina have a harder life than working-class people in the cities. Few people own their own farms. Much of the land is still tied up in huge individual estates of hundreds of thousands of acres. A recent census showed that less than 6 per cent of Argentine farm owners held three-fourths of the nation's farm land.

Most rural workers are tenants on the large cattle ranches. Tenants with families are provided with a small house and a garden plot, and receive a large allotment of beef as well as a small yearly wage. Unmarried men and migrant families travel from wheat harvest to cattle round-up, looking for work. They have few of the social security benefits enjoyed by workers in the city.

Argentina is a major producer of livestock. Today, as in the 1800's, huge herds of cattle feed on the lush grass of the Argentine pampa. But the days when gauchos herded cattle on the open range are over. Pastures have been fenced in, alfalfa is grown to ensure year-round feed for the livestock, and windmills pump up underground water. Ranching now is a far more settled life than it was in the last century.

The cattle ranches are called *estancias* (ay-stahn' see-ahss). A wealthy rancher may spend only a few months of the year on his *estancia*. But he maintains a large comfortable residence there, with well-kept grounds. Small houses nearby provide living quarters for servants and overseers. Some distance from the big house are countless barns, machinery sheds, and feed bins, as well as a village of homes for the tenant families and an elementary school for their children.

Much of the acreage is planted in grain and alfalfa. The ranchers realize that the best roasts and steaks come from cattle that have been fattened in corrals. Over the last 60 years, careful breeding has doubled the weight of the average steer. The beef cattle are the "aristocrats" of Argentine livestock. They are descended from many generations of cross-breeding between wild pampa cattle and prize bulls from the best beef-producing breeds of England. To compete in the yearly championship shows, *estancia* owners must have their animals' pedigrees registered in the records of the Argentine cattle society.

Beef-slaughtering and packing is the major industry of Buenos Aires. Most of the large packing plants, called *frigoríficos* (free-goh-ree' fee-kohs), are operated by the Argentine government. Though the Argentines themselves eat a huge amount of beef, many cuts are frozen or canned for export to Europe. The *frigoríficos*

handle sheep and hogs as well as cattle. Hides and wool are among Argentina's most valuable export products.

Gauchos herding cattle are a typical sight on the vast Argentine pampa.

The livestock industry faced a crisis. By the early 1970's Argentina's beef industry was in serious trouble. A shortage of cattle on the pampa had raised the price of beef for the Argentine housewife, had forced the closing of several packing plants, thus throwing men out of work, and had reduced exports. The higher prices were a severe blow to people used to eating fine steaks every day. And the reduced exports threatened the entire country's prosperity.

The pampa also produces grain. Argentina is one of the world's major wheat exporters. On the river docks at Rosario, grain is stored in big elevators like those on the Great Lakes ports of the United States and Canada. The grain pours down the elevator chutes into the holds of large freighters. Today the huge wheat farms around Rosario use the most modern machinery —tractors, harrows, planters, and harvesters.

Corn is becoming more important as an Argentine export. The Indians of the pampa had never learned to grow corn. It was only after

1900 that it began to be raised in large quantities in Argentina for cattle feed and for export to Europe. Other important agricultural crops are sugar cane, cotton, rice, barley, and flax.

Industry is increasing. Many factories produce a variety of goods for use within Argentina. In fact, more Argentine workers are employed in industry (including the meat-packing plants) than in agriculture. But Argentina is not yet an exporter of manufactured goods. About 90 per cent of its exports in recent years have consisted of agricultural products. In trying to develop heavy industry Argentina is handicapped by lack of coal and iron. Argentina's steel industry uses iron ore imported from Brazil, Chile, and Peru. Coal is shipped from the United States. In the late 1950's oil was discovered off the coast of Patagonia. Now Argentina produces most of the oil it needs.

The literacy rate is high. In level of education, as well as in material wealth, Argentina ranks high in Latin America. In fact, Argentina claims

259

a literacy rate of over 90 per cent. Almost all Argentine children attend school at least long enough to learn to read and write. The percentage of young people who go on to high school, however, is much lower. Since most high schools charge tuition, generally only children of well-to-do families are enrolled.

Argentina has several public universities, the largest of which is in Buenos Aires. Argentine college students have always taken a keen interest in politics and used to have more voice in university affairs than American college students. In recent years student demonstrations and rioting have led to repressive measures on the part of the government.

The Argentines have high standards in literature.
Buenos Aires is the world's leading center for Spanish-language publishing. Argentines buy so many books that writers in their country, unlike those elsewhere in Latin America, can earn a living from their publications. Most Argentine books are published in paperback editions, which are sold in bookstores from Chile to Texas.

Argentina's leading newspapers, *La Prensa* and *La Nación,* are well-known throughout South America. Buenos Aires has more daily newspapers than any city in the United States. A number of excellent journals and magazines are also published there. One widely read literary magazine is called *Sur* ("South"). Its publisher and editor, Victoria Ocampo, is prominent in Argentine intellectual circles and is the country's most highly regarded woman.

Gaucho life was long a favorite theme of Argentine literature. The country's most famous poem is an epic about a fictitious cowboy, *Martín Fierro,* written by José Hernández in 1872. *Don Segundo Sombra* (1926), by Ricardo Güiraldes, is a popular gaucho novel. It tells about a young boy who idolizes a wandering gaucho, Don Segundo. At the end of the story, the boy goes to live in the city, while Don Segundo rides away on horseback. The book symbolizes modern Argentina's nostalgic fondness for its gaucho past.

The best-known of modern Argentine writers is Jorge Luis Borges (*bor'* hayss), called by one North American reviewer "a truly international author." Many of Borges' short stories, poems, and essays have appeared in English translations.

The other arts also flourish.
In Buenos Aires both native and foreign plays, films, soloists, orchestras, and opera companies find enthusiastic audiences. An Argentine composer of international fame is Alberto Ginastera (*hee'* nah *stay'* rah). One of his works, *Don Rodrigo,* was the first Latin American opera to be performed throughout the world. Another well-known Argentine gift to international music is the famous dance called the *tango.*

Argentine painters are also internationally recognized. One outstanding recent artist is Benito Quinquela Martín, who grew up as a foundling on the docks of Buenos Aires. As a little "wharf rat," he drew charcoal sketches of boats on the sides of packing boxes. After someone gave him paints and canvases, he began to sell his pictures of ships, stevedores, and the slums. Later in life, Quinquela Martín founded an elementary school which specialized in art. The students, many of them also from the waterfront slums, are encouraged to paint pictures of the common people of Argentina.

POLITICAL HISTORY

Conservative and liberal parties developed.
By 1900 Argentina was the most prosperous country in Latin America. But this prosperity was enjoyed by the wealthy few—the great landowners, bankers, and merchants. Very little of the "good life" trickled down to the needy masses. A middle class was growing but had little voice in running the country.

The struggle between federalists and *unitarios* (Chapter 8) had died out as Buenos Aires became the acknowledged capital of the nation. Now the two political forces that opposed each other were "liberals" and "conservatives." Members of a new liberal party called for fair elections and wider participation in voting. Their demands had results. In 1912 a law granted the right to vote to all male citizens and provided for a secret ballot.

Irigoyen was the first freely elected president.

Four years later the Argentine people for the first time freely elected a president. The election of Hipólito Irigoyen (ee-rih-*goh'* yayn) was considered a triumph for the common people. Celebrating crowds unharnessed the horse from his carriage and themselves pulled the new president through the streets of Buenos Aires. Irigoyen was dedicated to the ideals of justice and equality. He cared little what other people thought of him. Because of his shabby clothes and simple way of life, his enemies called him *El Peludo*, "the armadillo." During Irigoyen's presidency Argentina prospered by selling beef and wheat to the European nations fighting World War I.

But Irigoyen was a poor administrator and had no practical program for reform. In 1928, at the age of 78, he was elected president a second time. By that time in poor health, Irigoyen found it difficult to govern the country. When the world-wide depression of the early 1930's hit Argentina, beef exports fell off and the country suffered hard times. Irigoyen was forced out of office, and in 1933 he died friendless and alone. But thousands stood bareheaded outside the rooming house where he had died, to pay homage to a man they had regarded as their friend.

Conservatives regained control.

In 1930 a group of land-owning conservatives and army officers took control of the government. As World War II approached, the Argentine government leaned toward the Germans, though most of the people sympathized with the Allies. A group of army officers seized power in 1943, and the government became even more pro-German. University professors, students, and workers who demonstrated in favor of the Allies were thrown in jail. The United States and other Latin American nations continued to prod Argentina into taking an Allied stand. Finally, in 1945, when the war was almost over, Argentina declared war against Germany and Japan.

Perón rose to power.

One of the army colonels who had carried out the 1943 revolution was Juan Domingo Perón (pay-*rohn'*). The forceful and energetic Perón took on a job none of the other officers wanted—that of Secretary of Labor—and made a power base out of it. He settled strikes in the meat-packing plants by making friends with the strike leaders.

Perón's most effective ally in his rise to power was a young blond radio performer named Eva Duarte. Politically ambitious, Eva devoted herself to Perón's career and in 1945 they were married. By that time Perón had effective control of the Argentine government. His dictatorship became legal in 1946 when he won an overwhelming victory in a presidential election.

The workers idolized Perón and his wife.

It was the workers in the Argentine towns and cities who gave Perón his impressive victory. The dream of all these workers was someday to get a white-collar job, called in Argentine slang a *camisa*, from the word for "shirt." Perón and Eva told workers that the *camisa* jobs were not the important ones, that the *descamisados* (dayss-kah-mee-*sah'* thohss), those who wore no shirts, held the future of Argentina in their hands. Perón himself, speaking to crowds of workers, would take off his shirt and say, "I also am a *descamisado!*" Perón showed his gratitude for the workers' support by making new laws that guaranteed them higher wages, paid holidays, pensions, and other benefits.

Perón and Eva were snubbed by the conservatives. The wives of the wealthy landed aristocrats had always handled charity in Buenos Aires through their church organizations. These women did not care to have Eva join in their activities. But Perón appointed Eva Minister of Social Welfare. From that position she handled all the money for relief, charity,

An elaborate parade marked the inauguration of Juan Perón's second term as president in 1952 (left). Eva Perón, idol of the Argentine masses, rode at his side. Three years later a revolt drove Perón out of the country. Argentina's politics continue to be stormy. Right, in 1969 Buenos Aires police used tear gas to break up an anti-Yankee demonstration by young people.

and education. With this money and millions from so-called "contributions" from labor and business, she made the care of orphans, the aged, and other needy people a public responsibility. The people adored Evita, as she was called. A United States ambassador described her in this way:

The bitterness and adoration she aroused made her career so dazzling as to have been matched by few women in history. . . . Evita's desire to assert herself was matched by seemingly boundless energy. . . . It forced her to follow the rigorous diet that undermined her health. She wanted to have one of the loveliest figures in the world and to be the world's most expensively dressed woman. Constantly and astutely she told her *descamisados,* or shirtless followers, that she wore her elaborate wardrobe only in trust for them . . . and that some day they would have similar luxuries.[1]

The Peróns concentrated all power in their own hands. The Peróns made the working people of Argentina feel that they themselves had become a force in the nation. Gratefully

[1] James Bruce, *Those Perplexing Argentines* (New York: Longmans, Green, 1953), pp. 281–282.

the workers helped their representatives, Perón and Eva, stay in power. But the Peróns went even further in trying to control the nation. Eva forced the owners of three large newspapers to sell them to her, and freedom of the press was stifled in other ways as well. In 1949, Perón had a new constitution adopted, which made it legal for him to run two years later for a second term as president. The new constitution also provided for woman suffrage. The dictator confidently expected that all Argentine women would vote for him.

Eva planned to run for the vice-presidency in 1951, but the army officers who helped keep Perón in power balked. They would not support a woman—not even Eva Perón—for such a high position. By this time Eva was already ill with cancer. Perón easily won his second term but Eva died in July, 1952. Thousands of *descamisados* were injured and some were trampled to death in the hysterical mourning that marked her funeral.

Perón's economic policy was disastrous. In addition to the loss of his popular wife, Perón was facing other problems. He wanted to make Argentina a strong, self-sufficient state. With

this goal in mind, he had tried to build up industry and had downgraded agriculture. As part of his industrialization campaign, Perón bought the country's railroads from the English companies that had owned them. He also made elaborate plans for developing a merchant fleet and for building oil and gas pipelines and hydroelectric and steel plants. But Argentina lacked the capital, or financial wealth, to pay for these grandiose schemes. Some of them were never completed. Moreover, when the price of beef dropped on the world market, the country began to lose income. Inflation soon wiped out many of the benefits that Perón's rule had brought to workers.

Growing discontent forced Perón to resign. After Evita's death, Perón soft-pedaled his industrialization policy. But enemies were gathering courage to oppose him. Businessmen and middle-class Argentines began to show their resentment. Catholic leaders denounced laws that restricted the Church. Even army officers joined in opposition to the dictator. In September, 1955, all these forces combined to drive Perón out of power. Faced with open revolt, he escaped to a Paraguayan gunboat in the Rio de la Plata. Perón eventually became a guest of General Franco, dictator of Spain.

Though he had almost wrecked the country's economy, many Argentine workers look back with longing to the age of Perón. They remember that he brought them higher wages and other benefits and gave them a feeling of being important in Argentine politics. Nevertheless, Perón's attempts to return to power in Argentina failed.

Political disorder followed. Probably no president could have brought order out of the chaos left by the exiled dictator. Military conservatives were now in charge of the country. For three years provisional presidents held office. In 1958 an election was held in which the Peronista party (formed by those who still favored Perón) was not allowed to offer candidates. But Arturo Frondizi, a second-generation Italian lawyer, was elected president with the help of Peronista votes. Though Frondizi was a popular president, he was unable to do much about Argentina's economic problems. Moreover, the military disapproved of his leniency toward the Peronistas. Frondizi was ousted by a military revolt in 1962.

In 1964 a doctor named Arturo Illia (ill-*lee'* uh) became president, but neither conservatives nor workers supported him. After only two years, he too was ousted by the military. A general named Juan Carlos Onganía (ohn-gah-*nee'* ah) then declared himself president for an indefinite period.

A military dictatorship took charge. At an earlier time Onganía had supported constitutional government. But now he imposed a strict military dictatorship. Newspapers were censored, opposing political parties were outlawed, and universities were placed under oppressive government control. Onganía tried to stabilize the economy, but unpopular policies, such as strict wage levels, led to unrest and rioting. In 1970 Onganía was forced out in one of the country's traditional military revolts. Since then, two more generals have filled the office of president. The latest one has pledged to restore civilian rule. Observers, however, have seen little likelihood that Argentina will return to constitutional government soon.

THINKING ABOUT THIS SECTION

1. Explain or define the following words: pampa; *estancia; frigoríficos; descamisados.*

2. Why is southern Argentina colder than northern Argentina? How is the western part of the pampa different from the eastern region?

3. Fewer than 6 per cent of Argentina's farm owners hold three-fourths of the agricultural land. What conclusions can you draw from this fact?

4. What is Argentina's chief industry? Why? What handicaps has the country had in developing a steel industry?

5. Argentina's literacy rate is over 90 per cent. Yet a comparatively low number of young people go to high school. Why? Who are some of the outstanding figures in Argentine literature, music, and art?

6. How did Perón win control of Argentina? What mistakes did he make in his economic plans? What kind of government has Argentina had since Perón's overthrow?

2. Chile

GEOGRAPHY, ECONOMY, AND CULTURE

Chile is a long and narrow country. Argentina's neighbor to the west, Chile, stretches more than 2600 miles from north to south. This is a greater distance than from New York City to Seattle, Washington. But from east to west, Chile averages only a little over a hundred miles. Chileans themselves call their geography "crazy."

The northern coast is very dry. Chile's eastern border is the Andes mountain range, reaching south to the tip of the continent. Between this *cordillera* and the Pacific Ocean lies the narrow shelf of Chilean territory. Chapter 12 told how the Peru Current, flowing north from the Antarctic, keeps the coastal regions of both Peru and Chile very dry. At the "shoulder" of Ecuador the current turns west towards the mid-Pacific, so that the climate north from there is rainy. But especially from Lima south through northern Chile the land is extremely arid. In fact, in some places in the Atacama (ah-tah-*kah'* mah) Desert in northern Chile no rainfall has ever been recorded. The writer Peter Matthiessen called this desert "a dead, windless world of giant dunes and cones, half sand, half dust" (see picture, page 6).

Most Chileans live in central Chile. South of the Atacama Desert the Spaniards who came to Chile centuries ago found a fertile valley. Indians were already farming this land when the Spaniards arrived. Today the rich valley is one of the "garden spots" of South America.

Vineyards and fields of grain and vegetables alternate with orchards and green meadows where cattle and horses graze. All of Chile lives on food produced in this central valley, although some food is also imported. Chilean fruits and vegetables are quick-frozen for shipment to Peru and Bolivia.

The majority of Chileans live in and between the two major cities, Santiago and Valparaiso. Santiago, Chile's capital, is a metropolis. Majestic snow-crowned peaks of the Andes form a dramatic background for this city. Its public buildings, apartment houses, and business center are as modern as those of Caracas and Buenos Aires. But, also like those cities, Santiago has its slums, called *callampas* ("mushroom towns"). Here in makeshift huts live people who have no share in the country's prosperity. Valparaiso, 75 miles west of Santiago, is the largest Pacific port in Latin America. North and south of Valparaiso, beach resorts are crowded with people during the summer months of December, January, and February.

Southern Chile is cold and forested. As Chile extends southward toward the Antarctic, the climate becomes colder and wetter and the land more forested. This is a region of islands and deeply indented coastline. At the tip of the continent, the rocky sides of the Strait of Magellan form the southern end of the Andes *cordillera*. Punta Arenas (*poon'* tah ah-*ray'* nahss), lying on the strait, is the southernmost city in the world. South of the strait is the group of islands called Tierra del Fuego (*tyeh'* rah del *fway'* goh). Some of these islands belong to Chile and the rest to Argentina.

The population is a "melting pot." Though close to three-quarters of the Chileans are mestizos, the European strain dominates far more than in other mestizo countries. Most of the rest of the people are of all-European descent. Besides the usual Spanish surnames, many Chileans have names of English, German, Irish, Scottish, Italian, Slavic, or Arab origin. In southern Chile more than 100,000 Araucanian Indians have preserved their native way of life. They live in communities where they farm their lands in common.

Mining dominates Chile's economy. The Atacama Desert may look like a wasteland, but it is a treasurehouse of minerals. According to an old story, in the 1840's a Scottish businessman interested in gold mines planted a garden around his house in this desert. He watered the plants with drinking water brought in by boat. To his amazement, his flowers grew twice as fast as they would have in Scotland. He sent some of the desert soil to England to be tested. It was found to contain sodium nitrate. This mineral is a valuable fertilizer and at the time was also used in the manufacture of gunpowder. Since the Chilean desert proved to be rich in nitrates, mining boomed there. By the end of the 1800's nitrates made up three-quarters of Chile's export trade. After 1920, however, profits from nitrates fell because German chemists developed a different way of making explosives. Chile's nitrate industry did not die out entirely, however. Mining continued, and in recent years nitrates have made up about 5 per cent of the country's exports.

But copper is now "king" in the Chilean economy. In production of this metal Chile ranks among the world leaders. The great Chuquicamata (choo-kee-kah-*mah'* tah) mine in northern Chile is the largest copper mine in the world. Thousands of workers live nearby in a modern town. Originally this mine was owned by the Anaconda Copper Company of the United States. But the company's labor policies were resented by the Chileans. In the late 1960's the Chilean government bought large quantities of stock in the United States-based firms that operated the five largest copper mines in Chile. Then, in 1971, under Salvador Allende (page 269), Chile completely took over all the mines.

Chile also has important resources of iodine, coal, iron ore, and oil. A government-managed steel plant near the city of Concepción is one

The huge copper mine at Chuquicamata (left) was nationalized by the Chilean government in 1971. Here a gigantic loading machine lifts ore into waiting railroad cars. Right, Chilean students and rural workers guard a farm seized by their radical organization. The signs read (from left): "Bread, land, and socialism," "Revolutionary Farm Workers Movement," and (on the gate) "This farm is ours."

of the largest in Latin America. Among the chief non-mineral exports of Chile are wool, wine, fruit, paper products, and fish meal.

Goods and passengers are carried by land transportation, water, and air. Chile's peculiar geography has posed special problems in transportation. But today Chile has five railroad lines linking it with its neighbors, and government-owned railroads run north and south within the country. There also are some 30,000 miles of roads, mostly in northern and central Chile. Water transportation is important too. The government operates a fleet of vessels that carry both freight and passengers between the many small ports along the Pacific coast. A government-owned airline provides service both within the country and to foreign cities. But Chile has only a few good airports. Foreign airlines fly into Santiago's airport.

Chilean industrial workers have fared well. Miners and other industrial workers in Chile have long had a voice in determining their working conditions. The isolation and bleakness of the northern desert made it difficult for the mining companies to recruit workers. Since the

companies had to make it worthwhile for men to go to the mines, the Chilean workers were able to form strong unions and to demand higher wages. Today the mine workers live in houses much more comfortable than those of laborers on the farming estates in the central valley. By co-operating with the miners' organizations, unions in Santiago and Valparaiso also won higher wages and better working conditions.

Chilean labor unions have secured other kinds of benefits for workers too. These include pensions, loans for buying houses, health programs, and day nurseries for the children of working mothers. There are even workingmen's restaurants which serve meals at low prices. In recent years, however, continued inflation has cut down the purchasing power of wages, and discontent has increased.

Farm laborers have not shared in benefits. The rural poor of Chile have seen little of the benefits won by the labor unions. For years the landless farm workers have lived in poverty on great estates owned by a small group of wealthy aristocrats. Many rural Chileans have moved to the cities, hoping to find a better life. But

they have no skills to fit them for city jobs, and they cluster in the *callampa* slums on the edges of Santiago and Valparaiso.

In an effort to relieve rural poverty, the government started a program of agrarian reform in the 1960's. Privately owned land was bought up and sold to small farmers on long-term loans. Under the left-wing government that was elected in 1970, this program received new emphasis. But in some areas peasants grew tired of waiting for government aid. They organized in bands and seized and occupied private farms.

Chile is trying to upgrade education. Chile has a high literacy rate. More than three-quarters of the people have had enough schooling to read newspapers. By law all children are required to attend elementary school, but in practice there are just not enough schools available in some areas, especially outside the cities. Many children who do go to school leave after the eighth grade and go to work. For the small number who continue their education, high schools offer college preparatory courses or vocational training. In 1966 President Frei pushed a law through congress promising every Chilean child free education from kindergarten through the university level. The largest of the country's eight universities is in Santiago. Like the students at other Latin American universities, Chilean students take an active interest in politics.

Two Chilean poets are internationally famous. Chile has writers and artists as talented and sophisticated as those of Argentina. Two poets are especially well-known. One of them is Pablo Neruda, who won the 1971 Nobel Prize for Literature. Much of Neruda's work deals with revolutionary themes and faith in the common people. He has influenced younger poets throughout Latin America.

The other poet is Gabriela Mistral (mees-*trahl'*). This remarkable woman was the first Latin American to win the Nobel Prize for Literature (in 1945). Her real name was Lucila Godoy Alcayaga. As a young woman she began to publish her poetry under a pen name: Gabriela Mistral. Using this name, she entered a poetry contest in Santiago and won. Soon she became famous not only as a poet but also as a teacher. In Mexico during the 1920's, Gabriela Mistral trained young women to teach in the new rural schools. She also lectured at universities in the United States. As a member of cultural committees for the League of Nations, she was the only woman delegate from Latin America. The status and rights of women and children were of special interest to her. At the time of her death in 1957, Gabriela Mistral was one of the world's most renowned women. Today volumes of her poetry continue to sell throughout the Spanish-speaking world.

POLITICAL HISTORY

A reform period started in 1920. As late as 1920 the Chilean government was dominated by wealthy landowners and businessmen who made fortunes from nitrates. The year 1920, however, marked a peaceful revolution by the middle class against the traditional rulers. A new political group had formed. Made up of small landholders, shopkeepers, and professional men, it was the first true middle class to emerge in South America. This group, with help from miners and city workers, elected a reform president, Arturo Alessandri Palma. He had been a union leader among the nitrate miners.

During Alessandri's presidency Chile adopted laws that legalized labor unions. Over the next few years the unions gained the benefits mentioned earlier. A new constitution adopted in 1925 gave the vote to all men over 21, separated church and state, and established free public schools.[2] Chile became known throughout the world for its forward-looking legislation in the field of public welfare.

Since 1920, Chile's workingmen and middle class have continued to be influential in politics, and elections have generally been honest. But Chilean politics are by no means calm. Low prices in the world copper market, inflation, labor unrest, and continued rural poverty have all made for unsettled conditions. Such natural disasters as drought and earthquakes add to the problems that face Chile's presidents.

[2] In 1949, Chilean women won the right to vote in national elections.

President Salvador Allende proclaimed Chile's first "National Day of Voluntary Labor" and then, to set an example, pounded nails into the roof of an unfinished one-room house.

Frei supported reform programs. In 1964, Eduardo Frei Montalva won election as president. Frei (*fray' ee*), the son of Swiss immigrants, wanted to expand welfare programs and strengthen democratic participation in politics. He called for increased government control of large mines and other major industries. But he disagreed with politicians who demanded total nationalization of industries. Frei wanted to avoid the concentration of power that strangles democracy in Communist countries.

Frei's government did distribute land to small farmers and secured greater control of the large copper mines. But by the end of Frei's term Chile's economic difficulties were still sizeable.

A Socialist president was elected. In 1970 widespread discontent contributed to the victory of a Socialist candidate, Salvador Allende Gossens, in the presidential election. (Frei could not run again because Chilean presidents are not allowed to serve two consecutive terms.) Allende (ahl-*yen'* day) won with the help of Chile's Communist Party. On taking office, however, he declared that the Socialist and Communist parties would not dominate his administration. Allende said that he favored "a nationalist, popular, democratic, and revolutionary government that [would] move toward socialism." According to a *New York Times* report, "Chileans, publicly at least, tried to accept the world's first free election of a [Socialist] president as just another twist in their complicated political history."

The copper mines were nationalized. Soon after taking office the new president called for the nationalizing of all the country's copper mines. The Chilean congress unanimously approved the nationalization. This was the largest take-over of foreign property in Latin America since Fidel Castro's seizure of United States investments in Cuba. At first Chile said it would pay the United States-based companies for their investments in the mines. But later Allende ordered that "excess profits" received by the companies in the past be deducted from Chile's payments.

THINKING ABOUT THIS SECTION

1. Explain or define the following words: *callampas;* Tierra del Fuego; nitrates; socialism; nationalization.

2. Why is the weather along the Chilean coast dry and cool? What is the importance to Chile of the central valley? of the Atacama Desert?

3. Contrast working conditions and social benefits among Chile's industrial workers and farm laborers. Why have the former fared better? What is being done to help the rural workers?

4. How did Gabriela Mistral become one of the world's most renowned women?

5. How did Chile's middle class and workingmen achieve a peaceful revolution against the traditional rulers? What reforms were introduced during Alessandri's presidency? Compare Chile's politics since 1920 with those of Peru (Chapter 12).

6. What were the views of Presidents Frei and Allende on national control of the copper industry? What actions were taken by each in this respect?

3. Uruguay

GEOGRAPHY, ECONOMY, AND CULTURE

Tucked in between giant Brazil and Argentina is Uruguay, the smallest of the South American republics. Uruguay is somewhat larger in area than the state of Oklahoma.

Uruguay has a pleasant setting. The Uruguayan territory is a rolling, grassy, treeless plain resembling the Argentine pampa. This country enjoys a mild climate—a winter without snow and a summer cooled by sea breezes. A number of rivers flow across Uruguay. Ships can steam from the Plata estuary inland up the Uruguay River as far as the small city of Paysandú (py-sahn-*doo'*).

On the southern coast, about where the brown waters of the Plata estuary darken the

*Millions of sheep graze on Uruguay's grassy plains
and produce the country's major export, wool.
Here wool is being sorted and bagged for shipment.*

ocean, stands the capital city, Montevideo (mohn-teh-vih-*day'* oh). Almost half of the Uruguayans live in this city. The capital does not have the wretched slums that are found in every other large city in Latin America. But Montevideo no longer has the look of comfortable living that was characteristic only a few decades ago. Years of economic decline have left their mark, and the city now looks shabby.

Few Uruguayans own cars, but a network of modern bus lines carries passengers to every part of the city, into the interior of the country, and to the ocean resorts. The pleasant climate and miles of sandy beaches attract tourists,

especially from neighboring Argentina. In Uruguay's interior there are many small farming towns. These are reached by paved highways and have electric lights and modern sewer systems. Rural Uruguay is a vast sheep and cattle pasture.

Uruguay raises livestock. The lush pastureland is the mainstay of the Uruguayan economy. Millions of sheep and cattle are raised, and wool has long been Uruguay's chief export. Grains and fruits are also produced but chiefly for use by the Uruguayans themselves. The most important industry, as one might expect, is meat-packing. There are also small industries which manufacture consumer items.

The people of Uruguay are white and middle-class. Most of the Uruguayan people are of Spanish or Italian descent. About 1 per cent are blacks, and there are hardly any Indians. The country is free of the great social divisions found elsewhere in Latin America, since almost everyone is considered a member of the middle class. Unlike other Latin American countries, Uruguay is losing population. Many young Uruguayans have moved to other countries, and the birth rate is low. As a result, Uruguay has more people over the age of 50 than under.

Education is free in Uruguay, and the great majority of people can read and write. Uruguayan literature has produced some of Latin America's finest writers. Best-known was the essayist and philosopher José Enrique Rodó, who died in 1917.

POLITICAL HISTORY

Batlle brought basic changes to Uruguay. Before 1900, Uruguay had a long, unhappy history of political chaos. Between 1825 and 1900 some 40 revolutions took place. But stability was finally achieved under the leadership of José Batlle y Ordóñez, often called "the founder of modern Uruguay." Batlle (*bah'* jay) served two terms as president during the early 1900's and continued to influence Uruguay until his death in 1929. He was determined to raise the standard of living of the Uruguayan people. Thanks to the sweeping program of reforms that he started, this aim was largely achieved.

Batlle's reform programs were very advanced for that time. Measures adopted to aid workers included the eight-hour day, a minimum-wage law, and old-age pensions. Batlle also founded Uruguay's first free public schools and outlawed child labor. Moreover, these laws did not exist only on paper, for the government strictly enforced them. Under Batlle and later presidents, the Uruguayan government acquired ownership of banks, insurance companies, bus lines, and most housing projects. Uruguay also pioneered in giving women greater control over their own lives. Divorce was legalized, an unusual step for a Catholic country. Women workers were assured of leave with pay when they had babies. A new constitution adopted in 1919 reaffirmed many of Batlle's reforms

and also helped to strengthen political democracy.

Some Uruguayans opposed Batlle's program for social improvement. "Why should we, a small underpopulated country hardly known abroad, continue to astonish the other nations with the radicalism of our laws?" asked an opposition newspaper. A newspaper founded by Batlle answered: "You have not seen anything yet! We may be a poor and obscure little republic, but we can have forward-looking little laws!" These words about the "little laws" became a motto for Uruguay. One historian has said, "the spirit of Batlle engendered a touch of greatness in the Uruguayan people."

After Batlle's time, Uruguayans continued to emphasize social welfare. Other Latin Americans envied the Uruguayans their comfortable standard of living. Uruguay was by no means free of economic and political difficulties, but the Uruguayan people seemed able to deal with their problems in an orderly way.

Uruguay's prosperity and democracy are threatened. By the 1960's, however, economic crises posed a serious threat. The high cost of social security programs had overburdened Uruguay's national budget. But also the country was losing its share of the world's wool and meat markets. As the value of the Uruguayan peso plunged, the government was unable to pay pensions and workers' salaries. Runaway inflation threatened to wipe out savings, unemployment rose, and wages had to be cut. Consumer goods became scarce, and people grew poorer every year. In response to the wage cuts, workers' organizations called strikes which threatened to paralyze the nation. Economists in the United States predicted that Uruguay would "come apart at the seams." Some politicians in Montevideo began to call for military rule.

To make matters worse, a terrorist group called the Tupamaros harassed the government by robbing banks, throwing fire bombs, and kidnapping prominent people. The Tupamaro guerrillas even murdered one of their hostages, a United States adviser to the Uruguayan national police. In 1969 the president of Uruguay declared the country in "a state of emergency." This meant that he could suspend constitutional rights. Newspapers and radio broadcasts were censored, and Uruguay's democracy was obviously endangered. One observer commented: "If the Uruguayan system fails, what hope is there for anything but military dictatorships in Latin America?"

THINKING ABOUT THIS SECTION

1. Explain the following words: Batlle; Tupamaros.

2. Compare Uruguay and Chile with respect to (1) geography, (2) population, (3) economy, (4) programs for social improvement.

3. What problems have plagued Uruguay in recent years? Why? What is the outlook?

4. Paraguay

GEOGRAPHY, ECONOMY, AND CULTURE

North Americans sometimes confuse Uruguay with Paraguay, another of the Plata river countries. Both names come from words of the Guaraní Indian language. An ancient Guaraní legend called eastern Paraguay a "paradise on earth," and early European travelers praised the beauty of the land. Except for their names, however, Uruguay and Paraguay are utterly different. Paraguay has long been one of the poorest nations in Latin America.

Paraguay has two distinct regions. Paraguay seems small compared to neighboring Argentina and Brazil. Yet its area is almost as large as Kansas and Nebraska combined. The eastern part of the country is the "paradise" region. It enjoys a healthful climate, a good water supply, and fertile soil. Most Paraguayans live in this area. In western Paraguay the dry lonely plains of the Chaco (page 256) extend across the border from Argentina. During the rainy season the Chaco becomes a swamp.

Paraguay is warmer than the other Plata countries. Since Paraguay has more territory in the tropics than the other Plata countries, it is generally warmer. The "winter" months are mild, and summer temperatures range from the high 70's into the 90's. But occasional cold fronts from the south may cause temperatures to drop sharply.

Rivers provide a lifeline to the sea. Paraguay's landlocked situation has been a handicap. Asunción (ah-soon-*syohn'*), the capital city, lies on the Paraguay River, about a thousand miles inland from the Atlantic Ocean. The map on page 257 shows that this river flows into the Paraná River, which runs across Argentina and empties into the Plata estuary. This Paraguay-Paraná route is Paraguay's "lifeline," since it provides a vital connection with ocean trade. Until the 1900's, in fact, this was Paraguay's only link with the outside world. Now there are roads to Brazil and Bolivia, railroads to Argentina and Brazil, and air service to other South American nations. But the Paraguay-Paraná river route remains important.

Paraguay lives off the products of the land. The economy of Paraguay is almost totally agricultural. In fact, the majority of people grow most of their own food. Corn and manioc are the staples of the diet. Vegetables and oranges are also grown, and cattle are raised. Leading exports are meat products, *quebracho* wood (page 256), tobacco, and *yerba maté* (*yair'* bah mah-*tay'*) leaves. These leaves brew a tea which is popular in all the Plata river countries. Since Paraguayan ranchers have not adopted modern breeding methods or improved feed, their beef cannot compete with Argentine beef. Even the hides are inferior.

Few farmers own their own land. Most are "squatters" living on forest clearings of a few acres. Paraguay has an ample supply of land for its population, however, and squatters are seldom forced off their little farms. The country has few minerals worth working. Sawmills and meat-packing plants represent the chief industries.

Asunción is less "modern" than other capital cities. Asunción, the capital, is Paraguay's only large city. It was important in Spanish colonial history, for it survived in the interior when Buenos Aires was abandoned (page 86). Today the streets of Asunción are cobbled and many of the oldest houses date back to colonial days. But there is also a newer residential section. The city has electricity, a modern water system, and a small section of business and government buildings. Lying a little south of the tropics, Asunción has no winter season and outdoor markets are held year-round. Barefoot Indian women come in from the country to sell fruit and vegetables. The Paraná River at Asunción is full of riverboats carrying bales of cotton, loads of oranges, twists of tobacco, and logs of *quebracho* wood to Buenos Aires.

The Guaraní heritage survives. The great majority of Paraguayans are descended from Europeans and Guaranís. There are almost no Negroes in Paraguay and very few people of either "pure" Indian or "pure" European descent. Though Spanish is the official language, virtually all Paraguayans speak Guaraní. As noted in Chapter 5, the Jesuit missionaries helped keep this Indian language alive.

Education is not widespread. Many Paraguayans speak *only* Guaraní. This becomes a handicap for children who go to school, since classes are taught in Spanish. Though Paraguay has a law that says all children between the ages of seven and fourteen must attend school, the law

Originally an Indian drink, yerba maté or "Paraguayan tea," was adopted by the Spanish and is still popular throughout the Plata countries today. The beverage is brewed like tea and sipped through metal "straws."

is not enforced. Thousands of children never see the inside of a schoolhouse. Illiteracy in Paraguay is estimated at 25 per cent. But outside Asunción a much higher percentage of the people are unable to read or write. Of those young people who make their way through high school, a few thousand go on to attend the country's two universities.

POLITICAL HISTORY

Disastrous wars crippled Paraguay. Being landlocked is not Paraguay's only handicap. Devastating wars and bad government have also burdened the country. In the war fought with Brazil, Argentina, and Uruguay in the 1860's (page 165), Paraguay was almost destroyed. Most of its able-bodied men between the ages of 14 and 60 died in the savage fighting.

In 1932 Paraguay was plunged into yet another cruel war. It was fought with Bolivia over the northern Chaco, the territory between the Paraguay River and the Bolivian foothills (map, page 257). Bolivia wanted this land in order to get a route to the Paraguay River. This would have given Bolivia a trade outlet to the Plata estuary and the Atlantic. After several years of quarreling, the war formally began in 1932 and continued for three bloody years. Finally, the two exhausted countries yielded to pressure from other nations to stop fighting. In 1938 an international committee awarded most of the disputed area to Paraguay. But the war had cost "victorious" Paraguay some 36,000 lives and left the country poorer than ever.

Dictatorships have dominated Paraguay.
Throughout its history as an independent nation, Paraguay has been ruled by dictators as oppressive as any in Latin America. One president who took office in 1939 did try to begin desperately needed reforms. He was José Estigarribia (ay-stee-gah-*ree'* bee-yah), a hero of the Chaco War. Estigarribia hoped to get loans from the United States to modernize Paraguay's economy. He also helped write a new constitution. But after only a year in office Estigarribia was killed in an airplane crash.

Estigarribia was followed by one of the worst dictators in Paraguayan history, Higinio Morínigo (moh-*ree'* nee-goh). Any hint of criticism or opposition was ruthlessly silenced during Morínigo's reign. After eight years of tyranny, this dictator was forced out of office in 1948. In the confusion that followed, Paraguay had several different presidents.

In 1954 an army revolt brought into power Paraguay's current ruler, General Alfredo Stroessner (*stress'* ner). The son of a German immigrant, Stroessner has been described by journalists as the "last of the old-time *caudillo* dictators." Although Paraguay remains a police state, Stroessner has taken some steps toward economic modernization. A railroad was built to Brazil, roads were constructed in the Chaco, and oil was brought by pipeline from eastern Bolivia. Also, two hydroelectric plants were built. But the majority of the people feel little benefit from these projects. Meanwhile, General Stroessner has vowed that political unrest and rebelliousness will not be allowed in Paraguay. The only organized opposition to his rule in recent years has come from members of the Catholic clergy.

THINKING ABOUT THIS SECTION

1. Explain or define the following words: Chaco; *quebracho; yerba maté;* Guaraní.

2. Contrast the geography of eastern and western Paraguay. Why has the Paraguay-Paraná river route been important to the country?

3. What are Paraguay's chief exports? Why are these limited in number and amount?

4. What are some of the factors that may explain Paraguay's lack of progress in comparison to its neighbors? Consider geography, natural resources, colonial history, wars, government.

5. What kind of government has Paraguay had under General Stroessner?

Summing Up

The four countries of the southern triangle of Spanish-speaking South America have, for the most part, a temperate climate. But they do not experience the extremes of temperatures that are common in temperate North America. Since they lie south of the equator, their seasons are the reverse of those in the United States.

Three of these countries—Argentina, Chile, and Uruguay—are among the most advanced Latin American nations. Nevertheless, their economies reflect the "single-export" weakness typical of many countries in South and Central America. The fourth country, Paraguay, is poor and much less modern.

Each of these four countries has had a distinctive political history. Argentina's history seems to bear out the truth of a saying popular in that country: "Argentina grew great in spite of her governments." Since the army officers regard themselves as the guardians of public order in Argentina, many changes of government have come about as military revolts. This was true in the case of Juan Perón, who ruled Argentina from the mid-1940's to 1955. With the co-operation of his dynamic wife, Perón brought union organization, better wages, and other benefits to Argentine urban workers. But Perón weakened Argentina's economy by trying to force industrial development in a nation which lacked the necessary financial resources. Since Perón, Argentina has lived under a series of military dictatorships.

In Chile workers in the copper and nitrate mines demanded and won a better standard of living for themselves and for city workers. Rural Chileans have fared less well, though recent governments have tried to make land available to them. Despite periods of stormy politics, the democratic tradition has remained strong in Chile. In 1970 a Socialist candidate won the presidency with the support of the Communist Party. It remains to be seen how Chilean democracy and prosperity will fare under this government.

Until the 1960's, Uruguay, a small agricultural nation, had an enviable reputation as Latin America's most prosperous, democratic, and stable country. Extensive welfare programs ensured a comfortable life for all Uruguayans. But in recent years the rising burden of welfare costs and other economic problems have threatened the nation with bankruptcy. In trying to deal with outbursts of discontent, the government has moved away from the country's democratic tradition.

Paraguay has little in common with the other countries of temperate South America. A land-locked nation crippled by two disastrous wars and oppressive government, Paraguay has lagged in development. This country lacks important industry, and its economy depends almost solely on agriculture and forest products.

The Latin American Nations: Brazil

CHAPTER FOCUS

1. Brazilian Politics Since 1889
2. Cities and Regions
3. Brazil's Crops and Industries
4. Social Gains and Problems
5. Literature, Art, and Music

Seen above is the bowl-like structure where the Brazilian senate meets at Brasília. Behind the senate tower other government buildings.

The journalist John Gunther wrote about a place he visited in South America: "Everything has a note of the fantastic, and in general the town resembles some marvelous creation out of science fiction—a city on the far side of the moon. . . ." He was talking about Brazil's new capital city, Brasília, located in the backlands of west-central Brazil. Not long ago, this site was an untouched wilderness. Now Brasília is a spectacular modern city.

The idea of building a capital city in the interior of Brazil was not a new one. It had first been suggested in the 1820's, when Brazil became independent. The idea stayed alive through the years. Finally, in 1957 the construction of a new capital was approved by the Brazilian congress. Just three years later, the seat of the national government was officially transferred from Rio de Janeiro to Brasília.

A contest to provide the plan for the new capital was won by an architect named Lúcio

Costa. From the sky his design looks like a long airplane with outspread wings. Tall government buildings made of green glass blocks form the "nose" of the airplane. The Brazilian house of representatives meets in a massive concrete building that looks like a white bowl turned upside down. The senate meets in a similar huge bowl turned right side up. In the "wings" of the airplane are model apartment buildings for government workers. A four-mile mall, forming the "body" of the airplane, reaches from the government buildings to the city's central plaza. By 1970 the city had several hundred thousand people.

But Brasília's dazzling modern buildings are surrounded by slums on the city's outskirts. Here, as in other Brazilian cities, people live in crowded shanty-towns. They have no running water, no electricity, and no sewage system.

And there are no schools for their children. The sight of poverty near high-rise buildings and luxury apartments is typical of Brazil itself. Many of the country's people are not only poor but hungry. Probably more than half the Brazilian people survive on an income of less than a hundred dollars a year. Yet Brazil is a country of great potential wealth. It is almost as large as all the rest of South America. Brazil has two million square miles of land which has never been plowed and planted, although the soil is fertile and rainfall is plentiful. It has perhaps the greatest quantity of untapped iron-ore reserves of any country in the world. If Brazilians can solve their problems and realize the promise of their natural wealth, this country could become a world leader in the twenty-first century. Brazil has been called "a giant beginning to stir."

1. Brazilian Politics Since 1889

During the long reign of Emperor Pedro II (Chapter 8), Brazil had been spared the power struggles that kept other Latin American countries in turmoil. But after it became a republic in 1889, Brazil too suffered rebellions, regional rivalry, and military interference in the government.

Army officers controlled the government. Under Pedro, army generals had little political influence. But it was a military plot that overthrew the emperor, and it was an army officer who then took charge of the government. A new constitution, modeled on that of the United States, created a republic called the United States of Brazil.[1] But this constitution gave to the president the powers of a dictator. People had even less voice in public affairs than they had had under Pedro. In 1894 Brazil's first civilian president took office, but military men continued to be active in political matters.

[1] Today the country's official name is the Federative Republic of Brazil.

A rebellion in the northeast was crushed. During the early years of the republic, insurrections broke out in various regions. The most serious uprising was staged by backwoods settlers in the northeastern interior. There a religious fanatic named Antonio Maciel (mah-see-*ehl'*) had wandered from village to village preaching opposition to the republic. His fiery speeches attracted huge crowds of ragged people. With thousands of devoted followers, Maciel founded a religious community called Canudos.

The Brazilian government declared Maciel a rebel. But soldiers who were sent to destroy Canudos died from lack of water or were picked off by Maciel's guerrillas. It took almost three years for the Brazilian forces to crush the rebel community. There was no surrender. The defenders fought to the death.

A newspaper reporter named Euclides da Cunha (dah *koon'* yuh) wrote an eyewitness account of this siege. Da Cunha's book, called in English *Rebellion in the Backlands,* has become a classic of Brazilian literature. In it, da Cunha told how the Brazilian soldiers were shamed by the sight of the pitiful rebels they had been sent to destroy. Da Cunha's book questioned the point of a military campaign against primitive people who had been "abandoned by civilization."

Mineiros and paulistas vied for control of the government. By the early 1900's Brazil's federal government had succeeded in suppressing rebellions. But regional rivalry continued as a fact of Brazilian life. The rivalry was chiefly between the leading families of São Paulo, called the *paulistas,* and those of Minas Gerais, the *mineiros.* Thanks to its coffee plantations, the state of São Paulo was becoming prosperous. The *mineiros* had moved away from the gold mines at Ouro Preto and were settling around the new town of Belo Horizonte ("beautiful horizon"). Thousands of people were leaving the old sugar-producing coastal areas of Bahia and Pernambuco to settle in these more prosperous states farther south.

By the early 1900's the *mineiros* and *paulistas* held a monopoly on wealth and influence in Brazil. The politicians of São Paulo and Minas Gerais reached an understanding that the presidency of Brazil would be alternated between *paulista* and *mineiro* leaders. Political figures from the rest of Brazil had little chance of winning the top post in the federal government.

Brazil took part in World War I. Brazil was the only Latin American country to get involved in World War I (1914–1918). Brazil declared war on Germany and sold enormous quantities of food and raw materials to the Allies. Some Brazilian aviators and medical units saw service in Europe. By taking part in the peace conference after the war, Brazil gained a sense of participation in world affairs.

Hard times followed the war. An economic depression hit Brazil in the 1920's. The coffee growers of São Paulo were producing more coffee than could be sold to customers in other countries. Even though surplus coffee beans were burned or dumped at sea, the price of coffee fell lower and lower. The collapse of the coffee market almost ruined the state of São Paulo. Other parts of Brazil suffered too. Workers in both cities and rural regions went hungry, and even wealthy people were losing their fortunes. This crisis had political effects. It helped to break down the traditional monopoly on the presidency by the *mineiros* and *paulistas.*

Vargas seized power. In the election of 1930 another Brazilian state entered the race for the presidency. This was the cattle-raising province of Rio Grande do Sul, next-door to Uruguay. Although Rio Grande do Sul had its own powerful political machine, it had taken little part in the federal government. The governor of the state was Getúlio Vargas. As a boy, Vargas had worked on his father's cattle ranch. Later he bragged: "I grew up with a lasso in my hands and a horse between my knees." In 1930 the politicians of Rio Grande do Sul united behind Vargas as a candidate for the presidency.

According to the tradition of alternating presidents, it was time for a *mineiro* to take office. But a *paulista* was put forward as the "official" candidate, and he came out ahead in the government-controlled election. With the help of angry *mineiros,* army officers, and other supporters, Vargas overthrew the government and installed himself as president.

A small pleasant-faced man, Vargas hardly looked like the traditional *caudillo.* But he was a shrewd and able politician. Calling himself "the poor man's president," he lived simply in one wing of the Presidential Palace. Vargas worked sixteen hours a day at the presidency

Brazil

Modern Brazil includes 23 states and 3 territories, some of them huge and some small. Only the more important states are named on the map. Numbered areas are the regions described in this chapter. Note the route of the Trans-Amazon Highway, now being built.

ATLANTIC
OCEAN

VENEZUELA

GUYANA

SURINAM
(DU.)

FR.
GUIANA

COLOMBIA

EQUATOR

Rb

Manaus

Amazon

Belém

Ma

AMAZONAS

5

R

V

Lu

PARÁ

Ct

1

PERNAMBUCO

Recife

PERU

Rb

Lu

São Francisco R.

S

BAHIA

Cc

Salvador

GOIÁS

Ca

Brasília

4

MATO GROSSO

Ca

BOLIVIA

FEDERAL
DISTRICT

MINAS GERAIS

F

2

Belo
Horizonte

M

S

M

Cf

PARAGUAY

Cf

SÃO PAULO

Cf

GUANABARA

Rio de Janeiro

São Paulo

Santos

F

IGUASSU
FALLS

Ct

TROPIC OF CAPRICORN

Paraná R.

3

RIO
GRANDE
DO SUL

Wt

L

C

R

ARGENTINA

Pôrto Alegre

Ca

URUGUAY

1 Northeast
2 Southeast
3 South
4 West-Central
5 Amazonia

Cc Cacao
Ca Cattle
Cf Coffee
C Corn
Ct Cotton
F Fruit
L Industry
Lu Lumber
Ma Manioc
M Mining
R Rice
Rb Rubber
S Sugar cane
V Vanilla
Wt Wheat

▬ ▬ ▬ Trans-Amazon Highway
━━━━ Belém-Brasília Highway

0   100 200 300 400   500 Miles

279

and expected the same kind of hard work from his cabinet officers.

Vargas made himself a dictator.
In 1937, Vargas proclaimed a new constitution for Brazil. Under this constitution, he established what he called the *Estado Novo,* the "new state." Centralized control was the keynote. All state governors were dismissed, and Vargas tightened his control over almost every aspect of Brazilian life. Education was regulated by the central government; newspapers were censored; political parties were abolished. "Don't speak," went a saying, "Getúlio [Vargas] will do it for you; don't think—the DIP [the propaganda bureau] will do it for you." In short, Brazil had become a dictatorship.

Economic and social changes were ordered by Vargas.
The *Estado Novo* imposed a gigantic welfare plan on Brazil. Vargas introduced a number of programs and reforms intended to improve the life of the people. To strengthen the economy, the production of crops other than coffee was encouraged. At Volta Redonda, near Rio de Janeiro, the Brazilian government built a huge steel industry. For laborers Vargas established a minimum wage and an eight-hour work day. He promoted elementary education and restricted child labor. Schools offering vocational and technical training were opened. Railroad mileage doubled, and the government expanded the country's airlines. These policies did raise the standard of living for many Brazilians. Though there was resentment of his high-handed methods, Vargas enjoyed great popularity.

Brazil joined the Allies in World War II.
After flirting with both sides, Vargas took Brazil into World War II on the side of the United States. Five thousand Brazilians fought with the Allies in Italy, making Brazil the only Latin American country to send land forces abroad. As in the First World War, Brazil aided the Allied effort by supplying badly needed raw materials.

After a short retirement, Vargas again became president.
Vargas had used World War II as an excuse to keep himself in power. But by 1945, when the war was over, rising discontent and pressure from military leaders forced him to call an election. A general named Eurico Gaspar Dutra was elected president. Dutra's government introduced a new constitution in 1946. It restored to the individual states many of the powers which they had lost under the *Estado Novo.*

Vargas meanwhile served in the Brazilian senate as a representative of Rio Grande do Sul. In 1950 the popular "Uncle Getúlio" ran again for the presidency and easily won, this time legally. Now, however, Vargas was older and in ill health, and his control of the government was less complete than during the days of the dictatorship. In 1954 army leaders charged that some of Vargas' bodyguards were involved in the murder of an air force officer. They demanded that the president resign. The morning after a cabinet meeting, Vargas shot himself. His suicide note said: "To the wrath of my enemies I leave the legacy of my death. I take the sorrow of not having been able to do for the humble all that I desired."

Kubitschek promised economic progress.
Vargas' vice-president served out the remaining year of the dead president's term. Then in 1955 a *mineiro* of Czech descent, Juscelino Kubitschek (*koo'* bih-chek), was elected president in a peaceful and honest election. Kubitschek had worked as a telegraph operator to put himself through medical school. After working as a doctor among the poor in Belo Horizonte, he had given up his medical practice to become governor of Minas Gerais. As president, Kubitschek was determined to modernize the country —to "advance Brazil 50 years." One of his plans was to bring water and electricity to the parched northeast. This program was called SUDENE (Superintendency of the Development of Economics in the Northeast).

Another of Kubitschek's ideas was an "Operation Pan Americana," in which Latin American countries would co-operate with the United States in raising the capital needed to improve standards of living. The Alliance for Progress, launched by President John F. Kennedy in the early 1960's, was based on Kubitschek's idea (Chapter 17).

Brasília was built in the wilderness. Kubitschek also put into action the old idea of building a new federal capital in the interior. By locating the new federal district beyond the settled coastal region, he hoped to encourage Brazilians to push into the interior and develop new resources.

Kubitschek promised to have the capital moved to Brasília within three years and kept his promise by opening congress there in April, 1960. But many congressmen did not attend the meeting. Moreover, many people doubted that diplomats from other countries would ever leave Rio de Janeiro for a city in the wilderness. By the late 1960's however, Brazil's Foreign Affairs ministry had moved to Brasília. The Brazilian government made it clear to foreign embassies that they must move to Brasília soon or lose their diplomatic privileges.

Inflation threatened. Building Brasília was expensive. The country went deeply into debt to pay for the new city. For some time inflation had been a growing worry, and during Kubitschek's presidency the cost of living doubled. Moreover, industrialization was lagging, partly because of a shortage of skilled workers.

Quadros served briefly. Brazil's next president, Janio Quadros, was inaugurated with a big celebration at Brasília in January, 1961. Quadros had promised to wipe out corruption and check inflation. But stiff opposition to many of his policies frustrated the new president. A brilliant but moody man, Quadros resigned after only seven months in office.

The economy worsened. Vice-president João Goulart (goo-*lar'*) became president at a time when Brazil's economic situation was growing rapidly worse. As prices continued to soar, few Brazilians could live on income from a single job. Even university professors took second jobs in order to keep their children in high school. Hungry people in the cities stood in long lines waiting for bread to be handed out by relief organizations.

Goulart was forced out. Brazilian conservatives soon grew dissatisfied with President Goulart. Because he had praised Fidel Castro, Goulart was regarded as a dangerous radical. But, aside from political views, his dishonesty and corruption were well-known. With strong civilian backing, Brazilian army officers ousted Goulart in 1964. One of these officers, a general named Humberto Castelo Branco, became president. Honest and efficient, Castelo Branco had once favored constitutional rule. Now he felt that Brazil desperately needed to be ruled with a firm hand.

Castelo Branco imposed dictatorship. Through a series of so-called Institutional Acts, Castelo Branco tightened control over the country. The first of these laws gave military officers the power to hold people in jail without court action and to deny any individual the right to vote or hold office. Under the second Institutional Act, only the official government party and one approved opposition party could present candidates for an election. A third act declared that all national and state officials, including the president and the state governors, were to be chosen by the state and national legislatures. Still another measure legalized censorship of the press. One Brazilian newspaper declared that this step would "destroy, without doubt, whatever is left of the concept of Brazil as a democratic country."

Reform programs were planned. These dictatorial measures dismayed a great many Brazilians. Yet Castelo Branco thought of himself not as a military dictator but as a "caretaker." Some of his policies were aimed at improving

Students and other Brazilians gathered in Rio in 1968 to demonstrate against government policies. Signs called for freedom of the press.

life in Brazil. He started a fair program of collecting taxes, from the rich as well as from the poor. Unused land was taken over from large estates and distributed in small plots. Castelo Branco put the army to work building schools and teaching in them, paving roads, clearing swamps, and carrying out programs of immunization against smallpox and polio. He also tried hard to halt the galloping inflation.

Unrest mounted as dictatorship continued. In 1966 the government party's candidate, Artur da Costa e Silva, was "elected" president by the congress. No opposition was allowed. When he took office in 1967, Costa e Silva promised the Brazilian people that he would stress "social humanism." He meant that the problems of the people would receive serious attention and that he would listen to the dissatisfied, including students and members of labor unions. But increasing unrest led Costa e Silva to impose still stronger controls. The government outlawed political opposition, suspended the congress, and tightened censorship of newspapers. There were also reports that government police were torturing political prisoners.

In 1969 Costa e Silva suffered a stroke, and before the end of the year he died. Many Brazilians hoped that different leadership might relax the dictatorial policies of the government. But military leaders took charge and continued oppressive rule. General Emilio Garrastazú Médici (*may'* dee-see), who was named president, declared that Brazil would have a military government until long-range economic goals were achieved.

THINKING ABOUT THIS SECTION

1. Explain or define the following: Canudos; *Estado Novo;* SUDENE.

2. Why has regionalism been a problem in Brazil?

3. Why did hard times hit Brazil in the 1920's? What serious problem affected the economy in the years after World War II?

4. What were the goals sought by Vargas? by Kubitschek? What success did each have?

5. What changes did the Institutional Acts make in Brazil's government?

By the 1970's Brazil's population was approaching the hundred-million mark. Close to a half of the people live in towns and cities. And of these, over fifteen million are residents of the two great metropolises, only 200 miles apart, of Brazil's southern coastal region. But the frontiers of the vast interior regions are slowly being pushed back.

Rio de Janeiro is a busy, modern city. The people of Rio have a proverb: "God made the rest of the world in six days and saved the seventh for Rio de Janeiro." The city stretches along fifteen miles of beautiful coastline. From the mountains which rise behind the city, the visitor sees one of the most magnificent views in the world. Before Brasília was built, Rio was the "federal district." But now it is the state of Guanabara, named for Emperor Pedro's palace. (There is a separate state named Rio de Janeiro, which includes suburbs across the bay from the city.) Though it is no longer the capital city, Rio continues to be the nation's major port and a leading business center. Its year-round beach resorts attract many tourists.

Rio is a dynamic city with ultramodern apartment and office buildings designed by famous architects. Beautiful parks lie along the shore. But motor traffic in the city is hectic. A large percentage of middle-class Brazilians own automobiles.

Rio is famous for its Carnival, the last week before Lent. Everyone wears a costume and mask and joins in street merrymaking. Friends and strangers, Brazilians and foreigners, all sing and dance together. After the excitement of Carnival begin the quiet 40 days of Lent.

The urban poor live in favelas. Visitors to New York, Los Angeles, or Tokyo may fail to see the slums of those huge cities. But it is impossible to miss the slums of Rio de Janeiro. Called *favelas* (fah-*vay'* lahss), they cover the hillsides which rise just back of the tourist hotels. The hovels of the *favelas* are patched together from pieces of tin, palm thatch, plaster board, and other scraps. No streets, only burro trails, lead up to the *favelas*. The city pipes water to a faucet at the base of each hill. There are elementary schools for the children of the *favelas,* but only a small percentage of the children go to classes. The rest carry water, look after babies, collect trash for sale to junkyards, and deliver groceries to the apartment houses below. More than once, entire *favela* neighborhoods have been washed downhill by heavy floods.

The people of the *favelas* come to the city to find work. Incredible as it may seem, poverty in Brazil's rural areas is even more wretched than in the *favelas*. For many of the poor, life in the *favelas* is actually an improvement. But since they have no job skills, the men cannot find work.

São Paulo is Brazil's industrial center. The city of São Paulo lies south of Rio de Janeiro and about forty miles inland from the seaport of Santos. Even more than Rio, São Paulo is bustling and prosperous. *Paulistas* claim that a new skyscraper is started every month. Probably half of Brazil's industrial production is centered in or near this great city. Despite the city's prosperity, however, São Paulo also has its *favelas*.

Many immigrants have settled in São Paulo. About two-fifths of the *paulistas* are of Italian descent, and the Italian language is often heard. Other citizens of São Paulo are of Polish, Ukrainian, German, or Japanese descent.

São Paulo city is the capital of São Paulo state. The people of this state compare it to a locomotive pulling the freight cars of all the rest of Brazil. And it is true that they pay almost half of the nation's income taxes. A healthy balance of industry and agriculture has made this prosperity possible. While coffee continues to be the leading crop, São Paulo farmers also market dairy products, beef, cotton, soybeans, and many other commodities.

An aerial view shows Rio de Janeiro's spectacular setting (above). Note how tall buildings cluster between the harbor and jagged peaks. In stark contrast to the modern skyscrapers are Rio's favelas (left), where the city's poor live in huddled makeshift shacks.

Two important cities in the Northeast are Salvador and Recife. Chapter 4 told how Bahia became the first capital of Portuguese America. It was here that the sugar plantation system started. Today Bahia is called Salvador[2] and is still a busy port. From its wharves are shipped large cargoes of sugar, chocolate, rope fiber, and cotton. Before the air age, this city was isolated from Rio and São Paulo, both of which lie more than a thousand miles away. But today there is frequent airplane service between Salvador and the cities of southern Brazil.

Another large city on the northeastern coast is Recife, capital of the sugar-producing state of Pernambuco. Since Recife and its suburb of Olinda were held for half a century by the Dutch, many old Dutch colonial buildings are still found there.

Northeastern Brazil is desperately poor. The region inland from Recife has long suffered from drought. Refugees from the arid lands have swarmed into the city. Recife's *favelas* are even more depressing than those of Rio and São Paulo. The archbishop of Recife, Dom Helder Câmara (*kah'* mah-rah) has taken an active role in seeking help for the starving people of northeastern Brazil. The archbishop's forceful statements have made him known throughout Latin America. Dom Helder, as he is called, has become a symbol of Catholic churchmen in Latin American reform movements. A controversial figure, he is out of favor with the present military government in Brazil.

The government's answer for the plight of the Northeast is the agency called SUDENE (page 280). One goal of this agency is to build small local factories which will hire unemployed people from the countryside. SUDENE has also begun to irrigate land and to build power plants. But the latter programs have aided property owners far more than the hungry peasants who need immediate relief.

[2] The state of which Salvador is the capital is still called Bahia.

Drought in northeastern Brazil has forced rural people to abandon their land. This refugee family, on reaching a town or city, will probably make their home in a favela, *like that pictured on page 284.*

West-central Brazil is part of the sparsely settled interior. The western part of central Brazil is high plateau country. Within this region is the new capital city of Brasília. The area around Brasília has been designated as Brazil's Federal District (like our District of Columbia). The Federal District lies within the state of Goiás (goy-*ahss'*). To the west of Goiás is the state of Mato Grosso (*mah'* too *groh'* soo), which means "thick bush." As one might guess from the name, much of this thinly peopled state is scrub woodland. Parts of Mato Grosso have never been explored. Since Mato Grosso could be productive land if properly farmed, Brazilian leaders have urged people to settle there. A number of large cattle ranches have been started.

Amazonia is a challenging frontier. The huge expanse of northern Brazil is known as Amazonia, after the Amazon River, and includes several different states. The area drained by the Amazon and its many tributaries covers more than two million square miles. This is an area larger than Argentina, Chile, Paraguay, Uruguay, and Bolivia put together. Amazonia's vast expanse includes tropical rain forests, grassy plains, and high tablelands.

The Brazilian government is also encouraging development of Amazonia. As part of this effort, the government plans to penetrate the wilderness with a Trans-Amazon Highway. The road will cross northern Brazil, extending for some 3000 miles from Recife to the Peruvian border (map, page 279).

Belém is the Amazon system's ocean port. Another important wilderness road, already completed, links Brasília with the seaport of Belém. This city, also called Pará (pah-*rah'*), is 90 miles from the sea on the Pará River, which forms one of the mouths of the great Amazon delta. Many old houses are a reminder of Belém's colonial past. But Belém is also a busy port, shipping every year thousands of tons of mahogany, vegetable oils, coconuts, brazil nuts, and other tropical forest products.

Dom Helder Câmara is the best-known of the many Latin American priests who have challenged repressive governments and called for peaceful social reform and respect for human rights.

THINKING ABOUT THIS SECTION

1. Explain or define the following words: *favelas;* Mato Grosso; Amazon delta.

2. Look at the map on page 279. Are most of Brazil's large cities located in the north or in the south? Explain why.

3. How are Rio de Janeiro and São Paulo similar? What are the chief exports of São Paulo? of Salvador? of Belém?

4. Why is there great poverty in northeastern Brazil? What efforts are being made to improve the situation?

5. Why is west-central Brazil sparsely settled? How has the government encouraged development of this region? of Amazonia?

3. Brazil's Crops and Industries

Brazil has had a single-export economy. Brazil's economy has gone through a series of cycles, each of them centered around a particular export. The Brazilian tradition has been to concentrate on the commodity that was most profitable at a given time. As told in earlier chapters, brazilwood was the first export. Then sugar began to dominate Brazilian life. Next came gold, cotton for a while, then rubber, and finally coffee. Throughout these different economic periods, some parts of Brazil also produced tobacco, cacao, and cattle products for export. And, of course, food crops for local use were also grown.

The one-crop emphasis weakened economic development. Brazil has suffered from this heavy dependence on certain exports. There was always new land to move to when old land was exhausted. There was always some new crop or other raw material to sell when the market for the old product declined. It has been said that the Brazilians "collect the fruit without planting the tree." As a result of this attitude, land and resources were not developed in an orderly way. No thought was given to the future as natural resources were recklessly exploited. A region prospered as long as there was demand for a local product and then slumped into poverty when the land wore out or the demand fell off. Moreover, this dependence on a single export made Brazil "a slave of world markets."

Today Brazil is trying to get away from this pattern by diversifying its economy. (A diversified economy is one based on a variety of activities.) While coffee continues to lead Brazil's export trade, other agricultural products are becoming more important. Among these are cotton, chocolate, oranges, bananas, jute, pepper, and frozen and canned beef.

Coffee is king. It was coffee that made São Paulo such a prosperous state. The rich red soil, the hot wet growing season, and the cool rainless harvesting season were ideal for the raising of coffee trees. By the 1870's Brazil was producing about half the world's supply of coffee. Since then, coffee has continued to dominate Brazilian agriculture.

Coffee is grown on plantations. A big coffee plantation is called a *fazenda*. Much of Brazil's coffee crop is still grown by tenants on *fazendas* of 10,000 to 30,000 acres. Four or five thousand people may work on a single *fazenda*. A tenant agrees to care for several thousand trees. It is his responsibility to clear the land if necessary, to plant the seedling trees, and to tend them until they begin to bear fruit in about five years. Throughout this time the owner of the *fazenda* pays the tenant a small wage and provides a house for his family.

The small red coffee berries grow in clusters on the branches of the trees. Inside each berry are two green seeds or beans. On most *fazendas* the berries are picked by hand. They are then washed and carried to a mill, where machinery removes the red skin and the yellow pulp. The beans are spread on platforms for drying in the sun. Next the beans are sorted and loaded into sacks to be picked up by merchants from the port city of Santos.

Once the coffee trees are mature, they will bear fruit for 20 to 30 years. Naturally the *fazenda* owners value their investment in these long-lived trees. But some of the coffee-growers have begun to see the folly of depending too much on a single crop. Coffee production in other Latin American countries and in Africa has increased tremendously. To avoid economic disaster, a number of coffee-producing countries, including Brazil, have agreed to limit their production. The Brazilian government has uprooted some coffee trees and destroyed poor-quality coffee beans. In São Paulo, the state government has helped small farmers resettle on undeveloped lands near the Paraná River. There, after clearing the land, they plant cotton and soybeans or raise cattle and hogs.

Coffee trees produce first blossoms (top left) and then shiny red berries (left). An average five-year-old tree yields some 2000 berries, or about a pound of roasted coffee. Before the beans are roasted, they must dry for two or three weeks (above).

Industry is expanding. The new emphasis on variety in production applies to industry too. Brazil is already the most highly industrialized nation in South America. Brazilian industries produce most of the country's consumer items. Textile mills make cloth from Brazilian-grown cotton. Other factories turn out shoes, hats, window glass, inner tubes for tires, processed foods, and an endless variety of other articles.

Heavy industry is progressing as well. The government-owned steel mill at Volta Redonda is the largest in Latin America. It makes use of iron deposits north of Rio de Janeiro. But Brazil lacks large coal resources. About two-thirds of the coal used at Volta Redonda is imported.

The lack of natural fuels and the difficulty of controlling river waters have long been major problems in Brazil. A major hydroelectric project in the valley of the São Francisco River is aimed at tackling both of these problems. When the project is completed, a series of dams will make the river navigable over its entire length. Electricity will be produced cheaply, thus encouraging the establishment of factories in that region. So far, little petroleum has been discovered in Brazil. But the government is searching for oil in Mato Grosso.

Though Brazil's industrial growth has been impressive, for such a large country this is really only a start. Land reform and agricultural improvement, construction of more roads and railroads, and the extension of industry into the interior are important next steps. If these are achieved, the Brazilian economy will become the success story of the twenty-first century.

THINKING ABOUT THIS SECTION

1. Explain or define the following words: *fazenda;* Volta Redonda; heavy industry.
2. What various exports have at one time or another dominated Brazil's export trade? What has been the effect on the country's economic development? How has Brazil tried to cope with the problems stemming from overproduction of coffee?
3. Why is light industry booming in Brazil? Why has slower progress been made in heavy industry?

4. Social Gains and Problems

Race prejudice in Brazil is less intense than elsewhere in America. If Brazil is not yet an economic success, it is in some ways more of a social success than many other countries. Chapter 5 pointed out that color lines were less sharp in colonial Brazil than in the rest of America. This tradition has continued into modern times. Most Brazilians have little patience with the kind of race prejudice too often found in North America. A Brazilian's standing in society is based more on ability, economic status, education, and dress and manners than on race.

Nevertheless, it would be a mistake to assume that there is complete racial equality in Brazil. White domination of the government, business, and society in general has been the rule in that country as in almost all of the American nations.

The Indians of the interior are threatened. The most serious racial problem in Brazil is the effect on the Amazon Indians of the spread of modern life. Deep in the interior, many of these tribes live at a Stone Age level of civilization. General Candido Mariano Rondon, himself part Indian, devoted much of his life to helping Brazil's primitive peoples. To organize this work, he founded a government agency called the Indian Protection Service. One goal was to protect the Indians from cruel exploitation at the hands of rubber companies. The rubber merchants had enslaved great numbers of the jungle Indians and forced them to collect the sap of the wild rubber trees.

After General Rondon died in 1958, the history of the Indian Protection Service took a tragic course. An investigation in the late 1960's revealed that some agency officials had actually killed off whole communities of Indians in order to get control of their lands. This scandal led President Costa e Silva to reorganize the Brazilian Indian Service. But the outlook for the Indians of the interior remains bleak. They apparently face two choices: resisting white civilization and dying, or giving up their ancient way of life in an effort to adjust to modern ways.

The great waterway of the Amazon serves as a lifeline. Public-health launches ply up and down the river, bringing medical services to the towns and villages along its banks.

Public-health programs are needed. Sanitation and health always pose problems in the tropics. Rio de Janeiro used to be plague-ridden with yellow fever. In 1903 the Brazilian government asked a doctor named Oswaldo Cruz to do something about this terrible problem. Cruz organized a campaign to wipe out disease-carrying mosquitoes. Within a few years he had cleared the city of yellow fever and malaria. By purifying the public water supply, he also managed to control typhoid in Rio.

But much more needs to be done in the field of public health. "Brazil is finally learning," writes one historian, "that sick men do not dig in the fields, mine iron, cultivate coffee, and tend cattle." One public-health program has been set up to serve the Amazon basin. Working out of Belém, nurses and doctors travel by motor launch to the river towns. There they treat sick people and also carry out inoculation programs and organize malaria control. Such activities are worthwhile, but the country's health problems continue to be enormous. One-fifth of the rural population suffers from malaria, hookworm, or tuberculosis. Very few rural communities have running water and sewers.

Many people never get enough to eat. Since almost half of Brazil's doctors and nurses live in Rio de Janeiro and São Paulo, few people in the vast rural regions ever have professional medical care.

Only a small part of the population gets much schooling. More schools and teachers are also desperately needed. Probably only about half the Brazilian population can read and write. And millions of children continue to grow up without ever attending school. Of those who do go to school, only a tiny percentage reach the secondary level. Most of Brazil's high schools are in the cities of the south. Some of these schools prepare students for college, and others offer vocational training.

Each state in Brazil has at least one university, and most of these institutions are free and public. But very few young people get that far in their education. Among those privileged students who do go to college, a large proportion are enrolled in traditional courses such as engineering, law, and medicine. Few enter the newer fields of nursing, veterinary medicine, and scientific agriculture. Budgets for university education are so low that Brazilian students often go on strike, demanding better laboratories and library facilities.

Women are freer than in the past. For girls in Brazil education has been even more limited than for boys. It used to be that even daughters of well-to-do families rarely had any formal schooling. Today things are changing. Though many Brazilians still believe that woman's place is in the home, women are freer to enter the professions and the business world. Brazil has more women engineers than all the rest of Latin America. Since 1933, Brazilian women have had the vote, and several women have held important positions in the government.

THINKING ABOUT THIS SECTION

1. Compare relations between blacks and whites in Brazil and in the United States.
2. Why is the lot of the Amazon Indians in Brazil more difficult than that of blacks?
3. Why is public health an urgent problem in Brazil? Why is education also an urgent problem?
4. Contrast the status of women in Brazil and in the United States.

5. Literature, Art, and Music

Literature. Much of the work of modern Brazilian writers is unknown to the rest of the world. These authors write, of course, in Portuguese; and, outside of Brazil and Portugal, there are few people familiar with this language. But English-language translations are now bringing the best of Brazilian writing to readers in the United States.

In a remarkable book published in the 1960's a black woman named Carolina Maria de Jesus described life in a São Paulo *favela*. In vivid language she told of her struggle to raise three children in a one-room shack in the crowded slum. She barely managed to support herself and her children by collecting and selling old newspapers. "On good days I would make twenty-five or thirty cents," she wrote. "Some days I made nothing." Carolina had learned to write during two years of schooling in a rural town in Minas Gerais. On scraps of the paper that she collected in São Paulo, she wrote a daily diary. One day a newspaperman heard her mention the diary. After persuading her to let him read it, he arranged to have it published. The book is called in English *Child of the Dark*. It is an engrossing account of the struggle to survive in heartbreaking poverty.

An outstanding figure in Brazilian literature and scholarship is the historian-sociologist Gilberto Freyre (*fray'* ree). A major theme of his writing is Brazil's African heritage, which he has traced from the early settlements to the present. Freyre's two best-known books have been translated into English as *The Masters and the Slaves* and *The Mansions and the Shanties*.

Among leading Brazilian novelists, Erico Verissimo and Jorgé Amado are perhaps the best-known in English translations. In a series of novels Verissimo described life in the state of Rio Grande do Sul from colonial times onward. Jorgé Amado writes about life in Bahia.

Art. The artists and architects of Brazil are known throughout the world for their creative work. In fact, São Paulo is a leading center for modern art. Every two years this city holds a famous art show called the *Bienal*. Painters from all over the world enter their pictures, and to win a prize is a great honor.

Cândido Portinari, the son of Italian immigrants, painted scenes remembered from his childhood among Brazil's plantation workers. Above is his painting entitled Morro (1933).

As in Mexico, it has only been during the last 50 years that artists in Brazil began to look to their native land for themes and inspirations. The best-known of recent Brazilian painters was Cândido Portinari, who died in 1962. Black workers and the coffee plantations of the south were favorite themes in Portinari's colorful pictures.

Architecture. In the field of architecture Brazilians have been pace-setters. During the

1930's, Brazilian architects pioneered in the imaginative design of modern structures. The evidence of this appears today in the attractive buildings of Brazil's southern cities. The most startling result of Brazilian interest in modern architecture is, of course, Brasília.

Music. Brazil is a musical country. At carnival time especially, the streets are filled with music. Portuguese, African, and Indian rhythms and tunes mingle in this yearly outpouring of music. Such dances as the *conga,* the *samba,* and the *bossa nova* have become popular in North America.

Brazil's most famous composer of serious music was Heitor Villa-Lobos (*vee' luh-loh' boosh*), who died in 1959. As a young musician, Villa-Lobos visited many of the small towns of Brazil. Traveling up the Amazon, he heard the Indians play strange tribal music on primitive instruments. In Bahia he heard African songs remembered by descendants of the slaves. Villa-Lobos used the rhythms and melodies of these folk songs in his own compositions. Today Villa-Lobos's music is often performed in the United States, and he is ranked among the finest of the Western Hemisphere's composers.

THINKING ABOUT THIS SECTION

1. Identify the following: *Child of the Dark;* Gilberto Freyre; Cândido Portinari; Heitor Villa-Lobos.
2. Why are the writings of most Brazilian authors generally read in translation outside their own country?
3. How is Brazilian life reflected in the country's art and music?

Summing Up

As a republic, Brazil began to experience the same political difficulties that plagued other Latin American countries. Regional rivalry and military interference in the government enabled Getúlio Vargas to seize power in 1930.

Vargas launched programs aimed at economic improvement, but he also established a dictatorship. None of the presidents who followed Vargas succeeded in capturing the imagination of the people or in fulfilling hopes for both prosperity and democracy. In recent years a military government has tightened control and eliminated democracy from Brazil.

Chaotic economic conditions helped make the military take-over possible. Brazil's single-export tradition stood in the way of developing a balanced economy. While industrial expansion and advances in agriculture have improved life for the growing middle class in the southern states, most Brazilians continue to live in poverty. In the drought-stricken Northeast the situation is especially desperate.

There are great contrasts between Brazil's different regions—beef-producing Rio Grande do Sul, industrialized São Paulo, tourist-conscious Rio de Janeiro, sugar-producing Bahia, and the undeveloped Amazon valley and Mato Grosso. The new capital city, Brasília, is a symbol of Brazil's determination to develop the interior. But, like other Brazilian cities, Brasília has its *favelas,* huddled shanty-towns built by refugees from rural poverty.

Despite industrial growth and plans for developing untapped resources, Brazil faces many difficult problems. Among its greatest needs are improved transportation, control of inflation, more public-health programs, and better education.

Mexican Americans in the United States

CHAPTER FOCUS

1. Mexican Americans and the War of 1846–1848
2. Mexican Americans in the Southwest to 1900
3. Immigration from Mexico During the First Half of the 1900's
4. The Struggle for Equality: Mexican Americans in Recent Years

Farm-labor leader Cesar Chavez became a symbol to many Mexican Americans of the campaign to win equal opportunities and respect for Chicano culture.

Not long ago a student at the University of New Mexico wrote to the medical science division of a large eastern university. He wanted to know what financial help might be available if he were to apply for graduate study there. The answer he received was discouraging. It said that the course of study was a long one and that financial aid was not easy to get, "especially for foreign students." The university official who wrote the letter suggested: "It might be well for you to apply to a foundation in your own country." Why did the official think the student was foreign? Apparently because the young man had a Spanish last name! [1]

This story suggests how unaware many people are of this nation's second largest minority group. It has been estimated that United States

[1] Reported in the *Boston Sunday Globe*, May 2, 1971.

citizens of Mexican descent number well over eight million. Over four-fifths of the Mexican Americans make their homes in the southwestern United States. But a large number also live in the Chicago area and other midwestern industrial centers.

For many years the Mexican Americans were the most ignored large minority in the United States. More than any other ethnic group, they seemed to be "invisible" to the rest of the people of this country. Several things may account for this. Mexican Americans who have recently come to the United States from Mexico are still close to their native land. Americans of European, African, or Asian origin cannot easily go "home." But for many Mexican Americans the border is near, and to cross it is easy. The attachment to Mexico naturally remains strong. Probably, too, language has been more of a barrier than for some other minority groups.

But this "invisibility" does not mean that Mexican Americans lack a history and a culture or that they have not made important contributions to the United States. Chapter 6 told how people from Mexico explored and settled the Spanish borderlands which are now United States territory. The settlement of California and the Southwest up to the 1840's is a story of the founding of missions and ranches, the rise of the cattle industry, the development of mining, the opening up of new routes, and the birth of many towns and cities. Then the United States-Mexican War of 1846–1848 ushered in a new period. English-speaking North Americans became dominant in the Southwest, and Mexican Americans were pushed into the background.

After 1900, Mexican immigrants poured into the southwestern United States. They were attracted by job opportunities, mining, and railroading. But the turmoil of the Mexican Revolution of 1910–1921 also drove hundreds of thousands of people north seeking safety. Today the great majority of Mexican Americans are descended from the men and women who left Mexico for the United States during the great migration after 1900.

In recent years Mexican Americans have developed a new awareness of themselves as a minority group. More and more United States citizens of Mexican background are calling themselves *Chicanos* (chee-*kah'* nohz). The origin of this word is not certain, but it probably comes from the Aztec word for "Mexican." The name Chicano is cherished because it symbolizes the new self-awareness and pride in the Mexican heritage. Chicano activists are no longer willing to remain "invisible." They are pressing for equal rights and opportunities and are demanding full recognition of the value and importance of Mexican American culture.

1. Mexican Americans and the War of 1846–1848

By the 1840's there were perhaps 75,000 Mexicans living in that part of Mexico that today is part of the United States. There were about 7500 Mexicans in California, perhaps 1000 in Arizona, 5000 in Texas, and 60,000 in New Mexico. Throughout this area there were probably some 200,000 Indians.

Texas was lost to Mexico. Chapter 8 told how English-speaking Americans moved into Texas and in 1835 rebelled against Mexican rule. The Texan rebellion succeeded, and from 1836 to 1845 Texas was an independent republic, though Mexico refused to acknowledge the fact. During the years that Texas was independent, the Mexicans who continued to live there became a voiceless minority. This was in spite of the fact that many settlers of Mexican ancestry had fought for Texan independence from Mexico. In fact, two of the signers of the Texas Declaration of Independence were Mexicans.

Kearny took possession of New Mexico. In 1845 Texas won admission to the United

States. War soon broke out between the United States and Mexico in a dispute over the Texas-Mexico boundary. Even before the war began, the United States had been eyeing other parts of Mexican territory. In fact, on the day that war was declared in May, 1846, President Polk told his cabinet: "In making peace . . . , we shall acquire California, New Mexico, and other further territory as an indemnity [payment] for this war, if we can."

Trade had helped to stimulate this interest. When Mexico broke away from Spain in the early 1820's, its new government encouraged United States trade with Santa Fe, the chief town in New Mexico. Over the Santa Fe Trail, between Missouri and New Mexico, a long caravan of wagons filled with merchandise rolled every year (map, page 125). To Santa Fe the Yankee traders brought manufactured goods, including cotton and silk cloth, china dishes, iron pots and kettles, needles and thread. On the return trip the traders took back to Missouri mules, furs, gold, silver, and pottery. Many Yankees became convinced that the fertile land along the trail to Santa Fe should be part of the United States.

Soon after war broke out in 1846 a United States army officer, Stephen W. Kearny (*car' nih*), led a small force from Kansas to New Mexico. Though the people in the Mexican villages shot at the invaders, the governor of Santa Fe abandoned the town after only a show of resistance. In August, 1846, Kearny raised the United States flag in Santa Fe, thus taking possession of New Mexico. He then continued westward across southern Arizona[2] to California (map, page 153).

California was also seized. California was much farther from Mexico City than New Mexico and Texas. As a result, its ties with the Mexican central government were much looser. In 1821, when news reached the California Mexicans that Mexico had won independence from Spain, they called a meeting to choose a *junta*. After that, the Californians

[2] Arizona was then considered part of New Mexico.

practically governed themselves. The fertile lands of the missions were opened to private ownership, and large ranches were soon established. The Indians who had lived on the missions either returned to their tribal villages or became ranch hands.

Meanwhile, Yankee traders were busy in California. Ships from New England traded along the coast while fur traders and pioneers blazed new overland trails from the east. By the 1840's a number of English-speaking Americans had acquired land in California and had settled there. They and other Yankees interested in expansion were thinking of how to make California part of the United States.

John C. Frémont, an explorer for the United States government, was one of those interested in California. In 1845 he led a party of explorers from Missouri to northern California. There he became the supporter and instigator of revolts by English-speaking settlers against the Mexicans.

In 1846 the news that the United States and Mexico were at war soon reached California. About the same time a United States naval squadron occupied the ports of Monterey and San Francisco. Moreover, Stephen Kearny, having crossed Arizona, entered southern California. He met with determined resistance from Mexican Californians, especially at the Battle of San Pascual, near San Diego. After reinforcements were brought in, the Yankees finally defeated the Mexicans. Thus, the United States took possession of California, even before the war with Mexico came to an end.

The Treaty of Guadalupe-Hidalgo was supposed to guarantee property rights. Early in 1848 the Treaty of Guadalupe-Hidalgo officially ended the war between the United States and Mexico. Under the terms of this treaty Mexico ceded a huge part of its territory to the United States. Mexico also recognized the annexation of Texas.

But the treaty had other provisions as well. It specifically stated that Mexicans living in the ceded lands were to have the choice of moving to Mexico or staying in their homes and becoming United States citizens. (Only about 2000 decided to move to Mexico.) The treaty also guaranteed property rights. It stated:

In the said territories, property of every kind . . . shall be inviolably respected. The present owners, the heirs of these, and all Mexicans who may hereafter acquire said property by contract, shall enjoy with respect to it guarantees equally ample as if the same belonged to citizens of the United States.

The Treaty of Guadalupe-Hidalgo further indicated that the new United States citizens of Mexican descent were to be guaranteed all rights granted to citizens under the federal Constitution.

Statehood was delayed for New Mexico and Arizona. Nearly all of the southwestern United States was acquired in the Texas annexation and the Mexican Cession.[3] In addition to the state of Texas, the territories of California, Utah, and New Mexico were created from the former Mexican lands. The question of statehood for the new territories soon came up. California and Nevada (the latter carved out of Utah Territory) became states quickly because they filled up with Yankees who came to mine gold and silver. Statehood for Utah was delayed until 1896 because of prejudice against the Mormons, who had settled that area.

Arizona Territory was separated from New Mexico Territory in 1863. But these two territories did not win statehood until 1912, more than half a century after they became United States soil. One reason was resistance to the proposal, often repeated, to admit the two areas as a single state. Also, until the late 1800's raids by Apache and Comanche Indians made orderly government difficult and slowed up the growth of settlements. But prejudice against Mexican Americans, who outnumbered English-speaking residents in New Mexico, was also a factor. Despite the guarantees of the

[3] In 1853 the Gadsden Purchase added southern New Mexico and Arizona to the United States (map, page 153).

Mexican Californios like this colorfully uniformed lancer fought the Yankee forces, but California was ceded to the United States.

Treaty of Guadalupe-Hidalgo, some members of Congress questioned whether Mexican Americans were "fit" for full citizenship!

THINKING ABOUT THIS SECTION

1. Explain or define the following: Chicano; Santa Fe Trail; Battle of San Pascual.

2. How did the admission of Texas to the Union lead to war between the United States and Mexico? What evidence is there that the United States by 1846 was interested in acquiring additional Mexican territory?

3. What evidence is there that California's ties with Mexico had weakened after that country gained independence from Spain in 1821?

4. What rights did the Treaty of Guadalupe-Hidalgo guarantee to Mexicans living in lands ceded to the United States?

5. California became a state in 1850; New Mexico and Arizona, in 1912. Explain the long delay in statehood for the latter two states.

Mexican American patrones and Anglo-American businessmen controlled New Mexico. At the time New Mexico became United States soil, Spanish-speaking settlements there were about 250 years old. Santa Fe was the oldest non-Indian settlement in the United States. Most of the farmland and cattle range in New Mexico that was not owned by Pueblo Indians was held by a few wealthy Mexican families. On these lands thousands of mestizos and Spanish-speaking Indians lived and worked as shepherds, cowboys, and field hands. Just as peons in Mexico toiled without question for their landlords, so the poor in New Mexico worked for the landholders or *patrones* (pah-*troh'* nayss). When English-speaking Americans (called *Anglos* or *gringos*) settled in New Mexico, not much good land was available for purchase. The Anglos, therefore, tended to become businessmen and bankers in Albuquerque and Santa Fe. They joined with the wealthy Mexican *patrones* in controlling the territorial government.

Chaves and Larrazolo were spokesmen for Mexican Americans. Many of the *patrones* served as representatives of New Mexico Territory in Congress and as territorial governors and judges. One of these was J. Francisco Chaves (*chah'* vayss). As a boy he had been told by his father: "Go and learn English and come back prepared to defend your people." Young Chaves did just that. After going to school in St. Louis and New York, he studied medicine. During the Civil War, Chaves fought with the Union army. Later he won election as New Mexico's territorial representative to Congress. Chaves also served twelve years as president of the territorial senate and then as New Mexico's first superintendent of education. He insisted on public schooling for all the children in New Mexico, Mexican Americans and Indians as well as Anglos. This stand earned him many enemies among the Anglos and also among the *patrones*. They knew that widespread education might reduce the supply of cheap labor. In 1904 Chaves was mysteriously murdered.

Another spokesman for Spanish-speaking people was Octaviano Larrazolo (lah-rah-*soh'* loh). When New Mexico finally won statehood in 1912, it was Larrazolo who succeeded in getting guarantees of Mexican American rights written into the state constitution. These were the same guarantees that had been included in the Treaty of Guadalupe-Hidalgo. Larrazolo served as governor of New Mexico and later became the first Mexican American to be a member of the United States Senate.

Traditional ways of ranching and farming continued. After 1850 agriculture in New Mexico (and also in western Texas and Arizona) continued to follow long-established Spanish and Mexican patterns. Centuries before, the Moors had developed irrigation systems in southern Spain. When Spaniards came to New Mexico, they found that the Pueblo Indians in the Rio Grande valley also knew how to bring water to thirsty lands. Moorish and Indian methods of irrigation blended in the agriculture of New Mexico. "To prevent wastage of precious water, soils [had] to be carefully prepared and leveled; and the question of when to irrigate, and to what extent, are matters learned only from long experience. . . . After carefully leveling the land, the Mexicans blocked out their fields in squares, the sides of which were just high enough to hold the water. When one block was *soaked* —not flooded—a hole was made in the side wall of earth and the water was permitted to flow into the next square." [4] Such methods, as well as the use of dams, canals, branch ditches, and deep wells, spread throughout the West wherever land had to be irrigated.

In raising livestock Mexican methods were also followed. Branding as a way of identifying

[4] Carey McWilliams, *North from Mexico* (New York: Greenwood Press, 1968), pp. 157–158.

cattle had been used in Mexico since the 1500's. The roundup, the rodeo, and the long drive were all old traditions in Mexican cattle ranching. The sheep raisers likewise had their traditional ways. In summertime, when the lowlands were hot and dry, the Mexican American sheepherders drove the sheep up to higher pastures where green grass could be found. During the mild winters the shepherds and the flocks returned to the lowlands. Anglo-Americans who came to the Southwest knew little about raising large herds of cattle and flocks of sheep on open semi-desert range. Those who went into ranching learned what they needed to know from the Mexican Americans.

New Mexicans lost their land. Despite the guarantee of property rights, many people in New Mexico lost the lands that had been granted to them or their ancestors under Spanish rule. Some could not pay their taxes; others had no papers to prove ownership; sometimes boundaries were too vague. Also, in many cases dishonest Anglo-Americans cheated the rightful owners in fraudulent deals. Some present-day New Mexicans have cited these cases in demanding the return of lands that once belonged to their ancestors.

Mexicans in Texas resisted Anglo domination. The years after the Mexican-American War saw the decline of the Mexican and the rise of the Anglo in Texas as well. As in New Mexico, the Texan Mexicans lost much of their land. The period was also marked by the rise of Mexican resistance in protest against unjust treatment. The most famous Mexican resister in Texas was Juan Cortina, the "Red Robber of the Rio Grande." The Texas Anglos regarded Cortina as a *bandido* or outlaw, while the Mexicans saw his activities as compensating for the inferior status, lynchings, and other abuses to which they were subjected.

Arizona developed slowly. Arizona was the "orphan" of the Mexican Cession territories.

It was too far from Santa Fe to benefit from the trade over the Santa Fe Trail. And its ranches and settlements had never prospered like those in California. Raids by Apache Indians were a continuing problem. In fact, by the 1850's most Arizona settlers lived in or near Tucson, where there was a military garrison to hold off the Indians.

In 1863 Arizona became a separate territory. Its population, in addition to Indians, included about 1500 Mexican Americans, most of them poor. When the Civil War ended in 1865, a number of Anglo-Americans from the southern states moved to Arizona. They tended to settle near the new town of Phoenix. Many settlers also moved in from Mexico as the demand for labor grew in copper mines and on railroads and irrigation projects.

Arizona copper mining was based on Mexican skills. In 1875 rich copper deposits were discovered at Bisbee in the southeastern corner of Arizona. The Anglo-Americans who developed the Arizona copper mines went across the border to hire laborers, since Mexican miners were skilled in the techniques of separating metal from ore. The Mexican miners built adobe furnaces for smelting the copper ore, fired the furnaces with charcoal, and kept the fires hot with hand bellows. Thousands of Mexican Americans made a success of copper mines in Utah and Nevada as well as Arizona.

The discovery of gold built up California's population. United States history textbooks usually say that it was a man named James Marshall who discovered gold in California. Actually, six years before Marshall made his discovery in 1848, a cowboy named Francisco Lopez found gold in a canyon near Los Angeles. But the deposits that Marshall discovered in the tributaries of the Sacramento River proved to be far richer than those found by Lopez. The Sacramento valley was a part of California that had never been explored or settled by Spaniards or Mexicans. After news of Marshall's big find leaked out, thousands of gold seekers rushed to California. By 1849 the population had reached 100,000, and California Anglos were clamoring for statehood.

California's state government was organized by Anglos. At this time Spanish-speaking Californians, called *Californios,* numbered about 15,000. Most of them lived in southern California. Eight *Californios* were delegates to the convention that was called in 1849 to write a state constitution. At the convention, held at Monterey, the eight *Californios* were outnumbered by the 40 Anglo delegates from the new mining towns. Since three of the *Californio* delegates spoke no English, the proceedings of the convention were translated into Spanish.

At this meeting it became clear that the mining interests of northern California conflicted with the ranching interests of southern California. As ranchers, the *Californios* feared the Anglo miners would lay heavy taxes on cattle lands while gold taken from the mines would not be taxed. For many years this was to be an issue in California politics.

When California was admitted as a state in 1850, Anglos won control of the government. An Anglo was elected governor, and Anglos were also elected to California's two seats in the United States Senate. One of these senators was John Frémont (page 296), whom the *Californios* considered a spy and a personal enemy. Although Monterey had been the capital of California during the days of Spanish and Mexican rule, the Anglos soon made Sacramento the state capital. In southern California, where Spanish remained the common language, *Californios* ran the local governments for a time. But they took little part in the state government in Sacramento.

Mexican mining techniques were used in California. Mexicans as well as Anglo-Americans streamed into the California gold fields. The Mexicans were far more experienced in mining than the English-speaking forty-niners. It was easy to pan for gold in a running stream,
but the Mexicans knew how to extract the gold in dry diggings. Using what was called the "dry-wash" method, they separated gold from sand by blowing on the mixture or tossing it in the air. The Mexican miners also introduced the use of the *arrastra.* This was a heavy slab of granite pulled by a mule or an ox around a central post. The *arrastra* ground up the gold-bearing ore, thus making it possible to separate the metal from the gravel.

Mexican experience also proved valuable when silver was discovered near the California-Nevada line in 1859. A miner named Henry Comstock had found a vein of rock flecked with gold. He complained about the bluish clay that made the digging difficult. It was one of his Mexican laborers who told him that the "blue stuff" was silver. With the experienced help of his Mexican workers, Comstock developed the famous Comstock Lode, the richest silver mine in the world.

California mining codes were borrowed from Mexican experience. Still another Mexican contribution was the system of mining codes. These were rules or laws that regulated all aspects of mining. The codes dealt with such matters as the staking out of claims, the control of water rights, and the testing of ore to determine gold content. On the frontier where there was no organized government, such codes were needed to prevent chaos. The mining codes had their origin in practices developed over the years in Spanish America.

Mexicans were forced out of the mines. Mexican miners soon encountered unfair treatment in the California gold fields. Those who worked for wages were paid much less than Anglo laborers. Mexicans were also robbed and cheated out of their claims. Many were even lynched. The Anglos finally declared that "no foreigners" were wanted in the mines. This term was applied to all miners of Spanish or Mexican background, whether they had been born north or south of the Rio Grande.

In 1850 the new state legislature passed a law saying that all miners who did not speak English had to pay a monthly tax of 20 dollars. The Spanish-speaking miners then founded their own town, named Sonora, south of the main gold-rush area. When the tax collectors came to Sonora, the Mexicans staged a "revolt." But a mob of Anglo-American miners attacked the Spanish-speaking miners, lynched many, and drove the rest out of the area. Most of the surviving Mexicans took refuge in the southern part of the state. Others formed bands and struck back at the Anglo-American miners.

Spanish and Mexican land grants did not have precise boundaries. As in other parts of the borderlands, Mexican American landowners in California eventually lost much of their property to Anglo immigrants. Some of the *Californio* land grants dated back to the earliest Spanish settlements in southern California. Others had been made after Mexico became independent of Spain. Mission lands had been divided up and granted to individual ranchers. More than 600 of these land grants were made in California during the period of Mexican rule. They ranged in size from 4500 to 100,000 acres.

The boundaries of these land grants were seldom stated in exact terms. One deed stated that a parcel of land extended from "the line along a dry wash to a large oak tree." Another referred to a tract that reached from "the point where there are three sycamore trees to the top of the rise." At the time the grants were made, exact boundaries did not matter. The land was used for grazing, and the cattle were branded anyway.

The Anglos brought new ideas of land ownership. After California became part of the United States, however, different ideas of land ownership were introduced. In the United States, land was always surveyed so that exact boundaries could be established. Moreover,

An 1890 photograph shows a Californio *family outside their home in Los Angeles.*

the Anglo immigrants came from areas where a farm of 160 acres was considered large. They felt that ranchers who owned thousands of acres were not making good use of the land. Under the Anglo-dominated state government, land in California came to be taxed at a high rate. Even so, during the early years of statehood, the *Californio* ranchers prospered by selling cattle to the booming mining towns. Though they resented the high taxes, they were able to pay them.

Californios lost their lands. In the early 1860's, however, came two years of extreme drought. The semi-arid pasture lands turned into desert. Hundreds of thousands of cattle died. The *Californio* ranchers had no ready cash. After their taxes went unpaid for five years, their lands were taken over by county tax authorities and sold at public auction. Other *Californios* lost their lands in court cases because they were unable to prove their claims.

Many old *Californio* families were too discouraged to stay on in California. They sold out what land they had left and went to live in Mexico. Others started small businesses in hides or opened livery stables. By the late 1800's the Anglos had become the majority group in southern California. The big cattle ranches had been broken up, and the Anglos were planting orange groves and founding new towns. By buying and selling land, they started a real estate boom. Few Mexican American families remained.

Mexican culture was threatened. The cultural rights of the Mexican Americans also suffered. Among the Spanish-speaking people, the parish priests taught children whose parents wanted them to learn to read and write. When English-speaking Americans moved into California, they brought with them the concept of public schools supported by taxes. After the state government was organized, the legislature in Sacramento passed a law requiring every town to have a public school. It also ordered that all teaching in the public schools be done in English. Thus the Spanish language, which was basic to Mexican American culture, was downgraded.

The threat to Mexican American culture was fought by a newspaper editor named Francisco Ramirez. His newspaper, *El Clamor Público,* was published in southern California in the late 1850's. In this paper Ramirez urged the *Californios* to preserve their heritage by continuing Spanish-language schools. He reported thefts of land and lynchings and attacks on Mexican Americans by Anglos. Such events were often ignored by English-language newspapers. Ramirez urged the old families to become familiar with the new taxation system and to vote for candidates with Spanish names for public office. He also stressed the importance of serving on juries and encouraged young Mexican Americans to become lawyers. Only then could Mexican Americans be assured of

fair treatment in the Anglo courts. By 1860 an English-language paper had "squeezed" Ramirez out of business. He went to San Francisco and tried unsuccessfully to launch a Spanish-language weekly there.

The violation of Mexican American rights in the last half of the 1800's was a tragic development in the history of the Southwest. Laws, differences in customs, bureaucratic procedures, and sharp practices—all served to deprive Mexican Americans of their political, property, and cultural rights. Even violence was openly used. Many history books ignore this aspect of southwestern history. Other accounts seem to suggest that it was necessary in "taming the frontier." Thus the Anglo has been pictured as the "pioneer" while the Mexican who resisted and defended his rights became the *"bandido."*

THINKING ABOUT THIS SECTION

1. Explain or define the following: Anglos; *bandido; Californio;* mining codes.

2. Why did Anglos join with *patrones* in controlling the territorial government of New Mexico? What ethnic groups made up the labor force in New Mexico?

3. When Anglos settled in the Southwest, what traditional Mexican methods of ranching and farming did they adopt? Why?

4. How did many Mexican Americans in the Southwest lose their lands?

5. After the Civil War what kinds of settlers moved into Arizona Territory? Why?

6. What contributions were made by Mexican Americans to the mining industry? How were Mexican Americans forced out of the California gold fields?

7. In the last half of the 1800's Mexican Americans were deprived of their property and political and cultural rights. Give an example of how each of the following factors served to bring this about: new laws; differences in customs; bureaucratic procedures; sharp practices; violence.

After 1900 a great wave of immigration brought thousands of people from Mexico into the United States. Most of them came north to work on the railroads or in agriculture. The turmoil of the Mexican Revolution also drove many Mexicans across the border.

Railroad companies recruited workers in Mexico. There had been a great demand for unskilled labor in the Far West after the Civil War, especially in railroad construction. To meet this need, the railroads imported thousands of Chinese laborers and paid them very low wages. Many of the Chinese also worked in agriculture. But in 1882 Chinese immigration was prohibited by law. Agents for the railroads then began to recruit workers in northern Mexico.

During the early 1900's thousands of Mexicans were brought into the United States every year. In time many of them left the railroads and went to work building streetcar lines in the rapidly growing cities of the Southwest and Midwest. Others went to work in the Arizona mines or in the new fruit and vegetable farms that were laid out in the San Joaquin (wah-*keen'*), Salt River, and lower Rio Grande valleys. To replace men who found other jobs, the railroad companies simply recruited more Mexican workers. Since there was no immigration quota, the companies were free to bring in as many Mexican employees as they needed. Probably over a million Mexicans entered the United States between 1900 and 1930.

The Mexican railroad workers lived with their families in camps along the railroad lines, in tents behind freight stations in the towns, or in boxcars that were moved from siding to siding. A whole generation of young Mexican Americans was born and grew up in railroad boxcars scattered throughout the West and Midwest. In 1928 railroad boxcar labor camps in Chicago were "home" for almost a thousand Mexican Americans, about a third of them children.

Workers were needed to farm irrigated lands. By the early 1900's vast tracts of land once used as cattle and sheep range were being irrigated for large-scale agriculture. In Texas cotton had become especially important. One observer wrote that in middle and west Texas people "planted cotton, talked cotton, thought cotton, sold cotton, everything but ate cotton." Much of the labor in the Texas cotton fields was done by migrant workers brought in from Mexico.

The cotton harvest was in the late fall. But there was enough work in other kinds of crops to keep the Mexican field workers busy from April to November. Irrigation had turned the Rio Grande delta into a huge vegetable garden centered in Brownsville, Texas. In southern California a flood-control system near the mouth of the Colorado River made it possible to irrigate the Imperial Valley. Tomatoes, lettuce, and cantaloupes could be grown the year round. Huge numbers of workers were needed, since these crops must be planted, weeded, and picked by hand. This is not easy work. In 110-degree heat, the fast-ripening tomatoes must be picked as quickly as possible.

Many of the vegetable and fruit workers followed a certain schedule of seasonal work. From the Imperial Valley they headed north to the San Joaquin Valley to pick grapes and peaches; then farther north to the Sacramento River near Stockton to pick asparagus; and finally to Yakima, Washington, to pick apples. It was Mexican labor that made possible the large-scale production of these fruits and vegetables.

Migrant workers lived a bleak life. At first many of the migrant workers returned to Mexico for part of the year. But since the winter was short, many of them settled in California and Texas towns. Their wages when they had work were miserably low. And much of what they earned went back to the ranchers and growers as payment for food and rent. As a result, the Mexican families often had no money for the winter and would have to go on county relief. It seemed impossible for them to improve their lot. They were much too poor to buy farms of their own. Few of them were able to vote. And they could not bring pressure on growers to pay higher wages, since more low-paid workers could always be recruited in Mexico.

To make matters worse, Mexican Americans suffered discrimination throughout the Southwest. They were paid less for doing the same work as English-speaking employees. Schools and housing were segregated. Restrooms in public buildings and in filling stations from Brownsville, Texas, to Fresno, California, had signs reading "Closed to Mexicans." Moreover, Anglos who committed crimes against Mexican Americans were seldom prosecuted.

Young people of Mexican descent found it hard to get ahead. Many never stayed long enough in one place to make much progress in school. And they often had to drop out of school at an early age to go to work. Since they spoke Spanish at home, they did not learn to speak English well. In school they were often ridiculed for speaking Spanish or placed in "slow" classes.

The situation grew worse during the Great Depression. During the Depression years of the 1930's there was little work for anyone, whether they spoke English or Spanish. Because people were too poor to buy much food, crops rotted in the fields and canneries shut down. Many spinning and weaving mills also closed as cotton fields went untended. Railroads reduced maintenance crews by half. In the early 1930's local governments in California forced thousands of Spanish-speaking families who had been on relief to go to Mexico. Many of these Mexican Americans had been born in the United States and therefore were citizens. Nevertheless, they were deported in order to ease the load on relief agencies and to improve job prospects for Anglo-Americans.

The war years revived the need for labor. In the 1940's World War II drastically changed things. Hundreds of thousands of Mexican Americans joined the armed forces. Other Mexican Americans got jobs in defense industries, and more field workers were needed than ever before.

In 1942 the United States and Mexico reached an agreement concerning the employment of Mexican-born field workers. The workers were called *braceros* (brah-*sehr'* ohss), from *brazo,* the Spanish word for "arm." Under the terms of the agreement, the *braceros* were to receive free transportation to and from Mexico. They were to have decent housing, safe working conditions, and good food. Also, they were to be paid at the current rate for farm work. In other words, employers were not supposed to take advantage of the *braceros* in order to underpay or fire other workers.

When the first trainload of *braceros* arrived in Stockton, California, they were welcomed as "helpers in the war effort." From 1942 to 1945 more than 200,000 *braceros* went north to the United States. They harvested crops across the country, from California and the Southwest to Michigan and New York. *Braceros* also worked in industry and on the railroads.

Wetbacks entered illegally. While the *braceros* entered the United States legally, additional thousands of Mexicans crossed the Rio Grande illegally into Texas. These illegal immigrants were called "wetbacks," even though in many places they could wade across the river. The wetbacks worked in agriculture for less than the growers paid the *braceros*. Actually some *braceros* also were paid less than the fair rate. If they protested, the growers could threaten them with deportation.

The bracero program came to an end. Because of pressure from local labor, including Mexican Americans, the *bracero* treaty program was halted in 1947. But after the Korean War started, growers were again allowed to bring in *braceros* if no domestic labor was "available." The "prevailing wage" was to be paid. Over the decade of the 1950's more than three million *braceros* were imported. During all this time Mexican American leaders opposed the *bracero* program. Because the *braceros* were willing to work for low pay, the arrangement kept wages low for United-States-born labor and increased unemployment. The *bracero* program finally came to an end in 1964. One reason was that the greater use of farm machinery had drastically reduced the need for hand labor.

Mexican Americans fought for their country. While the *braceros* filled the manpower shortage during World War II, young Mexican Americans left the migrant camps and the *barrios* (the Spanish-speaking neighborhoods of the cities) to go off to war. In the lists of military casualties printed in southwestern newspapers, three or four out of every ten names were Spanish. Several Mexican American servicemen won Congressional Medals of Honor, and many others earned special citations for bravery. Meanwhile, Spanish-speaking men in the armed forces heard or read with disgust about attacks on Mexican American teenagers in Los Angeles by servicemen from nearby military bases.

Mexican Americans were attacked. During the war years many Mexican American teenaged boys wore "drape shapes" or "zoot suits." These suits had long coats with padded shoulders, high waistlines, and very tight trouser cuffs. The hair style then popular was called the "ducktail." Like any other adolescents, the Los Angeles groups took a special pride in their clothes and hair styles. Many of the Mexican American teenagers who wore drapes and ducktails tended to gather together in gangs. In cities all over the United States young people of minority groups have found in gangs a way of gaining status and developing a sense of "belonging." The different gangs in Los Angeles were competitive, and occasionally they

The back-breaking labor of Mexican American field workers has made possible abundant harvests in the irrigated valleys of the United States Southwest.

fought each other. The local newspapers gave big headlines to the gang-fighting and also played up stories about crimes committed by people with Spanish names.

Servicemen stopped this Los Angeles streetcar in June, 1943, and searched it for young Mexican Americans wearing zoot suits. Crowds of curious people watched.

Serious trouble started when bands of sailors on leave in Los Angeles began beating up zoot-suited teenagers. Egged on by the press and some Anglo citizens, and given a free hand by the police, servicemen attacked Mexican American youths nightly for more than a week in June, 1943. The police arrested large numbers of Mexican Americans but none of the Anglo-American servicemen who were involved in the fighting. The Mexican ambassador in Washington, D.C., and the United States Secretary of State made formal complaints to the city of Los Angeles. When the military command declared the city of Los Angeles off limits for servicemen, the attacks finally came to an end. But Mexican Americans long remembered the nights of terror in the *barrios*. News of the violence in Los Angeles aroused anger and resentment throughout Latin America.

Veterans demanded a better chance. When the war ended, returning Mexican American servicemen hoped to find a better life than the discrimination they had known in prewar days. "Mexican American soldiers shed at least a quarter of the blood spilled at Bataan. . . . What they want now is a decent job, a decent home, and a chance to live peacefully in the community. They don't want to be shot at in the dark," said one of them.[5] But when they came home, the veterans found that they were

[5] Quoted in Carey McWilliams, *North from Mexico,* p. 261.

still refused service in restaurants and forced to sit in the balconies in movie theaters. They were also denied good jobs. To protest against discrimination, they formed Mexican American veterans' organizations. Among these were the Community Service Organization (CSO) in Los Angeles and the GI Forum in Texas.

Organized action brought some results. The veterans' groups publicized cases in which Mexican Americans were unfairly treated. In Los Angeles the veterans who formed the Community Service Organization pressed for full civil rights for Mexican Americans. As part of this campaign, the CSO started voter-registration drives. The CSO members also organized free classes in United States history and government for foreign-born residents hoping to become citizens. Moreover, they succeeded in electing one of their members, Edward Roybal, to the Los Angeles City Council. He was the first person with a Spanish last name to serve on the Council since 1881. Later he was elected to the United States House of Representatives.

THINKING ABOUT THIS SECTION

1. Explain or define the following words: labor camps; *braceros;* wetbacks.
2. Why did the railroads begin to recruit labor in northern Mexico after 1882? How did the railroad workers live? What other types of jobs were open to Mexican American workers in the early 1900's?
3. Why did these workers find it difficult to get ahead? Why was this also true for their children? Why did the situation grow worse during the Depression years of the 1930's?
4. Why did the job situation for Mexican Americans change in the 1940's? Why did Mexican American leaders oppose the *bracero* program?
5. What were the circumstances of the clash between Mexican American young men and Anglo servicemen in Los Angeles in 1943? How was the news of this violence probably interpreted in Latin America?
6. What was the reaction of Mexican American veterans to discrimination following World War II? What steps did they take to change the situation?

4. The Struggle for Equality: Mexican Americans in Recent Years

The postwar years began a new period in Mexican American history. The determination of war veterans to win equal rights spurred other Mexican Americans to similar efforts.

Equality of education was one goal. Many of the veterans took advantage of the benefits offered by the government's GI Bill of Rights to get high-school diplomas. Some also went to college. All hoped that their younger brothers and sisters would have greater educational opportunities than they had had in the prewar years.

Mexican Americans fought segregated education. The town of Westminster, California, in the mid-1940's had two schools. One was a modern, well-equipped school for Anglo-American children. Mexican American children went to school in an older, shabbier building. A Westminster resident named Gonzalo Mendez thought it was wrong for the schools to be segregated. Why should his three children have to attend an inferior school just because their names were Spanish? In 1945 Gonzalo Mendez brought suit in the California courts against the local school officials. A number of organizations helped Mendez fight his case. These included the American Jewish Congress and the National Association for the Advancement of Colored People. The judge ruled in favor of Mendez, declaring that segregation of Mexican American students was illegal. But the school officials appealed this

"Green-carders" regularly cross the border from Mexico to work in United States fields and factories.

decision to a higher court. In 1947 the higher court upheld the ruling that segregation was illegal. After this victory Mexican Americans began to oppose segregation in other public facilities as well, including swimming pools and parks.

Political influence was another goal. One way for minority groups to bring about change is to build up political power. The way to do that is to get citizens to register, vote, and elect sympathetic candidates to office. In the past a number of Mexican Americans had never voted. Those who were migrant workers could not meet residency requirements. Foreign-born residents who had not learned English could not pass examinations for citizenship. Moreover, those with limited education were at a great disadvantage in trying to get politicians to listen to them.

The postwar generation of Mexican Americans set about changing this situation. As mentioned earlier, veterans' organizations carried on voting drives. The first group specifically formed for political action was the Mexi-

can American Political Association (MAPA). Its goal was to bring about social and economic improvement through political activities. "We have to learn to play the political game," said one MAPA official.

Victories came slowly. But some Mexican American candidates were elected to office. Henry B. Gonzalez won election to Congress as representative from San Antonio, Texas, and Joseph M. Montoya became United States senator from New Mexico. A few Mexican Americans were also elected to city councils and school boards. But still today Mexican Americans hold only a tiny percentage of local political offices. As a whole, the group is badly underrepresented in political life.

Over the years neither of the two major political parties took full notice of Mexican American needs. In the 1960's Chicanos began forming third parties and running their own candidates. One party in Texas, called *La Raza Unida* ("The United Race"), succeeded in electing some candidates. What long-range success these parties will have remains a question. "Our movement is changing from month to month," one Chicano leader said. "No one knows what political form it will take tomorrow. All we know is that it will be our own. We will no longer take orders from anyone." [6]

Green-carders undercut United States labor.
Economic betterment is a continuing goal of Mexican American leaders. Mexico has long provided a ready supply of cheap labor for employers in the southwestern United States. Though the *bracero* program has ended, thousands of Mexicans now work in the United States on a day-to-day basis. Each morning they cross the border to work in fields or factories and then return to their homes in Mexico at night. Because they carry green identification cards to show when crossing the border, they are called "green-carders." The green-carders will accept lower wages than United States workers and so are much sought after by employers in this country. This supply of cheap labor undermines the bargaining power of workers born in this country. It is especially damaging to Mexican Americans. For years it hampered efforts to organize labor unions in large-scale agriculture.

Cesar Chavez organized the grape workers.
By the late 1960's machinery was doing much of the field work once done by huge gangs of migrants. In the grape industry around Delano, California, however, the work was still done by hand. Many of the vineyard workers lived there the year round, since there was work to be done during ten months of the year. All the big vineyards, many of which produced wines and brandy, were owned by large growers. The workers were paid the lowest possible legal wage. They were not covered by Social Security, and they had no medical or accident insurance. Living conditions in the camps provided for the laborers were miserable.

The vineyard workers found a leader in Cesar Chavez, a field worker who had grown up in a migrant family. In 1965 Chavez organized the grape workers into a union and led them out on strike. The strikers met with bitter resistance from the growers, who said that Chavez was out to destroy the grape industry. The growers also charged that Chavez was putting the field laborers out of work and that he did not represent the majority of the workers. But the strikers gained widespread support. Contributions of food and money came from veterans' groups, Catholic clubs, and even grandmothers in the *barrios* who as children had worked in the vineyards. As an expression of support, many people stopped buying grapes.

Chavez had a strong commitment to nonviolence. He told one reporter: "Those of us who have seen violence never want to see it again. I know how it tears people apart. And in the end we lose. I'm not saying we should lie down and die. . . . But I think we can force meaningful change without the short cut of violence." [7] Finally most of the grape growers recognized the field workers' union and raised wages. The union next began a campaign to organize lettuce workers. Against heavy odds, Chavez's movement had established the right of farm workers to organize, a right long enjoyed by industrial workers in this country.

Tijerina fought for restoration of lost lands.
One of the most militant Mexican American organizations is the *Alianza Federal de Los Pueblos Libres* ("Federal Alliance of Free City States"). It is led by Reies Lopez Tijerina (tee-heh-*ree'* nah). The goal of the *Alianza* is to regain the lands lost by people who lived in New Mexico and other parts of the Southwest before these regions became United States soil. Tijerina and the *Alianza* base their campaign on the property-rights guarantee included in the Treaty of Guadalupe-Hidalgo.

In fighting for this cause Tijerina and his followers have carried on guerrilla warfare. In 1967 they raided a courthouse in northern New Mexico in an effort to kidnap a district attorney. They claimed that they wanted to

[6] Quoted in Stan Steiner, *La Raza: The Mexican Americans* (New York: Harper, 1969), p. 207.

[7] Quoted in *The New York Times,* April 20, 1969.

Chicano demands have resulted in some bilingual education. Left, a science teacher in a Texas school uses both English and Spanish. Political influence is also a goal. Congressman Henry B. Gonzalez (above) is one of the few Mexican Americans who have won important political office.

"arrest" him for "violation of our civil rights." When shooting broke out, Tijerina escaped. A small army of heavily armed national guardsmen, state police, sheriffs, and other lawmen set out after him. They finally captured Tijerina, and he was jailed. But he became a hero to many Mexican Americans who believe that their ancestors were cheated out of their lands.

Urban Chicanos are also demanding change.
Traditionally Chicano militancy and political activism have been associated with rural movements, such as those led by Tijerina and Cesar Chavez. Yet more than 80 per cent of the Mexican American population is urban and not rural. Most Mexican Americans live in such cities as Los Angeles, San Diego, San Antonio, El Paso, Phoenix, Tucson, Albuquerque, and Denver.

As the Chicano movement gathered strength during the 1960's, increasing numbers of urban Mexican Americans gave it their support.

Among the goals of the urban Chicanos are fair treatment by the police, a greater voice in politics, equal opportunities in employment and education, and recognition of Mexican American culture.

The growing use of the word *Chicano* symbolized the spirit of the movement. A member of a Chicano priests' organization told why he wanted to be called a Chicano: "I don't come from Spain, I wasn't born in Mexico. I don't see why I should be connected to either of these countries. I am a Chicano, a member of a new race and that is what I want to be called." [8]

In March, 1968, Chicano militancy played a part in a massive "blow-out" in several Los Angeles high schools. During the three-day strike a total of 15,000 Chicano students walked out of classes. The students demanded better conditions in the schools and courses

[8] Quoted in *National Catholic Reporter,* April 2, 1971.

on Mexican and Mexican American history and culture. Thirteen leaders, including a teacher, were jailed. But the "blow-out" set a pattern that was followed by Chicano students in other states.

Still another page in the history of the Chicano movement was written on a summer day in 1970. A huge antiwar rally was held by Mexican Americans in Los Angeles. It began as a peaceful protest against the high number of Mexican American casualties in the Vietnam War. But it ended in a night of burning, looting, and rioting in the *barrio* of East Los Angeles. The destruction of property totaled millions of dollars. Three persons lost their lives. One of them was a well-known Chicano journalist, Ruben Salazar, who had been covering the antiwar rally for the *Los Angeles Times*.

Ironically, in a speech not long before his death, Salazar had urged other Americans to listen to what the *barrio* Chicanos had to say. He had warned that many people in East Los Angeles felt that a massive riot was needed to make themselves heard.

Whether the Chicano movement now takes a violent path or makes use of peaceful, established channels will depend on the response of American society to Chicano efforts to gain equality and respect. Awareness of the Chicano movement does seem to be growing. Developments in education, for example, show that this is so. Chicano student groups have formed chapters in colleges and high schools. Through-

Three famous names on a fence in a California barrio *symbolize the pride of Mexican Americans in their cultural heritage.*

out the southwestern states Chicano Studies Departments have been organized in colleges and universities. Funds from the federal government now finance bilingual ("two-language") elementary programs in 31 states. In the bilingual classes supported by these funds teachers carry on lessons in both English and Spanish for students of all backgrounds. Special educational programs have also been started at the high-school and college levels. Thus, some progress has been made. But much more will be needed before Mexican Americans can be sure of equal opportunities and cultural recognition.

THINKING ABOUT THIS SECTION

1. Explain or define the following: MAPA: *La Raza Unida;* bilingual.
2. Why did Mexican Americans fight segregation in schools and other public facilities? What success did they have? How have they increased their political influence?
3. Who are the "green-carders"? How have they affected wage rates?
4. How was Cesar Chavez able to organize grape workers? Why was this victory of significance to farm workers in general?
5. What was the goal of the *Alianza* headed by Tijerina?
6. Why is the urban Chicano movement gaining strength? What are its goals?

Summing Up

Mexican Americans are this nation's second largest minority group. As a group, Mexican Americans are predominantly an urban people. They are concentrated in the large cities of the southwestern United States.

Mexican Americans have played an important role in the history of California and the Southwest. Long before these areas became United States soil, Spanish-speaking pioneers blazed new routes, developed mines, and founded towns. As a result of the war of 1846–1848, Mexico's border areas were annexed by the United States. Anglo-American culture then began to push Mexican American culture into the background. Although the Treaty of Guadalupe-Hidalgo stated that property rights and citizens' rights were to be protected, these guarantees were frequently violated. Thus was laid the groundwork for the discrimination experienced by Mexican Americans since 1848.

After 1900 began a mass migration of Mexicans into the United States. The upheavals of the Mexican Revolution drove many refugees north across the border. Many of these newcomers found work on the railroads and in large-scale agriculture. Later, during the Depression years of the 1930's, jobs became scarce and Mexican workers were no longer wanted. Thousands of Spanish-speaking people, both Mexicans and United States citizens, were forced to leave the Southwest and go to Mexico.

With the coming of World War II, the situation drastically changed. The manpower shortage in the United States led to a large-scale importation of Mexican *braceros* to work in this country's fields and factories. Many citizens of Mexican descent fought in the United States armed forces. Meanwhile, attacks on *barrio* teenagers in Los Angeles dramatized the existence of prejudice against Mexican Americans.

After World War II and especially since the 1960's Mexican Americans have begun to press for equal rights and opportunities. A union movement led by Cesar Chavez sought to win for field workers the rights already enjoyed by industrial workers in this country. More militant has been the *Alianza Federal* in its fight for recognition of old land claims in New Mexico. Meanwhile, urban Chicanos are demanding better opportunities and a greater voice in politics. All of the new Mexican American groups are stressing a new self-awareness and pride in the Chicano heritage.

The rolling hilly interior of Puerto Rico is seldom seen by the North American tourists who vacation in San Juan. The small farmers who live in this part of the island raise food crops, tobacco, or coffee.

Puerto Rico and the Puerto Ricans

CHAPTER FOCUS

1. Puerto Rico as a Spanish Colony
2. Puerto Rico as a United States Territory
3. Operation Bootstrap
4. Puerto Rico as a Commonwealth Associated with the United States
5. Puerto Ricans on the Mainland

If someone were asked to name the world's major Spanish-speaking cities, he would surely include in his list such places as Mexico City, Buenos Aires, Madrid, Lima, and Caracas. Probably few people would think of naming New York City. Yet this metropolis has approximately two million Spanish-speaking residents. By themselves these people would form the population of a huge city. Among the Spanish-speaking residents of New York City are Mexican Americans and people from Spain and the Latin American countries. But the largest group of Spanish-speaking New Yorkers are of Puerto Rican background. In fact, after the Mexican Americans, the next largest group of Spanish-speaking United States citizens is the Puerto Ricans. Both the people who live on the island of Puerto Rico and those Puerto Ricans who have moved to the North American mainland are citizens of the United States.

Puerto Rico has a unique political status. It is not a colony and not a state; nor is it an independent nation. It is a self-governing Commonwealth associated with the United States. In Spanish the Puerto Ricans call their homeland *Estado Libre Asociado,* a "Free Associated State." The voters of Puerto Rico do not send representatives and senators to Congress, and they do not vote for president. But they have an elected legislature and governor. Of course, those Puerto Ricans who have permanently moved to the mainland vote for congressmen and for president just like other citizens of the United States.

Puerto Rico is the most easterly of the large islands of the Antilles, lying 75 miles east of the Dominican Republic (map, page 214). Though it is the fourth largest island in the Caribbean, it is not very big, measuring about 100 by 35 miles. By air Puerto Rico is just about three hours from New York City.

The island has a beautiful natural setting. The word "paradise" is overworked in descriptions of Puerto Rico, but for centuries people have been calling it that. An English sailor wrote about Puerto Rico in the 1700's: "It is one of the finest islands I ever saw. . . . It abounds in oranges, lemons, limes, etc., in such plenty that they are not worth the gathering. There are [huge] quantities of bananas, plantains, coconuts, pineapples, mountain cabbage, with a great many other fruits and vegetables. . . . In short, there is not anything for the support of human nature but may here be found or cultivated."

Much of the island is a lush green, with sandy beaches along the deep blue Caribbean. In the interior of the island there are mountains and foothills, but no peak is higher than 4400 feet. During much of the year the temperature stays in the 70's and low 80's. On only about five days during the average year is there no sunshine. The island's climate and natural beauty have made it a favorite vacation spot for tourists from the mainland United States. Puerto Rico does have one geographical handicap. Lying in the Caribbean hurricane belt, it is occasionally hit hard by tropical storms.

Because of the rough terrain in the interior, only about half of the island's land is good for commercial agriculture. The soil, however, is lushly fertile. Still today, as in the 1700's, Puerto Rico grows abundant quantities of fruits, but sugar cane is the most important crop. As on other Caribbean islands, the cane is grown in the coastal lowlands. In the hilly regions tobacco and coffee are produced; and many basic food crops are raised by small farmers throughout the island. But since so much of the land is devoted to sugar cane, a large part of the island's food supply has to be imported.

Far more important than agriculture in the island's economy today are its many industries. Only a few decades ago, Puerto Rico had almost no industry. As the result of a self-help campaign called Operation Bootstrap, the situation has changed, and hundreds of manufacturing plants now provide jobs for many skilled workers.

1. Puerto Rico as a Spanish Colony

Peaceful Indians lived on Puerto Rico. The Indians who lived on Puerto Rico when the Europeans came to the New World were Tainos (*ty'* nohz), a branch of the Arawaks. The Indians called their island Boriquén (spelled Borinquén by the Spanish). Even today Puerto Ricans are proud to be called Borinqueños, and their national anthem is "La Borinqueña." The natives of Boriquén were peaceful farming people. They tilled little plots of manioc and also gathered wild yams and caught fish. Their only enemies were the fierce Carib Indians, who occasionally raided the coastal villages of Puerto Rico.

Ponce de León founded a European settlement. Columbus was the first European to see Puerto Rico. He anchored off the island, exactly where is uncertain, for several days during his second voyage (1493). Juan Ponce de León was a member of this expedition. In 1508 Ponce de León received permission from the Spanish Crown to return to the island and explore it. The next year he founded a town at Caparra (kah-*pah'* rah) in low hills near a protected bay on the north coast of the island. He called the bay Puerto Rico or "rich port." [1] Colonists from Santo Domingo came to the new settlement with Ponce de León and brought along cattle and horses.

Caparra proved to be an unhealthful spot, damp and swarming with insects, so in 1521 the Spaniards moved to a small island in the harbor. There they founded a new town and named it *San Juan Bautista* for Saint John the Baptist. The Spaniards called the town San Juan (sahn *hwahn'*) for short, and the entire island came to be known as Puerto Rico.

The Indian population dwindled. The colonists who came with Ponce de León to San Juan were granted tracts of land. As in other parts of the Americas that were conquered, the Indian villagers had to work for the Spaniards. Overwork and European diseases soon killed off great numbers of the Puerto Rican Indians. Others lost their lives in rebellions against the Spanish conquerors. Most Indians who survived gradually blended into the general population.

San Juan became a fortress. The Spanish community at San Juan did not grow quickly. Few Spaniards wanted to settle there permanently. In fact, so many colonists left San Juan to seek gold in Mexico and Peru that the governor forbade people to leave Puerto Rico. But the island had strategic importance since it provided an excellent harbor on the direct route between Mexico and Spain. Properly fortified, the island could play a major role in fighting off British and French attempts to share the wealth of the New World.

In the early 1500's the governor of Puerto Rico appealed to Spain for funds to build a strong fortress. The funds were granted, and workmen began building the large castle called *La Fortaleza.* (Today *La Fortaleza* is the governor's residence.) Later in the century the Council of the Indies set aside a yearly share of the silver mined in Mexico to maintain San Juan's defenses. This money made possible the building of *El Morro,* a powerful fortress which guarded the entrance to San Juan's harbor. "This fort will be the strongest that his majesty hath in all the Indies," declared the Spanish governor.

El Morro was completed in the early 1590's. In 1595, when a Spanish treasure ship was anchored there for repairs, Sir Francis Drake sailed into San Juan harbor and tried to capture the town. But the gunners of El Morro fought off the English attack. Drake gave up and sailed away. Three years later an English admiral attacked San Juan with a fleet of eighteen ships. An epidemic was raging in the Puerto Rican port when the Englishmen landed. Soon they began to sicken also. Indians from the interior highlands joined with the Spaniards to drive the English forces out of San Juan. After losing 600 men, the English commander loaded his ships with hides, ginger, and sugar, and set sail. "It was not God's pleasure that this island should be inhabited by the English," wrote his chaplain.

Over the next century English, French, and Dutch pirates regularly plundered the Puerto Rican coast. In fact, these raids continued into the 1700's. But El Morro stood strong against all attempts to capture San Juan.

African slaves were brought to the island. Slavery came to Puerto Rico in its earliest days as a European colony. In 1509 the first African slaves were sold on the island, and the slave traffic continued over the next 300 years. The sugar planters of Puerto Rico did not use as many slaves on their plantations

---

[1] "Porto Rico" is a mispronunciation of the name.

El Morro still guards the entrance to San Juan harbor, though the threat of English pirates ended long ago. Today the old fortifications are maintained as a historic site.

with a total population of 45,000 people. Of these, about 5000 were slaves.

Despite the importance of El Morro, Puerto Rico was a neglected island. The regular Spanish fleet seldom called there and then only to supply the garrison. At one time in the mid-1600's the governor complained that eleven years had passed without a visit from any Spanish merchant vessels. A century later the same sort of complaint was being voiced by the islanders. Puerto Rico did not lack European goods, however. Portuguese, English, French, Dutch, and Danish traders were smuggling along the coast all the time.

It has been said that Spanish neglect of the island may have served to develop a quality that remained part of the Puerto Rican character. This was a strong love of freedom and a respect for individual dignity and rights.

Puerto Rican culture developed. By 1800 attacks by European powers on Puerto Rico had ended. Entering a period of peace, the islanders were better able to give attention to cultural development. Among educated Puerto Ricans there was considerable interest in literature, history, and public problems. Puerto Rican authors began producing a literature distinct from that of Spain, and artists, musicians, and dramatists also became active. In 1849 Manuel Alonso described in his novel *El Jíbaro* (hee' bah-roh) the sad life of the country peasants. Since Alonso was critical of Spanish rule, the police were ordered to watch him. *El Jíbaro* now ranks as the first major work in Puerto Rican literature.

Education during the 1800's was similar to schooling in Spain. Secondary education was provided by private tutors or in schools run by the Catholic Church, and was limited to upper-class children. According to census figures for 1860, about 17 per cent of the male population and 12 per cent of the female population could read. These figures were much the same as for Spain at the time. There was no university on the island throughout the period of Spanish rule.

as did those of Cuba and Hispaniola. Nevertheless, there was a time when blacks accounted for half of the island's population. On the whole, slaves were treated less harshly in Puerto Rico than elsewhere in the Caribbean. In fact, many runaway slaves from Cuba and Santo Domingo fled to Puerto Rico. There they lived in the hills or became fishermen along the coast.

San Juan failed to prosper. Throughout the years of attacks by foreign enemies and pirates, San Juan remained a small town. Many of the original settlers had left to seek their fortunes in Mexico. Compared to Cuba, Puerto Rico was sparsely populated and undeveloped. In 1765 a royal Spanish commissioner visited the island. He reported that Puerto Rico had 24 towns

Puerto Rico remained loyal to Spain. When Spain's American colonies began to break away in the early 1800's, Puerto Rico did not join in this movement. There were liberal Puerto Ricans who wanted independence, but Spain was determined to hold on to its Caribbean possessions. Under a capable governor, Puerto Rico did gain a small measure of self-government. Moreover, the islanders won the right to trade legally with the ships of all nations. Before this, only Spanish ships had been allowed to enter San Juan harbor.

New settlers swelled the population. Immigration was also liberalized, and people from many lands began to settle in Puerto Rico. Refugees from the wars in Mexico and South America came to the island, as did French Catholics from Louisiana after that territory was sold to the United States. Other newcomers were French planters fleeing from slave rebellions in Haiti and wealthy loyalist families opposed to the new governments in Venezuela, Colombia, and Peru. Some Irish Catholics from the United States also sought a friendlier atmosphere in Catholic Puerto Rico. Many black people were brought to the island as house servants by French and Spanish immigrants. But some black immigrants came to Puerto Rico as refugees seeking a safe home.

Puerto Rico's population today reflects a blending of the many peoples who migrated to the island. As one writer has put it, the Puerto Rican "is not a Negro, though 20 per cent of the population is Negro. He is not an Indian, yet the golden skin, the high cheekbones, [and] the aquiline nose . . . of the Indians are a common trait all over the island. He is not a Spaniard, yet he may have the blond hair of northern Spain and the white skin of Barcelona." [2]

With so many new arrivals, the Puerto Rican population mushroomed. In 1800 there were reported to be 155,000 people on the island. This was a startling increase over the estimate

[2] Ruth Gruber, *Puerto Rico: Island of Promise* (New York: Hill and Wang, 1960), p. 26.

for 1765 mentioned on the previous page. This growth continued until the island had 900,000 people in 1898.

Meanwhile, sugar and coffee plantations grew in size and number, and Puerto Rican planters were selling much of their output to the United States. With increased emphasis on plantation agriculture, two classes of society emerged—landowners and workers.

Some Puerto Ricans were dissatisfied with Spanish rule. During the 1800's a series of revolts, dictatorships, and counter-revolutions kept Spain in turmoil. As a result, Spain's few remaining American colonies suffered from bad government and restrictions on personal freedoms. Some Puerto Ricans continued to think their island should break away from Spain. They also believed the slaves should be freed. One reform leader was Ramón Betances (bay-*tahn'* sayss).

Betances was born in 1827 to a poor family of part-African descent. As a boy, Ramón managed to get a little schooling. A well-to-do family, impressed with his ability, sent him to Paris to study medicine. After completing his studies, Betances returned to Puerto Rico. One day, seeing a Negro child offered for sale, Dr. Betances bought the little slave for 25 pesos. This ridiculous price for a human being so troubled him that he began working to free the slaves. During a period in the 1860's when liberals controlled the Spanish government, Betances traveled to Spain and pleaded for emancipation. A measure was passed decreeing that from then on, all children born to slave mothers were to be free.

An uprising failed. But soon the Spanish liberals were ousted from power. Betances returned to Puerto Rico and in 1868 started a revolt. A handful of rebels seized the town of Lares (*lah'* rayss) and proclaimed the Republic of Borinquén. Spanish soldiers soon captured the rebels, and the uprising collapsed. But that early call for freedom is known today to all Puerto Ricans as the *Grito de Lares,* similar

SAN JUAN-NEW YORK 1600 MI.

ATLANTIC OCEAN

Aguadilla

TO DOM. REP.

Arecibo

Lares

Mayagüez

San Juan

Bayamon

CULEBRA

TO VIRGIN IS.

Caguas

Cayey

VIEQUES

Ponce

Guayama

Caribbean Sea

S Sugar cane
T Tobacco
Cf Coffee
⌐ Industry

0 10 20 30 40 Miles

Puerto Rico

to Father Hidalgo's *Grito de Dolores* in Mexico. And the Lares independence fighters are now Puerto Rican heroes. Betances went into exile and for many years lived in Paris.

Finally in 1873 the slaves in Puerto Rico won full freedom. Many of the freedmen became small farmers, raising food for themselves on tiny plots of land and doing seasonal work on the sugar and coffee plantations.

Muñoz Rivera won a promise of self-government. An important Puerto Rican leader in the late 1800's was Luis Muñoz Rivera (*moo' nyohss ree-vay' rah*). Muñoz was only a boy when the Lares Revolution failed. When he grew up, he became a poet. But he also decided to work for Puerto Rican self-government within the Spanish system. He edited a newspaper called *La Democracía* and founded a political party, the Autonomista Party. (*Autonomista* means "autonomy" or "self-government.") Liberal leaders in Madrid gave Muñoz support, hoping that his plans would satisfy the Puerto Ricans and preserve the island as a colonial possession. Despite his goal, Muñoz was critical of the Spanish governors. He once

pointed out that the government gave more attention to regulating cockfights than to providing schools. It also disturbed him that the wealthy planters made big money from sugar cane, while the *jíbaros,* or country people, lived in hopeless poverty.

After revolution broke out in Cuba in 1895, some leaders in the Spanish government realized that Puerto Rico as well as Cuba might be lost. So Muñoz Rivera was able to win promises of reform from Spain. His biggest victory was securing a document called the Charter of 1897. Under the terms of this Charter the Puerto Ricans were to have their own congress (partly elected and partly appointed). The governor was still to be appointed by the Spanish government, but the Puerto Ricans were to have their own citizenship, and the men of the island would not be required to serve in the Spanish army. Moreover, Puerto Rico was to have full freedom in carrying on foreign trade.

But these reforms came too late. No one will ever know whether the Charter of 1897 would have worked or not. In the spring of 1898 the United States declared war on Spain, and by mid-summer Puerto Rico had been occupied by United States troops.

THINKING ABOUT THIS SECTION

1. Explain or define the following words: *Estado Libre Asociado; El Jíbaro; Grito de Lares.*

2. Why was San Juan of strategic importance to Spain? Why did Puerto Rico fail to prosper? What were the consequences of Spanish neglect? What cultural advances were made in the 1800's?

3. How was Puerto Rico's loyalty to Spain rewarded in the early 1800's? Why was there a rapid increase in population?

4. What part did Betances play in Puerto Rican reform efforts? With what success?

5. What was the goal of the Autonomista Party? What were the provisions of the Charter of 1897?

Earlier in this book the story of how the United States' war with Spain affected Cuba was told. What did the war mean for Puerto Rico?

Puerto Rico was not a battleground. In 1898, Puerto Rico was not a prosperous or busy or thickly settled place. San Juan, the largest city, had a population of some 35,000, and eighteen other towns had more than 2500 people each. The island's total population was less than a million. The port at San Juan was fairly quiet, although the island was exporting sugar, coffee, wood, corn, oranges, leather goods, and rum to a number of countries. The only roads on the island had been built by the Spanish for military use, and even on horseback it was difficult to get from village to village. It has sometimes been said that Puerto Rico was "a happy little island" in 1898, but this description seems doubtful. Most of the people were very poor.

On the island of Cuba, rebel guerrillas had been fighting the Spanish for some time. But in Puerto Rico there had been little fighting since the Lares uprising. A number of leaders who openly sought independence had been forced into exile. Also, large numbers of Puerto Rican patriots had gone to Cuba to help liberate that island. They hoped to get Cuban help to liberate Puerto Rico afterwards.

Most of the Spanish troops in the Caribbean were involved in the fighting in Cuba. Consequently, when United States forces under General Nelson Miles landed in Puerto Rico in July, 1898, there was little resistance. In fact, many of the island's people received the landing soldiers courteously because they thought the United States would help them win their freedom from Spain.

Puerto Rico was ceded to the United States. Only about two weeks after General Miles' landing, the United States and Spain reached a peace agreement. Under the terms of the treaty formally signed in December, 1898, Spain turned the island of Puerto Rico over to the United States. The people of Puerto Rico were, of course, not consulted.

The Spanish governor had delayed organizing the island's promised new government until the war with the United States should be over. But when Puerto Rico became a possession of the United States, the Spanish plan for the island's self-government was dropped. For two years United States military officers ruled the island and were accepted with indifference by most Puerto Ricans. A few islanders, however, continued to demand home rule.

Since the United States was not really prepared to deal with a colony, Puerto Rico's future was a big question mark. Was it to remain a colonial possession? Or should it eventually become a state? What about independence?

The Foraker Act provided a civilian government for Puerto Rico. In 1900 the United States Congress passed an act which ended military rule in Puerto Rico and set up a new civil (nonmilitary) government. Under the Foraker Act the governor of the island was appointed by the president of the United States. The president also appointed the members of the upper house of the Puerto Rican legislature. The members of the lower house were elected by the islanders themselves, but this body had no power to pass laws. Thus, Puerto Rico remained a colony, the people having little voice in their own government.

The Foraker Act also said that the Puerto Ricans were to be considered "Americans," but they did not become United States citizens. (President Theodore Roosevelt felt this was wrong, and he repeatedly asked Congress to declare the Puerto Ricans citizens.) Elementary education was made compulsory, but nothing was said in the Foraker Act about the language to be used in the schools. The Foraker Act also provided that no single person or corporation could own more than 500 acres of land. This was to keep large sugar corporations from buying up more land and squeezing out small planters. But since the 500-acre law was not enforced for another 40 years, North American companies managed to buy up most of the good sugar-cane land.

The Jones Act revised the Puerto Rico government. All of the governors who served under the Foraker Act were men from the United States. The only voice to speak for Puerto Rico in Washington, D.C., was Luis Muñoz Rivera. As the island's Resident Commissioner, he reported to Congress on Puerto Rican problems. Again and again Muñoz Rivera urged more responsible government for Puerto Rico, but no action was taken.

Muñoz Rivera died in 1916. In the following year Congress passed an act which made all Puerto Ricans United States citizens. The Jones Act also empowered the islanders to elect the members of the upper house of their legislature. But the governor was still appointed by the United States president, and many of the high officials were chosen by the governor. Puerto Ricans were disappointed with the Jones Act, but they found little sympathy in Washington. One reason was that the United States entered World War I in 1917. Puerto Rico's problems were forgotten in the hectic atmosphere of wartime.

By making the Puerto Ricans United States citizens, the Jones Act also made the men of that island subject to this country's military draft. Since then, thousands of Puerto Ricans have died in wars fought by a country in whose government they have no representation.

Governor Roosevelt urged the recognition of the island's Spanish heritage. Few of the governors who came to Puerto Rico could speak Spanish. Most of them knew nothing about the island or the problems of its people. An exception was Theodore Roosevelt, Jr., son of the former president. Governor Roosevelt served in San Juan from 1929 to 1932. He recognized the value of Puerto Rico's Spanish heritage. "I see no reason," Governor Roose-velt said, "to continue the drive to remodel all Puerto Ricans so that they should become similar in language, habits, and thoughts to continental Americans." He was among the first to suggest that Puerto Rico have a sister-state relationship with the United States. This would have been similar to Canada's relationship with England at the time.

The sugar industry failed to benefit the island. To the casual observer Puerto Rico might have looked prosperous. The port of San Juan was busy shipping coffee and sugar. Sugar exports had climbed from a value of eight million dollars in 1900 to one hundred million dollars in 1930. Yellow fever had been wiped out, and public health programs were attacking other problems.

But four large companies owned by United States investors controlled most of the sugar-cane industry. Though the 500-acre law in the Foraker Act was supposed to have prevented this, the companies found ways to get around the law. It was estimated that 75 per cent of the people were dependent, directly or indirectly, on the sugar industry. Because many small food farms had been taken over by the big sugar companies, the island did not grow enough food to feed its population.

Coffee also had nearly become a monopoly. There were still many small growers, but they had to sell their coffee beans through a few large companies. Though they managed to hold on to their lands, the small coffee planters found it harder and harder to make a living. Their children left the hilly country in the interior and went down to the coastal plains. There they could get jobs harvesting sugar cane for a wage of ten or twelve cents a day. But even these jobs lasted for only five months of the year. During the "dead time," while the cane was growing, there was little work to be found.

Some women found employment in the needlework industry. This work was contracted out to Puerto Ricans by New York garment manufacturers. Working at home, the women hemmed and embroidered table linens, underclothing, and handkerchiefs. For a dozen embroidered handkerchiefs, the needleworkers might be paid three cents.

Most islanders continued to be very poor. Governor Roosevelt tried to stir up concern in the United States for the poverty in Puerto Rico. Roosevelt wrote in an article for the *New York Herald Tribune:* "Riding through the hills, I have stopped at farm after farm where lean, underfed women and sickly men repeated again and again the same story— little food and no opportunity to get more. From these hills the people have streamed into the coastal towns, increasing the already severe unemployment situation there." But after 1929 the United States itself was suffering hard times, as the Great Depression gripped the nation. Puerto Rico continued to be neglected by the government in Washington.

Education was inadequate. United States officials recognized the island's desperate need for schools. But they ignored the island's Spanish heritage. The University of Puerto Rico was founded in 1903 to train young Puerto Ricans to become teachers. When these teachers went into the schools, however, they were supposed to use English, not Spanish. "Children who had never in their lives heard any language but Spanish were suddenly expected, on entering the first grade, to master the three R's and other subjects, taught to them in a language they knew nothing about, by teachers who spoke it poorly and had difficulty expressing themselves in it." [3]

Padín tried to improve the schools. In 1930 a Puerto Rican educator named José Padín changed this system. Padín was appointed Commissioner of Education by Governor Roosevelt. As Commissioner, he set aside the rule that all teaching was to be in English.

[3] Earl Parker Hanson, *Transformation: The Story of Modern Puerto Rico* (New York: Simon and Schuster, 1955), p. 53.

Textbooks were printed in Spanish, and classes were held in the language that the children and teachers knew best. Commissioner Padín also established rural vocational schools which offered practical courses. Visiting congressmen from the United States found fault with the policy of not using English in the schools, however, and Padín resigned. Most of the schools returned to the practice of holding classes in English rather than Spanish.

The need for reform was recognized in the 1930's. By the 1930's Puerto Ricans were desperately unhappy with conditions on the island. Some leaders in the United States understood this feeling. During the administration of President Franklin D. Roosevelt, the United States government took a much greater interest in Puerto Rican problems. Food was provided for the hungry people on the island, and plans were outlined for long-range reform. Unfortunately none of these efforts had much effect on the island's deep-rooted poverty. Moreover, when the United States entered World War II in 1941, the administration in Washington had to concentrate on wartime emergencies.

Some Puerto Ricans sought a change in government. Meanwhile, the dissatisfaction of Puerto Ricans with their colonial status came clearly into the open. Some islanders called for statehood. Others demanded complete independence from the United States. Several times nationalist activists clashed with police. In 1937, at a demonstration in the city of Ponce, about twenty unarmed nationalists were shot to death by military police, and many more were wounded. Today this event is remembered as the "Massacre of Ponce."

Muñoz Marín emerged as a leader. One of the reform groups thought that progress could best be made if the island's association with the United States were continued, at least for the time being. The leader of this group was Luis Muñoz Marín (*moo'* nyohss mah-*reen'*),

In campaigning for political office, Luis Muñoz Marín traveled throughout Puerto Rico by bus and stopped frequently to speak to the voters.

the son of Luis Muñoz Rivera. Elected to the Puerto Rican senate in 1932, Muñoz Marín soon became a dynamic and popular leader. He had worked hard to get aid from Washington for the island, but he felt the New Deal programs had not gone far enough. Basic reforms that would speed the island's economic development seemed to him the most important need. As for the political issue, Muñoz Marín believed that the island could not survive if it broke away from the United States, and that economically it was not ready for statehood. Even so, he campaigned with the slogan "Independence is just around the corner."

In the late 1930's Muñoz Marín founded a new party, the Popular Democratic Party, and began campaigning for the 1940 elections. It was customary for the conservatives who had kept the sugar companies in power to buy the votes of sugar workers for two dollars apiece. Muñoz Marín urged the workers: "Don't sell your vote. Lend it to me." *Time* magazine described him as a man who could explain ideas in either English or Spanish "with literary dignity or colloquial directness . . . that can go straight to the heart and mind of the humblest and least educated hearer."

With the help of their votes, Muñoz told the workers, his party's candidates would work to make the island a better place to live. They would enforce the 500-acre law, make the sugar companies obey other laws as well, raise wages, extend electricity to rural areas, and bring new factories to the island. Muñoz and the other candidates of his party succeeded in making their message clear. The new party won control of the senate and gained many seats in the lower house. Muñoz Marín himself was chosen president of the senate.

Tugwell co-operated with Muñoz. Over the next six years Muñoz Marín worked closely with Rexford Tugwell, the North American who now lived in the governor's palace in San Juan. In 1941 President Franklin D. Roosevelt had named Tugwell governor, knowing that he was well-qualified and interested in Puerto Rico's needs. Tugwell had served as United States Undersecretary of Agriculture and knew much about the problems of rural poverty.

Piñero was the first governor of Puerto Rican background. When Tugwell resigned in 1946, he convinced President Harry Truman that a native of the island should hold the post of governor. Truman appointed Jesús Piñero (hay-*sooss'* pih-*nyay'* roh), who had been Resident Commissioner in Washington. Like

Tugwell, Piñero also worked closely with Muñoz Marín in attempts to solve the island's problems.

Revision of the Jones Act pointed toward self-government. By 1947 both President Truman and United States congressmen recognized that the Puerto Ricans should have more voice in their government. In that year the Jones Act was revised to allow Puerto Ricans to elect their own governor. In the election held the next year the Popular Democratic Party nominated Muñoz Marín. Despite opposition from some newspapers, Muñoz won over five other candidates, and in 1949 he was inaugurated as the island's first elected governor. The celebration was one of the most enthusiastic ever held in the island's history. But since Puerto Rico was still dominated by the United States, many of the people remained dissatisfied with their country's status.

THINKING ABOUT THIS SECTION

1. Explain or define the following: Muñoz Rivera; Muñoz Marín; 500-acre law.
2. Why was there little resistance when United States troops landed in Puerto Rico in 1898? How did the outcome of the war between Spain and the United States affect the island?
3. What were the provisions of the Foraker Act? What were its shortcomings? How did the Jones Act fall short of Puerto Rican hopes?
4. Why did most Puerto Ricans continue to be poor in the early 1900's even though sugar exports were rising? Why did education on the island fail to meet the needs of Puerto Rican children?
5. What were the goals stressed by Muñoz Marín and the Popular Democratic Party? What was the significance of the 1947 revision of the Jones Act?

3. Operation Bootstrap

Industrialization got under way. Meanwhile, a drive to lift Puerto Rico out of poverty had gotten under way in the early 1940's. When the Popular Democratic Party came to power, it focused on industrialization as the key to a better life. To build more factories on the island, the government created the Puerto Rican Industrial Development Company. This company was commonly called *Fomento* (the Spanish word for "development.") Under *Fomento,* factories were set up to produce cement, paper, glass bottles, clay products, and shoes. But over the first few years *Fomento* lost money, and the few jobs it created did little to relieve the massive unemployment.

Fomento recruited manufacturers. Muñoz Marín decided to try a new approach. Instead of building factories itself, the Puerto Rican government used its limited resources to provide services needed by factories—water, electric power, and transportation. The island has few mineral resources (except copper) that can be used in heavy industry. Therefore, *Fomento's* agents tried to recruit light industries—those that process agricultural products or make consumer goods.

Fomento offered a number of attractions to businessmen. First, a new factory would not have to pay taxes to the Commonwealth government for a period of from ten to seventeen years. Moreover, since Puerto Rico is not required to pay federal income tax, the factory would pay *no* taxes at all to the United States government. Secondly, *Fomento* offered special cash grants to firms willing to build factories in villages where unemployment was especially high. *Fomento* even built factory buildings and rented them to businessmen at low rates. Third, Puerto Rico had a large population eager to work in the new industries at wage rates lower than those in the United States. The Puerto

Rican government helped pay for the training of islanders in special skills needed for the new industries. (Many job-seekers were disappointed, however, because they had to know English to qualify.)

Under "Bootstrap" the island's industrial output grew.

All these efforts brought results. Under "Operation Bootstrap," as *Fomento's* campaign was called, the number of factories in Puerto Rico rose from 82 to 723 in ten years (1950–1960). By 1970 the island had over 2000 industrial establishments. Pouring out of these factories were transistor radios, electric appliances, synthetic fabrics, clothes, toys, decorative tile, paper products, ballpoint pens, inexpensive watches, camera light meters, and other products. Most of the manufacturers ship into the island the raw materials used in the factories. Recently oil refineries and chemical plants have also begun operations on the island.

The factories opened up new job opportunities for the islanders. By 1968 the average Puerto Rican family income was four times greater than in 1950 (though it was still much lower than in the United States). As incomes rose, Puerto Rican workers were able to pay higher taxes. With this tax money the Commonwealth financed low-cost housing and built thousands of new schools. Health services too were improved. Electricity was brought to rural areas, and modern roads soon covered the island. Muñoz Marín's government also founded a bank to aid in the island's industrial development. The bank makes loans to Puerto Ricans who want to start small businesses. Most small businessmen in Puerto Rico, however, find it very difficult to compete with the huge North American concerns that have operations on the island.

Foreign visitors studied "Bootstrap."

Operation Bootstrap won attention all over the world. Officials, educators, and engineers from developing nations in Asia and Africa have visited Puerto Rico to see for themselves how Bootstrap programs have worked. By studying methods used there, they hope to map out similar programs for their own countries.

Rural life also improved.

Meanwhile, promises to reform agriculture were not forgotten. Steps were taken to put teeth into the law that forbade ownership of more than 500 acres. The government bought up land from large sugar companies, divided some of it into smaller plantations, and hired managers to run these plantations. Both the managers and the workers share in the profits. Smaller parcels of land were distributed to individual rural families. A variety of programs got under way to help farmers improve their output. The government encouraged rural people to stay on the land, hoping to slow down the steady migration to the slums of San Juan.

Tourism contributed to economic growth.

Still another factor in Puerto Rico's economic progress was the growth of tourism. In the 1940's the *Fomento* planners decided to build a large luxury hotel in San Juan, chiefly because the city didn't have one. To their surprise, the hotel was an immediate success. Tourists from the mainland flocked to the beaches to enjoy the agreeable climate of Puerto Rico. Many more tourist hotels were built to accommodate the mainland visitors who flew into San Juan's International Airport. The tourist industry not only provided jobs for islanders but also brought in millions of dollars of income that could be invested in other projects. In recent years, however, other islands in the West Indies have drawn tourists away from Puerto Rico, and some of the island's hotels have closed down.

Economic expansion continues but difficult problems remain.

In the 1960's, Puerto Rico continued on the course of economic growth. But with industrialization came new problems. One Puerto Rican official called them the "problems of an urbanized society so familiar to the mainland United States—problems of

Better homes for Puerto Ricans was one of the goals of Operation Bootstrap, which brought many industries to the island. New and old housing are seen in the photo above of a neighborhood in San Juan. Right above, these young women help assemble television sets in a Puerto Rican industry. The arts are also important in Puerto Rico. The Spanish cellist Pablo Casals (right) attracted world attention to the island's cultural life through his sponsorship of an annual music festival and his encouragement of Puerto Rican students.

325

mass civilization, of providing adequate nutrition for all citizens, of better education for the young, of dignity for older citizens, and of ways to increase the humanization of institutions dealing with individual problems." Some of the specific problems are slum housing, water pollution, traffic jams in San Juan, and inadequate roads in rural areas.

Poverty, moreover, is still a very real problem. According to a recent survey, half the island's people live below the poverty level as defined by the federal government. And many families cannot find decent housing. Within walking distance of San Juan's luxury tourist hotels are some of the worst slums in America. One slum, *El Fanguito,* stretches for five miles along a polluted, rat-infested swamp.

A high jobless rate continues to plague Puerto Rico. The modernization of agriculture makes the problem worse, since farm workers tend to be replaced by machines. Nor does a sharply rising population help the situation. With more than two and a half million people (as reported in the 1970 census), Puerto Rico is one of the world's most densely populated areas. It is true that the job market is vastly better than it was in the 1930's and 1940's. But at least 10 per cent of those looking for work fail to find jobs. Some say the unemployment rate is actually much higher—perhaps 30 per cent—because many job-hunters get discouraged and stop looking.

Does Puerto Rico have a colonial economy?
Some critics claim that Operation Bootstrap itself has deepened the cycle of poverty in Puerto Rico. They charge that Bootstrap is typical of a colonial economy. It provides bargains for North American investors while forcing Puerto Rico into endless dependency on the United States. In supporting this argument the critics point out that the average wages of a Puerto Rican industrial worker are one-half to one-third of those of a North American industrial worker. With those wages the Puerto Rican worker has to pay 25 per cent more for consumer goods, since the cost of living on the

island is 25 per cent higher than in New York and other mainland cities.

As a result of tax exemptions and the low wages paid in Puerto Rico, North American companies with operations on the island make very high profits. It has been estimated that the average gain on investments in Puerto Rico is well over double the gain that can be made in the United States itself. But for every dollar produced by the island's industries, only 17 cents remain in Puerto Rico.

Moreover, few of the industries established in Puerto Rico make goods for use by the island's consumers. Most consumer goods used on the island are imported from the United States. In fact, Puerto Rico is this country's fifth largest overseas market. Industries that would process local raw materials and produce goods for the home market could help relieve Puerto Rico of its dependence on outside markets. But very few industries of this kind have been established. In the words of one critic, "can we consider as industrialized a country which produces coffee and imports ground coffee? A country which produces sugar and imports refined sugar? A country which has big salt mines and imports salt? A country with plenty of fish in its water which imports canned and frozen fish and shellfish?" The same critic sums up by saying: "Puerto Rico as a colonial country does not have the power to develop its economy and prevent it from being controlled by foreign interests."

THINKING ABOUT THIS SECTION

1. How did *Fomento* seek to improve Puerto Rico's economy? What new approach was tried? Why?

2. What success did Operation Bootstrap have? How has rural life in Puerto Rico improved? How did tourism contribute to economic growth? What old problems continue? What new problems stem in part from industrialization?

3. What do critics of Bootstrap mean by saying it has established a colonial economy?

Puerto Rico secured its own constitution. In 1950 still another chapter in Puerto Rico's political history opened. Congress passed a law which authorized the Puerto Rican people to draw up a constitution of their own. After elected delegates wrote this constitution, it was submitted to the people of the island for approval. By a large majority they voted in favor of the new form of government. In 1952 Governor Muñoz Marín proclaimed the island to be the Commonwealth of Puerto Rico. Muñoz remained in office as governor until 1965.

Commonwealth government in many ways resembles state government. There is nothing quite like Puerto Rico's present form of government. As a Commonwealth or "Free Associated State," it is unique. Yet in some ways its government is similar to those of the 50 states. For example, the Puerto Rican people elect their own governor and legislature. Laws passed by the Puerto Rican legislature do not have to be approved by the United States president or Congress. But all laws passed by the United States Congress are in full force on the island. Like the states, Puerto Rico has its own courts and judges, but a disputed point of law may be appealed to the United States Supreme Court. The Puerto Rican people alone can amend their constitution. Since they are United States citizens, they are guaranteed the rights provided in the federal Constitution. United States citizenship also means that the young men of Puerto Rico can be drafted for service in this country's military forces. United States money and postage stamps are used on the island, and federal Social Security laws are in force there. Another important similarity between the Commonwealth and the states is that foreign trade and defense are controlled by the federal government.

But the people of the Commonwealth have no voice in the federal government. There is a very important difference, however, between the Commonwealth and the states. Although the islanders are United States citizens, they do not vote for president nor do they elect members of Congress. Puerto Rico has a Resident Commissioner in Washington, D.C., and he may introduce legislation in the House of Representatives. But he has no power to vote in Congress. Because Puerto Rico has no voting power in the federal government, many of the islanders feel that their island is still a colony. To call their country a "Free Associated State," they say, is dishonest, since Puerto

Puerto Ricans wanting independence demonstrated outside San Juan tourist hotels during a conference of the governors of the 50 states.

Rico is not free to rule itself, is not associated on equal terms with the United States, and is not a state.

Pressure has grown for a change in form of government. Puerto Rico's political status has become a heated issue as a growing number of islanders demand a change in government. Some Puerto Ricans want statehood; others want full independence. A good many prefer the Commonwealth government but think that some change in the relationship with the United States is needed.

Some want statehood. Those who favor statehood began pressing their case in the early 1960's. Alaska and Hawaii had become states in 1959. If Hawaii, a group of islands much farther from the mainland than Puerto Rico, could become a state, why not the Caribbean island? Members of the Statehood Party put stickers saying "51" on cars, buildings, and bicycles. This was to show that they wanted Puerto Rico to become the 51st state.

Luis Ferré, who became governor in 1968, has been a leading voice in the statehood movement. He pointed out that the Commonwealth status is a step that should lead naturally to statehood. He rejected the view that Puerto Rico as a state would lose its Spanish culture and heritage. Ferré argued that Puerto Rican industry must remain closely linked to the United States.

A *Fomento* information officer found fault with Ferré's arguments: "Under statehood we would not only lose our culture. Puerto Rico would be the only state in the Union that would be worse off the day after it became a state. It would immediately have to pay the federal treasury 188 million dollars a year [in taxes]. Where would we get the money? Statehood is an impossibility for the time being." Former Governor Muñoz Marín held that only when the per capita wealth of Puerto Rico equaled that of the poorest state in the Union could Puerto Rico afford to be a state. He thought that might happen in the 1990's.

Others press for independence. A vigorous new movement has demanded full separation from the United States. One spokesman said: "Independence is the logical solution to the status question. We are a Latin American nation. We want to govern ourselves, we want our independence." Those who disagree have claimed that without the Commonwealth's free trade privileges with the United States, Puerto Rico would become a "bankrupt sugar-cane republic." But the pro-independence campaign has gained many supporters, especially among young people. At the University of Puerto Rico's main campus near San Juan, pro-independence student demonstrations have disrupted classes and led to clashes with the police.

A 1967 referendum approved Commonwealth status. A referendum in 1967 gave the Puerto Rican people a chance to express their views on the island's political status. About two-thirds of the registered voters went to the polls. Of these, 60.5 per cent voted for the Commonwealth status and 39 per cent for statehood. Less than 1 per cent voted for independence. Many supporters of full separation from the United States made clear in other ways, however, that they had decided not to take part in the referendum. Since 1967 both the statehood campaign and the independence movement have picked up steam. Puerto Rico's political status is sure to be a key issue in the 1970's.

THINKING ABOUT THIS SECTION

1. In what respects are the rights of Puerto Ricans the same as those of citizens of the 50 states? In what respects are they different?

2. What different views about the future political status of Puerto Rico are held by islanders? What are the advantages claimed for each solution by those who favor it? What are the disadvantages of each, according to its opponents? What is your opinion on the subject?

Hundreds of thousands of Puerto Ricans have left the island and migrated to the mainland United States. As United States citizens they have as much right to fly to New York City as residents of any of the states, and modern air travel makes the trip easy. All they need is the money for their fare.

Migration to the mainland swelled from a trickle to a flood. From the earliest days of United States rule, there was some movement of Puerto Ricans to the North American continent. By 1930, according to the federal census, people of Puerto Rican birth lived in all the 48 states. During the 1930's, when the island's future seemed so bleak, more Puerto Ricans left home and traveled north. It was after World War II, however, that sizable numbers of Puerto Ricans began streaming to the mainland. Then, during the decade of the 1950's, when *Fomento* was bringing new hope to Puerto Rico, migration reached its peak. Conditions were improving on the island, but many Puerto Ricans hoped to find still greater opportunities in mainland cities.

By the mid-1960's, however, more Puerto Ricans were returning to the island every year than were migrating to the mainland. Even though pay was good in North American cities, jobs and good housing were not easy to find. Moreover, life in these cities was dreary, crowded, and impersonal, and the winters were much too cold for people used to a Caribbean climate. Nevertheless, many Puerto Ricans have chosen to remain in North America and have become integrated into mainland life.

Puerto Rican agricultural workers fly back and forth between the island and the mainland. Some Puerto Ricans come to the mainland with no intention of settling permanently. A number of agricultural workers, for example, take seasonal employment on farms in midwestern and eastern states. After the island's sugar harvest ends in June, cane-workers fly to the mainland, work through the summer and early fall, and then return to Puerto Rico. Many North American farmers have come to rely on seasonal laborers from Puerto Rico.

What has life in New York been like for Puerto Rican newcomers? Today, as in 1930, citizens of Puerto Rican descent live in all the states. But most of those on the mainland live in eastern cities. By the 1970's about a million people of Puerto Rican descent lived in New York City, a larger number than the total population of San Juan. Many women who have done needlework on the island get jobs in New York's garment industry. Men who have acquired skills in Puerto Rico's new factories often find employment in New York City's light industries. Those with no special skills may work in hotels, restaurants, and hospitals as service employees. It is said that New York's large hotels would have to shut down if their Puerto Rican employees were suddenly to quit. But Puerto Ricans have entered a great variety of other jobs as well. They work as chefs, taxi drivers, teachers, post-office workers, policemen, social workers, mechanics, secretaries, lawyers, and so on.

Many, though by no means all, Puerto Ricans living in New York are concentrated in the area called *El Barrio* in East Harlem. Newcomers to this neighborhood generally have little money and few job skills. From necessity they have had to make their homes in crowded apartments in shabby rundown buildings. But those who earn steady wages can buy television sets, kitchen appliances, and other conveniences they could not afford in Puerto Rico. As they get ahead, they make plans to move into better housing. From their savings, moreover, they may buy airplane tickets to send to brothers and sisters, cousins, or grandparents and godparents still on the island. When these people arrive in New York, they may move into the same flats with their relatives for a time.

In his book *The Puerto Ricans,* Christopher Rand described how newcomers might start life in New York City:

They go to a certain part of the city because they have friends or relatives there. . . . The friends meet them at [the airport] and take them in to live with them. The next thing is to find a job, and a friend can help there too. He will take the new man to the factory or wherever else he's working. That's the first approach, and if it doesn't succeed he'll try something else. In general he will know which factories are taking on help. For instance, in parts of the summer, the garment industry is busy on fall and winter wear. Then in the fall the toy factories are going great guns, and the makers of jewelry and novelties. There are lots of others too, and with any luck he should get a job soon.

Next, he should find a place to live. He really should leave his friend after a reasonable time, and he may want to bring his family up as well. Finding a place isn't easy, and in the end he will probably have to settle for a dump and pay good money for it. That will be just part of his troubles, though. He will have to get used to the rush-rush-rush here—to getting places on time. He will have to learn how to take criticism from his boss without feeling insulted. He will have to get used to the cold, and the city life, and all kinds of other things. It is a very big change.[4]

It should be remembered that the story of every newcomer from Puerto Rico is different. They come from various levels of prosperity on the island, and naturally they carry over their customary ways of life into the new environment. If in Puerto Rico people lived in a rural district and were quite poor, the move to New York will be an abrupt and startling change. On the other hand, if they come from San Juan or some other urban area, the adjustment to mainland life will be smoother. Those who had a middle-class standard of living on the island will fit into the same way of life on the mainland.

[4] Christopher Rand, *The Puerto Ricans* (New York: Oxford University Press, 1958), pp. 68–69. Reprinted by permission.

Several things make adjustment difficult. But real problems face the newly arrived Puerto Rican regardless of his background. One is dealing with an unfamiliar language. Spanish of course is the island's language, though English is widely spoken. All children in Puerto Rico study English in school, but, even so, most newcomers to the mainland have very limited knowledge of that language. Unawareness of local laws may also add to the Puerto Ricans' troubles. And dishonest landlords and employers may take advantage of the newcomers. Racial discrimination is still another difficulty. If the Puerto Rican is dark-skinned, he finds much more prejudice on the mainland than back home.

Second-generation youth have had a special kind of experience. For the young people of Puerto Rican descent who grow up in New York City, the problems have been similar to those of young Mexican Americans in the Southwest. Most Puerto Rican youth in New York are bilingual; that is, they speak two languages. Sometimes these young people may serve as interpreters for parents who speak only Spanish. Even a child of ten or twelve may have to help his Spanish-speaking mother deal with a landlord or social workers or teachers who speak only English. The second-generation children may never learn to read and write Spanish, at least not well. To their parents this is disappointing; they say that their children have "lost their language." Christopher Rand reported a Puerto Rican friend's views on the "Americanizing" of Puerto Rican youth:

"In school [said the friend] the teacher will say, 'Don't speak Spanish.' She really means 'Speak more English,' but she puts it in that negative way and the kids feel ashamed. Or a nutritionist will say, 'Tell your mother not to give you rice and beans.' She really means, 'Tell her to give you other things too,' but the way it is put sounds like criticism, and the kids get the idea their parents are in the wrong. And then they keep hearing all the city's ills blamed on the parents—you know how the talk against Puerto Ricans goes here. So of course they reject them. Or else they retreat into their own group." [5]

Like young people of other ethnic groups who have had to fend for themselves in hostile cities, many Puerto Rican boys have stuck together in gangs. Sometimes rival gangs fight each other or gangs of other ethnic groups. These fights are publicized in the newspapers and win a bad name for the entire community. But statistics have not shown that Puerto Ricans have a higher crime rate than other ethnic groups.

Puerto Rican organizations in New York City have urged young people to stay in school and earn high-school diplomas. By doing this, they can find opportunities open to them that were denied to many of their parents. "Aim high" was the message recently brought to Puerto Rican students in New York City by a group of visiting professional people from the island. A New York City congressman, who came to the mainland from Puerto Rico as an

[5] *The Puerto Ricans*, pp. 136–137. Reprinted by permission.

Puerto Rican culture flourishes in New York City. An art museum displays Puerto Rican paintings, and musicians and theater groups present professional performances. (Right, above) young members of the Alliance of Latin Arts gave a free performance of West Side Story *in a New York park. Light industries in New York rely heavily on the Puerto Rican community. (Right) Puerto Rican women operate sewing machines in a New York garment factory.*

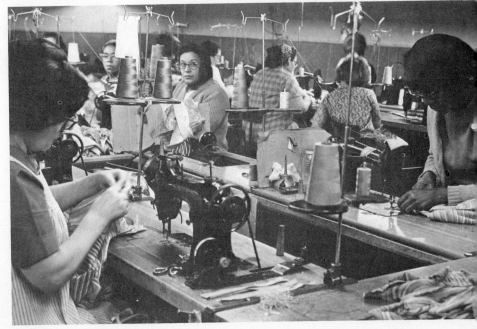

eleven-year-old orphan, made the same point in these words: "It is important that the Puerto Rican student here knows that there are Puerto Ricans who are bringing up a country by themselves. That will help the Puerto Rican students to recognize that they can be leaders in New York City too."[6]

THINKING ABOUT THIS SECTION

1. Explain or define the following words: seasonal employment; *El Barrio*.

2. Why have Puerto Ricans moved to the mainland? Why, by the mid-1960's, were there more people returning to the island than were leaving? Why do many Puerto Ricans who do not intend to settle permanently come to the mainland?

3. What types of jobs are filled by Puerto Ricans who move to New York City? What difficulties do many have to overcome?

4. In what ways are the experiences of second-generation Puerto Ricans in New York City similar to those of young Mexican Americans in Los Angeles?

Summing Up

Puerto Rico has been called the nearest thing there is to a blend of the Latin American and North American cultures. While taking pride in their island's dramatic modernization, Puerto Ricans also remain proud of their Spanish heritage. The beautiful Caribbean island was discovered by Columbus and its capital city founded by Ponce de León. Throughout the colonial era, the island's fortresses defended the Spanish Caribbean against the attacks of European raiders.

[6] Representative Herman Badillo, quoted in *The New York Times,* December 21, 1970.

In the early 1800's, when other American colonies broke away from Spain, Puerto Rico remained in the hands of the mother country. Though a few concessions were made by the Spanish government, Puerto Rico remained poor and was badly governed throughout the 1800's. Near the end of the century Spain agreed to self-government for the island. But before this reform got under way, the Spanish-American War broke out and United States soldiers occupied the island. In the peace treaty ending the war, Spain ceded Puerto Rico to the United States.

Under United States rule Puerto Rico remained a neglected island. Though sugar production became a big industry, the profits went to large companies while the islanders lived on the verge of starvation. During the 1930's and 1940's a new political party, led by Luis Muñoz Marín, launched a drive to lift the island out of poverty. The chief goal of Operation Bootstrap was to attract new industry to Puerto Rico. The effort was successful, with results that meant better health, education, and housing for many islanders. But critics charged that the industrialization program actually deepened Puerto Rico's economic dependence on the United States. Meanwhile, poverty remains a serious problem. Unemployment continues at a high rate, population threatens to outgrow natural resources, and economic expansion has brought the problems of modern life. Many Puerto Ricans have chosen to seek opportunities on the North American mainland. There they have faced problems of adjustment but have entered all walks of life.

As a Commonwealth associated with the United States, Puerto Rico has a unique status. But the question of the island's destiny has aroused controversy. Though in 1967 a majority of voters endorsed the Commonwealth form of government, growing numbers of Puerto Ricans favor a change in their island's political status.

17

The United States and Latin America: Politics and Diplomacy

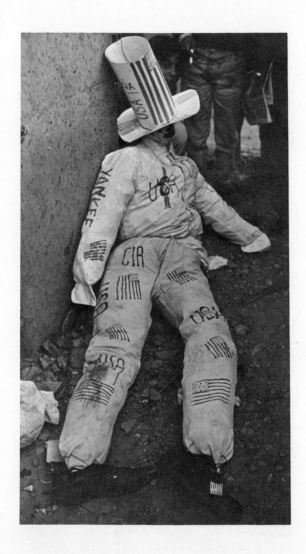

Anti-Yankee demonstrations in Latin American countries reveal the bitterness felt toward the United States by many people of the hemisphere. Colombian students paraded this effigy of Uncle Sam in protest against the visit of a North American official.

CHAPTER FOCUS

1. Latin American Attitudes Toward the United States
2. From the Monroe Doctrine Through the Good Neighbor Policy
3. The Pan American Movement
4. Inter-American Relations Since 1950

You are the United States!
You are the future invader. . . .
You hold that life is a fire, and progress an eruption;
That where your guns can reach, there you control the future.
No! . . . Beware! For Spanish America lives!
The Spanish Lion has a thousand cubs.
'Twere needful, Roosevelt, to be . . .
The terrible rifleman and the hunter strong,
Even to keep us in your iron grasp.[1]

[1] G. Dundas Craig, ed., *The Modernist Trend in Spanish American Poetry*. Originally published by the University of California Press; reprinted by permission of The Regents of the University of California.

The lines of poetry on the preceding page were written by a famous Nicaraguan poet named Rubén Darío. The poet was protesting against Theodore Roosevelt's part in helping Panama to secede from Colombia in 1903. As told in earlier chapters, the United States several times intervened in the affairs of Caribbean nations during the early 1900's. Perhaps people in the United States thought this kind of interference was necessary. They may have believed that they knew what was best for the people of the Caribbean nations and that their "assistance" would be welcomed. But no one likes to have an outsider tell him what to do. And Latin Americans bitterly resented Yankee interference in their affairs. The attitude expressed in Darío's poem suggests the bitterness toward the United States which still exists in Latin America today.

Latin Americans do not dislike individual North Americans. Every year Latin American countries welcome thousands of North American students, tourists, and other visitors. It is the policies of the United States government and of large North American businessmen that have been resented in Latin America.

It has often been pointed out that many Latin Americans have a two-sided feeling toward the United States. On the one hand, they admire this country's economic accomplishments and the progress it has made toward achieving democracy. But they also fear and resent the tremendous power of their northern neighbor.

1. Latin American Attitudes Toward the United States

Latin Americans fear United States power. It is not surprising that weaker countries should be wary of a neighbor as powerful as the United States. Memories of the past keep fear and distrust alive. Mexicans, for example, regarded the United States' annexation of the borderlands as robbery. Colombians still feel that this country stole Panama. In Cuba many people probably believe Fidel Castro when he claims that the United States has no legal right to its naval base at Guantánamo.

Intervention can be political. Latin Americans also fear North American interference in their governments. Intervention can take different forms. Sending in a military force is the most obvious kind of meddling. But there are also less direct ways. At times, for example, the United States has withheld diplomatic recognition in an effort to influence a country's internal affairs. By refusing to recognize a new government as legal, the United States could prevent that government from getting loans either in the United States or abroad. This could be a serious matter for a government in need of money. Even the threat of not recognizing a new government may discourage efforts to remove a dictator from power.

Another way of wielding influence without direct interference is to permit or refuse the sale of arms to countries where there is a threat of rebellion. The United States might sell arms to the government and refuse to sell them to the rebels. Or it might sell them to the rebels and *not* to the government. In these various ways a powerful nation can influence events in other countries.

Economic influence is also effective. Economic control can provide a basis for political influence. North American oil companies in Venezuela, the United Fruit Company in Central America, and the Anaconda Copper Company in Chile were among the large businesses that at times tried to influence Latin American governments. In a country where thousands of workers are dependent on a foreign-owned company for their livelihood, such a company has great power.

There is still another kind of economic control. Occasionally the United States government has taken charge of a country's financial affairs in order to prevent European nations from stepping in to collect unpaid debts. Examples of this kind of interference have been described earlier in this book.

Military occupation is most resented. The kind of intervention still most feared by Latin Americans is armed occupation. This happened several times in the Caribbean area during the early 1900's. But even as recently as 1965, United States marines were sent to "restore order" in the Dominican Republic.

In cases where United States forces occupied a Latin American country over several years, some material benefits usually resulted. Hospitals, schools, and roads, for example, may have been built or improved. Nevertheless, the people of the occupied land resented having foreigners in charge. Moreover, they were offended by United States paternalism,[2] an attitude which all but openly declared them inferiors. Resentment grew especially bitter when the behavior of the occupying troops showed a prejudiced attitude toward the local people. Unfortunately this was often the case during an occupation. Many Latin Americans continue to believe that North Americans think of them as lazy, ignorant, backward, and hot-tempered.

Latin Americans claim that the United States neglects them. Although Latin Americans accuse their northern neighbor of meddling, they

[2] *Paternalism* is treating people kindly but without giving them any responsibility.

Latin American Trade with the United States

Most Latin American countries depend heavily on trade with the United States. This can be seen in the figures below for representative countries in different parts of Latin America. The first column of figures shows the percentage of a country's imports that came from the United States in a recent year. The second column shows what percentage of the country's exports was bought by United States customers.

Country	Imports	Exports
Argentina	22%	9%
Bolivia	42	35
Brazil	32	33
Colombia	50	42
Dominican Republic	55	89
Mexico	63	57
Panama	39	79
Peru	34	39

also charge it with neglect. Since the 1940's, the United States has given billions of dollars of aid to foreign countries. But most of these funds go to other parts of the world. Latin American countries think they should get a larger share of this foreign aid.

They also charge that United States trade policies discourage the economic development of their countries. It is to the advantage of an industrial giant like the United States to buy raw materials and export manufactures. Many Latin Americans have accused this nation of blocking the industrialization of their countries in order to hold on to its markets there.

The United States is also charged with supporting dictators. Then, too, Latin Americans know that many dictatorial governments in their part of the world have received military aid and diplomatic approval from the United States. Yet the United States prides itself on having a democratic government. Many Latin Americans accuse the United States of being hypocritical. They believe that economic interests are more important to the United States than democratic ideals, and that the United States government will side with any Latin American government that safeguards North American investments.

Of course, in deciding on policy toward another country, United States leaders have to keep two things in mind: what is good for this country and what is good for the other country. The two things may often be quite different. But many Latin Americans think that no real improvement can be made in their countries as long as the United States plays such an influential role in their part of the Hemisphere.

THINKING ABOUT THIS SECTION

1. What are the various ways in which the United States has intervened in Latin American affairs? Why have these been resented by Latin Americans?

2. Look at the graph on page 347. What two regions of the world have received far more economic aid from the United States than Latin America? Why?

3. What is the basis for the charge that the United States neglects Latin America? for the charge that the United States is hypocritical in its dealings with Latin America? What is your opinion of these charges?

2. From the Monroe Doctrine Through the Good Neighbor Policy

The United States favored Latin American independence. The earliest relations between the United States and Latin America were commercial. Even while both areas were still colonial outposts of European powers, Yankee merchants traded in the Caribbean. This trade violated Spanish restrictions. But the Yankee captains cared little about that.

During the early 1800's the United States strongly sympathized with the Latin American independence movements. Officially the United States remained neutral. But Latin American agents had little trouble buying arms and other supplies in this country. Some North Americans even fought in the Latin American wars for independence. As soon as the Latin American states succeeded in ousting the Spanish, the United States became one of the first outside nations to recognize the new governments.

European intervention was rumored. The approval and sympathy of the United States were not enough, however, to make the new Latin American republics secure. In the early 1800's the United States itself was still a weak nation. Moreover, it was believed that some of the

European powers might try to help Spain recover its former American colonies. Great Britain opposed any such intervention in Latin America. At the time, Britain's navy "ruled" the sea, and the British wanted a free hand in trading with the Latin American nations.

Britain's proposal for a joint declaration was turned down. The British government suggested to the United States that the two countries make a joint declaration. The message would be to warn other European powers not to interfere with the new Latin American republics. After thinking this over, John Quincy Adams, who was then Secretary of State, gave his opinion to President James Monroe. Adams said that if any statement were to be issued, it should be made by the United States alone. There should be no commitment with Britain and no plan for joint action.

The Monroe Doctrine warned Europe to keep hands off. In December, 1823, President Monroe stated Adams' ideas in a message to Congress. This message became the basis of the famous Monroe Doctrine. The main points made in Monroe's statement were as follows:

(1) The United States did not intend to get involved in European affairs.

(2) The United States would not interfere with the existing colonies or dependencies of any European power.

(3) The American continents were not to be considered as subjects for future colonization by any European power.

(4) The United States would regard any European interference in the Western Hemisphere as dangerous to this country's safety.

The people of the United States were proud of this warning to Europe, but Europeans were less impressed. The British were annoyed because their proposal for joint action had been rejected. The Russian czar declared: "This document merits only the most profound contempt." A Mexican philosopher was alarmed, however, because he saw in the Doctrine a "threat of North American imperialism."

At first the Monroe Doctrine was not enforced. At that time, of course, the United States had no way of enforcing its bold new policy. The powerful British navy was a far more important factor in keeping other European nations out of Latin America. But Great Britain itself did not hesitate to violate the principles of the Doctrine. In 1833 the British occupied the Falkland Islands off Argentina and in other ways meddled in Latin America. But the United States could do nothing about it.

Polk put teeth into the Doctrine. In the 1840's the Monroe Doctrine took on new meaning. This was the era of "manifest destiny," when the United States was seeking to extend its frontiers west to the Pacific and south to the Rio Grande. In the early 1840's Great Britain was taking an interest in California, then part of Mexico. President James Polk of the United States made clear that the United States would frown on any transfer of territory from Mexico to Britain.

Of course, after the war with Mexico, the United States itself took over California as well as other Mexican territory. Thus it was the United States, not Europe, that encroached on Latin American territory. Polk's action suggested that, as far as territorial expansion was concerned, the Monroe Doctrine applied to Europe but not to the United States.

The United States tried to buy Cuba. North American expansionists also took an interest in Cuba. Southerners, anxious to add to the number of slaveholding states, looked longingly at this island that lay so close to Florida. In 1853 President Franklin Pierce tried to buy Cuba from Spain but was turned down. The next year three United States officials in Europe met at Ostend, Belgium, to work out a plan for acquiring Cuba. In a statement called the Ostend Manifesto, they proposed that Spain be offered 120 million dollars for the island. If Spain refused, suggested the document, the United States would be justified in taking Cuba by force. The Ostend Manifesto stirred up a storm of criticism, and the government in Washington denied that it was official policy.

French encroachment in Mexico tested the Monroe Doctrine. A serious challenge to the Monroe Doctrine came in the 1860's when the ruler of France installed an Austrian archduke, Maximilian, as "emperor" of Mexico. Chapter 8 told the unhappy story of Maximilian's short reign. For a while the United States was too busy with its Civil War to do anything about the French takeover of Mexico. Even so, the government at Washington protested. Then, as the Civil War drew to a close, this country demanded that France get out of Mexico. United States troops were even sent into Texas. Unwilling to risk war at a time when he already had trouble in Europe, the French emperor withdrew his forces. The luckless Maximilian was soon overthrown.

The United States declared itself "sovereign" in the Americas. Another dramatic incident involving the Monroe Doctrine developed from a border dispute between Venezuela and British Guiana. For years British surveyors had steadily encroached on Venezuelan territory. Venezuela appealed to the United States for help. In 1895 the United States warned Britain that it was violating the Monroe Doctrine in Venezuela. The Americans insisted that the question be decided by international arbitration. In other words, an outside party should decide the rights and wrongs of the dispute, and Venezuela and Britain should agree beforehand to accept the decision whatever it might be. Britain at first ignored the proposal but finally agreed to arbitration. (Most of the disputed territory was eventually awarded to Great Britain.)

During the negotiations with Britain, an important statement was issued by the United States Secretary of State, Richard Olney. In a letter to the British foreign secretary, Olney declared: "The United States is practically sovereign on this continent." These words showed that the United States regarded itself as master in the Americas.

The Spanish-American War made the United States a colonial power. By 1898 the United States stretched across North America from Atlantic to Pacific and was looking beyond its borders. This was a period of rapid economic growth, and a self-confident, nationalistic spirit prevailed in the United States. Pride in the principles of the Monroe Doctrine was strong. This pride was offended by the fact that Spain still held the island of Cuba. The suffering of the Cubans who were fighting to free themselves from Spain aroused much sympathy in the United States.

Chapter 11 told how rebellion broke out in Cuba in 1895. Exiled Cuban rebels had gathered supplies and made their plans in the United States. When these rebels landed in Cuba and launched a guerrilla war, North American sympathy was on their side. Big-city newspapers in the United States rivaled each other in printing stories of Spanish cruelty in Cuba. The press played a major role in whipping up a sense of outrage against Spain's treatment of the Cuban people.

In February, 1898, anti-Spanish emotions reached a peak when the United States battleship *Maine* blew up in Havana harbor. More than 250 American seamen were killed. Obviously it was not in Spain's interest to blow up an American battleship. But North American newspapers blamed the Spanish. "Remember the Maine!" blared out the headlines.

Over the next two months the Spanish government assured the United States that it would meet American demands. Nevertheless, in April the United States declared war on Spain. In three months the fighting was over. The American navy won decisive victories in both the Pacific and the Caribbean. United States ground forces occupied Cuba, Puerto Rico, and the Philippines. In the peace treaty Spain reluctantly agreed to give up these colonies.

Cuba had to accept United States control. United States forces stayed on in Cuba for several years to help rebuild that war-ravaged country. Puerto Rico and the Philippines were also occupied. In fact, those two areas became United States possessions, but the United States promised not to make Cuba a colony. Nevertheless, some North Americans urged that the United States keep some kind of control over Cuban affairs even after the occupation ended.

In 1901 this control was ensured when Congress tacked on the so-called Platt Amendment to a military appropriations bill. The Platt Amendment required Cuba to include the following guarantees in its constitution:

(1) Cuba was not to make any treaty whereby it would give up its independence, and it was not to turn over any Cuban territory to a foreign power.

(2) Cuba was not to borrow any money that it could not repay from "ordinary revenues."

(3) Cuba was to lease naval stations to the United States.

(4) Cuba was to grant the United States the right to "intervene for the preservation of

Cuban independence [and for] the maintenance of a government adequate for the protection of life, property, and individual liberty."

The Cuban assembly that was writing a constitution at first rejected these provisions. But the United States said it would not withdraw its occupying forces until the Cubans accepted the Platt Amendment. The assembly had no choice but to include the North American demands in the Cuban constitution. In this way Cuba became the first of several *protectorates*[3] of the United States in the Caribbean area. Under the terms of the Platt Amendment, the United States leased land on Guantánamo Bay and built a large naval base.

Although the North Americans helped Cuba in its first years of independence, the roots of bitterness and mistrust had been firmly planted. On several occasions the United States did take a hand in Cuban affairs. Not until 1934 was the Platt Amendment repealed. But still today the United States maintains the Guantánamo naval base in Cuba.

Panama became a protectorate. Panama was another area that came under the "protection" of the United States. The Spanish-American War had made clear the need for an interocean canal through Central America. About half a century earlier the United States and Great Britain had signed a treaty in which the two nations agreed to joint control over any canal built in the area. But in 1901 the United States secured a new treaty on the subject. In this treaty Great Britain gave the United States the right to build a canal. After Panama was selected as the location for the canal, the next step was to deal with Colombia, since Panama was still part of that country.

Chapter 10 told the story of how the United States helped Panama break away from Colombia. President Theodore Roosevelt quickly recognized the new republic of Panama. A treaty was signed, by which Panama leased the Canal Zone to the United States, and construction of

[3] A *protectorate* is a country that is dominated and "protected" by a stronger country.

the canal soon began. Panama thus became another protectorate of the United States, and remained one for some thirty years. Several times the United States sent in troops to maintain order. Still today, of course, the United States controls the Canal Zone.

The United States' role in the Panama rebellion provoked much resentment, not only in Colombia but throughout Latin America. There was a growing feeling that the United States could not be trusted. In 1914, however, during the presidency of Woodrow Wilson, the United States in effect apologized to Colombia. A treaty was drawn up in which the United States agreed to pay Colombia 25 million dollars and expressed regret for its action in Panama. Friends of Theodore Roosevelt blocked approval of this treaty in the Senate. But seven years later a similar treaty was ratified.

Theodore Roosevelt enlarged the Monroe Doctrine. The Panama incident was typical of United States policy toward Latin America during the presidency of Theodore Roosevelt. A fervent nationalist, Roosevelt sought to build up this country's power and prestige. In 1904 he significantly expanded the Monroe Doctrine. In a message to Congress Roosevelt declared:

Chronic wrongdoing . . . may in America, as elsewhere, ultimately require intervention by some civilized nation, and in the Western Hemisphere the adherence of the United States to the Monroe Doctrine may force the United States, however reluctantly, . . . to the exercise of an international police power.

Roosevelt meant by this that if there had to be any intervention in Latin America, it would be the United States that did the intervening and not any European nation. This addition to the Monroe Doctrine came to be called the Roosevelt Corollary.

Reaction to the Roosevelt Corollary was mixed. In the United States Congress it was both praised and denounced. European bankers felt that the United States was guaranteeing the payment of Latin American debts. There was no official reaction from Latin American

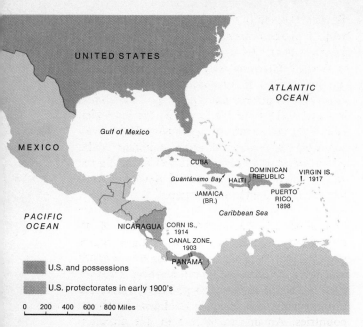

United States Domination of the Caribbean in the Early 1900's

U.S. and possessions

U.S. protectorates in early 1900's

0 200 400 600 800 Miles

governments, but some people in these countries were fearful of North American "protection." They listened to Rubén Darío's warning that the United States was "the future invader" and that Roosevelt was "a strong hunter."

The Dominican Republic became the next protectorate. Regardless of foreign opinion, the United States soon took action under the Roosevelt Corollary. In 1905 President Roosevelt sent officials to the Dominican Republic to manage that country's financial affairs (Chapter 11). Later, armed forces also landed in the Dominican Republic, and so the occupation became military as well as financial. Still another small Caribbean country had become a United States protectorate.

Two more protectorates were established. Altogether, the United States extended its control over five small Caribbean countries during the early 1900's. Besides Cuba, Panama, and the Dominican Republic, the nations of Nicaragua and Haiti also came under United States dom-

ination. How the last two nations came to be occupied by United States troops was told in Chapters 10 and 11.

In establishing these protectorates the United States was not trying to add to its own territory. The chief motive was one of security. The United States wanted to prevent European powers from getting a foothold in the Western Hemisphere. Moreover, after the Panama Canal was built, there was the need to safeguard that waterway. Another reason was to protect North American investments in the Caribbean. But there was also a genuine interest in helping small countries build honest and efficient governments. Unfortunately the chief outcome of the protectorate system was to make Latin Americans more hostile to the United States. For many years this fact seemed to go unnoticed in this country.

The "big stick" was followed by "dollar diplomacy." Theodore Roosevelt was responsible for establishing only two of the Caribbean protectorates—Panama and the Dominican Republic. But his attitude toward Latin America was typical of the entire protectorate era. Roosevelt's policy of showing United States strength was often called the "big stick" policy. This term came from a proverb that he liked to quote: "Speak softly and carry a big stick."

During the presidency of William Howard Taft, who followed Roosevelt, Latin Americans bitterly called United States policy "dollar diplomacy." By this they meant that the safeguarding of North American investments seemed to be the chief goal of the United States government as far as Latin America was concerned.

Wilson rejects "dollar diplomacy" but continues intervention. By the time Woodrow Wilson became president in 1912, the attitude toward Latin America was changing. An idealist, Wilson sincerely wanted to promote democracy in the Latin American republics without having to take an active hand. He denounced "dollar diplomacy." While he was president, Wilson said, the United States would not support any "special group of interests," meaning North American investors in Latin America. Despite his words, Wilson several times did take a hand in Latin American affairs. For example, he sent marines into Haiti, expanded the protectorate over the Dominican Republic, and intervened in Mexico.

The situation in Mexico during Wilson's first years in office was so turbulent that he probably could not have avoided involvement. Wilson refused to recognize the government of Victoriano Huerta, who had used violence to gain power (page 174). "We have no sympathy," said Wilson, "with those who seek to seize the power of government to advance their own personal interests or ambition."

In 1914 a crisis developed when seamen from a United States ship were arrested in the Mexican port of Tampico. Although the sailors were soon released, their admiral demanded an apology and a 21-gun salute to the United States flag. Huerta was willing to apologize but refused to order the salute. The situation was complicated by the fact that a German ship was bringing munitions to the port of Veracruz. To prevent landing of the munitions, Wilson ordered an armed fleet to Veracruz. United States troops landed and occupied the Mexican port for six months.

When Venustiano Carranza came to power in Mexico, Wilson recognized his government. But trouble broke out again in 1916 when Pancho Villa raided a town in New Mexico and murdered several people (page 175). Wilson sent cavalry into Mexico to pursue Villa, but called off the hunt early in 1917. During the 1920's relations between the United States and Mexico continued to be strained.

The United States renounced the right of intervention. A real change in United States policy toward Latin America became evident during the presidency of Herbert Hoover (1929–1932). Hoover was genuinely interested in improving relations with the Latin American countries. An important step in this direction was publication of a paper called the Clark Memorandum. This document had been written in the United States Department of State. It declared that intervention in the affairs of another nation was not justified under the terms of the original Monroe Doctrine. In effect, the United States said that the Roosevelt Corollary

An old photograph shows United States marines in Haiti during the 1915 occupation.

was no longer official policy. Hoover also made plans for ending the protectorates in Haiti and Nicaragua.

The United States declared it would be a "good neighbor." President Franklin D. Roosevelt carried on the policy of noninterference. In his inaugural address in 1933 he said: "I would dedicate this nation to the policy of the good neighbor—the neighbor who . . . respects the rights of others—the neighbor who respects his obligations and respects the sanctity of his agreements in and with a world of neighbors."

Roosevelt soon showed that he meant to carry out this Good Neighbor Policy. In 1934 the United States agreed to Cuban demands that the Platt Amendment be canceled. In that same year the last marines were withdrawn from Haiti. Moreover, the United States gave up its "right" to intervene in Panamanian affairs. As told in Chapter 9, when Mexico took over the oil properties of United States businesses, Roosevelt refused to yield to pressure for intervention.

Still other steps were taken to further the Good Neighbor Policy. During the 1930's the United States reduced tariffs on imports from Latin America. Large sums of money were lent to Latin American governments. Moreover, the United States launched programs of agricultural assistance. In various ways the Roosevelt administration showed a co-operative spirit in its relations with Latin Amerca.

THINKING ABOUT THIS SECTION

1. Explain or define the folowing words: manifest destiny; sovereign; protectorate; "big stick" policy; dollar diplomacy.

2. Why did the United States issue the Monroe Doctrine rather than make a joint declaration with Britain? What points were made in the Monroe Doctrine? Did it guarantee that the United States would not seek territorial expansion in this hemisphere? Explain.

3. In each of the following, explain why the United States acted as it did: (a) the United States' reaction to French intervention in Mexico; (b) the claim during the Venezuelan boundary dispute that "the United States is practically sovereign on this continent"; (c) the United States' insistence on the Platt Amendment; (d) the United States role in the Panama revolt from Colombia; (e) the Roosevelt Corollary and instances of intervention that followed from it. In the last three cases what was the reaction in Latin America?

4. Look at the map on page 340. Why could it be said that the United States "dominated" the Caribbean in the eary 1900's? Which areas were protectorates of the United States? Which were possessions?

5. Why did relations with Mexico worsen during Wilson's administration?

6. What was the Clark Memorandum? What significance did it have for United States policy toward Latin America? How did the Roosevelt administration show that it wanted to be a "good neighbor" to Latin American countries?

3. The Pan American Movement

The new spirit of good will in the 1930's revived interest in the Pan American movement. This movement dated back to the time of Bolívar but had accomplished little.

Bolívar was disappointed in his hope for inter-American co-operation. One of Simón Bolívar's most ambitious dreams was to create an inter-American league. He realized that the nations of Latin America were too different to unite under a single government. But Bolívar did hope that they could join in a league or federation and work together to advance common interests.

For the purpose of launching such a league, Bolívar invited all the newly independent Spanish American states to a meeting at Panama City in 1826. Brazil, the United States, and Great Britain were also invited, though Bolívar did not intend for them to become members of the new league. It soon became clear that the invited nations did not share Bolívar's enthusiasm for inter-American action. Of the Latin American governments, only Mexico, Central America, Colombia, and Peru sent delegates. Great Britain sent an official representative. Two delegates were appointed by the United States, but one died on the way and the other arrived in Panama after the meeting was over. Nevertheless, the Congress of Panama was significant as the first effort to hold a meeting of American nations. Over the next sixty years several inter-American conferences were held. But at none of them were all the nations represented.

Commercial interest led to the first Pan American Conference. By the 1880's United States interest in Latin America was growing. This was a time of economic and industrial expansion for the North American giant. With an abundance of manufactured goods to sell, the United States was looking for new customers. Secretary of State James G. Blaine realized that Latin America could provide new markets. To promote friendlier relations and greater trade, Blaine invited the Latin American nations to meet at Washington, D.C., in 1889. All but the Dominican Republic sent representatives.

The most important outcome of this conference was the creation of the Commercial Bureau of American Republics, with headquarters at Washington. The purpose of the Bureau was to circulate useful business information among the member nations. In 1910 this organization was renamed the Pan American Union.

Pan American meetings in the early 1900's achieved little. Pan American conferences were also held in 1901–1902 at Mexico City, in 1906 at Rio de Janeiro, and in 1910 at Buenos Aires. But not much was accomplished. This was the period when the Roosevelt Corollary, the "big stick," and "dollar diplomacy" dominated United States policy toward Latin America. Naturally the Latin Americans were wary of their northern neighbor. Inter-American co-operation was meaningless if the United States did not respect its neighbors to the south. There were always differences of opinion about the problems to be discussed at the Pan American meetings. The Latin Americans wanted to talk about such political issues as intervention and national independence. But United States representatives were chiefly interested in business and trade.

Some Latin American nations joined the Allies in World War I. There had been little need to discuss the defense of the Western Hemisphere at the Pan American meetings. When the United States entered World War I in 1917, therefore, there was no plan for common action involving the Latin American republics. But the United States sought Latin American co-operation, and some of the nations responded. Brazil and seven of the Caribbean countries declared war on Germany. Five other American nations broke off diplomatic relations with Germany, and the rest maintained a position of neutrality.

Latin American nations joined the League of Nations. After World War I, Brazil took part in the peace conference, and all of the Latin American countries joined the League of Nations. They hoped that this international organization would become strong enough to safeguard the interests of weak nations. Naturally they had in mind their own relations with their powerful northern neighbor. But the United States refused to join the League, and the League was in no position to question the policies of this country or those of North American businesses. As the weakness of the League of Nations became more apparent, the Latin American nations dropped out of the organization.

President Franklin D. Roosevelt attended an inter-American Conference for the Maintenance of Peace held at Buenos Aires in 1936.

Pan American meetings in the 1920's were deadlocked over the issue of intervention. At two Pan American conferences held in the 1920's, Latin Americans sought to take up the issue of United States domination of the hemisphere. In fact, at the 1928 conference in Havana the Latin American delegates proposed the following resolution: "No state has a right to interfere in the internal affairs of another." But the United States delegates firmly rejected the resolution. They said that the right of intervention was justified under international law. With this deadlock the future of the Pan American movement seemed bleak.

A spirit of good will appeared in the 1930's. As pointed out earlier, United States policy toward Latin America took a new direction during the presidency of Herbert Hoover. By this time the United States had learned that telling weaker nations what to do only made for bitterness and hostility. The Clark Memorandum made clear that the United States no longer claimed the right of intervention. This view was reaffirmed in Franklin D. Roosevelt's Good Neighbor Policy.

This shift in policy made possible a much friendlier atmosphere at Pan American meetings held in the 1930's. At the Montevideo Conference in 1933, United States Secretary of State Cordell Hull supported a non-intervention proposal like the one rejected at Havana just five years earlier. Thus, the United States recognized the equal rights of all American nations. In 1934 the United States Senate ratified this resolution without a single vote against it. As a result of this meaningful change, the Pan American movement took on greater importance in the eyes of Latin Americans.

Western Hemisphere nations co-operated during World War II. As the world moved toward war in the 1930's, the United States became concerned with plans for safeguarding the Western Hemisphere. At the 1938 Pan American Conference in Lima, all the 21 republics declared they would stand together in resisting any foreign threat. This idea was made more definite at a foreign ministers' meeting at Havana in 1940. The delegates agreed that their countries would regard an attack on any of the American nations as an attack on them all.

After the United States entered World War II in 1941, most of the Latin American states joined the Allies. Two of the nations, Brazil and Mexico, contributed men to the armed forces. Brazilian soldiers fought in Italy, and Mexico sent an air squadron to the Pacific. The Latin American nations also allowed the Allies to use air and naval bases within their borders and contributed essential raw materials. Hemispheric solidarity had come a long way since World War I. Chile and Argentina alone remained neutral. But they too declared war in 1945.

All the American nations joined the United Nations. Even before the end of the war, plans were made by the Allies to create a world body that would work for peace. As the idea grew, the Latin American nations wondered whether Pan American solidarity would begin to be overshadowed by the much larger international organization.

When the United Nations was organized at San Francisco in 1945, all the American nations became members. A series of meetings was held at which Latin American representatives urged that their regional union be recognized. Finally it was agreed that such bodies could function outside the United Nations. A provision of the UN charter allows a regional group of nations, acting independently of the United Nations, to repel an armed attack.

At first, the 20 Latin American nations made up about a third of the UN membership. As a large bloc, they had considerable influence on issues decided by a majority vote in the General Asembly. But the membership of the United Nations has steadily grown, and the Latin American bloc now is less powerful. In issues voted on by the General Assembly the Latin American nations often, but not always, side with the United States.

The Organization of American States was launched. The interest in collective defense carried over into the postwar years. At a 1947 conference held in Rio de Janeiro, the American nations agreed to a defensive military alliance. The Rio Pact declared that if any American nation was attacked, whether from outside or inside the hemisphere, the other nations would come to its aid. This was in accordance with the regional defense provision of the United Nations charter referred to earlier.

The 1948 inter-American conference, held at Bogotá, proved to be a stormy and eventful meeting. At this time, Colombia was undergoing serious political unrest. While the conference was meeting, a left-wing leader was assassinated, and rioting broke out in Bogotá. Views on the reasons for the rioting differed. The United States saw the violence as part of a campaign to spread Communism. Latin American delegates, on the other hand, believed that frustrating economic problems were chiefly responsible.

Despite the turbulent atmosphere, the Bogotá delegates did manage to accomplish something. They reorganized the Pan American Union and gave it a new name—the Organization of American States (often shortened to OAS).[4] The major goals of the OAS were agreed to be mutual security, the peaceful settlement of disputes between nations, and the promotion of hemispheric welfare. The OAS was to have a permanent council with a chairman who was preferably to be a Latin American. Agencies were set up within the OAS to deal with economic, social, and cultural matters.

The OAS charter was revised. By 1970 the range of OAS problems and activities had grown so varied that the member nations agreed to revise the charter adopted at Bogotá in 1948.[5] Many of the changes concerned the

[4] The name *Pan American Union* now applies to the main administrative offices of the Organization of American States and to its clearinghouse for information. Both are based in Washington, D.C.

[5] OAS membership in the early 1970's included all the Latin American republics, the United States, Barbados, Jamaica, and Trinidad-Tobago. Cuba, though a member, was excluded from OAS activities.

structure of the organization. But one important change called for more frequent general meetings. Before 1970, Inter-American Conferences were held every five years. Now the OAS General Assembly meets every year. (There are of course, frequent smaller meetings of OAS officials to discuss specific problems and issues.)

In his special message about the reorganization the OAS Secretary General, Galo Plaza, said: "The amended charter reflects the fact that in recent years the member states have given the OAS an important new mission: to support overall economic and social development and regional integration."

THINKING ABOUT THIS SECTION

1. Why did Secretary of State Blaine in 1889 invite Latin American nations to a conference in Washington, D.C.? What came of it?
2. Why was little accomplished at Pan American conferences during the early 1900's?
3. What was the basic issue raised at Pan American meetings during the 1920's? Why did the Pan American movement begin to take on more importance during the 1930's?
4. What important decisions were reached at the 1947 Rio de Janeiro conference and the 1948 Bogotá conference?

4. Inter-American Relations Since 1950

After 1950 cold-war tensions came to dominate United States foreign policy. In its stand against Communism the United States appealed for inter-American support. The Latin American nations, however, regarded the cold war as chiefly a North American worry. They were far more concerned with their own long-standing economic and social problems. It was their hope that their wealthy and powerful northern neighbor would help them with these problems. Since 1950, this difference of opinion over goals has shown up time and again in hemispheric affairs.

Latin Americans were disappointed in their hopes for a "Marshall Plan." In the years after World War II, the United States had seen the importance of rebuilding Europe. Under the Marshall Plan this country contributed billions of dollars to the war-torn countries of western Europe, including the former enemy Germany. Since the Latin American countries had problems of poverty and economic stagnation that dated from long before the war, they felt ignored when the United States spent huge sums on Europe. To make matters worse, just after the war the United States had actually cut down the amount of aid that went to Latin America. No wonder the Latin Americans asked, "Where is *our* Marshall Plan?"

The United States emphasized the Communist threat at the Caracas Conference. The Tenth Inter-American Conference was held at Caracas, Venezuela, in 1954. At this time the United States was worried about the left-wing government of Jacobo Arbenz in Guatemala. Some officials of the Arbenz government were Communists. At Caracas, United States Secretary of State John Foster Dulles urged the Latin American nations to take a strong stand against the Arbenz government. But the Latin Americans argued that the situation in Guatemala was not a serious threat. A few months after the conference, Guatemalan exiles overthrew Arbenz (page 197). Despite a denial by the United States government, Latin Americans believed that the Yankees had a hand in ousting Arbenz.

Cuba became the main concern. Several years later Cuba became the focus of United States

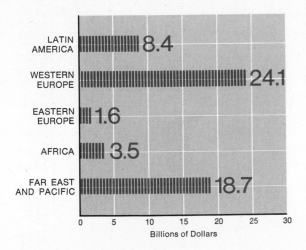

	Billions of Dollars
LATIN AMERICA	8.4
WESTERN EUROPE	24.1
EASTERN EUROPE	1.6
AFRICA	3.5
FAR EAST AND PACIFIC	18.7

0   5   10   15   20   25   30
Billions of Dollars

U. S. Foreign Aid, 1945–1969

Since 1945, Latin American countries have received roughly 15 per cent of the total amount of economic aid given to foreign countries by the United States. About half of the Latin American aid has been military — for example, weapons and airplanes.

concern about Communism in Latin America. Chapter 11 told how Fidel Castro came to power in Cuba. At first, the United States did not consider Castro a threat, and President Eisenhower's administration recognized the new Cuban government. Soon, however, Castro began to confiscate North American holdings, established close ties with the Soviet Union, and denounced the United States. President Eisenhower finally broke off relations with Cuba.

In dealing with Cuba, the United States wanted the backing of the other American governments. So it asked the Organization of American States for support. At a meeting of OAS foreign ministers in 1960, the United States urged that collective action (that is, action by all the OAS members) be taken against Castro. But the Latin American delegates refused to approve intervention in Cuba.

The Bay of Pigs invasion failed. The United States government decided to go ahead on its own. A small force of Cuban exiles was secretly trained and equipped with arms. In April, 1961, this force landed at the Bay of Pigs on Cuba's southern coast. The exiles hoped that Cubans on the island would join them and rise up against Castro. But the invaders found no support on the island and were quickly captured by Cuban troops. The United States was bitterly criticized for its part in the Bay of Pigs adventure. Latin Americans charged that it had violated a provision of the OAS charter which forbade intervention by one state in the affairs of another.

The OAS isolated Cuba. At a meeting of OAS foreign ministers held in 1962, the United States managed to get limited collective action against Cuba. By a two-thirds vote the OAS decided to exclude Cuba from "participation in the inter-American system." (Six nations refused to vote on the issue—Argentina, Bolivia, Brazil, Chile, Ecuador, and Mexico.) The effect of the vote was that Cuba remained an OAS member but was not allowed to take part in OAS affairs.

Kennedy won collective support for a blockade of Cuba. Gradually it became clear that the Soviet Union was planning to establish a base in Cuba. Soviet ships and airplanes brought "technical advisers" and supplies to the island. In October, 1962, photographs taken by United States airplanes showed that missile launching sites were being set up in Cuba. The photographic evidence made clear that the missiles would be capable of delivering nuclear warheads to distant targets in North and South America.

In a television address President John F. Kennedy revealed his knowledge of the missile sites. He also declared that the United States navy and air force would blockade Cuba to prevent Soviet delivery of any more military equipment. Meanwhile, Soviet ships continued to steam toward the Caribbean. People everywhere wondered what a showdown between the Soviet Union and the United States might bring.

OAS foreign ministers met at Punta del Este, Uruguay, in 1967. A round table symbolized the spirit of co-operation on which the OAS is based.

In this crisis the United States government realized that the collective support of the OAS was essential. At an emergency meeting the OAS member nations unanimously approved a resolution supporting the blockade of Cuba. Argentina sent two destroyers to aid in the blockade, and a number of Latin American countries offered troops or the use of bases. The firm stand of the American nations led the Soviet government to agree to remove the missiles. The United States, in turn, promised not to invade Cuba.

OAS members broke relations with Cuba. In 1964 the OAS again met to discuss a problem involving the Castro regime. It had been discovered that Cuba had supplied arms to anti-government guerrillas in Venezuela. As punishment for this interference in the affairs of another nation, all the OAS members except Mexico broke relations with Cuba and ended trade with that country.[6]

[6] Chile re-established relations with Cuba in 1970. By that time many Latin Americans thought Cuba should be readmitted to full participation in the OAS.

The United States sent troops into the Dominican Republic. The United States' fear of Communism also played a part in the Dominican crisis of 1965 (page 225). President Lyndon Johnson suspected that Cuban Communists were helping one of the rebel groups trying to seize control in the Dominican Republic. Within a few days of the outbreak of fighting, some 20,000 United States troops landed in Santo Domingo.

Other OAS nations raised a storm of protest. As in the Bay of Pigs episode, the United States had ignored the OAS charter by acting unilaterally (by itself). Those who supported the United States action pointed out that Communists were involved in the rebel cause. But critics of the United States declared that the Communist danger had been greatly exaggerated. Of greater concern to Latin Americans was the fact that the United States seemed to have returned to its "big stick" policy of intervening in the affairs of Caribbean republics. What was the value of the OAS, asked the critics, if the United States ignored it during a hemispheric crisis?

The United States government claimed that there had simply not been time to call the OAS into action. When reports from the island had warned of Communist involvement, President

Johnson had sent in troops with the aim of preventing "another Cuba." Nevertheless, this hasty action badly damaged United States prestige throughout Latin America.

An OAS peace army was formed to police Santo Domingo. Within a few days after the landing of United States troops, President Johnson did call a meeting of the OAS foreign ministers. At this meeting the United States asked the other countries to create an inter-American army to take over the policing of Santo Domingo. Despite this appeal for collective action, most of the delegates remained angry that the "deed had been done" before their approval was sought. But after a few days of debate, they agreed to establish the peacekeeping force.

The OAS peace force was the first such body ever to be formed in the Western Hemisphere. Within a few weeks soldiers from six Latin American nations landed in Santo Domingo, and military doctors and nurses from Panama joined them. A Brazilian general was chosen to command the OAS army. The United States withdrew its marines but left its army units, which became part of the peacekeeping force. José Mora, an Uruguayan statesman then serving as Secretary General of the OAS, said: "The purpose of this Inter-American Peace Force is clearly not one of intervention but rather one of rendering assistance to people of a sister nation."

Both Mexico and Chile, however, opposed the idea of an inter-American peace force. At an OAS conference at Rio de Janeiro in late 1965, the United States' suggestion for a permanent peace force was voted down. The delegates did agree to give greater emergency "peacekeeping power" to the OAS Council. This would make it possible for the Council to call together another OAS army if one should be needed again.

The Alliance for Progress seemed to promise a new era in hemispheric relations. Meanwhile, what was the United States doing about the Latin American appeal for financial help? During the 1960's many leaders in this country came to realize that perhaps the greatest threat to peace in the Western Hemisphere was poverty. Communism was a danger because desperately poor people would listen to any plan that seemed to promise a better way of life. The countries of Latin America, like developing countries in other parts of the world, were faced with a "revolution of rising expectations." Thanks to radio, television, and movies, the Latin American masses had become aware that people in some countries (especially the United States) lived far more comfortably than they. No longer would they be content with slum housing, ill health, too little food, and lack of schools for their children. Said José Mora: "Our people have developed a taste for fast answers and urgent change."

When John F. Kennedy became president of the United States in 1961, he recognized the justice of the Latin American appeal for a "Marshall Plan." President Kennedy made clear his sympathy with those Latin Americans who wanted to make fundamental changes in a democratic manner. He had read with interest the plan of Juscelino Kubitschek, president of Brazil, for a joint financial effort to bring social improvement to the Latin American people (page 281). Soon after taking office, Kennedy announced a ten-year program called the Alliance for Progress (*Alianza para el Progreso* in Spanish). This was to be a "vast co-operative effort . . . to satisfy the basic needs of the [Latin] American people for homes, work and land, health and schools . . . a plan to transform the 1960's into a historic decade of democratic progress." Both North Americans and Latin Americans had high hopes as planning for the Alliance got under way.

Financing was to come from several sources. President Kennedy proposed that the program be financed by both the United States and the Latin American countries themselves. It was thought that spending during the ten years

President Kennedy attended a ceremony in Bogotá, Colombia, marking the construction of school buildings with Alliance for Progress funds.

of the program would amount to 100 billion dollars. The United States promised to contribute one billion dollars a year and to make long-term loans at low interest to the participating countries. Investments by European, Japanese, and North American businessmen were also expected.

But the bulk of the needed funds was to come from private investors in Latin America itself. A major goal of the Alliance was to encourage well-to-do Latin Americans to invest in their own countries. Traditionally wealthy Latin Americans have preferred to invest their money abroad, where supposedly it was safer. Now the Alliance urged these Latin Americans to take an active part in helping their own countries develop.

Social reforms were envisioned. The Latin American countries were expected to work

out long-range development plans. These were to include not only economic improvements but social reforms as well. Sweeping changes in housing, land ownership and use, education, and public health as well as tax reforms were envisioned. Advisers from the United States would assist in working out the specific programs. It was hoped that all of these changes would help build a solid foundation for political democracy. The Alliance was to be a co-operative venture. The United States would provide economic and technical aid while the Latin American countries would take the major responsibility for planning.

The Alliance for Progress fell short of its goals. Perhaps in 1961 ten years seemed a reasonable period for such an ambitious program. But by the end of the 1960's it was realized that only a miracle could have accomplished much in so short a time. Assessments of the Alliance for Progress have ranged from "a disappointment" to "a shattered dream." At any rate, the high hopes for the program did not work out.

Before going into the reasons for its failure, however, it must be pointed out that the Alliance did score some real achievements. The journalist John Gunther, after visiting South America in 1965, wrote about the Alliance: "Miscellaneous good works . . . can be cited by the hundred. In half a dozen countries I saw roads, dams, tunnels, hydraulic plants, irrigation projects, normal schools, agricultural laboratories, constructed or installed by the *Alianza*. The project has built new schoolrooms for a million children, put up more than 220,-000 homes, improved 7000 miles of road, irrigated 136,000 acres of farmland, helped finance 5000 industrial firms, and assisted 36 universities." [7]

Unfortunately, when one considers the total needs of Latin America, the above figures seem pitifully small. Since 1960, unemployment has grown, millions of children have no schools to attend, the housing situation is worse, and people still go hungry. The population explosion has made all these problems more acute. In 1969, Nelson Rockefeller, governor of New York, made a fact-finding visit to Latin America for President Richard Nixon. In his report to the president, Rockefeller said about the food supply in Latin America: "While overall food production is going up, food production per person, due to the population explosion, is estimated at 10 per cent less than it was at the end of World War II. And each year there are eight million more mouths to feed." [8]

Why did the Alliance fail? The assassination of President Kennedy in 1963 was a great blow to the Alliance. Kennedy's belief in the future of the Alliance had been a life-giving force. After his death, the spirit of optimism that had surrounded the program faded. But even before 1963 the problems that would strangle the Alliance had begun to appear.

[7] John Gunther, *Inside South America* (New York: Harper & Row, 1966, 1967), p. 162.

[8] *The Rockefeller Report on the Americas* (Chicago: Quadrangle Books, 1969), p. 120.

Latin Americans in Antarctica

Two Latin American countries, Argentina and Chile, are among the nations of the world that take an active interest in Antarctica. In 1959 these two countries, along with ten other nations, signed a treaty aimed at preventing any "looting" of Antarctica's natural resources. The twelve nations agreed to postpone for 30 years any territorial claims on the ice-bound continent. Bases for research and exploration have been established in Antarctica, however, and there is much co-operation among the teams of scientists and other experts sent by different countries. Among the things being studied are fossil remains of ancient animals, mineral resources, ocean plant and animal life, weather and climate, ocean currents and tides, and the nature and movement of Antarctica's thick covering of ice.

Financing was one of these problems. Private investors simply failed to give the Alliance as much financial support as had been hoped for. Both in the United States and in Latin America investments lagged far behind goals. Moreover, not as much investment money came from Europe and Japan as had been expected. Also, as the fear of Castroism lessened in the United States, Congress became less willing to vote billions of dollars in aid for Latin America.

Still another problem was inefficient planning. Large amounts of money were poured into Alliance projects that never proved their worth. Critics in the United States thought the money was distributed too freely, with not enough guarantees that programs would be carried out. On the other hand, Latin Americans charged that United States funds had too many strings attached. The result was increased distrust of Alliance aid.

Opposition from conservative Latin Americans also handicapped efforts at reform. The Alliance for Progress had to make the idea of agrarian reform "respectable." No longer was the breaking up of huge estates into smaller

UNITED STATES

Gulf of Mexico

MEXICO

Mexico City

Havana

Nassau

BAHAMA IS. (BR.)

CUBA

Caribbean Sea

BR. HOND.
Belmopan

GUATEMALA
Guatemala City

HONDURAS
Tegucigalpa

San Salvador

EL SALVADOR

NICARAGUA

Managua

CANAL
ZONE
(U.S.)

San José
COSTA
RICA

PANAMA

Panama City

JAMAICA HAITI

Port-au-
Prince

DOMINICAN
REP.

Santo
Domingo

PUERTO
RICO
(U.S.)

San Juan

VIRGIN IS. (U.S.)

BARBADOS

Port-of-Spain

TRINIDAD-
TOBAGO

Caracas

VENEZUELA

Orinoco R.

Bogotá

COLOMBIA

Georgetown
GUYANA

Paramaribo
SURINAM
(DU.)

Cayenne
FRENCH GUIANA

*ATLANTIC
OCEAN*

TROPIC OF CANCER

EQUATOR

GALÁPAGOS
(ECUADOR)

ECUADOR

Quito

Amazon R.

PERU

Lima

*PACIFIC
OCEAN*

La Paz

BOLIVIA

Sucre

BRAZIL

Brasília

PARAGUAY

Asunción

Paraná R.

TROPIC OF CAPRICORN

Santiago

CHILE

ARGENTINA

Buenos
Aires

URUGUAY

Montevideo

Río de la Plata

FALKLAND IS.
(BR.)

STRAIT OF MAGELLAN

Pan American Highway System
Unfinished section

0   200   400   600   800   1000 Miles

holdings only the promise of radical parties. The governments themselves were now pledged to the goal of fair distribution of land. Nevertheless, wealthy landholders blocked such efforts. As earlier chapters have shown, land distribution has made headway in some countries. But millions of poor farmers continue to scratch out a meager living on land they cannot call their own.

Tax reform was also a major goal of the Alliance. Wealthy Latin Americans had seldom paid their fair share of taxes. Ex-president Alberto Lleras Camargo of Colombia wrote in 1963: "Not a single Latin American, whether of high standing or of the underworld, has ever been imprisoned for not paying his taxes or for sending in a fraudulent income tax report." Like the land-reform programs, plans for fair tax systems were stubbornly resisted by wealthy Latin Americans.

The democratic ideal on which the Alliance had been based was also neglected. The Alliance planners had hoped that its reforms would insure popular support for stable civilian governments. Yet United States money continued to go to non-democratic governments. Some of these governments spent Alliance money on their armed forces rather than on needed reforms. Several times in the 1960's, moreover, the United States intervened in Latin American countries, most notably in the Bay of Pigs episode and the Dominican crisis. These events added to Latin American disenchantment with the Alliance.

The Alliance for Progress had started out as a bold new venture in which Latin Americans and North Americans would co-operate as equals to solve urgent problems. But it became just another aid program, bogged down in red tape and hampered by motives of self-interest. As one author has put it, "the Alliance could neither reach the people nor involve them in its goals."

Nixon offered a different approach. When President Richard Nixon took office in 1969, he began what one observer called "a cooler approach" to Latin America. He seemed to formulate a policy of letting Latin Americans do the long-range planning and then offering to help specific projects. A promise was made to remove the strings often attached to aid programs and to make it easier for Latin American exports to enter United States markets. But many observers suspected that the new policy really meant a return to indifference toward Latin American problems. Nixon also moved to increase the amount of military aid provided by the United States to Latin American governments.

What will future policy be? Formulating policy toward Latin America is obviously no easy matter for United States leaders. In his book *Inside South America*, John Gunther summed up the challenge to United States policy-makers in three brief questions and answers. Though Gunther referred to South America, his evaluation can be applied to all of Latin America:

Do we own South America?
No, but we often behave as if we did.

Do we take more out of South America than we give?
Probably.

Are we finished in South America?
No, but we should watch our step.[9]

Whatever the policy of the United States may be, it is clear that Latin Americans themselves must determine their own futures. Felipe Herrera, a Chilean scholar and banker, has spoken for all Latin Americans on this point: "Latin America is rapidly coming to the realization that it must arrive at its own determination. . . . The most important thing is for us to begin convincing ourselves that the solution to our fundamental problems lies only with us."

Latin America Today

[9] John Gunther, *Inside South America*, p. 163.

1. Explain or define the following words: cold war; Marshall Plan; unilateral action.

2. Since 1950, how has the United States disagreed with Latin American nations about priorities in hemispheric affairs?

3. How has this difference of opinion shown up in the following: (a) the overthrow of the Arbenz regime in Guatemala; (b) United States policy toward Castro; (c) United States intervention in the Dominican Republic? In the last two, what actions of the United States were criticized by Latin Americans? How did the United States government answer these criticisms?

4. In the Cuban and Dominican situations, in what ways did other Latin American countries co-operate with the United States?

5. What were the goals of the Alliance for Progress? How was it to be financed? What was achieved? Why did the Alliance fall far short of its goals?

Summing Up

In trying to be a "big brother" to the Latin American nations, the United States has often been accused of being a "bossy uncle." This nation has been feared and resented by its neighbors to the south. The chief reason for such feeling has been the United States' interference in the affairs of Latin American countries. In the Caribbean this interference has sometimes taken the form of outright occupation. But power and influence can also be exercised in other ways. Latin Americans long have resented the economic power held by North American businesses, and the United States government's policy of dollar diplomacy has been equally hated. Yet Latin Americans have also accused their northern neighbor of taking them for granted.

After the United States won independence, this country looked with sympathy on the efforts of Latin Americans to win freedom from Spain. Once this was achieved, the United States in the Monroe Doctrine expressed the view that Europe should stay out of the Western Hemisphere. The United States itself, however, encroached on Latin American territory when it annexed a large part of Mexico. By the end of the 1800's the United States had become a colonial power. After the defeat of Spain in 1898, Puerto Rico became an outright possession, while Cuba was made a protectorate.

Then came the era of the "big stick" as Theodore Roosevelt made clear to the world that the United States ruled the Caribbean. To protect the Panama Canal, the United States interfered freely in the affairs of several small countries. A sincere desire to help the people of these countries played a part in the United States' Caribbean policy. But later presidents realized that the chief result of intervention was to stir up resentment and ill will.

In the 1930's Franklin D. Roosevelt started a new era in inter-American relations with the Good Neighbor Policy. This policy contributed a great deal to effective hemispheric co-operation during World War II. After the war the founding of the Organization of American States reflected the same spirit of co-operation. The purposes of the OAS were collective defense and mutual problem-solving. But there was disagreement over which problems were most urgent. The United States asked for a solid stand against Communism while the Latin Americans appealed for help in solving difficult economic problems.

In launching the Alliance for Progress, President John F. Kennedy aimed at both goals. It was his belief that Communism could best be checked by supporting Latin American economic development and social reform. Solid achievements were made during the ten years of the Alliance. But Latin America's problems proved to be far too deep-rooted to be solved in a single decade. Moreover, the Bay of Pigs invasion and the Dominican intervention re-awakened Latin American distrust of the United States. It remains to be seen what course inter-American relations will follow next. But one thing is certain: This country can no longer take Latin America for granted.

18

The United States and Latin America: Economic, Social, and Cultural Co-operation

CHAPTER FOCUS

1. Efforts to Liberalize Trade
2. Improving the Quality of Life
3. Efforts to Improve Health
4. Cultural Exchange

Among the agencies that have carried out assistance programs in Latin America is the United States Peace Corps. This Peace Corps volunteer, photographed with two friends in Salvador, Brazil, helped families in that city rebuild their homes in a community-development program.

During a recent spring, a group of British geographers, researchers, writers, and photographers boarded a hovercraft in the Brazilian port of Manaus and headed upstream on the Rio Negro, an Amazon tributary. A hovercraft is a boat that travels over land or water just a few inches above the surface. Fans on the bottom of the hull create a cushion of air over which the hovercraft glides. The hovercraft expedition had been sponsored jointly by a London geographical journal and the British royal family.

The expedition had two purposes. One was to prove that this kind of boat could travel from the headwaters of the Amazon tributaries to the headwaters of the Orinoco river system. If this could be done, the expedition would

355

have charted a possible all-water route between Brazil and Venezuela. The second goal was to study plant and animal life in this almost untouched region. Knowledge of the environment would be useful in planning its future development.

As the hovercraft left Manaus, aboard as part of the staff were two Brazilian scientists. Even before this, the expedition had traveled on Amazon tributaries in Peru, with a visiting staff of Peruvian scientists. Then, when the hovercraft crossed the Brazilian border into Venezuela, a biology professor from Caracas joined the expedition. Throughout the journey the scientists lived on board the hovercraft. They took samples of the water and soil, caught specimens of small animals, insects, and birds,

and collected plants and fruits. Thus three South American countries and one European country pooled scientific skills in a joint effort to plan for future development.

Stories of this kind are typical of the many international projects carried on in Latin America during recent years. These joint endeavors have been organized and sponsored by a variety of groups—scientific societies and universities, charitable foundations, business corporations, national governments. International bodies such as the OAS and United Nations agencies have also been active. This chapter will describe only a few of the many joint efforts that have improved conditions in Latin America and spread appreciation of its culture.

1. Efforts to Liberalize Trade

The Latin American countries recognize that they themselves must work more closely together to make life better for their people. One co-operative effort has as its goal the expansion of Latin American trade.

LAFTA was formed to encourage trade. With the idea of reducing tariff barriers among themselves, seven countries founded the Latin American Free Trade Association in 1960. The original members were Argentina, Brazil, Chile, Mexico, Paraguay, Peru, and Uruguay. Later Ecuador, Colombia, Bolivia, and Venezuela also joined LAFTA. The LAFTA members hoped eventually to create a common market that would unite Latin America from Mexico to Argentina in one mammoth free-trade area.

Like the Central American Common Market (described in Chapter 10), LAFTA was supposed to help the individual countries expand their markets. Since most Latin American countries produce chiefly raw materials (minerals, sugar, coffee, fruits, etc.), they have bought

very little from each other. What these countries need most in foreign trade is manufactured articles—clothing, automobiles, farm machinery, electrical appliances, and so on. If each nation could concentrate on the manufacture of certain of these items, and if the goods could be sold freely throughout the LAFTA area, industry in all the countries would prosper. The LAFTA countries also hoped that some day the entire area would have a common currency and passport system.

Problems slowed down the progress of LAFTA. The founding members of LAFTA realized that it would take years to make the common market a reality. At the founding meeting in 1960, the members agreed to lower tariffs on 2500 small manufactured items. The plan was that tariffs would be further reduced, a little more each year, until a full common market would be achieved in 1985.

By 1968 trade among the LAFTA members had increased by 85 per cent. That figure seems impressive until one realizes that this trade was still only a tenth of the total trade carried on by these countries. In other words, the bulk of the LAFTA countries' trade continued to be with non-LAFTA nations.

One problem handicapping LAFTA is the fear of the smaller members that they will be dominated by the larger countries. Ecuador and Peru, for example, have feared the competition of processed frozen foods from Chile and Argentina. These countries could probably sell their products so cheaply across free-zone borders that frozen-food industries could never survive in Ecuador and Peru. Basically, LAFTA seems to be unworkable because the member countries are at such different levels of economic development. Some are far more industrialized than others. Moreover, nationalistic interests constantly clash.

By the late 1960's it was clear that progress toward a LAFTA common market was much slower than had been expected. The member countries agreed to postpone the original target date of 1985. The timetable for achieving complete free trade has been left indefinite.

Regional market areas are foreseen. Now the emphasis is on forming free-trade areas of smaller size. We have already seen that the Central American Common Market made steady progress in the 1960's, at least until the war between El Salvador and Honduras confused the picture. Other countries that decided to form a free-trade group were the Andean nations of Bolivia, Chile, Colombia, Ecuador, and Peru. These nations have begun to liberalize trade restrictions among themselves. Since Bolivia and Ecuador are the poorest of the five members, it has been agreed that they will have a special status within the group. Sometime before the end of the century the five Andean nations hope to have removed all trade barriers within their common market area.

Still another trade region within South America is the Rio de la Plata group of countries. Argentina, Bolivia, Brazil, Paraguay, and Uruguay are the members, since all have territory bordering on the Paraná-Paraguay river system. One goal of the organization is to explore the natural resources of the Plata region. This will help the countries plan for its efficient development.

The Caribbean Free Trade Association is yet another regional trade group. It includes Guyana, Jamaica, Trinidad, and a number of the West Indian islands that are still associated with Great Britain. Venezuela and Colombia have shown interest in co-operating with this group.

THINKING ABOUT THIS SECTION

1. What is the long-range goal of LAFTA? What progress has been made? What problems have been identified?
2. What regional "common markets" have been formed in Latin America? What is a special goal of the Plata organization? Why would Venezuela and Colombia have an interest in the Caribbean group?

2. Improving the Quality of Life

Many people have taken an interest in Latin America's hopes for social and economic betterment. By their own efforts and by working through organizations, these individuals have helped to bring these hopes closer to reality.

The OAS sponsors co-operative efforts. Through the committees, agencies, and conferences of the Organization of American States, the Latin American peoples have dealt with a wide range of "grass-roots" problems. In ceremonies marking the revision of the

OAS Charter in 1970, Secretary General Galo Plaza commented on this role of the organization: "The OAS . . . has been transformed into a more effective instrument to [speed] the process of economic development as a means of achieving social justice. Economic progress alone would be meaningless if it were not translated into a higher standard of living for the people."

Planning for co-operative activities is important. To enable experts from different countries to pool ideas and information, many conferences are held. During a single year, for example, 81 different OAS meetings were scheduled. The following were just a few of the topics discussed: tropical agriculture, rural education, archeology, weather forecasting, tourism, nutrition, treatment of tuberculosis, child psychology, eye diseases, city planning, earthquake resistance, and juvenile delinquency.

During a single month of this particular year, South American teachers of vocational subjects met at Guayaquil, and forest conservation experts got together at San José, Costa Rica. At the same time there was an OAS conference at the Center for Rural Education in Patzcuaro, Mexico. Meanwhile, the government of Ecuador had just chosen 200 locations for a project of the United Nations Children's Emergency Fund. Working through OAS agencies, the UN workers were to set up youth programs something like 4-H clubs. Each center was to have a school garden and a youth-club headquarters where cooking and sewing would be taught. OAS funds were to pay for seeds, kitchen equipment, and sewing supplies.

OAS study groups lead to action groups. Just the pooling of ideas and experience would be good reason for holding the OAS study groups. But useful action often results from these meetings. One of the ways in which OAS officials work with an individual nation is to organize a group of specialists to work with a certain department of the nation's government. The specialists are paid by the OAS to give advice and direction in planning new projects. The government of the country involved may finance the project itself, or funds may come from a variety of sources.

Slums surround virtually every city in Latin America. UN advisers helped the Chilean government plan new structures to replace the Santiago slum pictured at left. Not only housing but schools and teachers are needed. The teacher in this Colombian classroom (right) was trained at a Catholic university with Ford Foundation aid.

The OAS has worked for better housing. Because housing is desperately needed throughout Latin America, this problem has been the object of many efforts. Earlier chapters in this book described the miserable slums that have mushroomed in almost every Latin American city. The urgency of this situation has been clearly stated by Galo Plaza: "Most of the explosive problems of Latin America start precisely in the slums that surround the large modern city."

It has been estimated that Latin American cities would need to build two and a half million living units a year for the next 30 years to catch up with the need for decent housing. But good housing is expensive to build. To pay the costs of construction and still make a profit, private builders have to charge high rents for new apartments. Such rents are too high for people with low incomes. If new housing is to benefit the people who need it most, it must be paid for, in part at least, by governments or by grants from other sources.

In many slum-clearance projects, OAS committees have hired the architects and provided the city planners and social workers. Usually government agencies of the nations involved choose the sites for new low-rent apartment buildings. The Inter-American Development Bank (page 364) may supply the funds. One huge housing development on the outskirts of Bogotá, Colombia, was built with the help of Alliance for Progress funds. After the death of President Kennedy, the residents of this community insisted that it be renamed *Ciudad Kennedy,* or Kennedy City.

In Rio de Janeiro and Lima early plans for new low-cost housing proved to be impractical. The sites chosen were too far from the factories where the residents might hope to find work. Even if public transportation were available, the cost was too high and the travel time was too long. In Rio, housing projects now are being built on some of the sites cleared of *favela* slums.

Other projects aim at improving rural life. One discouraging thing about efforts to provide low-cost urban housing is that poor rural people continue to pour into the cities. In fact,

they move to the cities much faster than new apartments can be built. An obvious answer is somehow to encourage rural people to stay on the land. OAS experts, therefore, have sought ways of making farming more profitable. They study how to grow more corn per acre, how to get cows to give more milk, and how to fight diseases that attack plants and livestock. For example, the OAS asked sixteen botany professors from North American universities to study the planting of wheat in Colombia. New seed strains developed by these specialists doubled the yield of wheat per acre on model farms near Bogotá.

At Turrialba, Costa Rica, the old Pan American Union years ago started an Institute of Tropical Agriculture on land donated by the Costa Rican government. The OAS has continued this Institute. Here the United Fruit Company sent young Hondurans and Ecuadorians on scholarships to train as specialists in banana production. This was the North American company's answer to the criticism that it never hired local people for good jobs. OAS botanists at Turrialba also have done research on ways of fighting banana leaf disease.

In Mexico, OAS agricultural specialists have investigated hoof-and-mouth disease. This highly contagious disease can wipe out entire herds of beef and dairy cattle. In the early 1950's, a joint United States-Mexican team halted an epidemic by slaughtering infected cattle and burying the carcasses in quicklime. Cattle that were still healthy were vaccinated. An OAS team in Brazil adopted these methods and taught them to local veterinarians. In the 1960's European veterinarians traveled to Brazil to study these ways of controlling a disease long dreaded by cattlemen.

Alliance funds aided Mexican villages. The previous chapter gave a gloomy account of the Alliance for Progress. But many individuals in Latin America realized improvements in their lives as a result of Alliance projects. Of all the Latin American nations, probably Mexico has done most to help its own rural villages. But by itself Mexico can only afford to do so much. The following story shows how Alliance funds helped one Mexican community to help itself.

The families of the village of San Francisco Tepeyecac (tay-pay-*yay'* kahk) owned their own little farms, but they could not make a decent living because the land was too dry and not fertile. Unlike the village of Santa Cruz Etla (page 184), this village had no mountain stream running close by.

With funds provided under the Alliance for Progress, a deep well was dug for San Francisco Tepeyecac and a pump powered by a diesel motor was bought. This enabled villagers to pump up water from deep in the earth. Pipes were laid to carry the water to 90 small farms. Because they now could irrigate their land, the farmers got credit to buy seed and fertilizer. Aided by another grant from the Alliance for Progress, they set up a credit union. (Credit unions are co-operative organizations that make loans to members at low interest rates.) From the credit union the farmers borrowed money to buy small tractors. An expert from Mexico City came out to show the villagers how to use the tractors in preparing the land for seed.

Over a four-year period (1963–1967), the farmers of San Francisco Tepeyecac increased by four times the amount of corn grown on their land. With the profits from selling their surplus corn, they started to pay off their debts and bought more seed and fertilizer. They also had some cash left over to spend on their families and houses. The wives had cement flooring laid and bought new clothes for their children. Some of the kitchen equipment they bought had never been seen in the village before.

The changes carried out in San Francisco Tepeyecac served as a model for projects in nearby valleys. Feeder roads were built to link the villages with each other and with the nearest market town. In this town food-storage and food-processing plants were built to handle the surplus crops brought in by the villagers. Besides corn and vegetables, the farmers were now raising chickens and pigs to sell to the food-processing plants. The meat could be quick-frozen in these plants and sold to townspeople. Thus, within a few years the people of these valleys significantly raised their standard of living. A number of young people decided to stay in the villages rather than move to the slums of Mexico City. In 1968 President Díaz Ordaz sent "special thanks to the Alliance for Progress which helped us increase our yield of corn per acre."

Peace Corps volunteers have done valuable work in Latin America. The Peace Corps was another aid program launched by President John F. Kennedy. It was designed to help developing countries meet their desperate need for trained manpower. Many of the Peace Corps volunteers in Latin America taught English, science, and mathematics to high-school students. They also taught reading and writing in Spanish to illiterate adults. But Peace Corps efforts have covered a wide range of activities. In fishing villages the volunteers have shown how more fish can be caught with improved nylon nets. They have also introduced the idea of credit unions in farm villages. Still other volunteers have trained machinists, plumbers, masons, and carpenters. They have also organized public-health clinics; taught fruit and vegetable canning; surveyed routes for new roads; and shown farmers how to improve crops and livestock.

Peace Corps workers who speak only English are taught the language of their assigned country in a crash program. Naturally volunteers who already speak Spanish are especially qualified for projects in Latin America. Since 1961, some 10,000 Peace Corps volunteers have served in Latin American countries. Their efforts have done much to create good will for the United States. Almost all of the Latin American countries have requested and received Peace Corps teams.

One Peace Corpsman worked among Indians in southern Chile. The story of Pat, a young man from Sioux City, Iowa, illustrates what Peace Corps workers can accomplish. At the age of 20, Pat left home to work in California. There he found a job stocking shelves in a Los Angeles supermarket. Persuaded by friends to take classes in the evening, he enrolled in East Los Angeles Junior College. Pat soon changed his job to evening hours and began taking daytime courses. Before long he was promoted to night-shift manager at the store.

On a field trip for a geology class Pat made his first visit to Mexico. Finding the country interesting, he began taking bus trips farther into Mexico. Meanwhile, he improved the Spanish he had picked up from Spanish-speaking friends. When Pat graduated from junior college, he found that his experience as a store manager and his smattering of spoken Spanish made him a good candidate for the Peace Corps.

The Peace Corps accepted Pat's application and asked him if he would like to go to southern Chile to work among Araucanian Indians on "community organization." Though not sure what "community organization" was, he welcomed the chance to see more of Latin America.

With a group of 83 other applicants, Pat was sent to the University of Illinois for intensive training. There he spent long hours learning about such things as rural credit unions, forestry problems, and road surveying. Of course he also worked hard on his Spanish.

After eight weeks of rigorous training, the candidates were sent to Mexican villages in the state of Michoacán, home of the still-tribal Tarascan Indians. Here Pat made a survey of one small village. He studied the political set-up, ways of making a living, social relationships of the village people, and the villagers' attitude toward the blond stranger in their midst. Of the 83 original members of the training group, only 59 "survived" the period of their village study projects.

As one of the "survivors," Pat was now ready for his Chilean assignment. After taking a direct flight to Santiago, Pat reached the Araucanian reservation on the third morning after leaving the United States. The Chilean Bureau of Indian Affairs was in charge of the Peace Corps workers and chose the areas where they would work. Pat learned that he was assigned to a community of 400 Indians, where there was already a school run by Catholic missionaries from Germany. The Germans were chiefly interested in teaching Spanish and religion to the younger Indian children. The head of the mission gave Pat a bed and co-operated with him throughout the following two years. Since Pat was blond, the Indians assumed that he was also a German.

The Indian village was in cold, bleak southern Chile. Thick forests had once covered the area, but overcutting had long since stripped it bare. The village consisted of ramshackle wooden buildings along a muddy street. A dirt road with deep ruts linked the village with a town called Temuco (tay-*moo′* koh), 40 miles away. Scattered around the village lived the Mapuche (mah-*poo′* chay) Indians. They were a subdivision of the Araucanian group but spoke their own dialect. Only a few of the men spoke Araucanian, and even fewer spoke Spanish. Many family groups of 10 or 20 people lived in isolated spots outside the village. There were no roads from the village out to these families.

As soon as Pat arrived, he began studying the village. Forestry was one of his first concerns. He tried to convince the Mapuche that it would be worthwhile to plant trees. But the trees would have to grow for ten years before they could be cut for firewood. People whose food supply is uncertain from one day to the next find it difficult to look that far ahead. Before the first year was out, however, Pat had persuaded the Mapuche to plant small seedling trees in the area that had once been forest. During the two years Pat spent in Chile, he and the "Committee" he organized among the Indians planted 40,000 seedling trees.

Pat also gave thought to the problem of a cash crop. The only marketable crop grown by the Mapuche farmers was wheat. But the land where they lived was not favorable for wheat farming. Every time they harvested a crop, they had to save a fourth of the wheat to provide seed for the next year's sowing. Since they needed most of the rest of the wheat for bread to feed their families, the Indians seldom had much surplus to send to market. It was clear that the Mapuche farmers needed more good land and a different cash crop.

The village straggled along the edge of a marshy lake which had once been an inlet of the Pacific Ocean. Carrying a bed roll and dry provisions, Pat made several overnight hikes to explore the marshland. He realized that if the marshes could be drained, some useful farmland might be recovered. With this idea in mind, Pat marked out certain marsh areas for drainage. He then persuaded the Mapuche headmen to organize volunteer workers to dig out a channel to the sea. Much of the drained land proved to be too salty for crops. But on a tract that had been covered with fairly fresh water, Pat urged the Committee to plant a new crop—potatoes.

Some of the men drove their oxcarts into Temuco, where they were able to buy seed potatoes through a newly organized credit union. The potatoes were planted and eventually yielded a crop which the Committee sold in Temuco for cash. Instead of dividing the profits into a bit of cash for each family, the Committee used the money to buy more picks and shovels. They also made "bulldozers" by attaching scoop-shovels to their oxcarts. With this home-made equipment, the Committee started a road-building campaign. More than a hundred men now belonged to the Committee. By clearing brush and draining and filling mudholes, they built more than 65 miles of good dirt road. Now the isolated families had easy access to the village and also could use the road to Temuco. More people were planting potatoes and marketing their crops in Temuco. Impressed with what the village had done, the governor of the state provided a real bulldozer. With this, the Committee dug a deeper channel to the sea. Now they could be sure of keeping the new cropland drained.

With his first efforts successful, Pat went on to other activities during his second year. Other Peace Corps people came to help set up a health program. Better nutrition and infant care were taught. In the garden of the tiny public school, Pat planted spinach, lettuce, and tomatoes. When the vegetables ripened, he showed the Mapuche women how to can the tomatoes as well as local apples. Pat also helped train Peace Corps men and women for work in other Araucanian villages. By the time he left, Pat felt he would be well-satisfied if the draining channel stayed open, if the lakebed continued to produce potatoes, and if the roads were kept in good shape.[1]

Peace Corps workers in Uruguay had varied experiences. The Peace Corps does not send volunteers to a country unless the government of that country specifically requests them. The Uruguayan government asked the Peace Corps for recreation directors and community organizers. In response a group of ten volunteers flew to Montevideo. This, of course, was a far

[1] Pat returned to the grocery store in East Los Angeles and to college. After earning an advanced degree, he joined the State Department's Latin American Affairs section and was assigned to a post in Guatemala City.

more developed locality than the Mapuche country. One of the Peace Corps workers organized a program of competitive sports for girls in a town 30 miles outside Montevideo. These girls had never played games in public before. Another volunteer demonstrated to women in a country town how to preserve tomatoes and fruits.

A third Peace Corps woman worker moved into an unfinished apartment building in Montevideo. For two years squatters had occupied the building after a strike had halted construction. The families living there had no heat or running water, the sewer system didn't work, and there was no school for their children. By appealing to the authorities for days on end, the Peace Corps volunteer got some action. Water was finally turned on at a central faucet, and sanitary outhouses were built. Meanwhile, the volunteer started a school. To protect her living quarters from the cold winter wind off the Atlantic, she had sealed it up with flattened packing boxes. Her cardboard-walled apartment became the social center of the "squatters' housing project."

Another worker in this Uruguayan group was assigned to help with a juvenile court. On this assignment he found out about a government orphanage for delinquent boys who had been rejected by their parents. A few of these boys attended a nearby public school, but many refused to go. The Peace Corps worker persuaded a number of the boys to give the school a try. He walked with them to class, talked with their teachers, helped the boys with their homework, and tutored those who could barely read and write. Every afternoon he organized sports at the orphanage. To boys who still refused to go to school, the Peace Corpsman, himself the son of a carpenter, gave training in woodworking. Soon he got the Uruguayan Welfare Department to provide tools and scrap lumber for the carpentry classes. He also won a promise from local government officials that jobs would be guaranteed for those boys who became good carpenters by the age of sixteen.

Some aspects of the Peace Corps programs were criticized. Although soccer is the most popular sport in Uruguay, some Peace Corps workers organized basketball leagues throughout the little farm villages that surround Montevideo. Several of the young Corpsmen who taught basketball in "soccer country" felt they were doing nothing of real value. For various reasons other Peace Corps workers have been dissatisfied. In Guatemala, Peace Corpsmen were bitter because Indian villagers lived in hopeless poverty while the United States provided large amounts of military aid to an unpopular government in Guatemala City. A married couple teaching English in Brazil were critical of their own program because so many Brazilian teachers were underpaid or even jobless. Moreover, they felt their students needed instruction in more practical subjects.

In recent years the Peace Corps has found that the needs of developing nations have become more specialized. With the aim of meeting these advanced needs, the Corps has sought to recruit more experienced people with specific skills and talents.

The Inter-American Development Bank aids progress. Still another friend to self-help projects is the Inter-American Development Bank. This institution, often called the Latin Bank, was created at an economic conference held at Buenos Aires in 1959. It serves as an international lending agency. Through the Bank's Social Progress Fund, national governments have secured loans for low-cost housing, pure-water and sewage projects, land resettlement programs, and the construction of schools and hospitals. The United States has given sizable financial support to the Latin Bank, but the Latin American countries themselves have put up two-thirds of the total cost of the projects.

Private foundations have sponsored intercultural exchange. Many worthwhile improvements in Latin America have been sponsored by nonprofit private organizations. Examples of these are the Rockefeller Foundation and

Latin America has long been a "man's world," but that may be changing. Representative of women's improved status are (top) a Mexican woman voting and (right) an Ecuadorian Indian mother who has learned how to read. Some women even hold high government office, like Señora Haydee Castillo de Lopez Acosta, Venezuela's Minister of Development (above).

the Ford Foundation. Both were set up by wealthy United States families for the purpose of financing good works (not only in Latin America).

One project sponsored by the Ford Foundation involved intercultural exchange between Chile and California. The Foundation asked the University of California and the University of Chile to see what they could do, working together, to improve agriculture and education in the poorer areas of Chile. The project made its headquarters at the university in Santiago. North American professors and graduate students assembled there to study Chilean problems and to co-operate with Chilean university people in working out solutions. Chilean graduate students, in turn, went to the United States and studied veterinary medicine, plant diseases, and milk production at branches of the University of California. After completing their courses, the students who had studied the plant diseases went home to work in the orchards of central Chile. There they investigated leaf diseases of apricot, plum, and apple trees. While these students worked on the spot, samples of insects, infected leaves, and soil were shipped to California laboratories for analysis.

As another phase of the exchange program, engineering students from California traveled to Chile to study earthquake-proof buildings. With them they took seismographs as gifts to Chilean scientists. Meanwhile, Chilean rural teachers attended training sessions at California campuses. On their return home, the teachers were provided with such useful equipment as audio-visual aids and microfilm, copying machines, and tape recorders.

THINKING ABOUT THIS SECTION

1. Look up in a recent almanac or encyclopedia the per capita income (average income per person) in the United States. Compare with the figures given for Latin American countries in the table on page 375. Which of the countries rank the highest in this category? Which are the lowest? Also look at the life expectancy figures in the table. Do you see any relationship between these figures and the per capita income figures? Explain. Note that the table also lists the chief exports of each country. What generalization can you make about these products?

2. Why is housing an urgent problem in Latin America? How has the OAS contributed to efforts aimed at relieving this problem?

3. Why would the improvement of rural life help to solve the problem of urban housing? What sort of effort is being made in this direction? Evaluate the case of San Francisco Tepeyecac.

4. How have Peace Corps workers helped developing countries cope with urgent problems? Why have Peace Corps workers occasionally been critical of the programs in which they were involved?

5. What other kinds of organizations have aided self-help projects in Latin America?

3. *Efforts to Improve Health*

Better health has been the goal of joint efforts. One of Latin America's most urgent needs continues to be the improvement of health. Through the Pan American Health Organization (PAHO), all of the American nations co-operate in working toward this goal. Also involved are the World Health Organization (WHO, a branch of the United Nations), the OAS, and agencies of the national govern-

ments. Private foundations and public-spirited businesses also make important contributions. The joint efforts of these groups generally concentrate on the problems of nutrition, contagious disease, sanitation, medical education, and population control.

Safe water is needed. Simply purifying drinking water would help greatly to improve the health of millions in Latin America. This need is urgent both in poor rural areas and in the cities. The journalist Tad Szulc has told of a pure-water project in a Peruvian village. Funds provided by the Inter-American Development Bank enabled the community to drill wells. The local public-health doctor was enthusiastic over the result: "You wouldn't believe it," he said, "but in the eighteen months since the pure-water system was installed, gastric diseases have fallen off by more than half. And the kids are healthier, tougher and have the kind of joy of living that I haven't seen in a long time in these mountains." [2] Szulc also reported that in 1963 fewer than half of Latin America's towns and cities had municipal water systems and sewer services.

The problem has not been neglected. Alliance for Progress funds provided safe water supplies for many Latin Americans during the 1960's. Moreover, the Pan American Health Organization has launched a 1.7-billion-dollar program to construct water systems in the 1970's.

People need adequate food, and the right kind of food, to have the energy to work. Good nutrition is also important, as the following story illustrates. A North American construction company was building stretches of the Pan American Highway in Central America. The company foremen were not satisfied with the rate of progress. They felt the local mestizo laborers were not working hard enough, but they couldn't get the men to work any faster.

During the early weeks of the project, the men were laying highway in an area close to their homes. Every night they returned to their huts to eat the evening meal of beans and tortillas with their families. But as the work slowly advanced, the crews had to eat in camp. The company brought in a nutrition expert to talk with the camp cooks. On the advice of this expert, the cooks prepared meals that included high-protein foods—meat, cheese, and

[2] Tad Szulc, *Latin America* (New York: Atheneum, 1965), p. 63.

UN experts have worked with the Argentine government in efforts to improve health in the Chaco region. As part of the program, visiting nurses regularly check on the health of expectant mothers.

eggs. Vitamin-rich foods such as fresh vegetables and oranges were also given the workers.

After a few weeks on this body-building diet, the laborers were clearing twice as much brush and handling twice as much concrete and asphalt. Work on the new highway now progressed at a rapid rate. The company officials realized that poor diet, not laziness, was the reason the men had worked slowly at first.

The real problem, of course, is that poor people in most countries cannot afford foods like meat and eggs. With this in mind, experts of the UN World Health Organization developed a cheap high-protein food from cottonseed meal, yeast, and sorghum. In the form of a tasteless powder, this food can easily be added to soups and stews.

But another problem is to get people to accept and use a food that is strange to them. Peruvian Indians threw away the powdered milk airlifted into their villages after the earthquake of 1970. Perhaps no one told them that the milk would make their children stronger and healthier. In Guatemala the WHO food workers persuaded Indian women to put the new protein-powder into a traditional soup made from meat bones, corn, and squash. The result was far more nourishing meals for the Indian families.

The United States has also helped in the campaign to raise food standards in Latin America. Millions of dollars were put into the Food for Peace program. Under this program, surplus food from the United States was distributed to eighteen Latin American countries in a school-lunch project called *Operación Niños*. (*Niños* means "children.") One outcome of this program was greatly increased attendance at school. For many of the students the lunches were the best meals they had ever eaten.

Joint efforts combat disease. The major causes of death in Latin America are still communicable diseases. This was the concern of the Pan American Sanitary Bureau, one of the first branches of the Pan American Union. With the help of specialists and money from the Rockefeller Foundation, this Bureau helped to save hundreds of thousands of lives even before World War II. Yellow fever and bubonic plague were wiped out in the New World, and outbreaks of cholera were greatly reduced.

Another goal was to eliminate hookworm disease. This is a disease that people get by walking barefoot on soil containing human waste. Worms in the soil burrow into the soles of the feet and make their way into the intestines. There they become parasites. As the worms feed off the victim's blood, anemia and malnutrition result. Hookworm disease, as

much as poor diet, makes a person listless and lacking in vitality.

In rural areas without modern sanitary facilities, hookworm has been a serious problem. In one district studied in Paraguay medical workers found that 80 per cent of the population was infected. Educating the people in hygiene and building sanitary facilities have made it possible to control this disease.

The Pan American Sanitary Bureau and the Rockefeller Foundation also moved to control typhus. This disease is caused by bacteria carried by lice, fleas, or ticks. Bolivian and Peruvian Indians in the cold Andes highlands seldom change their many layers of wool clothing and so have often fallen victim to typhus. A campaign to eliminate lice was carried on by Pan American agents with support from the Rockefeller Foundation. Over a period of 35 years the number of cases of typhus was cut in half. But efforts cannot lag. A few fleas or lice from a family infected with typhus can start an epidemic.

There are never enough doctors, nurses, and public-health specialists in any of the less developed countries to get rid of hookworms, lice and fleas, flea-carrying rats, and malaria mosquitoes. Such campaigns demand inter-American efforts and money. A World Health Organization specialist has estimated that ten billion dollars and the co-operation of all countries would make it possible to wipe out tuberculosis, venereal diseases, and malaria in the New World.

River-launch clinics brought health programs to Amazonia. During World War II the United States State Department set up a Committee on Inter-American Affairs to offer technical assistance to the Latin American nations. Because the Committee was headed by Nelson

Latin America — Population

Population experts predict that by 1980 twelve Latin American cities in addition to the ones shown here will have more than a million people.

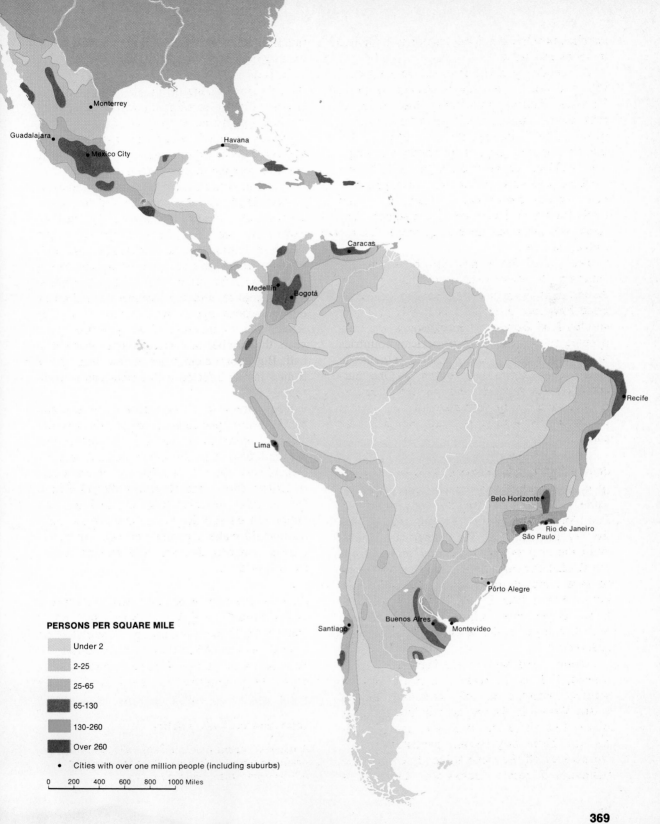

PERSONS PER SQUARE MILE

- Under 2
- 2-25
- 25-65
- 65-130
- 130-260
- Over 260

• Cities with over one million people (including suburbs)

0   200   400   600   800   1000 Miles

Monterrey

Guadalajara

Havana

Mexico City

Caracas

Medellín

Bogotá

Recife

Lima

Belo Horizonte

Rio de Janeiro

São Paulo

Pôrto Alegre

Santiago

Buenos Aires

Montevideo

Rockefeller, it was often called the Rockefeller Committee. Brazil asked the Rockefeller Committee to help organize a health program for the Amazon basin. To prepare for the program, young Brazilian doctors were sent for a year to Johns Hopkins Medical School in the United States to study tropical diseases. Nurses in Rio de Janeiro and São Paulo were given "crash" training programs in rural health. A year's training, all expenses paid, was offered to girls with an eighth-grade education to prepare them to work as nurse's aides. The young women of the Amazon River towns proved eager to make use of this opportunity.

By 1944 ten river launches had been fitted out as "health-mobiles" at Belém, the Amazon system's ocean port. Each launch had one doctor, one nurse, two aides, and a supply of medicines and equipment. The health teams began making regular runs up and down the Amazon, stopping at many little riverports between Belém and Manaus. They treated countless cases of hookworm, tuberculosis, venereal disease, and other illnesses. They also gave inoculations, set broken bones, delivered babies, and performed operations for appendicitis and tonsilitis. Serious cases were carried downriver to hospitals in Belém. Most of all, the medical teams tried to teach prevention—how to avoid hookworm, how to keep a wound clean, what to feed small children, how to care for newborn babies.

Did the river launches bring good health to the people of the Amazon basin? The most optimistic observers would not claim that. But when United States funds for the project ended in 1954, the Brazilian government itself decided to continue it. The medical teams had at least made a start toward solving health problems. The river-clinic idea was also adopted in the São Francisco valley in southern Brazil and on the Amazon tributaries in Peru.

Will population growth outrun progress? Because of great strides in health improvement, Latin America's population is growing at a rapid rate. Experts have warned that the tremendous increase in numbers of people threatens to undo all the gains that have been made in health services. At a meeting held in 1970, the director of the Pan American Health Organization named population growth as Latin America's biggest problem.

THINKING ABOUT THIS SECTION

1. Why are each of the following of great importance in Latin America: (a) providing safe water supplies; (b) improving nutrition; (c) wiping out hookworm disease; (d) controlling typhus?
2. How have medical clinics been brought to the people of Amazonia?
3. Why does rapid population growth threaten to cancel the progress made in health programs?
4. On the map on page 369, what do you notice about the location of most of the cities over one million in population? Explain. What connection do you see between large river systems and density of population?

4. Cultural Exchange

Latin Americans have looked to the United States for financial help in raising living standards. But in the fields of literature, art, and music, Latin American leaders traditionally have looked to Europe for inspiration. Now this is changing.

Latin Americans have learned more about their neighbors to the north. The Rockefeller Committee that was set up during World War II tried to encourage greater understanding between the peoples of North and Latin America. This agency of the United States Department of

Among notable Latin American artists whose paintings can be seen in the United States are Pedro Figari of Uruguay and Fernando Botero of Colombia. In pictures like Creole Dance *(1925) Figari showed how Uruguayan villagers might spend an evening (above). Botero's* The Presidential Family *(1967) poked fun at some of Latin America's ruling dynasties (right).*

371

State was responsible for many temporary and some permanent programs of cultural exchange.

Since the 1940's, many more Latin Americans have had contact with United States projects or have come to know North American individuals. More than 50 cultural centers connected with United States embassies in Latin America have held free classes in English. Thousands of students have taken advantage of this opportunity to learn a second language.

A number of young Latin Americans have learned about the United States from first-hand experience in this country. They may, for example, attend special summer schools held at North American colleges. It is not unusual for Latin American music students to study in New York City.

No longer are Latin Americans unaware of United States literature. Latin American professors have studied and written about the literature of this country. For the common reader many books by North American writers have been translated into Spanish and circulated as paperbacks in Latin America. English rather than French is now the most popular second language in Latin American cities.

And vice versa. Cultural exchange, of course, works both ways. North Americans have begun to learn more about the accomplishments of Latin American writers, artists, and musicians. Many United States teachers have attended Spanish-language summer schools in Mexico City, Lima, and other Latin American cities. By the 1970's more students in this country were studying Spanish than were studying French or German. Portuguese, however, is seldom taught in United States high schools.

Meanwhile, an increasing number of Latin American books have been translated into English and published in paperback editions in the United States. As a result, more North Americans have read books by such writers as Octavio Paz, Mariano Azuela, Jorge Luis Borges, Gabriel Garcia Marquez, Carlos Fuentes, and Jorge Amado. The names of Heitor Villa-Lobos and Carlos Chávez are well known to concert-goers in the United States, and the bewitching rhythms of Latin American dances continue to influence North American popular music. Performers from both the United States and the Latin American countries frequently tour other hemisphere countries. And North American artists travel south to see the work of Latin American artists or to show their own works at São Paulo's famous exhibits.

Still another kind of exchange is the kind of program described on page 366. Sponsored by the Ford Foundation, this co-operative effort between universities in Chile and California had practical "grass-roots" results and also increased understanding.

The Pan American Union offers information on the Americas. The Pan American Union has greatly helped in stimulating cultural exchange. For the first few decades of its existence, the Union published a monthly *Bulletin*. This journal was full of statistics on such things as trade and public health.

During World War II the Nelson Rockefeller Committee distributed throughout Latin America a picture magazine about the United States. Following the example of this slick-paper publication, the Pan American Union turned its *Bulletin* into an attractive monthly called *Américas*. This magazine prints articles on a wide range of interesting subjects. Excellent photographs, drawings, and reprints of old pictures illustrate the articles. Many issues include a short story by a modern Latin American writer. The last section of *Américas* is devoted to current news items and announcements: art exhibits to be held at the Pan American Union building, conferences for teachers and scholarships for students, OAS activities for the coming year, and similar items. Each issue appears in English, Spanish and Portuguese editions.

The Pan American Union also publishes inexpensive booklets on a variety of subjects. The American Nations Series, for instance, offers descriptive booklets on the individual countries of the hemisphere. Other booklets

Person-to-person encounters may be the most effective kind of cultural exchange. Left, U.S. folk dancers touring Latin America had a chance to talk with Panamanian dancers wearing traditional lace-and-pearl headdresses. Below, "the King" is what Latin American soccer fans call Pelé, the great Brazilian athlete. Here Pelé leaps as he adds another goal to his record-breaking total.

provide biographies of Latin American leaders, recipes for Latin American dishes, pictures of the various national flags, travel information, native songs, and so on.[3]

National governments promote exchange activities. The governments of the American nations themselves try to make friends among the different peoples of the hemisphere. Almost all Latin American nations have some kind of cultural center in the United States. Some of these centers operate through the consulates that the governments maintain in large cities. The United States has long had cultural centers in the national capitals of Latin America. Sometimes anti-Yankee hotheads have burned the centers down. But the United States has rebuilt them, realizing that most people found the centers interesting and useful.

Understanding also comes through sports. Since people everywhere enjoy sports, this is an obvious field for strengthening inter-American friendship. Tennis stars from Latin America have played in top United States tournaments. Yachtsmen of several nations compete in sailboat races held off the coast of Venezuela. A number of Latin American

[3] For information about these publications, write to Sales and Promotion Division, Pan American Union, Washington, D.C. 20006.

baseball players have starred in the United States' major leagues. Every year in Miami, Florida, an international Tournament of the Americas is held for bowling champions.

Latin American sports fans love soccer most of all. When championship soccer games are

373

played, people from all over Latin America fly to the cities where the matches are held. Chapter 10 told how rivalry over a soccer match played a part in the 1969 war between El Salvador and Honduras. This match was played in neutral Mexico City. It was one of the play-offs that determined who would compete in the World Cup finals in 1970. World Cup Tournaments are played every four years, and Latin American nations have always been among the finalists. By defeating Honduras, El Salvador became one of the sixteen finalists to compete for the 1970 World Cup.

As the World Cup tournament got under way, El Salvador was eliminated in the early matches. But another Latin American country went all the way. In the final match, played in Mexico City, the Brazilian team met the Italian team. The star of the Brazilian team was Pelé (pay-*lay'*), a black athlete who is one of the most celebrated figures in Latin America. With Pelé's spectacular playing, Brazil defeated Italy and won the world championship. Not only Brazil was thrilled by the victory. All of Latin America cheered the triumph of the Brazilian team, and Mexican fans carried Pelé on their shoulders through the streets of Mexico City.

THINKING ABOUT THIS SECTION

1. How have cultural exchange programs helped Latin Americans to learn more about the way of life of people in the United States? What evidence is there of growing interest among the people of this country in Latin America?

2. How were inter-American contacts encouraged by the wartime Rockefeller Committee? How have they been encouraged by the Pan American Union? through programs sponsored by the various countries? through sports events?

Summing Up

This book has made it all too clear that the Latin American nations have serious problems. Poverty and unemployment, the population explosion, poor education, bad health, economic stagnation, and undemocratic governments—all these problems demand solutions. Most people hope that solutions can be found and carried out in peaceful ways. Miracles cannot be expected, but Latin American political leaders, younger military officers, reform priests, schoolteachers, frontier settlers, and idealistic students are attacking these problems, each in their own way.

Grass-roots improvements have also been carried forward through international action. These useful programs have had a variety of sponsors—the Latin American governments themselves, the United States government, private foundations, businesses, and international bodies. Through health, educational, and social work projects the OAS and United Nation agencies are achieving more than they are in the broad area of world peace. Meanwhile, energetic individuals, such as farm experts, public health advisers, Peace Corps volunteers, and others, help make the United States respected rather than feared throughout Latin America.

In the end, people of both North and Latin America have much to learn from each other. And increased understanding will help to build mutual respect. It would be well for both the people and the government of the United States to realize, as the historian Robert J. Alexander has said, "that Latin America will no longer remain what it was during the nineteenth century and much of the first half of the twentieth—an isolated area more or less off the stage upon which the future of the world was being played out. It is moving out of the wings and onstage."

Independent Nations of Middle and South America

Country	Area (sq. miles)	Population* (in millions)	Capital	Chief exports	Per capita income* (est. in U.S. dols.)	Life expectancy* (years)
Argentina	1,072,749	24.3	Buenos Aires	Meat, grain	800	65
Barbados	166	3	Bridgetown	Sugar	428	63-68
Bolivia	424,163	4.6	La Paz	Tin	165	50
Brazil	3,287,195	93	Brasília	Coffee	350	55
Chile	286,396	9.8	Santiago	Copper	465	59
Colombia	439,519	21.4	Bogotá	Coffee	262	55
Costa Rica	19,575	1.8	San José	Bananas, coffee	380	63
Cuba	44,218	8.4	Havana	Sugar	310	(Not available)
Dominican Republic	18,703	4.3	Santo Domingo	Sugar	212	58
Ecuador	104,506	6.1	Quito	Bananas, coffee	183	54
El Salvador	8,061	3.4	San Salvador	Coffee	245	58
Guatemala	42,042	5.1	Guatemala City	Coffee	264	50-60
Guyana	83,000	.7	Georgetown	Sugar, bauxite	250	70
Haiti	10,714	5.2	Port-au-Prince	Coffee, bauxite	75	47
Honduras	44,480	2.7	Tegucigalpa	Bananas	209	49
Jamaica	4,411	2	Kingston	Bauxite	431	65
Mexico	760,337	50.7	Mexico City	Cotton, sugar, coffee	600	60
Nicaragua	54,864	2	Managua	Cotton	347	54
Panama	28,753	1.5	Panama City	Bananas	477	61
Paraguay	157,047	2.4	Asunción	Timber, meat	192	58
Peru	496,223	13.6	Lima	Copper, fish meal	241	53
Trinidad and Tobago	1,980	1.1	Port of Spain	Oil	515	65
Uruguay	72,172	2.9	Montevideo	Wool, meat	537	71
Venezuela	352,146	10.8	Caracas	Oil	902	66

*Figures for latest years available.

Sources: OAS publications; *1971 Britannica Book of the Year; The New York Times Encyclopedic Almanac, 1971.*

General

Arciniegas, Germán, ed., *The Green Continent: A Comprehensive View of Latin America by Its Leading Writers,* translated by Harriet de Onís and others. Knopf, 1967. Readings on many different aspects of Latin American life.

Bailey, Helen Miller, and Abraham P. Nasatir, *Latin America: The Development of Its Civilization,* 3rd ed. Prentice-Hall, 1972. A leading college textbook.

*Gunther, John, *Inside South America.* Harper, 1967. A very readable account of a famous journalist's travels in South America.

Herring, Hubert, *A History of Latin America from the Beginnings to the Present,* 2nd rev. ed., Knopf, 1968. Another leading college text.

James, Preston E., *Introduction to Latin America: The Geographic Background of Economic and Political Problems.* Odyssey, 1964. A readable survey by the leading authority on Latin American geography.

*Keen, Benjamin, ed., *Americans All: The Story of Our Latin American Neighbors.* Dell, 1966. A readable collection of original accounts. Covers all periods from the ancient Indian civilizations to the present.

*Keen, Benjamin, ed., *Readings in Latin American Civilization, 1492 to the Present,* 2nd ed. Houghton Mifflin, 1967. This collection is a longer anthology than the preceding title and is designed for college use.

*Kingsbury, Robert C., and Ronald M. Schneider, *An Atlas of Latin American Affairs.* Praeger, 1965. Maps of different regions, with explanatory text.

*Pendle, George, *A History of Latin America.* Penguin, 1963. A brief but interesting survey, written in a lively style.

Wilgus, A. Curtis, *A Historical Atlas of Latin America.* Cooper Square, 1967. Detailed but easy-to-read historical maps from the pre-Columbian era to modern times.

*Starred books are available in paperback editions.

Chapter 1
The Makers of Latin America: The Indians

*Brandon, William, *The American Heritage Book of Indians.* Simon & Schuster, 1961. Covers the native peoples of all the Americas. The hardcover edition has excellent illustrations.

Coe, Michael, *America's First Civilization.* Van Nostrand, 1968. A fascinating account of the Olmec people. Clearly written and richly illustrated.

Leonard, Jonathan Norton, *Ancient America.* Time, Inc., 1967. A beautifully illustrated and readable account of the pre-Columbian Indians.

*Mason, J. Alden, *The Ancient Civilizations of Peru.* Penguin, 1969. One of the best books on the Incas. Scholarly style.

Sutton, Ann and Myron, *Among the Maya Ruins.* Rand McNally, 1967. Describes the life and work of John Lloyd Stephens, the man who discovered many Maya ruins. Written for junior high school readers.

*Vaillant, G. C., *Aztecs of Mexico.* Penguin, 1962. A classic account of the Aztecs. Scholarly style.

Chapter 2
The Makers of Latin America: The Europeans

*Atkinson, William C., *A History of Spain and Portugal.* Penguin, 1960. Iberia from ancient times to the present. Scholarly style.

Chubb, Thomas Caldecott, *Prince Henry the Navigator and the Highways of the Seas.* Viking, 1970. An easy-to-read account of the man who revolutionized navigation.

Dos Passos, John, *The Portugal Story: Three Centuries of Exploration and Discovery.* Doubleday, 1969. An illustrated account.

Kubler, George, and Martin Soria, *Art and Architecture in Spain and Portugal and Their American Dominions, 1500–1800.* Penguin, 1959. An illustrated history of Iberian and colonial art.

*Morison, Samuel Eliot, *Christopher Columbus, Mariner.* New American Library, 1956. A brief and interesting biography of Columbus. The author retraced much of Columbus' route.

*Penrose, Boies, *Travel and Discovery in the Renaissance 1420–1620*. Harvard, 1955. A scholar's account of the great explorations in Asia, Africa, and America. Detailed but readable.

Thomas, Hugh, *Spain*. Time, Inc., 1962. A beautifully illustrated book on Spain, past and present.

Chapter 3
The Makers of Latin America: The Africans

*Burke, Fred, *Africa*. Houghton Mifflin, 1970. A well-written high school text with many interesting illustrations.

Davidson, Basil, *African Kingdoms*. Time, Inc., 1966. A beautifully illustrated survey of the great kingdoms of the past.

Davidson, Basil, *Discovering Our African Heritage*. Ginn, 1971. An interesting account written for high school students.

Howard, Thomas, *Black Voyage*. Little, Brown, 1971. Eyewitness accounts of the Atlantic slave trade. Easy to read.

Kennedy, Karen, *The Slave Who Bought His Freedom: Equiano's Story*. Dutton, 1971. This edition of Olaudah Equiano's autobiography has been shortened and adapted for modern readers.

*Mannix, Daniel P., with Malcolm Cowley, *Black Cargoes: A History of the Atlantic Slave Trade, 1518–1865*. Viking, 1962. A standard account of the slave traffic.

*Oliver, Roland, and J. D. Fage, *A Short History of Africa*. Penguin, 1966. A scholarly but brief history.

*Tannenbaum, Frank, *Slave and Citizen*. Vintage, 1946. Shows how black slavery was different in Latin America and North America.

Thompson, Elizabeth Bartlett, *Africa Past and Present*. Houghton Mifflin, 1966. A vivid account of Africa, with a chapter on the Atlantic slave trade.

Chapter 4
The European Conquest

*Bannon, John Francis, ed., *The Spanish Conquistadores, Men or Devils?* Holt, 1960. Presents views of conquistadors themselves as well as opinions of modern writers.

Blacker, Irwin R., *Cortés and the Aztec Conquest*. American Heritage, 1965. Written for young adult readers, this volume has excellent illustrations.

*Díaz del Castillo, Bernal, *The Discovery and Conquest of Mexico,* translated by A. P. Maudslay. Noonday Press, 1965. A first-hand account by a soldier who served under Cortés.

Howard, Cecil, *Pizarro and the Conquest of Peru*. American Heritage, 1969. Excellent illustrations highlight this book for young adult readers.

*Kirkpatrick, F. A., *The Spanish Conquistadores*. World, 1946. A standard book on the Spanish conquest.

*Leon-Portilla, Miguel, ed., *The Broken Spears*. Beacon Press, 1962. Original Indian accounts of Cortés' conquest of Mexico.

Chapter 5
Life in Colonial Latin America

*Bourne, Edward G., *Spain in America 1450–1580*. Harper, 1968. An old book (first published in 1904) but still a standard and readable narrative.

*Clissold, Stephen, *Latin America: A Cultural Outline*. Hutchinson, 1965. A brief outline of Indian and Iberian ways of life and thought and how they became the mestizo culture of Latin America.

*Gibson, Charles, *Spain in America*. Harper, 1966. A scholarly but clearly written account of colonial life.

Kubler, George, and Martin Soria, *Art and Architecture in Spain and Portugal and Their American Dominions, 1500–1800*. Penguin, 1959. Covers both Spanish America and Brazil during the colonial years.

*Leonard, Irving A., *Baroque Times in Old Mexico: Seventeenth-Century Persons, Places, and Practices*. University of Michigan Press, 1959. An excellent account of colonial Mexican life.

Chapter 6
Spanish Roots in the United States

*Bolton, Herbert Eugene, *Coronado, Knight of Pueblos and Plains*. University of New Mexico Press, 1949. The author reconstructs the Coronado expedition. Scholarly, but good reading.

Bolton, Herbert Eugene, *The Spanish Borderlands: A Chronicle of Old Florida and the Southwest*. Yale University Press, 1921. Though old, this is still a good account for the general reader.

*Gibson, Charles, *Spain in America*. Harper, 1966. Includes material on the borderlands.

*Horgan, Paul, *Conquistadors in North American History*. Farrar, Straus, 1963. A vividly written account of the Spanish explorers in what is now the United States.

O'Dell, Scott, *The King's Fifth*. Houghton Mifflin, 1966. Historical novel about the search for the "Seven Cities of Cíbola" as told by a young map-maker who accompanied Coronado. Written for young adults.

Shepherd, Elizabeth, *The Discoveries of Esteban the Black*. Dodd, Mead, 1970. An illustrated account of the life of Estevanico (also called Esteban). Written for teen-agers.

Wise, Winifred, *Fray Junípero Serra and the California Conquest*. Scribner, 1967. A biography written for teen-agers.

Chapter 7
The Independence Movements in Latin America

*Humphreys, R. A., and John Lynch, eds., *The Origins of the Latin American Revolutions 1808–1826*. Knopf, 1965. Readings by 27 authorities examine the forces behind the independence movement in Spanish and Portuguese America. Scholarly.

*James, C. L., *The Black Jacobins: Toussaint L'Ouverture and the San Domingo Revolution*. Vintage, 1963. Tells how Haiti won its independence.

*Lieberman, Mark, *Miguel Hidalgo: Father of Mexican Independence*. Praeger, 1970. The story of the man who started Mexico on the road to independence. Written for teen-agers.

*Simpson, Lesley Byrd, *Many Mexicos*. University of California Press, 1966. One of the best standard histories of Mexico. Authoritative but written in a lively style.

Vandercook, John W., *Black Majesty: The Life of Christophe, King of Haiti*. Scholastic, 1963. Fictionalized but accurate story of the Haitian ruler. Written for teen-agers.

Young, Bob and Jan, *Liberators of Latin America*. Lothrop, Lee & Shepherd, 1970. Biographical accounts of Toussaint, Bolívar, San Martín, Hidalgo, and others. Written for teen-agers.

Chapter 8
Outstanding Leaders of the Nineteenth Century

*Blancke, W. Wendell, *Juárez of Mexico*. Praeger, 1971. The story of one of Mexico's most noted leaders. Written for teen-agers.

*Hamill, Hugh M., Jr., ed., *Dictatorship in Spanish America*. Knopf, 1965. Eighteen articles by different authors analyze the role of *caudillos* in Latin America. Scholarly.

*Haring, C. H., *Empire in Brazil: A New World Experiment with Monarchy*. Harvard, 1958. A well-written account of nineteenth-century Brazil. Scholarly.

*Scobie, James R., *Argentina*. Oxford, 1964. A good history, though loosely organized. Emphasizes social and economic factors.

*Simpson, Lesley Byrd, *Many Mexicos*. University of California Press, 1966. (See Chapter 7 list.)

*Whitaker, Arthur P., *Argentina*. Prentice-Hall, 1964. A brief standard history. Includes two chapters on the nineteenth century.

Williams, Mary Wilhelmine, *Dom Pedro the Magnanimous, Second Emperor of Brazil*. Octagon, 1966. A sympathetic biography of the last emperor of Brazil.

Chapter 9
The Latin American Nations: Mexico

*Azuela, Mariano, *Two Novels of Mexico: The Flies; The Bosses*, translated by Lesley Byrd Simpson. University of California Press, 1956. *The Underdogs*, translated by E. Munguía, Jr. New American Library, 1963. Each of Azuela's classic novels is set in the period of the Mexican Revolution.

Bailey, Helen Miller, *Santa Cruz of the Etla Hills*. University of Florida Press, 1958. This readable account tells more about the village described in the chapter.

*Cline, Howard F., *The United States and Mexico*. Harvard, 1963. Most of the book deals with the period after 1910.

*Guzmán, Martín Luis, *The Eagle and the Serpent*, translated by Harriet de Onís. Doubleday, 1965. A classic novel of the Revolution written by a journalist who served under Pancho Villa.

Johnson, William Weber, *Mexico*. Time, Inc., 1966. Beautifully illustrated account of Mexico, past and present.

*Parkes, Henry Bamford, *A History of Mexico*. Houghton Mifflin, 1970. An updated edition of a standard authoritative work.

*Simpson, Lesley Byrd, *Many Mexicos*. University of California Press, 1966. (See Chapter 7 list.)

Chapter 10
The Latin American Nations: The Central American Republics

Lavine, Harold, *Central America*. Time, Inc., 1968. A richly illustrated look at the Central American countries, past and present.

May, Charles Paul, *Central America: Lands Seeking Unity*. Nelson, 1966. The countries of Central America are surveyed individually and as a whole in this book for teen-agers.

*Rodríguez, Mario, *Central America*. Prentice-Hall, 1965. A good survey history.

West, Robert C., and John P. Augelli, *Middle America: Its Lands and Peoples*. Prentice-Hall, 1966. Covers Mexico, Central America, and the Antilles.

Chapter 11
The Latin American Nations: The Latin West Indies

*Fagg, John Edwin, *Cuba, Haiti, and the Dominican Republic*. Prentice-Hall, 1965. A general survey of these three countries, with emphasis on Cuba.

*Freidel, Frank, *The Splendid Little War*. Little, Brown, 1958. A history of the Spanish-American War, based on primary sources.

Harman, Carter, *The West Indies*. Time, Inc., 1966. A beautifully illustrated look at all the West Indian islands.

Logan, Rayford W., *Haiti and the Dominican Republic*. Oxford, 1968. A brief but scholarly comparative study of the two neighboring nations.

Chapter 12
The Latin American Nations: The Northern Andean Republics

Beck, Barbara, *Colombia*. Franklin Watts, 1968. A good introduction for teen-aged readers.

Belaúnde Terry, Fernando, *Peru's Own Conquest*. Blaine Etheridge, 1965. The former president of Peru gives an optimistic account of his country.

*Bernstein, Harry, *Venezuela and Colombia*. Prentice-Hall, 1964. Brief but authoritative and readable history.

Galbraith, W. O., *Colombia*. Oxford, 1966. Surveys the country's history, economy, culture, society, politics, etc.

Johnson, William Weber, *The Andean Republics: Bolivia, Chile, Ecuador, Peru*. Time, Inc., 1965. Excellent coverage of modern life and historical backgrounds. Beautifully illustrated.

Linke, Lilo, *Ecuador: Country of Contrasts*. Oxford, 1960. A good basic survey.

MacEoin, Gary, *Colombia and Venezuela and the Guianas*. Time, Inc., 1965. A richly illustrated look at the present-day countries and their historical backgrounds.

Osborne, Harold, *Bolivia, A Land Divided*. Oxford, 1964. A good standard work.

Pike, Frederick B., *Modern History of Peru*. Praeger, 1967. One of the best recent histories, particularly good for the national period.

Chapter 13
The Latin American Nations: Southern South America

*Dana, Doris, translator and editor, *Selected Poems of Gabriela Mistral*. Johns Hopkins, 1971. A collection of the Chilean poet's best work.

Ferguson, J. Halcro, *The River Plate Republics: Argentina, Paraguay, Uruguay*. Time, Inc., 1968. A fine survey, beautifully illustrated.

*Güiraldes, Ricardo, *Don Segundo Sombra: Shadows on the Pampas*, translated by Harriet de Onís. New American Library, 1966. A classic Argentine novel.

Hernández, José, *Martín Fierro*, translated by Harriet de Onís. Doubleday, 1960. This epic poem, also an Argentine classic, tells the story of the gauchos.

May, Charles Paul, *Chile: Progress on Trial*. Nelson, 1968. This readable survey of Chile includes sections on the Mapuche Indians, the country's struggle for independence, and daily life.

Pendle, George, *Paraguay: A Riverside Nation*. Oxford, 1967. A brief but interesting account of Paraguay's history, culture, and present condition.

Pendle, George, *Uruguay*. Oxford, 1963. A similar treatment of Uruguay.

*Scobie, James R., *Argentina*. Oxford, 1964. A good general history, though loosely organized. Emphasizes social and economic factors.

*Silvert, Kalman H., *Chile: Yesterday and Today*. Holt, 1965. A good introduction for high-school students.

*Whitaker, Arthur P., *Argentina*. Prentice-Hall, 1964. A political history with special focus on the twentieth century.

Chapter 14
The Latin American Nations: Brazil

Bishop, Elizabeth, *Brazil*. Time, Inc., 1967. Tells the story of Brazil, past and present. Excellent illustrations.

Clark, Leonard, *The Rivers Ran East*. Funk & Wagnalls, 1953. In the mid-1940's the author journeyed along the Amazon from Brazil to Peru, penetrating unmapped regions. This is a young people's edition of his classic narrative.

*Freyre, Gilberto, *New World in the Tropics*. Knopf, 1959. A famous Brazilian writer and anthropologist shows how the culture of modern Brazil developed.

*Jesus, Carolina Maria de, *Child of the Dark*, translated by David St. Clair. New American Library, 1962. This diary by a *favela* resident presents a realistic portrait of life in the São Paulo slums. Recommended for mature students.

*Poppino, Rollie, *Brazil: Land and People*. Oxford, 1968. One of the best surveys of Brazil for students. Concentrates on the economic, social, and political aspects of Brazilian history.

Chapter 15
Mexican Americans in the United States

*Galarza, Ernesto, Herman Gallegos, and Julian Samora, *Mexican Americans in the Southwest*. McNally & Loftin, 1969. Three authorities on Mexican American affairs survey the situation of the Spanish-speaking people of the Southwest.

Landes, Ruth, *Latin Americans of the Southwest*. McGraw-Hill, 1965. An anthropologist analyzes Mexican and Spanish cultural elements in the southwestern states.

Moquin, Wayne, ed., *A Documentary History of the Mexican Americans*. Praeger, 1970. These readings record the history and accomplishments of the Mexican Americans.

*Simmen, Edward, ed., *The Chicano: From Caricature to Self-Portrait*. New American Library, 1971. Selections from Anglo authors of the 1800's and from Anglo and Mexican American writers of today show how the image of the Mexican American has changed. For mature readers.

*Steiner, Stan, *La Raza: The Mexican Americans*. Harper, 1970. An impressionistic history, vividly written.

*Terzian, James P., and Kathryn Cramer, *Mighty Hard Road*. Doubleday, 1970. A biography of Cesar Chavez. Easy to read.

Weinger, Sandra, *Small Hands, Big Hands*. Pantheon, 1970. Seven Chicano migrant workers tell what their life is like. Easy to read.

Chapter 16
Puerto Rico and the Puerto Ricans

Brau, M. M., *Island in the Crossroads*. Doubleday, 1968. An easy-to-read and informative history of Puerto Rico.

Gruber, Ruth, *Island of Promise*. Hill and Wang, 1960. An optimistic and readable account of Puerto Rican life.

*Mayerson, Charlotte, ed., *Two Blocks Apart: Juan Gonzales and Peter Quinn*. Holt, 1965. Records the views of two New York boys of very different backgrounds. Written for high school students.

Padilla, Elena, *Up from Puerto Rico*. Columbia University Press, 1958. An interesting study of how newcomers adjust to life in New York City.

Rand, Christopher, *The Puerto Ricans*. Oxford, 1958. Very readable account written for the general public.

*Senior, Clarence, *The Puerto Ricans: Strangers — Then Neighbors*. Quadrangle, 1965. A study of the problems that confront Puerto Ricans on the mainland.

*Sterling, Philip, and Maria Brau, *The Quiet Rebels: Four Puerto Rican Leaders*. Doubleday, 1968. The quiet rebels include José Celso Barbosa, Luis Muñoz Rivera, José de Diego, and Luis Muñoz Marín. For junior high readers.

*Wagenheim, Kal, *Puerto Rico: A Profile*. Praeger, 1970. An excellent overview of Puerto Rican history, society, culture, geography, economy, etc. Written for the general reader.

Wakefield, Dan, *Island in the City: Puerto Ricans in New York*. Houghton Mifflin, 1959. A sympathetic and readable account of life among Puerto Ricans in Spanish Harlem.

Chapter 17
The United States and Latin America: Politics and Diplomacy

*Abel, Elie, *The Missile Crisis*. Lippincott, 1966. A journalist's account of the Cuban missile crisis.

*Lieuwen, Edwin, *U. S. Policy in Latin America: A Short History*. Praeger, 1965. Scholarly but readable and short.

*Stoetzer, O. Carlos, *The Organization of American States: An Introduction*. Praeger, 1965. A good introduction to the OAS. Geared to students.

*Szulc, Tad, *Dominican Diary*. Dell, 1965. An account of the 1965 crisis by a reporter who was there.

*Wood, Bryce, *The Making of the Good Neighbor Policy*. Columbia University Press, 1961. Traces the history of the Policy. For able readers.

Chapter 18 The United States and Latin America: Economic, Social, and Cultural Co-operation

*Alexander, Robert J., *Today's Latin America*. Anchor, 1968. Discusses Latin American politics and development against a background of history, geography, and culture. Readable style.

*Castedo, Leopoldo, *A History of Latin American Art and Architecture*. Praeger, 1969. This richly illustrated book covers Latin American art from the pre-Columbian Indians to the present.

*Cohen, J. M., ed., *Latin American Writing Today*. Penguin, 1967. Stories and poems by 32 outstanding modern writers.

*Rockefeller, Nelson, *The Rockefeller Report on the Americas*. Quadrangle, 1969. This report on a fact-finding visit to Latin America surveys the state of Latin America in the 1960's.

*Szulc, Tad, *Latin America*. Atheneum, 1966. A survey of Latin America and its problems in the 1960's by a journalist who knows the region well. Very readable.

*Tannenbaum, Frank, *Ten Keys to Latin America*. Knopf, 1962. Delves into such subjects as race, religion, politics, leadership, and U. S. relations. A valuable book and one that is easy to read.

Acknowledgments

Thanks are extended to the persons and organizations listed below for making pictures available for reproduction. The following abbreviations have been used: Bettmann—The Bettmann Archive; Culver—Culver Pictures, Inc.; FPG—Freelance Photographers Guild; HPS—Historical Picture Service, Chicago; NYPL—New York Public Library; OAS—Organization of American States; UPI—United Press International Photos.

3 Peabody Museum, Harvard

6 (top) FPG; (lower right) Kerwin B. Roche/FPG; (lower left) Charles Marden Fitch/FPG

9 Lee Boltin

12 Lee Boltin

13 Lee Boltin

19 (left) Library of Congress; (right) The Metropolitan Museum of Art, Dick Fund, 1962

21 Courtesy of The Museum of Primitive Art, New York

24 (top) Courtesy of the American Museum of Natural History; (bottom) Helen Miller Bailey

26 Jacques Jangoux

28 Herbert Lanka/Black Star

31 Foto Mas, Barcelona

34 The Metropolitan Museum of Art, Purchased with Purchase Fund and special contributions bequeathed or given by Friends of the Museum

35 © Josip Ciganovic/FPG

40 HPS

43 Braniff Airways

45 Jay Datus

47 (top) Photo by Tomas D. W. Friedmann © 1970; (bottom) Helen Miller Bailey

49 Courtesy of the Trustees of the British Museum/Douglas R. G. Sellick

51 NYPL

55 Museum voorland-en volkenkunde, Rotterdam

58 (top) NYPL; (bottom) Hulton Picture Library

61 Bettmann

63 Selden Rodman

65 Photograph Courtesy of The Museum of the American Indian, Heye Foundation

67 Giraudon

71 Courtesy of The American Museum of Natural History

74 Biblioteca Medicea Laurenziana/Fotografia Guido Sanson

79 (top) Courtesy of the Trustees of the British Museum/Douglas R. G. Sellick; (bottom) Culver

81 © Weston Kemp

83 Culver

85 HPS

89 Fotos de Arquitectura Colombia

91 Bettman

95 Bettman

100 (top) HPS; (bottom) OAS

105 Rare Book Division, NYPL—Astor, Lenox and Tilden Foundations

111 OAS

113 California State Library, Sacramento

116 HPS

119 Brown Brothers

123 (top) Western Ways Photo; (bottom) Charles W. Herbert/Western Ways Photo

128 Religious News Service

129 Henry E. Huntington Library and Art Gallery

131 HPS

133 Culver

140 HPS

145 HPS

149 San Jacinto Museum of History Association

157 OAS

158 HPS

161 HPS

164 HPS

166 HPS

169 Lawrence Cameron

174 Archivo Casasola

181 (top) Mexican Government Tourist Department; (bottom) Photo Courtesy RCA Corporation

184 Owen Franken

187 (left) Hurok Concerts Inc.; (right, both) Barney Burstein

190 OAS

197 Rayes Juarez/Courtesy Guatemala Tourist Commission

199 (top) United Fruit Company; (bottom) OAS

205 United Nations

208 (top) UPI; (bottom) OAS

211 Association for Sugar Production of Puerto Rico

This index includes references not only to the text of the book but also to maps and pictures. These may be identified as follows: *m* refers to a map; *p* refers to a picture.

O

Oaxaca (wah-*hah'* kah), 8, 20, 155, *m* 153, *m* 178
Obregón (oh-bray-*gohn'*), Alvaro, 174, 176, 177, 185
Obsidian, 15, 16
Ocampo, Victoria, 260
Ogé (oh-*zhay*), Vincent, 132
O'Higgins, Bernardo, 138–139, 141, 146
Oil, in Mexico, 158, 171, 178–179; in Guatemala, 196; in Panama, 207; in Colombia, 234; in Venezuela, 238–239, 240; in Peru, 243, 248; in Bolivia, 249; in Ecuador, 252; in Argentina, 259; in Chile, 265; in Brazil, 289
Oklahoma, 116, *m* 153
Olid, Cristobal de, 75
Olmec people, 8
Olney, Richard, 338
Oñate (ohn-*yah'* tay), Juan de, 120–121; route, *m* 117
Onganía (ohn-gah-*nee'* ah), Juan Carlos, 264
O'Reilly, Alejandro, 126
Orellana (oh-ray-*yah'* nah), Francisco de, 83; route, *m* 69
Organization of American States (OAS), 201, 224, 226, 345–346, 347–349, 356, 357–358, 360, 361
Orinoco River, 41, 65, 84, 237, *m* 7, *m* 17, *m* 38, *m* 69, *m* 96, *m* 233
Orozco (oh-*rohss'* koh), José Clemente, 186; painting by, *p* 157
Otavalo Indians, 252
Ouro Preto (*oh'* roo *pray'* too), 109, 112, *m* 96

P

Pachácamac (pah-*chah'* kah-mahk), 20, 80, *m* 17, *m* 69
Pachacuti (pah-chah-*koo'* tee), 21
Pacific Ocean, 42, 43, *m* 38, *m* 257
Padín, José, 321
Palenque (pah-*layn'* kay), 10, *m* 17
Palmares (pahl-*mah'* rays), 62, *m* 52
Pampa (*pahm'* pah) Indians, 25–26, 85, *m* 17
Panama, Spaniards in, 42, 93; and Colombia, 146, 207, 208, 234, 334; and Canal Zone, 206, 209, 339; geography and economy, 207; and U.S., 208–209, 339; government, 209–210; *m* 38, *m* 52, *m* 69, *m* 142, *m* 193, *m* 340
Panama Canal, 206–209, 236, 340, *m* 193
Panama City, 90, 206, 209, *m* 96, *m* 193
Pan American Health Organization (PAHO), 366, 367, 370
Pan American Highway, 179, 184, 192, 198, 207, 367, *m* 352

Pan American Union, 342, 343, 345, 360, 368, 372. *See also* Organization of American States
Pará, *m* 279
Paraguay, Spaniards in, 85–86; missionaries in, 104, 273; independence, 146; in wars, 165–166, 273–274; geography, economy, and people, 272–273; government, 274; *m* 142, *m* 257
Paraguay River, 85, 272, 274, 357, *m* 7, *m* 38, *m* 257
Paraná River, 104, 109, 256, 258, 272, 357, *m* 7, *m* 38, *m* 257
Park, Mungo, 57
Patagonia, 256, 259, *m* 257
Paz, Octavio, 372
Paz Estenssoro (*pahss'* es-ten-*sor'* oh), Víctor, 250
Peace Corps, 361–364
Pedrarias (pay-*drah'* ree-ahss), 77
Pedro I, 143, 159
Pedro II, 159, 162, 277
Pelé (pay-*lay'*), 374, *p* 373
Pendle, George, 147
Pensacola, 118, 119, *m* 125
Peralta Barnuevo (pay-*rahl'* tah bar-*nway'* voh), Pedro, 108
Peralta, Pedro de, 121, 122
Pérez Jiménez (*pehr'* ess hee-*may'* nayss), Marcos, 240
Pernambuco (pair-nahm-*boo'* koh), 87, 285
Perón (pay-*rohn'*), Eva Duarte de, 261–262, *p* 262
Perón, Juan Domingo, 261–263, *p* 262
Peru, Pizarro in, 77–82; colony, 93; independence, 139, 146; war with Chile, 168; Indians of, 232–233, 243–246; geography, 242–243; economy, 243; Vicos project, 246–247; government, 247–248; and trade groups, 357; *m* 69, *m* 142, *m* 233
Philip II, 33, 36, 109, 118–119, 121
Philip V, 94
Philippines, 43, 121, 338
Phoenix, 299, 310
Pierce, Franklin, 337
Pineda (pee-*nay'* thah), Alonso de, 124
Piñero (pih-*nyay'* roh), Jesus, 322
Pirates, 54, 103, 118, 315
Pizarro (pee-*sar'* roh), Francisco, 77–82, 93; route, *m* 69; *p* 79
Pizarro, Gonzalo, 78, 82, 83
Pizarro, Hernando, 78, 81, 82
Pizarro, Juan, 78, 82
Pizarro, Pedro, 78, 82
Plácido (*plah'* see-thoh), 216
Plantations, 99, 110, 199–200, 215, 287, 317
Plata. *See* Rio de la Plata
Plaza (*plah'* sah) Lasso, Galo, 253, 346, 358, 359, *p* 254
Polk, James, 339
Polo, Marco, 37
Popayán (poh-pah-*yahn'*), 84, 85, *m* 69

Popé (poh-*pay'*), 122
Popocatepetl (poh-*poh'* kah-*tay'* petl), Mount, 171, *m* 7
Popol Vuh (poh-*pol' voo'*), 12
Population growth, 172, 194, 201, 271, 283, 317, 370, *m* 369
Portales (por-*tah'* layss), Diego, 167–168
Port-au-Prince (*port'* oh-*prans'*), 226, 227, *m* 214
Portinari, Cândido, 292; painting by, *p* 292
Porto Bello, 90, 102, *m* 96
Portolá, Gaspar de, 127–128; route, *m* 125
Portugal, 29, 34–36, 51–53, 86–88, 109–110, 143, *m* 33, *m* 52
Portuguese language, 1–2, 30, 36, 291
Potatoes, 22
Prehistoric Americans, 4–8; migrate from Siberia, 5, *m* 17
Press, 165, 260, 262, 264, 272, 302
Prester John, 35, 36
Pueblo (*pweb'* loh) Indians, 115, 122, 124, 298
Puerto Limón (*pwehr'* toh lee-*mohn'*), 204, 205, *m* 193
Puerto Ricans, in New York, 313–314, 329, 330–331; citizens of U.S., 314, 320, 327, 329
Puerto Ricans, The (Rand), 330
Puerto Rico, as Spanish colony, 146, 314–318; geography, 314; independence movements, 317–318, 321, 328; relationship to U.S., 319–323, 326–328; Operation Bootstrap, 323–326; present government, 327; statehood movement, 328; *m* 38, *m* 142, *m* 214, *m* 318, *m* 340
Punta Arenas (*poon'* tah ah-*ray* nahss), 265, *m* 257

Q

Quadros, Janio, 281
Quechua (*kay'* choo-ah) language, 22, 25, 244
Quesada (kay-*sah'* dah), Jiménez de, 84, 85; route, *m* 69
Quetzalcoatl (kayt-sahl-*koh'* atl), 9, 13, 19, 70
Quinquela Martín, Benito, 260
Quiroga (kee-*roh'* gah), Facundo, 165
Quito (*kee'* toh), 80, 84, 90, 92, 94, 252, 253, *m* 69, *m* 96, *m* 233
Quitu (*kee'* too) people, 22, 252

R

Race relations, compared with North American race relations, 62–63; in colonial period, 95, 97, 98; in Brazil, 110, 289; in Central America, 193, 205, 207; and Puerto Ricans on mainland, 330
Railroads. *See* Transportation

Rainfall, in Mexico, 170, 171, *m* 171; in Central America, 191, 202, *m* 171; in Caribbean, 212–213, 222, *m* 171; in Colombia, 232; in coastal desert, 242, 264; in Argentina, 256; in Paraguay, 272; in Brazil, 285, 286; in South America, *m* 242
Raleigh, Walter, 65
Ramirez, Francisco, 302
Rand, Christopher, 330
Rebellion in the Backlands (da Cunha), 277
Recife (ray-*see'* fay), 87, 109, 285, *m* 69, *m* 96, *m* 279, *m* 369
Reed, Walter, 217
Religion, Indians, 10, 12, 14, 18, 23; festivals, 29, 105, *p* 28; Islam, 30; in Africa, 49–50; in Haiti, 227. *See also* Catholic Church
Repartimiento (ray-par-tih-*myen'* toh), 97
Rimac (ree-*mahk'*), 80
Rio de Janeiro (*ree'* oo duh zhuh-*nay'* roo), 87, 109, 159, 283, 359, *m* 69, *m* 96, *m* 279, *m* 369, *p* 284
Rio de la Plata (*plah'* tah), 42, 85, 249, 256, *m* 7, *m* 38, *m* 69, *m* 257
Rio Grande, 116, 120, 125, 154, 303, *m* 7, *m* 117, *m* 125, *m* 153, *m* 178
Rivera (ree-*vay'* rah), Diego, 186; painting by, *p* 187
Roads. *See* Transportation
Rockefeller, Nelson, 351, 368
Rockefeller Committee, 370, 372
Rockefeller Foundation, 364, 368
Rodó, José Enrique, 271
Rojas (*roh'* hahss) Pinilla, Gustavo, 236–237
Rondon, Candido Mariano, 289
Roosevelt, Franklin D., 179, 203, 229, 321, 322, 342, 344, *p* 344
Roosevelt, Theodore, 209, 223, 319, 334, 339–340
Roosevelt, Theodore, Jr., 320, 321
Rosario, 258, 259, *m* 142, *m* 257
Rosas (*roh'* sahss), Juan Manuel de, 163–165
Royal African Company, 54
Roybal, Edward, 307
Ruiz Cortines (roo-*eess'* kor-*tee'* nehss), Adolfo, 179

S

Sacramento, 299, 300, *m* 153
Sagres (*sah'* gresh), 35, *m* 33
Sahagún, Father, 70
St. Augustine, 119, *m* 96, *m* 117, *m* 125
Salazar, Ruben, 311
Salt River, 303, *m* 153
Salvador, *m* 279. *See also* Bahia
San Antonio, 113, 126, 308, 310, *m* 125, *m* 153

San Diego, 113, 118, 121, 127, 128, 296, 310, *m* 125, *m* 153
Sandino, Augusto, 203
San Francisco, 113, 118, 121, 127, 128, 129, 296, *m* 125, *m* 153, *p* 129
San Gabriel, 129
San Joaquin River, 303, *m* 153
San José, Calif., 127, *m* 125
San José, Costa Rica, 192, 205, *m* 193
San Juan, New Mexico, 120, *m* 117
San Juan, Puerto Rico, 92, 315, 319, 320, *m* 96, *m* 214, *m* 318
San Luis Obispo, *m* 125
San Martín (*sahn'* mar-*teen'*), José de, Buenos Aires junta, 138; in Chile, 139; in Peru, 139; and Bolívar, 139–141; *p* 140
San Pascual, Battle of, 296, *m* 153
San Salvador (island), 40, *m* 38
San Salvador, El Salvador, 201, *m* 193
Santa Anna, Antonio Lopez de, 149, 151–155, *p* 149
Santa Barbara, 113, 127, *m* 125
Santa Clara, 127, *m* 125
Santa Cruz Etla, 184–185
Santa Fe, 120, 121, 122, 296, 298, *m* 117, *m* 125, *m* 153
Santa Fe Trail, 296, *m* 125
Santander, Francisco de Paula, 137
Santa Rita Durão (thoo-*rown'*), José de, 111
Santiago, Chile, 84, 265, *m* 69, *m* 96, *m* 142, *m* 257, *m* 369
Santiago de Cuba, 94, 213, *m* 69, *m* 96, *m* 214
Santo Domingo, 66, 93, 222, 223, *m* 38, *m* 52, *m* 69, *m* 96, *m* 142, *m* 214
San Xavier del Bac, 124, *m* 125
São Paulo (sown *pow'* loo), 109, 159, 283, *m* 96, *m* 279, *m* 369
São Tomé (*sah'* oon too-*may'*), 51, *m* 52
São Vicente (sown vih-*sayn'* tay), 87, *m* 69, *m* 96
Sarmiento (sar-*myen'* toh), Domingo, 165–167
Scott, Winfield, 154; expedition, *m* 153
Serra (*sehr'* rah), Junípero, 127–128, *p* 128
Shadow of the Chieftain, The (Guzmán), 188
Silver, 76, 80, 171, 300
Siqueiros (see-*kay'* rohss), David, 186
Slavery, general history of, 50–51; in Africa, 49, 57; in Latin America, 53–63, 76, 97–98, 104, 110, 161–162, 315–316; abolition movement, 55–56, 97, 144, 162, 216, 317–318; slave revolts, 61, 62, 127, 132
Solis (*sohl'* eess), Juan de, 42, 85; route, *m* 38
Somoza (soh-*moh'* sah), Anastasio, 203, *p* 208
Songhai (sahn-*guy'*), 46, *m* 52

Sonoma, *m* 153
Soto, Hernando de, with Pizarro, 78, 80; in North America, 116–117, 124, *m* 117
Souza (*soo'* zah), Martím Alfonso de, 87
Souza, Thomé de, 87
Soviet Union, and Cuba, 219, 347
Spain, geography, 29; in Roman Empire, 30; Muslims in, 30–31, 33; unified, 32; religion, 33, 104; Golden Age, 33–34; administration of colonies, 93–94, 97, 102–103, 104; decline of, 103; *m* 33, *m* 96
Spanish-American War, 208, 216, 318–319, 338
Spanish language, 1–2, 28, 30, 34, 196, 244, 302, 313, 320, 321, 330
Sports, 373–374
Steel industry, in Mexico, 180; in Venezuela, 239, 240; in Argentina, 259, 263; in Chile, 265; in Brazil, 280, 288
Stephens, John Lloyd, 3–4, 10
Stockton, Calif., 303, 304
Stroessner (*stress'* ner), Alfredo, 274
Sucre (*soo'* kreh), 249, *m* 142, *m* 233
Sucre, Antonio José de, 141
Sugar, and slavery, 60, 212; trade, 88, 110, 160; Cuba and, 213–215, 220; Puerto Rico and, 320
Szulc, Tad, 219, 367

T

Taft, William Howard, 340
Tainos (*ty'* nohz) Indians, 314
Tannenbaum, Frank, 2, 63
Taos, *m* 125
Tarascan people, 76, 362; language, 20
Taylor, Zachary, 154; expedition, *m* 153
Tegucigalpa (teh-*goo'* sih-*gahl'* pah), 198, *m* 193
Tehuantepec (teh-*wan'* teh-pek), Isthmus of, 170
Tello (*tay'* yoh), Julio, 25
Tenochtitlán (tay-nohch-tee-*tlan'*), 15–16, 74, *m* 7, *m* 17, *m* 69
Teotihuacán (tay-oh-tee-wah-*kahn'*), 9, 10, 14, *m* 7, *m* 17
Texas, Spaniards in, 115, 116, 124, 126; French in, 125; republic, 151–152, 295; after U.S. annexation, 299; *m* 153
Tiahuanaco (tyah-wah-*nah'* koh), 21, *m* 17
Tierra caliente, templada, and *fría,* in Mexico, 170, *m* 171; in Central America, 191, *m* 171
Tierra del Fuego (*tyeh'* rah del *fway'* goh), 265, *m* 257
Tijerina (tee-heh-*ree'* nah), Reies Lopez, 309–310
Tikal (tee-*kahl'*), 10–11, *m* 17
Tlaloc (*tlah'* loc), 18